TWENTIETH-CENTURY
RUSSIAN POETRY

Twentieth-Century Russian Poetry

Reinventing the Canon

*Edited by Katharine Hodgson,
Joanne Shelton and Alexandra Smith*

https://www.openbookpublishers.com

© 2017 Katharine Hodgson, Joanne Shelton and Alexandra Smith.
Copyright of each chapter is maintained by the author.

This work is licensed under a Creative Commons Attribution 4.0 International license (CC BY 4.0). This license allows you to share, copy, distribute and transmit the work; to adapt the work and to make commercial use of the work providing attribution is made to the authors (but not in any way that suggests that they endorse you or your use of the work). Attribution should include the following information:

Katharine Hodgson, Joanne Shelton and Alexandra Smith (eds.). *Twentieth-Century Russian Poetry: Reinventing the Canon.* Cambridge, UK: Open Book Publishers, 2017. https://doi.org/10.11647/OBP.0076

In order to access detailed and updated information on the license, please visit https://www.openbookpublishers.com/product/294#copyright

Further details about CC BY licenses are available at http://creativecommons.org/licenses/by/4.0/

All external links were active at the time of publication and have been archived via the Internet Archive Wayback Machine at https://archive.org/web

Digital material and resources associated with this volume are available at https://www.openbookpublishers.com/product/294#resources

The contributions to this volume were developed as part of a project funded by AHRC, 'Reconfiguring the Canon of Twentieth-Century Russian Poetry, 1991–2008' (AH/H039619/1).

Every effort has been made to identify and contact copyright holders and any omission or error will be corrected if notification is made to the publisher.

Anna Akhmatova and Moisei Nappelbaum are represented by FTM Agency, Ltd., Russia

ISBN Paperback: 978-1-78374-087-1
ISBN Hardback: 978-1-78374-088-8
ISBN Digital (PDF): 978-1-78374-089-5
ISBN Digital ebook (epub): 978-1-78374-090-1
ISBN Digital ebook (mobi): 978-1-78374-091-8
DOI: 10.11647/OBP.0076

Cover image and design: Heidi Coburn

All paper used by Open Book Publishers is SFI (Sustainable Forestry Initiative), PEFC (Programme for the Endorsement of Forest Certification Schemes) and Forest Stewardship Council(r)(FSC(r) certified.

Printed in the United Kingdom, United States, and Australia
by Lightning Source for Open Book Publishers (Cambridge, UK)

Contents

Notes on Contributors   vii

1. Introduction: Twentieth-Century Russian Poetry and the Post-Soviet Reader: Reinventing the Canon   1
   Katharine Hodgson and Alexandra Smith

2. From the Margins to the Mainstream: Iosif Brodskii and the Twentieth-Century Poetic Canon in the Post-Soviet Period   43
   Aaron Hodgson

3. 'Golden-Mouthed Anna of All The Russias': Canon, Canonisation, and Cult   63
   Alexandra Harrington

4. Vladimir Maiakovskii and the National School Curriculum   95
   Natalia Karakulina

5. The Symbol of the Symbolists: Aleksandr Blok in the Changing Russian Literary Canon   123
   Olga Sobolev

6. Canonical Mandel'shtam   157
   Andrew Kahn

7. Revising the Twentieth-Century Poetic Canon: Ivan Bunin in Post-Soviet Russia   201
   Joanne Shelton

8. From Underground to Mainstream: The Case of Elena Shvarts   225
   Josephine von Zitzewitz

9. Boris Slutskii: A Poet, his Time, and the Canon 265
   Katharine Hodgson

10. The Diasporic Canon of Russian Poetry: 289
    The Case of the Paris Note
    Maria Rubins

11. The Thaw Generation Poets in the Post-Soviet Period 329
    Emily Lygo

12. The Post-Soviet Homecoming of First-Wave Russian Émigré 355
    Poets and its Impact on the Reinvention of the Past
    Alexandra Smith

13. Creating the Canon of the Present 393
    Stephanie Sandler

Bibliography 425

Index 471

Notes on Contributors

Alexandra Harrington is Senior Lecturer in the School of Modern Languages and Cultures at Durham University. Her research focuses primarily on modern Russian poetry and literary culture, in particular the career of Anna Akhmatova, and she is currently writing a monograph on Russian literary fame and the phenomenon of literary celebrity. Alexandra is also working on a longer-term project, *The Poem in the Eye: The Visual Dimension of Russian Poetry*, which investigates Russian poetry from the seventeenth century to the present, with a focus on the different ways in which poems prompt the reader to visualise, and the varied relationships that exist between Russian poetry and the visual arts. Her publications include *The Poetry of Anna Akhmatova: Living in Different Mirrors* (2006) and 'Anna Akhmatova', in Stephen M. Norris and Willard Sunderland (eds.), *Russia's People of Empire: Life Stories from Eurasia, 1500 to the Present* (2012). Email: a.k.harrington@durham.ac.uk

Katharine Hodgson's research focuses on twentieth-century Russian poetry, particularly the complexities faced by writers during the Soviet period, and how attitudes towards the cultural legacy of the USSR have evolved since 1991. Katharine has published extensively on the topic, including with Alexandra Smith, *The Twentieth-Century Russian Poetry Canon and Post-Soviet National Identity* (2017) and *Voicing the Soviet Experience: the Poetry of Ol'ga Berggol'ts* (2003). Between 2010 and 2013 Katharine led a project funded by the Arts and Humanities Research Council (AHRC), 'Reconfiguring the Canon of Twentieth-Century Russian Poetry, 1991–2008' (http://humanities.exeter.ac.uk/modernlanguages/russian/research/russianpoetrycanon), which has enabled her to examine how the twentieth-century poetry canon has been revised in recent years. This book is the fruit of this productive collaboration. Email: K.M.Hodgson@exeter.ac.uk

Aaron Tregellis Hodgson is currently writing his doctoral thesis, entitled 'From the Margins to the Mainstream, or the Mainstream to the Margins? Joseph Brodsky's Canonical Status in the West and Russia in the post-Soviet Period'. His doctoral research is funded by the AHRC as part of the project 'Reconfiguring the Canon of Twentieth Century Russian Poetry, 1991–2008.' Email: aaron.hodgson87@gmail.com

Andrew Kahn is Professor of Russian Literature at the University of Oxford. He has written widely about Russian Enlightenment literature, Pushkin, and modern poetry. He is completing a book about Mandel'stam's late poetry called *Mandelstam and Experience: Poetry, Politics, Art*. He has edited and introduced new translations of Mikhail Lermontov, *A Hero of Our Time* and Leo Tolstoi, *The Death of Ivan Ilyich and Other Stories*, both for Oxford World's Classics. Email: andrew.kahn@seh.ox.ac.uk

Natalia Karakulina completed her PhD at the University of Exeter. Her thesis 'Representations of Vladimir Maiakovskii in the Post-Soviet Russian Literary Canon' assembled evidence from a range of post-1991 publications to show how Maiakovskii's position has been affected by the wide-ranging rejection of writers strongly associated with the official Soviet culture. The thesis contributes to the body of research analysing the development of the Russian literary canon in the post-Soviet period. Email: N.Karakulina@exeter.ac.uk

Emily Lygo is Senior Lecturer in Russian at the University of Exeter. Her main research interests are Russian poetry especially of the Soviet period, Soviet literary politics and policy, literary translation in Russia and Anglo-Soviet relations. Her translation of Tatiana Voltskaia's *Cicada: Selected Poetry & Prose* was published in 2006. She is also the author of *Leningrad Poetry 1953–75: The Thaw Generation* (2010), and *The Art of Accommodation* (2011). Email: E.F.Lygo@exeter.ac.uk

Maria Rubins is Senior Lecturer in Russian Literature and Culture at the School of Slavonic and East European Studies of University College London. She works on Russian literature and cultural history of the nineteenth to the twenty-first centuries, from a comparative and interdisciplinary perspective. In particular, her research interests include modernism, exile and diaspora, national and postnational cultural identities, the interaction between literature and other arts, canon formation, postcolonial, bilingual and transnational writing, Russian-French cultural relations, and Russian-language literature in Israel. Her most recent book is *Russian Montparnasse: Transnational Writing in Interwar Paris* (2015; a revised and expanded Russian translation is forthcoming from the NLO Publishing House, Moscow). Email: m.rubins@ucl.ac.uk

Stephanie Sandler is Professor of Slavic Languages and Literatures at Harvard University. Her research centres mainly on poetry and cinema. Stephanie has written about Pushkin and myths of Pushkin in Russian culture, and about the contemporary poetry of Russia and of the United States. She has a long-standing interest in women writers and in feminist theory, and her work also draws on psychoanalysis, philosophy, visual studies, and post-modernist theories. Stephanie is also a translator of Russian poetry. Her publications include *Distant Pleasures: Alexander Pushkin and the Writing of Exile* (1989); *Commemorating Pushkin: Russia's Myth of a National Poet* (2004); and three edited collections: *Rereading Russian Poetry* (1999); *Self and Story in Russian History* (2000; with Laura Engelstein); and *Sexuality and the Body in Russian Culture* (1993; with Jane Costlow and Judith Vowles). Email: ssandler@fas.harvard.edu

Joanne Shelton has undertaken research into the role of educational institutions and publishers in the canon formation process. She has collated information for entry in the searchable bibliographical database of the 'Reconfiguring the Canon of Twentieth Century Russian Poetry, 1991–2008' project, which was designed to show quantitative changes in the prominence of a given poet in post-1991 publications, and the extent of his or her appearances in textbooks and literary histories.

Alexandra Smith is Reader in Russian Studies at the University of Edinburgh. Her research interests include literary and film theory, critical theory, Russian literature of the nineteenth to the twenty-first centuries, and the history of ideas and the interaction between literary and visual modes of artistic expression. Alexandra is the author of *The Song of the Mockingbird: Pushkin in the Works of Marina Tsvetaeva* (1994) and *Montaging Pushkin: Pushkin and Visions of Modernity in Russian*

Twentieth-Century Poetry (2006). She has also written numerous articles on Russian literature and culture, as well as European and American literature. Currently she is working on several publications related to the AHRC project 'Reconfiguring the Canon of Russian Twentieth-Century Poetry, 1991–2008', in which she participated as Co-Investigator. Email: Alexandra.Smith@ed.ac.uk

Olga Sobolev is a Senior Lecturer in Russian and Comparative Literature at the London School of Economics and Political Science. She researches Russian and European culture of the nineteenth and twentieth centuries. Olga's recent publications include *From Orientalism to Cultural Capital: The Myth of Russia in British Literature of the 1920s* (with Angus Wrenn, 2017), 'Reception of Alfred Tennyson in Russia', in Leonee Ormond (ed.), *The Reception of Tennyson in Europe* (2016), 'The Only Hope of the World': George Bernard Shaw and Russia* (with Angus Wrenn, 2012), *The Silver Mask: Harlequinade in the Symbolist Poetry of Blok and Belyi* (2008) and articles on Leo Tolstoi, Fedor Dostoevskii, Vladimir Nabokov, Anton Chekhov, Boris Akunin and Viktor Pelevin. Email: o.sobolev@lse.ac.uk

Josephine von Zitzewitz is presently Leverhulme Early Career Fellow at the Department of Slavonic Studies, Cambridge University, having previously held a lectureship at Oxford University. She is working on Leningrad *samizdat*, with a particular focus on *samizdat* journals, the networks that formed around them and their function as early social media. Her monograph on *samizdat* poetry, *Poetry and the Leningrad Religious-Philosophical Seminar 1974–1980: Music for a Deaf Age* was published in 2016, and she has written several articles on poetry and late Soviet culture. Her second interest is translation, and she envisages a new project bringing together young Russian poets, scholars and translators. Email: jhfv2@cam.ac.uk

1. Introduction: Twentieth-Century Russian Poetry and the Post-Soviet Reader: Reinventing the Canon

Katharine Hodgson and Alexandra Smith

The aim of this collection is to investigate the state of the Russian twentieth-century poetic canon in the context of socio-political changes triggered by the collapse of the Soviet Union in 1991.[1] This introductory essay sets out the larger context of cultural evolution in which the alterations to the poetry canon, to be discussed in the chapters that follow, took place. It explores developments in Russian culture during a period which has seen both the dramatic disruption of links with the past, as well as the rediscovery of neglected aspects of the twentieth century's cultural legacy.

The process of reshaping the poetry canon is complex and multifaceted. This Introduction will focus on three main aspects related to canon change. It will start by considering the particular challenges posed by the mass of forgotten or previously unknown poetry from different parts of the century which became available over a short period

---

1 The chapters in this book grew from a series of workshops at which contributors gathered to share their ideas and discuss how they might develop their work for publication. These workshops, held at the University of Exeter in December 2011, the University of Edinburgh in July 2012, and the University of Exeter in January 2013, were supported by a grant from the Arts and Humanities Research Council, which the editors of this volume gratefully acknowledge.

of time. The following section will explore the relationship between the poetry canon and identity, looking at the influence of nostalgia on shaping perceptions of poetry associated with the Soviet past, as well as of the modernist poetic legacy of the early years of the century. After focusing the discussion on poets and poetic groups, the introduction then explores the role of literary criticism in canon change, considering how particular strands in twentieth-century Russian criticism have helped to form the poetry canon. Just as has been the case for the poetry canon, the canon of literary criticism has seen considerable change in recent years with the recovery of formalist thought, which has in turn influenced the way twentieth-century poetry has been perceived. The concluding part of the Introduction outlines the diversity of the emerging canon, as illustrated in the individual chapters that follow, and considers the more inclusive, less dogmatic approach to canon formation that seems to have developed since the early 1990s.

Raw Materials for Revising the Canon

During the last century the Soviet state sought to exercise far-reaching control over all aspects of culture, with unprecedented levels of state intervention in education and scholarship, literary criticism, and the publication and distribution of reading matter. Activity across all these fields contributes to the shaping of literary canons as a set of works and authors that are accorded exemplary status by, for example, their inclusion in educational syllabuses, literary histories, and anthologies. In the Soviet Union censorship meant that at any given time the works of certain authors could be deemed unpublishable, withdrawn from libraries, excluded from critical and scholarly discussion. The work of authors who had emigrated became largely inaccessible to most readers inside the country; some who remained in the Soviet Union were made subject to publication bans, while others preferred not to engage in the negotiations with editors and censors which were an unavoidable part of the process of getting their work published. The return to 'pre-Gutenberg' era culture in the 1920s and 1930s, when manuscripts were hidden, or shared only with a few trusted friends, was followed by the post-Stalin development of underground seminars, writers' circles, and journals, and the growth of self-published *samizdat* literature.² In the last decades of the Soviet Union's existence there were steps towards creating a more inclusive poetry canon as some previously marginalised figures were brought back into the mainstream. From the late 1980s, however, as a result of the relaxation of censorship, and then its complete abolition, readers were faced with a hugely expanded accessible canon of twentieth-century works.³ Émigré poets were published once more and countless texts emerged from the archives and the underground, at the same time as the state relinquished its monopoly control over cultural life.

Now that the mechanisms that had maintained the reputations of some, suppressed others, and permitted only a partial knowledge of other poets' output had been dismantled it was plain that the late-Soviet poetry canon, as expressed in literary histories and textbooks of the previous decade, was in need of an overhaul. In the Soviet Union the process of forming selective canons was monopolised by official state-controlled institutions; attempts to propose an alternative view of the canon through different channels were severely restricted, and were possible only in the later Soviet period among a small number of poets and readers active in unofficial underground culture. As the state set aside its role as cultural policeman, and so removed the underground's reason for existing, the task of defining the shape of the poetry canon was now open to all comers. Whatever their opinions on the content of the canon, they had a common goal: to reshape a canon that had been constructed to serve the state's narrow ideological ends.

While this process is still at a relatively early stage, it is possible that individuals are able to exercise particular influence, though this is likely to decrease as more numerous and varied agents become involved. Partisan promoters of certain schools of poetry, of particular

---

2   Nadezhda Mandel'shtam refers to the 1930s as a 'pre-Gutenberg era' in her memoir *Hope Against Hope*, translated by Max Hayward (New York: Atheneum, 1970), p. 192.

3   The terms 'accessible canon' and 'selective canon' (below) are taken from Alastair Fowler, 'Genre and the Literary Canon', *New Literary History*, 11: 1, Anniversary Issue: II (Autumn 1979), 97–119 (pp. 98–99). For more on Fowler's approach to categorising types of canon, see Olga Sobolev's chapter in this volume, pp. 123–56 (p. 130).

individuals, and of rival ideological outlooks were able to enter the arena alongside experts and enthusiasts who were concerned to present a broadly inclusive picture of the century's poetry, as well as publishers who were facing new market conditions and having to deal with the question of what readers might be prepared to buy. The spread of the internet in Russia has made it possible for anyone with online access to read and respond to a wide range of material. Educational institutions also have their part to play, as do the state educational authorities who issue guidance on what is to be studied, in influencing ideas about which poets and works should be considered canonical. Participants in the process of canon formation are far more numerous and diverse than they were before 1991.

The canon-forming process in Soviet Russia involved only limited numbers of agents; it was, moreover, disrupted and delayed by the effects of decades of censorship. Significant legal and institutional changes at the start of the 1990s helped to clear a path for major cultural shifts. One particularly important development was the emergence of free speech, legitimised by a new media law approved by the final Soviet Parliament in 1990 and by the new Russian government in 1991. In the words of prominent Russian media expert Nadezhda Azhgikhina, this law 'represented the greatest achievement of the liberal legal experts of the *perestroika* era'. The emergence of free speech in the Russian media paved the way for a large-scale rediscovery of previously censored or suppressed works of literature and cinema, as well as artefacts created in the Russian underground and by émigré artists. In the opinion of Frank Ellis, the official abolition of censorship was the most important factor in accelerating the collapse of the Soviet Union and in changing the role of literature and of the author in Russian society. The Russian literary landscape changed significantly once readers could gain legitimate access to a wide range of different voices, especially when extensive online resources grew up alongside print culture, to create a vast, integrated information space.[4]

A particular challenge confronting those involved in reconfiguring the canon was presented by the great number of poems that had emerged many years after they had been written, to be received in a dramatically

---

4   Frank Ellis, *From Glasnost to the Internet: Russia's New Infosphere* (Basingstoke: Macmillan, 1999), pp. 125–137.

changed cultural context. In the process of canon formation it is hardly unusual to see the reputations of authors change significantly over time. Aleksandr Pushkin, though celebrated in his own lifetime, was relatively neglected in the mid-nineteenth century, and his position as Russia's ultra-canonical writer was secured only after a revival of his reputation starting in the 1870s.[5] It is much less common to see unknown authors, or formerly well-known poets whose work has been forgotten, brought in to the canon after several decades in obscurity. Some poets, such as Mariia Shkapskaia and Zinaida Gippius, made a brief re-appearance in the late 1980s and early 1990s, but it seems that they have yet to establish themselves in the canon, while those who, like Anna Akhmatova, had secured their canonical status in the later Soviet period, have retained it. Other, younger poets, for example Dmitrii Bobyshev, seem to have remained on the margins for reasons that are difficult to explain; Bobyshev may simply have been overshadowed by his famous contemporary, Iosif Brodskii. Part of the problem may be the fragmented way in which the 'unknown' poets have been received, separated from the context in which they created their work. The large twentieth-century poetic legacy that had come to light by the 1990s had not been subject to the kinds of processes involving contemporary would-be readers, publishers, and critics that contribute to the formation of canons. The task of assimilating such a volume of material went beyond simply integrating unknown or forgotten poets into an existing literary-historical narrative; the emergence of so much 'new' material made it clear that the existing narrative was fragmented, disjointed, and full of gaps caused by the deliberate suppression of information, or by straightforward lack of knowledge.

The state of affairs in literary history that became clear by the 1990s mirrored the situation in broader accounts of the nation's history. The process of rediscovering suppressed aspects of twentieth-century Russian history had made a tentative start during the post-Stalin Thaw period. This process resumed in the mid-1980s and quickly gathered pace, revealing numerous omissions and distortions in the official version. Attempts to supplant a familiar and reassuring version of the past with one that offered strange and disturbing perspectives were

---

5   Andrew Kahn, 'Introduction', in *The Cambridge Companion to Pushkin*, edited by Andrew Kahn (Cambridge: Cambridge University Press, 2006), pp. 1–7 (p. 5).

not perceived as the straightforward matter of establishing an objective and accurate historical account. How the past is remembered within a culture involves not just the need to preserve knowledge of it, but the emotional connections that exist with the culture of that past. The encounter with an unsettling history in the late 1980s and early 1990s evoked conflicting emotional responses: this 'new' past did not always sit comfortably with people's memories of their own lived experience. Moves towards reshaping the previous century's poetry canon have elicited a similarly mixed reactions from post-Soviet readers. There is an ambivalent attitude towards the poetry of the socialist realist tradition, in which nostalgia sits alongside unease about its open didacticism and aesthetic of accessibility. The poetry canon is one of the constructions that represents what a society considers worthy of being remembered, and contributes to the creation of a shared identity in the present. As the canon evolves in a shifting and unpredictable landscape, it expresses a complex relationship between the present and past as elements are foregrounded, neglected, or discarded. The canon has its own part to play in a wider social process of constructing collective memory, which is pieced together through the countless actions of individuals and institutions as they respond to cultural change, and, in turn, stimulate further such change. For a nation undergoing a reshaping of its recent history, at the same time as experiencing dramatic social and political change in the present, it is not surprising that such extensive upheavals have contributed to anxieties about modernity as much as they have encouraged excitement about the creative possibilities of cultural transformation.

The sheer quantity of material that became available to Russian readers in a post-censorship, digitally connected world presented its own problems. In the early 1990s they were able to access a mass of virtually unknown literary texts from various decades of the twentieth century, but had little help in making sense of their relative cultural significance, particularly when works of high literature appeared on the same internet sites as texts aimed at mass entertainment. The ever-increasing volume of materials available online created an environment in which an expanding archive of digital cultural artefacts offered the resources from which selective canons might be drawn, rather than selective canons as such. At the same time, the role of literature, and of the poet in particular, began to change significantly. Michael Wachtel aptly identifies as a defining feature of Soviet-era culture the special role that was ascribed to poets: 'in a society that controlled all sources of information, people looked to literature as a secret source of wisdom and a moral compass', and the dissident poet, capable of outwitting the totalitarian regime, was often perceived 'as a cultural hero unimaginable in the West'.⁶ In the post-Soviet period, however, the familiar roles of the poet as martyr and prophet withered away, paving the way for a new role for the post-Soviet poet as an entertainer competing with television sitcoms and Hollywood films.⁷ There was a proliferation of performances of Russian poetry both on television channels and internet sites, but no clear guidance for viewers about the cultural value of these recordings, or whether they should be treated purely as an eccentric collection of archival materials. Nevertheless there are indications that the Soviet notion of culturedness continued to make itself felt, even in the new, commercially focused world.⁸ Twentieth-century Russian poets often featured in advertisements for services, goods, and restaurants, signalling to consumers that at least some of the companies involved in the post-Soviet market valued high culture. For example, several advertisements for Slavianskii Bank contains references to the poetry of famous Russian modernist poets including Aleksandr Blok, Boris Pasternak, and Osip Mandel'shtam, and were nominated for a prize for the best video advertisements of the last twenty years.⁹

While the boundary between high and mass cultural products became blurred, so too did temporal boundaries, when works created during the Revolutionary period emerged alongside writing from the Soviet underground of the late 1960s and 1970s, together with new texts by contemporary authors. Mark Lipovetsky recognises the difficulties created by the simultaneous appearance of the work of

---

6   Michael Wachtel, *The Cambridge Introduction to Russian Poetry* (Cambridge: Cambridge University Press, 2004), p. 10.
7   *Ibid.*
8   As Vadim Volkov points out, in 1936 the Komsomol press in the Soviet Union launched a campaign promoting the notion of culturedness that was linked not only to attending the theatre and cinema but also to the 'mastery of a correct, literary speech — manner' associated with reading good literature. See Vadim Volkov, 'The Concept of *Kul'turnost'*: Notes on the Stalinist Civilizing Process', in *Stalinism: New Directions*, edited by Sheila Fitzpatrick (Routledge: London and New York, 2000), pp. 210–30 (p. 223).
9   'Bank Slavianskii, Poety: Mandel'shtam, Pasternak, Blok, Pushkin', http://www.sostav.ru/columns/mmfr20/nominantCard.php?IDNominant=125

'at least three different generations', which made it much harder for readers to draw nuanced distinctions between different, but perhaps related trends, or to appreciate the particular features of various modes of writing.[10] Yet this simultaneous encounter with the literary legacy of different periods of the twentieth century also prompted critics and scholars to start redrawing the map of the century's literary culture so as to reveal the connections between the present and the past which linked modernist works of earlier decades and more recent writing. The façade of socialist realism, it turned out, had obscured developments including postmodernist modes of expression that had taken place in the underground of the 1960s onwards, and had now finally come out into the open. From the 1960s until the late 1980s, in Lipovetsky's view, 'Russian postmodernist aesthetics was taking place underground, in constant confrontation not only with official aesthetics and ideology, but also with society as a whole'.[11] Lipovetsky rightly points out that many established practitioners of Russian postmodernism did not feel opposed to the modernist tradition but 'rather dreamed of revival of this tradition which has been interrupted by the aggressive nature of totalitarian culture'.[12]

The massive influx of new and forgotten texts in the 1990s may be seen as an explosive event in Russia's cultural evolution, of the kind discussed by Iurii Lotman in his 1992 study *Culture and Explosion*. According to Lotman, Russian cultural development has been marked over several centuries by repeated sudden dramatic ruptures with the past which should be viewed as 'an integral element of the linear dynamic process'. He draws a distinction between the effects of explosive change in Russian culture, structured according to a binary model 'oriented towards notions of polarity and maximalism', and in Western culture, which is characterised by a ternary structure 'which strives to adapt the ideal to reality'.[13] Lotman maintains that in ternary social structures 'the core structure can survive an explosion so powerful and catastrophic that its echo can be heard through all

---

10 Mark Lipovetsky, 'Russian Literary Postmodernism in the 1990s', *Slavonic and East European Review*, 1 (2001), 31–50 (pp. 31–32).
11 Ibid.
12 Ibid., p. 32.
13 Juri Lotman, *Culture and Explosion*, edited by Marina Grishakova, translated by Wilma Clark (Berlin and New York: Mouton de Gruyter, 2009), p. 171, p. 166.

the levels of culture'.[14] While in the West historical connections are not entirely broken even by a major rupture, in Russian culture, due to the prevalence of binary structures, 'moments of explosion rupture the continuous chain of events, unavoidably leading not only to deep crises but also to radical renewals'.[15] In the light of Lotman's comments, Russian cultural developments of the 1990s may be interpreted as part of such a radical renewal, since he understands explosions not solely as destructive events, but also as events which bring about opportunities for 'creative transformation'.[16]

There is a place in Lotman's thinking for gradual processes of cultural change, which he understands as 'relatively predictable', unlike explosive processes.[17] Certainly, the gradual post-Stalin evolution of the canon to re-admit Sergei Esenin, Anna Akhmatova, and Marina Tsvetaeva, for example, can be defined as a non-explosive, gradual process. In Lotman's understanding, the artistic consciousness tends to be governed by two different tendencies that shape the dynamic relationship between preservation and change:

> In the phenomenon of art it is possible to isolate two opposing tendencies: the tendency toward the repetition of that which is already known and the tendency toward the creation of that which is fundamentally new. Does the first of these theses not arise from a contradiction to the thesis that art, as the result of explosion, always creates a text that is initially unpredictable?[18]

The explosive, rather than gradual process of change manifested in the simultaneous reception of three generations of poets in the 1990s presented readers with masses of new material which had the potential to reshape the canon, changing poets' reputations and dismissing some writers, while welcoming others. It was far from evident, at the start of the final decade of the twentieth century, how the canon might change in response to the new situation. What did become clear, however, was that there was little interest in abandoning the idea of canon construction altogether. The immediate post-Soviet years were disordered and

---

14 Ibid., p. 166.
15 Ibid., p. 169.
16 Ibid., p. 10.
17 Ibid., p. 59.
18 Ibid., p. 154.

marked by anxiety about the prospect of growing chaos. The idea of a literary canon held the promise of order and hierarchy, something that could serve as a stable point of reference, even as it evolved. As well as offering a model of order, the canon also provided a means of creating narratives about the past which could propose possible identities and future directions. As Paul Lauter notes, 'A canon is, to put it simply, a construct, like a history text, expressing what a society reads back into its past as important to its future'.[19]

Poetry and Nostalgia: The Canon and Identity

The type of catastrophic evolutionary patterns that Lotman sees as being typical for Russian culture give rise to a complex relationship with the past. This section will consider two aspects of Russian twentieth-century culture which have evoked powerful nostalgic responses: works strongly identified with mainstream Soviet culture, and the legacy of the modernist culture of the Silver Age.[20] In both cases the nostalgic attachment to particular cultural phenomena may be seen as a reaction to a society's experience of far-reaching disruption. Galina Rylkova sees the fascination with the Silver Age as a 'cultural construct of retrospective origin brought to life as a means of overcoming the existential anxieties unleashed by the Bolshevik Revolution, the civil war, and the Stalinist terror'.[21] Fondness for the remembered culture of the Soviet Union grew as Russians experienced the prolonged uncertainty and repeated crises of the 1990s. This section will show how attitudes towards both Silver Age and mainstream Soviet poetry, which form a significant proportion of the century's accessible canon, have been influential in shaping the process of post-Soviet canon formation.

In the early post-Soviet period it was clear that mainstream Soviet culture evoked an ambivalent response. Adele Barker notes the tensions

---

19 Paul Lauter, *Canons and Contexts* (New York and Oxford: Oxford University Press, 1991), p. 58.
20 The term loosely denotes Russian cultural developments in the 1880s–1910s. On the latest usage of this term see Alexandra Smith, 'Silver Age Studies: The State of the Field', in *The AATSEEL Newsletter*, 56: 2 (April 2013), 2–4, http://www.aatseel.org/100111/pdf/aatseelapril13nl.pdf
21 Galina Rylkova, *The Archaeology of Anxiety: The Russian Silver Age and its Legacy* (Pittsburgh: University of Pittsburgh Press, 2007), pp. 6–7.

that characterised Russian popular culture emerging in the late 1980s and early 1990s, and describes this culture as being 'torn between its own heritage and that of the West, between its revulsion with the past and its nostalgic desire to re-create the markers of it, between the lure of the lowbrow and the pressures to return to the elitist pre-revolutionary past'.[22] Barker describes post-Soviet popular culture as 'heavily nostalgic' and marked by a complex relationship between the past and the present:

> Although much cultural production — from rave parties to anecdotes and art installations — in the new Russia deals with the past, it does so not merely to remember and to mourn but to rewrite the nostalgic text, often by domesticating, familiarizing, and even trivializing outworn symbols of oppression or by returning to what is familiar from a safe enough distance to preclude any real return to what is both mourned and despised.[23]

William Havlena and Susan Holak see mass media and education as channels which have purveyed virtual nostalgia, imbued with emotions based on shared indirect experience, which enables recipients to create a new cultural identity for themselves.[24] Barker notes that while many consumers of the new Russian popular culture in the 1990s had direct experience of the later decades of Soviet socialism, their nostalgia was shared by younger people who had only brief encounters with Soviet reality. The older generation's lived experience, suggests Barker, helped to shape 'the imaginations of the young' through Russian cultural production which transmitted collective memory from one generation to the next.[25] The sense of nostalgia experienced by younger audiences should be defined as virtual nostalgia because it was evoked not by their memories of personal experience but, for example, by television and radio programmes such as 'Starye pesni o glavnom' ('The Main Songs

---

22 Adele Marie Barker, 'Rereading Russia', in *Consuming Russia: Popular Culture, Sex, And Society Since Gorbachev*, edited by Adele Marie Barker (Durham, NC, and London: Duke University Press, 1999), pp. 3–11 (p. 5).
23 Barker, 'The Culture Factory: Theorising the Popular in the Old and New Russia', in *Consuming Russia*, pp. 12–48 (p. 19).
24 Susan Holak, Alexei Matveev, and William Havlena, 'Nostalgia in Post-Socialist Russia: Exploring Applications to Advertising Strategy', *Journal of Business Research*, 60 (2007), 649–55 (p. 650).
25 Barker, 'The Culture Factory', p. 19.

of the Past'), 'Rodivshiesia v SSSR' ('Born in the USSR'), and 'Staroe radio' ('Old Radio'). The post-Soviet upheavals which affected many people's lives dramatically intensified a need for a sense of identity, both for individuals and the wider nation, and the recent past, imagined as a time of relative stability and national prestige, could be mined for memories which would evoke pleasantly nostalgic feelings of a shared history informed by personal and emotional significance.[26]

The appeal of nostalgia in relation to Soviet culture was heightened because it offered a version of the past which was far more reassuring than the accounts of Russia's twentieth-century history that spilled out of the archives from the late 1980s onwards. Jay Winter and Emmanuel Sivan declare that 'public and private modes of remembering were severed in the Soviet period'.[27] Bringing the two together once more raised awkward questions about how the disparate, often conflicting memories of individuals and society might be brought together in some kind of collective memory and shared identity. The task was made more complicated by the collapse of the grand narrative of the inevitable triumph of communism over capitalism, which meant that the project of nation-building and post-Soviet identity construction was being conducted against the background of multiple and conflicting views of Russia's past, and its possible future direction.

Nostalgic representations of the Soviet past offered an attractive, emotionally satisfying solution which simplified an otherwise complex picture. For example, Leonid Parfenov's television programmes about famous historical and literary figures in Russia, and also his entertaining programme *Namedni* (*Not So Long Ago*), featuring news reports from the past, have contributed considerably to the shaping of Russian collective

---

26 This tendency can be illustrated by the popularity of the 2015 television series loosely based on Vasilii Aksenov's novel *Tainstvennaia strast'* (*Secret Passion*). It features famous Soviet poets of the 1960s, including Evgenii Evtushenko, Bella Akhmadulina, Robert Rozhdestvenskii and Andrei Voznesenskii. Igor' Virabov reports that the thirteen-episode television story about popular poets of the 1960s attracted an incredible amount of interest among post-Soviet spectators eager to learn more about the Thaw: 'Vakson vo mgle', *Rossiiskaia gazeta*, 2 November 2016, https://rg.ru/2016/11/02/serial-tainstvennaia-strast-novye-pohozhdeniia-poetov-shestidesiatnikov.html

27 Jay Winter and Emmanuel Sivan, 'Setting the Framework', in *War and Remembrance in the Twentieth Century*, edited by Jay Winter and Emmanuel Sivan (Cambridge: Cambridge University Press, 1999), pp. 6–39 (p. 6).

nostalgia. The perceived gap between the past (remembered as former happy days) and the unsatisfactory present can stir up powerful emotions. Oleg Gorbachev, commenting on Parfenov's programmes, makes an important distinction between the notion of cultural memory as the preservation of knowledge of the past and nostalgia as an embodiment of emotional experience: 'The difference between nostalgia and collective memory is not merely the presence of emotion but also its intensity'.[28] Gorbachev notes that over the last twenty years in Russia, as a result of active state involvement 'there has occurred a gradual displacement of the ironic, reflexive nostalgia of which Parfenov is a purveyor, by a nostalgia of restorative type, which is distinguished by much greater simplification and a drive to mythologization'.[29]

The tendency towards simplification of the past is often linked to the desire of famous post-Soviet cultural figures to promote their own literary canons. In 2011 the writer Dmitrii Bykov, actor Mikhail Efremov and newspaper editor Andrei Vasil'ev, acting as producer, embarked on a joint project *Grazhdanin poet* (*Citizen Poet*), which combined elements of nostalgia with an attempt to de-mythologize both past and present. The project consisted of a series of videos, broadcast first on television, then on the internet, in which Bykov's parodies of work by well known poets were performed by Efremov. The opening episode featured Efremov as Nikolai Nekrasov, the nineteenth-century classic poet and editor whose poem 'Poet i grazhdanin' ('The Poet and the Citizen') gave the project its title.[30] A majority of the poets whose work featured in the project were prominent figures in the literary canon of the Soviet era; many were famous poets of the Soviet period, including Vladimir Maiakovskii, Aleksandr Tvardovskii, and Evgenii Evtushenko. *Grazhdanin poet* blends the old and the new. Its attitude towards the past is highly ambivalent, while its treatment of the present day is unmistakably satirical.

The project's title implies that a poet should play a civic role, gesturing as it does to Nekrasov's poem in which the Citizen instructs the Poet that being a poet may be a matter of choice, but being a citizen

---

28 Oleg Gorbachev, 'The *Namedni* Project and the Evolution of Nostalgia in Post-Soviet Russia', *Canadian Slavonic Papers*, 3–4 (2015), 180–94 (p. 181).
29 Ibid.
30 Moritz Gathmann, 'Satire Against Cynicism', *Russia Beyond the Headlines*, 13 March 2012, http://rbth.com/articles/2012/03/13/satire_against_cynicism_15054.html. For all the *Grazdanin poet* episodes, see http://ongar.ru/grazhdanin-poet

is a matter of obligation, a dictum taken up by official Soviet culture.³¹ Many of the poets subjected to Bykov and Efremov's treatment, from Pushkin to Soviet children's classic Sergei Mikhalkov, were celebrated in Soviet-era literary histories as appropriately civic-minded poets fulfilling their prescribed role of enlightening and guiding their readers. Bykov's own handling of his material suggests a less didactic and more playful stance. Nina Barkovskaya comments on the ambivalent nature of this project, saying:

> Undoubtedly, the aim is to shame those in power. [...] At the same time, the project has been performed publicly in front of a huge audience. Poet and Citizen are just roles here; satire is theatricalised as a show. Make-up, sets, props (the discrepancy with historical realities emphasises the absurdity of what is happening on the stage and created [sic] an effect of defamiliarisation) are important.³²

The selection of poets who feature in *Grazhdanin poet* is unquestionably canonical, perhaps necessarily so, as the effectiveness of the satire depends to a considerable extent on the audience's ability to recognise the poet, and, often, the particular poem which is being parodied. Parody need not be seen as an attack on the work or author selected for imitation; satirical poets often make fun of poems that have genuine artistic merit and are popular among readers. As Linda Hutcheon points out, despite being a threatening and anarchic force 'that puts into question the legitimacy of other texts', parody reinforces existing conventions: 'parody's transgressions ultimately remain authorized [...] by the very norm it seeks to subvert'.³³ *Grazhdanin poet* has a dual focus: contemporary realities are satirised using poetic personas which evoke the culture of the Soviet era, an approach which calls attention to discontinuity and incongruity. Neither the past nor the present is

---

31 'Поэтом можешь ты не быть, / Но гражданином быть обязан' ('You do not have to be a poet, but you are obliged to be a citizen'), Nikolai Nekrasov, 'Poet i grazhdanin', *Izbrannye sochineniia* ((Moscow: OGIZ, 1945; 1st edn 1938), pp. 47–51 (p. 49).
32 Nina Barkovskaya, 'Poet and Citizen: Canon Game in Contemporary Russian Poetry', in *Russian Classical Literature Today: The Challenges/Trials of Messianism and Mass Culture*, edited by Yordan Lyutskanov, Hristo Manolaked and Radostin Rusev (Newcastle upon Tyne: Cambridge Scholars Publishing, 2014), pp. 110–25 (p. 114).
33 Linda Hutcheon, *A Theory of Parody: The Teachings of Twentieth-Century Art Forms* (Urbana and Chicago: University of Illinois Press, 2000), p. 75.

immune from mockery, and so Bykov keeps nostalgia at arms length. Bykov's recourse to the literary canon can be seen as a contrast to the actions of the current leadership, which, as Svitlana Malykhina points out, 'is using everything it can extract from history to boost the country's imperial traditions' and to promote 'a geopolitical strategy that puts Russia in the centre'.[34] One can see *Grazhdanin poet* as an attempt to keep many established Soviet poets, including Esenin, Tvardovskii, Maiakovskii, Evtushenko, and Sergei Mikhalkov in a newly emerging poetic canon which is much more inclusive than the socialist realist canon was.

While *Grazhdanin poet* may cater to the contemporary Russian appetite for nostalgia, it refuses to wallow in uncritical enjoyment of familiar works from the Soviet past. Nina Barkovskaya characterises Bykov's relationship towards the literary canon as 'attraction-repulsion towards the literature of the past'.[35] Bykov's parodic renderings of the Soviet canon may express a certain affection for particular poets and works, but they mock the notion of universal truths and hierarchical orders that are part of the outlook that this body of work represented. Bykov's parodies contain strong post-utopian overtones and the suggestion that official attempts to create new master narratives are based on outdated views and doomed to failure. Bykov's frequent ironic references to the poetry of Maiakovskii and Evtushenko, poets often perceived as advocates of modernisation and the utopian restructuring of Soviet society, provide a playful critique of their views as idealistic and naïve. In drawing attention to his predecessors' shortcomings Bykov does not portray himself as a poet-prophet, assuming instead the role of a poet-critic who playfully reassembles different fragments of the Soviet canon in order to subvert utopian understandings of modernisation and of the idea of progress.

Bykov addresses the demise of the role of the poet-prophet in Russian contemporary culture in his 2011 poem 'Skazka prodolzhaetsia' ('The Fairy Tale Continues').[36] The poem alludes to Maiakovskii's 1929 poem, a classic of Soviet 'production literature', 'Rasskaz Khrenova

---

34 Svitlana Malykhina, *Renaissance of Classical Allusions in Contemporary Russian Media* (Lanham, NY: Lexington Books, 2014), p. 47.
35 Nina Barkovskaya, 'Poet and Citizen', p. 111.
36 https://www.youtube.com/watch?v=f6zxSQny4Bg

o Kuznetskstroe i liudiakh Kuznetska' ('Khrenov's Story about the Construction of Kuznetsk and Its Citizens'). Maiakovskii's poem declares that a new garden city will be constructed in Siberia thanks to the selfless efforts of Soviet workers and engineers to overcome the challenges presented by the climate. As Karen McCauley notes, the authors of production literature saw themselves as engineers whose texts were constructed with the help of aesthetic devices which they used like mechanical tools. They viewed the literary text 'as an object or artefact capable of being dismantled and reproduced independent of the psychology of authorial genius'.[37] Bykov's text 'Skazka prodolzhaetsia' appropriates Maiakovskii's declaration that 'there will be a garden city here in four years', using it as a refrain throughout the whole parody. It also playfully applies Maiakovskii's utopian vision of modernisation to Bykov and his contemporaries who believed in a radical transformation of Russian society in the early 1990s. Bykov takes an ironic view of the idealistic and naïve dreams of a radiant future in Moscow that he and his fellow writers once cherished. Bykov's poem prophesies glumly that in four years time the Russian capital will come to resemble ruins, and advises the reader not to expect help from anyone else in order to secure his own survival: 'Ni goroda, ni sada ne budet nikogda [...] Cherez chetyre goda zdes' budesh' tol'ko ty' ('There will never be any city or any garden. In four years time the only thing here will be you'.)[38]

The *Grazhdanin poet* project expresses the shared experience of a nostalgic longing for the past, combined with a reminder that this past cannot serve as a model for the future. It relies on the capacity of Russian and Soviet poetry as a mnemonic tool which can be used for re-organising individual and collective memories. The project's episodes are readily available to be viewed online. Bykov and Efremov's enterprise contributes, therefore, to the representation of poetry both as a source of memory containing collective and personal knowledge and as a wellspring of nostalgia associated with a repository of cultural myths and emotions.

Although the Silver Age is something few, if any, Russians in the 1990s had personal memories of, it nevertheless occupied a significant

---

37 Karen A. McCauley, 'Production Literature and the Industrial Imagination', *The Slavic and East European Journal*, 42: 3 (Autumn 1998), 444–66 (p. 462).
38 https://www.youtube.com/watch?v=f6zxSQny4Bg

position in the collective memory. There are powerful emotional associations and cultural myths connected with the early decades of the twentieth century, seen by many literary scholars as 'a charmed lost era' marked by a flowering of the arts, and brought to a premature close by the Soviet state's imposition of cultural control.[39] The nostalgic appeal of Russia's rich modernist culture, which developed rapidly in this period, was already evident in Soviet times, when modernist writing was attractive because it offered something very unlike standard socialist realist fare and because of its marginal position. The growth of the cultural underground in the 1970s marked a revival of modernist aesthetic principles that asserted the autonomy of cultural activities from the state. Pre-revolutionary models of small-scale poetry performances, among people who were striving to create a collective identity as devotees to high art and aiming to transcend reality, proved attractive in an era of stagnation, when hopes for far-reaching change that had been kindled by the Thaw were largely extinguished. In the late-Soviet cultural space, non-conformist poetry, represented by such poets of the 1970s and 1980s as Elena Shvarts, Leonid Gubanov and Ol'ga Sedakova, occupied a peripheral position in comparison to the work of popular Thaw-era poets such as Evtushenko: their work can be interpreted as an alternative modernism which was at odds with, and resisted by, official cultural policies.

A defining characteristic of modernism, in Andreas Huyssen's view, was the belief in the transcending powers of art. The late-Soviet underground was able to use its peripheral position outside the official cultural hierarchy to create works of art and literature oriented towards pre-revolutionary modernist culture. The end of the Soviet Union presented new challenges: culture was released from its ideological shackles, but it was faced with the pressures of the marketplace, something that the early twentieth-century modernists had also confronted. Huyssen explains the rise of modernism as a radical response to the division between high culture aimed at the elite, and commercialised culture for the masses: 'Modernism was by and large the attempt to turn the traditional European postulate of high culture against tradition itself and to create a radically new high culture

---

39   Rylkova, *The Archaeology of Anxiety*, p. 3.

that opened up utopian horizons of social and political change'.[40] To create this new high culture 'that would shun the commercialization of capitalism' and appeal to a mass audience, says Huyssen, both modernist and avant-garde artists, such as Bertolt Brecht, Walter Benjamin and Sergei Tret'iakov appropriated and reworked elements drawn both from popular and mass culture.[41] In the Soviet Union this kind of modernist experimentation was short-lived; artists and writers escaped commercial pressures but found themselves subject to the state's requirements for ideologically acceptable literature.

In the early post-Soviet years, figures emerging from the underground found themselves in an environment where they risked being marginalised as representatives of high culture unable or unwilling to respond to new commercial pressures. This state of alienation is captured effectively in Aleksei German Junior's 2005 film *Garpastum*, set at the start of World War One, which represents the growing gap between artist and audience through the figure of leading modernist poet Aleksandr Blok (played by Gosha Kutsenko). Blok is presented as a tragic hero who feels excluded from the society he had hoped to transform. German's image of Blok as a tragic hero alludes also to the anxieties of Russian writers in the 2000s who felt displaced in a new environment driven by commercial success.

Timur Kibirov, a conceptualist poet from Moscow who became popular in the 1990s, expresses just such anxieties in his work of the early post-Soviet years, alongside a certain nostalgia for the lost universe of Soviet popular culture. His early work, such as his 1984 collection *Kogda byl Lenin malen'kim* (*When Lenin Was a Little Boy*), is full of parodic appropriations of clichés found in official Soviet culture. The works of Russian conceptualists, including Kibirov, have been associated with the use of heteroglossia (plural language) which is opposed to a unique poetic language. In the words of Mikhail Aizenberg, 'in conceptualist art it is not the author who is expressing himself in his own language but languages themselves, always someone else's, conversing among

---

40 Andreas Huyssen, 'Geographies of Modernism in a Globalizing World', in *Geographies of Modernism: Literatures, Cultures, Spaces*, edited by Peter Brooker and Andrew Thacker (London and New York: Routledge, 2005), pp. 6–18 (p. 11).
41 *Ibid.*

themselves'.⁴² Sergei Gandlevskii described Kibirov's poetry as 'a priceless encyclopaedia of a dead language', in recognition of the value it would acquire once the 'newspeak' of the Soviet era retreated from living memory.⁴³ Thomas Lahusen's remark that, with the disappearance of the Soviet state, the socialist realist heritage might be seen as a repository of cultural myths which 'truthfully represents the Soviet past' is helpful for understanding contemporary intertextual and parodic poetry.⁴⁴ It would be safe to say that works of Soviet official poetry of the kind that Kibirov drew on are now perceived not only as an embodiment of Soviet everyday life and values, which may provoke nostalgic reactions, but also as containing striking aesthetic features based on an eclectic mixture of various nineteenth- and twentieth-century poetic trends. While socialist realism as a mode of artistic expression is now perceived by contemporary Russian readers as monological and reductive, some features of socialist realist art were successfully appropriated by literary and artistic experiments of the 1990s and 2000s, including the kinship metaphor and the ethics of communal support and shared experience which were adopted by the Mit'ki group; Bykov's project *Grazhdanin poet*, and Kibirov's elegiac 1994 collection of poetry *Santimenty* (*Sentiments*), to name but a few. It could be argued that Kibirov's poetry offers something more than a reference work which preserves the culture of a long-lost civilisation: it gives some insight into the ambivalent relationship the inhabitants of that civilisation had with their culture, and into the painful but necessary process of separation from it. Certainly Kibirov's 1987 long poem 'Skvoz' proshchal'nye slezy' ('Through Tears of Parting'), features multiple ironic allusions to, and quotations from Soviet songs and poems, but also reveals the poet's nostalgic attachment to this already vanishing culture.

Sofya Khagi detects in Kibirov's poetry two competing tendencies: it is oriented on the one hand towards an ironic detachment from the

---

42   Mikhail Aizenberg, 'In Lieu of an Introduction', *Russian Studies in Literature*, 4 (1993), 8–24 (p. 10).
43   Sergei Gandlevskii, 'Sochineniia Timura Kibirova', *Poeticheskaia kukhnia* (St Petersburg: Pushkinskii fond, 1998), pp. 18–22 (p. 22).
44   Thomas Lahusen, 'Socialist Realism in Search of Its Shores: Some Historical Remarks on the "Historically Open Aesthetic System of the Truthful Representation of Life"', in *Socialist Realism Without Shores*, edited by Thomas Lahusen and Evgenii Dobrenko (Durham, NC, and London: Duke University Press, 1997), pp. 5–26 (p. 5).

past, and on the other, towards the desire to convey 'a meaningful sentimental nostalgia experienced by an average post-Soviet citizen'. Khagi concedes that Kibirov's poetry 'has found its niche in modern Russian poetry' because it aspires both 'to repudiate "the other's word"' and 'to dis-alienate the culture of the past'.[45] The ambivalent attitude shown by Kibirov towards Soviet culture and literature is in keeping with the post-Soviet trend towards creating a more inclusive canon of Russian twentieth-century poetry, replacing the binary opposition between official and unofficial poetry with a different, more nuanced vision of the past. Kibirov's treatment of the post-Soviet present is no less ambivalent than his handling of former times. His 1992 poem 'Letnie razmyshleniia o sud'bakh iziashchnoi slovesnosti' ('Summer Reflections on the Fate of Belles Lettres') addressed to Igor' Pomerantsev, a former dissident writer from Ukraine now resident in Prague, offers witty musings on the predicament of the artist in a newly emerged consumer society, a topic Kibirov addresses in other poems of the 1990s.

Khagi's analysis of 'Letnie razmyshleniia' suggests that the setting for the poem, Kibirov's summer cottage in Shil'kovo, should be viewed as the location of the poet's internal exile which empowers him with a sense of moral authority. In the poem the lyric hero uses the device of estrangement in order to voice his criticism of Moscow as the centre of economic reforms. The poet represents authors who, like Kibirov, once belonged to unofficial Soviet culture but are now are excluded from and ridiculed by the new social order; similarly marginalised are nineteenth-century ideals of freedom and artistic harmony. The poet's longing to acquire symbolic power is entwined in his poetry with an ironic depiction of cultural and ideological changes, yet it is not satire that enables him to overcome his sense of displacement, but the recourse to the early nineteenth-century genre known as the friendly epistle. This was usually a friendly letter in verse written to a fellow poet, often seen as a hybrid form of the prose letter and the elegy. One of the most popular Golden Age genres, it promoted the cult of friendship and was associated with the development of dialogic devices and the

---

45 Sofya Khagi, 'Art as Aping: The Uses of Dialogism in Timur Kibirov's "To Igor" Pomerantsev. Summer Reflections on the Fate of Belles Lettres', *The Russian Review*, 4 (2002), 579–98 (p. 592).

incorporation of prosaic elements into poetic language.⁴⁶ Kibirov's epistle evokes Pushkin's conversational style of the 1820s and promotes a spirit of unity with other poets who, like the author himself, wish to depart from the imitation of popular styles and genres that seems to have become a requirement for success in the new cultural marketplace.

By situating himself on the geographical periphery, on the margins of contemporary society, and by adopting a peripheral and temporally distant genre through which to address the problems of the present day, Kibirov points to the potential value of re-imagining the relationship between what is considered central and peripheral. His poem, cast as a private letter to a friend, becomes a marker of friendliness not only to the addressee but also to the world at large. It contributes to a strand of Russian cultural discourse over the last three decades or so which relates to questions of identity and imagined geographies, explored in Edith Clowes's recent study *Russia on the Edge*. Clowes concludes that Russian intellectuals' current discourse about peripheries was developed as early as the 1970s with a view to rethinking the geopolitical *realia* of the Soviet empire and challenging Moscow's self-justifications as the centre of that empire.⁴⁷ Clowes aptly acknowledges that the crisis of identity experienced by Moscow in the early 1990s is rooted in late Soviet culture when the 'conceptual oppositions of centre and periphery' became popular among Russian intellectuals and artists who eagerly constructed imagined geographies in which Moscow featured as an insignificant 'hinterland' of other, stronger empires.⁴⁸ In late Soviet unofficial poetry and in early post-Soviet poetry this tendency manifested itself both in the revival of neo-classical themes (found, for example, in the works of Brodskii, Shvarts, and Sedakova) and in the appropriation of oriental

---

46   The term 'Golden Age' is usually applied to Russian poetry and fiction of the 1800s to the 1830s but many scholars extend the usage of this term to Russian novels published in the 1840s to the 1880s. See, for example, the description of Russian nineteenth-century canonical works as 'the "Golden Era" of the 19th century', in Jonathan Stone, *Historical Dictionary of Russian Literature* (Lanham, Toronto, Plymouth: The Scarecrow Press, 2013), p. ix. Ivar Spector also suggests that it is customary to speak of the nineteenth century either as the classical or the golden age of Russian literature. See Ivar Spector, *The Golden Age of Russian Literature* (New York: Scholastic Press), 1939, p. 11.

47   Edith W. Clowes, *Russia on the Edge: Imagined Geographies and Post-Soviet Identity* (Ithaca and London: Cornell University Press, 2011), pp. 7–9, p. 171.

48   *Ibid.*, p. 12.

and Eurasian themes shaped by the legacy of Russian romanticism and modernism (a trend evident in the works of Bella Akhmadulina, Bulat Okudzhava, Gennadii Aigi, Inna Lisnianskaia, and Russian song writer and performer Boris Grebenshchikov). Such alternative aesthetic trends developed in late Soviet culture almost simultaneously, coinciding with the emergence of conceptualism and the revival of lyric poetry which became increasingly oriented towards the use of intertextuality and palimpsest, as well as parodic and metaphysical overtones. Perhaps it was due to their peripheral position in relation to Soviet mainstream literature that unofficial Soviet poets felt a need to find their ideal interlocutors not in contemporary society but in the past. Their engagement with modernist poets who were victimised and destroyed by the Communist regime — such as Tsvetaeva, Akhmatova, Nikolai Zabolotskii, Kharms, and Mandel'shtam — also provided them with a sense of moral authority and empowered them as witnesses to the truth about Russian historical developments.

As the Soviet official canon, and its underground counterpart, were made redundant by the end of the Soviet era, it was inevitable that the process of creating a new canon would involve looking backwards to discover what might be appealing to readers in the new Russian Federation, and might provide some sense of cultural continuity in the face of sudden and far-reaching change. Paradoxically, perhaps, nostalgia was evoked both by the poetry of modernism which had been suppressed by the Soviet state, and by the poetry which the same state had then enlisted for its own purposes. The coexistence of these strands of twentieth-century Russian poetry in the emerging canon demonstrates the profound ambivalence with which the changes of the 1990s were greeted.

Beyond Russian Formalism: The Poetry Canon in the Context of Changes to the Canon of Literary Criticism and Theory

In her Introduction to *Rereading Russian Poetry*, Stephanie Sandler praises the efforts of the editors of the journal *Novoe literaturnoe obozrenie* (*New Literary Review*), which began publication in 1992, for their promotion of new approaches to Russian culture. She recognizes the valuable work the journal had done in making available to Russian readers many previously unknown texts and memoir accounts by Russian and Western authors, as well as the writings of Western critics whose works had been ignored in Soviet times, including Jacques Derrida, Roland Barthes and Gilles Deleuze. Sandler comments that the journal 'made even methodologically conservative publications significant and exciting by the choice of the subject matter, for example, publications about Kuzmin, clustered accounts of Petersburg and Moscow avant-garde poets, and essays on contemporary poetry'.[49] Sandler readily acknowledges the influential work carried out by literary scholars based in the Soviet Union, such as those associated either with the Tartu or Moscow groups of semioticians, including Roman Timenchik, Vladimir Toporov and Tamara Tsivian, who pursued subtext-based work on Acmeism and had 'a powerful effect on the canon of twentieth-century Russian poetry'.[50] In Sandler's view, not only did they succeed in bringing the poetry of Akhmatova and Mandel'shtam to the attention of readers and scholars with the help of subtext theory, they also provided the tools for understanding 'the apparently obscure verse of Mandel'shtam and the later Akhmatova'.[51] While she praises the impact of these scholars' subtext theory outside Russia, Sandler nevertheless identifies an enduring division among literary scholars based inside Russia, separating semioticians, structuralists and poststructuralists, as well as historically and textually based scholars. This forms a striking contrast with the kind of training received by Western interpreters of Russian poetry, which takes in both formal and historical methods, allowing researchers to blend 'interpretative argument with careful contextualization in biography, culture and history'.[52]

During a large part of the Soviet era the literary academy was unable to access or to apply the legacy of Russian formalist thinking that had made a considerable impact in the 1920s. Starting in the 1930s the

---

49 Stephanie Sandler, 'Introduction: Myths and Paradoxes of the Russian Poet', in *Rereading Russian Poetry*, edited by Stephanie Sandler (New Haven and London: Yale University Press, 1999), pp. 1–28 (p. 16).
50 Ibid., p. 13.
51 Ibid.
52 Ibid., p. 14.

works of the Russian formalists were no longer systematically studied and were not widely available even to specialist readers. When, in the post-Stalin period, scholars interested in formalism or structuralism began to publish, their work appeared in highly specialised journals or collections of articles published in Estonia, Latvia, or Moscow, rather than in journals or collections aimed at a broader readership.[53] It is important to remember in this context that scholars in the West had access to formalist works which were not available to their Soviet counterparts. Foreign scholars' rediscovery of Russian modernist poets whose works were suppressed in the Soviet Union was prompted in part by the publication of formalist works in which quotations from Russian poetry of the 1900s to the 1920s were often to be found, as well as by émigré memoirs and essays on Russian modernism.

Although a serious examination of the legacy of Russian formalism was under way in the West as early as the 1950s, the integration of its main ideas into western scholarship was rather slow. In a 1954 article Victor Erlich states: 'The linguistic barriers, as well as the cultural isolation of the Soviet Union, prevented the bulk of Western literary scholars from taking cognizance of the achievement of the Russian formalist School, indeed of its very existence'.[54] Curiously, as Erlich's article suggests, although Russian formalism was often seen as 'a specifically Russian phenomenon', 'a reaction against symbolist metaphysics', and 'a mouthpiece of the Futurist movement', some scholars viewed it as 'a body of critical thought' inseparable from the global trend of the re-examination of methods of literary study especially evident in European literary criticism.[55] Erlich says that the formalist, while fighting local battles with critics and educationalists, was unaware that he 'found himself asking the same questions and giving practically the same answers as did some of his *confrères* in Germany, France, England, and the United States'.[56] Erlich's list of similarities between the formalist

---

53   Uil'iam Mills Todd III [William Mills Todd III], 'Otkrytiia i proryvy sovetskoi teorii literatury v poslestalinskuiu epokhu', in *Istoriia russkoi literaturnoi kritiki*, edited by Evgenii Dobrenko and Galin Tikhanov (Moscow: Novoe literaturnoe obozrenie, 2011), pp. 571–607 (pp. 579–83).
54   Victor Erlich, 'Russian Formalism: In Perspective', *Journal of Aesthetics and Art Criticism*, 2 (December 1954), 215–25 (p. 215).
55   Ibid.
56   Ibid.

School and the Anglo-American 'new criticism' is compelling. He also asserts that 'the emphasis on the organic unity of work of literature', advocated by both approaches, can be described as 'organistic'[57] because critics of both schools viewed literature as a linguistic system of devices that evolved in accordance with its own set of rules. In the wake of the collapse of the Soviet Union, it became clear that many insights of the Russian formalists had outlived totalitarian cultural policies and found their way into Russian poetic practices and theoretical approaches during the late-Soviet and post-Soviet periods.

The full rediscovery of the formalist legacy in Russia took place only in the post-Soviet period thanks to the efforts of such journals and publishing houses as *Novoe literaturnoe obozrenie*, *Znamia* (*The Banner*), *Iazyki russkoi kul'tury* (*Languages of Russian Culture*), and *Kriticheskaia massa* (*Critical Mass*).[58] The disrupted reception of formalist scholarship left its mark on twentieth-century Russian literary studies. William Mills Todd III points out that many important tenets of Russian formalist theory were largely suppressed due to the severe censorship of, and ideological pressures on, Soviet critics in the 1930s to the 1950s. Although Todd does mention the rediscovery of Russian formalism during the post-Stalin period, he states that its reception in the remaining Soviet period was patchy and idiosyncratic: while Boris Eikhenbaum's 1929 book *Moi vremennik* (*My Chronicle*) was republished only in 2001, his 1923 essay 'Melodika russkogo liricheskogo stikha' ('The Melody of Russian Lyric Verse') was published in a collection of his articles in 1969.[59] According to Todd, the publication of the proceedings of the Tynianov conferences organised in the early 1980s by Aleksandr Chudakov and Marietta Chudakova triggered an interest in Tynianov and his contemporaries. Yet the circle of scholars from Latvia, Estonia and Russia who contributed to these conferences did not occupy a position at the centre of the Soviet establishment; the conferences took

---

57   *Ibid.*, p. 217.
58   Among the most important monographs the following are especially worthy of mention: Oge Khanzen-Lieve, *Russkii formalizm: metodologicheskaia rekonstruktsiia razvittiia na osnove printsipa ostraneniia* (Moscow: Iazyki russkoi kul'tury, 2001); I. Iu. Svetlikova, *Istoki russkogo formalizma: traditsiia psikhologizma i formal'naia shkola* (Moscow: Novoe literaturnoe obozrenie, 2005); Katrin Depretto, *Formalizm v Rossii: predshestvenniki, istoriia, kontekst* (Moscow: Novoe literaturnoe obozrenie, 2015).
59   Todd, 'Otkrytiia i proryvy sovetskoi teorii literatury v poslestalinskuiu epokhu', pp. 571–607, p. 579.

place in Latvia, a peripheral location. Although these scholars may have occupied a marginal position in the Soviet academy, they should not be seen, Todd suggests, as being completely separate from the established field of Russian literary studies: they succeeded in 'constructing a semiotic version of the traditional heroic description of Russian authors' and in promoting many traditional values of high culture.[60]

The study of poetry in Russia usually tends to oscillate between two poles: the aesthetic and the sociological. The formalists are well known for their significant contribution to the study of structural features and aesthetic functions of devices used in Russian verse. The range of issues explored in their works include rhythmical impulse and rhythmical-syntactic word combination (explored by Osip Brik); the role of intonation in the lyric (studied by Boris Eikhenbaum); rhythmically organised speech and changes in the metrical system (analysed by Boris Tomashevskii), and the peculiarities of poetic speech and poetic genres (examined by Iurii Tynianov).[61] According to Roman Jakobson, who believed that 'poetry is language in its aesthetic function', in any poem, 'different levels blend, complement each other or combine to give the poem the value of an absolute object'.[62] Arguably, the renewed post-Soviet reception of Russian formalist thought has promoted the emergence of a new artistic sensibility oriented towards the complexity of poetic language and an appreciation of the experimental aspects of pastiche. It has also prepared the Russian reader for a considerable re-evaluation of Russian modernist poetry of the early twentieth century, including émigré writing, as well as of the neo-avant-garde poetry of the 1960s to the 1980s. The belated re-acquaintance with formalist thinking marked a complete departure from the socialist realist aesthetic which had produced no adequate theoretical tools for the analysis of texts that deviated from its norms. Such criteria as mass accessibility, an ideologically driven belief in a radiant future, and simplicity, were at

---

60 *Ibid.*, p. 584.
61 O. M. Brik, 'Ritm and sintaksis (Materialy k izucheniiu stikhotvornoi rechi)', *Novyi LEF*, 3 (1927), 15–20; 4 (1927), 23–29; 5 (1927), 32–37; 6 (1927), 33–39; B. M. Eikhenbaum, *O poezii* (Leningrad: Sovetskii pisatel', 1969); Boris Tomashevskii, *O stikhe* (Leningrad: Priboi, 1929); Iurii Tynianov, *Arkhaisty i novatory* (Leningrad: Priboi, 1929).
62 Quoted in Clare Cavanagh, *Lyric Poetry and Modern Politics: Russia, Poland, and the West* (New Haven and London: Yale University Press, 2009), p. 9.

the core of socialist realist dogma. As Evgeny Dobrenko points out, the aesthetic agenda of socialist realism 'boiled down to the defeat of modernism' and its utopian character manifested itself in the desire to jump out of history 'by creating a premodernist aesthetic'.[63]

Dobrenko's comment about the suppression of the modernist tradition during the Soviet period can be supported by a few examples that highlight the negative attitude towards modernist lyric poetry, associated by Soviet critics with individualism and stylistic complexity. As early as 1920, Maksim Gor'kii, one of the main precursors of socialist realism, attempted to canonise the notion of simplicity and artlessness of poetry in his reminiscences about Lev Tolstoi. According to Gor'kii, Tolstoi was critical of Konstantin Bal'mont's poems: he defined them as 'charlatanism', 'rubbish', 'a nonsensical string of words', and went on to say that new poets are 'inventing' rather than writing poems 'straight from the soul' in the style of Afanasii Fet who 'expressed a genuine, real, people's sense of poetry'.[64] It is clear that, in his memoirs, Gor'kii uses the authority of Tolstoi in order to promote his own vision of Soviet literature as something rooted in a premodernist aesthetic.

In his 1935 survey of Soviet poetry, Andrew Steiger puts forward the widespread view that he encountered in the Soviet Union: the role of poetry should be primarily educational, it should embody the spirit of national life and make the wealth of Russian folklore accessible to a wider public. Steiger writes:

> The new Soviet poetry roots in the life of the people. A dynamic exchange of harmonic poetic verse is heard. Primitive illiterate bards come from remote regions to recite unwritten songs in the enlightened capital. Cultured modern poets send their voices pulsating on radio waves to the farthest corners of the land. Poetry is written to be heard and is heard even before it is read and the reading public of the Soviet poet is like an ocean compared to the inland sea of the revolutionary days.[65]

---

63 Evgeny Dobrenko, *The Making of the State Writer: Social and Aesthetic Origin of Soviet Literary Culture*, translated by Jesse M. Savage (Stanford: Stanford University Press, 2001), p. xv.
64 Maxim Gorky, *Reminiscences of Lev Nikolayevich Tolstoy*, translated by S. S. Koteliansky and Leonard Woolf (New York: B. W. Huebsch Inc., 1920), p. 8.
65 Andrew J. Steiger, 'Soviet Poetry-Dynamized Incarnate Sound', *Books Abroad*, 3 (1935), 247–50 (p. 249).

As can be inferred from Steiger's article, the Soviet poet was expected to be a spokesman of his nation and a platform orator who contributed to the popularisation of poetry through public performances and radio broadcasts. Unlike the former minstrel or folk bard, asserts Steiger, the Soviet poet 'uses the rich heritage of Russian classical poetry to make his spoken verse more varied in style, more cultured in content, more moving in effect'.[66] In the 1930s, this orientation towards a mass audience went hand in hand with the tendency to produce depersonalised lyric verse and songs which created the impression of shared collective experiences and thereby limited the expression of erotic emotions, individual experiences of love, and a subjectivised vision of the self.[67] Sandler rightly identifies a strong trend in the 1930s to the 1950s to promote narrative poetry that would 'pursue plots of successful integration into the new socialist order' and suggests that 'the requirements for lyric poetry were hotly debated'.[68] The principal task of Soviet poetry was to help readers develop their own identity as Soviet citizens. Aesthetic considerations were secondary, yet this does not mean that the poetry that was written to fulfil this task was necessarily lacking aesthetic merit, a fact recognised by Stephanie Sandler, who says: 'Poets who participated in tasks of identity formation for the new citizen produced poems in praise of Stalin and odes extolling the heroic Soviet people during World War Two. These poets were in many cases as sincere as marginalized poets, and the quality was not always inferior'.[69]

The emphasis placed by the Soviet state on the importance of collective values and contemporary themes in literature did not wither away after the death of Stalin, or even after the vigorous discussions on lyric poetry which took place at the 1954 Writers' Union Congress. A resolution of the Central Committee of the Communist Party of the Soviet Union, published in 1959, declares:

---

66 Ibid.
67 Irina G. Tazhidinova, '"Declaration of Emotional Independence" in Soviet Poetry in the 1930s: A Historical-Sociological Analysis', *History and Historians in the Context of the Time*, 12: 1 (2014), 48–54, http://oaji.net/articles/2014/5-1413287078.pdf
68 Stephanie Sandler, 'Poetry after 1930', in *The Cambridge Companion to Twentieth-Century Russian Literature*, edited by Evgeny Dobrenko and Marina Balina (Cambridge: Cambridge University Press, 2011), pp. 115–34 (p. 116).
69 Ibid., p. 115.

> The high calling of Soviet writers is to unfold truthfully and imaginatively the beauty of the heroic toil of the people, the grandeur and majesty of the struggle for Communism, to be impassionate propagandists of the Seven Year Plan, to uproot the survivals of capitalism in the consciousness of the people, to assist in removing all that still hinders our movement forward.[70]

Not all Soviet writers were enthused by the optimistic tone of this resolution, and questioned the validity of the notions that writers should 'varnish' reality and peddle artificial optimism. In an article published in *Literaturnaia gazeta* (*Literary Gazette*) in May 1959, Konstantin Paustovskii, a talented post-war writer, courageously attacked the 'burdensome tradition' of having to avoid writing about the shortcomings of Soviet life and the necessity 'to demonstrate to every Soviet reader the superiority of our system over the capitalist'. He also pointed out that the unwillingness to write about suffering due to 'the fear of a mere hint of sadness' constitutes 'another harmful tradition' because it suggests that the entirety of Soviet life takes place beneath 'azure skies, to the accompaniment of the strong and optimistic laughter of "active" men and women'.[71]

The discussions of the 1950s about the main tenets of socialist realism and their applicability to post-Stalin literary production attracted the attention of many poets, too. Nikolai Aseev urged publishers to produce small editions of poetry (a print run of between 500 and 1000 copies); Il'ia Sel'vinskii accused Soviet critics of favouring only Mikhail Isakovskii's patriotic song-like poetry, Tvardovskii's poems with their folksy style, and Aleksei Surkov's poetry, which was conservative in form and full of clichés. Sel'vinskii thought that Soviet critics should promote diversity and recognise the right of poets to produce experimental and difficult poetry as opposed to accessible and highly simplified verse. Semen Kirsanov also voiced his concerns about the long-standing habit of Soviet critics to label as 'naturalists' or 'formalists' any poets who wanted to use 'in addition to grey, the other colours of the spectrum'.[72]

---

70 *Pravda*, 23 May 1959. Quoted in English in Maurice Friedberg, 'Socialist Realism: Twenty-Five Years Later', *The American Slavic and East European Review*, 2 (1960), 276–87 (p. 281).
71 *Literaturnaia gazeta*, 20 May 1954, p. 4. Quoted in English in Friedberg, 'Socialist Realism', p. 283.
72 Quoted in *ibid*.

As a result of such debates, as Emily Lygo demonstrates in her book on Leningrad poetry of the Thaw period, many liberal writers of the time contributed to the restoration of lyric poetry to the Soviet canon. 'The fashion for poetry', writes Lygo, 'was not only a response of young people to the Thaw [...], [it] was also cultivated by the authorities: in the early 1950s, the Kremlin issued instructions to all local branches of the Writers' Union to improve the state of Soviet poetry, which was deemed to have fallen behind other genres in its development'.[73] The Soviet government's imperative to enable lyric poetry to develop in the 1950s created several opportunities for young people to get their work published in various journals, including the periodical *Iunost'* (*Youth*), to enrol in the creative writing courses offered by the Gor'kii Literary Institute in Moscow, and to become members of literary associations supported by local branches of the Union of Writers in many cities. At the same time, underground and alternative groups of poets emerged in Moscow and in Leningrad too.[74]

Undoubtedly, the cultural policies of the post-Stalin Thaw created a favourable environment in which the socialist realist approach to poetry could challenged by poet-performers such as Evtushenko and Voznesenskii, whose stadium recitals attracted mass audiences in the 1960s. Their performances may be seen as an attempt to create a kind of mass culture that offered an alternative to mainstream Soviet culture. Their recitals of poetry formed an intense emotional and intimate bond between the reader and the poet. It was very different from the rigid and highly controlled relationship between the mass reader and the Soviet poet that existed before the Thaw. A different alternative model was developed by poets such as Shvarts who, in the 1970s, 'created a lively poetic underground' in which authors turned away from the broader public in order to focus their attention towards 'each other's small audiences' and circulate their works in a '*samizdat*-like atmosphere'.[75]

While poets were, in different ways and to a greater or lesser degree, distancing themselves from socialist realism, pioneering scholars and

---

73 Emily Lygo, *Leningrad Poetry 1953–1975: The Thaw Generation* (Oxford: Peter Lang, 2010), p. 3.
74 *Ibid.*, p. 7.
75 Sandler, 'Poetry after 1930', p. 117.

critics were starting to formulate new approaches to literary texts, with the aim of overcoming the socialist realist orientation towards the production of accessible mass literature and seeking a more nuanced interpretation of modernist writing. It is an aim exemplified by the efforts of Soviet critic Aleksandr Dymshits to publish a collection of Mandel'shtam's poetry as part of the series *Biblioteka poeta* (*The Poet's Library*). It took him more than ten years to do so because many established poets, censors and officials were opposed to such a publication. As Tvardovskii noted in 1961, it might be useful to publish Mandel'shtam's poetry in the Soviet Union but not as part of such a prestigious series. Tvardovskii's reservations were rooted in his anxiety about whether Mandel'shtam's lyric poetry, with its highly subjectivised poetic persona, was suitable for the Soviet mass reader. Not only did Tvardovskii define Mandel'shtam's poetry as being too narrow (describing it as 'chamber poetry' ('kamernaia poeziia')) but he also characterised its author as being mentally ill.[76] The volume that eventually appeared thanks to Dymshits's persistence brought at least a selection of Mandel'shtam's poems back into the accessible canon, helping to fill a gap which had lasted for decades.

The example of the profound difference of opinion over publishing Mandel'shtam's poetry indicates the complexity of cultural developments in Russia during the 1950s and 1960s. Many liberally minded writers and poets were unwilling to consider a departure from socialist realism. Literary critic Andrei Siniavskii, on the other hand, advocated a turn to the grotesque as an appropriate mode for new art in the post-Stalin period in his seminal 1957 study *Chto takoe sotsialisticheskii realizm* (*What Is Socialist Realism*) available only in *samizdat* and *tamizdat* forms under the pseudonym Abram Terts until the late 1980s. Siniavskii proclaimed Soviet literature of the 1950s to be a peculiar hybrid of different styles: neither classical, nor realistic. In an ironic way, he defined it as a 'half-classical half-art of not very socialist definitely not realism'.[77] According to Mikhail Epstein, Siniavskii's reinterpretation of socialist realism

---

76 Viacheslav Ogryzko, '"Vosslavim, bratsy, sumerki svobody", ili kak dogmatik Aleksandr Dymshits dobil partiinye vlasti i vypustil v "Biblioteke poeta" tomik poluzapreshchennogo Osipa Mandel'shtama', *Literaturnaia Rossiia*, 11 March 2016, http://litrossia.ru/item/8721-vosslavim-brattsy-sumerki-svobody

77 Abram Terts, *Chto takoe sotsialisticheskii realizm* (Paris: Syntaxis, 1988), p. 60.

created a playful distance from the ideological content of its products and laid the foundation for the emergence of Russian Sots Art and conceptualism in the 1970s and 1980s.[78] The artists linked to those movements became interested in the appropriation of the signs and images of socialist realism for use in a new socio-political context. As Epstein noted, Siniavskii

> is not only sensitive enough to grasp the inherently parodic element in socialist realism, but he goes so far as to advise the self-conscious exploitation of parody as an enhancement of Soviet heroic art. He regrets that the eclectic mixture of realism and classicism that was officially promoted from the 1930s through the 1950s lacks the genuinely phantasmagoric proportions capable of transforming dull, didactic imitations of life into inspirational imitations of didacticism and teleology itself.[79]

Epstein does not mention, however, that most of the examples of Russian poetry used in Siniavskii's treatise *Chto takoe sotsialisticheskii realizm* were drawn not from Socialist realist classics, but from the verse of Pasternak and Maiakovskii, poets who were also at the centre of attention of the Russian formalists' analysis of poetic form. Like the formalists, Siniavskii was interested in the Russian futurists, including Maiakovskii and early Pasternak, because they, like the Acmeists, were preoccupied with the concept of poetry as a craft. The cult of craftsmanship among futurists, as Kristina Pomorska reminds us, enabled them to sweep away the symbolist notion of poetry 'as ridiculous mysticism'.[80]

One scholar with strong connections to the formalist tradition who played a significant role in training new generations of critics and poets was Lidiia Ginzburg, the author of the 1964 book *O lirike* (*On Lyric Poetry*)

---

78   As Konstantin Kustanovich explains, the term 'Sots Art' was coined in 1972 by the unofficial Russian artists Vitalii Komar and Aleksandr Melamid. They used it to define their own mode of artistic expression. Subsequently the term was used to describe Soviet unofficial visual artefacts and literary texts produced in 1972–1985 that aspired to deconstruct totalitarian language and to subvert the style of socialist realism with the help of irony and parody. See Konstantin Kustanovich, 'The Unbearable Lightness of Being the Other: Myth and Nostalgia in Sots Art', *Slavonica*, 9: 1 (2003), 3–18 (p. 3).

79   Mikhail Epstein, 'The Philosophical Implications of Russian Conceptualism', *Journal of Eurasian Studies*, 1 (2010), 64–71 (p. 67).

80   Krystyna Pomorska, *Russian Formalist Theory and Its Poetic Ambiance* (The Hague: Mouton, 1968), p. 92.

which focused, in the style of her mentor Tynianov, on the historical development of literary modes and styles. As Richard Gustafson rightly notes, it would be wrong to see Ginzburg as a living embodiment of Russian formalist theory. Gustafson asserts that Ginzburg 'transcended formalism', known for its striking grounding in linguistics, because she was not interested in writing 'a summa of devices'. For Gustafson, Ginzburg was a humanist 'trained in the school of close analysis'. According to Gustafson, Ginzburg, while basing her study on a theory of contextuality, locates her 'concern for human values' 'at the centre of her work and of her theory of the lyric'.[81] Her theory of contextuality suggests that the poetic word depends heavily on the context in which it is perceived. She writes:

> Outside of a dictionary a word lives in a context; it is defined by the context. The fate of the poetic word, furthermore, depends especially strongly on the context. The context narrows the word, displaces it, dynamizing some of its meanings to the detriment of others. At the same time, however, the context expands the word, grafting onto it various layers of associations. Poetic context is a loose concept. It goes from the sentence to the immediately given rhythmic and syntactical unit, to the poem itself, to the cycle of poems, to the oeuvre of the writer and finally to the literary movements and styles of the time. One or other of these contexts dominates in different periods or in different individual systems.[82]

In her book on the lyric Ginzburg considered the work of both nineteenth- and twentieth-century poets. The list of poets she discussed includes Pushkin, Mikhail Lermontov, Fet, Fedor Tiutchev, Blok, Maiakovskii, Annenskii, Pasternak, Valeri Briusov, Blok, Vladimir Solov'ev, Fedor Sologub, and Andrei Belyi. Together with Zara Mints, whose contribution is discussed below, Lotman, Siniavskii and Dymshits, Ginzburg should be remembered today as one of the critics who aspired to broaden the Russian poetic canon by breaking the mould of socialist realist dogma.

---

81 Richard F. Gustafson, 'Ginzburg's Theory of the Lyric', *Canadian-American Slavic Studies*, 2 (1985), 135–39 (p. 136).
82 Lidiia Ginzburg, *O lirike* (Leningrad: Sovetskii pisatel', 1964), p. 270. Quoted in English in Gustafson, 'Ginzburg's Theory of the Lyric', p. 136.

The Tynianov conferences held between 1982 and 2012 provided a platform for developing new approaches to the study of Russian modernism, including poetry. Many innovative perspectives on the study of Blok in the context of Russian symbolist culture were incorporated into a series of publications known as the Blok volumes, founded by University of Tartu professor Zara Grigor'evna Mints in 1964. Articles in these volumes explored semiotic, formalist and intertextual approaches to literature. In contrast to the Tartu scholars who worked on Blok and his contemporaries in a contextualised manner, many established Soviet scholars had created their own image of Blok, moulding him into a precursor of socialist realism. As Aleksandr Lavrov puts it, in the 1960s Soviet scholars saw Blok not as a real person but as a hero who spent his life fighting the decadents and symbolists. In their eyes, Blok was a subversive poet, 'who did not live, did not create, but carried out his "heroic feat", struggling against decadence, symbolism, religious obscurantism, while soaring like a heavenly bird above his worthless fellow-countrymen and contemporaries'.[83]

Towards the end of her life, Mints, the founder of the series of Blok volumes, having achieved recognition as one of the leading experts on Russian symbolism, developed a strong interest in the poetry that had been suppressed by Soviet officials, reinforcing thereby her political commitment to the recovery of authors and works from the Soviet literary periphery. For example, in the 1988 Blok volume she published an article by B. V. Pliukhanov about Elizaveta Kuz'mina-Karavaeva (known usually as Mat' Mariia), an important Russian émigré poet, playwright and religious thinker who, early in her career was associated with the Russian symbolist movement. In 1990, shortly before her death, Mints wrote an article about Iurii Gal', an unknown poet who died young in one of the Gulag camps, but whose manuscripts were preserved by his relatives. In addition to publishing her article about Gal', Mints suggested organising a panel on the legacy of Russian symbolism and Soviet Gulag poetry for a conference planned in Tartu in 1991.[84]

---

83   A. V. Lavrov, 'Neskol'ko slov o Zare Grigor'evne Mints, redaktore i vdokhnovitele taruskikh "Blokovskikh sbornikov"', *Blokovskii sbornik*, 12 (1993), 6–10 (pp. 7–8).
84   Ibid., p. 10.

Both Mints and Lotman (her husband) are well known in Russia and abroad as founders of the Tartu School of Semiotics which included a circle of scholars active in the 1960s to the 1980s whose approach was consciously non-Marxist. As Maxim Koupovykh points out, Soviet structuralists and semioticians went against the grain of Soviet Marxist humanities:

> [they] were criticised not so much for their non-Marxism as for challenging established disciplinary borderlines, as well as a web of Romantic and Realist assumptions in the foundation of both Russian and Soviet 'Marxist' humanities: the work of art is a unique image, or even a 'reflection', of reality in its 'typical features', created by the unique artistic genius, who, like Hegelian 'great personality', is granted with the ability to sense the *Zeitgeist* and express it by means of his unique mastership (*masterstvo*).[85]

These critics' willingness to venture beyond officially sanctioned ways of thinking helped to make room for models of literary evolution which view the canon in more flexible terms. The understanding of canon that dominated in Russia during the nineteenth and twentieth centuries was informed by Romantic notions of the unique artistic genius and of literature as an expression of the spirit of a given nation. The canon, therefore, tended to be constructed as a linear, teleological demonstration of how the way was prepared for the advent of writers of genius who would express the national spirit most fully. Formalist critic Viktor Shklovskii's vision of cultural evolution focused not on authors or nations, but on the dynamics at work in the realm of literary form. Shklovskii's vision of art was influenced by the eminent Russian nineteenth-century scholar Aleksandr Veselovskii (1838–1906) who, as Richard Sheldon observes, 'demonstrated the possibility of studying literature as a construct of discrete verbal norms'. Veselovskii, along with his brother Aleksei, believed that European literature had evolved in part through the adoption of literary devices and genres imported from the Orient or from folk ritual.[86] While Veselovskii envisaged this

---

[85] Maxim Koupovykh, *The Soviet Empire of Signs: A Social and Intellectual History of the Tartu School of Semiotics* (unpublished doctoral thesis, University of Illinois at Urbana-Champaign, 2005), p. 53.

[86] Richard Robert Sheldon, 'Viktor Borisovich Shklovsky: Literary Theory and Practice, 1914–1930' (unpublished doctoral thesis, University of Michigan, 1966), p. 2.

process as gradual and continuous, Shklovskii's view was that literary evolution was a dialectical process driven by distinct shifts, a notion that may have laid the foundation for Lotman's idea of explosions as part of evolutionary cultural processes. Shklovskii appropriated Broder Christiansen's concept of the quality of divergence triggered by a deviation from the usual, 'from some sort of operative canon' ('canon' used here in the sense of a set of norms of style and form, rather than exemplary texts) and resulting in 'an emotional impression of special quality' which is inaccessible to sensory perception.[87] It was Shklovskii's view that new forms arise from unnoticed and unrefined forms that are already in existence on the cultural margins. The suggestion that literary evolution might develop in eccentric and non-linear ways creates the possibility that arbitrary changes could become influential in the construction of a literary canon and that works, authors, and approaches considered as peripheral might in due course play a significant role in bringing about cultural change.

When canon formation is not restricted to a small number of officials and state-controlled bodies, as it was in the Soviet Union, the actions that contribute to a poet's canonisation are distributed among a variety of agents, including critics, scholars, and editors, who present and explain his or her work to readers. Bearing in mind the complexity of any literary text, Rachel Schmidt argues that canonising authorities often rely on critical annotations, visual images, and other devices that enable the reader to interpret a given work as suitable for inclusion in the canon as a classic text.[88] Schmidt sees an important role for commentary that accompanies a text and shows how it meets the criteria of the canonising authority. Many post-Soviet anthologies and recently published volumes of the prestigious series *Biblioteka poeta*, as well as post-Soviet biographies of Russian twentieth-century dissident and émigré poets including Tsvetaeva, Brodskii, and Georgii Ivanov, have provided extensive commentaries on previously marginalised poets and contributed to their canonisation. The role of visual culture in the process of canonisation is also immense. Internet sites such as RuTube, Vimeo and YouTube enabled post-Soviet subjects in Russia

---

87 *Ibid.*, p. 141.
88 Rachel Schmidt, *Critical Images: The Canonization of Don Quixote through Illustrated Editions of the 18th Century* (Montreal: McGill-Queen's University Press, 1999), p. 22.

and outside Russia to watch documentaries and films produced in the 1990s–2000s: these films deal with the lives and works of prominent Russian twentieth-century poets, especially those who, like Akhmatova, Mandel'shtam and Tsvetaeva, are interpreted in the Russian popular imagination as martyrs of the Soviet regime.

In the case of late-twentieth-century Russia, previously marginalised or peripheral spaces such as underground culture, émigré literature and semi-official cultural landscapes both in Moscow and the provinces were already becoming more visible as coexisting traditions with the help of Evtushenko's landmark 1994 anthology of Russian poetry *Strofy veka* (*Stanzas of the Century*), initially serialised in the popular weekly periodical *Ogonek* (*The Little Light*).[89] An examination of the various coexisting traditions of Russian poetry was also undertaken by numerous documentaries about Russian modernist poets and post-war poets and by internet sites such as *Vavilon* (*Babylon*), *Samizdat veka* (*The Century's Self-Publishing*), *Neofitsial'naia poeziia* (*Unofficial Poetry*), *Russkaia poeziia 1960kh gg.* (*Russian Poetry of the 1960s*); theatrical productions about the lives of twentieth-century Russian poets, and anthologies dedicated to poetry of the Silver Age also contributed to revealing a broader picture of the century's poetry.[90] In addition to the changes in the Russian literary landscape oriented towards the recovery of forgotten poets and traditions, Semen Vilenskii's 2005 anthology of poetry written by Gulag prisoners presented a challenge not only to historians of Russian literature but also to the promoters of a new educational syllabus in schools and universities.[91] Vilenskii's anthology suggested that the existing canon of Soviet poetry should include Gulag poetry as a genre in its own right, and implied that Evtushenko's anthology *Strofy veka* was not as all-inclusive as the title suggests. While Evtushenko's anthology does offer readers many works that were previously excluded from the mainstream of Soviet published literature, it is nevertheless the case that

---

89 *Strofy veka. Antologiia russkoi poezii*, edited by Evgenii Evtushenko (Moscow: Polifakt, 1994).
90 http://www.vavilon.ru, http://rvb.ru/np, http://www.ruthenia.ru/60s; *Poeziia Serebrianogo veka*, compiled by Boris Akimov (Moscow: Eksmo, 2007); *Poety Serebrianogo veka*, http://slova.org.ru; *Antologiia poezii Serebrianogo veka: 1890–1940*, compiled by Karen Dzhangirov, http://anthology.karendjangirov.com/sereb.html; *Russkaia poeziia: Stikhi serebrianogo veka*, http://rupoem.ru/silver.aspx
91 *Poeziia uznikov Gulaga. Antologiia*, compiled by Semen Vilenskii (Moscow: Mezhdunarodnyi fond Demokratiia/Materik, 2005).

a large portion of it is made up of the work of poets who were published during the Soviet period.

Multiplicity and Diversity: Facets of the Emerging Canon in the 1990s–2000s

The present collection explores several examples of how the contemporary process of overcoming the many constraints created by socialist realist critics, censors and poets is starting to reshape the canon of twentieth-century Russian poetry. It points to the exciting diversity of the post-Soviet literary landscape and uncovers its links with the Thaw period as well as with the unofficial poetry of the 1970s to the 1980s. The volume also highlights the ongoing creative dialogue between the centre and the periphery, be it the provinces, Gulag prisons, or émigré communities of poets and writers. Not only do the contributors to the present volume analyse different coexisting versions of the poetic canon in contemporary Russia, they also concern themselves with identifying some significant gaps in the Russian collective memory.

The poetry of the Russian diaspora is one area that was relatively unfamiliar to readers in the Soviet Union; its reception in Russia has been gradual, with numerous gaps in readers' knowledge still to be filled. Maria Rubins draws attention to the second generation of émigré poets who remain largely unknown to the post-Soviet reader in Russia. Taking her cue from Russian émigré critic Georgii Fedotov, she illustrates how the original and distinct voice of the Paris Note group of poets was shaped by their engagement with the Russian national canon but also by their experience of living in the diaspora where they encountered other influences which promoted a cross-cultural, transnational sensibility. Other chapters also consider the twentieth-century poetry canon as something that has developed across national boundaries. Aaron Hodgson's chapter on the reception of Brodskii in Russia in the 1990s–2000s suggests that the rise of popular culture and the influence of the Russian media on the literary imagination contributed to the formation of a mythologised image of the poet as a martyr and an authority who bridges the gap between Russian national and Anglo-Saxon traditions. Alexandra Smith also identifies the impact of extra-literary factors on the reception of such important émigré poets as Marina Tsvetaeva, Vladimir Nabokov and Georgii Ivanov. Their experiences of exile and displacement seems to appeal to the post-Soviet reader engrossed in a nostalgic imaginary construction of the past. Joanne Shelton examines the legacy of émigré writer Ivan Bunin as a poet rather than a prose writer in contemporary Russia and explores the role played both by institutions, such as museums and schools, and by other poets, in securing his place in the post-Soviet poetic canon. In his insightful chapter 'Canonical Mandel'shtam', Andrew Kahn investigates the role played in Mandel'shtam's canonisation in the West and in post-Soviet Russia by established poets, who acted as critics and canon-makers; he concludes that several important post-Stalin poets, including Sedakova and Brodskii, downplay such biographical factors as Mandel'shtam's martyr-like fate, and engage with the poet's aesthetic ideas about defamiliarisation as well as his unique appreciation of reality in its visual and sound polyphony. Stephanie Sandler's informative examination of various innovative trends in Russian contemporary poetry, not all of it written in Russia, or, indeed, in Russian, highlights its eclectic nature and its strong orientation towards experimentation. Her examples include the visual poetry of Gennadii Aigi and Elizaveta Mnatsakanova (b. 1922); the emphasis on narrative which may be found in many poems written by Maria Stepanova, Elena Fanailova, and Fedor Svarovskii; and performative traits of Dmitri Prigov's poetry. The main goal of Sandler's analysis 'has been to look at those who are at the boundaries, who offer new ways to see the changing totality that is Russian poetry today'. Elena Shvarts, the subject of the chapter by Josephine von Zitzewitz, was a poet active in the late-Soviet Leningrad literary underground rather than in the diaspora. Shvarts is unique among her fellow Leningrad underground poets in having successfully made the transition from being known only in this restricted milieu to becoming part of mainstream literary culture. Von Zitzewitz explores the ways in which Shvarts's poetry and persona have made her someone who is able to stand in for the entire underground and take her place as an established figure in the contemporary twentieth-century poetry canon.

Other chapters focus on ways in which the reputations of particular poets or groups of poets whose work was, to a greater or lesser extent, officially published in the Soviet Union, have been changing since the 1990s. Katharine Hodgson demonstrates successfully how Boris Slutskii, one of the poets most strongly identified with the Soviet establishment, has been liberated from his Soviet captivity and rediscovered not as an influential war poet but rather as a philosophical poet who became a role model for many unofficial poets interested in Jewish themes and in the poetry of trauma. As Hodgson notes, Slutskii's poetic career 'demonstrates the inadequacy of simplistic divisions between "official" and "unofficial" poetry as a way of understanding twentieth-century Russian poetry, and the power of poetic innovation'. Olga Sobolev also urges the post-Soviet reader to liberate the poet from the dubious tradition embedded in Soviet scholarship that portrayed Blok as a supporter of revolutionary changes in Russia and as a precursor of socialist realist poetry. She suggests that Blok's reception in the 1990s–2000s started shifting away from political aspects of Blok's poems and essays towards an exploration of the philosophical and metaphysical concerns embedded in his works. Blok's vision of creativity based on the dynamic relationship between the irrational and the rational, Sobolev asserts, accords well with contemporary debates about the role of poetry as a tool for understanding reality. Alexandra Harrington's engaging discussion of Anna Akhmatova's cult in contemporary Russia reveals the emergence of glamour ideology. This trend has given rise to a new type of biographical writing in Russian that accommodates popular culture's preoccupation with stardom. Harrington examines Tamara Kataeva's highly controversial books about Akhmatova — *Anti-Akhmatova* (2007) and *Abolition of Slavery* (2012) — and explains their immense popularity by the tendency of post-Soviet readers to demythologise idols of the past and to reassess canonical authors. Emily Lygo's contribution provides a very useful examination of poets who are strongly identified with the post-Stalin Thaw; it examines what recent work by influential critics, as well as the contents of poetry anthologies, textbooks and educational syllabuses can tell us about the place that poets of the Thaw generation occupy in the contemporary canon.

All of the case studies included in the present volume suggest that many living Russian poets have successfully integrated themselves into new cultural and social developments and explored new opportunities for forging their identities as performers, philosophers, entertainers, critics, translators, and multimedia figures. This volume also illustrates how the re-configuration of the Russian poetic canon has encouraged many educationalists and critics to reassess their traditional views about lyric poetry and civic poetry. It certainly prompts the reader to re-examine the simplistic division between official and unofficial poetry which existed in the western scholarship of the Cold War period. The present collection also shows that views of the twentieth-century Russian poetry canon as an expression of nation are not sufficient to encompass the complexities of verse written in different diaspora communities, or poetry that was composed in the same geographical space, but one that was profoundly divided, with only certain texts reaching a readership soon after being created. The national canon is, meanwhile, being promoted with increasing energy by the Russian authorities hoping to construct a new Russian identity beyond borders based on the logocentric world view and on the idea of shared national values. A conservative approach to the Russian literary canon can be found in a 2014 interview with Dmitrii Livanov published in *The Times Educational Supplement*. Livanov, the Russian minister of education and science, suggested that all nations, including Britain, should follow Russia's example by compelling students to study their own literary canon. Livanov said that all students in Russia were expected to acquire a golden repository of cultural values by the time they left school. He went on to say: 'You can't leave a Russian school without having read poetry by Pushkin, novels by Tolstoy and Dostoevsky or short stories by Chekhov'.[92]

As Livanov's list of authors indicates, the national literary canon that he would like to preserve in Russia is still very much oriented towards nineteenth-century literature written in Russian and widely translated outside Russia. The present collection demonstrates that notions of constructing a poetic canon around the cult of Pushkin as supreme national poet appear to be rapidly crumbling away, and are being replaced by multiple coexisting canonical traditions. It also suggests that the process of reassessment of Russian poetry understood during the Soviet era as 'official' and 'unofficial' has resulted in a new configuration of the canon. Lotman's aforementioned association of poetry with cultural memory (both personal and collective) appears to be highly productive for contemporary poetic experiments and creative engagements with the past. Dmitrii Bykov, whose collaborative project *Grazhdanin poet* has been discussed above, seems to represent a different approach to the literary canon. He clearly has no interest in overturning or dismissing the canon as such, and recognises its role as one of the elements that make up collective identity. Yet he also acknowledges the importance

---

92 Quoted in Richard Vaughan, 'Literature — Why Dostoyevsky is One of Russia's Best Teachers', *The Times Educational Supplement*, 24 January 2014, p. 8.

of personal associations that individual readers or, indeed, critics, may have with particular writers and their works. His 2012 collection of essays *Sovetskaia literatura: kratkii kurs* (*Soviet Literature: A Short Course*), and indeed the expanded version published two years later with the subtitle *rasshirennyi kurs* (*Extended Course*) offers a highly individual and playful account of Soviet canonical literature which mocks the solemn didactic tradition, and, indeed, the Stalin-era *Short Course of Soviet History* which was compulsory reading for Soviet citizens.[93]

Bykov treats his texts and authors with the same kind of ambivalence evident in *Grazhdanin poet*: he is neither reverent nor unequivocally dismissive. The keynote of his *Short Course* is familiarity, both in the sense of informality and of extensive knowledge. His take on the canon, both here and in his parodies, is to re-animate past writers, not to treat them as monuments to be politely admired. Bykov's playful approach should not be seen as trivialising though it may not be to everyone's taste, like Siniavskii's *Progulki s Pushkinym* (*Strolls with Pushkin*, 1975), which caused scandal because of its admiring but less than reverent treatment of the most canonical or Russian poets.[94] His contribution to the reassessment of the poetry canon is to appeal to a mass audience as a populariser. He may be trenchant in the way he delivers opinions, but he does not lay claim to have the one correct understanding of the issues. As an informed observer, but one who does not set himself up as ultimate arbiter, he offers a vision of the literary canon as something on which we can all have our opinions. This is a view of canon on a human scale rather than canon as monument: a resource to be drawn on, not a sacred object. While there are still scholars who seem to be attracted to the Soviet-era understanding of the canon as monolithic and authoritative, Bykov's idiosyncractic approach suggests that a more democratic, flexible, and inclusive understanding of the literary canon is starting to take root.

---

93 Dmitrii Bykov, *Sovetskaia literatura: kratkii kurs* (Moscow: Prozaik, 2012); Bykov, *Sovetskaia literatura: rasshirennyi kurs* (Moscow: Prozaik, 2014); *Istoriia VKP (b): kratkii kurs* (Moscow: OGIZ, 1945; 1st edn 1938).

94 Andrei Siniavskii, *Progulki s Pushkinym* (London: Overseas Publications Interchange, 1975). For an analysis of the responses to Siniavskii's book, see Stephanie Sandler, 'Sex, Death and Nation in the "Strolls with Pushkin" controversy', *Slavic Review*, 51: 2 (1992), 294–308.

2. From the Margins to the Mainstream: Iosif Brodskii and the Twentieth-Century Poetic Canon in the Post-Soviet Period

Aaron Hodgson

The biography of Iosif Brodskii is at once completely unique and yet simultaneously representative of the Soviet experience for many writers. Born in Leningrad in 1940, by the time he was twenty-four he had already been attacked in the press, arrested and tried for social parasitism, and then sent into internal exile in the Arkhangelsk region of Russia. Although his sentence was commuted in 1965 following protests by various Russian and Western cultural figures, harassment by the KGB continued and he was eventually exiled from the country in 1972, sent to the West less than a month after his thirty-second birthday. During the next fifteen years in exile Brodskii rose to the summit of the US intelligentsia, receiving the Nobel Prize for Literature in 1987 and later being appointed as American Poet Laureate in 1991. Yet for all his awards and honours in the West, Brodskii was not published in his native country until late 1987 during the twilight of the Soviet Union, save for some of his children's poems in the 1960s. His death followed shortly after in 1996, aged only fifty-five, 'after a life that seemed in many ways tailor-made for the prophetic model, as Akhmatova had foreseen'.[1]

---

1   Clare Cavanagh, *Lyric Poetry and Modern Politics: Russia, Poland, and the West* (New Haven: Yale University Press, 2009), p. 274.

Famously, he never returned to Russia following his expulsion from his native country.

As David Bethea notes, 'it is a virtual topos in such preliminaries to claim that one's subject has been "neglected" or unfairly passed over by literary history. Not so in Brodsky's case'.[2] By my reckoning, up to early 2013 there have been at least twenty-seven books published in the West that are specifically about Brodskii, and this information is supplemented by a search on ProQuest Dissertation Abstracts and Theses, which revealed that his name is mentioned in 1389 dissertation abstracts, with 20 theses written specifically about him. These books and dissertations have been produced across a sustained period of time, mainly after the poet's death, and continue to appear up to this day, which demonstrates a continued scholarly interest in Brodskii in the West.

But what about Brodskii's status in Russia during the post-Soviet period? John Glad notes in the acknowledgements to his book *Conversations in Exile: Russian Writers Abroad* that Glad's file of Russian writers in exile at the end of the Soviet period numbered some 2500, and this was not an exhaustive list.[3] The late Soviet period, from 1987 when Gorbachev introduced his *perestroika* and *glasnost'* policies to the dissolution of the Soviet Union in December 1991, can best be characterised, from a literary point of view, as thirsty; there was a thirst for the works of all those who were deemed unpublishable by the state, from throughout the Soviet period until the present day. Consequently, the following period, which saw a revision of the literary canon that brought together poets and their works from the Soviet mainstream, underground and émigré literature, can be understood best as an attempt to quench this thirst. This leads to the questions: how has Brodskii's position in the canon changed in the post-Soviet period, and can we consider him to be a canonical figure in the newly reshaped literary canon? This chapter will contextualise the rise of Brodskii in Russia during the post-Soviet period and investigate the literary and extra-literary mechanisms behind his canonisation there,

---

2   David Bethea, *Joseph Brodsky and the Creation of Exile* (Princeton: Princeton University Press, 1994), p. xiii.
3   *Conversations in Exile: Russian Writers Abroad*, edited by John Glad (Durham, NC: Duke University Press, 1993).

both immediately following the dissolution of the Soviet Union and after Brodskii's death in 1996.

The title of this chapter, 'From the Margins to the Mainstream' ('ot okrainy k tsentru'), is an allusion to one of Brodskii's early poems, written in 1962, which seems to prophesy his rise from near obscurity in his native country to fame in the post-Soviet period.[4] This stands in stark contrast to his status in the US, where he was already famous upon his arrival in 1972, thanks to a secret transcript of his 1964 trial that had been smuggled out of the Soviet Union and printed in the West eight years before his exile. This gave him a reputation in America as a dissident and symbol of artistic resistance in a totalitarian society.

This chapter will assess Brodskii's canonisation across a range of criteria, utilising a quantitative and qualitative methodology, in order to demonstrate objectively, in this instance, that Brodskii is indeed now a part of the Russian canon. It is composed of two sections, mirroring Brodskii's canonisation in Russia in the post-Soviet period. The first focuses on the poet's initial reception in the late- and immediate post-Soviet period (1987–1995), when the process of revision of the literary canon was beginning. It traces his initial reception and notes the importance of Brodskii's biography and awards in the context of the move away from the Soviet cultural inheritance that was evident during this time. A useful comparison to the poet Andrei Voznesenskii and his Soviet and post-Soviet reception will help to highlight the different factors at play in the reconfiguration of the canon at this time.

The second section of the concentrates on Brodskii's posthumous reception and canonisation in Russia between 1996 to 2012, and explores the ways in which he has been incorporated into the post-Soviet poetic canon since his death in 1996. This section is further divided into two broad parts. The first deals with scholarly and critical interest in the poet, and traces his posthumous critical reception in Russia by providing quantitative analysis of primary and secondary sources written by, or about, him, which reveal a sustained academic interest in Brodskii. The second part will investigate the cultural manifestations of that interest: the posthumous phenomenon sometimes described as 'Brodskiimania'. This chapter proposes to define the cult of Brodskii in a broader context

---

4   Brodskii, Iosif, 'Ot okrainy k tsentru', *Sochineniia* (Ekaterinburg: U-Faktoriia, 2002), pp. 18–23.

by looking at the ways in which a growing interest in the biography and works of the poet has manifested itself in Russia over the last two decades, and considering why this has happened. Cultural narratives about Brodskii are inevitably composed of literary and non-literary elements; this chapter will analyse how the poet has been adopted by various aspects of popular culture, noting films and documentaries about him, as well as songs that use his poetry in their lyrics, and other cultural manifestations of 'Brodskiimania'.

Thus, the chapter aims to contextualise the rise of Brodskii in post-Soviet Russia, arguing that his posthumous canonisation grew from his earlier reception in Russia and the West. It is important to note the complexity of his essentially unique transnational canonisation. The present discussion aims to contextualise both the literary and the sociopolitical aspects of Brodskii's reception in Russia by examining his canonisation chronologically in order to determine the specific combination of factors at play in his post-Soviet canonisation.

Brodskii's Initial Reception, 1987–1995

Brodskii's initial reception in Russia can be traced through the pages of the scholarly journal *Voprosy literatury* (*Questions of Literature*). Of all the journals examined, *Voprosy literatury* offers the most representative picture of the various factors involved in Brodskii's transnational narrative. Founded in 1957, *Voprosy literatury* is an authoritative literary critical journal that publishes articles and transcripts of roundtable discussions that explore Russian and world literature, and the history and theory of literature. The journal first appeared soon after the Twentieth Party Congress that marked the beginning of the Thaw in the cultural life of the Soviet Union. It soon evolved into a major discussion platform for literary critics and scholars.

G. S. Smith noted the appearance

> of a selection of Brodsky's poetry in the last issue of 1987 of the venerable Soviet literary journal *New World* (*Novyi mir*). This was the first time Brodsky's poetry had been published in his native country following his exile in 1972, and indeed the first ever substantial publication of it there. Of greater general significance was the fact that this was also the first publication in the seventy-year history of the USSR by a major living Russian writer who was a citizen of a foreign country. Brodsky

thus lived long enough to see his work overcome all the prohibitions the Soviet system had piled up against it.[5]

Consequently, one would not expect to see Brodskii's name appear in print in any Soviet literary journal before 1987, and certainly not while he might still be considered as an exile in the West. The data collected from *Voprosy literatury* upholds this theory. Brodskii is first mentioned in its pages in 1989, and appears there 123 times up until the end of 2011. Most of these mentions (anything between a full-blown article and a single-word reference) are concentrated in the periods 1989–1990 and 1994–1995, immediately prior to his death. These figures help to demonstrate an initial awareness of Brodskii, but, as Andrew Kahn notes, 'a proper assessment of the stature of a poet naturally depends on the content of their reception as much as its frequency'.[6]

These nineteen mentions of Brodskii in the journal fall into two distinct categories. The first category, which comprises the majority, discusses Brodskii in the context of the revision of the literary canon, and focuses on his exile, biography, or awards. An example of this can be found in a 1989 issue in which Efim Etkind discusses the metaphorical return of writers to Russia:

> From France and America a crowd of shadows burst into Russia. Among them were authors of varying stature and merits, but each one of them was significant in his own way: from Bunin and Kuprin to Averchenko and Don Aminado, from Marina Tsvetaeva to Irina Odoevtseva, from Bal'mont, Georgii Ivanov and Khodasevich to Viacheslav Ivanov and Adamovich, from Zamiatin and Remizov to Nabokov, from Igor' Severianin to Kuz'mina-Karavaeva. Merezhkovskii, Aldanov, Zinaida Gippius, Boris Poplavskii, Il'ia Zdanevich and many others still await their time. Exiles, still living, were already starting to return in the form of their works: the first one to be published was Joseph Brodskii.[7]

Here, within a broader discussion of the reshaping of the canon, Etkind notes that by 1989 the first works by Brodskii had already been published

---

5   G. S. Smith, 'Joseph Brodsky: Summing Up', *Literary Imagination*, 7: 3 (2005), 399–410 (p. 401).
6   See Andrew Kahn's contribution to the present volume, 'Canonical Mandel'shtam', p. 157.
7   Efim Etkind, contribution to roundtable discussion 'Kopengagenskaia vstrecha deiatelei kul'tury', *Voprosy literatury*, 5 (1989), 14–20 (p. 17).

in Russia. This is indicative of the wider trend of mentions of Brodskii in *Voprosy literatury* between 1989 and 1995. The second category, in which there are fewer examples, is composed of texts that tend to use Brodskii in a discussion of contemporary poetics. The best example of this category can be found in a 1994 issue of the journal:

> And here even Joseph Brodskii is praised to the skies, sometimes called 'the best, most talented poet of our epoch' (in more intellectual formulations, of course, such as 'a major figure among Russian poets living today'), but he has still not been studied at all in connection with his poetic contemporaries.[8]

This passage discusses the role and place of Brodskii in contemporary poetry; Vladimir Novikov argues that Brodskii is the most postmodern Russian poet. These examples illustrate the two distinct categories that form Brodskii's initial reception in Russia in the late Soviet and early post-Soviet period.

At no point in the period up until the end of 1995 does the journal offer any textual analysis of Brodskii's works. This, to a certain extent, is to be expected. The period of the reconfiguration of the canon, which coincided with Brodskii's initial post-Soviet reception, can be best characterised, as has been suggested above, as *thirsty*. Generally speaking, the literary public were eager to read any works that were deemed unpublishable during the Soviet period. This was a time of generalisations, not specifics. There were too many writers trying to be heard, and it would take time for individuals in this crowded arena to rise to the top. Therefore, general collected works were published in abundance, rather than individual cycles of poems, to try to quench this thirst. Works previously unpublished during the Soviet period did not always receive the critical and scholarly attention that they would later be given.

The reception of the poet Andrei Voznesenskii in *Voprosy literatury* during this period provides a useful and illuminating comparison with that of Brodskii, which highlights the different factors at play in the canonisation process and in the evolution of the canon in the late Soviet and early post-Soviet period. The differences in their reception

---

8 Vladimir Novikov, contribution to roundtable discussion 'Puti sovremennoi poezii', *Voprosy literatury*, 1 (1994), 9–16 (p. 15).

were initially noticeable in the West. While Brodskii was Akhmatova's protégé, Voznesenskii was Pasternak's. According to Reuters, when Voznesenskii sent Pasternak some early verse asking for his opinion, the response from the future Nobel Prize winner to the fourteen-year-old was: 'Your entrance into literature was swift and turbulent. I am glad I've lived to see it'.[9] Famously, Robert Lowell once referred to Voznesenskii as 'one of the greatest [living] poets in any language'.[10] Although Brodskii and Voznesenskii were contemporaries, the latter was published and favoured in the Soviet Union, whereas the former was arrested and exiled for his art. While Brodskii received awards and honours in the West, Voznesenskii was given the USSR State Prize in 1978, as well as the Order of the Red Banner of Labour in 1983, and other notable prizes.[11] While Brodskii rose to the summit of the American intelligentsia, Voznesenskii matched his achievement in his native country.

Voznesenskii travelled to the West during the Thaw period, and, like Brodskii after his trial and internal exile, was the darling of the Western press and one of the most acclaimed poetic voices of his day. Yet ultimately it was Brodskii, not Voznesenskii, who became known in the West as the greatest Russian poet of his generation. One explanation for these differing fortunes may be found in Cold War attitudes towards the Soviet Union, which created a favourable atmosphere for Brodskii's reception as an exiled poet. This was a time when writers officially out of favour with the Soviet authorities were often perceived in the West as having greater talent and creative integrity than those such as Voznesenskii who were published in the Soviet Union and therefore part of its official culture. Voznesenskii's poems were, by and large, published widely in his native country during the Soviet period, but his works ultimately received less critical attention in the West than Brodskii's. Yet the situation is more complex than this. Voznesenskii was not a Soviet lackey. However, perhaps the most interesting aspect of Brodskii's reception in the West is his elevation from being ranked

---

9   Dmitry Solovyov, 'Poet of post-Stalin thaw Voznesensky Dies at 77', *Reuters Online*, 1 June 2010, http://in.reuters.com/article/2010/06/01/idINIndia-48968820100601
10 [N.a.], 'Poets at Peace', http://www.ikewrites.com/tag/jack-kerouac
11 For a list of awards he received see Michael Pushkin's entry on Voznesenskii in *Reference Guide to Russian Literature*, edited by Neil Cornwell (London and Chicago: Fitzroy Dearborn Publishers, 1998), p. 888.

among the best Russian poets, along with Voznesenskii and Evtushenko, to being hailed as *the* best Russian poet alive following his exile.[12] Was this change due to the prestige that attached to his status as exile, or perhaps to greater exposure of his work and his newly published poems? Certainly, Brodskii's work was more widely published in the West after he left Russia. The importance of literary quality in building a writer's reputation should never be underestimated, but in this case there are extra-literary factors to be considered. It is likely that the Cold War political agenda helped to shape Brodskii's reception in the West, which saw the victimisation and expulsion of Brodskii as evidence of the USSR's oppressive nature.

During the later Soviet period, one would expect to find the name of such a widely-published poet as Voznesenskii frequently mentioned in literary journals in Russia. This is exactly what we see in *Voprosy literatury*. Between 1960 and 1987, Voznesenskii's name is mentioned thirty-nine times, appearing at least once in most years, while Brodskii is not mentioned once in this period.[13] Between 1987 to 1995, Voznesenskii's name is mentioned five times in *Voprosy literatury*, in comparison to Brodskii's nineteen.[14] Voznesenskii's apparent marginalisation during the post-Soviet years may be explained by the widespread rejection of

---

12 For evidence of the former opinion, see Olga Carlisle, 'Speaking of Books: Anna Akhmatova', *New York Times*, 11 September 1966, section VII, 2, 28, 30; A. Alvarez, 'From Russia With Passion', *The Observer*, 9 July 1967, 21; Olga Carlisle, 'Speaking of Books: Through Literary Russia', *New York Times*, 26 May 1968, section VII, 2–7; Sidney Monas, 'Poets on Street Corners: Portraits of Fifteen Russian Poets', *New York Times*, 26 January 1969, section VII, 6, 40; and K. Van Het Reve, 'Samizdat: The Sudden Flowering of Underground Literature in Russia', *The Observer*, 29 March 1970, 21. For the latter, see Anthony Astrachan, 'Powerful, Beautiful and Incomplete: Book World. The Living Mirror', *The Washington Post*, 29 November 1972, B11; Anthony Astrachan, 'Requiem Service for W. H. Auden', *The Washington Post*, 5 October 1973, B13; Vadim Medish and Elisavietta Ritchie, 'Writers in Exile: Planting New Roots — Planting Roots in Foreign Soil', *The Washington Post*, 24 February 1974, C1, C5; 'A Selected Vacation Reading List', *New York Times*, 2 June 1974, F31–37; Robert Kaiser, 'Panovs Have 5 Days to Leave', *The Washington Post*, 9 June 1974, A13; and John Goshko, 'The Exiles: No Escaping Literary Wars', *The Washington Post*, 29 December 1974, B5.
13 The exceptions being 1961, 1963, 1968, 1971, 1979, 1984, 1985, and 1987. The main flurry of activity for Voznesenskii seems to occur in the early- to mid-1960s, and then between 1974 and 1983.
14 To give a further comparison, between 1957 and 2011 Voznesenskii's name is mentioned 62 times on the pages of *Voprosy literatury*, whereas Brodskii (over a much shorter period, between 1989 and 2011) is mentioned 123 times.

figures identified with official culture. Voznesenskii, a published Soviet writer, was sidelined to make room for the massive influx of work by the 'crowd of shadows' from abroad, to paraphrase Efim Etkind. By contrast, Brodskii's biography aided his canonisation, which was further supported by the awards and honours that he had received abroad.[15] Ultimately, the comparison of Brodskii to Voznesenskii shows the importance of extra-literary factors in the post-Soviet reconfiguration of the canon. In effect, Voznesenskii was doubly marginalised: in the West, following Brodskii's exile, and in the early years of post-Soviet Russia, when the 'returnee' Brodskii received far more attention than he did.

Brodskii's Posthumous Reception and Canonisation in Russia

Brodskii died in January 1996 in New York, famously never having returned to Russia, and was initially interred in a crypt there before being buried in Venice in 1997. His death brought his name to the fore in Russia, and there it has remained. In the period following his death to the end of 2011, Brodskii is mentioned 104 times on the pages of *Voprosy literatury*, compared to the nineteen mentions he received in the period between 1989 and 1995. On average during the period of Brodskii's initial reception we see there were just over three mentions per year, whereas after his death there were nearly seven mentions a year, over a twofold increase. These figures reflect the sustained interest in Brodskii's work between 1996 and 2011, but with an initial flurry of mentions in the years immediately following his death and in the period between 2005 and 2011.[16] During this time, those articles that appear in *Voprosy literatury* can be divided into five broad categories which all help to demonstrate how Brodskii's place in the canon was by that time an accepted fact. These categories are as follows: articles about contemporary literature that feature Brodskii; articles that use a

---

15 Efim Etkind, contribution to roundtable discussion 'Kopengagenskaia vstrecha deiatelei kul'tury', *Voprosy literatury*, 5 (1989), 17.
16 The only year without a single mention of Brodskii's name in the journal was 2002. The results can be broken down thus: five mentions in 1996, six in 1997, eight in 1998, seven in 1999, three in 2000, three in 2001, none in 2002, five in 2003, two in 2004, fifteen in 2005, twelve in 2006, eleven in 2007, five in 2008, five in 2009, seven in 2010, and ten in 2011.

quotation from his work to facilitate a discussion not otherwise directly related to the poet; articles that examine his place in the canon in general; articles about different aspects of Brodskii's poetic career that discuss his biography and awards, or his works; and articles that engage in close textual analysis of Brodskii's poetry.

The most important trend to note is that gradually the journal devoted increasing attention to the poet's life and work, and particularly to the analysis of his poetry. For instance, in the period of his initial reception, of the nineteen mentions of Brodskii on the pages of *Voprosy literatury*, none of the articles were about him specifically. In general, he featured in broader discussions about the reshaping of the canon or about contemporary poetics. This changed in the years between 1996 and 2011, when eighteen articles specifically about Brodskii were published in *Voprosy literatury*, a significant increase in scholarly and critical interest that was not evident during the period of his initial reception.[17] His name is mentioned predominantly (on 86 out of 104 occasions) in articles that can be classified under the first two of my categories, which is indicative of a paradigm shift in the poet's reception.

An example of the first category of articles, which mention Brodskii in the context of contemporary literature, is a piece by by Kathleen Parthé, in which Brodskii is mentioned at various points in a discussion of the so-called 'Russification' of the nation's literature since the decline of the USSR and the struggle to preserve the cultural history of Russia.[18] Articles of this kind which situated Brodskii within the broader context of contemporary poetry were rare in the earlier stages but became much more frequent after the poet's death. Over time, Brodskii became an integral part of the canon as a poet who is not just accepted as a major writer, but whose work may be seen as exemplifying, and even leading, broader literary trends.

Articles in the second category, using Brodskii, or a quotation from his works, to facilitate a discussion about a separate topic, did not appear

---

17 There was an initial flurry of articles specifically about Brodskii immediately after his death, with five published alone in 1997 and 1998. This was followed by a slight drought where only two articles were published between 1999 and 2004, however between 2005 and 2011 there were ten articles published in *Voprosy literatury* that were specifically about Brodskii.

18 Kaitlin Parte [Kathleen Parthé], 'Chto delaet pisatelia russkim? Puti sovremennoi poezii', *Voprosy literatury*, 1 (1996), 83–120.

in *Voprosy literatury* during the earlier phase of the poet's reception. Moris Bonfel'd's article about Tsvetaeva is an example of this trend, in which Bonfel'd writes that 'Joseph Brodsky, who considered Tsvetaeva to be a major twentieth-century poet, also includes Tsvetaeva's syntax among the most important content-bearing attributes of her poetry'.[19] Having noted Brodskii's opinion on the matter, Bonfel'd then engages in a textual analysis of Tsvetaeva's work. This is important because it indicates that Brodskii is deemed an authority on the subject, thus reinforcing his canonical status. Another example can be seen in the introduction to a set of three articles on English metaphysical poetry, where Brodskii is deemed an expert, and the person responsible for introducing this body of work to Russian readers:

> Our knowledge of English Metaphysical poetry and our interest in it changed thanks to Joseph Brodskii. He spoke of the significance Donne had for him and translated a number of poems by the Metaphysical poets [...].[20]

The introduction to an interview with Semen Lipkin is a further example. The interviewer, Ol'ga Postnikova, uses a quote by Brodskii to facilitate a reflection on Russian twentieth-century poetry in general, as well as on the place of Lipkin's poetry in the canon:

> In an interview for the newspaper *Russkaia mysl'* on 3 February 1983 Joseph Brodskii says: 'I have always been struck by how it happened that in the poetry of Russia, which has been destined to undergo such a unique, and in many ways catastrophic experience, an experience which brought people face to face with the very foundations of existence: the years of collectivisation, war, not to mention terror [...], this was barely reflected at all.[21]

The interviewer here uses Brodskii as a means of validating Lipkin's contribution to twentieth-century Russian poetry, presenting Lipkin as one poet who fills the gap identified by Brodskii. Lipkin goes on to refer to Brodskii himself later in the interview:

---

19 Moris Bonfel'd, 'Moshch' i "nevesomost"', *Voprosy literatury*, 5 (2003), 91–99 (p. 94).
20 [N.a.], 'Angliiskaia metafizicheskaia poeziia', *Voprosy literatury*, 4 (2004), 78–79 (p. 78).
21 Semen Lipkin, 'Iskusstvo ne znaet starosti', *Voprosy literatury*, 3 (1998), 253–77 (pp. 253–54).

> I have to begin with the fact that I was aware, having left the Writers' Union in January 1980, and was living, in my own country, forbidden to work in my proper profession, that a collection of my poems was due to be published by the American publisher 'Ardis'. But I could not have imagined that the book would have been produced on such a scale, nor that it had been compiled by such a major poet as Joseph Brodskii, with whom I was not acquainted.[22]

This quote is not only interesting because it suggests that Lipkin was aware of the émigré Brodskii in 1980, though not personally acquainted with him, but also because it demonstrates that by 2004, the year of this interview, Brodskii's canonisation can be considered to be well underway, since Lipkin retrospectively acknowledges Brodskii's canonical status as an authoritative figure who helped raise awareness of his own poetry abroad.

There are a number of articles in *Voprosy literatury* between 1996 and 2011 that discuss Brodskii's place in the canon after its post-Soviet revision. An example of this third group is an article by Svetlana Boiko, which examines the philological consciousness of poetry as a developed tradition in the second half of the twentieth century. Different poets of this tradition are discussed, including Brodskii:

> In actual fact, Joseph Brodskii was a teacher and historian of world poetry; David Samoilov was a leading theoretician of Russian rhyme; Andrei Voznesenskii and Aleksandr Kushner were authors of essays on poetry and aesthetic. All of them, as well as Bella Akhmadulina and Bulat Okudzhava, were translators of Soviet and world poetry into Russian, and poetic translation is a laboratory where aesthetic views are refined, and a concern for the genuine spirit and style of a poem is manifested.[23]

In this example, as in other articles of this category, Brodskii is placed alongside other well-established authors in a discussion of the literary canon, which has the effect of reinforcing the canonisation of each of the writers mentioned. Articles of this kind dominated Brodskii's initial reception in *Voprosy literatury*, but the tone changed after his death. Whereas initially Brodskii was discussed in the context of the changing canon, with particular attention given to his exile, his biography, or his

---

22 *Ibid.*, p. 254.
23 Svetlana Boiko, '"Divnyi vybor vsevyshnikh shchedrot...": filologicheskoe samosoznanie sovremennoi poezii', *Voprosy literatury*, 1 (2000), 44–73 (p. 44).

awards, now the focus is on his place in the canon in general. He is no longer seen as an outsider and an exile; he is firmly accepted as a part of the canon.

The fourth category of articles appearing between 1996 and 2011 address Brodskii's poetic career, including his biography and awards, and his poetic output. Arina Volgina's article, entitled 'Iosif Brodskii/ Joseph Brodsky', is an example of this; it discusses Brodskii's English-language *alter ego*.[24] Vladimir Kozlov's article about the effect of exile on Brodskii's works between 1972 and 1977 is another such piece.[25] Such articles are indicative of a developed and sustained critical and scholarly interest and they demonstrate a change in how Brodskii is perceived in relation to the canon.

The fifth and final group of articles are those that focus on the textual analysis of his work, an approach absent from the initial reception of his poetry. Until 1996, no textual analysis of his work appeared in the pages of the journal, but after Brodskii's death a shift in perceptions occurred, and in 1997 and 1998 alone five articles engage in textual analysis of Brodskii's poetic output. One reason might be that the poet's death stimulated this turn towards a closer readings of his works. This may also have been combined with the slow, gradual process of Brodskii's assimilation into the canon as one of the many writers who were restored to the Russian literary mainstream. In other words, it took time for Brodskii's poetry to rise to prominence, but perhaps the poet's death was the trigger for this deeper critical engagement with his poetry.

The first textual analysis of Brodskii's poetry appeared in *Voprosy literatury* in 1997, in Sergo Lominadze's examination of Brodskii's 'Pis'mo v oazis' ('Letter to an Oasis').[26] Another early example includes Sergei Kuznetsov's article 'O poetike Brodskogo'('On Brodskii's Poetics'), which discusses the motifs and themes that can be found in Brodskii's works, including the effect of time on man.[27] A further example can

---

24 Arina Volgina, 'Sravnitel'naia poetika. Iosif Brodskii/Joseph Brodsky', *Voprosy literatury*, 3 (2005), 186–219.
25 Vladimir Kozlov, 'Neperevodimye gody Brodskogo: dve strany i dva iazyka v poezii i proze I. Brodskogo 1972–1977 godov', *Voprosy literatury*, 3 (2005), 155–85.
26 S. Lominadze, 'Pustynia i oazis', *Voprosy literatury*, 2 (1997), 337–44.
27 Sergei Kuznetsov, 'Raspadaiushchaisia amal'gama: o poetike Brodskogo', *Voprosy literatury*, 3 (1997), 24–49.

be found in Caterina Graziadei's article on the use of enjambments in Brodskii's poetry and how they help to convey the meaning of the poem:

> Death, Joseph Brodskii argued, was one of the possible ways in which time could be embodied. 'All my poems, more or less, are about the same thing: time'. It was not by chance that his two-volume collected works, published in Minsk in 1992, had the thoroughly eloquent title *A Form of Time*. For all poets, to some extent, have to measure themselves against time, and a song is, in itself 'Time reorganised'.[28]

Another instance can be seen in 2005, in M. Sverdlov and E. Staf'eva's textual analysis in which they attempt to uncover what they term the 'birth of the metaphysical Brodskii'.[29] These varied readings of Brodskii's work reflect the sustained and regular nature of this form of criticism, and suggest that Brodskii's canonisation is complete.

Posthumous 'Brodskiimania': Brodskii in Popular Culture

Having considered the critical interest in Brodskii as a literary phenomenon, I will now turn to the growth of a broader interest in the poet over the last two decades and how this interest has manifested in various forms of cultural production. The term 'Brodskiimania' here describes the cult of Brodskii in this broader context beyond the specifically literary sphere: in films, documentaries, television programmes, music, and in memorials dedicated to the poet.

Altogether, between 1990 and 2011, there have been fourteen documentary films and television programmes either specifically about Brodskii, or that feature him heavily. Of these, only one was filmed in 1991, i.e. during the early period of his reception in Russia. The production of the remaining thirteen is spread fairly evenly between 2000 and 2012, but with more of a flurry towards the end of the period, in particular in 2010 when Brodskii would have reached

---

28 Katerina Gratsiadei [Caterina Graziadei], 'Enjambement kak figura: bitva v predstavlenii Al'tdorfera i Brodskogo', *Voprosy literatury*, 3 (1998), 324–28 (p. 324).
29 M. Sverdlov and E. Staf'eva, 'Stikhotvorenie na smert' poeta: Brodskii i Oden. Rozhdenie "metafizicheskogo" Brodskogo iz stikhotvoreniia na smert' poeta', *Voprosy literatury*, 3 (2005), 220–44.

the age of seventy.³⁰ These films can broadly be assigned to one of two main categories: they are either about the poet and his views on certain topics, or about his works. In addition to these two groups, a number of programmes mention Brodskii as an authority on a certain topic, and can therefore be seen as constituting a third, supporting category.

The first group (films about Brodskii and his opinions) features the only documentary film from the period of Brodskii's early reception in Russia. This was entitled *Prodolzhenie vody* (*The Extension of Water*, 1991), and was directed by Natan Fedorovskii and Harald Luders.³¹ The film was shot over the Christmas holiday period in Venice, as a joint production with German television. In the documentary Brodskii talks about his knowledge of Venice and its history, reads verses about Venice and Petersburg, and talks about himself. There is also a recording of Brodskii's conversation with Thomas Krentsem, director of the Guggenheim Collection in Venice, about the dialogue between Russian and Western culture and the ways in which they interact. Many of the films that feature Brodskii (six out of fourteen) belong in this category, and they are produced throughout the entire period under analysis. A later example can be found in *Iosif Brodskii: razgovor s nebozhitelem* (*Joseph Brodsky: A Conversation with a Sky Dweller*, 2010), edited by Roman Liberov. This is a documentary film based on a recorded conversation that took place in New York in 1993 between the critic Solomon Volkov and Brodskii. The frankness of this dialogue make this film a key resource to understand Brodskii's personality and his perception of himself, his fate, his own poetry, and his place in the world.

The second category includes films and television programmes about Brodskii's poetic output. This category is larger than the first (eight out of fourteen films), and includes works produced after the poet's death, mirroring the textual analysis that was published during this period on the pages of *Voprosy literatury*. Works in this category include recordings of poetry readings of Brodskii's works, such as *Potomu chto iskusstvo poezii trebuet slov: vecher-posviashchenie Iosifu Brodskomu* (*Because the Art of Poetry Requires Words: An Evening Dedicated to Joseph Brodsky*) broadcast on 24 October 2010. This was a recorded literary-theatrical performance

---

30   For the sake of clarity, two were produced in 2000, one in 2002, one in 2003, one in 2006, one in 2009, four in 2010, two in 2011, and one in 2012.

31   The running time of the film is thirty minutes.

in which Brodskii's verses were read on stage by various actors from the theatre, and it took place in the Moscow Arts Theatre on the day that would have been Brodskii's seventieth birthday. The other main type of work to be found in this category are feature films that engage with Brodsky's works. Included here are two films by Andrei Khrzhanovskii. The first is *Poltora kota* (*A Cat and a Half*, 2003), an animated film that focuses on Brodskii's life before his exile in 1972. The film is based on Brodskii's works and drawings, and on the materials of a unique photographic archive. The second film by Khrzhanovskii is his *Poltory komnaty, ili sentimental'noe puteshestvie na Rodinu* (*A Room and a Half, or a Sentimental Journey to the Homeland*, 2009). A film that portrays the imagined journey of Brodskii back to St Petersburg, it is a fantasy based on his verses and essays, as well as the poet's biography.

These two categories are supplemented by many programmes that mention Brodskii, often as an authority on a certain topic. An example of this category can be found in Aleksandr Zholkovskii's recorded lecture 'O poniatiiakh invariant i poeticheskii mir: 1-ia lektsiia' ('On Notions of the Invariant and the Poetic World: Lecture 1'). In his lecture, Zholkovskii analyses lyrics by Pushkin and Pasternak, Okudzhava and Brodskii, Aleksandr Kushner and Sergei Gandlevskii from the point of view of their thematic and structural invariants.[32] Although this lecture is not solely about Brodskii's work, programmes such as this contribute to the poet's canonisation because of his proximity to other canonical figures such as Pushkin and Pasternak. Similarly, in Igor' Volgin's series *Igra v biser* (*A Game of Beads*), Volgin uses a quote by Brodskii to initiate a discussion on Sergei Dovlatov's *Zapovednik* (*Pushkin Hills*).[33] These three types of visual representation of the poet show the renewed significance of Brodskii's poetry in the post-Soviet period, and demonstrates a wider interest in his works.

Brodskii's place in popular culture is cemented not only by films, documentaries, and television programmes, but also through music. The earliest example is Andrei Makarevich's song 'Pamiati Iosifa

---

32 Aleksandr Zholkovskii's recorded lecture 'O poniatiiakh invariant i poeticheskii mir: 1-ia lektsiia', http://tvkultura.ru/video/show/brand_id/20898/episode_id/156605/video_id/156605

33 Volgin quotes Brodskii when he says: 'Dovlatov's prose was measured in verse'. See Igor Volgin, '"Igra v biser" c Igorem Volginym. Dovlatov. "Zapovednik"', http://tvkultura.ru/video/show/brand_id/20921/episode_id/154989/video_id/154989

Brodskogo' ('In memory of Brodskii', 1997) from his album *Dvadtsat' let spustia* (*Twenty Years Later*). Brodskii's lyrics have also been set to music, for example in the song by the band Surganova and Orchestra 'Neuzheli ne ia' ('Surely, it was me...'), which appeared on their 2003 album of the same name. The lyrics for this song are taken from the same poem from which this chapter takes its title: 'Ot okraini k tsentru' ('From the margins to the centre', 1962). The poem 'Niotkuda s liubov'iu' ('Out of nowhere with love...') appears as a ballad sung by Gennadii Trofimov in the film *Niotkuda s liubov'iu, ili Veselye pokhorony* (*Out of Nowhere with Love, or The Merry Funeral Party*, 2007), an adaptation of Liudmila Ulitskaia's novel *Veselye pokhorony* (*The Funeral Party*). Other musicians including Konstantin Meladze, Elena Frolova, Evgenii Kliachkin, Aleksandr Mirzaian, Aleksandr Vasil'ev, Diana Arbenina, Petr Mamonov, and Leonid Margolin have also turned the verses of Brodskii into songs. Others have been inspired by Brodskii and his works to create musical compositions which go beyond setting his poetry to music. In 2008 Viktoriia Poleva wrote *Summer Music*, a chamber cantata for violin solos, children's choirs, and string instruments based on verses by Brodskii. She has also written *Ars moriendi* (1983–2012), which is composed of twenty-two monologues about death for sopranos and piano, with two monologues based on verses by Brodskii ('Song' and 'Empty circle'). Another example is the 2011 contemporary classical album *Troika*, which includes Eskender Bekmambetov's critically acclaimed song cycle 'there...', his setting of five of Brodskii's Russian language poems and his own translations of the poems into English.[34]

The wider public interest in Brodskii is also demonstrated by memorials commemorating the poet, and by efforts to embody a collective memory of him. In 2002 a competition was launched to design the first monument to Brodskii in Russia, which was timed to coincide with what would have been his sixty-fifth birthday in 2003. The winning monument, by sculptor Vladimir Tsivin and architect Feliks Romanovskii, was due to be erected in St Petersburg, on the Pirogovskaia Embankment, in time for what would have been the poet's seventieth birthday. However, there is still no sign of it. Instead, the

---

34　See Vivien Schweitzer, 'Poetry and Song to Plumb the Russian Soul's Depths', *The New York Times*, 14 February 2008, http://www.nytimes.com/2008/02/14/arts/music/14krem.html

first public monument to Brodskii in Russia was sculpted by Konstantin Simun and unveiled in November 2005 in the courtyard of the Faculty of Philology of the State University of St Petersburg. It depicts Brodskii's head placed on a suitcase with the poet's name on the tag, and is entitled *Brodskii priekhal* (*Brodskii Arrived*). The title underlines the fact that this was the first monument to Brodskii in Russia, and was meant to signify the poet's metaphorical return to his home city. In 2011, the sculptor Georgii Frangulian and architect Sergei Skuratov unveiled their monument to Brodskii outside the US Embassy in Moscow. This design had lost out in the 2002 competition in St Petersburg. In an interview with Galina Masterova, Frangulian exaplined that his composition represented 'how a poet is alone but with a circle of followers'.[35] The choice of the location for this monument is significant, pointing to the cultural rapprochement between Russia and the United States in the post-Soviet period.

There are of course other minor monuments dedicated to Brodskii. In 1997 a memorial plaque was placed on the house in St Petersburg in which he lived until his exile in 1972. Another memorial plaque was unveiled in the courtyard of 19, ulitsa Stakhanovtsev, in St Petersburg on 1 December 2011. It takes the form of a huge boulder from Karelia that bears a line from the poem 'Ot okrainy k tsentru' ('From the Margins to the Mainstream'): 'Vot ia vnov' probezhal Maloi Okhtoi skvoz' tysiachu arok' ('Here I ran again across Little Okhta / through a thousand arches').[36] Other memorials to Brodskii have been created in smaller cities outside his native Petersburg and Moscow. One such example can be seen in Vilnius, where a memorial plaque has been fixed to a house in which Brodskii frequently stayed between 1966 and 1971. Another is to be found in Voronezh, where there is a street named after Brodskii, 'pereulok Brodskogo' ('Brodskii Lane'). Perhaps the most ironic example involves Aeroflot, the very company which flew Brodskii to his Western exile, and which has named one of their planes after him ('I. Brodskii', an A330, side number VQ-BBE).[37] Like the monument to Brodskii near

---

35   Galina Masterova, 'Sculpture of Exiled Poet Brodsky Graces U.S. Embassy', 4 July 2011, http://rbth.com/articles/2011/07/04/sculpture_of_exiled_poet_brodsky_graces_us_embassy_13113.html
36   'Ot okrainy k tsentru', *Sochineniia* (Ekaterinburg: U-Faktoriia, 2002), p. 18.
37   For a picture of the plane, see http://farm8.static.flickr.com/7038/6881456042_dcc9a91d57_m.jpg

the American Embassy in Moscow, the choice of an aeroplane to bear the poet's name suggests that in the popular imagination Brodskii is seen as a figure who connects Russia and the West.

Yet the most compelling evidence that cultural interest in Brodskii has been increasing is the opening of a Brodskii flat-museum in May 2015 in St Petersburg.[38] There was already a Brodskii room in the Akhmatova museum, a recreation of his study in New York, which contained numerous typewriters, his desk, and other possessions, but the flat-museum places Brodskii beside other canonical figures, including Pushkin, who are similarly remembered. This museum is arguably the culmination of 'Brodskiimania'. The prolonged public interest in Brodskii since his death is indicative of, and has contributed to, the poet's canonisation in post-Soviet Russia.

The arguments I have developed through this examination of Brodskii's posthumous critical reception are supported by quantitative analysis of both primary sources by Brodskii and secondary sources about the poet that have been published in Russia between 1987 and 2012. During the early period of Brodskii's reception in Russia there were 19 books published that bear his name. Of these, 18 were individual general collections of his poetry or works. This is indicative of the tendency during this period to publish large collections of a writer's literary output rather than individual cycles of poetry. In comparison, during the years following Brodskii's death there were 144 books published. Of this number only 20 were collected works and 124 were individual cycles of poetry. This indicates a deeper interest in the individual works of Brodskii and demonstrates an increased awareness of the poet among readers of Russian literature.

A similar trend is revealed by quantitative analysis of secondary sources about Brodskii. During Brodskii's early reception there were only three books published about him in Russia. Of these, only one contained any textual analysis. In comparison, after his death eighty-eight books about Brodskii were published. Of these, forty-five included textual analysis of his poetry. A further thirty-five belong to a broader category that includes collections of interviews and addresses topics

---

38 'News: Joseph Brodsky's flat opens as museum in St Petersburg', *Russian Art + Culture*, 24 May 2015, http://www.russianartandculture.com/news-joseph-brodskys-flat-opens-as-museum-in-saint-petersburg

as capacious as Brodskii's influence on metaphysical poetry and his effect on Romantic poetry. A further two books comprise collections of photographs, and five deal specifically with Brodskii's place in the Russian canon.

On average, during his early reception 2.1 books of Brodskii's poetry were published per year, whereas after his death that number rose to 8.47 books per year. This represents an increase in commercial demand for the works of Brodskii of over 300%. An even more sizeable increase can be seen in terms of secondary sources, with an average of 0.3 books published per year during the poet's early reception, and, in comparison, an average of 5.17 books published per year after his death. This represents an increase of over 1454%. Yet, most importantly, there is also a shift towards more in-depth textual analysis, which demonstrates academic and scholarly interest in Brodskii's works, rather than just his biography.

As this chapter has shown, Brodskii's canonisation in Russia can be considered as a narrative. In this way we can see that Brodskii's posthumous canonisation was only possible due to his early reception, which was shaped by the process of literary canon revision together with wider changes in the cultural narrative. Whether or not Brodskii stands the test of time as a canonical poet in Russia remains to be seen, but at present his canonical narrative is comprised of a balance between literary and extra-literary factors. Brodskii can be situated in several coexisting canons: popular culture, world literature, Russian twentieth-century poetry, Russian émigré literature and prison writing. Even as Brodskii has been embraced by many different cultural forms in Russia, however, there is no shortage of established authors who reaffirm his status as a classic literary figure, and thereby emphasise his centrality to a logocentric culture. In Ol'ga Sedakova's obituary of Brodskii she states that he should be considered a 'poet of our time', the Virgil and Dante of Russian twentieth-century poetry.[39]

---

39   Ol'ga Sedakova, 'Konchina Brodskogo', http://olgasedakova.com/Poetica/239

3. 'Golden-Mouthed Anna of All the Russias': Canon, Canonisation, and Cult[1]

Alexandra Harrington

> The widespread worship of her memory [...], both as an artist and as an unsurrendering human being, has [...] no parallel. The legend of her life and her unyielding passive resistance to what she regarded as unworthy of her country and herself, transformed her into a figure [...] not merely in Russian literature, but in Russian history in our century.
>
> Isaiah Berlin[2]

In theoretical discussions of the canon, there is perceptible slippage between canonical *authors* and canonical *works*.[3] Anna Akhmatova (1889–1966) qualifies not only as the canonical author of a range of canonical texts, but also as a major cultural icon. The Akhmatova museum at Fontannyi Dom is one of Petersburg's most important post-Soviet cultural sites relating to literary history, attracting on average 30,440 visitors a year, and the city now boasts 4 monuments to the poet.[4]

---

1   I should like to express my thanks to the organizers of, and participants at, the enjoyable and productive project workshops for their invaluable comments on drafts of this essay, and also to Tom Wynn for his. The title incorporates a phrase from Marina Tsvetaeva, 'Zlatoustoi Anne — vseia Rusi' (1916), *Sochineniia*, edited by Anna Saakiants, 2 vols. (Moscow: Khudozhestvennaia literatura, 1988), I, 79.

2   Isaiah Berlin, 'Anna Akhmatova: A Memoir', in *The Complete Poems of Anna Akhmatova*, edited by Roberta Reeder, translated by Judith Hemschemeyer (Boston: Zephyr Press, 1997), pp. 35–55 (p. 53).

3   Tricia Lootens, *Lost Saints: Silence, Gender, and Victorian Literary Canonization* (Charlottesville and London: University Press of Virginia, 1996), p. 6.

4   Details available at http://www.russianmuseums.info/M127

Berlin's words, written before the collapse of the Soviet Union, certainly still apply in twenty-first-century Russia — and in themselves constitute an element in Akhmatova's canonisation.

How and why did Akhmatova, a poet whose work was enormously popular in the pre-revolutionary period, but then became apocryphal (non-canonical, hidden away) in the Soviet era, become a key presence in the poetic canon and a figure of such significance in post-Soviet society? Akhmatova is an instructive example of a poet whose canonical status and international renown were by no means guaranteed or inevitable.[5] Her trajectory sheds revealing light on the mechanics of, and strategies involved in, literary canonisation, offering ways of productively bringing together and testing different theoretical perspectives on canonicity and canon formation, as well as exploring how these relate to popular phenomena such as secular sainthood and celebrity. As Berlin's remarks indicate, Akhmatova's canonical position is not explicable solely in terms of the intrinsic qualities of her poetry, but is also linked, as canonicity is generally, to 'complicated considerations of social and cultural history'.[6] One of the foremost among these in the Russian context is the tendency to view literature, and especially poetry, as a surrogate, or secular religion — Berlin characterises the popular attitude towards Akhmatova as one of 'worship' and, as Boris Gasparov notes, in Russia 'the sanctification of literature (an attitude that often included the sanctification of the writer as well) became a conscious element of society in the nineteenth century'.[7] This elevation of the author to secular sainthood extends across Eastern Europe, where 'serious literature and those who produce it have traditionally been overvalued', according to a recent cultural definition.[8]

---

5   Catriona Kelly, 'Anna Akhmatova (1889–1966)', *A History of Russian Women's Writing 1820–1992* (Oxford: Clarendon Press, 1994), pp. 207–23 (p. 210).
6   Robert Alter, 'Introduction', in Frank Kermode, *Pleasure and Change: The Aesthetics of Canon* (Oxford: Oxford University Press, 2004), pp. 3–12 (p. 12).
7   Boris Gasparov, 'Introduction', in Iurii M. Lotman, Lidiia Ia. Ginsburg, Boris A. Uspenskii, *The Semiotics of Russian Cultural History: Essays*, edited by Alexander D. Nakhimovsky and Alice Stone Nakhimovsky (Ithaca: Cornell University Press, 1985), pp. 13–29 (p. 13). See also: Catriona Kelly, *Russian Literature: A Very Short Introduction* (Oxford: Oxford University Press, 2001), p. 26; G. S. Smith, 'Russian Poetry: The Lives or the Lines?', *The Modern Language Review*, 95 (2000), xxix–xli (p. xl); Svetlana Boym, *Death in Quotation Marks: Cultural Myths of the Modern Poet* (Cambridge, MA and London: Harvard University Press, 1991), pp. 15–16.
8   Andrew Baruch Wachtel, *Remaining Relevant After Communism: The Role of the Writer in Eastern Europe* (Chicago and London: University of Chicago Press, 2006), p. 4.

This essay begins by exploring some of the extra-literary factors which contributed to Akhmatova's popular appeal and canonicity, such as her iconography, her strategies of charismatic self-presentation, and the vast industry of adulatory biographies and canonising memoirs devoted to her. It goes on to address how these relate to and combine with more strictly literary and aesthetic factors; in particular, her insistent textual practices of auto-canonisation and self-mythologisation, and her poetry's mnemonic qualities. It demonstrates that much of her success rests on the extent to which she was sensitive to cultural expectations of writers, composing her poetry and creatively shaping her biography to create the impression of herself as a unique, extraordinary individual. Roland Barthes famously sought to reduce the author to a function of the text, claiming in 1968 that the cultural image of literature was 'tyrannically centred on the author, his person, his life, his tastes, his passions'.[9] An anti-biographical critical stance is completely unsuited to the case of Akhmatova, who has entered the canon as a biography and personality — a literary celebrity and 'figure [...] in Russian history', as Berlin puts it. As this essay shows, the 'passive resistance' that he highlights made her a particularly important role model and emblematic figurehead for the Russian intelligentsia.

Iconography, Biographical Mythmaking, and the Hagiographic Epitext

In his historical study of fame, Leo Braudy observes:

> To understand why some are remembered with more force than others, we need to investigate the process by which fame becomes a matter of premeditation, a result of media management as much as of achievement, as well as how the great of the past behaved in such a way as to project larger-than-life images of themselves.[10]

Akhmatova made explicit attempts to impose herself upon the imaginations of others from the outset. To invoke Pierre Bourdieu's

---

9 Roland Barthes, 'The Death of the Author', in *Authorship: From Plato to the Postmodern*, edited by S. Burke (Edinburgh: Edinburgh University Press, 1995), pp. 125–30 (p. 126).

10 Leo Braudy, *The Frenzy of Renown: Fame and its History* (New York: Vintage Books, 1997), p. 15.

analogy, she entered the literary field with an instinctive feel for the game and played her trump cards with consummate skill.[11] Born Anna Gorenko, she adopted the exotic pseudonym which Iosif Brodskii later called 'her first successful line' and Marina Tsvetaeva (the only other plausible contender for the title of greatest Russian woman poet) characterised as an 'immense sigh' ('ogromnyi vzdokh').[12] When Akhmatova entered literary life, it was virtually unknown for women to make their way into the canon of great writers, but modernity offered new opportunities upon which she capitalised, carefully shaping her persona and expertly assimilating a tradition of women's writing that she simultaneously disavowed. She later claimed in an epigram that she 'taught women how to speak'.[13] Her restrained, unsentimental treatment of the theme of love, combined with her studiedly self-possessed, imperial bearing, soon earned her the canonising titles of 'Sappho of the North' and 'Anna of All the Russias'.[14]

Akhmatova's lyrics were immediately recognizable, bearing a distinctive stylistic stamp, or 'imprimatur'.[15] They had a confessional quality, presenting laconic narratives arranged 'narcissistically [...] around her persona', creating what Tom Mole terms a 'hermeneutic of intimacy' — the impression that they could only be understood fully through reference to their author's personality, to which they gave the illusion of access.[16] This, along with the biographical fact of her marriage to another prominent poet, Nikolai Gumilev, helped

---

11   Pierre Bourdieu, *The Field of Cultural Production: Essays on Art and Literature*, edited by Randal Johnson (Cambridge: Polity Press, 1993), p. 150.
12   Joseph Brodsky, 'The Keening Muse', in *Less Than One: Selected Essays*, edited by Joseph Brodsky (London: Penguin, 2011), pp. 34–52 (p. 35); Tsvetaeva, 'Zlatoustoi Anne' (see note 1).
13   Anna Akhmatova, 'Mogla li Biche slovno Dant tvorit'...' (1958), *Sochineniia*, edited by M. M. Kralin, 2 vols. (Moscow: Pravda, 1990), I, 280. See also Kelly, 'Anna Akhmatova' and Alexandra Harrington, 'Melodrama, Feeling, and Emotion in the Early Poetry of Anna Akhmatova', *The Modern Language Review*, 108 (2013), 241–73 (pp. 267–68) on Akhmatova and other women poets.
14   Andrew Baruch Wachtel and Ilya Vinitsky, *Russian Literature* (Cambridge: Polity Press, 2009), p. 181; Tsvetaeva, 'Zlatoustoi Anne' (see note 1).
15   Aaron Jaffe, *Modernism and the Culture of Celebrity* (Cambridge: Cambridge University Press, 2005), p. 20.
16   Aleksandr Zholkovskii, 'The Obverse of Stalinism: Akhmatova's Self-Serving Charisma of Selflessness', in *Self and Story in Russian History*, edited by Laura Engelstein and Stephanie Sandler (Ithaca and London: Cornell University Press, 2000), pp. 46–68 (p. 50); Tom Mole, *Byron's Romantic Celebrity: Industrial Culture and the Hermeneutic of Intimacy* (Basingstoke: Palgrave, 2007), pp. 22–23.

elevate Akhmatova to literary stardom. An adept self-marketer, she engineered a comprehensive move from the periphery into mainstream Russian culture by downplaying her Ukrainian heritage and emphasising her connections with aristocratic Tsarskoe Selo and metropolitan Petersburg.[17] As her career developed, Akhmatova reacted to contingency, moving away from her pre-revolutionary persona of demure yet decadent *femme fatale* and cultivating the (equally paradoxical) image of victimized martyr and triumphant survivor of Stalinism, thereby successfully inscribing herself in a hitherto exclusively male tradition of the Russian poet as heroic fighter against tyranny.

Akhmatova was an immediate heir to — and particularly skilled practitioner of — the neo-Romantic notion of *zhiznetvorchestvo* (life creation), developed by her older contemporaries, the symbolists, which conceived of life as art form in its own right and produced concerted efforts to impose an aesthetic pattern on behaviour and biography.[18] Numerous observations made by Akhmatova's contemporaries suggest that she often acted in accordance with a biographical imperative and shaped her conduct according to aesthetic criteria. Natalia Roskina recalled that 'she generally spoke to affirm her own conception of her life' and Nadezhda Mandel'shtam observed, 'She lived always aware of her own biography'.[19] She was in the habit of repeating anecdotes she was keen to have remembered, thereby creating a mythology, or body of stories about herself.[20] Although Akhmatova could hardly have single-handedly generated the interest in her that followed her death in 1966 or influenced the reintegration of her work into Russian literature in subsequent decades, she was extremely keen to control

---

17 See Alexandra Harrington, 'Anna Akhmatova', in *Russia's People of Empire: Life Stories from Eurasia, 1500 to the Present*, edited by Stephen M. Norris and Willard Sunderland (Bloomington and Indianapolis: Indiana University Press, 2012), pp. 255–63 (p. 256) and Aleksandr Zholkovskii, 'Anna Akhmatova: Scripts, Not Scriptures', *Slavic and East European Journal*, 40 (1996), 135–41 (p. 137).

18 See *Creating Life: The Aesthetic Utopia of Russian Modernism*, edited by Irina Paperno and Joan Grossman (Stanford: Stanford University Press, 1994); Alexandra Harrington, 'Anna Akhmatova's Biographical Myth-Making: Tragedy and Melodrama', *Slavonic and East European Review*, 89 (2011), 455–93 (pp. 455–59).

19 Natalia Roskina, 'Goodbye Again', in *Anna Akhmatova and Her Circle*, edited by Konstantin Polivanov, translated by Patricia Beriozkina (Fayetteville: University of Arkansas Press, 1994), pp. 162–98 (p. 175); Nadezhda Mandel'stam, 'Akhmatova', in *Anna Akhmatova and Her Circle*, pp. 100–29 (p. 121).

20 Anatoly Naiman, *Remembering Anna Akhmatova*, translated by Wendy Rosslyn (New York: Henry Holt, 1991), pp. 81–82.

representations of herself and to lay down an official, coherent version of her life and career for posterity. Biography in Russia had long involved 'setting out an author's creative path, according to a Romantic model' and representing the writer's life as a 'saintly path of suffering and triumph'.[21] Akhmatova's tendency to 'live biographically' and to shape the narrative of her life according to traditional models is revealing of the extent to which she both understood, and responded to, dominant cultural expectations.[22]

As Braudy notes, 'Whatever political or social or psychological factors influence the desire to be famous, they are enhanced by and feed upon the available means of reproducing the image'.[23] Similarly, Chris Rojek observes that celebrities seem 'superhuman' because 'their presence in the public eye is comprehensively staged'.[24] When Akhmatova published her first collection, *Vecher* (*Evening*, 1912), contemporary readers were already inclined to confer celebrity status upon literary figures and to recognise them through visual images (postcards of Aleksandr Blok had been on sale from at least 1909, for instance).[25] Akhmatova exploited her own striking physical appearance, becoming one of the most frequently photographed, painted, and sculpted of cultural figures during her lifetime.[26]

Among the best-known portraits of Akhmatova is a stylised photograph of 1924 by Moisei Nappel'baum (Figure 3.1) which displays her distinctive profile complete with fringe and aquiline nose. The pose, as well as the sculptural sharpness of the image, is reminiscent of a monarch's head on a coin, and automatically connotes power and authority. Of all the photographs published in the Ardis collection of Nappel'baum's portraits (of which it is the cover image), this is the only one in complete 180-degree facial profile.[27] Akhmatova's pose, this suggests, was not typical of Nappel'baum's practice. It proceeded from

---

21 Kelly, *Russian Literature*, p. 58.
22 Sophie Ostrovskaia, *Memoirs of Anna Akhmatova's Years 1944–1950*, translated by Jesse Davies (Liverpool: Lincoln Davies & Co., 1988), p. 48.
23 Braudy, p. 4.
24 Chris Rojek, *Celebrity* (London: Reaktion Books, 2001), p. 13.
25 Gregory Freidin, *A Coat of Many Colors: Osip Mandelstam and his Mythologies of Self-Presentation* (Berkeley and Los Angeles: University of California Press, 1987), p. 44.
26 See M. V. Tolmachev, 'Akhmatova v izobrazitel'nom iskusstve', in *Tainy remesla*, Akhmatovskie chteniia 2, edited by N. V. Koroleva and S. A. Kovalenko (Moscow: Nasledie, 1992), pp. 158–97.
27 Moisei Nappel'baum, *Nash vek*, edited by Il'ia Rudiak (Ann Arbor: Ardis, 1984).

what was already an established way of representing the poet from the side, as with Natan Al'tman's portrait of 1914, Osip Mandel'shtam's poem 'Vpoloborota, o pechal'...' ('Half-turning, o grief...', 1914), and her own auto-description, 'a profile fine and cruel' ('profil' tonok i zhestok'), in a lyric of 1912.[28] While her lyrics invite intimacy, her portraiture creates distance — she exemplifies the combination of the 'fantasy of intimacy' and 'reality of distance' that is a feature of celebrity.[29]

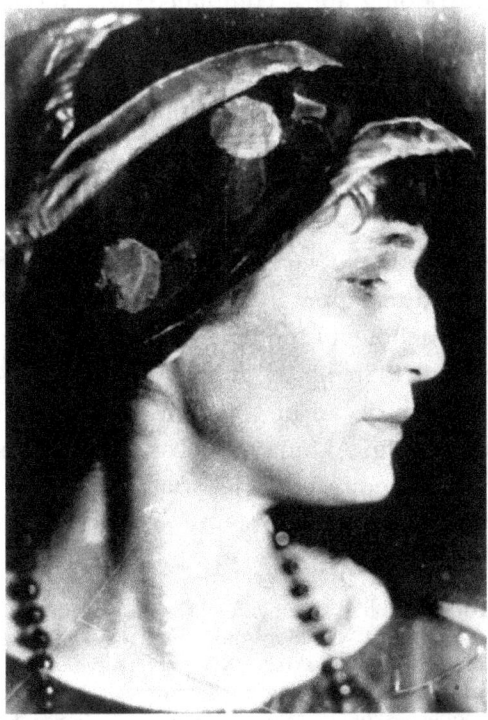

Fig. 3.1 Among the best-known portraits of Akhmatova is a stylised photograph by Moisei Nappel'baum (1924). © E. Tsarenkova and E. Nappel'baum, all rights reserved.

In Nappel'baum's picture, Akhmatova wears a bead necklace evoking her greatest critical success, the collection *Chetki* (*Rosary*, 1914), and lyric self-portrait, 'Na shee melkikh chetok riad...' ('On the neck a string of fine beads', 1913). As well as the necklace — presented simultaneously

---

28 'Protertyi kovrik pod ikonoi', Akhmatova, *Sochineniia*, I, 70.
29 David P. Marshall, *Celebrity and Power: Fame in Contemporary Culture* (Minneapolis and London: University of Minnesota Press, 1997), p. 178.

as religious artefact and item of female jewellery — Akhmatova wears a cloche hat, which on the one hand announces her as modern and bohemian, but on the other serves to cover her hair demurely. All this visually articulates the famous nun/harlot dichotomy which was used by Boris Eikhenbaum in 1923 to highlight the oxymoronic characteristics of Akhmatova's heroine, then appropriated in 1946 by Andrei Zhdanov, whom Stalin had placed in charge of cultural policy, as condemnation.[30] In this respect, the photograph accumulated meanings over time, so that its symbolic value as icon shifted correspondingly. Other photographs and portraits of Akhmatova similarly testify to her 'sophisticated understanding of self-presentation'.[31]

Visual portraits can be 'linked to the contexts of narratives about personal qualities that constitute a body of myth and a hagiography'.[32] Akhmatova's 'meaning' as major writer is generated and organised not only by her portraits, poetry, and fragmentary prose, but also by a substantial epitextual apparatus (epitext being the term used by Gérard Genette to denote all the material surrounding a text, but not appended to it, which circulates 'in a virtually limitless physical and social space' and which can be 'overwhelmingly authorial', even if compiled by others).[33] In Akhmatova's case, this epitext is comprised of the biographies, memoirs, critical studies, and so on devoted to her, with which her iconography and poetry interact in complex ways.[34] In

---

30 Boris Eikhenbaum, 'Anna Akhmatova: Opyt analiza', *O poezii* (Leningrad: Sovetskii pisatel', 1969), pp. 75–147 (p. 136); Andrei Zhdanov, 'O zhurnalakh "Zvezda" i "Leningrad": Iz postanovleniia TsK VKP (b) ot 14 avgusta 1946 g.', in *Sovetskaia pechat' v dokumentakh*, edited by N. Kaminskaia (Moscow: Gosudarstvennoe izdatel'stvo politicheskoi literatury, 1961), pp. 94–98. On the nun/harlot representation of women in the Silver Age, see T. A. Pakhareva, 'Obraz "monakhini-bludnitsy" v kul'turnom kontekste serebrianogo veka', *Anna Akhmatova: epokha, sud'ba, tvorchestvo: Krymskii Akhmatovskii nauchnyi sbornik*, 9 (2011), 227–37.

31 Helena Goscilo, 'Playing Dead: The Operatics of Celebrity Funerals, or, the Ultimate Silent Part', in *Imitations of Life: Two Centuries of Melodrama in Russia*, edited by Louise McReynolds and Joan Neuberger (Durham, NC, and London: Duke University Press, 2002), pp. 283–319 (p. 294).

32 James F. Hopgood, 'Introduction', in *The Making of Saints: Contesting Sacred Ground*, edited by James F. Hopgood (Tuscaloosa: University of Alabama Press, 2005), pp. xi–xxi (p. xiii).

33 Gérard Genette, *Paratexts: Thresholds of Interpretation*, translated by Jane E. Lewin (Cambridge: Cambridge University Press, 1997), pp. 344 and 351.

34 The texts comprising the epitext are too numerous to list here, but they include: Amanda Haight, *Anna Akhmatova: A Poetic Pilgrimage* (Oxford: Oxford University Press, 1976); Lidiia Chukovskaia, *Zapiski ob Anne Akhmatovoi*, 3 vols. (Moscow: Vremia, 1987; 2013); and works in other media, such as the documentary film

combination, these materials possess a phenomenal extra-literary power and — as is increasingly acknowledged — in large part reproduce an image of Akhmatova that the poet herself consciously constructed and promoted, reinforcing her own biographical mythmaking, and glossing over any detail that threatens to destabilise the received image of moral exemplar and persecuted genius.[35] They thus perpetuate a hagiographic, adulatory version of Akhmatova's biography and personality, creating a one-sided, monumental image that is both 'larger and leaner' than life.[36] Literary scholars have also contributed to the hagiographic discourse on Akhmatova, perhaps because she conforms to an elitist model of authorship that produces what Rebecca Braun calls 'creator fetishism' — the elevation of authors to the status of an intellectual and moral ideal.[37]

Akhmatova as Canon-Maker

Robert Alter suggests, however, following Frank Kermode, that it is not academics, but 'writers, resuscitating and transforming and interacting with their predecessors, who both perpetuate and modify the canon', so that the canon is somehow 'intentional, possibly on the part of writers who aspire to enter it'.[38] This is largely borne out in the case of Akhmatova, who exhibited what might be termed a canon mindset. From early on, she and her fellow Acmeists were concerned with protecting the high literary achievement of the past. Initially the greatest challenge came from avant-garde futurist contemporaries who advocated throwing her cherished Aleksandr Pushkin and Fedor Dostoevskii overboard from the 'Steamship of Modernity'.[39] Later, a more serious threat was posed

---

     directed by Semen Aranovich, *Lichnoe delo Anny Akhmatovoi* (Lenfil'm, 1989); and John Tavener's musical setting, *Akhmatova: Requiem* (1980).

35 Solomon Volkov describes her as the 'master par excellence of self-fashioning': *The Magical Chorus: A History of Russian Culture from Tolstoy to Solzhenitsyn*, translated by Antonina W. Bouis (New York: Vintage Books, 2009), p. 161.

36 Zholkovskii, 'Scripts', p. 14 and 'Obverse', p. 46. See also his 'Anna Akhmatova: Piat'desiat let spustia', *Zvezda*, 9 (1996), 211–27 and 'Strakh, tiazhest', mramor (iz materialov k zhiznetvorcheskoi biografii Akhmatovoi)', *Wiener Slawistischer Almanakh*, 36 (1996), 119–54; Harrington, 'Biographical Myth-Making', pp. 469–73.

37 Rebecca Braun, 'Fetishising Intellectual Achievement: The Nobel Prize and European Literary Celebrity', *Celebrity Studies*, 2: 3 (2011), 320–34 (pp. 322–23).

38 Alter, pp. 7 and 4.

39 Available at http://feb-web.ru/feb/mayakovsky/texts/mp0/mp1/mp1-399-.htm

by the Soviet regime with its dislike of modernism, limited canon, and prescriptive attitude towards literary production, so that perpetuating a non-official counter-canon became a matter of cultural preservation.

Akhmatova was herself prescriptive in her recommendations (she pronounced that 'two hundred million people' should read Aleksandr Solzhenitsyn's *Odin den' Ivana Denisovicha* (*One Day in the Life of Ivan Denisovich*), and displayed a pronounced tendency to list, rank, and use superlatives (Dostoevskii is 'the most important'; Franz Kafka is 'the profoundest and most truthful of modern authors', etc.).[40] Her view of the poetic canon was conservative, with Pushkin at its apex, and the only significant revisions she made were in the realm of prose: she disliked Anton Chekhov, and also demoted Ivan Turgenev and Lev Tolstoi.[41] These idiosyncrasies (which indicate a pronounced anxiety of influence) aside, her personal canon, insofar as it can be constructed on the basis of her poetry and recorded observations about literature, resembles a reduced version of Harold Bloom's.[42] She admired Homer, Hesiod, Sophocles, Euripides, Horace, Virgil, Ovid, Dante, and Shakespeare, among others, and would presumably have agreed with T. S. Eliot, whom she also revered, that a poet must embody 'the whole of the literature of Europe from Homer'.[43]

Of major significance for Akhmatova's canonical status is the position she assumed as a living relic and guardian of the Silver Age of Russian culture. Something of a 'fallacy' and 'cultural construct of retrospective origin', this period, which saw the first explosion of Russian modernism across the arts, came to be regarded as a charmed, legendary era in the Russian collective consciousness.[44] Akhmatova undertook a large-scale poetic reflection on the Silver Age in the latter part of her career, asserting her right to act as its chronicler, and placing herself at its centre. Various poems reminisce about the 1910s and its denizens, and

---

40 Roberta Reeder, *Anna Akhmatova: Poet and Prophet* (London: Allison & Busby, 1994), p. 372; Roskina, p. 187; Berlin, p. 42.

41 See Olga Tabachnikova, 'Akhmatova on Chekhov: A Case of Animosity?', *Russian Literature*, 66: 2 (2009), 235–55.

42 Harold Bloom, *The Western Canon: The Books and School of the Ages* (New York: Riverhead Books, 1994).

43 T. S. Eliot, 'Tradition and the Individual Talent', in *Points of View* (London: Faber & Faber, 1941), pp. 23–34 (p. 25).

44 Omri Ronen, *The Fallacy of the Silver Age in Twentieth-Century Russian Literature* (Amsterdam: Harwood Academic, 1997); Galina Rylkova, *The Archaeology of Anxiety: The Russian Silver Age and its Legacy* (Pittsburgh: University of Pittsburgh Press, 2007), p. 6.

they often take the form of subjective summaries of their individual achievements which are given an objective, authoritative character. Blok is thus characterised as the 'tragic tenor of the epoch' and 'monument to the beginning of the century'.[45]

Akhmatova's most concerted attempt to mythologise the Silver Age and establish her own place in it is her sprawling, multilayered *Poema bez geroia* (*Poem Without a Hero*, 1940–1965). The poem blends different modernist idioms and combines diverse material from memory in the manner of *bricolage* (the term used by Claude Lévi-Strauss to characterise the typical patterns of mythological thought).[46] It presents Akhmatova as self-appointed expert and commentator on, and evaluator of, the Silver Age, as well as a key participant. In this respect the poem both contributes to Akhmatova's biographical legend and has a particular canon-making thrust. The poem itself lays claim to canonical status for its innovative daring and unique formal structure, and can legitimately be regarded as one of the first Russian postmodernist texts. It interacts closely with modernism, from which its principles of composition are derived, but succeeds and exceeds it, celebrating modernism and evaluating it with hindsight. The poem proved timely: it both pre-empted and, in its late stages of composition, was energized by a resurgence of interest in the Silver Age that remained strong from the mid to late 1960s into the post-Soviet era. Akhmatova wrote:

> Time has worked upon *Poem Without a Hero*. Over the last 20 years, something amazing has happened; that is, before our very eyes an almost complete renaissance of the 1910s has taken place. [...] Mandel'shtam, Pasternak, Tsvetaeva are being translated and coming out in Russian. [...] Almost no-one has been forgotten, almost all are remembered.[47]

Akhmatova's remark indicates her awareness of the incompleteness of the Silver Age canon and of the role that chance — a neglected factor in discussions of canonicity — can play in canon creation.[48] She went to considerable lengths to ensure her own place through a form of intertextual auto-canonization. One of her late poems, 'Nas chetvero'

---

45 'Tri stikhotvoreniia' (1944–1960), in Akhmatova, *Sochineniia*, I, 289.
46 R. D. Timenchik, 'K semioticheskoi interpretatsii "Poemy bez geroia"', *Trudy po znakovym sistemam*, 6 (1973), 438–42 (p. 439); Lévi-Strauss developed the concept of *bricolage* in *La Pensée sauvage* (Paris: Librarie Plon, 1962).
47 Anna Akhmatova, *Sobranie sochinenii*, 6 vols. (Moscow: Ellis Lak, 1998), III, 255.
48 Alter, p. 4.

('The Four of Us', 1961), part of the cycle 'Venok mertvym' ('A Wreath for the Dead'), is a particularly blatant exercise in self-promotion and canon formation, and operates according to the assumption that — as Kermode puts it — each member of the canon 'fully exists only in the company of others; one member nourishes or qualifies another'.[49] It reads:

Нас четверо
Комаровские наброски

Ужели и гитане гибкой
Все муки Данта суждены.
О.М.

Таким я вижу облик Ваш и взгляд.
Б.П.

О, Муза Плача.
М.Ц.

…И отступилась я здесь от всего,
От земного всякого блага.
Духом, хранителем 'места сего'
Стала лесная коряга.

Все мы немного у жизни в гостях,
Жить — это только привычка.
Чудится мне на воздушных путях
Двух голосов перекличка.

Двух? А еще у восточной стены,
В зарослях крепкой малины,
Темная, свежая ветвь бузины…
Это — письмо от Марины.[50]

---

49 Kermode, p. 33. Akhmatova was not the first Russian modernist to compose poetic wreaths — Viacheslav Ivanov's 'Venok sonetov' (1909) was written in memory of his wife. On 'Venok mertvym', see N. L. Leiderman and A. V. Tagil'tsev, *Poeziia Anny Akhmatovoi: ocherki* (Ekaterinburg: Slovesnik, 2005), pp. 67–87.

50 Akhmatova, *Sochineniia*, I, 253, reproduced with permission. The translation is my own.

There are Four of Us
Komarovo Sketches

Is the lithe gypsy really also fated to experience
All Dante's torments?
O. M.

This is how I see your face and glance.
B. P.

O, Muse of Weeping…
M. Ts.

…And here I renounced everything,
All earthly blessings.
The forest tree stump became
The spirit, guardian of 'this place'.

We are all a little like guests in life,
To live — is just a habit.
It seems to me that on the airy highways
Two voices call to one another.

Two? But still, by the eastern wall,
In a thicket of sturdy raspberry bushes
There's a dark, fresh branch of elder…
It's — a letter from Marina.

Akhmatova identifies the major Russian poets of the twentieth century as herself, Mandel'shtam, Tsvetaeva, and Boris Pasternak. She effectively operates according to the axiom that there is strength in numbers — it would have been an act of extreme hubris to name only herself, but in celebrating her famous contemporaries and including herself in a poetic quartet, the self-aggrandizement of the gesture is somewhat mitigated. Nonetheless, Akhmatova still makes herself the central, focal point of interest by quoting lines from poems addressed to her.

The main body of the lyric enters into intertextual contact with the other poets, most notably Pasternak and Tsvetaeva (the fact that allusion to Mandel'shtam is less in evidence is in itself revealing — of all three, Akhmatova held him in the highest regard and they were on the closest personal terms). On the face of it, Akhmatova pays particular homage to Pasternak: the key phrase 'airy highways' ('vozdushnye puti') is drawn from his 1924 short story of that title, and Akhmatova's own title immediately recalls his lyric 'Nas malo. Nas, mozhet byt', troe' ('We are few. There are, perhaps, three of us...', 1921).[51] The original three were Pasternak himself, Vladimir Maiakovskii, and Nikolai Aseev, his fellow futurists, so that Pasternak's poem also has a canon-making dimension.

Underlying Akhmatova's surface homage it is possible to detect a pronounced degree of polemic. She had a tense, competitive relationship with Pasternak, from whom she became somewhat estranged towards the end of his life. There are strong indications in memoirs that she was jealous of his Nobel Prize — a marker of his own canonization — and she was offended by what she saw as his neglect or imperfect knowledge of her poetry and apparent demotion of her as an important figure of twentieth-century Russian verse.[52] Her line 'To live — is just a habit' ('Zhit' — eto tol'ko privychka') is both an echo and refutation of Pasternak's maxim, from 'Gamlet' ('Hamlet', 1946) — the most well-known of the Zhivago poems and key component of Pasternak's own self-mythology (it was read at his graveside): 'Life isn't a stroll across a field' ('Zhizn' prozhit' — ne pole pereiti').[53] 'Nas chetvero' thus offers a covert challenge and corrective to Pasternak, while purporting to cement his position in Russian poetry alongside Akhmatova's own.

Roman Timenchik points to the complex origins of this lyric, which arose from a chance confluence of impressions and reminiscences.[54] In 1961, Akhmatova was in hospital reading Tsvetaeva. In 'Nas chetvero', she alludes to Tsvetaeva's work through the image of the *buzina* (elderberry branch), the central motif of the lyric 'Buzina tsel'nyi sad zalila!' ('Elderberry filled the entire garden!', 1931–1935) and a prominent image in an essay of 1934, from which Akhmatova's rhyme

---

51 Boris Pasternak, *Vozdushnye puti: Proza raznykh let* (Moscow: Sovetskii pisatel', 1982), pp. 123–35.
52 Reeder, pp. 360–66.
53 Boris Pasternak, *Izbrannoe*, edited by A. Pikach, 2 vols. (St Petersburg: Kristall, 1998), II, 518.
54 Roman Timenchik, 'Rozhdenie stikha iz dukha prozy: "Komarovskie kroki" Anny Akhmatovoi', in *Analysieren als Deuten: Wolf Schmid zum 60. Geburtstag*. Edited by L. Flejshman, C. Gölz and A. A. Hansen-Löve (Hamburg: Hamburg University Press, 2004), pp. 541–62 (p. 541).

maliny/Mariny also derives. In the essay, Tsvetaeva states her wish to be buried 'under an elderberry bush' ('pod kustom buziny').⁵⁵

Akhmatova reacted contemptuously to Tsvetaeva's essay, describing it as 'terrifying stupidity' ('strashnaia glupost"').⁵⁶ The negative tone of this appraisal is also perceptible in other remarks about Tsvetaeva, in relation to whom Akhmatova displays a pronounced anxiety and rivalry.⁵⁷ There is evidence to suggest that Tsvetaeva was equally ambivalent about Akhmatova, and that the latter sensed this: she perceived Tsvetaeva's 1916 poems dedicated to her as 'not altogether benevolent'.⁵⁸ Alyssa W. Dinega argues cogently that Tsvetaeva's cycle is far from being the 'adoringly eulogistic' tribute that it appears. Instead, its poems constitute 'interlocutionary minibattles' in which Tsvetaeva engages in a 'contest of competing mythologies'. Dinega concludes that the cycle constitutes an attempt 'ironically [to] canonize' Akhmatova as pre-eminent female poet of all Russia in order to allow Tsvetaeva to 'stake out her own poetic domain' in contrast.⁵⁹

Although the final stanza appears to be a tribute and expression of kinship, when considered against the biographical context of Tsvetaeva's suicide, the line 'To live — is just a habit' in the previous stanza seems singularly glib and unfeeling. Moreover, while the two (male) voices of Pasternak and Mandel'shtam intersect on the 'vozdushnye puti', Tsvetaeva is denied this triumphant overcoming of time and space: she is less audible ('Two?' ('Dvukh?')), and the elderberry branch is likened to a letter, not a poem. She is given an inferior position in the quartet and effectively discarded in the undergrowth, not quite-but almost-buried, albeit not under an elderberry bush according to her wishes, but in a thicket of raspberry bushes.

Akhmatova's poem is paratextually heavy.⁶⁰ A twelve-line lyric, it is bolstered by a grandiose set of title, subtitle, and three epigraphs (which

---

55 'Kirillovny', in Tsvetaeva, *Sochineniia*, 2 vols. (Moscow: Khudozhestvennaia literatura, 1980), II, 77–84 (pp. 83 and 84).
56 Timenchik, 'Rozhdenie stikha', p. 544.
57 Tamara Kataeva, *Anti-Akhmatova* (Moscow: Ellis Lak, 2007), pp. 400–06 and *Otmena rabstva: Anti-Akhmatova 2* (Moscow: Astrel', 2012), pp. 37; *Akhmatova bez gliantsa*, edited by Pavel Fokin (St Petersburg: Amfora, 2008), p. 235.
58 Timenchik, 'Rozhdenie stikha', p. 554.
59 Alyssa W. Dinega, *A Russian Psyche: The Poetic Mind of Marina Tsvetaeva* (Madison: University of Wisconsin Press, 2001), pp. 37–38.
60 For a definition of the paratext see Genette, p. 1.

together are about a third as long as the main text). Genette identifies four distinct functions of an epigraph, all of which are in operation here. The first is to 'elucidate and justify' the title: here the epigraphs reveal the identity of the 'four' in question. The second is to comment on the text, 'whose meaning it indirectly specifies or emphasizes': Akhmatova's epigraphs serve primarily to signal the idea of dialogue between poets, and they also articulate and reinforce key aspects of her personal mythology, arguably the poem's real theme.[61] The epigraphs from Pasternak and Mandel'shtam recall her charismatic, youthful physical image, and the quotations from Mandel'shtam (again) and Tsvetaeva convey the idea of tragic suffering.[62] A third, more oblique function of an epigraph is to give 'indirect backing' ('the main thing is not what it says but who its author is'): this is clearly a key motivation for Akhmatova. Last but not least, the fourth function is what Genette calls 'the epigraph-effect', whereby an epigraph is intended as a sign of culture. With it, an author 'chooses his peers and thus his place in the pantheon'.[63]

Martyrdom and Martyrology

Rekviem (*Requiem*, 1935–1961), probably Akhmatova's best-known work, is a compelling and instructive example of a canonical poem which led a precarious, 'furtive, underground' mode of existence — relying exclusively on human memory for its survival, as it was too dangerous to keep a written version.[64] The story is well known: Akhmatova entrusted the poem to the memories of a small group of friends, scribbling lines down on a scrap of paper so that they could be silently memorised (to avoid detection by the microphones installed in her apartment), at which point the scrawled words were immediately burnt over an ashtray. The poem's preservation therefore involved a combination of chance and

---

61 Genette, p. 160.
62 On the mythologising function of epigraphs, see David Wells, 'The Function of the Epigraph in Akhmatova's Poetry', in *Anna Akhmatova 1889–1989: Papers from the Akhmatova Centennial Conference, Bellagio*, edited by Sonia Ketchian (Oakland, CA: Berkeley Slavic Specialties, 1993), pp. 266–81 (p. 273).
63 Genette, p. 160.
64 Clare Cavanagh, *Lyric Poetry and Modern Politics: Russia, Poland, and the West* (New Haven and London: Yale University Press, 2009), p. 112.

individual acts of heroism (as with other non-conformist classics, such as Mandel'shtam's *Voronezhskie tetradi (Voronezh Notebooks)*).

In many respects, the conditions in which non-official poetry existed in the Soviet Union of the 1930s resemble older, oral traditions: Nadezhda Mandel'shtam called this the 'pre-Gutenberg era' of Russian literature.[65] Mandel'shtam's Stalin epigram, 'My zhivem, pod soboiu ne chuiia strany…' ('We live without feeling the country beneath us…', 1933), the most notorious example of an 'oral' work of the Soviet 1930s, was not written down until the poet transcribed it at his police interrogation.[66] The form of the poem — rhyming couplets — seems expressly designed for ease of oral transmission, and it duly bypassed the entire state censorship apparatus before it came to the attention of the authorities: it was apparently recited from memory by deputy GPU and future NKVD head, Genrikh Iagoda.[67]

John Guillory observes that 'there can be no general theory of canon formation that would predict or account for the canonization of any particular work, without specifying first the unique historical conditions of that work's production and reception'.[68] This is manifestly the case with *Requiem* (which was composed secretly, circulated widely in *samizdat* during the Thaw, and was published in the Soviet Union for the first time during *perestroika*, a period which produced what one commentator calls 'an altogether curious historical phenomenon — the *swift transformation of elite culture into mass culture*').[69] These culturally-specific historical and contextual factors also have a bearing on the intrinsic, aesthetic qualities of the text, because it was designed for memory.

---

65 Nadezhda Mandelstam, *Hope Against Hope*, translated by Max Hayward (London: Collins and Harvill Press, 1971), p. 192.
66 Cavanagh, p. 115.
67 The *Gosudarstvennoi Politicheskoi Upravlenie* (GPU) was the State Political Directorate, the intelligence service and secret police of the Soviet Union. The *Narodnyi Komissariat Vnutrennikh Del* (NKVD) was the People's Commissariat for Internal Affairs, which oversaw the work of the GPU. Mikhail Gronas, *Cognitive Poetics and Cultural Memory: Russian Literary Mnemonics* (New York and London: Routledge, 2011), p. 7.
68 John Guillory, *Cultural Capital: The Problem of Literary Canon Formation* (Chicago and London: University of Chicago Press, 1993), p. 85.
69 Konstantin Azadovski, 'Russia's Silver Age in Today's Russia', http://www.pum.umontreal.ca/revues/surfaces/vol9/azadovski.htm

Mikhail Gronas's study *Cognitive Poetics* offers a compelling way of accounting for *Requiem*'s canonical status through its mnemonic qualities. Gronas likens aesthetic pleasure to sexual pleasure, suggesting that it, too, possesses an evolutionary logic, and hypothesising that 'what sexual pleasure is to genes, aesthetic pleasure is to memes' (the minimal units of cultural evolution or transmission first postulated by Richard Dawkins in 1976).[70] Gronas continues:

> What we subjectively experience as being thrilled, elated, soothed, moved, or inspired by a poem is in fact the poem's (or, rather, its memes') way to make sure that it replicates and propagates in human memory, the only medium that matters for things immaterial.[71]

In other words, according to this view, the great works of the literary canon are the mnemonically fittest and, to survive culturally, a text must possess 'certain mnemonic qualities [...]: it must comply with the demands of individual readers' memories and fit in with the mechanisms of institutionalized cultural memory, also known as the literary canon'.[72]

Gronas identifies Akhmatova in passing as a mnemonic poet.[73] Certainly, her concise, metrically traditional poetry has a strong mnemonic quality. To give an anecdotal piece of evidence: her second collection gave rise to a game, 'telling *Rosary*', whereby one person would begin to recite a poem and the next would complete it.[74] Brodskii observes that Akhmatova's poems 'could be committed to memory in a flash, as indeed they were — and still are — by generations and generations of Russians'.[75]

Although the text of *Requiem* as a whole is relatively long, its component parts, particularly the ten lyric poems that form its core, are all fairly brief (the longest has twenty lines). The second and third poems read:

---

70 Gronas, p. 1; Richard Dawkins, *The Selfish Gene*, 30th Anniversary Edition (Oxford: Oxford University Press, 2006), p. 192.
71 Gronas, p. 3.
72 *Ibid.*
73 *Ibid.*, p. 122.
74 Haight, p. 30.
75 Brodsky, p. 40.

II

Тихо льется тихий Дон,
Желтый месяц входит в дом.

Входит в шапке набекрень —
Видит желтый месяц тень.

Эта женщина больна,
Эта женщина одна,

Муж в могиле, сын в тюрьме,
Помолитесь обо мне.

III

Нет, это не я, это кто-то другой страдает.
Я бы так не могла, а то, что случилось,
Пусть черные сукна покроют,
И пусть унесут фонари.
     Ночь.[76]

II

Quietly flows the quiet Don,
Yellow moon enters a home.

He enters with hat aslant —
Yellow moon sees a shadow.

This woman is ill,
This woman is alone,

Husband in the grave, son in prison,
Pray for me.

---

76 Akhmatova, *Sochineniia*, I, 198, reproduced with permission. The translation is my own.

III

No, it's not me, it's someone else suffering.
I couldn't, and what happened,
Let them cover it in black cloth,
And let them take away the lanterns...
Night.

This brevity is highly successful in artistic terms — the fragmentary quality mirrors the persona's psychological breakdown and conveys the inadequacy of words to describe her experience. At the same time it has a more practical function: the cycle is broken down into short units, making it more readily memorisable. The folk metre of poem two assists in this process, as does the allusion to Blok's lyric 'Noch', ulitsa, fonar', apteka' ('Night, street, lantern, pharmacy', 1912) in poem three, because these features give further hooks for memorisation. Akhmatova's prevalent use of intertextuality is, in general, highly relevant to the issue of mnemonics. As Gronas writes, 'a mnemonic poet's mind is filled with preexisting poetic utterances that serve as material or background for the ones being newly created': it is significant that, for Akhmatova, allusion to other texts is not merely a prevalent device, but is frequently the primary principle of composition.[77] In one poem, she even suggests that poetry is nothing other than 'one magnificent quotation' ('odna velikolepnaia tsitata').[78] It is also worth noting that memory is arguably the major theme of Akhmatova's later poetry, and that *Requiem* itself is explicitly an act of memory which presents *remembering* as a moral imperative.

In taking a Darwin-inspired memetic approach to literary canon formation, Gronas sees himself as occupying the middle ground between the two poles of the canon debate — the 'aesthetic' (which, like Kermode, holds that canonicity arises from intrinsic qualities of texts) and the 'institutional' (which, like Guillory, stresses academia and curricula as sites of power in canon formation). The mnemonic approach complements these, defining canonicity as a 'measure of how often a text is read, reread, mentioned, cited, and analyzed over

---

77 Gronas, p. 82.
78 Akhmatova, 'Ne povtoriai — dusha tvoia bogata' (1956), *Sochineniia*, I, 301.

a historically significant slice of time; that is, as a yardstick of textual recurrence or reproducibility within a culture'.[79] According to this criterion, *Requiem* probably emerges as Akhmatova's most canonical text, not least in the West, where it has gained a secure foothold in Russian literary studies. Donald Loewen, analysing data collected from forty-six North American universities in 2006, noted that since 1982 *Requiem* had featured increasingly prominently on curricula: in 1982 it was the twelfth 'most frequently used' work, in 1992 the tenth and, in 2002, the seventh (the six works which the respondents used more are all works of prose). The most common reason given for the choice of text was 'literary merit'.[80] On this basis, *Requiem* undoubtedly deserves its place in the canon. It is, as Catriona Kelly contends, 'a work of artistic skill dedicated to a morally impeccable purpose'.[81] Clare Cavanagh remarks similarly that *Requiem* is 'internationally acknowledged as both a masterwork of modern writing and one of the past century's greatest testaments to an age of mass terrors'.[82]

Brodskii notes that the fact that Akhmatova's poetry is easily memorized is not in itself enough to make people want to commit it to memory — its appeal lies in its sensibility, the poet's treatment of her theme.[83] Both Kelly and Cavanagh point to *Requiem*'s unimpeachable moral credentials and Terry Eagleton, in a discussion of the relationship between poetry and morality, suggests that poems 'are moral statements [...] not because they launch stringent judgements according to some code, but because they deal in human values, meanings and purposes'.[84] While this is perhaps debatable as a general definition of poetry, *Requiem*'s humanity and powerful clarity as moral statement undoubtedly help to account for its enduring popularity and memorability. Kermode, in a reflection on aesthetic response, argues that canonical works produce in readers a complex form of pleasure that combines happiness with dismay.[85] Commenting on this view,

---

79 Gronas, pp. 8 and 52.
80 Donald Loewen, 'Twentieth-Century Russian Literature and the North American Pedagogical Canon', *Slavic and East European Journal*, 50 (2006), 172–86 (pp. 176–78 and 179).
81 Kelly, *Russian Literature*, p. 88.
82 Cavanagh, p. 126.
83 Brodsky, p. 40.
84 Terry Eagleton, *How to Read a Poem* (Oxford: Blackwell, 2007), p. 29.
85 Kermode, p. 23.

Alter suggests that in reading certain texts, 'We feel a keen sense of exhilaration in the magisterial power (and the courage) of the poetic imagination together with a wrenching experience of anguish over the vision of suffering or gratuitous evil or destructiveness articulated in the work'.[86] Again, the problems with Kermode's argument (and with Alter's sweeping use of 'we') notwithstanding, this description would probably encapsulate many readers' immediate responses to *Requiem*.

Requiem is not only aesthetically successful and morally satisfying, but contributes significantly to the image of Akhmatova as suffering martyr or survivor dissident (Anatolii Naiman calls it a 'martyrology').[87] It cannot be adequately appreciated without reference to the political context in which it was composed and which it indicts, or to the circumstances of Akhmatova's own biography, which gave her the authority to write it (it was directly inspired by the arrests of her son Lev Gumilev and common-law husband Nikolai Punin during the Ezhov Terror). It is thus central to Akhmatova's personal mythology and to her prevailing image as moral exemplar, staunch patriot, and implacable opponent of Stalinism. In it, she equates herself with both Mary, mother of Christ, and Russia itself, metonymically standing for all Russian women and assuming the role of 'chief mourner for a stricken people'.[88] Her words in the epigraph, 'I was with my people then' ('Ia byla togda s moim narodom'), are spoken more like a monarch than a silenced and disgraced poet.

Akhmatova as Secular Saint and Charismatic Leader

In Russia, a significant role in canon formation has historically been played by the intelligentsia (who influence public opinion through its members' roles in publishing houses, editorships of journals, and, latterly, television, radio and the internet).[89] This culturally-specific situation makes wholesale application of some Western theories of the canon problematic. In Guillory's understanding, for instance, the canon

---

86 Alter, p. 9.
87 Anatoly Naiman, *Remembering Anna Akhmatova*, translated by Wendy Rosslyn (New York: Henry Holt, 1991), p. 135.
88 Cavanagh, p. 126; Wachtel and Vinitsky, p. 181.
89 Rosalind Marsh, *Literature, History, and Identity in Post-Soviet Russia, 1991–2006* (Bern: Peter Lang, 2007), p. 17.

is not formed by a particular community of readers or social group. Rather, he emphasises the role of academia, the educational syllabus, in the reception and reproduction of literature and the canon.[90] These ideas can be productively applied to Russia only with some context-sensitive modifications: if 'institution' is taken to mean the cultural intelligentsia, the main propagators of the idea of literature as religion (who are not exclusively academics or educators), it becomes possible to understand more clearly why Akhmatova has achieved such cultural prominence, and how hagiographic, canonising memoirs like Lidiia Chukovskaia's have played a key part in this process.

The genre of memoir itself, as 'a mode of bestowing power', focused on a shared experience of a historical period ('stories of intimate life embedded in catastrophic history'), assumed a major role in the historical construction of the identity and community of the Russian intelligentsia.[91] Chukovskaia's record of her conversations with Akhmatova is a prime Soviet-era example, which forms part of a larger body of memoir literature that 'basically expresses the viewpoint of the old Russian intelligentsia and tends to be a literature of moral protest, either against the Soviet regime as such or against the abuses of the Stalin period'.[92] These memoirs provide a means of rationalising a paradoxical situation which involved compliance with the regime in terms of behaviour, coupled with non-compliance in viewpoint.[93] From the early 1930s onward, despite their ideological opposition to Soviet power, intellectuals were powerless actively to resist it.[94] Moreover, the intelligentsia — especially the cultural intelligentsia — constituted a highly privileged group within Soviet society. As Sheila Fitzpatrick points out, Stalin's regime made 'the basic decision to put its money on

---

90   Guillory, p. vii.
91   Beth Holmgren, 'Introduction', in *The Russian Memoir: History and Literature*, edited by Beth Holmgren (Evanston: North Western University Press, 2003), pp. ix–xxxiv (p. xxii); Irina Paperno, *Stories of the Soviet Experience: Memoirs, Diaries, Dreams* (Ithaca: Cornell University Press, 2009), p. 11; see also: Holmgren, *Women's Works in Stalin's Time: On Lidiia Chukovskaia and Nadezhda Mandelstam* (Bloomington: Indiana University Press, 1993).
92   Sheila Fitzpatrick, 'Culture and Politics under Stalin: A Reappraisal', *Slavic Review*, 35 (1976), 211–31 (p. 211).
93   Vladimir Shlapentokh, 'The Justification of Political Conformism: The Mythology of Soviet Intellectuals', *Studies in Soviet Thought*, 39 (1990), 111–35 (p. 114).
94   Smith, pp. xxiv–xxxv.

kul'turnost' (culturedness) [...] and to honor the old non-Communist, nonproletarian cultural intelligentsia'.⁹⁵ The *zhdanovshchina*, the major 'disciplinary operation against the cultural intelligentsia' (of which Akhmatova was the most prominent literary victim in 1946), caused widespread fear, but did not threaten the intelligentsia's existence or result in arrests.⁹⁶ Prominent cultural figures, although harried by censorship and consumed by dread of imprisonment, were generally afforded a degree of protection when it came to their physical fates, and Stalin intervened directly in the cases of famous non-conformist poets. In relation to Mandel'shtam, the greatest literary martyr of the period, his initial order was to 'isolate, but preserve'.⁹⁷ Similarly, he exhorted officials to leave Pasternak, 'that cloud-dweller' in peace, and he personally approved the list of cultural figures, including Akhmatova, to be evacuated from wartime Leningrad.⁹⁸ The power relations between party leadership and intelligentsia, which tend to be framed in terms of repression and purging, are thus more complex: 'the party had the political power to discipline the intelligentsia, but lacked the will or resources to deny its cultural authority'.⁹⁹ The intelligentsia was fragmented (many had emigrated, others were physically destroyed) and terrified, but was nonetheless largely able to maintain its traditions and separate sense of identity throughout the Stalin period.¹⁰⁰

After Stalin's death in 1953, intellectuals were increasingly able to confront the regime without fear of instant arrest, but only a minority dared to do so, so that a by-product of political conformism in the 1960s and especially the 1970s (the period following Akhmatova's death) was the intelligentsia's need to develop 'a special mythology capable of exculpating passive intellectuals as well as those who collaborated with the authorities'.¹⁰¹ Chukovskaia's memoirs play a role in this, because they vividly describe the 'anatomy and physiology of the fear which was deeply rooted in the minds of intellectuals after 1917' and provide a

---

95 Fitzpatrick, p. 229.
96 *Ibid.*
97 Mandel'stam, *Hope Against Hope*, p. 63.
98 See Simon Sebag Montefiore, *Young Stalin* (London: Phoenix, 2008), p. 59; Constantin V. Ponomareff, *The Time Before Death: Twentieth-Century Memoirs* (Amsterdam: Rodopi, 2013), p. 48.
99 Fitzpatrick, p. 230
100 *Ibid.*, pp. 230 and 219.
101 Shlapentokh, p. 113.

positive model of 'passive resistance' (as Berlin expresses it) in the figure of Akhmatova, who held sharply critical views of the system privately but was never flagrantly disobedient publicly.[102] Her occasional acts of conformism — most notably the publication of her pro-Stalinist 'Slava miru' ('In Praise of Peace', 1950) — were performed under duress, to protect her son. Akhmatova's 'passive resistance' (which maps onto what Aleksandr Zholkovskii characterises as her exercise of 'power through weakness', a strategy available as a result of her gender) proved less self-destructive than the active opposition of Mandel'shtam.[103] As Zholkovskii observes, it is 'precisely as a "survivor dissident" that she has been so representative of and, therefore, acceptable to the Soviet (now post-) intelligentsia'.[104] This view, he suggests elsewhere, conforms to a broader liberal approach to non-conformist classic authors that sees them either as innocent victims of the regime or penetrating critics of it (and sometimes both) who, despite being forced into certain compromises, did not espouse its ideology.[105]

Irina Paperno points out that belonging to the intelligentsia 'implies allegiance to values associated with nineteenth-century tradition: alienation from the establishment; rejection of accepted living forms, valorization of poverty, suffering, and self-denial; [...] staunch belief in literature as a source of moral authority [...]'.[106] These are central elements of the mythology surrounding Akhmatova — consider, for instance, her uncompromising stance in relation to Soviet authority, her unconventional household arrangements, the homelessness *topos* of her biography, her poverty and nun-like image, stoicism and poetic theme of renunciation, the role of the execution of Gumilev and imprisonments of her son and Punin in her biography, her dedication to her vocation.[107] This mythology conforms absolutely to the culturally-ingrained view of literature as a quasi-religion, according to which the poet's life is seen as a martyrdom and the literary text as gospel.

---

102 *Ibid.*, p. 125.
103 Zholkovsky, 'Scripts', p. 138.
104 *Ibid.*
105 Aleksandr Zholkovskii, 'K pereosmysleniiu kanona: sovetskie klassiki nonkonformisty v postsovetskoi perspektive', http://www-bcf.usc.edu/~alik/rus/ess/reth.htm
106 Paperno, p. 60.
107 On Akhmatova's asceticism, see Rylkova, p. 85.

The values listed by Paperno strongly echo the Christian conception of Christ's passion and by extension, narratives of saints' lives. Saints — religious or secular — are important as a focal point for identity building, providing a resource to turn to for wisdom in the face of hardship, bestowing 'sacred meaning on certain types of conduct and experience'.[108] Rojek observes that celebrities, as secular icons, 'simultaneously embody social types and provide role models', and argues that celebrity has a political as well as a social function, in that it 'operates to articulate, and legitimate, various forms of subjectivity that enhance the value of individuality and personality'.[109] Max Weber's classic definition of charismatic authority is apposite here:

> Charisma is a certain quality of an individual personality by virtue of which he is set apart from ordinary men and treated as endowed with supernatural, superhuman, or at least specifically exceptional powers or qualities. These are such as are not accessible to the ordinary person, but are regarded as of divine origin or as exemplary, and on the basis of them the individual concerned is treated as a leader.[110]

Akhmatova's emblematic importance for the intelligentsia (Paperno calls her its 'sacred cow') arises from the way in which she provides a role model that embodies its key values and reflects its own self-mythology, validating and bolstering its sense of identity.[111]

Iconoclasm and Mass Culture

In recent years, Akhmatova's image has suffered as a result of what Kermode calls the 'effect of monumentalization that is always the risk of […] elevation to the status of canonicity'.[112] He refers specifically to the annulment of pleasure in a particular literary *work*, but in Akhmatova's case it is the *author* that has been subject to this process of monumentalisation, so that a distinctly iconoclastic trend has entered discourses about her in the post-Soviet era.

---

108 Hopgood, pp. 15–16.
109 Rojek, pp. 16 and 53.
110 Max Weber, *On Charisma and Institution Building*, edited by S. N. Eisenstadt (Chicago: University of Chicago Press, 1968), p. 48.
111 Paperno, p. 60.
112 Kermode, p. 75.

Zholkovskii makes what is arguably the most significant critical intervention in Akhmatova studies since the 'semantic poetics' of the 1970s or formalist studies of the 1920s — although his focus is not primarily her poetry — in a series of articles which argue that Akhmatova's life-creating strategies are uniquely Soviet but, because of her anti-Soviet stance, produce the 'obverse of Stalinism', making her a paradox of 'resistance-cum-replication'.[113] He repeatedly emphasizes the Stalinist key of Akhmatova's behaviour, concluding that her careful manufacture of her image reveals her to be a 'power-smart' contemporary of Stalinism.[114] While he refutes the established view of Akhmatova as martyr, presenting her instead as a totalitarian ideologue whose capricious exercise of control over others was symptomatic of a form of Stockholm Syndrome, he does not contest her right to a position in the canon, although the grounds for her inclusion are significantly revised. Akhmatova's value, he asserts, resides not in her critical view of Soviet life but rather the opposite: her close identification with its fears and typical strategies.[115] He observes: 'The indisputable force of her poetry and persona lays a strong claim on a lasting place in the Russian literary canon — as perhaps the most durable specimen of the siege culture of her time', noting that she succeeded in establishing a cult that not only rivalled Stalin's, but proved to have greater staying power.[116]

However provocative and controversial Zholkovskii's thesis may appear in connection with a poet who is synonymous with moral protest and symbolises the suffering of the entire Soviet Union of the 1930s, it is difficult to ignore some striking parallels with Stalin's personality cult. Beth Holmgren, citing dissident historian Roy Medvedev's evidence on Stalin, observes:

> His opinions on every topic and in every discipline were cited as sacred scripture; his image proliferated as the icon of the great Leader [...]. At least on the public surface of Soviet society an almost religious, enraptured atmosphere prevailed in which '[t]he social consciousness of the people took on elements of religious psychology'.[117]

---

113 Zholkovsky, 'Obverse', p. 68.
114 Zholkovsky, 'Scripts', p. 141.
115 Zholkovsky, 'Obverse', pp. 62 and 68.
116 *Ibid.*, p. 68; Zholkovskii, 'Piat'desiat let spustia', p. 211.
117 Holmgren, *Women's Works*, p. 5.

A similar phenomenon is certainly observable in relation to Akhmatova. However, to make extended comparisons between her and Stalin is, as Galina Rylkova remarks, irresponsible.[118] Moreover, the Soviet period of Akhmatova's career sees not so much an emulation of Stalin's cult of personality as the development of mythmaking and self-advertising strategies that were shaped prior to the revolution by the theatrical, neo-Romantic cultural milieu in which she was formed as poet and which built upon nineteenth-, and even eighteenth-century traditions.[119] Boris Groys highlights Stalinist culture's fundamental Romanticism, expressed in its aspiration to extend art into life, so that modernist and avant-garde life-creation were transformed into Stalinist world-creation.[120] To over-emphasise the Stalinist influence on Akhmatova's behaviour (as Zholkovskii does), is to downplay the extent to which Stalin — who in his youth was a published Romantic poet — had himself assimilated the cultural traditions upon which Akhmatova drew.[121] It is entirely possible to turn Zholkovskii's argument on its head, making Stalin the imitator, and Akhmatova, and other modernists, the originals.[122]

Zholkovskii's deconstruction project has had a discernible impact on popular writing on Akhmatova, notably in two books by Tamara Kataeva: *Anti-Akhmatova* (2007) and *Otmena rabstva* (*Abolition of Slavery: Anti-Akhmatova 2*, 2012) — the slavery in question being the perceived obligation to venerate Akhmatova.[123] Unlike Zholkovskii, who does not dispute the quality of Akhmatova's poetry, Kataeva aims to demote her in the canon.[124] She goes much further than Zholkovskii in debunking the prevailing image of Akhmatova as unimpeachable moral authority and victim of Stalinism, presenting her as an egotistical, fame-obsessed and lazy drunkard, as well as a terrible mother, who did not actually suffer at all.

---

118 See Rylkova's article 'Saint or Monster? Akhmatova in the 21st Century', *Kritika: Explorations in Russian and Eurasian History*, 11: 2 (Spring 2010), http://muse.jhu.edu/article/379896
119 Harrington, 'Biographical Myth-Making', p. 458.
120 Boris Groys, *The Total Art of Stalinism: Avant-garde, Aesthetic Dictatorship, and Beyond*, translated by Charles Rougle (Princeton: Princeton University Press, 1992).
121 On Stalin as poet, see Sebag Montefiore, pp. 56–59.
122 Harrington, 'Biographical Myth-Making', pp. 488 and 492–93.
123 See note 57 in this chapter.
124 Kataeva, *Anti-Akhmatova*, pp. 455–87.

Kataeva's books are tendentious hatchet-jobs, yet despite their manifest flaws, they contain some astute observations and have been highly popular — *Anti-Akhmatova* went to three large print runs in two years. Predictably enough, they have prompted various outraged reactions from members of the intelligentsia keen to 'defend geniuses from mass culture'.[125] After the publication of *The Abolition of Slavery*, the poet Iunna Morits published a strident poetic defence of 'the great Anna Akhmatova' entitled 'Defekatsiia defektologa K' ('The Defecation of Speech Therapist K').[126]

These demythologising and iconoclastic interventions are unlikely to do Akhmatova's reputation any serious damage or topple her from her pedestal. In fact, they are a paradoxical indication of her continued celebrity and cultural dominance: as Dmitrii Bykov suggests, her 'unforgiven-ness' ('neproshchennost') and the mixture of strong emotions that she evinces are 'the guarantee of her immortality'.[127]

Secular Sanctification and the Power of Legend

A particularly noticeable feature of the debate generated by the Zholkovskii/Kataeva challenge to the received image of Akhmatova is the prominence of rhetoric drawn from religion and relating to religious canonisation. This clearly both arises from and reacts to the conception of literature as a form of surrogate religion and the elevation of Akhmatova to secular sainthood (the 'widespread worship' that Berlin observes). Zholkovsky charges scholars with writing 'hagio-biographies', and Kataeva objects strenuously to the idea of Akhmatova's 'saintly feat' ('podvig') and to the public 'veneration' ('blagogoveli pered Akhmatovoi') of her.[128] Viktor Toporov praises Kataeva for the fact that she 'took on the sacred' ('pokusilas' na sviatoe'), remarking that Akhmatova's poetic significance has been exaggerated and that her

---

[125] Natal'ia Ivanova, 'Mythopoesis and Mythoclassicism', *Russian Studies in Literature*, 45: 1 (2008–2009), 82–91 (pp. 85–86); Natal'ia Lebedeva, 'Gil'otina dlia zvezdy: kak zashchitit' geniev ot masskul'ta', *Rossiiskaia gazeta*, 446 (February 2007), http://www.rg.ru/printable/2007/08/22/chukovskaya.html

[126] Kataeva is a *defektolog*, or speech therapist. See http://www.morits.ru/cntnt/ne_dlya_pe/defekaziya.html

[127] Available at https://www.youtube.com/watch?v=_oKxZkqKsIs

[128] Kataeva, *Anti-Akhmatova*, p. 127.

life was far from being the 'great martyrdom' ('velikomuchenichestvo') that it is generally perceived to be: 'there is a place for her in the literary pantheon, although not the main one', he writes, 'but in the saints' calendar, hardly' ('a vot v sviattsakh — edva li'). All this, he continues, is obvious to anyone with any serious knowledge of Russian poetry, and yet it is perceived as 'blasphemy' ('koshchunstvo') to say so.[129]

The analogy between literary and religious canonisation is not wholly superficial or frivolous, for all that literary canonisation is a secular process.[130] Moreover, as the case of Akhmatova demonstrates, there appears to be a strong relationship (as well as confusion) between what, in religious terms, are two distinct categories: canonisation and sanctification. Canonisation is technically a formal process of adjudication (the closest analogy in literary terms is the Nobel Prize, which Akhmatova was never awarded, although she did receive a major Italian literary prize and an honorary doctorate from Oxford). Sanctification, on the other hand, is a popular process. The immense symbolic capital of authors in Russia has led to figures like Akhmatova becoming objects of worship. Even literary museums, like the one at Fontannyi Dom — as secular shrines complete with relics — seem to borrow from popular cults of saints. This secular sainthood resembles its religious counterpart in so far as it engenders strong emotions of identification or devotion: Akhmatova's grave in Komarovo is permanently adorned with flowers, icons, votive candles, and other offerings from members of the public.

There is inevitably a certain circularity to canonicity: Akhmatova is popular because she is in the canon, and in the canon because she is popular. She successfully constructed a larger-than-life persona, which was then promoted and embellished by others, particularly the late and post-Soviet intelligentsia, but also Western commentators like Berlin. Scrutiny of Akhmatova's assumption of canonical status proves instructive because, although various theoretical explanations for canonicity help to illuminate what lies behind her place in the canon — be they institutional, aesthetic, mnemonic — they clearly operate alongside factors that bear more closely on the phenomena of

---

129 Viktor Toporov, 'No, Bozhe, kak ikh zamolchat' zastavit'!', *Vzgliad*, 18 August 2007, http://vz.ru/columns/2007/8/18/101677.html

130 Lootens, p. 3.

literary celebrity and secular sanctification and which tend to feature less prominently in theoretical discussions of canonicity.[131] The case of Akhmatova is indicative not only of the extent to which religious conceptions and practices permeate Russian attitudes towards literature but also of how mythmaking and legend formation can shape the canon.

---

131 A noteworthy exception is Lootens.

4. Vladimir Maiakovskii and the National School Curriculum

Natalia Karakulina

> Склонится толпа,
> лебезяща,
> суетна.
> Даже не узнаете —
> я не я:
> облысевшую голову разрисует она
> в рога или в сияния.[1]
>
> The crowd will bow, fawning, fussing.
> You won't ever know if it's me or not:
> as it will paint over my balding head
> maybe with horns or maybe with a halo.

Russians study the works of the Soviet poet Vladimir Maiakovskii throughout their time at school. In this chapter I examine the national school curriculum, focsing on the material covered in the final grade of school education. While this might seem limiting, as students are first introduced to Maiakovskii at a much earlier age, this approach enables me to draw conclusions about the image of the poet that students take

---

1   Vladimir Maiakovskii, 'Deshevaia rasprodazha', in *Polnoe sobranie sochinenii*, 13 vols. (Moscow: Gosudarstvennoe izdatel'stvo khudozhestvennoi literatury, 1955), I, 116. Unless noted otherwise, all translations from Russian are my own.

with them when they leave secondary education. In order to analyse what this image is, and how it changed after the collapse of the Soviet Union, I shall discuss the approach to teaching literature in both Soviet and post-Soviet schools. After establishing the framework in which Maiakovskii was and is studied, I will draw conclusions about which of the poet's works receive most attention in the classroom, what aspects of his life are particularly highlighted, and, ultimately, what role the study of Maiakovskii plays for students who are in their final year of education.

The chapter is divided into four sections. The first establishes the approach to the study of literature in Soviet schools from the 1960s to the 1980s. As I will show, literature as a subject became increasingly dogmatic, consisting mainly of learning information by heart and repeating interpretations suggested by textbooks. A major aim of literary education was to instil moral and ideological principles in the students, and topics were presented with little room for individual interpretation. Both the dogmatic nature of teaching and the focus on cultivating timeless values resulted in students and teachers who were uncomfortable with independent analysis, favouring instead the repetition of information given in the textbook, which, in turn, reinforced the dogmatism of literary studies.

The second section of the chapter is dedicated to an analysis of how Maiakovskii was represented in the Soviet classroom. Stalin's resolution in 1935 proclaimed that Maiakovskii was 'the best, most talented poet' of the Soviet era,[2] and since one of the focuses of literary studies was to provide positive moral and ideological examples to emulate, Maiakovskii's image had to be flawless. Any details which might be perceived as contradictory to the established code of morality were represented as obstacles that the poet was able to successfully overcome as he developed greater maturity. Similarly, any inconvenient biographical facts (including the poet's complex personal life and his eventual suicide) were glossed over to present a narrative of his

---

[2] Iosif Stalin, 'Rezoliutsiia I. V. Stalina na pis'me L. Iu. Brik', in Svetlana Strizhneva, 'V tom, chto umiraiu, ne vinite nikogo'?... Sledstvennoe delo V. V. Maiakovskogo (Moscow: Ellis Lak, 2000 and 2005), p. 317.

linear progression towards becoming the most talented Soviet poet, and therefore end the representation of Maiakovskii on a high note. It is difficult to tell whether the majority of students believed in this interpretation, as most of their written output reproduced material that they had memorised.

In the third section I examine the changes that took place in literary education in schools after 1991. One of the main differences was that, whereas in the Soviet Union there was a single textbook used by all teachers and students, after 1991 numerous textbooks were published, often presenting different views and covering different material. Furthermore, during *perestroika* many new names appeared in the school curriculum — a process which continued throughout the 1990s. Such an increase in material led to a dramatic decrease in the number of study hours dedicated to any one author. However, the one aspect of school education that remained largely unchanged from the Soviet era was the importance of cultivating moral and ideological values in students, and this aspect continues to shape the nature of post-Soviet literary education.

Finally, the last section of this chapter analyses how Maiakovskii is represented in post-Soviet secondary education, and what are the differences and similarities between the Soviet and post-Soviet representations of the poet. This proved to be a far from straightforward task, as a multitude of available textbooks resulted in many different, and, in some cases, contrasting representations. However, the majority of textbooks offer a similar interpretation of Maiakovskii's biography, but one that is in stark contrast to the Soviet image of the poet: the idea that the poet was overall a tragic and lonely figure. Post-Soviet representations of Maiakovskii evolved throughout the 1990s: while accounts presented in the early years of the decade resemble in many aspects the Soviet-era canonical image of the poet, by the late 1990s the similarities almost disappear. The single common aspect shared by Soviet and post-Soviet textbooks is the authors' reluctance to go into the details of Maiakovskii's private life. It would appear that in an area of school education which aims to cultivate positive traits in students, some aspects of Maiakovskii's personality still remain too controversial to be discussed.

Literature in Soviet Russian Schools

For the Soviet government, literature was a tool for propagating certain behaviours and values. When it came to the study of literature at school, the aim was not only to introduce students to authors and literary works, but also, and perhaps more significantly, to provide an example of morals and good behaviour that students were invited to emulate. Literature, therefore, became a primary tool to educate students in how to live their lives. There was little place for ambiguity — textbooks contained all the examples to be studied and emulated, and the students had to demonstrate that they had absorbed them. In this section I will mainly focus on the period between the 1960s and 1980s, as during this time Maiakovskii's official canonical image was already well established.

On the first page of the 1989 edition of *Russkaia sovetskaia literatura* (*Soviet Russian Literature*), a textbook for final grade students, we see the slogan: 'Beregite knigu!' ('Take care of the book!').[3] A book (particularly a textbook) had a very high status in the Soviet system of values:

> Books help us to determine our future careers, teach us to think and to act, to develop our best moral qualities. The whole history of mankind, its ideals and aspirations are reflected and captured in books. Through literature we understand the past and the present, the life of our people and people from all around the world. A. Tvardovskii called literature a 'kind guide' in answering the main question for young people: who to become in future? Love your book! Let it be your constant companion. Treat the book with respect, as a source of knowledge and a textbook for life, take care of it.[4]

Throughout the history of the Soviet Union literature was often referred to as *chelovekovedenie* (the study of men).[5] This term has a two-fold meaning: first of all, literature as a school subject was designed to aid pupils in understanding the social realities of the day, and thus to contribute to students' ideological education so that they could become worthy, active members of society. Of equal importance to the ideological education of the students was their moral development. Ivan

---

3 Valentin Kovalev, *Russkaia sovetskaia literatura*, 11th ed. (Moscow: Prosveshchenie, 1989), p. 2.
4 *Ibid.*, p. 2.
5 Noah Norman Shneidman, *Literature and Ideology in Soviet Education* (Toronto: University of Toronto, 1973), p. 57.

Ogorodnikov, in his textbook *Pedagogika* (*Pedagogy*), lists those values and principles which are key for any builder of a communist society. Among the expected devotion to the cause of communism, collectivism and a high consciousness of one's social duties, are such universal moral values as respect for others, honesty, truthfulness, moral purity, modesty in public and in private life, mutual respect in the family, and concern for the education of children.[6] While the list of positive traits and qualities might seem extensive, the method of introducing students to these qualities was strictly defined and left no room for ambiguity: the texts included in the school curriculum depicted desirable values and personality traits; the teacher's task was to enable students to recognise those traits and values as positive. In turn, the students had to aspire to become as worthy as the protagonists they learned about in their literature classes.

Graduation from secondary school was the end of literary education for all those who did not specialise in the field. Therefore the objective of the education system was not only to familiarise pupils with selected authors and their literary heritage, but also to give them the necessary tools for understanding and interpreting any works of literature they might encounter in future. In Noah Shneidman's words,

> the pupil must be taught to approach and analyse a work of art from the Leninist point of view. He must learn to appreciate and to like what is necessary to like, and to criticise what the official party line requires him to criticise. It is a difficult task and for many years literature has been taught as a dogma: a subject in which all the answers are given and the pupil has just to remember them.[7]

The texts included in the final grade programme were carefully selected with the main focus on the 'strong ideological level of the texts, their educational meaning for students'.[8] This resulted in a fairly limited number of texts and authors studied over a reasonably large number of teaching hours. The bulk of the final-year programme consisted of the study of the lives and legacies of Maiakovskii and Maksim Gor'kii.

---

6   Ivan Ogorodnikov, *Pedagogika* (Moscow: Prosveshchenie, 1964), p. 52.
7   Shneidman, *Literature and Ideology in Soviet Education*, p. 16.
8   *Skhema programmy po literature dlia srednei shkoly. Proekt. Dlia obsuzhdeniia na biuro otdeleniia didaktiki i chastnykh metodik* (Moscow: Akademiia pedagogicheskikh nauk SSSR, 1983), p. 2.

In 1970, Maiakovskii was studied over fifteen school hours and Gor'kii over sixteen hours. The third most important Soviet author was Mikhail Sholokhov with his text *Podniataia tselina* (*Virgin Soil Upturned*), to which twelve hours of study time were dedicated. The rest of the authors, including Aleksandr Blok, Sergei Esenin, Aleksandr Fadeev, Konstantin Trenev, Nikolai Ostrovskii, Aleksei Tolstoi and Aleksandr Tvardovskii, were studied for three to five hours each, with the exception of Tolstoi, who was studied for eight hours, largely due to the fact that his work was represented with the rather weighty novel, *Petr I* (*Peter the First*). Many of the later Soviet poets, such as Aleksei Surkov, Konstantin Simonov and Pavlo Tychina, were all studied together under the banner of patriotic works from the period of the Great Patriotic War.[9] Thus students had more than a month to familiarise themselves with the works of Maiakovskii and the way he was represented in textbooks to accord with the image of 'the best, most talented poet'[10]—a positive character for students to emulate.

Maiakovskii in Soviet Russian Schools

An analysis of Maiakovskii's representation in school textbooks will reveals a number of key aspects on which the poet's image is built: the general description of the poet and his legacy; the description of the poet's upbringing; Maiakovskii's relationship with futurism and the avant-garde; the authors with whom Maiakovskii is associated and by whom his work was allegedly influenced; love and work; and finally, his suicide. After analysing the image of the poet which was built on these key points, I will consider how this information was meant to be used by students to fulfil given tasks, and how the students responded to these guidelines.

---

9   Ministerstvo prosveshcheniia RSFSR, *Programmy vos'miletnei i srednei shkoly na 1969/70 uchebnyi god. Russkii iazyk i literatura* (Moscow: Ministerstvo prosveshcheniia RSFSR, 1969), pp. 59–64. Also in Shneidman, *Literature and Ideology in Soviet Education*, pp. 91–92. The portion of World War Two in which the Soviet Union was involved (1941–1945) is known in Russian as 'Velikaia otechestvennaia voina', translated either as the Great Patriotic, or the Great Fatherland War. The use of this name connects the 1941–1945 war with Russia's participation in the Napoleonic wars, known to Russians as 'Otechestvennaia voina' (the Fatherland, or Patriotic War).
10 See note 2 in this chapter.

I will begin by outlining the canonical Soviet image of Maiakovskii, as presented to Soviet children. I am mainly using one source — the literature textbook *Russkaia sovetskaia literatura* (*Soviet Russian Literature*) by Valentin Kovalev[11] as during the Soviet period there existed only one official textbook on Soviet literature, which was used in all schools. Although I refer here to the eleventh edition published in 1989, this book is in keeping with the image of the poet presented to several generations of Russian children.

The first thing students learned about Maiakovskii (besides the fact that he was the most talented Soviet poet) was his biography, starting with his childhood. Students were presented with an idyllic picture of the poet's early life, with accounts of the young Maiakovskii's early revolutionary activities, fully supported by his loving parents, set against a backdrop of breath-taking Georgian scenery.[12] Unlike the poet's childhood, his early adulthood and the dawn of his career as a poet is under-represented. This is because futurism and left-wing art movements were viewed in a highly negative light after the initial post-revolutionary period, and therefore Maiakovskii's association with them were topics with which teachers and textbook authors preferred not to touch upon. Thus David Burliuk and Velimir Khlebnikov, both of whom were crucial to Maiakovskii's development as a poet, are not mentioned anywhere in the textbook. The authors do suggest, however, that the young poet was somehow tricked into following the futurist movement: 'The youth [Maiakovskii], whose world view was not yet fully formed, found himself surrounded by artistic bohemia and its typically unstable social ideas and moral principles'.[13] Maiakovskii is therefore forgiven for his involvement in futurism, as he was too young to know any better, and other members of the group used his tender age to entice the talented poet under their banner. According to the textbook authors, the works Maiakovskii produced at that time are inferior to his post-1917 works, but nevertheless show great potential:

> In his earlier works we can find various kinds of experimentations in rhyme, the structure of the poem and poetic language, deliberately harsh

---

11   Valentin Kovalev, *Russkaia sovetskaia literatura*, 11th ed. (Moscow: Prosveshchenie, 1989).
12   Kovalev, *Russkaia sovetskaia literatura*, pp. 121–22.
13   *Ibid.*, p. 123.

'lowered' ['snizhennye'] images [...]. At the same time we can see more distinctively the poet's own voice, a growing interest in social topics, a critical attitude towards the bourgeois world.[14]

Even though Maiakovskii's actual artistic mentors were not included in the textbook, it was important to establish the poet within the accepted literary system, to show his positive relationships with other artists who were accepted and canonised during the Soviet period. 'During the war the futurist group came apart. A closer relationship with Gor'kii, meetings with [...] Blok, A[leksandr] Kuprin, V[alerii] Briusov, the artist I[l'ia] Repin, the literary critic K[onstantin] Chukovskii enhanced Maiakovskii's social and literary interests'.[15] Particularly important is the influence of Gor'kii, who was considered the leading author of the Soviet prose canon, and became the first President of the Union of Soviet Writers. Parallels are drawn between the two authors' works, particularly between Gor'kii's short story 'Chelovek' ('Human'), and the later long poem of the same title by Maiakovskii.[16] Maiakovskii is also compared with Mikhail Saltykov-Shchedrin, Nikolai Nekrasov and Aleksandr Blok.[17]

Of particular importance for Soviet literary education was the idea of post-revolutionary literature as a legitimate and worthy successor to early Russian literary tradition. Authors were therefore keen not only to draw parallels between Maiakovskii and his contemporaries, but also with canonical figures of the nineteenth century. However, it is far from easy to draw parallels between the poet who turned away from literary traditions proclaiming: 'Throw Pushkin, Dostoevskii, Tolstoi, etc., etc. overboard from the Ship of Modernity' and the predecessors he so vehemently rejected.[18] According to Soviet textbooks, one of the highlights of Maiakovskii's art is his long poem 'Vladimir Il'ich Lenin',

---

14 *Ibid.*, p. 124.
15 *Ibid.*, p. 125.
16 *Ibid.*, p. 126. Gor'kii wrote his short story 'Chelovek' in 1903, Maiakovskii completed his long poem 'Chelovek' in 1917. Note that Gor'kii's short story is traditionally translated into English as 'Human', and Maiakovskii's long poem as 'The Man'.
17 *Ibid.*, p. 126.
18 David Burliuk, Aleksandr Kruchenykh, Vladimir Maiakovskii, Viktor Khlebnikov, 'Poshchechina obshchestvennomu vkusu', http://www.futurism.ru/a-z/manifest/slap.htm

written in 1927. By that time, futurism and its manifestos were a thing of the past. The authors claim that in this long poem:

> [Maiakovskii] continues the traditions of classical literature, especially the long poems of Pushkin and Nekrasov in which major problems of history and of the life of the common people found an artistic incarnation. Maiakovskii created a deeply innovative text, which became a milestone in his artistic development and in the development of all Soviet poetry.[19]

Another problematic aspect of Maiakovskii's biography was the poet's relationship with his lovers, particularly his controversial relationship with Lili and Osip Brik (for many years the three of them lived together in a *ménage à trois*). Similarly to the awkward question of his relationship to Russian literary tradition, this part of the poet's biography is also glossed over by the authors: 'he had complicated relationships, each case different in its own way, with some of his friends (N. Aseev, B. Pasternak, the Briks and others)'.[20] However, and this is a key feature of the Soviet image of the poet, which students were invited to emulate: 'Maiakovskii courageously fought against difficulties, overcoming temporary misconceptions, and openly discussing them'.[21] In this way, even the poet's shortcomings helped to build his image and students were invited to treat Maiakovskii's life as an example — to be courageous and stoic and to be prepared to discuss and acknowledge any mistakes they might make.

So far, the textbook's depiction of Maiakovskii's life and progress as an artist is fairly linear: the talented young man is supported by his loving family despite the difficulties they faced; as he grows up he is faced with challenges of his own and makes some mistakes, however, he outgrows those mistakes and becomes both a better poet and a better man: 'the revolutionary poet's many-sided talent developed and strengthened. In his works, the principles of partisanship and national spirit became firmly established'.[22] Eventually, the poet writes masterpieces of Soviet literature, including the long poems 'Vladimir Il'ich Lenin' and 'Khorosho!' ('Good!'), which change not only his own art, but the whole of Soviet literature. And then comes Maiakovskii's

---

19 Kovalev, p. 147.
20 *Ibid.*, p. 131.
21 *Ibid.*
22 *Ibid.*

sudden death. However, suicide does not work as a culmination of the poet's development. The description of the poet has to end on a positive note if his life is to be treated as a positive example to follow. Yet again, Soviet textbook authors deal with this problem by glossing over this part of Maiakovskii's biography:

> *At the Top of My Voice* is the last work by Maiakovskii. On 14 April 1930, he departed from this life. Artistic projects were left unfinished, tours and meetings with readers were never realised, the poet 'did not finish arguing' with his opponents, who tried to alienate him from the working class. However, Maiakovskii's poems, infused with ideas of communism, remained.[23]

In this way, the authors accomplish the near-impossible task of ending the retelling of Maiakovskii's biography on a high note.

There is one aspect that is entirely missing from this biographical account of the poet's life: Maiakovskii's personal relationships with women. Despite this, several of Maiakovskii's love poems were studied: 'Pis'mo Tat'iane Iakovlevoi' ('Letter to Tat'iana Iakovleva'), 'Pis'mo tovarishchu Kostrovu iz Parizha o sushchnosti liubvi' ('Letter from Paris to Comrade Kostrov on the Nature of Love'), 'Lilichka! Vmesto pis'ma' ('Lilichka! Instead of a Letter') and the long poem 'Pro eto' ('About This'). Students were directed to approach these works with no particular woman in mind, instead, the focus was on the social nature of love lyrics: 'Maiakovskii [...] dreams of a time when personal feelings would become part of the universal harmony, the happiness of one man would become the happiness of mankind'.[24] Thus, even Maiakovskii's personal feelings turn out to be part of his national spirit and desire for partisanship. Indeed, Soviet textbook writers did not need to go far in their search for facts to support this approach to the poet's love lyrics: Maiakovskii himself provided them a great source to work with in his poem 'Pis'mo Tat'iane Iakovlevoi':

---

23 *Ibid.*, p. 160. The citation within the quote refers to the poet's suicide note, where he mentions his argument with Vladimir Ermilov, a literary critic who wrote several negative articles about the poet's last play *Bania*. For further details see Vasilii Katanian, *Maiakovskii. Khronika zhizni i deiatel'nosti* (Moscow: Sovetskii pisatel', 1985), p. 491.

24 *Ibid.*, p. 138.

> В поцелуе рук ли,
>   губ ли,
> в дрожи тела
>   близких мне
> красный
>   цвет
>   моих республик
> тоже
>   должен
>   пламенеть.²⁵

In the kiss to the hands, or the lips, in the quiver of the body of those close to me, the red colour of my republics also has to blaze.

Maiakovskii's own desire to shape his public image provided countless possibilities for adaptations and retellings, and his wish to be seen only as a poet of the people, working for the betterment of the Soviet state gave plenty of material for textbook writers to portray Maiakovskii's life and art in precisely this way.

In order to complete the image of Maiakovskii in the Soviet school curriculum, I have found it helpful to look not only at accounts of his life, but also at the works which are referred to and analysed in *Russkaia sovetskaia literatura*. The book names sixty works by Maiakovskii, fifteen of which are analysed to varying degrees. However, out of this group of fifteen only two works, 'Oblako v shtanakh' ('A Cloud in Trousers') and 'Chelovek' ('The Man') were written before 1917. Both of them are treated briefly, 'Chelovek' mainly in relation to Gor'kii's story of the same name. Of the rest of the works mentioned, two stand out and claim the most attention: 'Khorosho!' and 'Vladimir Il'ich Lenin', with separate chapters dedicated to the analysis of each. Of the twenty-nine revision questions on Maiakovskii, seven relate to the analysis of 'Khorosho!' and eight to the analysis of 'Vladimir Il'ich Lenin'. There is only one question on the poet's love lyrics and no questions on his pre-revolutionary works.²⁶ Of the twenty-nine questions suggested, only four invite any form of independent analysis, while the majority

---

25   Vladimir Maiakovskii, 'Pis'mo Tat'iane Iakovlevoi', *Polnoe sobranie sochinenii*, IX, p. 386.
26   Kovalev, pp. 162–63.

(fifteen) are memory tasks. The remainder require students either to copy the material given to them, to explain the titles of Maiakovskii's works, or to trace how his poetic style and topics develop over time.

To find out whether remembering information was all that was expected from students, or whether there was an element of independent analysis which students were expected to demonstrate, I have looked at a selection of essay compositions by school leavers. This task is not only helpful for tracing the extent of the students' ability to present independent arguments, but also allows us to pinpoint exactly which of the facts relating to Maiakovskii's life students were expected to remember after they had left school. In his chapter 'Literaturno-tvorcheskie sochineniia v starshikh klassakh' ('Creative Literary Compositions in Senior Grades') Vladimir Litvinov discusses the type of composition in which students are invited to present their own opinions on a text.[27] An example of such an 'open' topic, according to Litvinov, would be 'My favourite poem by Maiakovskii'.[28] It is notable that, according to Litvinov, only a small minority of students attempted to write such compositions, most preferring topics which showcased their knowledge of core and supplementary material, but which did not require them to present their own opinions.[29] This preference for a lower-risk strategy is an understandable response by students who might have been unsure about a teacher's reaction to their personal opinions. Despite this, Litvinov states that such topics are necessary, and even suggests that students should not be marked down if their opinions are wrong: 'it is inadmissible to reduce the mark to a student who produced the answer in good faith, even though he seriously "lost his footing"'.[30] The willingness to consider answers from students based on their personal opinion rather than on the textbook created the dangerous possibility that there would be written evidence that students liked what they were not meant to like, and vice-versa.

---

27 Vladimir Litvinov, 'Literaturno-tvorcheskie sochineniia v starshikh klassakh', in Nikolai Kolokol'tsev, *Sochineniia v obshcheobrazovatel'noi politekhnicheskoi shkole (iz opyta raboty uchitelei-slovesnikov)* (Moscow: Gosudarstvennoe uchebno-pedagogicheskoe izdatel'stvo ministerstva prosveshcheniia, 1961), pp. 54–63 (p. 54).
28 *Ibid.*, p. 54.
29 *Ibid.*, p. 56.
30 *Ibid*, p. 63.

It is apparent that topics which invited students to share their opinions could be awkward, not only for the students, who could not be sure of being able to express their ideas effectively, nor of how teachers might react to their opinions, but also (and perhaps mostly) for the teachers themselves: how should one mark such a composition? After all, the student's opinion might not only be different from the teacher's personal view (and sometimes unsupported by the core text or ideologically unacceptable), but these works might not present a good opportunity for students to actually show their full knowledge of core material. Perhaps this is the reason why so many tasks in the textbook focused on memorising information and only a few on analysing it. Thus, even though it is fair to say that at least some teachers encouraged independent thinking and analysis, school assessments were overall based on the students' ability to memorise and reproduce given facts in order to answer the question correctly.

In summary, Soviet students left school with the impression that Maiakovskii was 'the best, most talented poet' of the era, a view supported by an array of memorised quotations.[31] Students would have been aware of Maiakovskii's large poetic corpus, and would have been able to discuss (and quote from) a fair number of poems. Maiakovskii's best known verses would have been 'Vladimir Il'ich Lenin' and 'Khorosho!'. Of his early works, the most successful was considered to be his long poem 'Oblako v shtanakh', in which he heralds the future revolution. His final work would have been 'Vo ves' golos' ('At the Top of My Voice'). The students would have known that Maiakovskii knew a number of literary figures (though these relationships were complex), and also that he had some good mentors (mainly Gor'kii). Despite the fact that the young Maiakovskii rejected the Russian classics, his legacy was viewed as a continuation of Russian literary traditions. Students would have learned that Maiakovskii lived a very rich life, always vigilant towards enemies of the young state and always busy creating socialist art; why he died was something of a mystery, but students were not encouraged to consider it too deeply, as the poet left a large volume of immortal works.

---

31   See note 2.

Literature in Post-Soviet Russian Schools

Post-Soviet school education, in contrast to Soviet-era education, is characterised by the availability of a large number of different textbooks. However, all of them to a greater or lesser extent reflect the most obvious change — the school curriculum itself. Many names have disappeared from the curriculum; however, what is more crucial is the fact that a large number of new names have made it into post-Soviet school textbooks. While the 1989 edition of *Russkaia sovetskaia literatura* lists just nine authors whose works were studied extensively in the final grade, two years later, in 1991, the number of texts included in the school curriculum had become so large that the textbook now comprised two volumes. In an article published by *Russkaia slovesnost (Russian Literature)*, Natal'ia Volchenko notes these changes: 'in the years of *perestroika* [...] "new names" poured into the school programme like a never-ending stream'.[32] By 2000, the list of authors represented in school readers exceeded seventy. Similarly, by this period the majority of textbooks included separate chapters on major literary groups of the twentieth century. Many anthologies also included letters and memoirs.[33] With such a drastic increase in the material to be covered and no change in the number of the lessons, the depth in which any one particular author could be studied decreased dramatically. This is a pressing concern for post-Soviet Russian literature teachers. As Volchenko points out in her review of 2004, there are now fewer teaching hours in the final grade than the number of topics presented in the literature exam.[34]

Equally challenging was the fact that there was no longer a single textbook that was adopted by teachers. The rapid increase in available textbooks and study aid materials after 1991 meant that schools had now to decide which ones to use in the classrooms. Furthermore, as textbooks vary in terms of the information provided and in the tasks

---

32 Natal'ia Volchenko, '"A vy noktiurn sygrat' mogli by na fleite vodostochnykh trub?" O probleme vypusknogo sochineniia' in *Russkaia slovesnost'*, 6 (2005), 2–7 (p. 5).

33 Anatolii Barannikov, *Russkaia literatura XX veka. 11 klass. Khrestomatiia dlia obshcheobrazovatel'nykh uchrezhdenii*, 2 vols. (Moscow: Prosveshchenie, 2000). An overview of the material supposed to be covered in lessons can be gained by viewing the contents pages: I, 379–81; II, 349–51.

34 Volchenko, p. 2.

set for students, discrepancies are likely to arise between the content of textbooks and what is actually covered in final-year examinations. Volchenko presents an example of such a discrepancy in her analysis of the teaching of Blok's poetry: not only do three textbooks have a different way of presenting the poet and his works, but none includes an analysis of the poem 'Na zheleznoi doroge' ('On the Railway'), which appeared in the 2004 examination.[35]

Another textbook author, Gennadii Belen'kii, warns that this abundance of recommended reading in the final grade curriculum means that some of the material has to be studied in earlier years, when students are too young to develop a full understanding of the literary material, in particular its complex moral and aesthetic significance.[36] Belen'kii argues that a central aim of the study of literature at school should be the cultivation of moral values. This view is shared by the majority of his colleagues, who 'are certain of the immense educational significance of literature, of its unique role in the process of the formation of individuals, their artistic potential and moral inclinations'.[37] Later, Belen'kii elaborates on what he sees as the purpose of literary education at school: 'it is the task of the literature teacher to shape the students' attitudes to moral values, patriotism, national duty, work, family, religion, love, language, nature and their own individuality'.[38] Many of the textbooks reiterate the importance of moral education to the study of literature, which suggests that while the material taught in the classroom changed after *perestroika*, the aims of literary study remained the same. Here is, for example, what Galina Lazarenko says in the foreword of her textbook:

> I doubt that one can overestimate the importance of the main subject in school — literature, especially in the final year of secondary education, because for the majority of young people the formal study of Russian literature comes to an end at that time. The lessons they have drawn

---

35 *Ibid.*, pp. 2–3.
36 Gennadii Belen'kii, '"Informoprobezhka" ili izuchenie?' in *Literatura v shkole*, 9 (2003), 26–29 (p. 26).
37 *Ibid.*, p. 27.
38 *Ibid.*

from their work [...] (aesthetic, philosophical, moral ideals) will stay with them throughout their adult lives.[39]

Although Lazarenko is very critical of the Revolution, the idea that literature should provide students with a moral education in preparation for adult life remains firmly in place.

The authors of school textbooks find a variety of ways to bring together canonical Soviet writers with a plethora of authors who were not admitted to the official canon in the USSR. Such an attempt to sketch out a broader and more inclusive version of the canon that integrates official and unofficial Soviet literature might be driven by the attempt to provide a sense of unity, in spite of the contrasting legacies of the authors studied. One way to accomplish this task is to draw parallels between work of established canonised authors, such as Maiakovskii, and authors not commonly associated with the official Soviet canon, such as Andrei Platonov or Anna Akhmatova. In addition, textbooks often attributed to them timeless moral values which remained unchanged after the collapse of the Soviet Union, thus reinforcing the idea of common ground between traditionally polarised writers. For example, Anatolii Barannikov writes that:

> The numerous and multifaceted [people of] Russia brought forward authors from all social classes; they had polarised opinions on the events of the time, including the revolution, but they were all united in their sincere love for Russia, their reflection of its fate and their desire to better the life of the people.[40]

This desire to present authors as positive moral examples is reminiscent of the way in which literature was taught during Soviet times. This approach used to mean that there was generally one 'correct opinion' and the majority of questions encouraged students to reproduce information they had learned. However, when we look at post-Soviet textbooks, we see that more value is placed on the students' personal opinions. In a textbook edited by Feliks Kuznetsov in 1991 we read that 'the book invites us to think, to develop an independent opinion in the

---

39 Galina Lazarenko, *Khrestomatiia po otechestvennoi literature XX veka* (Moscow: Metodicheskii kabinet zapadnogo okruga g. Moskvy, 1995), p. 5.
40 Anatolii Barannikov, *Russkaia literatura XX veka. Khrestomatiia dlia 11 kl. sr. shk.*, 2 vols. (Moscow: Prosveshchenie, 1993), I, p. 4.

analysis of various literary phenomena'.⁴¹ In 1998, in the foreword to his textbook, Iurii Lyssyi wrote: 'the material presented is not for learning by heart. Reading is a dialogue with the author: agreement, disagreement, sometimes even an argument'.⁴² This suggests that literature is starting to be taught in a less dogmatic way, with teachers and examiners more interested in students expressing their own opinions about the works they encounter.

However, in the final examinations, the notion that an author or a work of literature can inspire a variety of opinions is seemingly forgotten. Each year, publishing houses release booklets on how to write final-year compositions effectively. These booklets provide suggested answers to the most common questions, and in one such publication Evgeniia Basovskaia writes that:

> Most importantly [...] one has to adhere to certain 'safety measures' during the exam. As your work is going to be marked by a certain 'Mr X', it is advisable to remain neutral. You cannot know whether your examiner prefers prose or poetry, Nekrasov or Fet, [...] long compositions or short ones... Thus in order to not find yourself in an irreconcilable contradiction with your examiner, not to set yourself up against him, you should not express yourself too emotionally [...]. You should not come up with an unconventional compositional structure, create bold metaphors [...] Not to irritate your examiner — this is what is extremely important. Indeed, your composition will not be genius [...] But it will be what it should be — an entry ticket to university.⁴³

It seems that discussions and disputes are welcome during lessons, where, if teachers follow the textbooks' suggestions, students are encouraged to express their own opinions. However, when it comes to the examination, students are encouraged to ignore their own ideas and write an essay that conforms to established orthodoxies, so that it aligns with the examiner's presumed opinion, or at least does not conflict with it.

---

41 Feliks Kuznetsov, *Russkaia literatura XX veka. Ocherki. Portrety. Esse. Kniga dlia uchascshikhsia 11 klassa srednei shkoly*, 2 vols. (Moscow: Prosveshchenie, 1991), I, p. 3.
42 Iurii Lyssyi, *Russkaia literatura XX veka. 11 klass: praktikum dlia obshcheobrazovatel'nykh ucherezhdenii* (Moscow: Mnemozina, 1998), p. 3.
43 Evgeniia Basovskaia, *Literatura. Sochineniia. 11 klass. Kniga dlia uchenika i uchitelia* (Moscow: Olimp, 1997), pp. 9–10.

The apparent desire on the part of the examiners to read well-established views on literature suggests that there is a considerable mismatch between the method of assessment (still largely unchanged from the Soviet period) and the attempt to promote a less restrictive and prescriptive way of teaching literature seen in the textbooks. Part of the reason for the apparent reluctance to renounce this dogmatic approach may lie in the way in which the aims of literary study are formulated. As well as introducing the lives and works of authors and teaching students to present coherent arguments about what they read, the study of literature is ultimately seen as a moral education, and an important way to inculcate ideas of goodness, patriotism and civic duty. Students and teachers therefore struggle with the idea of voicing personal opinions because, as in the former Soviet Union, it is expected that students will offer up the single 'right' answer to questions of national identity and moral values.

Maiakovskii in Post-Soviet Russian Schools

When looking at the changes *perestroika* brought to the representation of Maiakovskii in post-Soviet Russian schools, I will focus on the characterisation of the poet and his works, his childhood and upbringing, his relationship with the Russian avant-garde and the futurist movement, and other persons considered influential during the formation of Maiakovskii's style. I will also consider the other poets to whom he is most commonly compared, the ways in which the textbooks address the poet's personal life and his love lyrics, and finally, how Maiakovskii's suicide is portrayed.

However, the main difference in post-Soviet representations of the poet is that there is no longer a single and uniform approach. While previously all students were required to study the same textbook, in post-Soviet Russia there is a growing list of authors whose work is read and no government control over the precise curriculum covered, so textbooks and supplementary materials have multiplied dramatically. This has resulted in some significant changes in the ways students are introduced to Maiakovskii. Multiple representations of the poet evolved throughout the 1990s and, as yet, no single dominant image has emerged.

The first difference is that the poet's childhood and upbringing is hardly ever mentioned in the post-1991 textbooks. It has been noted that in Soviet textbooks it was important to suggest that the poet had a stable and supportive family environment, in which his own views and beliefs, as well as his talent, were rooted. However, hardly any post-1991 textbook mentions the poet's family beyond the brief mention of biographical details. The studies therefore begin, not with Maiakovskii's childhood, but at the outset of his poetic career:

> Maiakovskii was a suffering and lonely youth when he began to emerge as a poet. In spite of this, from his first appearances in the press and on stage he was forced into the role of literary hooligan, and, in order to not sink into obscurity, he maintained this reputation with audacious pranks during readings.[44]

In fact, the motifs of loneliness and suffering have become key in post-Soviet representations of Maiakovskii.

Many aspects of Maiakovskii's representation evolved throughout the 1990s. In 1991, the futurist movement, with which the start of Maiakovskii's poetic career is associated, was still viewed in a negative light:

> Maiakovskii's antibourgeois mutiny in this long poem ('A Cloud in Trousers') was also a mutiny against salon art, which had been made anaemic by its exclusive concern for aesthetics. Thus, indirectly, acting on the instincts of a healthy, social conscious individual, Maiakovskii was also speaking against futurism with a concept of art which was, in essence, focused on the aesthetic.[45]

Equally, there is no mention of Burliuk or Khlebnikov and their influence on the poet's early works; instead, the authors draw parallels between Maiakovskii and other major Soviet writers such as Gor'kii and Blok. *Russkaia literatura XX veka* (*Twentieth Century Russian Literature*), on the other hand, proposes that the poet had a lot in common with authors who were not acknowledged during the Soviet era, but who became widely discussed during and after *perestroika*: 'Numerous satirical works by the poet (poems, feuilletons, plays) suggest that he saw clearly the

---

44 Kuznetsov, p. 136.
45 *Ibid.*, p. 142.

many difficulties in the cause of achieving great goals, in the same way as they were seen by [Andrei] Platonov, [Mikhail] Bulgakov, [Mikhail] Zoshchenko'.[46] Thus, since affiliation with futurism and the avant-garde was still considered detrimental to the poet's image, and so was his association with official Soviet culture, textbook authors required new relationships to justify Maiakovskii's high canonical status and distinguish him from many other Soviet writers who were no longer canonised by the emerging state.

Another similarity between this textbook and the example from the Soviet era is that they both have very little to say about the poet's personal life. We learn that when Maiakovskii was very young he fell in love with Maria Denisova, and this unsuccessful relationship resulted in the composition of 'Oblako v shtanakh'.[47] However, by the time this poem was finished, the poet was already in love with a different woman — Lili Brik, 'the character of another love drama, which filled many years, and was much more intense and destructive in its content'.[48] That is the only discussion of Lili Brik. Although considerable attention is dedicated to the analysis of Maiakovskii's love lyrics and the tragedy of the poet's love, the readers will have very little understanding of why Maiakovskii portrayed love as tragic, or what prevented his relationships from being successful. However, post-Soviet textbooks do not attempt to present Maiakovskii's personal feelings and lyrical poetry as part of his strong community spirit. Instead, the authors of *Russkaia literatura XX veka* separate Maiakovskii's love lyrics from his civic poetry:

> As much as the poet tried to 'tame' the intimate within himself in the name of the communal, the socially rational, as he was 'standing on the throat of his own song', 'the topic' (love) 'ordered' to write about itself.[49]

This is in stark contrast to the Soviet representation of the poet, in which Maiakovskii's love for women was an aspect of his love for life

---

46 *Ibid.*
47 *Ibid.*, p. 141.
48 *Ibid.*, p. 142.
49 *Ibid.*, p. 144. The quotations within the citation are from Maiakovskii's poems, the first two from 'Vo ves' golos', the last two from 'Pro eto'.

and humanity, and therefore his love lyrics were considered to have a civic aspect.

While we learn very little about Maiakovskii's complex relationship with Lili Brik, the textbook provides more substantial detail about Maiakovskii's later romantic entanglements with Tat'iana Iakovleva and Veronika Polonskaia. The tragic end to Maiakovskii's love for Iakovleva and the unstable nature of his relationship with Polonskaia are presented as among the reasons for the poet's suicide, a topic which, in post-Soviet textbooks, is openly discussed and analysed. In *Russkaia literatura XX veka*, it is suggested that the cause of Maiakovskii's decision to take his own life is not obvious, although the authors list a variety of unfortunate and tragic events that occurred in the months leading up to the poet's suicide.[50] One theory which the textbook disputes, however, is that the poet's psychological state contributed to his death. After the poet's suicide, this idea was cultivated by Maiakovskii's closest friend and ex-lover, Lili Brik, who suggested that even though Maiakovskii loved life, he was paranoid about getting old, and often had suicidal thoughts.[51] Despite the indisputable fact that Brik knew the poet very closely, the authors of *Russkaia literatura XX veka* suggest that her opinion was unfounded:

> What fear of old age when you are thirty-six! What suicidal tendency in a person, who so passionately rejected such action in the poem 'Sergeiu Eseninu' ('To Sergei Esenin'), so passionately, so impatiently looked forward into the future! In a person who was obsessed with the notion of immortality![52]

The authors present their view as correct, even though one does not have to spend long looking for evidence that supports Brik's arguments. 14 April 1930 was not the first time Maiakovskii attempted suicide.[53] In his work, the poet described thoughts of suicide and his fear of imminent old age. For example, in 1925 during his trip to America Maiakovskii wrote:

---

50 *Ibid.*, p. 165.
51 Lili Brik, *Pristrastnye rasskazy* (Moscow: Dekom, 2011), p. 181.
52 Kuznetsov, p. 169.
53 Maiakovskii attempted suicide in 1916, but the gun misfired. Lili Brik notes this in her diaries; see Brik, p. 181.

> жил,
>> работал,
>>> стал староват...
>> Вот и жизнь пройдет,
>>> как прошли Азорские
>> острова.⁵⁴
>
> I lived, worked, became a bit old... Thus life too will pass, just as the Azores have passed

And a year later he created these troubled lines:

> Все меньше любится,
>> все меньше дерзается,
> и лоб мой
>> время
>>> с разбега крушит.
> Приходит
>> страшнейшая из амортизаций —
> амортизация
>> сердца и души.⁵⁵
>
> I fall in love less, I dare less, and my brow is crushed by time as it runs at me. The most terrifying of erosions is coming — the erosion of heart and soul.

There are more examples to support Brik's idea that Maiakovskii was prone to suicidal thoughts, equally there is also evidence for the textbook's version that the poet despised such ideas. Maiakovskii's work was contradictory and it invites contrasting interpretations.

The vast majority of textbooks agree that Maiakovskii was a great poet: 'Maiakovskii was and remains one of the most notable figures of twentieth-century poetry... it is impossible to brush Maiakovskii aside, to categorise him as one of the poetic trimmers with little

---

54 Vladimir Maiakovskii, 'Melkaia filosofiia na glubokikh mestakh', *Polnoe sobranie sochinenii*, VII, p. 19.

55 Vladimir Maiakovskii, 'Razgovor s fininspektorom o poezii', *Polnoe sobranie sochinenii*, VII, p. 124.

talent'.⁵⁶ However, they do not praise him unreservedly. One striking example of a negative point of view can be found in Lazarenko's textbook, *Khrestomatiia po otechestvennoi literature XX veka* (*Twentieth Century Russian Literature Reader*). In her introduction, Lazarenko suggests that the social ills of contemporary Russia can be solved by providing students with Christian ideals to which they should aspire in their everyday life.⁵⁷ Maiakovskii's critical statements towards religion and God are well documented, so it is not surprising that he is not one of Lazarenko's favourite authors. Lazarenko's book does not provide biographical details about Maiakovskii, however, it does contain guidance notes and lesson plans to establish an image of the poet. Lazarenko's representation of Maiakovskii is therefore created substantially from her selection of his works, which are all focused on the ideas of violence and egocentrism, the two aspects of Maiakovskii's art that Lazarenko condemns:

> 'The butterfly of the poet's heart' should not hate. And in the long poem *Oblako v shtanakh* the grown-up poet goes to fraternise with the 'tongueless' street, in order to give it voice… Why not the Pushkin voice? ('For having awakened noble thoughts with my lyre' — for many decades keeps ringing on the lips and the ears of ancestors)? According to Maiakovskii, to give the street a voice means to arm it with the following slogans:
>
> 'Власть
>
>   к богатым
>
>   рыло
>
>   воротит —
>
>   чего подчиняться ей?!.
>
> Бей!!'⁵⁸
>
> The authorities turn their mugs to those who are rich — why follow them?! Strike!!

---

56   Anatolii Karpov, 'Vladimir Maiakovskii', in Vladimir Agenosov, *Russkaia literatura XX veka* (Moscow: Drofa, 1996), pp. 252–88 (p. 252).

57   Lazarenko, p. 5.

58   *Ibid.*, p. 21. The first citation within the quote refers to Maiakovskii's poem 'Nate!' (1913) and the image of the tongueless street is from 'Oblako v shtanakh' (1915); however, the final citation (the slogan: 'The authorities turn their mugs to those who are rich — why follow them?! Strike!!') is from 'Khorosho!' (1927). The line from Pushkin is from the poem 'Exegi Monumentum', *Pushkin: Selected Verse*, ed. and trans. by John Fennell (London: Bristol Classical Press, 2001), pp. 75-76 (p. 76).

Notably, this combines lines from three different poems: 'Nate!' ('Here you are!') (1913), 'Oblako v shtanakh' (1915) and 'Khorosho!' (1927), thus eliding different periods of the poet's career. Throughout her section on Maiakovskii, Lazarenko provides excerpts from poems without explaining when and why they were written, in order to support her image of the poet as a violent revolutionary without moral or aesthetic principles. It is possible that Lazarenko's opinion of Maiakovskii was influenced by the highly contradictory, widely known book by Iurii Karabchievskii, *Voskresenie Maiakovskogo* (*Maiakovskii's Resurrection*), which was first published in Russia in 1991. Karabchievskii argues that Maiakovskii's best poems are those in which the main theme is hate, and concludes that Maiakovskii is 'an anti-poet. His mission in this world is substitution: culture with anti-culture, art with anti-art and spirituality with anti-spirituality'.[59] Similarly to the authors of the 1991 textbook *Russkaia literatura XX veka*, Lazarenko finds Maiakovskii's life highly tragic. However, she claims that his was not the tragedy of being misunderstood and lonely, as other textbooks suggest, but rather that of a young poet severing his connections with the aesthetic roots of Russian literary traditions.[60]

Lazarenko's textbook is more the exception than the rule. In order to get a better idea of the image of the poet that students might have learned at school, I will focus on topics suggested for revision, starting with Karpov's chapter on Maiakovskii in the more commonly used *Russkaia literatura XX veka*, edited by Vladimir Agenosov, which was first published in 1996. The revision questions mainly focus on the historical background of various works by Maiakovskii, although we also find the following topic: 'the image of the poet in Maiakovskii's work (based on two or three poems, selected by the student)'.[61] While this question appears to seek the students' personal opinions, if we examine the textbook's presentation of Maiakovskii we will see the information on which their answers are based.

The motif of loneliness and the tragedies that the poet experienced are the central components of Karpov's presentation of Maiakovskii, as they were for other authors of post-Soviet textbooks. This sense of

---

59 Iurii Karabchievskii, *Voskresenie Maiakovskogo* (Moscow: Enas, 2008), p. 290.
60 *Ibid.*, p. 22.
61 Karpov, p. 286.

tragedy is related mostly to the latter part of Maiakovskii's life in the late 1920s: 'together with sharp criticism of the present, a certain anxiety about the future, which has no place for true humanity, is discernible. This anxiety becomes more and more prominent in the poet's work [...] which affirms [...] the motif of loneliness'.[62] The motif of loneliness identified by Karpov appears not to be supported by the biographical details he gives about Maiakovskii's life. For the first time, a plethora of the poet's friends and acquaintances are named, including Burliuk, Khlebnikov, Aleksei Kruchenykh, and his less well-known lover, Ellie Jones. His non-futurist acquaintances, who all praised his talent, are also mentioned within the chapter, such as Gor'kii, Repin, Akhmatova and Osip Mandel'shtam.[63]

Maiakovskii's feelings of loneliness and his eventual suicide therefore need some explanation, and Karpov supplies two main reasons. Firstly, he cites the political atmosphere in the country: 'the era in which revolutionary ideals got dimmer and dimmer was indeed understanding the poet less and less (to be precise, it accepted him less and less)'.[64] Secondly, in the months leading up to Maiakovskii's suicide the poet had an unhappy relationship with the actress Polonskaia, who, according to Karpov, refused to marry him despite Maiakovskii's love for her:

> the poet's demand to immediately unite their fates provoked a highly nervous reaction from Polonskaia. The final discussion happened in the morning of 14 April 1930: Polonskaia refused to choose a single role — that of the poet's wife — over everything else.[65]

Like many textbook authors, Karpov tends to gloss over the intricacies of Maiakovskii's relationships with women, and he does not mention Brik's or Polonskaia's husbands, since this compromises Maiakovskii's reputation and does little to promote the image of the tragic, lonely and misunderstood poet.

In the step-by-step guidebooks for using Agenosov's textbooks, Maiakovskii is allocated four study hours, which would have taken just

---

62   *Ibid.*, pp. 256–57.
63   *Ibid.*, p. 255.
64   *Ibid.*, p. 258.
65   *Ibid.*, p. 259.

over a week of classroom time. While this is much less than the month he was allocated during the Soviet period, this is still a good number of hours considering the density of the post-Soviet literary curriculum. Of other twentieth-century poets only Blok enjoys the same amount of classroom time, while the majority of authors are studied for just two or three hours. More time is dedicated to the study of prose: Gor'kii is given five hours, Bulgakov and Sholokhov, six.[66]

Looking at some typical exam questions, we discover that a considerable amount of attention is given to Maiakovskii's life and work. The questions are rather varied, from an analysis of Maiakovskii's earlier poetry (for example, the poem 'Skripka i nemnozhko nervno' ('A Violin, and a Little Nervous'), to images of the loudmouth ringleader (*gorlan-glavar*') that appear in Maiakovskii's works, to the place of revolution in his poetry.[67] Typically, Soviet exams omit the long poems 'Khorosho!' and 'Vladimir Il'ich Lenin' — instead, questions on his pre-revolutionary works are much more common. Students are thus much more likely to be familiar with these poems, in which Maiakovskii's emotions and personal tragedies take centre stage. Feelings of loneliness, which are often expressed in the early poetry, therefore became key aspects of Maiakovskii's life and legacy. Other characteristics of the poet might vary from textbook to textbook, but these aspects are commonly highlighted.

Maiakovskii's portrayal in post-Soviet Russian schools is shaped by several factors. Literature is viewed not only as a subject designed to enhance students' knowledge of texts and authors, but to cultivate their moral and civic values, so protagonists and authors are depicted with virtues to which students are encouraged to aspire. Although in post-Soviet education there appears to be an understanding of the importance of the students' own opinions, the final examinations are still structured in much the same way they were during the Soviet period — students are actively discouraged from saying anything that does not conform

---

[66] Aleksandr Arkhangel'skii, Vladimir Agenosov, *Metodicheskie rekomendatsii po ispol'zovaniiu uchebnikov 'Russkaia literatura XIX veka' pod redaktsiei A. N. Arkhangel'skogo, 'Russkaia literatura XX veka. pod redaktsiei V. V. Agenonosova* (Moscow: Drofa, 2006), pp. 61–62.

[67] Aleksandr Kniazhitskii, *Metodicheskie rekomendatsii i prakticheskie materialy k provedeniiu ekzamena po literature*, 2 vols. (Moscow: Mezhdunarodnaia shkola distantsionnogo obucheniia, 2003), *passim*.

to the ideas set down in textbooks and supplementary materials. The post-Soviet representation of Maiakovskii, however, differs from his Soviet-era image as 'the best, most talented poet'.[68] *Perestroika* brought an end to the single, unified image of the poet and the various textbooks that appeared after 1991 createdseveral images of Maiakovskii, some of them contradictory. On the basis of these presentations it is difficult to identify the place in the canon that Maiakovskii is thought to occupy. His is a key name in the curriculum, but the nature of his significance is unclear, as he does not easily fit the image of a role model for students. The only aspect that the majority of post-Soviet textbooks agree on (as well as the main difference from the Soviet-era image of the poet) is that Maiakovskii was a tragic poet, who, for large parts of his life, suffered from loneliness and misunderstanding. It was, according to the textbooks, largely, misunderstanding (whether by a single person, like Polonskaia, or a group of people, like the militant Russian Association of Proletarian Writers (RAPP), which was active in the late 1920s and early 1930s) that led to the poet's suicide, another topic which became widely discussed only after 1991.

There are also similarities between Soviet and post-Soviet representations of the poet. For example, Maiakovskii's association with futurism and the avant-garde was not evaluated positively until the second half of the 1990s. Other similarities persist today, and are rooted in the idea that literature is a source of moral improvement. Thus, even though his love lyrics are among those most studied, students still have little idea about the complexities of Maiakovskii's love affairs.

The understanding of Maiakovskii and his place in the school curriculum is still evolving, and different textbooks present contrasting opinions. Maiakovskii's place at the top of the poetic canon has certainly been challenged and largely revoked, however, at the same time we can see a more humanised and sympathetic image of the poet emerging. With literary education increasingly focused on the importance of discussion and differing views, perhaps it is only natural that no single image of the poet exists, and the post-Soviet generation of students will not necessarily believe Maiakovskii to be at the head of the poetic canon. They will, however, have a broader and more nuanced view of the poet's life and legacy.

---

68   See note 2.

5. The Symbol of the Symbolists: Aleksandr Blok in the Changing Russian Literary Canon

Olga Sobolev

> Прославленный не по программе
> И вечный вне школ и систем,
> Он не изготовлен руками
> И нам не навязан никем.
>
> Eternal and not manufactured,
> Renown not according to plan,
> Outside schools and systems, he has not
> Been foisted upon us by man.[1]

The turn of the twentieth century has always been regarded as a period of extreme dynamism in Russian culture — a time when many traditional values were questioned and transformed. During this period the genuine creative power in verse and prose came from the symbolists, who drew upon the aesthetic revival inaugurated in the 1890s by Dmitrii Merezhkovskii, and freed it of spuriousness and self-gratifying over-refinement. In turning their backs on civic ideals and echoing Stéphane Mallarmé's saying that poetry 'yields the initiative to

---

1   Boris Pasternak, 'Veter', *Izbrannoe*, 2 vols. (Moscow: Khudozhestvennaia literatura, 1985), I, 439; Boris Pasternak, 'The Wind', *Poems of Boris Pasternak*, translated by Lydia Pasternak-Slater (London: Unwin, 1963), p. 90.

words',[2] the symbolists brought fascinating resources of language and craftsmanship to their metaphysical preoccupations. Often termed the Silver Age of Russian art, this trend produced a whole host of illustrious authors, including such figures as Valerii Briusov and Konstantin Bal'mont, Zinaida Gippius and Viacheslav Ivanov, Andrei Belyi and the most celebrated poet of the movement — Aleksandr Blok. Quite a few factors may account for Blok's special position in the constellation of these eminent authors, one of which is directly related to the notion of a poetic canon, considered in the broadest sense of this cultural term. Whether one looks at the idea of canonisation within the framework of institutionalised aesthetics or simply as a literary art of memory (as suggested by Harold Bloom[3]), Blok stands apart from the cohort of symbolist poets. Not only does he appear to be the only symbolist who was ever accepted in the Soviet-era literary canon, but he retained his status later, when the country was keen to dismiss anything related to the fallen Soviet regime. By analysing Blok's critical reception throughout the twentieth century and beyond, this study will attempt to establish what aspects of his oeuvre made it central to the country's literary agenda, as well as by what mechanisms this long-standing cultural value became firmly associated with the corpus of his works. Given that the formation of a canon is necessarily related to the questions of nationhood and self-determination, such an analysis will shed more light on some key issues faced by contemporary post-*perestroika* Russia, such as the shaping of national identity, and the ways of overcoming the division between the two cultures that was created by the policies of the Soviet authoritarian state.[4]

The word 'canon' was originally used to designate a rule, measure or standard; and many subsequent uses of the term similarly invoke

---

2   Stéphane Mallarmé, 'Crise de vers', in *Divagations* (Paris: Bibliotèque Charpentier, 1897), pp. 235–51 (p. 246); translated in Rosemary Lloyd, *The Poet and his Circle* (Ithaca: Cornell University Press, 1999), p. 55.
3   Harold Bloom, *The Western Canon* (New York: Riverhead Books, 1995), p. 17.
4   Russian dissident culture emerged in the 1950s and the 1960s as intellectual opposition to Communist rule in a form of grassroots practice; it was largely associated with *samizdat*, a key dissident activity in the dissemination of censored cultural production (classified as a criminal anti-government activity), and it became a potent symbol of the rebellious spirit and resourcefulness of the Soviet intelligentsia; see for instance, Ann Komaromi, 'The Material Existence of Soviet Samizdat', *Slavic Review*, 63 (2004), 597–618.

the notion of restrictive authority, as when literary critics speak of the need 'to open' the canon, 'to expand' the canon, or 'to dispense' with the canon.[5] In actuality, scholars agree that there neither is, nor has there ever been, any such thing as an inherent, strictly defined literary canon, and it is not 'the reproduction of values but of social relations'[6] that should be associated with canonical form; as John Guillory puts it, 'canonicity is not a property of the work itself, but of its transmission, its relation to other works in a collocation of works'.[7] While recognising 'the historicity of the cultural category of literature itself', recent theorists of canon formation have begun to examine the interaction of literary taste (or even fashion[8]) with some larger structures of social and economic power.[9] Pierre Bourdieu, for instance, offers the concept of cultural capital to describe how, within a given socio-economic setting, the knowledge of certain literary texts (or art, music and so forth) can be used to describe social competition and stratification, and he points out some ways by which this knowledge is obtained and enhanced: through direct experience and education; through popular culture, and through secondary or tertiary contacts (book reviews, study guides, etc).[10] The work of Bourdieu and other scholars on nineteenth-century texts suggests that similar mechanisms might be at work within Russian post-revolutionary culture, although, of course, these must be carefully specified and analysed in relation to that particular socio-historical setting.

The Soviet notion of culture, far from being based on a simplistic Marxist conception of the ideological sphere as little more than a

---

5 John Guillory, *Cultural Capital: The Problem of Literary Canon Formation* (Chicago: University of Chicago Press, 1993), pp. 34, 81.
6 *Ibid.*, p. 56.
7 *Ibid.*, p. 55.
8 Isaac D'Israeli, an early promulgator of this view, claimed that 'prose and verse have been regulated by the same caprice that cuts our coats and cocks our hats […] and every age of modern literature might, perhaps, admit of a new classification, by dividing it into its periods of *fashionable literature*' (Isaac D'Israeli, 'Literary Fashions', in *Curiosities of Literature* (Boston: Lilly, Wait, Colman & Holden, 1833), III, 35–39 (pp. 35, 39), quoted in Alastair Fowler, 'Genre and the Literary Canon', *New Literary History*, 11: 1, Anniversary Issue II (Autumn 1979), 97–119 (p. 97)).
9 John Guillory, *Cultural Capital*, p. 60; Alastair Fowler, 'Genre and the Literary Canon', pp. 97–119.
10 Pierre Bourdieu, *Distinction: A Social Critique of the Judgement of Taste*, translated by Richard Nice (London: Routledge, 1984).

reflection of the social material base, emphasised the centrality of the cultural field in shaping and facilitating economic development. Moreover, from the early years of the Soviet state's existence, literature was considered an effective weapon of class warfare, and all interventionist post-revolutionary cultural campaigns (against illiteracy, religion and bourgeois morality) were conducted precisely in pursuit of this agenda. The official line was set out in a series of articles by Lenin, one of the most significant of which was *Pamiati Gertsena* (*In Memory of Herzen*, 1912) that outlined three stages in the history of the Russian revolutionary movement, and effectively defined both the periodisation and the methodology in all branches of the Soviet literary field.[11] The first stage was that of a liberally-minded nobility, from the Decembrists to Aleksandr Herzen (1825–1861); it was followed by the Populist period of 1861–1895, and culminated in the so-called 'proletarian' era, dating from 1895, the year in which Lenin's Union for the Emancipation of Working People was founded. When mapped onto the domain of scholarship and education, this later stage was commonly exemplified by the works of Maksim Gor'kii, and by the poetic writings of the Revolutionary Populists, such as Vera Figner, Petr Iakubovich, Nikolai Morozov, and German Lopatin, as well as by the group of certain younger proletarian authors with a distinct political concern. Chronologically, the major part of the symbolist movement also coincided with the 'proletarian' period, which immediately made it strictly out of bounds for Lenin and his supporters: symbolism was declared ideologically impoverished, aesthetically subversive, stimulating an unnecessary predilection for decadent romanticism that led away from the reality of socialist goals.[12]

---

11 Vladimir Lenin, *Pamiati Gertsena* (Moscow: Politizdat, 1980).
12 As early as 1896 Gor'kii characterised symbolist literature as 'the songs of decaying culture', impregnated with the feeling of 'pessimism and complete apathy regarding actual events' (Maksim Gor'kii, *Sobranie sochinenii*, 30 vols. (Moscow: Khudozhestvennaia literatura, 1949–1955), 23 (1953), 122, 136); Trotskii in his *Literature and Revolution* (1924) speaks of symbolism as an expression of old Russia's 'landlords and intelligentsia [...] disgusting environment' (Leo Trotskii, *Literature and Revolution* (Chicago: Haymarket Books, 2005), p. 105); and the chapter on symbolism, in the academic edition of *The History of Russian Literature*, entitled 'Poetry of the Bourgeois Decay (Symbolism, Acmeism, Futurism)' speaks for itself (*Istoriia russkoi literatury*, 10 vols., edited by N. F. Bel'chikov (Moscow-Leningrad: Akademiia Nauk SSSR, 1941–1956), X (1954), pp. 764–99).

Two authors, nonetheless, presented a rare exception to the accepted canon. From the early 1920s, Blok and Briusov began to feature in the *Narkompros* circulars and the lists of 'indicative reading'.[13] The choice of these two poets was far from coincidental, mainly because they were the only symbolists of the older generation who expressed a certain degree of sympathy (at least at the beginning) for the Bolshevik cause. By 1924 most of the major figures of the Silver Age had already fled the socialist country, and did not miss the opportunity to express their critical attitude towards the newly established regime: Gippius and Merezhkovskii had been residing in Paris since 1920, where they were soon joined by Bal'mont; Ivanov was the last to depart for Rome in 1924.[14]

Out of Blok and Briusov, who chose not to emigrate, Briusov seemed to be the most consistent supporter of the October upheaval, in which he saw a transformative historic event. In 1920 he became a member of the Communist Party and was very active in the People's Commissariat for Education, acting as the head of its printing and library divisions. Under Commissar Anatolii Lunacharskii, he became the head of Moscow's Public Libraries and the Chairman of the Union of Poets, and later on served as the Director of the Moscow Institute of Literature and

---

13 *Narkompros* (the People's Commissariat for Education) was charged with the administration of public education and most other issues related to culture, until it was transformed into the Ministry of Education in 1946. Since the early days of its formation (November 1917) *Narkompros* gained control over the content of libraries accessible to the mass reader. Its series of circulars drew attention to the role of books as a main source of dissemination of mass literacy and culture, while emphasising the importance of political control over such a large-scale undertaking, 'so that the flow of these books was channelled in the right direction' (N. K. Krupskaia, 'O plane raboty po BD Vneshkol'nogo otdela Narkomprosa', *Narodnoe prosveshchenie*, 6, 1918). In the context of Soviet official attitudes towards symbolist writers, it is interesting to note that the 1937 issue of the journal *Literaturnoe nasledstvo* dedicated to Russian symbolism was focused exclusively on three authors, Briusov, Blok and Andrei Belyi, who appeared in the spotlight because of his close connections with Blok.

14 Fedor Sologub also had a distinctly anti-Bolshevik orientation; in July 1921 he received permission to leave the country, but his wife's death, just two months later, left him in such a profound state of mourning that he gave up any thoughts of leaving Russia and died in Leningrad in 1927. Hundreds of Russian intellectuals were also expelled from the country in 1922–1923, and transported abroad on the so-called 'Philosophers' boats'; see Lesley Chamberlain, *Lenin's Private War: The Voyage of the Philosophy Steamer and the Exile of the Intelligentsia* (New York: St Martin's Press, 2007).

Arts until his death in 1924. Briusov edited the first edition of the Soviet Encyclopaedia and supported young proletarian writers (such as, for instance, Andrei Platonov), prioritising their work over the aestheticism of his fellow modernist authors (Osip Mandel'shtam's *Second Book* of poems (1923) was reviewed by Briusov in a very negative way[15]). In the words of Clarence Brown, 'his embrace of Bolshevism and the new order of things was more fervent by far than that of Maiakovskii, the unofficial poet-laureate of the Revolution'.[16] Briusov's own writing, on the other hand, never moved away from the elaborate symbolist experimentation of his pre-1917 work. Even his later post-revolutionary poems, such as the collections *Dali* (*Horizons*, 1922) and *Speshi!* (*Hurry up!*, 1924), were too sophisticated and too formalistic for the working masses. Classified as sheer 'academic avant-gardism' by Mikhail Gasparov,[17] they presented little material for the enlightenment and instruction of the working people. Blok's position in this respect was of a different order.

Surprisingly for his admirers, as well as for his closer literary circle, Blok also welcomed the proletarian coup. Gippius recalls that it was utterly frustrating to think of him as a friend of the Bolsheviks, to the extent that she was reluctant to shake hands with the poet when they accidentally met on a tram journey in Petrograd in September 1918.[18] Unlike the majority of his fellow symbolists, Blok refused to emigrate from Russia, claiming that he had to support the country during these difficult times. Never before able to cooperate with society (as he wrote in 1909 to his mother, 'either one should not live in Russia at all [...], or

---

15 In Briusov's words, Mandel'shtam's poetry, 'cut off from contemporary life, from social and political interests, cut off from the problems of contemporary science, from the search for contemporary world view', had nothing to offer. Valerii Briusov, 'Vtoraia kniga', *Pechat' i revoliutsiia*, 6 (1923), 63–66 (p. 66); quoted in Donald Loewen, *The Most Dangerous Art: Poetry, Politics, and Autobiography after the Revolution* (Plymouth: Lexington Books, 2008), p. 40.
16 Clarence Brown, *Mandelstam* (Cambridge: Cambridge University Press, 1973), p. 111.
17 Mikhail L. Gasparov, *Akademicheskii avangardizm: priroda i kul'tura u pozdnego Briusova* (Moscow: RGGU, 1995). Mandel'shtam viewed the late Briusov in a very negative way, saying in 1922 that 'such a vacuity is not to be ever repeated in Russian poetry' (Osip Mandel'shtam, 'O prirode slova', *Sobranie sochnenii*, 4 vols., edited by P. Nerler (Moscow: Artbiznestsentr, 1993), I, 217–31 (p. 230)).
18 Zinaida N. Gippius, *Stikhotvoreniia. Zhivye litsa* (Moscow: Khudozhestvennaia literatura, 1991), pp. 248–49.

else isolate oneself from *humiliation* — that is to say politics and "social activities"'), he now accepted several administrative posts.[19] From 1918 to 1921 he worked as a lecturer at the Journalism School, as the head of the German Section of the World Literature publishing house, as the deputy head of the Literature Department of *Narkompros* in Moscow, and as the chairman of the Petrograd Section of the All-Russia Union of Poets; he served on the State Committee on the publication of Russian classics; in the repertoire section of the Petrograd Theatre Department of *Narkompros*; on the editorial board of the journal *Repertuar*; and quite a few others.[20] However, he quickly became disillusioned with the Bolsheviks and their methods — as he once put it in a conversation with Gor'kii, his 'faith in the wisdom of humanity' had ended.[21] He did not write a single line of poetry for three years: 'All sounds have stopped for me', he mentioned to Kornei Chukovskii, 'Can't you hear that there are no sounds any longer?'.[22] From time to time he performed his verse for audiences in Petrograd and Moscow. His last public speech, 'O naznachenii poeta' ('On the Poet's Calling', January 1921), was dedicated to the anniversary of Aleksandr Pushkin's death. Centred on the conflict between freedom of expression and the absolutism of the Tsarist authoritarian state, it contained unmistakable references to the contemporary agenda;[23] and sounded like a doom-laden prophecy for literature in the oppressive climate of the socialist regime.

Nevertheless, taking into account Blok's initially liberal (albeit only fleeting) attitude towards the Soviet state, and the fact that he was undoubtedly a major poet of his age, it was his legacy which was appropriated by the system, and for years to come was preserved,

---

19 Aleksandr Blok, letter to his mother, 13 April 1909, in Aleksandr Blok, *Sobranie sochinenii*, 8 vols., edited by V. N. Orlov, A. A. Surkov and K. I. Chukovskii (Moscow-Leningrad: Khudozhestvennaia literatura, 1960–1963), VIII, 281.

20 V. L. Shepelev and V. N. Liubimov, '"On budet pisat' stikhi protiv nas". Pravda o bolezni i smerti Aleksandra Bloka (1921)', *Istochnik*, 2 (1995), 33–45 (pp. 34–42). For a more detailed account of Blok's life and work see Avril Pyman, *The Life of Aleksandr Blok*, 2 vols. (Oxford: Oxford University Press, 1979).

21 Maksim Gor'kii, 'A. A. Blok' (1923), in *Sobranie sochinenii*, XXIV, 425–27 (p. 427).

22 Kornei Chukovskii, 'Vospominaniia o Bloke', in *Sobranie sochinenii*, 6 vols. (Moscow: Khudozhestvennaia literatura, 1965–1969), II (1965), p. 311.

23 At this time Blok was already terminally ill (and died eight months later); his application for permission to leave the country in order to obtain the required medical treatment in Finland was rejected by the *Politburo* (and more specifically by Lenin) in spring 1921; see Shepelev and Liubimov, pp. 34–42.

reproduced and disseminated as an expression, or more precisely as an artefact, of the state approved culture. This fact in no way compromises the value of Blok's oeuvre; but the mechanism of his canonisation requires a more in-depth consideration in this context: firstly, because it consists of much more than a simple text-to-reader relation (as a carrier of cultural capital, a canonical work can become a vector of ideological motifs not necessarily embedded within the work itself); and secondly, because there may be several different canons circulating within a specific culture during a particular historical stage. When speaking of the formation of boundaries to existing literary knowledge or expression, Alastair Fowler describes six major types of literary canons: the *potential* canon would theoretically contain all works of written and oral literature; the *accessible* canon, in contrast, would consist of those works readers would actually come into contact with. Different criteria further narrow the *accessible* canon to produce *selective* canons. Some of these include the *official* canons shaped by mechanisms of patronage, education or censorship; the *critical* canons evidenced in trends in literary scholarship; and the *personal* canons of any individual reader's tastes and knowledge.[24] Below we shall examine Blok's position within the spectrum of the given canonical strands.

Considering the *official* canon, shaped through the mechanisms of censorship and education, it is worth bearing in mind that starting from the mid-1920s, Soviet Russia had begun to reconfigure the platform of its cultural agenda. Trotskii's idea of a world-wide revolution had been gradually phased out; and in 1925 the Party Conference put forward a different aim of constructing socialism in one country.[25] The emphasis was on building the nation, which involved creating a new ethnic entity — the Soviet people. This required a radical shift in the government's ideological policies: a step back to conservative values, a

---

24 Alastair Fowler, 'Genre and the Literary Canon', p. 98.
25 The resolution was read by Lev Kamenev, who claimed: 'By pursuing the right policy, namely reinforcing the socialist elements in our economics, we will show that despite the reluctant tempo of the international revolution, socialism must be built, can be built together with the representatives of peasants in our country, and it will be built'; *XIV konferentsiia Rossiiskoi Kommunisticheskoi partii (bol'shevikov): stenograficheskii otchet* (Moscow and Leningrad: Gosizdat, 1925), p. 267.

vindication of the past and a re-establishment of the concept of cultural heritage.²⁶

The new focus referred to continuity and tradition, and Blok fitted nicely into the scheme. Due to his considerable output and the broad thematic spectrum of his oeuvre, his legacy presented a vast store of material for the Soviet principle of selective reading.²⁷ His first cycle of poems, *Stikhi o Prekrasnoi dame* (*Verses on the Beautiful Lady*, 1904) saturated with the religious mysticism of Vladimir Solov'ev, was completely sidelined; and attention was fixed entirely on the patriotic pathos of his writings, exemplified, for instance, by the cycle *Rodina* (*Native Land*, 1907–1916) or *Na pole Kulikovom* (*On the Field of Kulikovo*, 1908). The description of St Petersburg that Blok crafted for his earlier collection *Gorod* (*The City*, 1904–1908), was both impressionistic and eerie. Representing his idea of an 'artificial hell', it was often based on the conflict between the Platonic theory of ideal beauty and the disappointing reality of perilous industrialism ('Neznakomka' ('The Unknown Woman', 1906)). *Gorod* was read as an expression of disapproval and interpreted along the lines of social criticism of the Tsarist regime.²⁸ Generally speaking, Blok was seen as a useful resource for filling the gaps in the newly established cultural progression, since he was a generic example of a transitional author who highlighted the decay of the capitalist order in such poems as 'Fabrika' ('The Factory', 1903), 'Rossiia' ('Russia', 1908), or 'Na zheleznoi doroge' ('On the Railway', 1910). Due to his origins and imperfect class orientation,

---

26 David Elliot, *New Worlds: Russian Art and Society 1900–1937* (London: Thames and Hudson Ltd., 1986), pp. 22–26.
27 Within the framework of *partiinost'* (party-mindedness), any literary work was considered from a purely political perspective, comprising such aspects as a selective approach to the content, which was supposed to direct its readers towards interpreting a text along the lines of the Party aims; an appreciation of the characters as representatives of a specific social stratum, and a class-defined viewpoint on the analysis of the form: 'Our analysis, conducted in a Marxist way, will open our eyes not only on the characters, but also on their author, who does have the power to guide them and who does determine everything in literature, but whose mentality, in turn, is preconditioned by his class-related psycho-ideology'; V. V. Golubkov and M. A. Rybnikova, *Izuchenie literatury v shkole II stupeni. Metodika chteniia* (Moscow: Gosizdat, 1929), p. 36.
28 *Programmy srednei obshcheobrazovatel'noi shkoly. Literatura 4–10 klassy* (Moscow: Prosveshchenie, 1983), p. 54.

however, he lacked the necessary political consciousness to embrace the principles of socialist art.

It is true that Blok's poetry was by nature less esoteric, simpler, and, perhaps, less abstract than that of some other Silver Age authors. Over the years he evinced an extraordinary ability to evoke life as it is in both its happy moments ('O, vesna bez kontsa i bez kraiu' ('Oh, spring without an end and without a limit', 1907), 'I vnov' — poryvy iunykh let' ('And again — the impulses of youth', 1912)) and its most depressive manifestations, represented in such poems as 'Pliaski smerti' ('Dances of Death', 1914), 'Golos iz khora' ('A Voice from the Chorus', 1914) or 'Miry letiat. Goda letiat' ('Worlds fly past. Years fly past', 1912), which, thanks to their doomed and negative perspective, were often seen as an expression of the ruthless realism of the poet's nib. Like many Russian intellectuals of the time, Blok was aware of the real gap separating the intelligentsia and the Russian people, as he put it in his famous speech *Narod i intelligentsia* (*The People and the Intelligentsia*, November 1908):

> There is a line between two camps — the people and the intelligentsia [...] these two camps still do not see each other and do not want to know each other; and those who are looking for peace and concurrence are still treated as traitors and deserters by both the majority of people and the majority of the intelligentsia.[29]

Blok challenged the intelligentsia's assumption of their shared identity with, and their leading position towards, the Russian people, and appealed to them to surrender their high culture to the popular *stikhiinost'* (element). He himself also tried to break out of the artificially created world of aestheticism towards the uncomplicated, down-to-earth life of simple people. 'I still live very quietly, on my own', he wrote to Belyi, 'I work a lot and everything is profoundly simple'.[30] Russia became a major focus of his writing at the time — a theme in which he found his vocation, his civic responsibility as a creator:

> I face my theme — the theme of Russia [...]. To this theme I consciously and irrevocably dedicate my life. This is the most significant question,

---

29 First published as 'Rossiia i intelligentsia', *Zolotoe runo*, 1 (1909); *Sobranie sochinenii*, V, 321–27 (p. 324).
30 Blok, letter to Andrei Belyi, 5 April 1908, in *A. A. Blok-Andrei Belyi: Perepiska* (Munich: Wilhelm Fink Verlag, 1969), p. 229.

the most vital, the most real. I have been approaching this question for a long time from the beginning of my conscious life, and I know that my road in its basic aspiration is as straight and as purposeful as an arrow.[31]

Although he pursued this vocation with almost suicidal sincerity, fervour and dedication (for his world had always been the world of absolutes), his yearning for a simple life was constantly undercut by profound depression and despair, his feeling of spiritual emptiness and isolation, as well as his disgust in the face of the society he lived in. This is not to say that the element of social concern in his writings was entirely contrived, but it was clearly generated by both his repulsion with the world and a horror at his own condition. To a certain extent he always remained the poet of intoxication: whether in surrendering himself to the flow of the popular *stikhiinost'*, or drowning in the ecstasy of oblivion in poems such as 'V chas, kogda p'ianeiut nartsissy' ('In the Hour when Narcissi are Intoxicated', 1904) and 'Ia prigvozhden k traktirnoi stoike' ('I am nailed to the bar in the tavern', 1908).

As regards the Revolution, during the last period of his creative work, Blok did put forward some political comments, pondering on the messianic destiny of the country, in *Vozmezdie* (*Retribution*, 1910–1921) and 'Skify' ('The Scythians', 1918). Influenced by Solov'ev's doctrines, he had vague apocalyptic apprehensions and often vacillated between hope and despair: 'Behind the storm, there opened a ferocious void of the day, menacing, however, with a new storm and concealing within itself a promise of it. These were the inter-revolutionary years that have exhausted and worn out body and soul. Now there is another storm', he wrote in his diary during the summer of 1917.[32] Quite unexpectedly (at least for his close circle) he accepted the October Revolution as the final resolution to these apocalyptic yearnings. The official Soviet stance on Blok, however, was configured in a somewhat different way. Blok was presented as a severe critic of bourgeois society, who displayed a suffocating picture of Tsarist Russia and revealed its social injustice with a strong emphasis on the motif of retribution — hence the title of his major cycle of seventeen poems (1908–1913), as well as his verse epic *Vozmezdie*. The Revolution was seen as a cathartic power, which ignited

---

31 Blok, letter to Konstantin Stanislavskii, 9 December 1908, *Sobranie sochinenii*, VIII, 265.
32 Blok, diary entry, 15 August 1917, *Sobranie sochinenii*, VII, 300–01.

Blok's poetic inspiration, manifesting itself in his two best-known poems 'Skify' and *Dvenadtsat'* (*The Twelve*, 1918).

In *Dvenadtsat'*, Blok included some eloquent poetic speculation on the meaning of the Revolution in the relentless spiral of human history. It depicts a group of twelve Red Army soldiers (a clear allusion to the twelve apostles) marching through revolutionary Petrograd, led by the mysterious figure of Jesus Christ ascendant at the end (an image whose symbolism defied a straightforward interpretation and which was therefore commonly disparaged by the critics who held sway after the Revolution).[33] Ambivalence pervades the poem, and contrast is its structural principle, analysed in great detail in Sergei Hackel's monograph *The Poet and the Revolution*.[34] The opening line 'Black night. / White snow' sets out the polarising framework for the poem's discourse, which alternates revolutionary marching songs with the orthodox liturgy for the dead, colloquial slang, and popular folk songs; clear and chopped rhythms and repetitive array of symbols all help to capture the mood of the time, as well as the poet's own uncertain view of the events.[35] In the words of Maiakovskii, who was one of the most faithful admirers of Blok's talent: 'two contrasting apprehensions of the Revolution linked fantastically in his poem *Dvenadtsat'*. Some read in this poem a satire on the Revolution, others a celebration'.[36]

Despite all its controversy (Kamenev and Trotskii, for instance, always denied the revolutionary content of Blok's writings: 'To be sure, Blok is not one of ours', wrote Trotskii in 1924, 'but he reached towards us. And in doing so, he broke down'), the poem became popular straight after its first publication on 3 March 1918: it was widely recited and publicly performed.[37]

---

33 For a modern interpretation of the finale of *Dvenadtsat'*, see Sergei Averintsev *et al.*, 'Final "Dvenadtsati" — vzgliad iz 2000 goda', *Znamia*, 11 (2000), 190–206.

34 Sergei Hackel, *The Poet and the Revolution: Aleksandr Blok's 'The Twelve'* (Oxford: Clarendon Press, 1975).

35 Blok, *Sobranie sochinenii*, III, 347–59. In her bilingual edition of *Dvenadtsat'* (Durham, UK: University of Durham Press, 1989), Avril Pyman lists seventeen translations of the poem available to date; for the purposes of this chapter a more literal translation of the text by Hackel (pp. 205–29) is preferred.

36 Vladimir Maiakovskii, 'Umer Aleksandr Blok', in *Sobranie sochinenii*, 13 vols., edited by E. I. Naumov (Moscow: Khudozhestvennaia literatura, 1955–1961), III (1957), 474.

37 Leo Trotskii, *Literature and Revolution* (Chicago: Haymarket Books, 2005), p. 111; V. N. Orlov, *Zhizn' Bloka* (Moscow: Tsentrpoligraf, 2001), p. 544.

A veil was drawn over the inconvenient fact that it was first published not by the Bolsheviks, but in the oppositional Socialist Revolutionary newspaper *Znamia truda*.³⁸ The text was configured along the lines of the Soviet state's current ideological aims and at times censored to the extent of turning into self-parody. The best example of this would be the version which, according to Evgenii Evtushenko, was read in the Red propaganda units, and in which the unwanted figure of Jesus was substituted with that of a proletarian sailor, who nevertheless still kept the garland of white roses: 'V belom venchike iz roz — / Vperedi idet matros' ('With a garland of white roses spliced — / Up in front is a sailor'). Having realized how ridiculous this image, verging on caricature, was, the post-war Stalin-era censors made an executive decision and simply cut out the baffling episode altogether.³⁹

Dvenadtsat' entered the school curriculum as 'the first poem of the October Revolution in Soviet literature'.⁴⁰ For years it became a trademark of the poet; and for many it remained the only piece of Blok's writing that they actually knew. It was largely due to *Dvenadtsat'* that Blok has never been effaced from the palette of recommended canonical reading and escaped the condescending remarks directed towards his fellow symbolist authors: 'Our contemporary literature is also full of outstanding literary influences', wrote the author of a teachers' handbook of 1928:

> There are organic trends coming from the past (Pushkin, Gogol', Tolstoi, Dostoevskii); there are examples of influences of contemporary poets on each other (Maiakovskii-Bezymenskii-Zharov; Blok-Esenin-Aleksandrovskii), and there are some instances of temporary accidental literary imitations such as the 'bal'montism' of Gerasimov.⁴¹

In this context, the name of Maria Rybnikova deserves special consideration. As a leading methodologist in the field of Soviet secondary education and the author of numerous school anthologies and teachers'

---

38 Blok, 'Dvenadtsat", *Znamia truda*, 3 March 1918, p. 2. From spring 1918 the newspaper was in active opposition to the Bolsheviks and Lenin's politics, and was closed down after the Socialist-Revolutionary uprising in July 1918.
39 *Strofy veka. Antologiia russkoi poezii*, edited by Evgenii Evtushenko (Minsk-Moscow: Polifakt, 1995), p. 82.
40 *Programmy srednei obshcheobrazovatel'noi shkoly. Literatura*, p. 54.
41 M. A. Rybnikova, *Russkaia literatura. Voprosnik po russkoi literature dlia zaniatii 7, 8 i 9 grupp shkol 2-i stupeni i dlia pedtekhnikumov* (Moscow: Mir, 1928), p. 120.

handbooks (republished in the 1980s), she expended significant effort in securing Blok's place in the canon through education. Rybnikova was a long-term admirer of the Russian symbolist poets, and her particular sphere of interest was focused on Blok. She wrote a number of scholarly articles on his poems, the most prominent of which was the essay *A. Blok—Hamlet*, published as early as 1923.[42]

Within the canon shaped by the framework of scholarship and so-called Blok studies, Blok's poetic output has always enjoyed a vast amount of attention, despite the fact that the poet himself expressed his utmost dismay at the prospect of becoming a subject of scholarly concern. In his poem 'Druz'iam' ('To My Friends', 24 July 1908) he writes:

> Печальная доля — так сложно,
> Так трудно и празднично жить,
> И стать достояньем доцента,
> И критиков новых плодить...
>
> Зарыться бы в свежем бурьяне,
> Забыться бы сном навсегда!
> Молчите, проклятые книги!
> Я вас не писал никогда![43]

> Depressing fate: to live a life,
> So complex, hard and festive,
> Only to end as young dons' prey,
> And serve to breed new critics...
>
> Let me delve deeper into weeds,
> And sleep oblivious forever!
> Be silent cursed books!
> I never wrote you, never!

In terms of his impact on the art of poetic composition, Blok was undoubtedly one of the most influential authors of the symbolist movement, and as regards this branch of literary research, it is worth

---

42 M. A. Rybnikova, *A. Blok — Gamlet* (Moscow: Svetlana, 1923).
43 Blok, *Sobranie sochinenii*, III, 125–26; translated in Hackel, p. vii.

mentioning the works of Viktor Zhirmunskii and Vladimir Orlov, Pavel Gromov and Dmitrii Maksimov, and the detailed analysis of his prosody and poetics by Mikhail Gasparov, as well as the works of the Tartu-Moscow Semiotic school, namely those of Iurii Lotman, Aleksei Losev, and Zara Mints. It is important to bear in mind, however, that for many years Soviet scholarship was predominantly centred on the textual analysis of Blok's writings (conducted within the framework of literary theory, semiotics, poetics, and topical research), while the metaphysical basis of his oeuvre remained, broadly speaking, a marginal and largely unexplored field (the only systematic study of the philosophical aspects of Russian symbolism in the Soviet period was carried out by Valentin Asmus).[44] Two main factors account for this restricted approach. Firstly, up until the late 1950s, there was a sheer lack of material and information. Blok's letters, notebooks and diaries were published in a more or less complete and systematic form only in the 1960–1963, eight-volume edition of the poet's *Collected Works*. Prior to this date these materials were released only sporadically and with considerable omissions. As highlighted by Orlov in his major review article on the legacy of the poet, the two volumes of Blok's *Diaries* published in 1928 were largely incomplete and contained the following explanation for editorial interventions:

> Our ambition was, of course, to publish the diaries in their authentic and comprehensive form. However, due to the fact that many of the records refer to the living members of our society, we were obliged to make certain textual omissions, which, nonetheless, are of very little significance [...]. Moreover, we had to encode a number of proper names; and in order to avoid any unnecessary guessing, they were substituted by asterisks rather than initials.[45]

---

44 V. F. Asmus, 'Filosofiia i estetika russkogo simvolizma', *Izbrannye filosofskie trudy*, 2 vols. (Moscow: Moscow University, 1969), I, 187–237; Iu. N. Davydov, *Begstvo ot svobody. Filosofskoe mifotvorchestvo i literaturnyi avangard* (Moscow: Khudozhestvennaia literatura, 1978) also contributed to the area.

45 V. N. Orlov, 'Literaturnoe nasledstvo Aleksandra Bloka', *Literaturnoe nasledstvo* (Moscow: Zhurnal'no-gazetnoe ob"edinenie, 1937), XXVII–XXVIII, 505–74 (p. 559). The first volume of Blok's diaries contained the diaries of 1911–1913 and the second those of 1917–1921: *Dnevnik Al. Bloka*, edited by P. N. Medvedev (Leningrad: Izdatel'stvo leningradskikh pisatelei, 1928); the diaries of 1901–1902 were published by Orlov later in 1937: 'Iz literaturnogo naslediia Aleksandra Bloka. Iunosheskii dnevnik', edited by V. N. Orlov, in *Literaturnoe nasledstvo* (Moscow: Zhurnal'no-gazetnoe ob"edinenie, 1937), XXVII–XXVIII, 299–370.

In practice, these omissions went far beyond the designated frame and, according to Orlov's scholarly analysis, resulted in a significant distortion of the author's text. Blok's notebooks, printed by *Priboi* (*The Surf*) in 1930, were subjected to even more severe excisions, so that, in the words of the editor, 'certain notebooks had to be omitted in their entirety, and the material of the others was drastically reduced'.[46] The same practice applied equally to Blok's letters and continued all way through the Khrushchev Thaw.[47] Although in the mid-1960s Orlov pointed out that it was time to release a new, comprehensive academic edition of Blok's works and correspondence, and in 1973 Zil'bershtein reiterated the matter, no such edition was issued until 1997.[48]

The second reason was directly related to the dominance of state censorship in the Soviet cultural field, which meant that scholarly works that focused primarily on textual analysis and literary techniques enjoyed a somewhat higher degree of freedom of expression, remote from ideological and political concerns. This partly explains the prominence of semiotic and structuralist analysis in Blok studies. Apart from the enormous power and grace of his writing, where formality merged with freedom, elevated language with vulgarity, public discourse with personal reflections and with song, his greater innovation was the emancipation of Russian metrics. The regular syllabic-accentuated scheme elaborated in the eighteenth century, and used almost without exception thereafter, was in many of his poems shifted to a purely stress metric — a development, of course, with close parallels in the history of modernist Western prosodies. Such major scholars as Lotman, Mints, Losev and Gasparov presented an in-depth examination of Blok's style

---

46 Orlov, 'Literaturnoe nasledstvo Aleksandra Bloka', p. 560.

47 Prior to the 1960s edition of Blok's collected works (8 vols.), his letters were released sporadically and in various editions: *Pis'ma Aleksandra Bloka*, edited by S. M. Solov'ev, G. I. Chulkov, A. D. Skaldin and V. N. Kniazhnin (Leningrad: Kolos, 1925), with four introductory articles by the editors, who were also the addressees of the letters; *Pis'ma Aleksandra Bloka k rodnym*, 2 vols., edited by M. A. Beketova (Moscow-Leningrad: Akademiia, 1927–1932); *Pis'ma Al Bloka k E. P. Ivanovu*, edited by T. S. Vol'pe (Moscow-Leningrad: AN SSSR, 1936).

48 V. N. Orlov, *Blokovskii sbornik, Trudy nauchnoi konferentsii, posviashchennoi izucheniiu zhizni i tvorchestva A. A. Bloka, mai 1962*, edited by Iu. M. Lotman et al. (Tartu: Tartusskii gosudarstvennyi univesitet, 1964); I. S. Zil'bershtein, *Literaturnaia gazeta*, 4 April 1973, p. 8, quoted in Hackel, p. 237; *Polnoe sobranie sochinenii i pisem v 20 tomakh*, edited by A. N. Grishunin (Moscow: Nauka, 1997–1999).

and poetics, drawing attention to his daring rhymes and innovative versification, to the intricate language of his symbols, and to the vast connotative spectrum of his verse.[49] Having added an extra layer of complexity to the subject of their studies, these works (together with some other factors) conjured a complementary image of the poet, opening up new avenues in the reception of his oeuvre, accessible to those who were prepared to extend their reading beyond the limits of prescriptive curriculum lists.

As regards Blok's position and function within this kind of alternative, and essentially dissenting canon, these can be best understood by looking closely into the processes of its configuration and the contingencies of its subsequent transmission and preservation. One of the factors to be taken into account is the history of publishing in the Soviet Union. Curiously enough, the cultural activities of the elite were less directly touched by state-led initiatives than those of the masses (specifically in education). As Anthony Kemp-Welch describes it, 'NEP permitted considerable freedom to Russia's brilliant elites [...] cultural experiments were [...] exuberant — constructivism, suprematism, utopian architecture and innovative theatre — offering an artistic counterpart to the political revolution'.[50] The Bolsheviks understood that what influenced the political outlook of the masses was far more significant than writings aimed at the refined taste of the elite. Although in the first decade of Bolshevik control private publishing houses printed only a small and ever-diminishing share of the total output of the literary material, they nonetheless made a contribution to the variety of texts available to the Soviet reader, bringing out a significant proportion of editions on philosophy, the works of fiction and translations. For instance, authors whose pro-Bolshevik credentials were not remotely flawless, such as Merezhkovskii, Nikolai Berdiaev, Semen Frank and Nikolai Losskii, were still published (by private publishers) in the mid-1920s; the same

---

49   Zara Mints, *Poetika Aleksandra Bloka* (St Petersburg: Iskusstvo, 1999); Iurii Lotman, 'A. A. Blok. Anne Akhmatovoi'; 'Blok i narodnaia kul'tura goroda'; '"Chelovek prirody" v russkoi literature XIX veka i "tsyganskaia tema" u Bloka', in Iurii Lotman, *O poetakh i poezii* (St Petersburg: Iskusstvo, 1996), pp. 211–20, pp. 653–69, pp. 670–75.

50   Anthony Kemp-Welch, *Stalin and the Literary Intelligentsia, 1928–1939* (Basingstoke: Macmillan, 1991), p. 34.

can be said about the symbolist poems of Blok that were produced in Petrograd by the Alkonost publishing house.

Another relevant factor is that up until the 1960s, quite a few people who knew Blok personally were still active on the Soviet literary scene. Through their social conversations and published records (for instance, those of Anna Akhmatova, Marina Tsvetaeva, Iurii Annenkov and many others), they moulded and passed on their own image of the poet — that of a refined aesthete, a herald of divine beauty — an *echt* embodiment of poetic inspiration itself. The reminiscences of Chukovskii, and more specifically his description of Blok reading *Neznakomka* at one of the gatherings in Ivanov's 'tower', are particularly exemplary in this respect:

> And Blok, sluggish, looking calm, young and sunburnt (he always got his tan already in early spring), climbed up some huge iron armature, connecting telephone wires, and in response to our unceasing begging, for the third, and even for the fourth time in a row read this everlasting ballad with his measured, muffled, monotonous, docile and tragic voice. And, while absorbing its ingenious phono-scripture, we have been suffering in anticipation that this enchantment would come to an end, whereas we all wanted it to last for hours.[51]

The fact that Blok was one of the most influential poets of his time is difficult to overlook. The richness of his images, which he conjured out of the most banal surroundings and trivial events (e.g. 'V restorane' ('In the Restaurant') or 'Na zheleznoi doroge' ('On the Railway')) inspired generations of younger poets: Sergei Esenin, Akhmatova, and Boris Pasternak. Compare, for instance, Blok's poem 'Rus'' ('Russia', 1906) with the poem of the same title written by Esenin (1914), which effectively invokes the same metaphor of an impenetrable and ghostly land:

> Русь, опоясана реками
> И дебрями окружена,
> С болотами и журавлями,
> И с мутным взором колдуна.[52]

---

51 Kornei Chukovskii, *Sovremenniki. Portrety i etiudy* (Moscow: Molodaia gvardiia, 1967), p. 250.
52 Blok, *Sobranie sochinenii*, II, 99.

Rus' is embraced by rivers
And surrounded by thick forests,
With marshes and cranes,
And with a hazy look of a sorcerer

И стоят за дубровными сетками,
Словно нечисть лесная, пеньки.
Запугала нас сила нечистая,
Что ни прорубь — везде колдуны.⁵³

And behind the array of oaks, there
Stand tree-trunks, like wood demons.
We were all scared by these evil spirits,
A sorcerer looks out of every ice-break.

Likewise, one can find numerous echoes of Blok's patterns in Akhmatova's poems. Zhirmunskii — one of the first major scholars of Russian symbolism — once pointed out that this was not a case of imitation in its most traditional sense, but rather a kind of 'contamination' of her writing with Blok's means of expression, imagery and certain metrico-syntactic structures.⁵⁴

И такая влекущая сила,
Что готов я твердить за молвой,
Будто ангелов ты низводила,
Соблазняя своей красотой.⁵⁵

And it is such an appealing power, that
I am happy to follow the rumour, acting
As if you brought angels down from heaven,
seducing them by your beauty.

---

53 Sergei Esenin, *Sobranie sochineni*, 7 vols., edited by Iu. L. Prokushev (Moscow: Nauka-Golos, 1995–2002), II (1997), 17.
54 V. M. Zhirmunskii, 'Anna Akhmatova i Aleksandr Blok', in *Izbrannye trudy. Teoriia literatury. Poetika. Stilistika* (Leningrad: Nauka, 1977), pp. 323–52 (p. 339).
55 Blok, 'K muze' (1912), *Sobranie sochinenii*, III, 7.

> И такая могучая сила
> Зачарованный голос влечет,
> Будто там впереди не могила,
> А таинственной лестницы взлет.[56]

> And such a compelling power
> Draws the bewitched voice on,
> As if ahead there were no grave,
> But a flight of mysterious stairs.

Maiakovskii, whose own style and convictions were hardly comparable to Blok's vision of aesthetics, was absolutely enthralled by the mastery of the poet's writing; and, according to the memoirs of David Burliuk, could easily recite from memory the vast majority of Blok's poetic collections.[57] These examples are manifold and stretch far beyond the literary domain. In music, Blok inspired Arthur Lourie's choral cantata *Dans le temple du rêve d'or* (*In the Sanctuary of Golden Dreams*, 1919), Shostakovich's lyric song cycle for soprano and piano trio, *Seven Romances of Aleksandr Blok* (1967), and Sergei Slonimskii's cantata *A Voice from the Chorus* (1963–1976); in art one might immediately think of the series of eye-catching illustrations to Blok's poems created in the early 1980s by the then oppositional artist Il'ia Glazunov.[58] All these primary, and in the case of art and music, secondary references to Blok's writings are, of course, of major cultural importance: they affirm the canonical status of the original, and constitute an effective mechanism of attaching value to the poet's oeuvre.[59] This aspect, however, has an extra political dimension in the Russian context. Curiously enough, the majority for whom Blok provided an inspiration were, in one way or another, at

---

[56] Anna Akhmatova, *Sochineniia*, 2 vols., edited by M. M. Kralin (Moscow: Tsitadel', 1997), I, 284; translated by Judith Hemschemeyer, *The Complete Poems of Anna Akhmatova*, edited by Roberta Reeder, 2 vols. (Somerville: Zephyr Press, 1990), II, 685.

[57] Burliuk, quoted by E. I. Naumov in his commentary to Maiakovskii's obituary 'Umer Aleksander Blok', in Maiakovskii, *Sobranie sochinenii*, III, 653.

[58] *Aleksandr Blok v illiustratsiiakh I. Glazunova* (a set of 16 postcards) (Moscow: Iskusstvo, 1982).

[59] The representation of Blok in Soviet cinema as an affirmation of the canon delivered to the mass viewer is a matter of separate investigation: Olga Sobolev, *Appropriated by the Revolution: Blok and the Socialist Realist Cinema*, presented at the AAASS Conference, Boston, November 2013.

odds with the Soviet system (the aforementioned authors are exemplary in this respect), which in itself, and not without a reason, had some bearing on the ideological reputation of their source.

In other words, the representation of Blok in Soviet culture can be characterized by a so-called double exposure. The first layer, configured by the school curriculum, firmly wedded the poet to the Revolution. It highlighted the patriotism of his lyrics; the revolutionary echoes in *Dvenadtsat'*; and associated his legacy with the notion of socially engaged writing. One can say that as an object of cultural capital, Blok's oeuvre was clearly appropriated by the dominant class. The second layer was available only to 'the happy few' — those who (through superior judgement or benefit of learning) were prepared to go beyond this artificially created frame. For all its greatness, *Dvenadtsat'* could not be made to stand for all of Blok; and for many he essentially remained a lyric poet in the Romantic tradition — one of the last heirs of the nineteenth-century Russian intellectual elite. By the mid-1950s Blok had become a canonical emblem of this elite — an epitome of poetic refinement, of sublime aestheticism, and spiritual elevation, but always with the double connotation of an angel fallen from grace. Gradually (from the early seventies and throughout Brezhnev's years), these particular undertones acquired a distinctly political dimension, which, in a way, reflected the overall status of the intelligentsia in the Soviet state. Leonid Trauberg, an eminent Russian film director, testified that he and his fellow artists secretly preferred Blok to Maiakovskii: 'he was much closer to our hearts', he reckoned, 'but we were deeply ashamed to voice these thoughts'.[60] At that time the Russian intelligentsia saw itself as a hostage of the system, and such qualities of Blok's writings as their charming sadness and vulnerability, the sense of spiritual isolation and sacrificial suffering were profoundly internalized (the circumstances of his death were widely known among cultural circles).[61] He became an

---

[60] V. Shcherbina, 'O gruppe estetstvuiushchikh kosmopolitov v kino', *Iskusstvo kino*, 1 (1949), 14–16 (pp. 14–15).

[61] A vivid reflection of this atmosphere can be found in Stanislav Rostotskii's 1972 film *A zori zdes' tikhie* (*And the Dawns Here Are Quiet*). The film is set in 1942: five young girls from the division of the anti-aircraft gunners are sent on a doomed mission to stop a detachment of German paratroopers. During her night-watch duty, Sonia, the only heroine with a university background, characteristically recites Blok's poem 'Rozhdennye v goda glukhie' ('Those Born in the Years of Stagnation'), which is charmingly mistaken for a prayer by her village-man commander Vas'kov.

echo of the hopeless cry of a trapped generation, bidding farewell to the end of the liberal Thaw. As Pasternak claimed in his 1956 poem:

> Но Блок, слава Богу, иная,
> Иная, по счастью, статья.
> Он к нам не спускался с Синая,
> Нас не принимал в сыновья.
>
> Прославленный не по программе
> И вечный вне школ и систем,
> Он не изготовлен руками
> И нам не навязан никем.[62]

> But Blok is, thank Heaven, another,
> A different matter for once,
> He did not descend from Sinai
> And not accept us as sons.
>
> Eternal and not manufactured,
> Renown not according to plan,
> Outside schools and systems, he has not
> Been foisted upon us by man.

The fact that Blok was canonised by the Russian intelligentsia as an expression of its self-image is in no way coincidental. The poet had always identified himself with and had a troubled attitude towards the intelligentsia, which effectively made him a typical representative of this social group. In his diary entries for January 1918, he repudiates 'the intelligentsia', referring to its negative view of the revolution, its instinctive 'hatred of parliaments, institutional gatherings and so on', and bitterly remarks that 'the smart alecks of the intelligentsia do not want to get their hands dirty with work'. In the same entries, however, he identifies with that very intelligentsia, calling it 'dear' and 'native' scum.[63] He claims that the removal of the gap between the intelligentsia and the people requires the former to love Russia as 'a mother,

---

62 Pasternak, 'Veter' (see note 1 above; the reference to 'his adopted sons' in the fourth line is an allusion to Stalin, who was regarded as the father of the Soviet people).
63 Blok, diary entry, 5 January 1918, *Sobranie sochinenii*, VII, 315; diary entry, 18 January 1918, *Sobranie sochinenii*, VII, 321.

sister and wife', and places himself in the role of that wife's lover by repeatedly stressing his status as 'a member of the intelligentsia'.[64] According to Mints, the same type of identification is reflected in his poetic compositions, namely in the cycle *Rodina* and his verse drama *Pesnia sud'by* (*Song of Fate*, 1908); in these writings the poet-protagonist is repeatedly presented as Russia's suitor or her promised husband, which, Mints maintains, irrevocably leads the reader to interpret him as a synecdoche for the intelligentsia.[65] At the same time, in a series of articles and speeches at the end of 1908, Blok argued that the intelligentsia was simply obsolete as a driving social force.[66] He accused it of pursuing a fatally individualistic course, expending its energies in literary novelties, nebulous philosophical speculations, and mechanical political activities, which had no connection with the needs and desires of the Russian people. Intellectuals, he wrote, loving 'individualism, demonism, aesthetics, and despair', were imbued with the 'will to die', thus becoming fundamentally opposed to the people, sustaining 'from time immemorial — the will to live'.[67] This, for Blok, was the cornerstone of the problem, making the intelligentsia incapable of national advocacy and moral leadership.

The feelings of self-doubt, ethical questioning, and reflection are, evidently, a constant factor in intellectual life, not least in that of the Russian intelligentsia. During the decades of Soviet power their old task of moral criticism and articulating national ideals acquired a new vitality in opposition to the regime. Moreover, throughout the apathy of the Brezhnev era, this was enhanced by the profound sense of disillusionment of many who had by and large been prepared to carry out the role allotted to them — a metaphysical rejection of the present and a psychological denigration of the possibility of change became the mode.[68] Effectively, each element of this quintessential array — spiritual

---

64 Blok, 'Rossiia i intelligentsia', *Sobranie sochinenii*, V, 321; 319; 327.
65 Blok, *Sobranie sochinenii*, III, 251–54; IV, 148–49; Mints, *Poetika Bloka*, p. 351.
66 His critical essays on the topic include: 'Russia and the Intelligentsia' (1908) and 'Nature and Culture' (1908); for a more detailed analysis of Blok's views on the Russian intelligentsia see Jane Burbank, *Intelligentsia and Revolution: Russian Views of Bolshevism, 1917–1922* (Oxford: Oxford University Press, 1986), pp. 9–11.
67 Blok, 'Rossiia i intelligentsia', *Sobranie sochinenii*, V, 327.
68 For a more detailed account of the changes in the intelligentsia's views in the Soviet period see Catriona Kelly, 'New Boundaries for the Common Good', in *Constructing Russian Culture in the Age of Revolution 1881–1940*, edited by Catriona Kelly and David Shepherd (Oxford: Oxford University Press, 1998), pp. 238–55.

abandonment, introspective reflection, despair and self-loathing — had a distinct parallel in Blok's own social and cultural position, turning him *ipso facto* into a canonical icon of the intelligentsia's views. His legacy (as well as his own image) began to function as a symbol of an alternative culture, and in this sense offered a perfect example of social conceptualisation brought about entirely by the grassroots activities of a particular group.

The first years of the post-Soviet period were characterised by a distinct reconfiguration of the country's cultural agenda. The abolition of state censorship and, consequently, of the *official* canon, the changes in the educational system and a tremendous increase in the number of privately printed books gave a new impetus to the debates on the function and value of literature, as well as on the formation of a canon of important works. When looking at the position of Blok (and the cohort of symbolist authors) in this newly developed context, two main issues should be considered. Firstly, the beginning of the 1990s was characterized by an unparalleled growth of interest in the legacy of the Silver Age. This can be demonstrated by the publication of such rare volumes as the collected poems of KR (the Grand Duke Konstantin Konstantinovich Romanov), edited by Askol'd Muratov, as well as a series of critical articles concerning his artistic output; the selected poems of Konstantin Sluchevskii, Solov'ev, Semen Nadson, Konstantin Fofanov, and Gippius; and, for the first time since 1914, an edition of poems by Merezhkovskii.[69] Moreover, the emphasis had now shifted considerably: it was transferred onto the philosophical platform of the symbolist authors, with a distinct attempt to establish an interdisciplinary approach to the field.[70] An increasing number of

---

69 D. S. Merezhkovskii, *Sobranie sochinenii*, 4 vols., edited by O. Mikhailov (Moscow: Pravda, 1990).

70 S. N. Broitman, *Russkaia lirika XIX — nachala XX veka v svete istoricheskoi poetiki* (Moscow: RGGU, 1997); *Vladimir Solov'ev i kul'tura Serebrianogo veka*, edited by E. A. Takho-Godi (Moscow: Nauka, 2005); S. P. Bel'chevichen, *Problema vzaimosviazi kul'tury i religii v filosofii D. S. Merezhkovskogo* (Tver': Izdatel'stvo Tverskogo universiteta, 1999); E. Andrushchenko, *Vlastelin 'chuzhogo': tekstologiia i problema poetiki D. S. Merezhkovskogo* (Moscow: Vodolei, 2012); S. Sapozhkov, 'Russkaia poeziia 1880–1890-kh godov: "konstruktivnost" khaosa ili "esteticheskii immoralizm"?', *Novoe literaturnoe obozrenie*, 75 (2005), 338–47; G. Obatin, *Ivanov-mistik: Okkul'tnye motivy v poezii i proze Viacheslava Ivanova* (Moscow: NLO, 2000); E. A. Takho-Godi, 'Vladimir Solov'ev i Konstantin Sluchevskii. K istorii vzaimootnoshenii', in *Kontekst: 1993. Literaturno-istoricheskie issledovaniia* (Moscow: Nasledie, 1996), 323–40.

works were released by a variety of specialists in literature, philosophy and cultural studies, and in this respect the studies of Efim Etkind and Aleksandr Etkind are particularly notable.[71] Symbolism started to be treated as a complex and far-reaching movement, which set out the framework for exploring the interaction between philosophy and art. The analysis of such interactions contributed to the appreciation of the philosophic theories of such major thinkers as Solov'ev, Nietzsche, and Schopenhauer, and their impact on the creative output of the symbolist writings of Merezhkovskii and Ivanov, Belyi, Feodor Sologub and Blok.

The second issue is related to the tendency to denigrate virtually the entire artistic output promoted in Soviet Russia before Gorbachev's years of *perestroika* and *glasnost'*. It became fashionable for iconoclastic critics to attack 'liberal' or 'dissident' writers of the socialist realist tradition from various different angles: either because of the conventional style of their work and the conservative nationalist viewpoint espoused by some, or because of the political and cultural compromises the artists were obliged to make with the system. In the 1990s vociferous adherents of alternative literature belittled virtually any cultural product of the post-Stalin era which displayed the moral or political concerns of its creator.[72]

One would think that the interaction of both trends would undermine Blok's position in the newly configured canon. The so-called *accessible* canon became broader, the competition in the field became stronger, and attention should have been drawn to the newly emerging, previously unknown names rather than to established figures. The mechanisms of the *selective* canon also should not have worked (at least in theory) in favour of a formerly classic writer, recommended and promoted by a now denigrated regime. This rather ill-fated combination, however, did not seem to weaken the poet's viability within the post-Soviet canon: his name still has the same weight in secondary education and features in literary anthologies with a considerably wider spectrum of verse. As far as indirect references to Blok's oeuvre are concerned, in the 1990s

---

71   E. G. Etkind, *Tam vnutri: O russkoi poezii XX veka* (St Petersburg: Maksima, 1997); A. M. Etkind, *Sodom i psikheia. Ocherki intellektual'noi istorii Serebrianogo veka* (Moscow: Its-Garant, 1996), A. M. Etkind, *Eros nevozmozhnogo: Istoriia psikhoanaliza v Rossii* (St Petersburg: Meduza, 1994); A. M. Etkind, *Khlyst: Sekty, literatura i revoliutsiia* (Moscow: NLO, 1998).

72   See, for instance, V. Erofeev, 'Soviet Literature: In Memoriam', *Glas*, 1 (1991), 225–34; M. Kharitonov, 'Apologiia literatury', *Literaturnaia gazeta*, 19 June 1991, 11.

his writings reached an even wider audience through popular culture, when his poem 'Devushka pela v tserkovnom khore' ('A Girl Sang in a Church Choir', 1905) was used by Slavianskii Bank in a series of its commercials *Poeziia v reklame* (*Poetry in Advertising*), shown in the cinema and on the major Russian TV channels.[73] Initially the series was based on four authors, Blok, Mandel'shtam, Pushkin and Pasternak — all with a distinctly non-conformist attitude towards the system; the advertisements using poems by Esenin and Daniil Kharms, added later, made these undertones even more pronounced. At first glance Blok's legacy appears simply inexhaustible, but on closer consideration one cannot fail to notice that its reproduction and representation remain largely defined by the poet's perceived social connotations. In the school curriculum, followed universally throughout Russia as a major mechanism of engraving cultural views, Blok is indeed no longer classified as a revolutionary poet,[74] but it is nonetheless the motif of Mother Russia and the elements of his socially engaged writing which still dominate the questions offered in the exams (bearing witness to the prevailing priorities).[75] This, of course, ties in well with the nationalistic drift in Putin's current policies; and curricular intervention in this context simply reaffirms the concept of desirable cultural assets, embodied in or associated with canonical works.[76]

---

73 The text in the clip using Blok's poem (shot by Timur Bekmambetov) is read by Vladimir Mashkov, a cult figure in Russian cinema, which added to the public appeal of the venture. The initiative of using poetry in advertising has now been picked up by another major company Mobile Tele-Systems (MTS), which in 2005 created its own clips based on poems by Blok ('Night, street and streetlamp, drugstore' (1912)) and Igor' Severianin.

74 This absurd attempt to turn Blok into a revolutionary poet (prevalent in the Soviet era) was parodied in Viktor Pelevin's widely read novel *Chapaev i Pustota* (1996): to heighten his pro-Bolshevik credentials the poet himself amends the finale of *The Twelve*, using the infamous image of a 'sailor' (see note 39): 'With a garland of white roses spliced — / Up in front is a sailor' (Viktor Pelevin, *Chapaev i Pustota* (Moscow: Vagrius, 1999), p. 36).

75 The list of Blok's poems specified in the programme of the Unified State Examination in literature (EGE) speaks for itself. It includes: 'The Twelve', 'The Unknown Woman', 'Russia', 'Night, Street and Streetlamp, Drugstore', 'In the Restaurant', 'On the Field of Kulikovo', 'On the Railway', 'Factory', 'Russia' ('Rus''), 'On Courage, Heroic Deeds and Glory': *Kodifikator elementov soderzhaniia i trebovanii k urovniu podgotovki vypusknikov obshcheobrazovatel'nykh uchrezhdenii dlia edinogo gosudarstvennogo ekzamena 2010 goda po literature* (Moscow: Federal'nyi institut pedagogicheskikh izmerenii, 2010), p. 7.

76 Bourdieu, *Distinction*, p. 310.

As regards scholarly studies of Blok, this domain represents, perhaps, the most interesting terrain in terms of reconfiguration of the canon, and provides some noteworthy material on the interaction of the sociopolitical and cultural currents in the absence of any direct steer from the state. Russian literary scholarship continues to be overwhelmingly based on the conviction that the value and quality of any major work are in inverse proportion to the level of political interference in the conditions of its production. Furthermore, despite the removal of the *official* Soviet-era canon, and the achievement of freedom of intellectual expression, one can, nonetheless, demonstrate that the emphasis in the scholarly response to Blok studies is still related, though less conspicuously, to the overall drift in the social agenda, and that the course of its re-orientation is largely directed by the changing political priorities.

The general socio-political atmosphere of the early 1990s, with its prevailing nihilism, its critical attitude towards the dying system and its destructive tendencies towards communist art, facilitated a series of works that highlighted the apocryphal motifs in Blok's writings, centred on the notion of theodicy, and on the subversive spirit of his poems, intended to desecrate everything concerning the accepted order. In this context, it is worth mentioning the works of Al'bert Avramenko and Irina Prikhod'ko, who argued the importance of Manichean philosophy in Blok's oeuvre; the monographs of Sergei Slobodniuk and Gennadii Glinin, who looked at Blok's poetry from the gnostic perspective; and the writings of Oleg Smola and Valentin Nepomniashchii, who highlighted the elements of Satanism and demonism in his verse.[77] One of the most prominent characteristics of these studies is a completely different interpretation of *Dvenadtsat'*, which (in order to outline the researchers' platform) can be best illustrated by a comparative reading of the following extract from the poem: 'Freedom, freedom, / Yeah,

---

77 A. Avramenko, *A. Blok i russkie poety XIX veka* (Moscow: MGU, 1990); G. G. Glinin, *Avtorskaia pozitsiia v poeme A. Bloka 'Dvenadtsat''* (Astrakhan': Izdatel'stvo Astrakhanskogo pedagogicheskogo instituta, 1993); V. Nepomniashchii, 'Pushkin cherez dvesti let', *Novyi mir*, 6 (1993), 230–38; S. L. Slobodniuk, *Idushchie putiami zla* (St Petersburg: Aleteia, 1998); I. S. Prikhod'ko, *Mifopoetika A. Bloka* (Vladimir: Vladimirskii pedagogicheskii universitet, 1994); O. Smola, *'Chernyi vecher. Belyi sneg...'. Tvorcheskaia istoriia i sud'ba poemy Aleksandra Bloka 'Dvenadtsat''* (Moscow: Nasledie, 1993).

yeah, without a cross! / Rat-a-tat-tat!' ('Svoboda, svoboda, / Ekh, ekh, bez kresta! / Tra-ta-ta!').[78]

In Soviet literary scholarship the reading of this passage was traditionally centred on the second line; the alienation from the holy cross ('Yeah, yeah, without a cross!') was seen as a manifestation of the poet's atheism and anti-religious views. Orlov argued that: 'everything that was established as a Christian dogma was alien to him', and Leonid Dolgopolov maintained that Jesus, leading the Red soldiers, as it appears in the ending of the poem, represented 'the ultimate objective of the Revolution' ('sverkh zadacha revoliutsii').[79]

By contrast, the scholars of the 1990s saw *Dvenadtsat'* in the light of a demonic canto — a text which positioned the Revolution within the framework of a black mass.[80] The title was read as an allusion to the 'twelfth hour' — the time of Satanic *shabash*, which, according to the Russian folk tradition, takes place between midnight and four o'clock in the morning (as, for instance, in Gogol''s short story *Vii*). The setting of the opening also contributed to the point: the bewildering combination of the night, the wind and the snow storm created the atmosphere of a nightmarish orgy, with a clear intertextual reference to Pushkin's poem 'Besy' ('Demons').[81]

> Черный вечер.
> Белый снег.
> Ветер, ветер!
> На ногах не стоит человек.
> Ветер, ветер —
> На всем божьем свете![82]

---

78 Blok, *Sobranie sochinenii*, III, 349.
79 V. N. Orlov, *Gamaiun: Zhizn' Aleksandra Bloka* (Leningrad: Sovetskii pisatel', 1980), p. 190; L. K. Dolgopolov, *Poema Bloka 'Dvenadtsat''* (Leningrad: Khudozhestvennaia literatura, 1979), p. 79.
80 Prikhod'ko, *Mifopoetika A. Bloka*, p. 106, p. 118; Nepomniashchii, 'Pushkin cherez dvesti let', p. 230; M. Petrovskii, '"Dvenadtsat'" Bloka i Leonid Andreev', in *Aleksandr Blok: Literaturnoe nasledstvo* (Moscow: IMLI, 1987), IV, 226.
81 Petrovskii, '"Dvenadtsat'" Bloka i Leonid Andreev', p. 226; Smola, 'Chernyi vecher. Belyi sneg...', p. 77; Nepomniashchii, 'Pushkin cherez dvesti let', p. 238.
82 Blok, *Sobranie sochinenii*, III, 347.

Black night,
White snow.
Wind, wind!
Knock you flat before you know,
Wind, wind!
Filling God's wide world!

Мчатся тучи, вьются тучи;
Невидимкою луна
Освещает снег летучий;
Мутно небо, ночь мутна.[83]

Clouds are whirling, clouds are swirling;
Though invisible, the moon
Lights the flying snow while blurring
Turbid sky and night in one.

Finally, the actions of the protagonists also tied in well with the proposed reading. The disposing of the cross in the passage quoted above ('Yeah, yeah, without the cross! / Rat-a-tat-tat!'), was seen by some scholars as an essential attribute of the satanic service, complemented by the blasphemous sayings and actions of the characters, such as 'Pal'nem-ka pulei v Sviatuiu Rus'' ('Let's put a bullet into Holy Russia').[84] Slobodniuk, for instance, pointed out that the shooting sounds reverberating in the air may well refer to characteristic rituals widespread among demonic sects and known as 'shooting the Invisible [Christ]' (also involving gunning down a crucifix, as a symbol of the demise of the Holy Spirit).[85]

---

83 A. S. Pushkin, 'Besy', *Sobranie sochinenii*, 10 vols. (Leningrad: Nauka, 1977), III, 167. Translated as 'Demons', in Aleksandr Pushkin, *Complete Works*, 15 vols. (Downham Market: Milner & Co. Ltd, 1999–2003), III (2000), 160.
84 Blok, *Sobranie sochinenii*, III, 349.
85 Slobodniuk, *Idushchie putiami zla*, p. 297.

> Трах-тах-тах! — И только эхо
> Откликается в домах...
> Только вьюга долгим смехом
> Заливается в снегах...
> Трах-тах-тах!
> Трах-тах-тах...[86]

> Rat-a-tat-tat! Only the echo
> Bounces round the buildings there...
> Only the blizzard, laughing, laughing,
> Roaring with laughter in the snows...
> Rat-a-tat-tat!
> Rat-a-tat-tat...

According to Slobodniuk and others, all of the above highlighted the destructive spirit of the Bolsheviks' venture, and related them to a group of the Devil's disciples.

The beginning of the twenty-first century witnessed yet another change in the canon. With the proliferation of authoritarian trends and consolidation of power in Putin's Russia, and with the instrumentalisation of religion as an additional mechanism of state manipulation, Blok's writings now tend to be configured towards the idea of an all-embracing unity. Following the new political direction, the accent is placed on Blok's theosophical reflections, on the symbolist concept of the omnipresent divinity of Sophia, as well as on his syncretic metaphysical doctrine.[87]

Very much along these lines, the new trend in Blok studies consists of apprehending his creative output in its entirety: for instance, the three volumes of his poems are seen as an overarching epic work equivalent to a novel (following Blok's own comment in the preface to the first edition of his *Collected Verse*: 'every poem is necessary to

---

86 Blok, *Sobranie sochinenii*, III, 359.
87 T. V. Igosheva, *Ranniaia lirika A. A. Bloka (1898–1904): poetika religioznogo simvolizma* (Moscow: Global Kom, 2013); S. L. Slobodniuk, *Solov'inyi ad. Trilogiia vochelovecheniia Aleksandra Bloka* (St Petersburg: Alataia, 2002); I. V. Grechanik, 'Osobennosti liriki Bloka: filosofskie osnovy, stil'', *Religiozno-filosofskie motivy russkoi liriki rubezha XIX–XX vekov* (Moscow: Sputnik, 2003), pp. 59–111.

form a chapter; several chapters make up a book; every book is part of a trilogy; and this trilogy can be called a "novel in verse"').[88] These studies argue that the entire set of Blok's poems can be characterized by a polyphonic structure of voices in its Bakhtinian, novelistic sense.[89] The focal point is the analysis of the first person narrative in its formal grammatical terms (the so-called lyrical self) and its conceptual dependence on, and correspondence to, the variety of different subjects of poetic consciousness, which even in the setting of the first volume of the *Stikhi o Prekrasnoi dame* can be interpreted as a whole spectrum of literary characters. As a result, the three volumes of Blok's poems are regarded as a novelistic trilogy in verse, unified through a number of specific elements of his poetics. Among these elements one can name the overarching *fabula*, which differs from the notion of the lyrical plot in the traditional cycle of poems, as well as a set of well-defined poetic-personae with a clear line of character-building throughout the cycle.

Another interesting line of inquiry, which has recently come under the spotlight, concerns the unity of the Apollonian and Dionysian in Blok's writings — the interaction of philosophy and the arts, of the rational and irrational in the process of creativity.[90] This dichotomy was one of the fundamental concerns of the Russian symbolist movement, and is now regarded as a useful lens for reflection on contemporary cultural thought.

Summarizing all of the above, it is worth pointing out that Blok's poetry, his works for the theatre, his literary criticism, and his prose, have always been a subject of extensive literary investigations; and the very fact that their appeal does not seem to be on the wane brings to mind the idea of 'exclusive completeness'[91] often seen as quintessential

---

88 Blok, *Sobranie sochinenii*, I, 559; the same idea is mentioned in his letter to Belyi of 6 June 1911 (*Blok-Belyi: Perepiska*, p. 261).

89 A. I. Il'enkov, 'O skrytoi kompozitsii liricheskoi trilogii Aleksandra Bloka', in *Arkhetipicheskie struktury khudozhestvennogo soznaniia*, edited by E. K. Sozina (Ekaterinburg: Izdatel'stvo Ural'skogo Universiteta, 2002), pp. 124–38; G. G. Glinin, *Avtor i geroi v poemakh Bloka* (Astrakhan': Izdatel'stvo Astrakhanskogo universiteta, 2006); A. F. Burukina, 'Formy avtorskogo prisutstviia v proze A. Bloka', *Gummanitarnye issledovaniia*, 4 (2007), 56–62.

90 A. V. Korniukhina, 'Misticheskii anarkhizm kak stadia formirovaniia russkogo simvolizma', *Vestnik Moskovskogo Gosudarstvennogo oblastnogo universiteta. Seriia Filosofskie nauki*, 2 (2006), 176–81.

91 Fowler, 'Genre and the Literary Canon', p. 98.

in the definition of a canonical work. When thinking of the reasons for such a persistent interest in the development of this domain, three main factors have to be brought into the discussion. Firstly, there is a vast amount of material that has only recently been released from the archives and that has been processed and examined in detail. There is, therefore, an expectation of a radical step forward, a long awaited breakthrough, which would bring the accumulated quantitative investigation onto a completely new qualitative level of research. Secondly, there is still a strong urge to revise the cultural legacy of the Soviet era, liberating this area, including Blok studies, from the tarnish of ideologically imposed compromise. Whether this can be achieved is highly debatable, because, as has been demonstrated, the newly shaped tendencies in the literary canon remain closely related to the overarching currents of the social and political agenda. It seems that the very idea of institutionalised critical thinking entails an obvious internal contradiction, but the current drift in itself is certainly welcome, for it is the desire for reification of a pluralistic critique that (in a liberal society) stands behind any form of canon revision.

Finally, when looking at this phenomenon from a more general perspective, one has to consider that, not unlike the post-*perestroika* years, the Silver Age represents a liminal stage in the history of Russian culture — a time which can be largely characterized as a deep existential crisis, and a time when poetry and art made a significant contribution to the development of the conceptual social doctrine.[92] Overcoming fragmentation, and moving towards the construction of a new sociocultural reality by virtue of their artistic creativity — these were the major concerns of the turn-of-the-century symbolist thinkers, which have their parallels and repercussions in the actuality of the present day. Having overcome the existential crisis of the 1990s, Russia is nowadays also making an attempt to construct a new national and cultural identity. Discussions on the value of literature, the new canon, its orientation and its function have become an integral part of the intellectual and literary

---

92 This crisis developed as a result of a series of failures in the socio-political structures of the time and encompassed a philosophical crisis (the disillusionment with positivism and with the cult of intellectual enlightenment); a religious crisis (Christianity was increasingly losing its standing as a dominant social authority); and a crisis in aesthetics (the shortcomings of realist art were becoming obvious) as well as politics (related to the failure of the Populists).

landscape; and any analysis of the reflective algorithms, elaborated within a similar context by the eminent generation of the turn-of-the-twentieth-century cultural elite, would have a meaningful impact on this process. As regards the position of Blok in this newly emerging canon, as Avril Pyman has put it in one of her latest articles on the poet:

> Blok has never lacked readers, but he has lacked objective critics. He has repeatedly been claimed or rejected for political or cultural-historical reasons which have little to do with his practice as a poet: innovative to the end, yet always mindful of tradition. Now that time is rolling him away, now that he stands roughly equidistant between us and Goethe, Byron, Derzhavin and Pushkin, it is enough to know his poetry has outlived the events to which it bore witness, just as the *Iliad* outlived Troy and the *Psalms* David.[93]

---

93   Avril Pyman, 'The Last Romantic', *Russian Life* (Nov.–Dec.2000), 34–43 (p. 43).

6. Canonical Mandel'shtam[1]

Andrew Kahn

Osip Mandel'shtam's recognition as a premier Russian poet developed posthumously and largely outside the Soviet Union. The creation of a canonical Mandel'shtam in world poetry is a case study in trans-cultural and trans-linguistic literary history and politics. This position stands in striking contrast to the history of his reputation in the Soviet Union where the period of his deletion from about 1934 lasted in effect well beyond his official rehabilitation in 1956 until the early 1970s. From the 1980s, absorption by a generation of Russian readers who came of age in the 1960s was gradual, nearly silent and clandestine, perhaps largely accomplished by the period of *glasnost'*.

Mandel'shtam's elevation to canonical status comprises an important story in the West. How did a poet who was unpublished at home, imperfectly published abroad, acknowledged as difficult, come to be absorbed into the mainstream of European literature as an indispensable poet?[2] This is not to confuse the West and the Russian emigration. Apart from Gleb Struve, the standard bearers for his poetic reputation were not émigrés of the second or third wave whose knowledge of Mandel'shtam for the most part ended in the early 1920s, but rather English and American writers galvanised by a combination

---

[1] For their comments and suggestions I would like to thank Jennifer Baines, Sasha Dugdale, Lazar' Fleishman, and Andrew McNeillie.

[2] Terry Eagleton, 'International Books of the Year for 1996', *Times Literary Supplement* (henceforth *TLS*), 29 November 1996, 12; Clive Wilmer, 'Song and Stone', *TLS*, 6 May 2005, 12.

of his poetic art in translation, literary politics and Cold War politics, and a liberal conviction in poets as truth-tellers.[3] This chapter seeks to tell that story with reference to the recovery and interpretation of Mandel'shtam's legacy; his place as a representative man of his cultural and historical situation; the contribution his critical writing made to his views as a literary thinker; and, centrally, the vexed question of the relation between moral daring, literary profile and political drama as the basis of his authority.

Over the last forty years a surge in interest via translations into French, Italian and German, has marked Mandel'shtam's discovery across Europe. This chapter will collect and analyse the most extensive, cumulative, and nuanced record of engagement to be found in the world of Anglo-American letters. As a description of the canonical and non-canonical Mandel'shtam, this history of Mandel'shtam's reputation constitutes a compelling episode full of implications for how we think about the mechanisms of canon formation and poetic afterlives. Dislocations affect literary history. Does literature belong to the time in which it is composed, or to the time when it reaches a readership? The question becomes even more complex, and potentially fascinating, when the reception is across languages and traditions, when a writer becomes almost fully known and recognized outside the mother tongue first.

My data set derives from a comprehensive analysis of the critical writing published in a range of quality literary reviews such as *The Times Literary Supplement* and *The London Review of Books*.[4] While I shall also

---

3 Gleb Struve, 'Soviet Poetry', *TLS*, 4 July 1958, 377.
4 A proper assessment of the stature of a poet naturally depends on the content of their reception as much as its frequency. But some comparative figures are of use in measuring the penetration of poetic presences and awareness among a readership. On the pages of the *TLS* for the period from 1930 until roughly 2000 Mandel'shtam (excluding Nadezhda Mandel'shtam) is mentioned about 350 times (for these purposes a mention means anything from a full-blown article to a single-word reference in passing). Khlebnikov is mentioned 79 times, mainly in the 1990s, Tsvetaeva occurs 145 times but only from the 1960s, Maiakovskii and Akhmatova are roughly on a par with Mandel'shtam, although Maiakovskii garners far fewer full-length pieces and is invoked more often within larger contexts such as futurism. Brodskii is mentioned 391 times from the 1960s. Zabolotskii, initially identified by Robin Milner-Gulland in 1967 as the other poet on the launch pad of rediscovery next to Mandel'shtam, occurs 36 times. Pasternak remains in public view from the 1920s, and earns 850 references over the duration. To Pushkin, of course, belong the laurels at 1000 hits. By comparison, Mallarmé stands at 745 references, Goethe a whopping 3000, and Paul Celan 160, the last an interesting

touch on the character and phases of Mandel'shtam studies as a scholarly enterprise, limitations of space mean that the academic side of the story, with its critical views on his poetic technique, and the question of his poetic difficulty, will feature only as subsidiary to the main narrative of reputation building. The abundant topic of Mandel'shtam's impact on Russian poets and their practice, both abroad and at home, remains a subject for separate study. One conclusion that needs to be stated outright is that the creation of a canonical Mandel'shtam in the broader world of literature developed in parallel to, and often independent of, scholarship about him. Yet both the scholarly and popular traditions created divisions between a canonical and non-canonical Mandel'shtam, the first represented largely by his first two collections, the second present in later poems that were off limits to exegesis such as 'Stikhi o neizvestnom soldate' ('Verses on an Unknown Soldier') or too hot to handle because of political controversy such as 'Oda' ('The Stalin Ode') or sometimes, as in the case of the Voronezh poems, even perceived as un-Mandel'shtamian because of a highly personal quality that looked alien to interpretations that stressed the poet of high culture.

My first section will present a thematic and broadly chronological account of Mandel'shtam's rediscovery by two literary traditions, and characterise the main elements of the poet's profile as a writer of lyric and a critic as they developed among American and British readers. The next two sections will argue that while the American and British stories overlap they also diverge in emphasis, and also through their implied understanding of what matters in poetry and why poets matter. What separates the two traditions is a difference in their relation of lives to lines, and the relation of life to context. The reputation of a foreign poet, extrinsic to the domestic literary canon, can depend on political circumstances. The first section proceeds thematically, with some deviation from chronological order. The next section will identify how the canonical Mandel'shtam has imposed an expectation of accessibility and an unwillingness to consider difficulty or political controversy; and finally, a brief section will provide a thumbnail sketch of the post-Soviet reception — an on-going story, to be sure.

---

counter to the expectation that Celan's reputation now eclipses that of the Russians hands down. Brodskii's status among the bean-counters looks impressive when we note that Seamus Heaney stacks up at 585 mentions and Derek Walcott 153 times.

While the present essay does aim to trace patterns in the story, and corroborate them amply, I would not want to insist that the divisions between biographical and poetic approaches, or between the English and the American receptions, are absolutely hard and fast. On both sides of these literary maps, readers were sensitive to the interplay of life and literature, text and context. Nevertheless, I would like to argue that the patterns that emerge in the history of reading Mandel'shtam reflect from decade to decade larger convictions about poetry and poets: the times shape Mandel'shtam's reception and Mandel'shtam was one voice shaping the times. At a narrower level, the story is part of the chapter of Russia Abroad and the recovery of silenced voices in the diaspora. But more broadly it is perhaps a rare case history of how a foreign poet became inextricably implicated in the idea of poetry across cultures, and included in other canons. Undoubtedly there was a feedback loop between Mandel'shtam's publication, critical reception, scholarly assimilation in the West, and writing about him by the likes of Iosif Brodskii, Seamus Heaney and many others, and the development of poetic craft in Russia.

Mandel'shtam Regained

Outside Russia, the reception of Mandel'shtam constitutes a multifaceted phenomenon, deeply embedded in different Anglo-American and European circumstances within the larger context of the Cold War and its associated literary politics.[5] Coming in the wake of Pasternak's plight and the Zhivago affair, readers invested the recovery of Mandel'shtam

---

5   A comprehensive scholarly treatment of this aspect of cultural politics and the Cold War is sorely needed, all the more so as embargoed archives and formerly classified documents become available. Hence as widely reported in the popular press and the *New York Times*, a newspaper of record (see Jeff Himmelman, 'Peter Matthiessen's Homegoing', *New York Times Magazine*, 3 April 2014, http://www.nytimes.com/2014/04/06/magazine/peter-matthiessens-homegoing.html) the personal files of contributors to the *Paris Review* such as Peter Matthiessen, a founder of the magazine, and George Plimpton its editor, have revealed ties to the CIA and the Congress for Cultural Freedom. For the broader context of how culture was weaponised, see David Caute, *The Dancer Defects: The Struggle for Cultural Supremacy During the Cold War* (New York and Oxford: Oxford University Press, 2003), especially Part V, 'Art Wars' (pp. 507–611). His discussion focuses on the performing art and Hollywood, and there are no entries in the index for literature and poetry, much less Mandel'shtam.

with a sense of historical urgency and moral imperative.[6] Initially the search was on for the instantiation of the Russian poet in its purest embodiment: an emblem of artistic innovation and traditionalism fully committed to the truth and autonomy of art and prepared to sacrifice him or herself for those values.[7] In the Soviet Union, the Thaw and the death of Akhmatova as the supreme relic of the Silver Age, and the efforts of individuals and small communities, stimulated the recovery of a lost tradition within which Mandel'shtam was reputed to be perhaps the greatest master.[8] The truncation of the Thaw did not check momentum on the Western side of the Iron Curtain among detractors and admirers of the Soviet Union, both sides having acknowledged Stalinism as a cultural and human tragedy.

Between 1930 and 1967 Mandel'shtam's name never appeared more than a handful of times in the *TLS*.[9] Maurice Bowra, then recognised as a translator of Russian verse, showed unusual awareness in reproaching anthologists such as Marc Slonim for omitting Mandel'shtam from his 1933 anthology, also lamenting the inadequate representation of Belyi, Khlebnikov, Gumilev, Pasternak, Tsvetaeva, Akhmatova, Maiakovskii, Esenin and Bagritskii in *The Oxford Book of Russian Verse*.[10] Reminiscing in 1995 about that span as a 'blackout period', Clarence Brown recalled a conversation he had in the 1950s with the composer Arthur Lourié about Mandel'shtam as a figure 'whom he [Lourié] deemed to have been irretrievably forgotten'.[11] By 1950, early research into acmeism had yielded some basic information about Mandel'shtam. Excerpts from the two collections published in his lifetime suggested to readers

---

6   See Magnus Ljunggren and Lazar' Fleishman, 'Na puti k Nobolevskoi nagrade (S. M. Bowra, N. O. Nil'sson, Pasternak)', in *Rossiia i Zapad: Sbornik statei v chest' 70-letiia K. M. Azadovskogo*, compiled by M. Bezrodnyi, N. A. Bogomolov and A. Belkina (Moscow: Novoe Literaturnoe Obozrenie, 2011), pp. 537–92. See more at http://www.nlobooks.ru/node/27#sthash.bzRqPhbQ.dpuf

7   For a vigorous account of the poet in Eastern Europe as a moral beacon, see most recently Clare Cavanagh, *Lyric Poetry and Modern Politics: Russia, Poland and the West* (New Haven: Yale University Press, 2010); for an alternative view that is sceptical or even antagonistic to the moral hero approach, see G. S. Smith, 'Russian Poetry: The Lives or the Lines?', *The Modern Language Review*, 95 (October 2000), xxix–xli.

8   See Emily Lygo, *Leningrad Poetry 1953–1975: The Thaw Generation* (Oxford and Berne: Peter Lang, 2010), p. 8.

9   R. D. Charques, 'Russian Poems', *TLS*, 9 January 1930, 23; idem., 'Soviet Literature', *TLS*, 19 October 1933, 707.

10 Maurice Bowra, 'Poets of Russia', *TLS*, 2 April 1949, 222.

11 Clarence Brown, 'Ashes and Crumbs', *TLS*, 7 January 1994, 8.

a poet of Parnassian perfection, an enemy of symbolism devoted to the supremacy of the object and a craftsman of the adamantine 'word'. First reputations are hard to dislodge. This picture of Mandel'shtam as the acmeist par excellence, mainly the poet of *Kamen'* (*Stone*), persists, discontinuous and unrevised, from the 1930s till the middle of the next decade. For Geoffrey Hill, whose knowledge of Mandel'shtam began around 1965, access to very few translations and scattered references in literary histories hardened the view of Mandel'shtam as an aesthete, an exquisitely private poet unable to adapt to the regime (rather than consciously being opposed to it or being persecuted by it) who was somehow pushed aside.[12] Further crumbs of information came via the English translation of Il'ia Erenburg's memoirs in which Mandel'shtam is mentioned alongside Georges Braque, Amedeo Modigliani, Guillaume Apollinaire and Gumilev. A review of an issue of *Den' Poezii* (*Poetry Day*, 1962) published in the *TLS* cites Tsvetaeva and Mandel'shtam as banned writers who have had a 'marked influence on young poets', a statement that looks more like wishful thinking based on the slightest sample.[13] Relatively little had changed between 1949 when Leonid Strakhovsky and Renato Poggioli published *Craftsmen of the Word: Three Poets of Modern Russia* and *The Poets of Russia*, respectively. The profile of Mandel'shtam is of a learned poet steeped in classical literature, a writer who believed in art for art's sake, an otherworldly figure. Each work essentially repackages a view based on Mandel'shtam's brief period as an acmeist. Among émigré critics, Vladislav Khodasevich's review of *Tristia* in 1924 consolidated the critical reception repeated by these later critics.[14] Yet Poggioli's thoughtful appreciation, based solely on the imperfect editions of the poems and incomplete prose published in 1952, does make two points of note. First, he disassociates Mandel'shtam from mainstream modernists like Eliot and Pound, and, while aware of his learning and his use of allusion, sees him as a visual poet whose use of image is reminiscent of Pablo Picasso and Giorgio de Chirico. This

---

12 Geoffrey Hill, 'Unpublished Lecture Notes', in Kenneth Haynes and Andrew Kahn, 'Difficult Friend: Geoffrey Hill and Osip Mandel'shtam', *Essays in Criticism*, 63 (2013), 51–80 (pp. 71–76).
13 Alexander Werth, 'New Russian Poetry', *TLS*, 22 March 1963, 200.
14 Vladislav Khodasevich, *Sobranie sochinenii v vos'mi tomakh*, edited by John Malmstad and Robert Hughes (Moscow: Russkii put', 2009–2010), vol. 2, 283 (review of O. Mandel'shtam, *Tristia*, 1922).

subjective point will resurface more frequently in literary criticism about his writing than in Mandel'shtam scholarship, focused throughout the 1970s and 1980s on textual allusion rather than visual values. Secondly, and more importantly, Poggioli conveys a rumour about a large body of manuscript poems still extant, suggesting how severely circumstances had hampered knowledge of Mandel'shtam. Unaware of the many poems with a broader contemporary dimension, Poggioli had heard about Mandel'shtam as an otherworldly and destitute figure, the image of him that survived in memoirs of contemporaries from the 1930s, abetted at least by publication of his later letters.

Among Russian readers who become aware of Mandel'shtam from the 1960s, the image of him as an outsider and alien to official literature — essentially the Mandel'shtam of *Chetvertaia proza* (*Fourth Prose*) — remained an article of faith, inseparable from how his legacy should be studied. At the Mandel'shtam Centenary Conference held in Moscow in 1991, an event attended by many hundreds even before his re-publication in Russia had occurred, a public debate broke out concerning the formation of a Mandel'shtam Society dedicated to the editing and publication of his works.[15] Opponents to the creation of such a society, forgetting that Mandel'shtam was an original member of the Tsekh Poetov (Guild of Poets), saw it as a betrayal of the belief that Mandel'shtam was permanently, in his own words, 'an outcast in the national family' ('otshepenets v narodnoi sem'e'), always marginal and about the marginal. At the 2009 events in Cherdyn', commemorating the seventy-fifth anniversary of his exile there, violent disapproval silenced advocates of the view that even in the late 1930s Mandel'shtam sought some sort of accommodation with Soviet power.

The émigré journal *Vozdhushnye puti* (*Aerial Ways*) featured in its single issue of 1961 an anthology of fifty-two poems Mandel'shtam wrote in exile in Voronezh, adding substantial material to the corpus of his work and also balancing out the range between the acmeist poet and the Soviet victim. By the late 1960s, following the publication of the Struve-Filippov edition and slightly ahead of the publication in English of Nadezhda Mandel'shtam's two volumes of memoirs, the view emerged that

---

15   Eyewitness account, Andrew Kahn, Moscow, January 1991.

Mandelstam's name is no longer only for cognoscenti and is known to most people in the West; his poetry already half-forgotten in the 1920s and misunderstood, without noisy adherents or even spectacular excellences of its own, has established itself next to that of Blok, Pasternak, Maiakovskii, Akhmatova and Khlebnikov as a major expression of the Silver Age of Russian verse'.[16]

By the 1970s, as David McDuff observed, generational interest had shifted from Pasternak to Mandel'shtam, a seismic change from the celebrated to the unknown.[17] Translations broke the ice of the Mandel'shtam revival from the early 1970s. While Struve and Filippov's single-volume edition of poems raised attention among émigré circles in the 1950s, there was a gap of about a decade between its appearance and a rippling out to wider circles.[18] Lasting literary reputations are not made quickly, especially across language barriers and an iron curtain. With the publication of successively more comprehensive editions, which hugely expanded knowledge of Mandel'shtam as both poet and critic in the West and eventually Russia, Mandel'shtam's reputation snowballed. Sidney Monas's translations of selected essays, containing accessible and learned expositions, were joined by landmark translations into English by Clarence Brown and W. S. Merwin, by James Greene and by Bernard Meares in the early 1980s; the appearance of Jane Gary Harris's compendious *Complete Prose and Letters* confirmed Mandel'shtam's reputation as a world-class critic worth perusal by Western readers for his observations on Western writers.[19] Whatever the merits of these translations as poetic acts, they made a discernible impact.[20] Guy Davenport's appreciation of Mandel'shtam, published in the *Hudson*

---

16 Robin Milner-Gulland, 'Mandelshtam and Zabolotsky: Two Russian Rediscoveries', *TLS*, 11 May 1967, 398.
17 David McDuff, 'The Prosody of Fate', *TLS*, 1 July 1983, 703
18 O. E. Mandel'shtam, *Sobranie sochinenii* (New York: Izdatel'stvo imeni Chekhova, 1955); superseded by O. E. Mandel'shtam, *Sobranie sochinenii v dvukh tomakh*, edited by G. P. Struve and B. A. Filippov (Washington and New York: Inter-Language Associates, 1964–1966); the second edition, expanded and revised, was republished in 1990–1991 as an immediate result of the *glasnost'* policy, and served in effect as the first comprehensive view of Mandel'shtam's oeuvre to be made available to Soviet readers.
19 John Bayley, 'The Dangerous Poet', *New York Times Book Review*, 4 March 1979, [n.p.].
20 For a review of a large number of translations along these lines, see Charles Newman, 'A People Does Not Choose its Poets', *Harpers*, 248 (1974), 83–84.

Review, a venerable organ of conservative literary taste, provided a round-up of critical work by Monas and Brown, and also articulated a distinct sense that despite repeated attempts to find reference points for him among canonical writers in Western literature, from François Villon to Pound, 'Mandelstam is not quite like any other poet so that analogies run into instant trouble'.[21] Time and again they garnered a great deal of critical attention, much of it overlapping between scholarly journals and highbrow literary magazines that were widely read, like the *TLS*, *New York Review of Books* (*NYRB*) and *London Review of Books* (*LRB*).[22] Clarence Brown, a pivotal figure in the restoration of Mandel'shtam literature in Russian and in English, spent a year in Hampstead (1969–1970) when he became something of an apostle for his cause among influential British literary critics such as Al Alvarez. Translation both spearheaded the reception of Mandel'shtam among poetry lovers, and also became a crucible for questions about translation technique. Brodskii's 'Introduction' to the Meares translations championed a poet he felt was still completely unknown in his native country. But in characterising Mandel'shtam's verse language for English-language readers, Brodskii also came down hard against renderings that traduced the original form. This occasioned a lively response from no less a poet and critic than Yves Bonnefoy who rejected Brodskii's argument by proposing a solution at the other extreme. Where 'world literature' was concerned, and there is an international and cross-linguistic demand for poets, Bonnefoy argued that the proper compensation for the inevitable loss of exact form could only be translation in free verse, a medium that, *pace* Brodskii, he regarded still as poetry and a viable form for phrases, images and ideas.[23]

By 1981, in Henry Gifford's estimation, Mandel'shtam was nothing less than 'a ferment in the minds of today'.[24] Another knowledgeable

---

21 Guy Davenport, 'The Man Without Contemporaries', *The Hudson Review*, 27: 2 (1974), 300.

22 For a review of translations by Brown and Merwin, Burton Raffael, David McDuff and others, see, for instance, Jennifer Baines's review in *The Modern Language Review*, 69: 4 (1974), 954. In a separate review Baines gave higher marks to Meares over Greene for selection and style; see Jennifer Baines, 'Mandelstam, Poems', *Slavonic and East European Review*, 57: 3 (1979), 439.

23 Yves Bonnefoy, 'On the Translation of Form in Poetry', *World Literature Today*, 53: 3 (1979), 374–79.

24 Henry Gifford, 'Surrounded with Fire', *TLS*, 19 June 1981, 700.

reader noted in 1967 that the lucky few who had already become aware of the poet of *Kamen'* would encounter an author who developed strikingly, whose poems become 'less cold and chiselled, more varied, allusive, personal and close to the life of his epoch'. More conclusively, he offered the view that despite its flaws, anyone with Russian will conclude that 'this is the sort of edition that should cause literary histories to be rewritten'.[25] When Brown showed Arkadii Raikin a copy of the Filippov-Struve edition on the train to London from Oxford, after Akhmatova received her honorary degree, he let Raikin, moved to tears at the Oxford Encaenia by the sight of Mandel'shtam's great friend, keep the copy.[26] Numerous comparable stories illustrate the incremental process of reputation creation and consolidation. Conviction about merit is an article of faith, but not absolute faith, because writers have opened a file on Mandel'shtam but not closed it: more editions, more texts, more translations are required as a matter of appreciation and appetite, and in order to establish the scale and shape of his œuvre.

Early attempts to place Mandel'shtam understandably looked to the Western canon for comparison, namely, among Anglo-American (rather than French) modernism, and sputtered fruitlessly. We find a commonplace assumption that as a poet of high culture Mandel'shtam must be like Eliot and Pound, yet there is some surprise to find that, as Donald Davie says, unlike his Western counterparts, Mandel'shtam prefers the bent-in, the rounded-upon-itself, favouring domes, the seashell's curvature, rather than the modernist preference for the discontinuous and asymmetrical.[27] One recurrent theme that moved to the fore as the Pound-Eliot comparison stalled was the recognition of the small scale, highly delineated and patterned quality of Mandel'shtam's images. In 1978, D. M. Thomas observed that 'few poets move so far as Mandelstam in so little space', yet George Steiner, a perennial promoter of affinities with Paul Celan, opined that while each poem might be sharply drawn there are reticulations, 'tenacious, elusive bonds' that form a poetic identity.[28] The reception of Robert Tracy's bilingual

---

25 Milner-Gulland, 'Mandelshtam and Zabolotsky: Two Russian Rediscoveries', 398.
26 Clarence Brown, 'Every Slightest Pebble', *LRB*, 25 May 1995, 24, 26–27 (p. 26).
27 Quoted in D. M. Thomas, 'The Weaponry of Poets', *TLS*, 17 February 1978, 186.
28 Thomas, 'The Weaponry of Poets', 186; see also John Pilling, 'Before Yesterday and After', *PN Review*, 82 (Nov–Dec 1991), 55–56; George Steiner, 'An Enclosure of Time', *TLS*, 4 February 1977, 132; see also these other pieces by Steiner: 'A Terrible

version of *Kamen'* consolidated the perception of Mandel'shtam as a Russo-Judaeo-Christian multicultural poet, whose voice combined a Pushkinian plasticity and solid verse architecture.[29] Images of stone, lace and enamel scattered through the entire collection revealed a permanent thematic tension between the precariousness of the spoken versus the silent, the lasting versus the ephemeral, the small versus the monumental. John Bayley praised Mandel'shtam as a poet as versatile as W. H. Auden with the same 'brilliance in gusto'.[30] Heaney, suspicious that Tracy's euphonious versions were only an echo of their original music ('Tracy's ear is not as gifted as Mandelstam's — whose is?'), sensed that Mandel'shtam possessed 'the high voltage of associative word-play which one understands to be so distinctive in Russian'.[31] The phrase 'one understands' we might read as a hint at the mentoring of his friend Brodskii, whose broadside against free verse translation of Russian poetry written in classical forms caused a stir. His 'Introduction' to Meares's translations also admired Mandel'shtam's prosody, observing that 'the presence of an echo is the primal trait of any good acoustics, and Mandelstam merely made a great cupola for his predecessors'.[32] Tracy's commentaries (highly derivative from work by Mandel'shtam scholars) convinced Heaney and other readers that Mandel'shtam's poems are 'as firmly rooted in both an historical and cultural context and in physical reality as Joyce's *Ulysses* or Eliot's 'The Waste Land'.[33]

'The recovery of Mandelstam has become something marvellous': Thomas is among the earliest to see in the survival of his work evidence

---

Exactness', *TLS*, 11 June 1976; 709; 'Songs of a Torn Tongue', TLS, 28 September 1984; 1093.

29 Stuart Hood, 'As if Winter Had not Touched', *PN Review*, 22 (Nov–Dec 1981), 62–63; Henry Gifford, 'The Staying Power of Russian Poetry', *TLS*, 24 May 1991, 9.

30 John Bayley, 'Nightingales'. Review of Ronald Hingley, *Nightingale Fever: Russian Poets in ~IRevolution*, Ronald Hingley, *Russian Writers and Soviet Society 1917–1978*; *The Cambridge Encyclopedia of Russia and the Soviet Union*, edited by Archie Brown; Edith Frankel, *'Novy Mir': A Case-Study in the Politics of Literature 1952–1958*, LRB, 15 April 1982, 5–7 (p. 6).

31 Seamus Heaney, 'Osip and Nadezhda Mandelstam', *LRB*, 20 August 1981, 3–6 (p. 5).

32 Joseph Brodsky, 'Introduction', *Osip Mandelstam: 50 Poems*, translated by Bernard Meares (New York: Persea Books, 1977), 14; and Henry Gifford, 'The Flinty Path', *TLS*, 20 October 1978, 1227.

33 Heaney, 'Osip and Nadezhda', 4, quoting from Robert Tracy's introduction to his translation of *Kamen'*, published in 1981.

of 'a miracle that the worst of times produced the best of poets'.[34] For many, Russian poets, and Mandel'shtam best of all, embodied an ideal of lyric that was further ennobled by the troubled circumstances of its production. Yet British critics show a clear priority in the ordering of art and life in which the value of a writer's art precedes interest in the life-story. It seems nearly axiomatic that admiration of great poets as victims must necessarily follows their rediscovery first and foremost as masters of the lyric. Appreciation of the life seems largely to have taken inspiration from the lines rather than vice versa. The miracle of recovery and rediscovery of a lost voice became a topos often recounted from the late 1960s until the early 1980s. Typically those who write about him also validate his personal importance to them. Virtually each time this happens the writer rehearses the story of the lost poetry, Nadezhda Mandel'shtam's loyalty and tenacity (Heaney calls her magnificently a 'guerrilla of the imagination'), how she kept the poetry alive, who it was that read clandestine copies, the writing of the *Voronezhskie tetradi* (*Voronezh Notebooks*), who it was that kept copies, Mandel'shtam's arrest and exile, and so on.[35] While the effect is one of awe, the propensity to repetition conveys an impression that writers with an interest in sharing their discovery recognise that establishing foreign poets abroad and in translation takes extraordinary effort. Within this frame narrative of miraculous poetic survival there is an underlying curiosity about the political relation between poetry and power, and a wish to know why they were victims, what sort of poetry incurs such sanction. But for the most part in the British context there also appears to be a lingering and long ungratified wish to appreciate the aesthetic dimension first. In 1992, Anatoly Naiman on the pages of the *TLS* sounded a note about sacrifice, rather than aesthetic worth, that had been mainly latent but unexpressed among British appreciations of Akhmatova, Pasternak, Mandel'shtam, as well as Platonov, that 'never has such a high price been paid for such a small handful of words that remained free, and never have so many lives been devoted to such a cause'.[36]

When, at a Cambridge gathering in 1981, a decade after the English publication of Mrs Mandel'shtam's *Hope Against Hope*, Monas pronounced

---

34 D. M. Thomas, 'The Weaponry of Poets', 186.
35 Heaney, 'Osip and Nadezhda Mandelstam', 3.
36 Anatoly Naiman, 'From Prayer to Howl', *TLS*, 4 September 1992, 4.

him 'the most sought-after poet of the twentieth century', the view that he is a central figure in the Russian poetic canon looks like a certainty, summed up by Gifford: 'By this time, many of the audience must have felt that Mandelstam may well be the supreme poet of this age — into which, after almost fifty years, we are still locked'.[37] One participant was Brodskii. He ended the meeting by reading the 'Stikhi o neizvestnom soldate' ('Verses on an Unknown Soldier'), a poem whose dense system of allusion, scientific reference, and formidable obscurity looks like a far cry from the beloved poet of *Kamen'* and *Tristia*. Brodskii's choice was clearly deliberate, a gesture at moving discussion on. Arguably, 1981 marks a point of closure in the first phase of Mandel'shtam's reception and an opening of the next chapter in which Brodskii played an important role in refocusing attention on Mandel'shtam as an engaged, difficult and rhetorically complex poet who had been misunderstood by critics, who were absorbed by sub-textual diversions, and by readers, who used Mandel'shtam to perpetuate a myth of poetic sacrifice.

Thanks to the publication of his prose in English in several instalments, culminating in Harris's comprehensive collection for Ardis, Mandel'shtam's work as an essayist became a more prominent part of his legacy.[38] The popularity of this part of his creation stands to reason. For readers such as Helen Vendler, reluctant to assume greatness on the basis of clumsy poetic translations, his prose offered compensation as well as a more secure touchstone by which to judge the quality of his thought, values and language.[39] Too tactful to comment directly on the poetry translations, Heaney, friend of both Vendler and Brodskii, drew amply on a prose which 'itself is bursting with eagerness to break out as a sequence of poems'.[40] In admiring Mandel'shtam's gift for metaphor and image, he turns Mandel'shtam's critical values back on to himself: 'What Mandelstam said of Darwin's style applies here perfectly to his own: the power of perception functions as an instrument of thought'.[41]

---

37 Quoted by Gifford in 'Surrounded with Fire', 700; *ibid*.
38 Henry Gifford, 'A Witness between two Worlds', *TLS*, 14 March 1980, 283.
39 Helen Vendler, 'False Poets and Real Poets', *The New York Times Book Review*, 7 September 1975, [n.p.]. This influential taste-maker concludes that the poems 'simply do not survive translation', with 'all color, weight and magnetism utterly lost' by McDuff.
40 Heaney, 'Osip and Nadezhda Mandelstam', 6.
41 *Ibid*.

Access to Mandel'shtam through his prose was, therefore, not seen as second best.[42] Furthermore, his critical writings came to serve quickly as a reliable source of opinion, and he is often invoked as an authority on the question of 'the use of poetry'. Lawrence Lipking has remarked that 'poets are the carriers of literary history'.[43] Mandel'shtam fulfilled that role. Unlike Khlebnikov, a 'poet of the future', Mandel'shtam appears both timeless and highly contemporary. Here is a Mandel'shtam who is a big-picture critic, who makes out of literature one of a set of coordinated cultural systems that includes architecture and philology, and that are about the preservation of 'a home for humanity' and the endurance of monuments to the human spirit. Elsewhere, readers of the poetry who are understandably concerned to find an analogous figure to Mandel'shtam, one recognisably modernist in technique yet traditionalist in outlook, will regularly reach for Eliot and W. B. Yeats. The former looks like a surer bet when seen from the viewpoint of these Eliot-like preoccupations with the mind of Europe and continuities of tradition under threat.[44] Mandel'shtam's criticism appealed to readers for a further reason. The immediacy with which he wrote about his poetic milieu was gripping. Writings about the connections between poetry and history and poetry and politics took the reader straight into the vortex of historical change in the 1920s. For poets like Christopher Middleton, Heaney, and especially Hill, Mandel'shtam's essays served as a hotline to history. Where Mandel'shtam scores over others is in conveying history as personal experience. Blok loomed magisterial and distant, Maiakovskii spoke to the world as though he were addressing a political meeting, but Mandel'shtam 'invokes the single reader alone with his conscience'.[45]

The appreciation of Mandel'shtam rode other trends in literary study. From the late 1970s, new criticism waned as both new historicism and critical theory revolutionised the academic study of literature. Mandel'shtam slotted into both trends outside the sub-discipline

---

42   The appreciative trend began auspiciously in a prominent revisionist journal with Sidney Monas, 'An Introduction to Osip Mandelstam's Essays', *New Literary History* 6: 3 (1975), 629–32.
43   Laurence Lipking, *The Life of the Poet: Beginning and Ending Poetic Careers* (Chicago: University of Chicago Press, 1981), p. 160.
44   *Ibid.*
45   Ruth Fainlight, 'Touching the String', *TLS*, 8 February 2002, 25.

of Russian poetic study where structuralist approaches focused on intertextual study became an entrenched methodology. In this broader context, two essays garnered repeated attention. 'O sobesednike' ('On the Interlocutor', 1913) and 'O prirode slova' ('On the Nature of the Word', 1922) offer a theory of poetry that fit the times like a hand and glove.[46] The first presented a version of a reader-response theory that looked timely in the context of the emergence of the Konstanz school of criticism. Many poetic treatments and tributes to Mandel'shtam, alongside the burst of translation activity, have a peculiarly personal quality. There was an appeal (and poetic justice) in the retrieval of a long-lost poet who was himself a theorist of reader-response as transhistorical conversation. As though they had absorbed the lessons of 'O sobesednike', writer after writer wished to enter into dialogue with him. Mandel'shtam's discussion of the interlocutor was the theory by which to judge his success as a poet and the value of ahistorical reader response. It was also one measure by which to describe what sort of poet he is. In this respect, he is more like Akhmatova than one might have expected, because his style and his story have a particularly personal and counter-cultural quality. It is also as a reader of Dante that Mandel'shtam earned most plaudits as a critic and literary theorist. As Gifford remarks, 'Mandelstam sends modern poets to school with Dante'.[47] Gabriel Josipovici instinctively brackets the 'Razgovor s Dante' ('Conversation on Dante') with Marcel Proust's *On Reading Ruskin*,[48] and Heaney named the 'Razgovor s Dante' one of his books of the year in 1996.[49] The essay seems repeatedly to have captured the interest of poets from Brodskii to James Fenton to Derek Walcott.[50] At the level of cultural theory, the essay triangulated the relationship between Mandel'shtam and Eliot, creating an equivalence of stature for the two moderns via Dante and generating stimulating, albeit imperfect, comparisons with

---

46 Henry Gifford, 'Origins and Recognitions', *TLS*, 25 July 1980, 827; Fainlight, 'Touching the String', 25.
47 Gifford, 'A Witness between two Worlds', 283.
48 Gabriel Josipovici, 'The Book of the Book', *TLS*, 17 June 1988, 684.
49 Seamus Heaney, 'International Books of the Year', *TLS*, 29 November 1996, 11.
50 James Fenton, 'Hell Set to Music', *The Guardian*, 16 July 2005, http://www.theguardian.com/books/2005/jul/16/classics.dantealighieri. Reviewing the reprint of Osip Mandel'shtam, *The Selected Poems of Osip Mandelstam*, translated by Clarence Brown and W. S. Merwin (New York: New York Review of Books, 2004), originally published in 1971.

Eliot's idea of Hebraic and Christian culture. These estimations paved the way for the reception of the 'Razgovor s Dante' as an instant classic (and published as such in the *NYRB Forgotten Classics* series) among several constituencies. For a readership without Russian, intrigued by the Russian tradition and its points of contact with the Western tradition, the link to Dante proved significant. According to the Oxford Italianist Martin McLaughlin, 'for that alone Mandelstam deserves to be remembered'. Furthermore, Mandel'shtam's experience as an exile lent authenticity to the role of poetry as a form of consolation. In a review of some new Dante translations, the *Economist* magazine quoted Heaney as observing that the Dante of Pound and Eliot is 'not quite the same as Osip Mandelstam's', whose jaggedly futuristic 'Razgovor s Dante' is also covered in the appraisal.[51] Persecuted by Stalin, he speaks from the bookless wastes of internal exile and identifies with the embittered Florentine, driven from his native city by political conflict. Mandel'shtam's Dante is vividly particular, local and spontaneous, his emotion resounding still in the sounds of his words. Eliot's Dante, by contrast, is Latinate and Olympian, evoking in 'the mind of Europe' a 'sublime vision of universal order'.[52] The review observes that the essay 'wasn't printed until three decades later, in 1967, when an edition of 25,000 copies appeared in Moscow and quickly sold out — the first of Mandelstam's works to appear after the Thaw', a point that was not lost on Fenton. He praises Mandel'shtam's view that a command of complex linguistic and intellectual resources ought to give poets credibility as good authorities even among the truly powerful. And while Fenton shies away from romanticising the martyrdom of Russian poets, he nonetheless speaks for many left-leaning intellectuals in using Mandel'shtam's authority (and the historic nature of his fate) to express the view that the Russians might be unique in appreciating poetry on an enviable scale, given the comparative enormity of print runs accorded the most famous poets. Mandel'shtam's Dante essay exercised a particular influence on Heaney, who appreciated it particularly as

---

51 [N.a.], 'An Underworld Classic: R. W. B. Lewis, *Dante: A Penguin Life*; *The Poet's Dante*, edited by Peter Hawkins and Rachel Jacoff; *The Inferno*, translated by Robert and Jean Hollander', *The Economist*, 17 February 2001, 125, http://www.economist.com/node/504945

52 *Idem*, 'An Underworld Classic', 125.

a discussion of inspiration articulated through the special phonetic rules of poetic craftsmanship. He also dwelled on it as a manifestation of poetry as an ethical defence of the non-utilitarian in life.[53] He sees a Mandel'shtam gripped by Dante's metaphorical genius rather than moved by self-identification with him as an exile; who demonstrates why poetic influence is not only about sound and allusion but also about poetic relationships as ethical touchstones: 'the Dante whom he would come upon in the Thirties and who would help him to live by the pure standard while false currency swirled all around him like blinding chaff'.[54] By pure coincidence, this conclusion comes very close to Lidiia Ginzburg's description seventy years earlier of how, in reading the essay, Mandel'shtam seemed to merge entirely with his poetic inspiration.[55] What Ginzburg calls 'creative realisation' ('tvorcheskaia realizovannost"') presciently identified the attraction of the essay to later generations.

A Special Relationship to Mandel'shtam: Divergences in the British and American Stories

However attuned to Mandel'shtam's historical period, the critical reception in Britain tended to dwell on the poetry and resist cult-building. Attention to the life and Mandel'shtam's status as a poet-martyr surfaces intermittently and late, mentioned with respect but overshadowed by interest in his work. From the early 1970s Mandel'shtam had become a formative poet for translators. Mick Imlah, well-placed in various editorial jobs, observed that 'fashion is certainly shifting in translation's favour; so much new British poetry alludes to Mandelstam, Montale, Trakl, Neruda and Seferis that it is unsophisticated as well as impoverishing not to know their work'.[56]

---

53 For a useful summary with attention to Mandel'shtam's presence in Heaney's poetry, see Stephanie Schwerter, *Northern Irish Poetry and the Russian Turn: Intertextuality in the Work of Seamus Heaney, Tom Paulin and Medbh McGuckian* (London: Palgrave Macmillan, 2013), esp. pp. 30–33.
54 Heaney, 'Osip and Nadezhda Mandelstam', 4.
55 See Andrew Kahn, 'Lidiya Ginzburg's Lives of the Poets: Mandel'shtam in Profile', in Lydia Ginzburg's *Alternative Literary Identity*, edited by Andrei Zorin and Emily van Buskirk (Oxford: Peter Lang, 2012), pp. 163–91 (p. 181).
56 Mick Imlah, 'Poetry Publishing and Publishers', *TLS*, 27 April 1984, 455.

If Mandel'shtam studies never took root in British graduate culture, it may be that the academic study of Mandel'shtam was inhibited by the degree to which public figures and men of letters such as Davie, Hill, Bayley and others had appropriated him to the ranks of poet as moral witness, the good antithesis to Pound.[57] Jennifer Baines was perhaps alone among her generation to pursue the course she took, sanctioned to a degree by the confidence and support of Nadezhda Mandel'shtam. Cold War rhetoric was far less extreme among the British intellectual classes of the 1960s, whose leftist sympathies were no secret, and this translated into a different sense of purpose for a journal like the *TLS*, which had a genuinely different editorial policy and mission by comparison with the *NYRB*. In that context, devotees of Mandel'shtam such as Davie, Donald Rayfield and the translator Greene pursued their initiative to broaden his readership.[58] Ronald Hingley's *Nightingale Fever* of 1981 took brickbats for enforcing groupthink among poets of a notably different cast. Yet the book provided evidence of the bond between Pasternak, Akhmatova and Mandel'shtam as three writers who shared integrity and a conviction that poetry must 'deal boldly with substantial things'.[59] This left an imposing question: how was it possible to write poetry in the adverse conditions of the 1920s and hardening ideological hostility of the early 1930s? Yet in the late 1970s caution remained about adopting a vocabulary of martyrdom and sanctification that might obscure links between writers and a context that, while fraught, required further investigation. Thomas argued that Akhmatova and Mandel'shtam were indifferent to failure and numb to the world around them, but Jeffrey Wainwright in *PN Review* took a different view, arguing that 'too much criticism of Soviet literature has been inevitably and crudely ideological, concluding complacently that these writers' fate demonstrates the natural and unalterable antipathy between socialism and artistic sensibility'.[60] British readers sidestepped

---

57 Claude Rawson, 'Escaping the Irish Labyrinth', *TLS*, 24 January 1992, 19; Wilmer, 'Song and Stone', 12; Charles Tomlinson, and John Bayley, 'An Involuntary Witness', *TLS*, 21 1986, 1295; Henry Gifford, 'Binocular Vision: review of Donald Davie, *Czeslaw Milosz and the Insufficiency of Lyric*', *PN Review*, 55 (May–June 1987), 83–84.
58 Donald Rayfield, 'The Great Unfathomable', *TLS*, 2 July 1999, 13.
59 Gifford, 'The Flinty Path', 1227.
60 Jeffrey Wainwright, 'On Anna Akhmatova', *PN Review*, 2 (Jan–March 1978), 1–2.

contentious issues of martyrdom that were part of the American reception from the start.

Instead, there is a pronounced tendency to portray Mandel'shtam as a poet of inner freedom able to sustain his own core values from the stoic simplicity he articulated in poems of the 1920s such as 'Umyvalsia noch'iu na dvore' ('I Am Washing Myself at Night in the Courtyard') well into exile. Perhaps optimistically, Gifford sees Mandel'shtam a decade later still 'faithful to that vision' when he appreciates the 'black earth' in 'Chernozem' ('Black Earth'): 'what he expressed here toward the end of his life arose from perceptions formed in that Tiflis courtyard'.[61] Similarly, Heaney and Brodskii buck the academic trend in Mandel'shtam studies by noting how much of his early poetry infiltrates the later poetry. While sub-textual criticism in this same span of about twenty years continued to move centrifugally out of the poems, amassing its vast body of external sources, readers more focused on a different idea of poetic and moral personality described a practice of self-allusion that sustained Mandel'shtam in the 'cultural and human wilderness in which he found himself in the 1930s'.[62] This was the poet saving himself as much as saving the European verse heritage obliterated by Soviet literary politics. That strategy was aptly summed up by Brodskii: 'Only a poem could permit itself to remember another poem'.[63] For these critics the resumption of poetic creativity was an assertion of power and also a posture of sanity, 'oases of calm strength and beauty in a mad and murderous world'.[64]

Can poetry resist tyranny with sanity and beauty? In 1974, an editorial in the *TLS*, offering solidarity, restated a traditional critical shibboleth about Russian writers and politics, opining that 'a Pushkin, a Turgenev, a Tolstoi, a Mandelstam, a Solzhenitsyn form a state within a state. Theirs is the haunting alternative conscience'.[65] Yet the tendency among

---

61 Henry Gifford, 'The Use of Poetry in Twentieth-century Russia', *PN Review*, 3 (April–June 1978), 4.
62 Mikhail Meilakh, 'Mandelstam in London', *TLS*, 6 September 1991, 13.
63 Joseph Brodsky, 'S mirom derzhavnym ia byl lish' rebiacheski sviazan...', in *Mandelstam Centenary Conference*, edited by Robin Aizlewood and Diana Myers (Tenafly: Hermitage Publishers, 1994), pp. 9–17.
64 Bayley, 'Nightingales', 6.
65 'Commentary', *TLS*, 15 February 1974, 159.

the poetry mavens was to wonder whether it would be more productive to write about a common commitment to culture and humanity:

> The use of poetry as Mandelstam sees it [...] is to keep a home for humanity, to make possible that lightness of allusion, that intimacy of tone, by which moral judgments are most successfully conveyed. [...] The most hopeful sign in our dark and criminal century has been the endurance of the word in the writing of the best Russian poets. They have raised a monument not so much to themselves as to the human spirit.[66]

The interchange of aesthetic and ethical values and their relative status is one intriguing element in the establishment of a canonical Mandel'shtam. Seamus Heaney exemplifies wariness about valorising the moral narrative over the poet's work in saying of Mandel'shtam and Zbigniew Herbert that 'the admirable thing about those lives is precisely that they demand to be read as lives, not just as literary careers'.[67] Geoffrey Hill, fully alert to, and persuaded by Mandel'shtam's example, is determined to argue that Mandel'shtam's greatness resides in an unfaltering capacity, once restarted in 1931, to sustain his art and voice, to produce words and rhythms that survive hauntingly on their own merit.[68] In the late 1970s, joyous delight greeted the publication in translation of Mandel'shtam's memoir *Shum vremeni* (*The Noise of Time*), and similarly the *Puteshestvie v Armeniiu* (*Journey to Armenia*), appreciated as evidence that the trip had set him free'.[69] Thomas regarded it as 'blackest comedy', while Heaney revelled in Mandel'shtam's 'pure happiness' and rejoiced to see that the poet of *Kamen'* had regained his faith in the durability of language, citing Mandel'shtam's own dictum in the *Puteshestvie v Armeniiu* that 'the Armenian language cannot be worn out because its boots are made of stone'.[70] If Bruce Chatwin, the most fashionable of all connoisseurs of beauty, was prepared to write about Nadezhda Mandel'shtam and to introduce the translation of the

---

66 Gifford, 'A Witness between two Worlds', 283; France, 'Songs of a Torn Tongue', 275.
67 Quoted in the Editorial, *PN Review*, 74 (July–August 1990), 4.
68 Kenneth Haynes and Andrew Kahn, 'Difficult Friend', 51–70.
69 Henry Gifford, 'Mandelstam Whole. Review of Sidney Monas, *Osip Mandelstam: Selected Essays*, Jennifer Baines, *Mandelstam. The Later Poetry*', *NYRB*, 25: 3, 9 March 1978, 32–33.
70 D. M. Thomas, 'Catching up — Poetry: 3: Poetry in translation', *TLS*, 18 January 18, 1980, 66; Heaney, 'Osip and Nadezhda Mandelstam', 4.

Puteshestvie v Armeniiu it was a sure sign that Mandel'shtam had become indispensable as a touchstone for certain values.[71] Chatwin found in the *Puteshestvie v Armeniiu* and the *Chetvertaia proza* together a remarkable instance of creative psychology, noting the genetic link between the 'angry, elliptical and cathartic'[72] essay and conversely the ebullient style of the *Puteshestvie v Armeniiu* in which 'Mandelstam's old trust in the resources of language, his identification with the clarity and Classical aura of the Mediterranean, his rejoicing in the "Hellenic" nature of the Russian inheritance, the ebullient philological certitude of his essay "On the Nature of the Word"' — all was revived by his physical encounter with the 'Armenian language and landscape'.[73]

We see among British critics a new consensus that the response of Russian poets to their difficult cultural situation is one of the highest sanity and courage rather than reckless martyrdom. If Mandel'shtam's reputation as a charismatic poet began in the early 1980s to emerge on the American side, no such characterisation attached to the equally sympathetic but differently nuanced reading of his actions, manner and, above all, poetry among British poets and critics.[74] The emphasis fell more on Mandel'shtam's rational choices, points of ambivalence (an approach also advanced in scholarship by Mikhail Gasparov that went unnoticed by most Russian language critics). John Bayley surmised that when Mandel'shtam republished 'Sumerki svobody' ('Let Us Praise the Twilight of Freedom') in 1928 he deleted the two references to the 'Soviet night' 'in the interests of discretion and concealment'.[75] Gifford argued that the poet who maintained that 'classical poetry is the poetry

---

71 Bruce Chatwin, 'Introduction', Osip Mandel'shtam, *Journey to Armenia*, translated by Clarence Brown (London: Next Editions in Association with Faber, 1980), pp. i–iii.
72 Heaney, 'Osip and Nadezhda Mandelstam', 5
73 *Ibid.*, 6.
74 Gregory Freidin, *A Coat of Many Colors: Osip Mandelstam and his Mythologies of Self-Presentation* (Berkeley: University of California Press, 1987); for a recent restatement of the position see Stephanie Sandler, 'Visual Poetry after Modernism: Elizaveta Mnatsakanova', *Slavic Review*, 67: 3 (2008), 610.
75 John Bayley, 'Nightingales'. Review of Ronald Hingley, *Nightingale Fever: Russian Poets in Revolution*; Ronald Hingley, *Russian Writers and Soviet Society 1917–1978*; *The Cambridge Encyclopedia of Russia and the Soviet Union*, edited by Archie Brown; Edith Frankel, *'Novy Mir': A Case-Study in the Politics of Literature 1952–1958, LRB*, 15 April 1982, 6; see also Aileen Kelly, 'Brave New Worlds', *NYRB*, 6 December 1990, pp. 60–67 (on Mandel'shtam, p. 64).

of revolution' was committed to 'changing continuity', to a form of repetition in which 'form counts for less than impulse'.[76] For those who read Mandel'shtam's understanding of culture not merely as a regret for the past but as expansive, this provided a view of history as dynamic change that could not be excluded from poetry and, if anything, was its proper subject matter. Seamus Heaney reminds us that Mandel'shtam's essay 'Gumanizm i sovremennost" ('Humanism and the Present'), published in 1923 in the Berlin émigré newspaper *Nakanune* (*On the Eve*) expressed hope for the post Civil War settlement; it is possible that Mandel'shtam was putting a brave face on it. While Heaney admits that in retrospect the piece 'takes on a tragic and ironical colouring', he entertains the possibility that Mandel'shtam, ambivalent or fooled, harboured an optimistic view of the Revolution, hedging and hoping that extremes would be reversed and the commitment to a socialist ideal might be attainable free of Bolshevik dictatorship.[77]

It is because such readers are aware of how difficult it is to decipher political intentions at such a distance, that they refrain from valorising a moral narrative that assigns clear-cut intentions. Reviewing Heaney's book *The Redress of Poetry*, the editorial in *PN Review* (1990) refers to his 'beloved Mandelstam' as one of a select set of poets 'show how poetry's existence at the level of art relates to our existence as tens of society — how it is of present use'. Yet this view is more communitarian than political or ideological; if anything it endorses a more aggressive retreat from any party programme by arguing that

> there should be no difference in kind between the 'artistic space' (as opposed to the political space) of Mandel'shtam and Sidney, of Herbert and Bishop; the differences are in the occasions the poets respond to, in the vigour and valour of the achieved artefact, the completeness or otherwise of the transfigurations through words.[78]

The tendency might also reflect a dominant leftist tilt to the politics of the British literary establishment. It takes an overtly right-wing anti-communist like A. L. Rowse to prove an exception to the rule by seeing

---

76   Henry Gifford, 'Dante and the Modern Poet', *PN Review*, 12 (March–April 1980), 13.
77   Heaney, 'Osip and Nadezhda Mandelstam', 3–6.
78   Editorial, *PN Review*, 74 (1990), 1. This is in fact an endorsement of Heaney endorsing Nadezhda Mandel'shtam whom he quoted on this point in *The Redress of Poetry*. Oxford Lectures (London and Boston: Faber & Faber, 1995), p. 193.

in Mandel'shtam a victim of Marxism, 'a Marxism that has spread to England's shores'.[79]

From the premise that Mandel'shtam should be valued primarily as a craftsman of verse language, other conclusions followed. It was felt that he had been harassed and marginalised because he followed his bent for aesthetic rather than political art. The willingness to acknowledge a moral dimension to his verse and behaviour was tempered by a fear that political statement would distort the meaning of his poems and overshadow his poetic greatness. Even from the start, then, a poet like Geoffrey Hill, alive to poetry as acts of witness and conscience, makes the 'Fedra' ('Phaedra') poem from *Tristia* his touchstone. In that connection, Hill and many others accord proper respect to Nadezhda Mandel'shtam's memoirs (which enjoyed dramatisation and staging in 1983), but wish to distance her testimony from the poems themselves.[80]

Because Mandel'shtam had acquired a readership and a profile of his own, discussions of Nadezhda Iakovlevna and Mandel'shtam within the British context tend to be separate, treating her as a great writer in her own right. To call him merely a victim is to group with him the anonymous millions caught up in the terror machine; yet to read him at the level of the 'bitch pack', Bayley's tart phrase for *publitsistika* focused on domestic detail and banal domestic rows, was in his view no great addition to the claims of his art.[81] We see that a distinct reluctance to make heroic claims, or to perpetuate the line that Mandel'shtam was a holy fool, followed from an aversion to moralizing about poetry. Most treat the Stalin epigram as a mistake rather than deliberately suicidal although, praised as 'brave and brilliant', it serves as a cornerstone of the defence of poetic free speech.[82] Donald Rayfield, unusually positioned as both scholar and gifted literary journalist, goes against the current in arguing that from 1910 Mandel'shtam had been spoiling for a fight against the state, and that his anti-Stalinism grew out of

---

79   A. L. Rowse, 'The Mandelstam Experience', *Contemporary Review*, 249 (1986), 21–26.
80   Andrei Rogatchevski, 'Staging the Unstageable: Casper Wrede's production of *Hope Against Hope* at the Royal Exchange Theatre (1983)', in *When the Elephant Broke Out of the Zoo: A Festschrift for Donald Rayfield*, edited by A. Schönle, O. Makarova and J. Hicks, Stanford Slavonic Studies, 39 (2012), pp. 108–28.
81   John Bayley, 'Mandelstam and the Bitch-Pack', *The Listener* (6 December 1973), 781.
82   Hugo Williams, cited in John Mole, 'Daisy chains and trains', *TLS*, 1 February 2002, 11; the poem was included for display in the Poems on the Underground exhibition.

antipathy for absolute regimes.[83] For Gifford, the careers of Pound and Maiakovskii presented the two most instructive counter-examples of political poets to Mandel'shtam as a poet of pure art as well as poet of conscience. He quotes Tsvetaeva's dictum that 'Mayakovsky does not forgive powerlessness', there is a sense in which their betrayal of art for the sake of political programmes spells a loss of a moral compass that whether tragic or farcical meant each writer forfeited some degree of respect in posterity.[84] On this argument, poetry vitiated by political delusion or principle loses its authority because it offers no outside perspective and can therefore not be taken too seriously as a critical judgement on the age. There are sins of commission as well as misjudgment. The explicitly anti-democratic stance Pound took in praising Mussolini, his contempt for the people, look objectionable when juxtaposed with Mandel'shtam's solidarity with the masses, and his alienation from literary life. As Gifford says, when much of Pound outside the *Pisan Cantos* and much of Maiakovskii are set against Akhmatova's *Requiem* and Mandel'shtam's 'Voronezh poems', they look marginal rather than like central statements made from the margins. Such an approach does not overplay the heroism; if anything it aims to anchor it in a commitment to literature and language that was betrayed and compromised by the times.

Such views come close to an understanding of Mandel'shtam as exceptional, but also exceptionally rational, shown by one of his most perceptive contemporary commentators. For Lidiia Ginzburg, who in the 1930s confined her most astute writings about Mandel'shtam to her notebooks, two forces were at play in Mandel'shtam's creative psychology and ethos. The ability to write poetry, even against his better judgement and sense of self-preservation, was an organic part of his personality that defined him as a genuine poet in the highest existential sense. Derek Walcott in a poem written for Brodskii, 'Forest of Europe', celebrates the 'divine fever' of Osip Mandel'shtam ('a fire whose glow warms our hands, Joseph'). Ginzburg, Hill and Walcott, to name a few, supported a view of Mandel'shtam as aware and

---

[83] Donald Rayfield, 'Stalin, Beria and the Poets', *PN Review*, 92 (July–August 1993), 22–30.
[84] Henry Gifford, 'Pound, Mayakovsky and the Defence of Human', *PN Review*, 6 (January–March 1979), 15–19.

dignified despite being trapped by the tide of history and circumstance. When confronted by political isolation and assailed by loneliness, Mandel'shtam's ethical worth, in this cumulative trend, lies in the record of honest responsiveness to the times; and in the conclusion that he remained true to himself by deliberate decision. All adherents of the 'noble victim' paradigm are close, but the distinctions they draw point to a significant and possibly fundamental difference of opinion. This idea of Mandel'shtam as a smart person — not just the poetic id to his widow's superego — challenges a very different portrait of Mandel'shtam, shaped by the larger idea of how poets should behave, as a 'fool figure', the latest instantiation of the Romantic ideal of poet as semi-insane visionary. More recently, Grigorii Kruzhkov expressed his consternation about a fashion of speaking of Mandel'shtam as an 'odd little man or urban lunatic', citing the monument to him in Voronezh as a grotesque piece of iconography, a monument to a distorted image.[85]

While the Anglo-Irish reception of Mandel'shtam diverges from the tendency observed by G. S. Smith, it is undoubtedly true that biography could be an irresistible narrative means when put to service of ideological ends. Peter France expressed his anxiety that hero-worship had come to overshadow Mandel'shtam's reputation, noting that 'Nadezhda Mandelstam's splendid memoirs have probably appealed far more to the English-speaking public than her husband's poetry even though this was their *raison d'être*'.[86] This reaction seems to convey a warning from the British perspective about the phenomenon of Mandel'shtam's reception among American readers. Smith's dictum about 'lives rather than lines' is borne out more on the American side of the equation. The American reception, largely as it can be traced through the pages of the *Paris Review*, the *New York Times* and the *NYRB*, is more monolithic. It is the story of a single poetic David versus the Soviet Goliath or a parable for the Cold War antagonism of the mass collectivised state and inhuman killing machine versus Western liberal democracy in which individuals are not done to death for their formal choices and love of art. That is putting it crudely, but there is a view of Mandel'shtam that coheres with the anti-Soviet posture of establishment culture in these years.

---

85 Personal communication (Moscow, May 2013).
86 Peter France, 'Four Troubled Lives', *TLS*, 12 March 1982, 275.

By contrast with the more apolitical English perspective, the American reception almost always began at the end of Mandel'shtam's life, firmly associated with anti-totalitarian values and heroic resistance. While he was never made into a spokesman for anti-communism, his widow's celebrity cast a long shadow. From the early 1960s until about 1981, Mandel'shtam as a victim overshadowed Mandel'shtam the poet. The selection of ten poems in translation made by Olga Carlisle and Robert (thoroughly hated by Nadezhda Mandel'shtam for their rewritings) published in December 1965 were landmarks, among the very first to appear in English.[87] The *NYRB*, perhaps the premier establishment literary and cultural highbrow magazine of the age gave Mandel'shtam top billing as the cover item and the subject of three stories. No more authoritative and passionate advocate could be found than in the dazzling essay Isaiah Berlin provided at the start, while a memoir by Akhmatova followed the translations. Berlin, Akhmatova and, above all, Robert Lowell, made the most powerful trifecta imaginable in adding a forgotten poet to the canon of world literature from outside his native land and language. But from the start, and even before the sensational publication of Nadezhda Mandel'shtam's memoirs in 1970, the biographical narrative tinges the literary image. Lowell and Carlisle commented that the poems were 'among the last by Ossip Mandelst'amm [sic], [and] written during the apocalyptic days of the great Stalinist purges in the Thirties'. The set included versions of 'Sokhrani moiu rech'' ('Preserve My Speech'), 'Net, ne spriatat'sia mne ot velikoi mury' ('No, I Cannot Escape This Grand Nonsense'), the Stalin epigram (said in the notes to have caused Mandel'shtam's arrest), 'My s toboi na kukhne posidim' ('We Will Sit in the Kitchen'), two poems ('Den' stoial o piati golovakh'; 'Ot syroi prostyni govoriashchaia') presented as two parts of a single lyric called 'Chapaev'.[88] Lowell invented and affixed titles, including 'The Future' as the rubric over 'Ne muchinistoi babochkoiu beloi' ('My Body, All that I Borrowed from the Earth'). That was the final poem chosen by Lowell and Carlisle who see it as a message from the Russian poet to those later readers who will be final comrades. Lowell and Carlisle gave emphasis to Mandel'shtam as the isolated outcast of totalitarianism well before the Parnassian poet of

---

87 Osip Mandel'shtam, 'Nine Poems', translated by Robert Lowell and Olga Carlisle, *NYRB*, 23 December 1965, 3–7.
88 Osip Mandel'shtam, 'Nine Poems', 7.

Kamen' appeared on the American poetic radar. This was the trend that the *NYRB* helped to establish and perpetuate. Their profile anticipated the wave of acclaim that followed on the publication of Nadezhda Mandel'shtam's first volume of memoirs in the early 1970s. In a banner review of *Hope Against Hope*, Christopher Lehmann-Haupt, the chief book critic of *The New York Times*, saluted the author's moral courage. But what he found most remarkable was the 'very idea that a man could be persecuted so for writing a poem'.[89]

We see two separate impulses, different in origin but complementary and compatible, joining forces on the pages of the *NYRB* from the 1970s. Clarence Brown's work set the academic seal on Mandel'shtam's reputation as a poet, picking up where Poggioli left off and conclusively establishing his claims on posterity. Yet this literary appreciation was subordinated to the role of poet-martyr that suited the firmly anti-Soviet and vocally pro-dissident editorial slant of the *NYRB*, who rightly celebrated the devastating accomplishments of his widow.[90] The joint article published by Brown and Nadezhda Mandel'shtam in October 1970 printed an account of the Stalin-Pasternak telephone call about Mandel'shtam. It takes up the story as published anonymously in 1958 in *The New Reasoner*, a version written by D. P. Costello. There was probably never any doubt that poetry mattered to Russians, an aspect of Soviet life that appealed to Western cultural commentators, especially on the Left. Michael Ignatieff comes close to glamorising oppression as an ideal creative state. He voices, perhaps unexpectedly, a nostalgia for the courage and daring bred by oppression:

> When one looks back at it now, the Stalin-Mandelstam story, terrible as it is, cannot fail to awaken a certain dubious nostalgia. For centuries, censorship was the deference the Western state offered to the only power which stood in the state's way, the power of the word. Dictatorship respected the word, even as it silenced it. The freedoms which have

---

89 Christopher Lehmann-Haupt, 'The Good Woman of Mandelstam', *Books of the Times*, 19 October 1970, []; see also Richard Pevear, 'On the Memoirs of Nadezhda Mandelstam', *Hudson Review*, 24: 3 (1971), 427–40; he argues that Mandel'shtam is the 'embodiment of poetry' and Stalin 'the embodiment of force', transvaluing 'poetry' into the 'language of freedom', a line of argument saturated in the Cold War dichotomy. For evidence of the persistence of this moral evaluation and narrative in mainstream literary circles, see, for instance, W. D. Erhart, 'An Indomitable Poetic Spirit', *The Virginia Quarterly*, 65: 1 (1989), 175–82.

90 Clarence Brown and Nadezhda Mandel'shtam, 'The Nature of the Miracle', *NYRB*, 22 October 1970, 24–27.

followed the abolition of censorship in Russia and the West seem bleak: the word has lost its power.[91]

In that respect Mandel'shtam's fate looked like an exemplary tale. What makes such a gloss tolerable, if it is, was the fact that readers considered it to have been authorised not only by the guardian of his legacy but by the poet himself. Nadezhda Mandel'shtam in her memoirs attributes to her husband a remark that has been widely reproduced after their English-language publication, 'Why do you complain?...Poetry is respected only in this country — people are killed for it. There is no place where more people are killed for it'.[92]

To be sure, the connection between inspiration and political repression can be contested. What was riveting, and might have constituted emotional proof of the claim that poetry was a life and death matter, was the drama of the Mandel'shtams' life in the 1930s as evidence became available: the players were Pasternak, himself a victim, Bukharin, Stalin, and Nadezhda Mandel'shtam, who recounted the story based on what Pasternak had told her. This version aimed to correct many fundamental misapprehensions about events; it was written in 1965 and the fact that it took a full five years to be published abroad was in itself a small detail that told a story about heroism and the effectiveness of the Iron Curtain. As Brown wrote, 'Stalin's telephone call to Pasternak on that summer evening in 1934 is probably, in certain circles, the most celebrated use of the instrument since Alexander Graham Bell asked his assistant what God had wrought'.[93] This was heady stuff in the context of Cold War politics, and it established the shape of Mandel'shtam's reputation among this influential readership. Vladimir Nabokov, who had in the 1930s sweetly celebrated pre-revolutionary Mandel'shtam in *The Gift*,

---

91 Michael Ignatieff, 'The Beloved'. Review of J. M. Coetzee, *Giving Offence: Essays on Censorship*, LRB, 6 Feb. 1997, 15.

92 Nadezhda Mandel'shtam, *Hope Against Hope*, translated by Max Hayward (New York: Atheneum, 1970), p. 190 (as reported by her in the chapter 'The Fatal Path' ['Gibel'nyi put']). Although essentially apocryphal and taken on trust, the comment has been often repeated, e.g., Osip Mandel'shtam, *Poems from Mandelstam*, translated by R. H. Morrison (London and Toronto: Associated University Press, 1990), p. 18, and used to frame the value of the poet's legacy ('a poet of towering proportions', p. 22), implicitly enhanced because feared by the state.

93 Brown and N. Mandel'shtam, 'The Nature of the Miracle', 24; the episode was repeatedly picked up by later commentators as clinching proof of the moral defence of art argument or the battle between 'poetry' and 'force'.

in his interview for the *Paris Review* (1967) expressed a scepticism that looks understandable when seen against this background: 'Today, through the prism of a tragic fate, Mandelstam's poetry seems greater than it actually is'.[94] The metropolitan literary base, defined by the journals cited here, continue to relate to Mandel'shtam primarily for his political value and status as a martyr. By contrast, American universities incubated increasingly active Mandel'shtam studies as a sub-field of Russian poetics. Yet discussion of the political and moral implications of Mandel'shtam's writings were virtually taboo in a field dominated by structuralist approaches.

The creation of a more rounded image of Mandel'shtam awaited the appearance of new translations such as offered by Brown and Merwin, and then Tracy's versions of *Kamen'*. Yet the initial martyr image survived reliably well into the 2000s.[95] For instance, numerous pieces in the *New York Times Book Review*, encompassing everything from Maia Plisetskaia's autobiography to Orlando Figes's cultural history, literature often spuriously invoke the 'grim fate' of Mandel'shtam.[96] His name became a byword for a certain exemplary fate. On 30 September 2001, Margo Jefferson included Mandel'shtam alongside Tom Clancy, Robert Ludlum and Doris Lessing as the author of one of the 'texts of our time' post- 9/11 for *Kamen*.[97] A translation of 'Pust' imena tsvetushchikh gorodov' ('Let the Names of Flowering Cities'), wrongly dated to 1917 (rather than 1914), cements his relevance as a poet to a besieged city. In 2010, Michael Scammell argued that the brilliance of Mandel'shtam,

---

94 Vladimir Nabokov, 'The Art of Fiction', *Paris Review*, 40 (1967), 99.
95 In connection with the Stalin epigram, Anne Carson accords Mandel'shtam a cameo appearance in her 'TV Men: Akhmatova (Treatment for a Script)', *PN Review*, 126 (March–April 1999), 14–15.
96 Orlando Figes, 'A Double Game with Stalin', *NYRB*, 12 January 2012, 33. Here and in other reviews Figes essentially perpetuates what might be called the '*New York Review of Books* narrative'. That trajectory of appreciation probably dates to a piece by Isaiah Berlin that raises the theme of the poet's sacrifice but pays equal attention to a remarkably insightful and vivid appreciation of Mandel'shtam's qualities as a writer, a balance that will recede as the political narrative comes to dominate (Isaiah Berlin, 'A Great Russian Writer'. Review, *The Prose of Osip Mandelstam*, translated by Clarence Brown, *NYRB*, 23 December 1965, 1–2. This text is followed by 'A Portrait of Mandelstamm [*sic*]' by Akhmatova that pays tribute to him as a 'tragic figure' who continued to write works of 'untold beauty and power until the very end of his life', works that were largely unknown and unavailable).
97 Margo Jefferson, 'On Writers and Writing: Texts for Our Time', *New York Times Books Review*, 30 September 2001, http://www.nytimes.com/2001/09/30/books/on-writers-and-writing-texts-for-our-time.html

Akhmatova and Pasternak was the product of the Russian philosophical and literary tradition rather than political pressure.[98] In journalistic criticism, this statement was more exception than rule.

The reception of Mandel'shtam and the story of his acceptance into a canon of great European writers occurred on a fault line between the American and British literary and academic establishments on the representation of his victimisation as the factor that determined his reputation. While from about 1981 champions like Heaney and Brodskii were perhaps going into overdrive to establish Mandel'shtam's reputation, it now looks clear that at least in the US and starting from the mid-1960s, martyrology had overtaken Mandel'shtam's art. As well as taking aim at academic scholarship on Mandel'shtam, about which he was publicly disparaging, Brodskii targeted the preference for lives over lines. The degree to which 'Mandel'shtam' had become a dissident brand assumed a degree of anecdotal absurdity in 1991 when the Modern Language Association rejected a proposal for a panel on Mandel'shtam at its annual convention. Grounds for refusal concerned the unsuitability of discussions built around single authors, seen as unfashionable at a moment when the death of the author as a theoretical premise was persuasive, at least to some. However, as a concession the committee recognized that Mandel'shtam was a rather special case, given his fate, and were prepared to allow a panel on Mandel'shtam and Nelson Mandela.

Non-Canonical Mandel'shtam

Within the English and American context, the poetry composed before 1926 constituted the canonical Mandel'shtam. In the early 1990s, nearly thirty years after Poggioli's speculation about imperfect editions, two decades after Baines's study, and a decade after Peter France's overview of later Mandel'shtam in his book chapter, the message about a different sort of poet began to get through. Thomas saw in both Akhmatova and Mandel'shtam 'new standards of poetic austerity and "hardness" with which to survive', and also detected a greater poise about history than could be found in Blok, and perhaps a degree of fatalism.[99] This idea of

---

98 Michael Scammell, 'Writers in a Cage', *NYRB*, 14 January 2010, 55.
99 D. M. Thomas, 'The Weaponry of Poets', p. 186.

poetic *sangfroid* would be taken up later by Heaney who spoke of the 'common sense of the craftsman',[100] and grouped Mandel'shtam with other poets (notably Rilke in his lecture 'The Sound of Poetry') whose poems are always rooted in real life, whose art does not exist for its own hermetic ends.[101] This sense of Mandel'shtam as an experiential poet both at odds with, yet within, Soviet life, increased with the publication of more late Mandel'shtam in the original and in translation.

Critical assessment of the poems faced resistance among three constituencies. For a variety of reasons impossible to discuss here, scholarly methods devised to analyse earlier poems made little headway with the later works, which in the minds of some devotees were of a difficulty bordering on madness. English language readers fond of the modernist poet of classical archetypes found it hard to identify, and identify with, Mandel'shtam's mature voices and changing poetics. And, finally, adherents to what I would call the 'moral valour school' had grave misgivings about poems on Soviet and national themes, most especially the controversial 'Oda'.

Attachment to the canonical reputation of Mandel'shtam as defined primarily by his earlier work was pervasive, further reinforced by a sense of poetic prudence from readers restricted to reading him in translation. Frank Kermode cast the dynamic of canon formation as question of aesthetic choice guided by the pleasure of change.[102] Conversely, modification to the canonical might occasion the displeasure of change. Negative reaction partly reflected hostility to the translations of Richard and Elizabeth McKane, which looked on a text-by-text basis more problematic than versions of the same poems as produced by the likes of Brown and Merwin who, for good or ill, had arguably created a single consistent style for Mandel'shtam.[103] Previously the proportion of late, difficult poems to familiar, earlier poems had remained relatively small in anthologies, whereas there was now a larger body of texts whose tone was hard to judge, whose moral resilience no longer looked absolute. The imperfect state of the texts, reflecting the absence of reliable Russian

---

100 Heaney's appraisal of Mandel'shtam's craft is taken up in the editorial of the *PN Review*, 63, September–October 1988, p. 1.
101 As reported in Harry Guest, 'Cantos at Kantô', *PN Review*, 62, July–August 1988, 23.
102 Frank Kermode, *Pleasure and Change: The Aesthetics of Canon* (Oxford: Oxford University Press, 2004), chapter 1 (pp. 15–35).
103 Pilling, 'Before Yesterday, and After', 56.

editions (a point importantly trailed by Baines) was compounded by the highly erratic quality of the translations. No stranger to difficult poetry, John Pilling, writing for the *PN Review* worried whether translation had made the *Voronezhskie tetradi* poems look more elusive than they might actually be, but also expressed a sense of deprivation brought about by poems that seemed only half finished, by writing that lacked the poise and finish associated with Mandel'shtam.[104] Resistance to the experiential poet or to a late style is a manifestation of the tug of familiarity with a writer the English poetic establishment thought it knew well. Even poems that Russian had internalised as classics, such as the Muscovite poems, 'K nemetskoi rechi' ('To the German Language'), 'Stikhi o russkoi poezii' ('The Verses on Russian Poetry'), in English engendered feelings of 'bafflement and elation at being granted this kind of intimacy with the mercurial laboratory of Mandel'shtam's sensibility'.[105] The reception is not uniformly blinkered. Pilling, for one, ekes out a more positive view of the second of the *Voronezhskie tetradi* in which 'most readers will look for the finesse they associate with Mandel'shtam, though this is different in kind from that found in the pre-1925 poetry'. Still, in 1991 Pilling clearly found it hard to overcome his sense of estrangement from a poet whose chief accomplishment was to preserve intact in the lyrics of *Tristia* both world culture and that longing for world culture, whereas the fragmentation of that culture with its uncomfortable alloying of the Soviet in the later poems confounds. By contrast, in a piece published in the *TLS* five years later, the poet Lachlan Mackinnon, while scathing about the translations which encouraged the view that Mandel'shtam had become an hysteric, clearly felt it was time to grasp the nettle and acknowledge that Mandel'shtam's poetry was 'notoriously difficult', 'allusive, elliptic and deeply attentive to both the acoustics and the etymology of its own language in ways that must defy translation'.[106] This cautious rowing back from first impressions of a late style possibly distorted through translation was a positive step. Moreover, Mackinnon relates none of this difficulty of the late lyric to biographical circumstance — he notes that the poems are 'encrusted by legend' — but adduces instead Brodskii's view that

---

104 *Ibid.*
105 *Ibid.*
106 Lachlan MacKinnon, 'A Last Testament', *TLS*, 6 September 1996, 6.

in the later poems, especially in the 'Stikhi o neizvestnom soldate', we witness an 'incredible psychic acceleration'. For Mackinnon, the appearance of Mandel'shtam's late style was a moment to celebrate an 'uncannily great poet, possibly the greatest of our century'.[107] By the late 1990s the moment was ripe for an adjustment to his reputation, if not a full-blown reconsideration of it in the context of his full oeuvre as well as a more dispassionate consideration of the impartiality of Nadezhda Mandel'shtam's memoirs. The disappearance of the authorities of the older generation, including Brodskii, and the rise of cultural studies, brought to a halt a new dynamic in the reassessment of Mandel'shtam.

For all groups of readers invested in Mandel'shtam as a certain type of poet, perhaps the greatest trial, and acid test, of received opinion surrounded attempts to understand the 'Oda'. Since its publication in 1975, the 'Oda' continues to cause consternation. Among Mandel'shtam scholars it is almost a no-go area, a toxic battle ground. In 1981, Heaney wisely guessed that any attempt to describe Mandel'shtam's politics of compromise as principled, rather than desperate, would unleash discord among his readers. Nobody should underestimate the degree to which, for reasons that remain mysterious and must be to a degree culturally determined, certain questions elicit almost elemental emotions rather than principled debate. Within the many pronouncements on Mandel'shtam's life and fate, differences in emphasis and vocabulary articulate two poles of opinion. The division concerns the degree of complicity and awareness that Mandel'shtam exhibited with respect to his own position, and therefore the degree to which the outcome was the result of heroic defiance or blindness. In other words, is Mandel'shtam a martyr or, like Pasternak and Khlebnikov, an example of the poet as fool (*iurodivyi*)?[108]

At just the moment when interest in the Stalin poems, epigram and ode, began to cause debate and real controversy in Anglo-American circles, we see a determined resistance among the hard-core *Mandel'shtamovedy* (Mandel'shtam specialists) of the 1980s to deliberating the place of these

---

[107] MacKinnon, *ibid.*, 6.; with the *Voronezhskie tetradi* (*Voronezh Notebooks*) also cited as definitive works by Helen Szamuely, review of Sonia Ketchian, 'The Poetic Craft of Bella Akhmadulina', *TLS*, 23 September 1994, 26.

[108] Czeslaw Milosz, 'On Pasternak Soberly', in *Emperor of the Earth: Modes of Eccentric Vision* (Berkeley: University of California Press, 1977), pp. 69–77.

poems in his oeuvre and evaluating their impact on his reputation. At the London conference, Gasparov opined that there was much more to be said about both the Stalin epigram and ode and Mandel'shtam's intentions, but that the time was not ripe. Even the suggestion that critics might discuss intentions, rather than list allusions, caused division and open hostility among the panellists, as recorded in the published transcription of the event.[109] Gasparov's illuminating, albeit incomplete, remarks acknowledged that nobody was prepared to face the possibility that Mandel'shtam's politics were more complex than the 'moral valour' school permitted.[110] On the grounds that such discussion would cause considerable pain, he curtailed his remarks. The value of his intervention lay in the powerful suggestion that it was simplistic to view the 'Oda' as a taboo subject because it was a craven or desperate act of submission. Instead, he went one step further in hinting that Mandel'shtam might have been struggling to keep faith with some forms of socialism. The second speaker to tackle the topic was Brodskii who throughout the proceedings adopted a consistently sceptical view of Mandel'shtam studies, at one point accusing the scholarship of simply missing out the poetry altogether and failing to pay attention to how Mandel'shtam's art worked because the obsession with subtextual sources had completely blinded it to elementary questions of critical reading. In the 1980s and the 1990s Brodskii's close readings of a large range of Russian, English and American poets made him a much lauded revivalist of the art of close reading in the New Critical style, and he clearly took a dim view of the gap between his style of interpretation and a critical school that in his view misunderstood how poetry was written and how it signified, and failed to appreciate its true power. He had allies such as the editor of the *PN Review*, who supported Heaney's similar *credo* that only through close encounters with poetic language and form would readers experience the living centre of poems, and that 'questions of expressive forms and diction, theme [...] lead towards the

---

[109] 'Stenogramma vystuplenii Brodskogo', in *Sokhrani moiu rech'*, edited by Pavel Nerler, 2 vols. (Moscow: 'Obnovlenie', 1991–2000), vol. 2, 17–58.

[110] M. L. Gasparov, 'Metricheskoe sosedstvo "Ody" Stalinu', in *Mandelstam Centenary Conference*, pp. 99–111 (p. 107).

larger questions that an intrepid reader might wish to call "moral"'.[111] The poets cited included Hill, C. H. Sisson and Davie, but once again Mandel'shtam provides the most challenging examples of the tense knot between the moral and the poetic. Pundits repeatedly adduce (and misquote) Mandel'shtam's dictum, as said to Akhmatova, that only in Russia is poetry taken seriously because only Russia truly persecutes its poets. At the London meeting Brodskii stated his view that the 'Oda' was one of Mandel'shtam's very greatest poems, and one of the greatest anti-Stalinist statements ever written, far more subversive than the notorious epigram. This statement was of a force and ostensible perversity — and Brodskii's authority and conviction too imposing to contest — as to reduce the group to a stunned silence (after tart exchanges between members of the audience, also recorded).

On the Anglo-American side of the fence, other impassioned life-long advocates of Mandel'shtam grappled with the question, properly recognising that the combined evidence of biography and psychology, historical circumstance, and the texts themselves opened the late political poems to multiple readings, all troubling but for different reasons. J. M. Coetzee reads the 'Oda' not as an abject self-abasement but as a genuine ode of praise written emphatically in the conditional tense, a hedging of bets that attempts, on the one hand, to perform the ritual tribute of the genre and, on the other hand, to maintain a stance of totally contradictory irony. Such an interpretation, I would argue, implicitly groups Mandel'shtam with the likes of other Russian poets such as Gavrila Derzhavin and Pushkin willing to produce rhetorical statements of praise that bear the risk of moral compromise in the hope of a political breakthrough. While this view stops short of Brodskii's compelling argument about the parodic and deadly subversiveness of the 'Oda', it advocates a need to start with the lines and read the poem as a complex verbal statement rather than to begin from the life and work inward. For at least one reviewer of Coetzee's essays his explanation — or expiation — was insufficient to draw the moral sting of an act of compromise, a 'desperate strategy' used 'to fabricate

---

111 Editorial, *PN Review*, 50 (1986), 1.

the body of an ode without actually inhabiting it'.[112] Davie, a lover of Mandel'shtam and an early champion in English, read the poem for the first time when reviewing Gregory Freidin's scholarly monograph *A Coat of Many Colors*.[113] Disillusioned by the 'Oda', he publicly lambasted Mandel'shtam and said he had lost all respect for him. The extreme response from a distinguished scholar of Pound, an expert reader of complex poetic statement and rhetoric, is disillusion in inverse proportion to erstwhile hero-worship.[114] It makes it clear that once Mandel'shtam was seen as a political poet, regard for him as a poet who remained ethical because his work was non-political, was a premise that might be open to question. Valentina Polukhina in a letter to the *TLS* had earlier hammered home the message that 'from the classic model lives of Mandelstam, Tsvetaeva and Akhmatova', we should all know 'that the degree of the poet's lack of well-being in Russia almost always directly depends on his or her non-conformism'.[115]

For Davie, Freidin's reading of Mandel'shtam as a kenotic poet could not be reconciled with the 'Oda' as an act of self-abasement. Mandel'shtam, whose art he cherished for its love of life, whose image he worshipped as a victim of involuntary suffering, had to forfeit his moral stature and relevance. The sentence Davie imposes upon Mandel'shtam as a charismatic poet of self-sacrifice, whose praise of Stalin he reads as betrayal, is revulsion and expulsion. This distinguished lifelong advocate of the cause of Russian poets and Russian poetry turns belatedly against what he calls on the same pages the 'inflation' with which 'groupies' invested the lives of Russian poets and no longer sees any point in reading their lines. Mandel'shtam 'cannot be so easily taken as a model by English language poets', and Davie in his disillusion warns that we should be 'prudently aghast at how Russian intelligentsia, before and

---

112 J. M. Coetzee, 'Osip Mandelstam and the Stalin Ode' in his *Giving Offence: Essays on Censorship* (Chicago: University of Chicago, 1993), pp. 104–16; and Michael Ignatieff, 'The Beloved', *LRB*, 6 February 1997, 14. Ignatieff accepts Coetzee's argument that in the end if the 'Oda' was meant as exculpation Mandel'shtam's language betrayed him into writing a highly subversive work.

113 Gregory Freidin, *A Coat of Many Colors: Osip Mandelstam and His Mythologies of Self-Presentation* (Berkeley, Los Angeles and London: University of California Press, 1987).

114 Donald Davie, 'From the Marches of Christendom: Mandelstam and Milosz', *PN Review*, 109 (May–June 1996), 13–24.

115 Valentina Polukhina, 'Poets of Protest', *TLS*, 11 September 1987, 987.

after the Revolution, accorded to their poets (and also their musicians, notably Aleksandr Scriabin) the privileges of the mystagogue, the sage, and the scapegoat'.[116] The outrage stands strikingly alongside the refusal to speak of the Stalin poem that marked the 1991 London conference, with the exception of Brodskii's reading of it as a highly subversive work and among Mandel'shtam's greatest poems. Davie was not alone in finding in one instance of disenchantment reasons to reconsider the equation of life and lines, and the potential cost to the proper appreciation of poetry on its own merits. Mandel'shtam's name is likely to continue to be used as shorthand for the victim of totalitarian ideology and repression — and enlisted in the ranks of firm anti-Communists.[117] At the other end of the spectrum, and in Russian but still on the this side of the vanished Iron Curtain, the poet Vladimir Gandel'sman read the 'Oda' as an experimental work, a defiant statement of poetic freedom almost detached from aspects of political content and risk.[118] But the forum for this type of reference may have shifted decisively to the realm of popular literature. Mandel'shtam continues, justifiably, to be seen as a poet devoured by the 'wolfhound age' that he so uncannily named.[119] Now the standard-bearers of this view are commercial writers like Laurent Binet, whose 2011 novel about Reinhard Heydrich, *HHhH*, bears an epigraph from 'Vek' ('Century'). The historian Anthony Beevor's edition of Vasily Grossman's war journalism begins similarly, while Robert Littell's 2010 *The Stalin Epigram* pits Mandel'shtam in a face-to-face encounter with Stalin himself. By 2005, this antagonism to poetry that must be tested for its value by stories of persecution and assaults on integrity has hardened into what has been called 'the Mandel'shtam syndrome', a damning tag for the hold that Eastern European poetry had on the minds and hearts of its readers.[120] It suggests that an appetite for lines over lives, a position I have described as the starting point in

---

116 Donald Davie, 'From the Marches of Christendom', 14.
117 Dennis O'Driscoll, 'Going A-roving', *TLS*, 12 June 1998, 24.
118 Vladimir Gandel'sman, '"Stalinskaia oda" Mandel'shtama', *Novyi Zhurnal*, 215 (1999), 133–41.
119 Nicholas J. Anning, 'The Wolfhound Age', *TLS*, 2 July 1971, 752; Henry Gifford, 'On Modesty and Boldness', *TLS*, 23 August 1985, 915.
120 Chris Miller, 'The Mandelstam Syndrome and the "Old Heroic Bang"', *PN Review*, 162 (March–April 2005), 14–22.

the previous cycle of appreciation, finally began to obtain in a more globalised literary field extended across borders.

Coda: Mandel'shtam at Home

There are numerous accounts of Mandel'shtam's disappearance from the printed page in Russia. In his *Paris Review* interview of 1982, Brodskii said that Mandel'shtam was

> still largely unpublished and unheeded — in criticism and even in private conversations, except for the friends, except for my circle, so to speak. General knowledge of him is extremely limited, if any. I remember the impact of his poetry on me. It's still there. As I read it I'm sometimes flabbergasted.[121]

On the basis of the documentary reception presented here, with strong evidence of a writer now firmly in the canon of translated European poets, this despairing outburst of frustration by Brodskii expressed the transcultural gap between appreciation at home and abroad. Yet Russian conversations about Mandel'shtam were taking place, texts were circulating, an invisible accumulation of regard was happening. Putting one's finger on his rescue from oblivion is more a question of disconnected dots on a timeline than the steady snowballing effect we see in the West. There comes a moment when, as he predicted in a famous letter to Yuri Tynianov of 1937, Mandel'shtam, while modestly summing up his poetic life as a mixture of the 'important and trivial', concluded that after twenty-five years of 'coming up against' Russian poetry (or 'forming a crust on' since the verb he uses can mean both) he felt that 'my poems will soon pour into and dissolve into it, changing something in its structure and composition'.[122] Mandel'shtam's afterlife abroad made him a canonical figure in America and the United Kingdom before that prediction came true in Russian. His stature as a classic of the Russian canon is perhaps an unfolding story, although that chemical reaction he predicted now seems irreversible. If in fact it seems

---

121 Joseph Brodsky, 'The Art of Poetry', *Paris Review*, 24 (1982), 83-126 (p. 104).
122 'Letter to Iu. N. Tynianov', 21 January 1937, Osip Mandel'shtam, *Polnoe sobranie sochinenii i pisem v trekh tomakh*, edited by A. G. Mets, 3 vols. (Moscow: Progress-Pleiada, 2011), vol. 3, p. 548 (no. 194).

almost more a matter of alchemy than the logic of literary history, it is obviously because political circumstances in Soviet Russia constrained the formation of a critical consensus before the 1990s.

The Khrushchev Thaw was too brief to be of more than limited benefit to the restoration of Mandel'shtam's work, especially his unpublished later poems. The year 1965, however, did see the first public readings of his poetry in thirty-two years held at Moscow University. Participants included not only veteran contemporaries such as Kornei Chukovsky and Il'ia Erenburg but the still unpublished Varlaam Shalamov, a *zek* (labour camp prisoner) who read Mandel'shtam in clandestine manuscript copies.[123] Nadezhda Mandel'shtam finally felt the time was ripe to publish new editions based on the substantial archive she had so remarkably preserved throughout the Soviet period. But the very substantial textual problems sorely tested the editorial abilities of Nikolai Khardzhiev, whose flawed *Biblioteka poeta* edition (1973; 1974) appeared well after the Thaw had ended and was quickly withdrawn as a political misjudgment and excoriated in the émigré press as textologically unreliable. As a result only handwritten or *samizdat* copies continued to circulate, making the question of Mandel'shtam's reception in late Soviet Russia a matter of random interest.[124] The children's writer and poet Marina Boroditskaia (b. 1954) records that Mandel'shtam, the last of the great Silver Age poets to become accessible because he was 'the most forbidden', eclipsed Pasternak and Akhmatova in her affections, and that numerous poems from *Tristia* were easily memorised by radio listeners even at a time when his name was still unprintable.[125] Grigorii Kruzhkov, the poet and gifted translator of English poetry, discovered Mandel'shtam's verse only in the late 1970s and came to see him as the equal of Pasternak, both classics worthy to stand alongside Pushkin and

---

123 'Posmotrim, kto kogo pereuptriamit...'. *Nadezhda Iakovlevna Mandel'shtam v pis'makh, vospominaniiakh, svidetel'stvakh* (Moscow: Izdatel'stvo ACT, 2015), 214.

124 Viktoria Schweitzer, 'Spustia pochti polveka', *Russica* (1981), 229–56. Many of the contributors to *'Posmotrim, kto kogo pereuptriamit...'* (above, n. 119) detail how their first encounter with Mandel'shtam's poetry in underground copies from the late 1950s and through the 1960s, in some cases thanks to access to Nadezhda Mandel'shtam who moved to Moscow in 1965. This handful of readers were inevitably from the urban intelligentsia and often, as it happened, trained scientists and mathematicians.

125 Marina Boroditskaia (personal communication, 11 May 2013, Oxford).

Evgenii Baratynskii, together with if slightly ahead of other beloved poets such as Blok, Georgii Ivanov, and Akhmatova.[126]

A generation later the phenomenon of Mandel'shtam as a quietly-absorbed revelation recurs, his reader base and place in the canon growing outside official literature from the ground up, almost reader by reader. The poet and academic Mariia Falikman first read some of Mandel'shtam's late and most difficult poems, and found the rhythmic irregularities disturbing (a topic for scholarly discussion by Iu. D. Levin at roughly the same time).[127] The publication of Nadezhda Mandel'shtam's memoirs, with quotations from Mandel'shtam's verse, expanded her awareness to a fuller range of poems and changes in his poetic vision and technique. By turning back to the earlier verse as texts became available during the *perestroika* period, Falikman began to make sense of the experimental quality of his later lyric and to acknowledge him as an influence on her own poetry.

Public events only served to formalise, and possibly expand, a truth hidden from distant advocates like Brodskii. Namely that, after his rehabilitation in 1956, Mandel'shtam steadily attracted the interest of a new generation of poetry readers despite the formidable obstacles they faced, including the absence of sound editions. By the time of the Mandel'shtam Centennial Celebration held in Moscow in 1991, a banned poet had become canonical even before most of his works could be published in his native country. To anyone who attended this particular event, however, it would have been very clear that among the large educated class of Russians-Muscovites and others Mandel'shtam was already a classic and much-loved figure; he was in the minds and on the tongues of hundreds of conference attendees who, often from the audience, fed speakers lines of his verse. With the newfound freedoms of *perestroika*, a generation of Mandel'shtam devotees such as Pavel Nerler and Iurii Freidin responded to obvious demand by producing new editions and making determined efforts to absorb a Western legacy of Mandel'shtam scholarship and foster home-grown studies. In the same year, a star of the new generation, Viktor Krivulin, provided an introductory essay to new English translations of poems from the

---

126 Grigorii Kruzhkov (personal communication, 11 May 2013, Oxford).
127 Mariia Falikman (personal communication, 13 May 2013, Oxford).

1930s, presented as *The Moscow Notebooks*, an invented title.[128] Less than twenty years later, *Vozdukh* (*The Air*), founded in 2006 and the most impressive contemporary journal to publish new poetry and poetic criticism, took its epigraph from Mandel'shtam, whose name appears frequently on its pages as an acknowledged master but also interlocutor for contemporary poets.

A detailed reconstruction of this internal reception of Mandel'shtam, as told more consecutively through memoirs and anecdotes, would, I surmise, multiply the reactions cited above in fascinating detail. While entities like the Mandel'shtam Society (*Mandel'shtamovskoe obshchestvo*) have used a questionnaire to collect data about Mandel'shtam's readership, including information about their preferences among his works, the evidence suggests that his canonical reputation remains uncontested among literary elites in both Moscow and St Petersburg, dovetailing with *perestroika* rather than being unleashed by political change. Within post-Soviet Russia, Mandel'shtam was inherited silently as part of a tradition that was being reconstituted because his life made him morally impeccable and his poems continued to strike a chord. While Nadezhda Mandel'shtam's own legacy has now become the subject of debate, the questions about image manipulation that now accompany studies of Akhmatova do not assail Mandel'shtam.[129] Even a slender sample of websites, interviews in poetry magazines and private correspondence strongly attests to the view that Mandel'shtam remains central and essential because he is both classical and experimental. It is these dual qualities that are seen to make a poet generative beyond his own time. In this sense, the idea of the canonical

---

128 Henry Gifford, 'Hearing Close-Knit Harmonies: Mandel'shtam's Essential Music Translated', *TLS*, 24 May 1991, 9.

129 From their original publication in Russian, Nadezhda Mandel'shtam's books were given classic status along with Solzhenitsyn for their look into the Soviet system as much as their contribution to poetry. See Gleb Struve, 'Nadezhda Mandelstam's remarkable memoirs', *Books Abroad*, 45: 2 (Winter 1971), 18–25. The 'cult' of Nadezhda Iakovlevna was more or less sanctioned in an anecdotal piece by Clarence Brown, 'Every Slightest Pebble', *LRB*, 25 May 1995, 24–27; inevitably her reputation, and Mandel'shtam's image, have subsequently become entangled in evaluations of other memoirists, most especially that of Emma Gershtein, on which see Rachel Polonsky, 'Beneath the Kremlin Crag', *TLS*, 14 May 2004, 9; Pavel Nerler, 'V poiskakh kontseptsii: kniga Nadezhdy Mandel'shtam ob Anne Akhmatovoi na fone perepiski s sovremennikami', in *Nadezhda Mandel'shtam, Ob Akhmatovoi* (Moscow: Novoe izdatel'stvo, 2007), pp. 7–108.

acquires another dimension to merely historical significance. In his manifesto for *Vozdukh*, the editor Dmitrii Kuz'min wrote eloquently about the relation between major and minor poets, and the work of literary histories to account for secondary and tertiary byways and even dead-ends. He cites Mandel'shtam as the measure of poetic greatness, a sound yet remarkable judgement when we think how little his poetry was known before the 1970s. By comparison, it is instructive to see how other poets interviewed in *Vozdukh* identify Brodskii as a classic, a great poet who, in the words of Aleksei Tsvetkov and Tat'iana Shcherbina, shut down traditions, unlike Nikolai Zabolotskii or Mandel'shtam who are cited as living sources for new poetry.[130] Mandel'shtam's reticulations to the Pushkinian tradition of lyric do not camouflage an avant-garde trend that leads Alexander Skidan to associate his later poetry with Velimir Khlebnikov and Konstantin Vaginov. Important poet-critics like Brodskii and Ol'ga Sedakova each in their own way anticipated the impasse by rooting the authority of the poet firmly in artistic genius. For Brodskii, the moral stature of a writer could only be a matter of consideration if it depended on aesthetic statements, and if poetry formulated ideas in ways that remained true to his ideals of poetry. For Sedakova, who, like Brodskii, admires the capacity of the poet to de-familiarise and make us see, the great moral stability of Russian poetry lay not in its martyrology but rather in its escapism to a greater appreciation of reality, in which few can compete with Mandel'shtam's 'intelligence of sight, of hearing' (umnost' samogo glaza, slukha).[131]

Arguably, the true measure of Mandel'shtam's post-Soviet reception, present of course in the now large body of scholarship, memoir-literature and biography of Russian *Mandel'shtamovedenie*, will be in his influence on poets and their lyric writing — in other words his contribution to the creation of a new canon. Meanwhile, outside the virtual reality of literature, physical landscapes now feature Mandel'shtam and tangibly

---

130 Dmitrii Kuz'min, 'Atmosfernyi front', *Vozdukh. Zhurnal poezii*, 1 (2006), 11; for some thoughts on the relation of literary 'overproduction' and the canon, see the 'state of the field' piece by G. S. Smith, http://www.aatseel.org/resources/stateofthefield/poetry.htm

131 Ol'ga Sedakova, 'Zametki i vospominaniia o raznykh stikhotvoreniiakh, a takzhe Pokhvala poezii', in *Proza* (Moscow: NFQ/Tu Print, 2001), p. 61.

bear witness to his newly established place. In a now famous letter to Tynianov, written just a year before his final arrest, Mandel'shtam declared that he was not a 'ghost' and was still 'casting a shadow'. Once he became a non-person, he was of course not even a shadow since his writings were left unpublished, unmentioned and unstudied. In the post-Soviet period, acts of commemoration have restored him to the cityscapes of St Petersburg and Moscow, his new textual presence in monuments and texture. Like Pushkin, whose celebrated imitation of Horace boasted that his posthumous fame would reach the entire extent of Russia's vastness, effigies of Mandel'shtam exist nearly at both ends of Russia. The first of three monuments erected to the poet was in Vladivostok, his final scheduled destination, and is located at 41, ulitsa Gogolia.[132]

In Moscow, the unveiling in late November 2008 of a statue commemorated the seventieth anniversary of Mandel'shtam's death in a transit camp on the way to the Far East; a bust of Mandel'shtam, undertaken at the initiative of a group led by the poet Oleg Chukhontsev, was unveiled at 5, ulitsa Zabelina. This is the site of the communal apartment block where the Mandel'shtams were frequent overnight guests of his brother, Aleksandr. The bust, on top of a slender black marble column, is the work of the sculptors Dmitrii Shakhovskoi and Elena Munts. It bears as an inscription the opening lines of the poem 'Za gremuchiu doblest' griadushchikh vekov' ('For the Ringing Renown of Future Ages'). The third statue is in Voronezh, a full-sized bronze statue by Lazar Gadaev unveiled in November 2008 near the house where the Mandel'shtams lived from 1934–1937. Like the other representations, the image of the poet fixes his characteristic gesture of tilting his head back, his eyes shut as though in a trance, a posture that contemporaries note in memoirs and even in poetry (Tsvetaeva, among others). The figure stands in front of a handsome stone on which his name and dates are inscribed in gilt letters. A number of historic plaques indicating the poet's places of residence have been installed in St Petersburg and Moscow. In June 2009, under the aegis of the Mandel'shtam Society of Moscow, a group travelled to Cherdyn', the original place of the

---

132 A concise timeline of the monument's history and its opening can be found online at http://polit.ru/article/2008/08/27/vladivostok.

Mandel'shtams exile before their transfer to Voronezh, to unveil a slate tablet on the outside wall of the hospital where Mandel'shtam broke his arm after jumping from a window.

Fig. 6.1 Memorial plaque on the outside wall of the hospital in Cherdyn'. © Andrew Kahn, CC BY 4.0.

7. Revising the Twentieth-Century Poetic Canon: Ivan Bunin in Post-Soviet Russia[1]

Joanne Shelton

Since 1991, revisions to the canon of post-Soviet literature have occurred, and poetry written during the course of the twentieth century has not escaped this process of re-assessment. Some writers have endured the re-evaluation of what it means to be canonical and they have succeeded in retaining the canonical status that they held prior to the collapse of the Soviet Union. The reverse of this is also true; some writers have been admitted to the canon of Russian poetry for the first time. However, any assessment of the changes to the Russian literary canon should not ignore the group of writers to which Ivan Bunin, émigré writer and first Russian winner of the Nobel Prize for Literature, belongs — that of the writer who has been in and out of the canon, even during the seventy years of Soviet rule. In the post-Soviet era, it seems that Bunin's position in the canon has finally been established, as a poet as well as a prose writer. This chapter will explore some of the ways in which Bunin's poetry has become established in the canon, and it will argue that, while the institutional model of canon formation appears to have had a more significant impact on Bunin's canonicity than the poet-based model of canonisation, the difficulty in drawing a distinction between the two models means that the contribution of poets to the process of

---

1   My thanks go to my colleague, Julia Kostyuk, for her suggested improvements to some of the Russian translations in this chapter. I am also grateful to the editors for their comments and feedback on this chapter.

canon formation cannot be ignored.² Furthermore, the chapter will examine how the 'Bunin institution', which encompasses such extra-literary factors as commemorations of Bunin's life, museums, or statues dedicated to his memory, has played a role in securing his place in the canon of post-Soviet poetry.

Paul Lauter suggests that a canon is the 'set of literary works, the grouping of significant philosophical, political and religious texts, the particular accounts of history generally accorded cultural weight within a society'.³ He goes on to attest that '[...] *literary* canons do not fall from the sky. They are constructed and reconstructed by people [...], people with certain ideas and tastes and definable interests and views of what is desirable'.⁴ This (re)construction of the canon according to the views of certain individuals can be seen in the Soviet context, where the literary canon was subject to ideological manipulation. Not only did the Soviet leadership decide what was acceptable for publication, it also sought to control the way in which the reader understood the text, thus explanatory notes and quotations from Karl Marx and Friedrich Engels, Stalin, or Lenin accompanied many works.⁵ Furthermore, the position of a writer and the assessment of his or her work were subject to change throughout the Soviet era.⁶ The canon management that took place in the Soviet period is one of the fundamental reasons why there has been a post-Soviet re-assessment of Russian poetry, and it seems that the processes more commonly associated with the canonisation of literary works are beginning to play a significant role in identifying the

---

2   Alan Golding, *From Outlaw to Classic: Canons in American Poetry* (Madison: The University of Wisconsin Press, 1995), p. 41. Golding suggests that the institutional model of canon formation is shaped by 'teacher-critics, [...] anthologies, the publishing industry [...], grant-giving agencies, and the structuring of [literary] studies according to "field"'. In contrast, the poet-based model 'holds that poetic canons are mainly the creation of poets themselves'. He goes on to argue that a synthesis of these models is 'the most useful' in the context of American poetry; such a model seems also appropriate in exploring the canonisation of Bunin's poetry.
3   Paul Lauter, *Canons and Contexts* (New York: Oxford University Press, 1991), p. ix.
4   *Ibid.*, p. 261.
5   Ludmila Koehler, 'New Trends in Soviet Literary Criticism', *Russian Review*, 27 (1968), 54–67 (p. 54).
6   Peter Yershov, 'Soviet National Literature in the New Soviet Encyclopedia', *American Slavic and East European Review*, 13 (1954), 89–99 (p. 93). Yershov details changes to the entry about Bunin in the *Great Soviet Encyclopedia*.

works to be established in the re-evaluated canon of twentieth-century Russian poetry.

The poet-based model of canon formation demonstrates the value that Bunin's contemporaries placed on his poetic works and marks out the position that they awarded him in the hierarchy of Russian literature. Furthermore, it enables us to see how his successors have accepted, or rejected, the assessments of their literary forerunners and the extent to which the poet-based model has been subject to Soviet-era manipulation. The precedence given to Bunin's prose may have obscured his poetry, yet it must be noted that he was the recipient of two Pushkin Prizes: the first awarded in 1902, followed by a second in 1909. In addition, reviews of his work by his fellow poets can be traced in Russian-language criticism from the late 1880s onward. Bunin's potential as a poet was recognised from his first published collection: 'this small book [*Stikhotvoreniia. 1887–1891* (*Poems. 1887–1891*)], where just thirty-nine poems are published, gives a complete understanding of his [Bunin's] talent, that is, that Mr Bunin is undoubtedly a talented poet'.[7] As might be expected when subject to the opinions of individuals, Bunin's poetry did not receive universal praise. Positive assessments of Bunin's early publications were tempered with assertions, such as those made by Ivan Ivanov, who suggested that Bunin should 'abandon the occupation of poetry', and such disparities in opinion were not restricted to Bunin's early collections.[8] In response to the collection *Stikhotvoreniia. 1903–1906* (*Poems. 1903–1906*), Sergei Solov'ev declared 'calling Bunin a poet should not be permitted. He is a verse-maker, and a bad one at that'.[9] These views were balanced by Aleksandr Blok who asserted the necessity of 'acknowledg[ing Bunin's] right to one of the chief positions among contemporary Russian poetry'.[10] Among those

---

7   Vladimir Lebedev, 'Rets.: Stikhotvoreniia. 1887–1891 gg. Orel, 1891', in *Klassik bez retushi: Literaturnyi mir o tvorchestve I. A. Bunina*, edited by N. Mel'nikov (Moscow: Knizhnitsa and Russkii put', 2010), p. 26 (first published in *Sever*, 9 (1892), 495).

8   Ivan Ivanov, 'Rets.: Stikhotvoreniia. 1887–1891 gg. Orel, 1891', in *Klassik bez retushi*, pp. 24–25 (p. 25) (first published in *Artist*, 20 (1892), 106).

9   Sergei Solov'ev, 'Rets.: Stikhotvoreniia 1903–1906 gg. (Sochineniia. T. 3). SPb.: Znanie, 1906', in *Klassik bez retushi*, pp. 92–93 (p. 92) (first published in *Zolotoe runo*, 1 (1907), 89).

10 Aleksandr Blok, 'Rets.: Stikhotvoreniia 1903–1906 gg. (Sochineniia. T. 3). SPb.: Znanie, 1906', in *Klassik bez retushi*, pp. 95–98 (pp. 95–96) (first published in *Zolotoe runo*, 6 (1907), 45–47).

poets who voiced their appreciation of Bunin's poetic talent, there was no hesitation about which poems most clearly demonstrated the writer's skill. Bunin's talent lay in depicting nature and the Russian countryside in his poems.[11] In response to the collection *Stikhotvoreniia. 1903–1906*, Valerii Briusov recognized that 'the best from [the collection], as before, are the pictures of nature [...]. The very weakest are all the verses where Bunin occasionally wants to moralize, or, even worse, to philosophize'.[12]

In spite of the consensus that Bunin's poems concerning nature were his best, his reviewers and his contemporaries were challenged to find him a suitable place in the pantheon of Russian literature. As Zinaida Gippius points out, critics of Bunin's work 'did not know what to do with him because they wanted "to put him on a certain shelf"'.[13] Some considered the fact that he did not follow the trends of the symbolists to be a positive attribute in his poetry. Petr Iakubovich was delighted by Bunin's collection *Pod otkrytym nebom. Stikhotvoreniia* (*Under the Open Sky. Poems*): 'With great pleasure, we bring to the attention of the readers, this small collection of poems; among the dead desert of all the symbolist rubbish, it can boldly be called, small as it is, a bright oasis'.[14] For others, Bunin's poetry was a relic of the past. Briusov highlights the fact that 'all the metrical life of Russian verse of the last decade [...] has passed Bunin by. His poems (according to their metre) could have been written in the [18]70s and [18]80s'.[15] The fact that Bunin acknowledged and corresponded with writers and poets belonging to other literary

---

11 See Apollon Korinfskii, 'Rets.: Stikhotvoreniia. 1887–1891 gg. Orel, 1891', in *Klassik bez retushi*, p. 25 (first published in *Vsemirnaia illiustratsiia*, 47 (1892), 402–03); Vasilii Korablev, 'Rets.: Listopad. Stikhotvoreniia. M.: Skorpion, 1901', in *Klassik bez retushi*, pp. 50–52 (first published in *Literaturnyi vestnik*, 2 (1901), 32–34). Korinfskii (p. 25) contends: '[Bunin] knows nature, in nature he senses life. In his poems nature is represented strikingly, colourfully, bewitching with its charm'. Korablev (p. 50) highlights the fact that Bunin's work is 'dedicated to the description of spring, autumn, and winter, of day and night, of the steppe, the sea and the river, the moon and the nightingale [...]'.

12 Valerii Briusov, 'Rets.: Stikhotvoreniia 1903–1906 gg. (Sochineniia. T. 3). SPb.: Znanie, 1906', in *Klassik bez retushi*, pp. 91–92 (p. 91) (first published in *Vesy*, 1 (1907), 71–72).

13 Gippius's comment attributed by Temira Pachmuss, 'Ivan Bunin through the Eyes of Zinaida Gippius', *The Slavonic and East European Review*, 44 (1966), 337–50 (p. 340).

14 Petr Iakubovich, 'Rets.: Pod otkrytym nebom. Stikhotvoreniia. M.: Izd. zhurnala "Detskoe chtenie", 1898', in *Klassik bez retushi*, pp. 45–46 (p. 45) (first published in *Russkoe bogatstvo*, 12 (1898), 46–47).

15 Briusov, pp. 91–92 (p. 92).

movements 'though in substance he was quite alien and even hostile to them' further complicated the matter for those who were seeking to identify a place for him in the hierarchy of Russian literature.[16] This inability to define neatly Bunin's place in the canon and the positive reaction to his nature poems are two elements that emerge most clearly from the pre-1917 assessments of Bunin's poetry publications.

Bunin's decision to emigrate meant that his work became unpublishable in the Soviet Union during his lifetime. After his death, this ban was relaxed, and between 1963 and 1967, a nine-volume *Sobranie sochinenii* (*Collected Works*), the introduction to which was written by Aleksandr Tvardovskii, was published in a print run of 210,000 copies.[17] In his assessment of Bunin's work, it is possible to see that the evaluations of earlier critics are reinforced. As commentators before him had observed, Tvardovskii sees 'the exquisite landscape painting of his native country, and the motifs of village and country-estate life' as the 'most viable feature' of Bunin's poetry, arguing that readers are 'less stirred by his poems about the exotic East, antiquity, biblical stories [...]' and he recognizes that the theme of 'impoverished and neglected "gentlefolk's nests", of the melancholy country estates and the wistfulness of autumnal decay' were 'by no means a pandering to the literary fashions of the day'.[18] However, Tvardovskii also signals to the reader that just because Bunin's poetry might appear to belong to the past, his contribution to Russia's literary heritage would be detrimental, and that it would 'lower [...] standards and cultivate a bleak, featureless, language in our poetry and prose'.[19]

As with his predecessors, it seems that Tvardovskii is keen to find a place in the canon for the poet and suggests that 'Bunin could not have become the poet he was if he simply followed the classical examples to the letter', and that 'it would be wrong to imagine that he did not adopt anything at all from the biggest poets of his day'.[20] Furthermore,

---

16 Gleb Struve, 'The Art of Ivan Bunin', *The Slavonic and East European Review*, 11 (1933), 423–36 (p. 424).

17 Aleksandr Tvardovskii, 'About Bunin', in *Stories and Poems by Ivan Bunin*, translated by Olga Shartse (stories and poems) and Irina Zheleznova (poems) (Moscow: Progress, 1979), pp. 9–29 (p. 9). The dates and print run of Ivan Bunin's nine-volume *Collected Works* are included as a note to Tvardovskii's introduction.

18 *Ibid.*, p. 28, p. 12.

19 *Ibid.*, p. 29.

20 *Ibid.*, p. 28.

Tvardovskii draws attention to the fact that 'the circle of writers and poets whose work is marked by an affinity to Bunin's aesthetic behests is very wide', and he even goes as far as to write himself into Bunin's poetic legacy.[21] Arguably, Tvardovskii was more eager to fit Bunin into the canon than pre-revolutionary commentators because Bunin and his work needed to be 'made safe' for the Soviet readership; by aligning Bunin with other poets that the leadership considered acceptable, Tvardovskii may have been attempting to make Bunin's works appear less threatening to the regime.[22] The desire to write Bunin into the canon and plot his position in relation to other poets was continued by other Soviet-era commentators. According to Valerii Nefedov, Nikolai Gribachev, Bella Akhmadulina, Valentin Berestov, Andrei Voznesenskii, Konstantin Vanshenkin, Evgenii Vinokurov, Sergei Narovchatov, Lev Ozerov, Evgenii Evtushenko, and Viktor Bokov were all helped by Bunin to 'find their individual creative writing style'.[23] In contrast, in the post-Soviet period, Iurii Azarov points out that 'it is difficult to compare the literature of different eras […]. Sorokin cannot be compared to Bunin', and he reiterates the common opinion that Bunin is the 'last representative of the "Golden Age" of Russian literature'.[24]

The desire not to disrupt Bunin's place in the canon as his contemporaries had defined it can be seen in the Soviet-era evaluations of Bunin's poetry. Tvardovskii's introduction highlights the way in which the canon promoted by the poet-based model is perpetuated. In order to validate his opinions about Bunin's poetry, Tvardovskii reiterates the observations made by Bunin's contemporaries, emphasising the fact that 'the recognition of [Bunin's] enormous talent and the importance of his contribution to Russian literature [was] not a present-day discovery',

---

21 *Ibid.*, p. 11.
22 Golding (p. 36) suggests that 'when a textbook anthology […] canonizes poetic outsiders, […] it renders their work culturally and intellectually harmless'. By allocating Bunin a place among acceptable writers, it appears that Tvardovskii is achieving the same ends as those compiling anthologies.
23 Valerii Nefedov, *Poeziia Ivana Bunina: Etiudy* (Minsk: Vysheishaia shkola, 1975), p. 132. See also Oleg Mikhailov, *I. A. Bunin. Ocherk tvorchestva* (Moscow: Nauka, 1967). In contrast to Nefedov, Mikhailov (pp. 4–5) suggests that 'Bunin completes the whole page in the development of Russian culture, although according to his social inclinations, he himself does not have successors'.
24 Iurii Azarov, 'Polnoe sobranie sochinenii Bunina nuzhno podgotovit' k ego 150-letiiu', *Russkii mir* (22 October 2010), para. 13, http://www.russkiymir.ru/publications/87865/?sphrase_id=704486

but was attributable to other writers, including Blok, Briusov, Anton Chekhov, and Maxim Gor'kii.²⁵ The assertions made by Bunin's contemporaries continue to be referenced later in the Soviet period. Oleg Mikhailov highlights Blok's praise for Bunin's depictions of nature, and Nefedov relies on Gor'kii to provide a reason why Bunin's poetry should not be omitted from the Russian literary scene.²⁶ The replication of criticism produced by Bunin's contemporaries has continued since 1991, with works such as *Klassik bez retushi: Literaturnyi mir o tvorchestve I. A. Bunina* (*A Canonical Author Without Retouch: The Literary World on the Creative Work of I. A. Bunin*), offering readers a clear picture of what other poets thought of Bunin's poetry at the time when it was written.²⁷

Arguably, the difficulties associated with where to place Bunin in the canon of Russian poetry have arisen from the fact that he tends to be somewhat forgotten as a poet. As N. G. Mel'nikov illustrates, this was common, even during Bunin's lifetime: 'Bunin, as a poet, was simply forgotten about, and it happened more than once. The names of Blok, [Innokentii] Annenskii, [Nikolai] Gumilev, [Anna] Akhmatova, [Vladislav] Khodasevich, [Osip] Mandel'shtam, [Boris] Pasternak, and several others were listed, and no one mentioned Bunin'.²⁸ The somewhat unfair lack of recognition that was afforded Bunin's poetry did not go unnoticed. Andrew Colin argues that 'there is no reason to penalize the man because he happened to combine two very rare gifts — that of a first-rate poet with that of a first-class novelist', and Gleb Struve feels that Bunin's poetry is 'an indispensable part of his artistic self-expression; and some of his best verse [...] is not inferior in quality to the best of his prose'.²⁹ Bunin himself continually felt the need to reassert his credentials as a poet, and his status as a poet is often reiterated in post-Soviet discussions about him.³⁰

---

25 Tvardovskii, p. 10. Tvardovskii points out that Bunin was held in great esteem by Blok and Briusov, by Chekhov, 'who spoke very favourably' of him, and by Gor'kii, who 'acclaimed Bunin's talent in the most lavish terms ever applied to him'.
26 Mikhailov, *I. A. Bunin*, p. 65; Nefedov, p. 131.
27 Mel'nikov, *Klassik bez retushi*, 2010.
28 Georgii Adamovich's comments attributed by N. Mel'nikov, 'Vvedenie — Izbrannye stikhi 1929', in *Klassik bez retushi*, pp. 333–39 (p. 333).
29 Andrew Guershoon Colin, 'Ivan Bunin in Retrospect', *The Slavonic and East European Review*, 34 (1955), 156–73 (pp. 167–68); Gleb Struve, pp. 423–36 (p. 423).
30 Nikita Struve's comment attributed by A. V.: 'In his soul, he was a poet, and not a novelist'. A. V., 'Novaia shkola — novye traditsii', *Nezavisimaia gazeta* (13 September

Although it appears to be something of a struggle to find a place for Bunin in the canon of Russian poetry, and the need to remind readers that he was a poet as well as a prose writer persists, it could be argued that without the contributions of Bunin's contemporaries and the critics and poets that have followed them, it would have been far harder to begin to identify where Bunin fits into the Russian poetry canon. Leaving aside the ideological dimension of the various assessments of Bunin's work, it is clear that Bunin was highly esteemed by other writers, even though their views on his poetry differed. It is on these arguments that canon formers are constructing the post-Soviet canon of twentieth-century Russian poetry, and it appears that they share the views of their predecessors: Bunin's poetry is worthy of note. Furthermore, it demonstrates the role that the poet-based model of canon formation plays in the process of establishing Bunin as a canonical figure. However, as noted in the introduction to this chapter, there is some difficulty in drawing a clear distinction between the poet-based model of canon formation and the institutional model. The next section of this chapter will outline the role of the institutional model in the process of canonisation.

In the context of the institutional model, the teaching of a writer or work at school or university level is fundamental to the reinforcement and the reproduction of a canon. Owing to the sheer quantity of texts that were no longer subject to state censorship and the publication of material printed in Russia for the first time, the school curriculum required substantial reworking in the early 1990s. In this instance, Bunin is not a straightforward example. In spite of his status as an émigré writer, some of his works had been available to Soviet readers since the mid-1950s and to Soviet students in the 1970s.[31] However, it was not until the first post-Soviet decade that Bunin's prose and poetry

---

2001), para. 1, http://www.ng.ru/education/2001-09-13/10_korotko.html; Vasilii Peskov, 'Buninskie mesta', *Komsomol'skaia Pravda* (25 October 2002), para. 31, http://www.kp.ru/daily/22662/21472; Liza Novikova, 'Poeticheskoe stolpotvorenie. Ob"iavleny pretendenty na Buninskuiu premiiu', *Kommersant'* (7 August 2007), para. 1, http://www.kommersant.ru/doc/793345

31 N. N. Shneidman, *Literature and Ideology in Soviet Education* (Toronto: Lexington Books. D. C. Heath & Co., 1973), p. 77, p. 95. Shneidman notes that Bunin's poem 'Gustoi zelenyi el'nik u dorogi' is included for independent reading at grade four, and 'Gospodin iz San Frantsisko', various poems, and 'Pesn' o Gaiavate' are included at grades eight to ten for home reading.

became a more permanent fixture of the school curriculum. In 1997, a number of Bunin's short stories and poems appeared on the syllabus for grades five to nine, when educational professionals had to teach two or three poems from ten suggested in the curriculum.[32] On the syllabus for the upper grades, Bunin's poetry and prose appeared in the section 'Literature of the end of the nineteenth century and beginning of the twentieth century', where five poems were suggested for study.[33] However, in 2004, there were substantial revisions to the inclusion of Bunin's poetry. In grades five to nine, Bunin's poems were omitted from the curriculum, and just two of his stories were to be studied.[34] In the upper grades, at both foundation and profile levels, a number of Bunin's poems had to be studied, along with a selection of stories.[35]

Despite the changes to the study of Bunin's poetry in the curriculum, his verse is included in a number of approved textbooks. At the lower

---

32 Ministerstvo obshchego i professional'nogo obrazovaniia RF, 'Ob obiazatel'nom minimume soderzhaniia obrazovatel'nykh programm osnovnoi obshcheobrazovatel'noi shkoly' (18 July 1997), section titled 'Iz literatury XX veka', http://www.businesspravo.ru/Docum/DocumShow_DocumID_52815.html. Children in grades five to nine of school are aged between ten and fifteen.

33 Ministerstvo obrazovaniia RF, 'Obiazatel'nyi minimum soderzhaniia srednego (polnogo) obshchego obrazovaniia' (30 June 1999), section titled 'Iz literatury kontsa XIX–nachala XX v.', http://www.businesspravo.ru/Docum/DocumShow_DocumID_71939.html

34 Ministerstvo obrazovaniia Rossiiskoi Federatsii, 'Standart osnovnogo obshchego obrazovaniia po literature', Federal'nyi komponent gosudarstvennogo standarta obshchego obrazovaniia. Chast' I. Nachal'noe obshchee obrazovanie. Osnovnoe obshchee obrazovanie (2004), section titled 'Russkaia literatura XX veka', http://window.edu.ru/resource/259/39259/files/09.pdf. The documents can be downloaded from Edinoe okno dostupa k informatsionnym resursam, http://window.edu.ru

35 Ministerstvo obrazovaniia Rossiiskoi Federatsii, 'Standart srednego (polnogo) obshchego obrazovaniia po literature. Bazovyi uroven'', Federal'nyi komponent gosudarstvennogo standarta obshchego obrazovaniia. Chast' I. Nachal'noe obshchee obrazovanie. Osnovnoe obshchee obrazovanie (2004), section titled 'Russkaia literatura XX veka', http://window.edu.ru/resource/276/39276/files/29.pdf. Ministerstvo obrazovaniia Rossiiskoi Federatsii, 'Standart srednego (polnogo) obshchego obrazovaniia po literature. Profil'nyi uroven'', Federal'nyi komponent gosudarstvennogo standarta obshchego obrazovaniia. Chast' I. Nachal'noe obshchee obrazovanie. Osnovnoe obshchee obrazovanie (2004), section titled 'Russkaia literatura XX veka', http://window.edu.ru/resource/277/39277/files/30.pdf. The documents can be downloaded from Edinoe okno dostupa k informatsionnym resursam, http://window.edu.ru. Taking a subject at 'profile level' in the final two years of secondary education indicates specialisation in particular subjects which are studied in greater depth; other subjects which pupils must follow, but in which they have not chosen to specialise, are taken at 'foundation level'.

grades, the discussion varies in its depth. The grade five textbook edited by Buneev and Buneeva includes a single poem by Bunin, 'Zmeia' ('Snake'), alongside a number of other single poems by other poets.[36] In the grade six textbook, edited by Aleksandr Kutuzov, seven of Bunin's poems are included. Six comprise part of the chapter titled 'Journey Three: To the Homeland' ('Puteshestvie tret'e, na rodinu') and the poem 'Sviatogor i Il'ia' ('Sviatogor and Il'ia') appears alongside Gumilev's 'Zmei' ('Dragon') in the section 'epic motifs of Russian poetry'.[37] By the time students reach grade nine, the textbooks contain far greater contextual detail about the events of the twentieth century and the impact that they had on literature. There is no criticism of Bunin's emigration; the decision to leave is attributed to the 'animosity' that Bunin felt for the Revolution; and in spite of his feelings toward the new regime, Bunin's love for Russia remained and the sadness which he felt on abandoning the country in 1920 is highlighted.[38] Despite the commentary on Bunin's life in emigration, there is no sense that his works should be read any differently from those penned by writers who remained in Russia after 1917: 'within the country Soviet literature was created; beyond Russia's borders was the literature of the abroad. [...] But the main thing not to forget is this non-unified sea of works carried the name of Russian literature'.[39] Indeed, according to the textbooks, the position that Bunin holds in twentieth-century Russian literature is that of the 'last Russian classic'.[40] Beyond grade nine, the study of

---

36 Rustem Buneev and Ekaterina Buneeva, *Shag za gorizont. Uchebnik-khrestomatiia po literature. 5 klass. Kniga 2*, 2 vols. (Moscow: Balass, 1998), II, 306–15; Buneev and Buneeva, *Shag za gorizont. Uchebnik-khrestomatiia po literature. 5 klass. Kniga 2*, 2 vols. (Moscow: Balass, 2004), II, 210–17.
37 *V mire literatury. 6 klass*, edited by Aleksandr Kutuzov (Moscow: Drofa, 1996), pp. 72–77, pp. 192–93; *V mire literatury. 6 klass*, edited by Kutuzov (Moscow: Drofa, 2005), pp. 87–92, p. 222.
38 *Literatura. Uchebnoe izdanie. 9 klass*, edited by Tamara Kurdiumova (Moscow: Drofa, 1998), p. 315; *Literatura. Russkaia klassika (izbrannye stranitsy). 9 klass. Uchebnik-praktikum dlia obshcheobrazovatel'nykh uchrezhdenii*, edited by Gennadii Belen'kii (Moscow: Mnemozina, 1997), p. 278; Buneev and Buneeva, *Istoriia tvoei literatury, Uchebnik-khrestomatiia po literature. 9 klass. Kniga 2*, 2 vols. (Moscow: Balass, 2005), II, 169. Belen'kii points out that 'even at the very beginning of his emigration, [Bunin] expressed his longing for his paternal home', p. 278, a sentiment echoed by Buneev and Buneeva, who emphasize that 'during his entire life, Russia was [Bunin's] greatest and fondest love', p. 169.
39 *Literatura*, edited by Kurdiumova, p. 313.
40 *Literatura. Russkaia klassika*, edited by Belen'kii, p. 279.

Russian literature is no longer compulsory. In the textbooks for those pupils who choose to continue studying literature, Bunin's poetry is, in many instances, included by the editors.[41] Unsurprisingly, the level of contextual material that accompanies Bunin's prose and poetry in the textbooks for pupils in grade eleven is far more detailed than it is at the lower grades. It is also interesting to note that there is emphasis on the fact that Bunin 'proved himself equally brilliant as a prose writer, a poet, and a translator', publishing his lyrics and prose in the same collections.[42]

In several textbooks, the promotion of Bunin as a canonical writer is supported by the use of critical assessments by scholars and by other authors. Just as Tvardovskii did in his introduction 'O Bunine' ('About Bunin'), Gennadii Belen'kii draws upon comments made by Bunin's contemporaries, thus he quotes Blok's assertion that 'the wholeness and simplicity of the verses and Bunin's outlook so valuable and unique that we have to [...] acknowledge his right to one of the chief positions in contemporary Russian poetry'.[43] Furthermore, by quoting from Tvardovskii's introduction, Belen'kii contributes to the process of canonising what Tvardovskii has said about Bunin: 'Bunin could not have become that which he became in poetry if he had only followed classical examples. And it is not correct, when it is said that his poems were one-dimensional and monotonous [...]'.[44] This further illustrates the challenge in distinguishing the boundaries between the institutional model of canon formation, and the poet-based process of canonisation. Clearly, the institutional model of canon formation draws upon the assessments of the poet-based model for validation thus revealing how the ideas promoted by individual writers are perpetuated.

---

41 A. V. Barannikov, *Russkaia literatura XX veka. 11 klass. Khrestomatiia. Chast' I.*, 2 vols. (Moscow: Prosveshchenie, 1997), I, 8–10; Iulii Lyssyi, *Russkaia literatura XX veka. 11 klass. Praktikum* (Moscow: Mnemozina, 1998), pp. 6–33; Sergei Zinin and Viktor Chalmaev, *Literatura XX veka. Khrestomatiia. 11 klass. Chast' I*, 2 vols. (Moscow: Russkoe slovo, 2005), I, 5–11.

42 Vladimir Agenosov, *Russkaia Literatura XX veka. 11 klass. Chast' I*, 2 vols. (Moscow: Drofa, 1996), I, 167; Lyssyi, p. 12.

43 *Literatura. Russkaia klassika*, edited by Belen'kii, p. 280. See also *Literatura*, edited by Kurdiumova, p. 315. Kurdiumova draws upon Tolstoi's words to exemplify the point that Bunin's contemporaries admired his work.

44 *Literatura. Russkaia klassika*, edited by Belen'kii, p. 281. (The translation of Tvardovskii's quotation here is mine, rather than that of Shartse and Zheleznova (1979)).

It is interesting to note that the critical work included in Belen'kii's textbook is all dated prior to 1991, which raises the question: does the inclusion of this material represent some sort of reconciliation with past assessments of Bunin's work, or is it simply a reflection of a lack of post-Soviet material about Bunin? Given that this particular textbook was published in the mid-to-late-1990s, it is not unreasonable to suppose that new works about Bunin were not widely accessible, especially given the declining print runs of the 1990s. However, continued recognition of Soviet-era criticism might suggest a form of compromise, whereby contemporary critics and textbook editors accept the limitations of works produced prior to 1991, and take from them sections that remain relevant, while rejecting those parts that no longer apply.[45] It might also suggest that post-Soviet editors are aware of the ways in which literary hierarchies develop and recognise that comments made by Bunin's contemporaries were reiterated by Soviet-era critics, who may themselves have been endeavouring to perpetuate a canon that was not distorted by ideology.

Mike Fleming points out that there are at least two reasons why a writer appears on the school curriculum.[46] In the first instance, there are the 'traditional criteria for forming the canon [that] have primarily been associated with notions of quality, selection of those texts or authors which are considered "the best"'.[47] Secondly, Fleming suggests that 'other related criteria were to do with selecting texts thought to be representative of a particular period, style or genre or those which have had an impact on culture historically and those which are thought to have a particular national significance'.[48] Arguably, Bunin's inclusion in the curriculum has more to do with Fleming's second point about

---

45 This rejection of Soviet-era assessments of Bunin's work can be seen in *Literatura*, edited by Kurdiumova, p. 315, when it is stated that 'abroad, the work of the writer did not lose its brilliance or its unbreakable connection with the Motherland. In emigration Bunin remained one of the most remarkable and brilliant of Russian writers', which is in direct contrast with Tvardovskii's suggestion that Bunin's emigration caused 'the premature and inevitable depreciation of his creative strength' (pp. 11–12).

46 Mike Fleming, 'The Literary Canon: Implications for the Teaching of Language as Subject', in *Text, literature and 'Bildung'*, edited by Irene Pieper (Strasbourg: Council of Europe, 2007), pp. 31–38, http://www.coe.int/t/dg4/linguistic/Source/Prague07_LS_EN.doc (p. 33).

47 Ibid., p. 33.

48 Ibid.

representation than it has to do with his comments about quality. Bunin fills a gap that might otherwise be empty at the beginning of the twentieth century. His works demonstrate a link between the poetry and prose of the nineteenth and twentieth centuries, following the traditions established by nineteenth-century writers, such as Aleksandr Pushkin, Mikhail Lermontov and Fedor Tiutchev.[49] Instead of following the 'aesthetic views and creative practices' of poets, such as Briusov and Blok, Bunin chose to 'put up an impenetrable wall against all fads and fashions […]', thus, the inclusion of his poetry provides an alternative to the experimentation that was taking place in literature at the beginning of the 1900s.[50] By selecting Bunin to represent the writers of the Russian emigration, his works help to fulfil the post-Soviet desire to bring together literature's different pasts and to overcome the division between émigré and Soviet literature.[51] The fact that he lived for an extended period outside Russia and continued to write in emigration provides an example of how Russian literature survived in exile. In addition, his rejection of Nazism and alleged contemplation of a return to the Soviet Union in the post-war period were no doubt in his favour when textbook and curriculum compilers came to evaluate which writer should represent the émigré community of the first wave.[52] In terms of being of 'particular national significance', Bunin was a prizewinner within pre-revolutionary Russia and internationally, when he became Russia's first Nobel Prize winner for Literature in 1933.[53] In spite of the Soviet-era condemnation of this award, a post-Soviet reconciliation with the honour appears to have taken place, demonstrated by the frequency with which Bunin's victory in this competition is mentioned. Whatever

---

49 Tvardovskii, p. 28. The suitability of Bunin's poems for children, the particular time in which he was writing, and the literary traditions that he sought to follow might also mean that he is used by those interested in the agenda of cultural elitism and the desire to promote pre-revolutionary values. My thanks go to the editors of this chapter for highlighting this point.
50 Tvardovskii, p. 10, p. 28.
51 My thanks go to the editors of this chapter for highlighting this point.
52 Sergei Shapoval, 'Otdushina dlia politika', *Nezavisimaia gazeta* (14 February 2003), para. 9 of 16, http://www.ng.ru/saturday/2003-02-14/13_lukyanov.html. It has been suggested that, when it comes to the inclusion of Bunin in poetry anthologies intended for a wider audience, Bunin's support of the Soviet Union during World War Two and his 'brilliant review' of Tvardovskii's 'Vasilii Terkin' are reasons to include him.
53 Fleming, p. 33.

the reasons for Bunin's inclusion in the school and university curricula, it is quite clear that the state and those responsible for education at all levels view him as a canonical writer, whose works, both prose and poetry, should be studied by younger generations.

The notion that Bunin's work should be considered part of a canon of Russian literature is further supported by the recognition that he received from elsewhere within the institutional model of canon formation. Although the spheres of influence of literary prizes, institutions of higher education, and publishers might be considered more limited than the school curriculum, each of these three components of the institutional model has a significant role to play in canon formation. The award of the Nobel Prize for Literature no doubt helped to reinforce any claim that Bunin might have had to a position in a canon of Russian literature. After all, as Horace Engdahl points out, 'the Nobel laureates have inevitably come to be seen as forming a kind of canon'.[54] Bunin's works came to be 'regarded as belonging to an elite order and ranked accordingly'; he 'no longer risked being forgotten'.[55] Although Bunin was awarded the Nobel Prize for Literature for 'the strict artistry with which he [...] carried on the classical Russian traditions in prose writing', it should be noted that his prose was widely recognized as having poetic elements, thus it could be argued that his prose would not have been so distinctive, and worthy of acclaim, if it had not been for his earlier poetry.[56]

In the awarding of prizes there seems to be something of a blurring between the institutional model of canon formation and the poet-based model. In the case of the Nobel Prize for Literature, once a writer has been awarded the accolade of Nobel Laureate, he or she is entitled to

---

54 Horace Engdahl, 'The Nobel Prize: Dawn of a New Canon?' (2008), p. 1.
55 *Ibid.*
56 'The Nobel Prize in Literature 1933: Ivan Bunin', Nobelprize.org, [n.d.], http://www.nobelprize.org/nobel_prizes/literature/laureates/1933. Tvardovskii (p. 27) suggests that Bunin's writing had a 'clearly pronounced individuality' and 'musical organisation'. He argues that 'the music of [Bunin's] prose cannot be mistaken for any other writer's' and that one possible reason he was able to achieve such a 'distinct rhythmical identity' was because 'he wrote poems all his life'. Tvardovskii (pp. 27–28) goes on to cite Bunin, who asserted that 'prose writing should adopt the musicalness and pliancy of poetry' and points out that Bunin had his poetry and short stories published together in his collections in order to 'emphasize the fundamental unity of poetry and prose'.

nominate other writers for future awards, yet the award is made by an institution. The awarding of literary prizes in the honour of a particular writer also distorts the boundaries of the canon-forming process. For example, in the case of the Ivan Bunin Literary Prize, founded in 2004, the awarding institutions seek to establish a winner in the contest for 'the revival of the best traditions of [Russian] literature'.[57] The institutions awarding the prize include *Moskovskii gumanitarnyi universitet* (the Moscow University for the Humanities), *Obshchestvo liubitelei rossiiskoi slovesnosti* (The Society of Lovers of Russian Literature), *Natsional'naia institut biznesa* (The National Institute of Business), *Natsional'nyi soiuz negosudarstvennykh vuzov'* (The National Union of Non-State Universities) and *Institut sovremennogo iskusstva* (The Institute of Contemporary Art), which clearly involves academic establishments as well as those that might include writers or poets.[58] In 2007, the committee awarding the Bunin Literary Prize decided that, because 'Bunin considered himself foremost to be a poet', the prize should be awarded to a writer whose achievements lay in the sphere of poetry, thereby perpetuating a particular aspect of Bunin's work.[59] Once again, the institutional model of canon formation draws on the poet-based model. While the use of literary prizes as a means of perpetuating a canon might be viewed as belonging to the institutional model of canonisation, the process followed in order to make such awards relies, at least in part, on the traditions of the poet-based model, whereby the assessment of, or a link to an individual writer, helps to shape the canon.

Although the role that universities play in shaping the canon might initially appear to be less influential than that of the school curriculum or literary prizes, on closer examination it is clear that such institutions contribute much to the development of the canon. A number of academic conferences have been held as part of commemorative events dedicated to Bunin and his work: a conference in 2010 was held

---

57 'V stolitse vruchili literaturnuiu premiiu imeni Ivana Bunina', Newsru.com (24 October 2005), para. 3, http://www.newsru.com/cinema/24oct2005/bunin.html
58 Aleksandr Alekseev, '350 tysiach rublei za talant: Ezhegodnaia Buninskaia premiia smenila format', *Rossiiskaia gazeta*, 15 April 2008, para. 7, http://www.rg.ru/2008/04/15/premia.html
59 Igor' Il'inskii, 'I. A. Bunin i sovremennaia poeziia: Press-konferentsiia, posviashchennaia ob"iavleniiu konkursa Buninskoi premii 2007 goda' (2007), para. 5, http://ilinskiy.ru/activity/public/bunin/2007

to commemorate the 140th anniversary of Bunin's birth, and followed earlier conferences; marking Bunin's 125th and 135th anniversaries, and another celebrating 75 years since Bunin was awarded the Nobel Prize for Literature. The occurrence of several Bunin conferences over a number of years demonstrates that there is continued scholarly interest in his work, and that he therefore has a legitimate claim to a place in the canon of Russian poetry.[60] Of course, the reach of such academic conferences is likely to be somewhat restricted, but the work at these gatherings is relevant to the process of canon formation on a wider scale because it contributes to other areas of the university's remit that have wider public influence. The activities of the centre 'Buninskaia Rossiia' ('Bunin's Russia'), established in 2010 at the I. A. Bunin Elets State University, exemplify the multifaceted role that institutions play in shaping the canon. In addition to the 2010 conference, the 'Bunin's Russia' was also involved developing a cultural programme.[61] While the academic study of a writer's works might be the point at which canon formation starts and the validation of a writer's place in the canon begins, it is the way in which this research is more widely disseminated that really demonstrates the role that universities play in the institutional model of canon formation. Indeed, the aims of the 'Bunin's Russia' to 'organiz[e] and coordinat[e] academic research and cultural enlightenment linked to the study of the creative legacy of I. A. Bunin, and other writers, academics and public figures from the region', perfectly encapsulate how academic establishments operate

---

60   *I. A. Bunin i XXI vek: materialy mezhdunarodnoi nauchnoi konferentsii, posviashchennoi 140-letiiu so dnia rozhdeniia pisatelia*, edited by E. Atamanova, N. V. Borisova, A. M. Podoksenov (Elets: Eletskii gosudarstvennyi universitet im. I. A. Bunina, 2011); *I. A. Bunin i russkii mir: materialy Vserossiiskoi nauchnoi konferentsii, posviashchennoi 75-letiiu prisuzhdeniia Nobelevskoi premii pisateliu*, edited by Elena Atamanova et al. (Elets: Eletskii gosudarstvennyi universitet im. I. A. Bunina, 2009); *Ivan Bunin: Filologicheskii diskurs: Kollektivnaia monografiia k 135-letiiu so dnia rozhdeniia I. A. Bunina*, edited by E. Atamonova (Elets: Eletskii gosudarstvennyi universitet im. I. A. Bunina, 2005); *I. A. Bunin i russkaia literatura XX veka: Po materialam mezhdunarodnoi konferentsii, posviashchennoi 125-letiiu so dnia rozhdeniia I. A. Bunina* (Moscow: Nasledie, 1995).

61   Nauchnyi tsentr 'Buninskaia Rossiia', 'Itogi deiatel'nosti nauchnogo tsentra "Buninskaia Rossiia" v 2010 godu', Buninskii tsentr (2010), p. 1, p. 13, http://www.elsu.ru/bunincnt_osnov_rezul.html The painting exhibition later moved to Moscow, see '"Khudozhniki-Buninu". Raboty sovremennykh khodozhnikov', Muzei Rossii (2011), http://www.museum.ru/N41906

within the institutional model of canon formation and how they seek to shape the canon using a variety of methods.[62]

The contributions of academics to events, such as those designed to commemorate the various anniversaries of Bunin's birth, help to generate interest in Bunin among non-specialists, which is particularly important in relation to the somewhat more commercial aspect of the institutional model of canon formation, that is, to publishers. The role that publishers play in terms of canon formation is further complicated because it is hard to identify whether publishers are responding to a demand from readers for a particular writer, or whether the publishing industry is choosing to make a particular writer more readily available. Bunin's poetry has been published throughout the 1990s and 2000s, though not as extensively as some of his prose works. The differences in print run since the mid-1980s are substantial, but unsurprising. In 1985, a collection of Bunin's poems was published in a print run of 500,000 copies, by 1990, this had dropped to 400,000 copies. In 1999, this figure had dropped to a mere 7000 copies, and by 2007, a collection of Bunin's poetry was published in just 5000 copies.[63] Although such a figure may appear very low when compared with the print runs of the late Soviet period, the average print run for a book in 2012 was 4624 copies.[64] Of course, the number of copies printed does not equate to popularity, neither does it guarantee that the material is read. However, in the post-Soviet period it is possible to assert that the figures for the print run do indicate the relative popularity of an author, not least because publishers want to make money, and achieve maximum sales figures. Publishers are also more readily able to reprint any texts that sell better than expected, ensuring a rapid response to reader demand.

---

62 Natalia Borisova, 'Buninskii tsentr', Eletskii gosudarstvennyi universitet im. I. A. Bunina, [n.d.], para. 2, http://www.elsu.ru/news/2899-o-centre-buninskaya-rossiya.html

63 For examples of print runs, see I. A. Bunin, *Stikhotvoreniia* (Moscow: Khudozhestvennaia literatura, 1985), http://www.ozon.ru/context/detail/id/4235774; I. A. Bunin, *Stikhotvoreniia* (Moscow: Molodaia gvardiia, 1990), http://www.ozon.ru/context/detail/id/5041243; I. A. Bunin, *Stikhotvoreniia. Perevody* (Moscow: Olma-Press, 1999), http://www.ozon.ru/context/detail/id/7446534; I. A. Bunin, *Stikhotvoreniia* (Moscow: Profizdat, 2007), http://www.ozon.ru/context/detail/id/5529353

64 'Uglubliaiushchiisia krizis: knigoizdanie Rossii v 2012 godu', Rossiiskaia knizhnaia palata, [n.d.], p. 2, http://www.bookchamber.ru/download/stat/stat_2012.zip (see file titled knigi_2012 in zip folder).

The relative popularity of Bunin's poetry can also be measured by the inclusion of his works in poetry anthologies. In 1994, Bunin's work was included in the section 'Vne grupp' ('No affiliation') in *Serebrianyi vek russkoi poezii* (*The Silver Age of Russian Poetry*), with the poet Marina Tsvetaeva.[65] Bunin's poems feature in *Strofy veka. Antologiia russkoi poezii* (*Stanza of the Century: An Anthology of Russian Poetry*); in *Russkaia poeziia. XX vek. Antologiia* (*Russian Poetry. Twentieth Century. An Anthology*); and more recently, in *Russkie stikhi 1950–2000 godov. Antologiia (pervoe priblizhenie)* (*Russian Poetry of the 1950s–2000s. An Anthology (The First Approximation)*).[66] However, the number of Bunin's poems included in each of these anthologies has varied. In *Strofy veka*, nine of Bunin's poems are included, whereas twenty-three appear in *Russkaia poeziia. XX vek. Antologiia*. In contrast, Bunin is represented in *Russkie stikhi 1950–2000 godov* by 'his twelve-line poem "Night" (Noch') and occupies one page', while other Nobel Laureates, Pasternak and Iosif Brodskii, are given seven and ten pages respectively.[67] Once again, when it comes to the compilation of anthologies, a blurring of the boundaries between the poet-based and institutional models of canon formation occurs. In instances where an anthology has been compiled by a poet, literary hierarchies are clearly at work. While the compiler's agenda might not be immediately obvious, the decision to include one poet over another, or the relative space allotted to each poet may give the reader an understanding of the compiler's personal view of poetry and poets within the hierarchy of Russian literature. Of course, this assumes that the poet-compiler (or the academic-compiler) has enjoyed the freedom to create the anthology as he or she sees fit. In reality, there may be greater input from the publisher, who might have an understanding of

---

[65] *Serebrianyi vek russkoi poezii*, edited by K. F. Nesterova (Moscow: IMA-Kross, 1994), pp. 419–27.

[66] *Strofy veka. Antologiia russkoi poezii*, edited by Evgenii Evtushenko (Minsk and Moscow: Polifakt, 1997), pp. 46–53; *Russkaia poeziia. XX vek. Antologiia*, edited by Sergei Fediakin et al. (Moscow: OLMA Press, 1999), pp. 48–52; *Russkie stikhi 1950–2000 godov. Antologiia (pervoe priblizhenie)*, edited by I. Akhmet'ev et al. (Moscow: Letnii sad, 2010), p. 4.

[67] Sergei Mnatsakanian, 'Bratskaia mogila', *Literaturnaia gazeta*, 35 (8 September 2010), para. 8, http://www.lgz.ru/article/N35--6289---2010-09-08-/Bratskaya-mogila13774/. Of course, numerous factors might affect a poet's inclusion in an anthology. Perhaps each poet is given a certain number of pages, or the anthology might focus on work written between certain dates or on certain themes.

which poets a reader likes and who he or she expects to be included in an anthology dedicated to a particular era or subject.

In addition to the views of individuals and the actions of institutions, Bunin's place in the canon is supported by extra-literary material and events, i.e. by the 'Bunin institution', including museums and statues, commemorations of his life, and articles about Bunin that appear in the current press.[68] Bunin's establishment in the wider canon of Russian literature has been reflected in material printed in newspapers. It is possible to categorize the articles into three groups: articles which inform the reader of some anniversary and/or event commemorating Bunin's life; articles that use Bunin or his work as the starting point to discuss a topic that is not directly associated with the poet or his publications; and finally, articles that appeal to the general interest of readers.[69] Articles, such as 'Otkrylas' vystavka, posviashchennaia 140-letiiu so dnia rozhdeniia Ivana Bunina' ('The Opening of an Exhibition Dedicated to Ivan Bunin's 140th Anniversary'), 'Buninskie iabloki' ('Bunin's Apples'), and 'Gospodin iz Efremova: BUNIN 140' ('The Gentleman from Efremov: Bunin is 140'), simply detail events linked with the 140th anniversary of Bunin's birth.[70]

For some writers, Bunin's works provide a source from which they can explore other newsworthy stories. Vladislav Korneichuk's article

---

68 For details of museums dedicated to Bunin, see Inna Kostomarova, 'Muzei I. A. Bunina v Orle', Bunin Ivan Alekseevich (1870–1953), [n.d.], http://bunin.niv.ru/bunin/museum/museum-orel.htm and 'Muzei', Bunin Ivan Alekseevich (1870–1953), [n.d.], http://bunin.niv.ru/bunin/museum/museum.htm. Details of statues and other memorials to Bunin can be found on the Russian-language Wikipedia page, sections 4 and 5: 'Bunin, Ivan Alekseevich', Wikipedia, http://ru.wikipedia.org/wiki/Бунин,_Иван_Алексеевич

69 This does not include all of the instances when Bunin, or references to him, are quoted in an unrelated context, such as being an example of a famous person who received mostly '2s' at school: 'Kak pravil'no delat' uroki', *Izvestiia* (16 February 2006), para. 25, http://izvestia.ru/news/311276. However, even such references are relevant because of the way in which they demonstrate an assumed familiarity with who Bunin was.

70 'Otkrylas' vystavka, posviashchennaia 140-letiiu so dnia rozhdeniia Ivana Bunina', *Rossiiskaia gazeta* (22 October 2010), http://www.rg.ru/2010/10/22/bunin-anons.html; Ol'ga Glazunova, 'Buninskie iabloki', *Rossiiskaia gazeta* (28 October 2010), http://rg.ru/2010/10/28/reg-roscentr/bunin.html; 'Gospodin iz Efremova', *Literaturnaia gazeta*, 42–43 (27 October 2010), http://www.lgz.ru/article/N42-43--6297---2010-10-27-/Gospodin-iz-Efremova14296/

about reading in the provinces of Russia provides one such example.⁷¹ His article 'Kniga v provintsii i ee chitateli' ('Books in Russian Provinces and their Readers') is about the announcement made by the *Federal'noe agenstvo po pechati i massovym kommunikatsiiam* (Federal Agency for Press and Mass Communications) about the adoption of a national programme of reading, but he bases his investigation into what is being read and how it differs from the Soviet period in Elets, Bunin's hometown. An article such as this, or those which mention events commemorating Bunin, serve his canonical status in an interesting way — they reinforce his biography in the mind of the reader, reminding him or her about Bunin: who he was, what he wrote, and his key achievements. In contrast, an article written by Sergei Baimukhametov does little to reinforce Bunin's biography and instead relies upon the reader's knowledge of Bunin and his works to understand the main points raised in the article.⁷² Writing in 2000, Baimukhametov acknowledges the tenth anniversary of the first publication in the Soviet Union of Bunin's *Okaiannye dni* (*Cursed Days*) and uses it to discuss the responsibility that the Russian aristocracy should have taken for the 1917 Revolution.⁷³ Arguably, such an article demonstrates just how strong Bunin's place in literature already is. Baimukhametov relies on readers to understand the reference to Bunin's *Okaiannye dni* in the title of the article 'Ekho okaiannykh stoletii' ('The Echo of Cursed Centuries'), and to see how it relates to the argument he is presenting.⁷⁴ Tat'iana Marchenko's article details the Russian writers nominated for the Nobel Prize between 1914 and 1937, and why, in most cases, they did not win.⁷⁵ The focus of the article is not Bunin, but the Nobel Prize and the Russian nominees prior to World War Two, yet Bunin's victory no doubt provides the impetus for the article and offers the reader interesting details about the selection process for the prize, as well as identifying other Russian writers who could have been the first Russian winner.

---

71 Vladislav Korneichuk, 'Kniga v provintsii i ee chitateli', *Nezavisimaia gazeta* (3 August 2006), http://www.ng.ru/tendenc/2006-08-03/4_kniga.html
72 Sergei Baimukhametov, 'Ekho okaiannykh stoletii', *Literaturnaia gazeta*, 28–29 (12–18 July 2000).
73 Ibid.
74 Ibid.
75 Tat'iana Marchenko, 'Izbranie i ne', *NG Ex Libris* (11 May 2000), http://www.ng.ru/ng_exlibris/2000-05-11/3_nobellius.html

Of those articles that are of interest to the general reader and focus primarily on Bunin and his life or work, that by Sergei Fediakin marks the 130th anniversary of the writer's birth and discusses a selection of reviews of Bunin's work from the 1920s and 1930s.[76] Veronika Chernysheva's article also looks back at the different reactions that Bunin's contemporaries had towards him.[77] In these two articles, the reader is shown that Bunin commented on other writers and their work, and was reviewed himself. Just as others involved in the formation of the canon draw upon the comments of Bunin's contemporaries, so too do journalists, further reinforcing the significance of the poet-based model in shaping and perpetuating a particular canon. Yet, it is interesting to note that both of these articles present a relatively balanced view of Bunin, allowing the reader to choose which of the poets' arguments they would rather follow. In contrast to these articles which draw on comments made by other authors to deliver a particular picture of Bunin, the article 'Buninskie mesta' ('Bunin's Places') details journalist Vasilii Peskov's trip to various villages where Bunin spent his formative years and discusses the efforts that those living in these places are making in order to ensure that Bunin and his connection with these towns is not forgotten.[78] The personal element of recounting a relationship with Bunin and his work also comes through in 'Moi Bunin' ('My Bunin'), which details how Mikhailov's interest in Bunin arose and how this influenced his future research.[79] Mikhailov concludes by saying that he 'always strove to write books about Bunin not as a "dry herbarium" directed at a small group of specialists, but for a wide readership', demonstrating his passion for Bunin's texts and reinforcing the sense that they should be read.[80] Perhaps the more personal element of these stories encourages readers to see Bunin not as inaccessible, as the 'last of the Russian classics', writing about a time far removed from

---

76 Sergei Fediakin, 'Dali Ivana Bunina', *Nezavisimaia gazeta* (24 October 2000), http://www.ng.ru/culture/2000-10-24/7_bunin.html
77 Veronika Chernysheva, 'Nesovremennyi i nesvoevremennyi', *Nezavisimaia gazeta* (12 November 2004), http://www.ng.ru/style/2004-11-12/24_bunin.html
78 Peskov.
79 Oleg Mikhailov, 'Moi Bunin', *Literaturnaia gazeta*, 50 (14 December 2011), http://www.lgz.ru/article/N50--6350---2011-12-14-/Moy-Bunin17885/
80 *Ibid.*, para. 20.

contemporary Russia, but as a writer whose work remains relevant and enjoyable in the twenty-first century.

The discussion of Bunin in newspaper articles suggests that, to a part of society, he has become a relatively well-known figure. However, Bunin is not recognizable only to those who read the paper. In 2008, viewers of the television programme *Imia Rossiia* [sic] (*The Name: Russia*) voted Bunin among the top fifty most notable Russian personalities.[81] From an initial list of 500 names, Bunin scored more than 76,000 votes.[82] However, the question must be asked: does selection from a list of 500 names mean that Bunin is finally established in the canon, or does it mean that his name is simply familiar to people who may or may not be interested in his work? It is possible that films of Bunin's life, such as *Dnevnik ego zheny* (*The Diary of His Wife*) and the documentary *Okaiannye dni. Ivan Bunin* (*Cursed Days. Ivan Bunin*), went some way to raising his profile with screen audiences who later voted in the *Imia Rossiia* [sic] poll.[83] Any commentary that covered the seventy-fifth anniversary of Bunin's Nobel Prize victory might also have reminded viewers of his relevance to the history of Russian literature.

The relative success of Bunin in a televised poll suggests that the activities of the 'Bunin institution', along with the various canon-forming models, to secure him a place in the minds of the public, have been effective. But to what extent can Bunin's place in the canon of post-Soviet Russian poetry be attributed solely to the processes of canon formation discussed in this chapter? Although the institutional model of canon formation appears to hold the widest influence over

---

81 '*Imia Rossiia* [sic]. Istoricheskii vybor 2008', Telekanal 'Rossiia' (2008), http://top50.nameofrussia.ru
82 'Bunin Ivan Alekseevich', Telekanal 'Rossiia' (2008), http://top50.nameofrussia.ru/person.html?id=62; 'Blok Aleksandr Aleksandrovich', Telekanal 'Rossiia' (2008), http://top50.nameofrussia.ru/person.html?id=106; 'Vysotskii Vladimir Semenovich', Telekanal 'Rossiia' (2008), http://top50.nameofrussia.ru/person.html?id=63; 'Esenin Sergei Aleksandrovich', Telekanal 'Rossiia' (2008), http://top50.nameofrussia.ru/person.html?id=68. Blok received 86,991 votes, Vysotskii 429,074, and Esenin 781,042 to achieve places in the top 50. No twentieth-century writers or poets were among the top twelve. Pushkin and Fedor Dostoevskii were the only writers, coming fourth and ninth respectively. See 'Rezul'taty Internet golosovaniia', Telekanal 'Rossiia' (2008), http://www.nameofrussia.ru/rating.html
83 *Dnevnik ego zheny*, dir. by Aleksei Uchitel' (Goskino Rossii, 2000); *Okaiannye dni. Ivan Bunin*, dir. by Aleksei Denisov (Vserossiiskaia gosudarstvennaia televizionnaia i radioveshchatel'naia kompaniia; Studiia istoricheskogo dokumental'nogo kino, 2007), http://russia.tv/brand/show/brand_id/10345

Bunin's place in the canon of post-Soviet Russian poetry, it is clear that the comments made by other poets play a fundamental role in Bunin's canonisation. The function of the Bunin Institution has also changed. In the first instance, it appeared to operate as a means of canonising Bunin, of highlighting him as a poet whose work was worth noting. Over time, this role has evolved into one of maintenance, ensuring that Bunin does not lose his position in the literary hierarchy. In addition, the more the canonisation of Bunin has to do with the events of his life and less to do with the works that he wrote, the more complex the discussions become.[84] It is hard to deny that the various canon-forming models play a significant part in the canonisation of Bunin, yet it seems that other factors are relevant. Was it simply that the time at which Bunin was living and the circumstances of his life make him relatively unique, and thus his inclusion in the canon has been by default rather than by selection? If such an assertion, which ignores his literary output, were true, it would be unlikely that Bunin's works would have retained a place in the canon of twentieth-century Russian poetry. For many, Bunin fills something of a gap at the end of the nineteenth and beginning of the twentieth centuries; he occupies a niche as the unrivalled 'last of the Russian classics'. His refusal to follow the literary trends of his contemporaries sets him apart and this is clearly one of the reasons why he is included in the school textbooks. Furthermore, he has been constructed as a representative of the first wave of the emigration. In the search for reconciliation between 'returned' literature and that written within the Soviet Union, Bunin represents a certain aspect of Russian literary history that post-Soviet academics and critics are trying to renegotiate. The fact that he was sympathetic toward the Soviet cause during World War Two and allegedly considered returning to the Soviet Union may have strengthened his position as the chosen representative

---

84   See Aleksandr Kondrashov 'Gody okaianstva, ili Zagadka N.B.I', *Literaturnaia gazeta*, 33–34 (27 August 2013), para. 13, http://www.lgz.ru/article/-33-34-6427-27-08-2013/gody-okayanstva-ili-zagadka-n-b-i. Kondrashov provides something of a review of the series of programmes about Bunin broadcast by the television channel *Kul'tura*, in which he highlights the points where he disagrees with the way in which Bunin's life is discussed by the narrator of the programme, Natal'ia Borisova Ivanova. For example, in response to Ivanova's suggestion that much fell to Bunin's lot, including the 1905 revolution, World War One, and the events of 1917, Kondrashov argues that 'considerably fewer trials fell to Bunin than to the majority of the Russian people'.

of this first wave of Russian émigré literature. However, in this instance, as Azarov points out 'Bunin is of course considered the "first" Russian émigré writer, but here we could also name a few others who were no less significant to Russian culture: Alexander Kuprin, Dmitrii Merezhkovskii, Boris Zaitsev, Ivan Shmelev...'.[85] Arguably, all of these factors have also contributed to his canonisation. Clearly, the processes of canon formation are complicated and there can be little doubt that other factors have an influence on those responsible for forming the canon, as well as those who perpetuate it. It seems impossible to attribute successful establishment in the canon to just one process, and while the works of the writer are significant, they cannot be considered in isolation from the writer's life and the point in time in which he or she lived, nor indeed, from the lives of those responsible for (re)evaluating literary works included in the canon.

---

85 Azarov, para. 13.

8. From Underground to Mainstream: The Case of Elena Shvarts

Josephine von Zitzewitz

This chapter examines the popularity of Elena Shvarts (1948–2010) in the 1990s and 2000s. Shvarts began her poetic career in the literary underground that flourished in Leningrad in the 1970s and 1980s. Experimentally minded poets, many of whom had made their first steps inside official structures designed to promote the evolution of Soviet poetry, were then largely excluded from the official cultural process.[1] Their creativity found an outlet in the underground, variously known as second or unofficial culture, an alternative structure that grew into an extremely fertile creative environment, and in the practice of *samizdat*. The organisational structures of literature in the underground often closely emulated the official literary process. Periodicals, the most popular form for circulating *samizdat* from the mid-1970s onwards, resembled 'thick' literary journals, down to organisational details such as dedicated section editors and submission procedures.[2]

---

1   Emily Lygo's *Leningrad Poetry 1853–1975: The Thaw Generation* (Berne and New York: Peter Lang, 2010) details the interdependence of the 1970s underground and efforts undertaken by the literary authorities to foster young talent.
2   The 'thick' journals, so called because each issue consisted of several hundred pages, began to appear in the nineteenth century. They were periodicals which appeared several times a year, combining the publication of new works of literature with articles on a range of topics including literature and the arts, social and political questions, and comment on current events.

The Leningrad underground quickly established its own canon of household names. The members of this canon were often also its makers: many of those who performed their work at innumerable semi-private happenings were involved in the editing of the *samizdat* journals in which these works were subsequently published.³

This chapter argues that apart from Shvarts, none of the poets from her circle fully succeeded in making the transition from being a poet of the 1970s who found retrospective recognition but was mostly read and studied for her connection to the underground, to an agent in the literary process of the new Russia. I take 'Shvarts's circle' to mean a group of poets of the Leningrad underground whose style can be defined as neo-modernist. Several features unite them: their understanding of the role of the poet essentially follows the Romantic model, where the poet is an outsider to society with prophetic gifts and poetry is a quasi-spiritual activity. They strove to be recognised as belonging to the classical Russian tradition, which they regarded as part of the European cultural heritage. Their style exhibits many similarities to that of leading Silver Age poets, with whom these representatives of the Leningrad underground were in intense intertextual dialogue. Moreover, the unofficial Leningrad poets formed a tightly-knit group the members of which promoted each other through *samizdat* journals and readings, in allusion to the practice of the Silver Age poets (and indeed that of nineteenth-century Russian writers before them).

In the appendix to this chapter I have collated comparative data for Shvarts and four poets who, aesthetically and institutionally, belonged to the same circles of the Leningrad underground: Viktor Krivulin, Aleksandr Mironov, Oleg Okhapkin and Sergei Stratanovskii. They were established in the underground canon of the 1970s and 1980s, a status that is now confirmed by multiple scholarly works and repeated inclusion in anthologies. Stanislav Savitskii, following Efim Etkind, refers to Shvarts, Stratanovskii, Okhapkin and Krivulin as the

---

3   A full list of Leningrad journals and information about their authors and editors can be found in *Samizdat Leningrada 1950e-1980e. Literaturnaia entsiklopediia*, edited by D. Severiukhin, V. Dolinin, B. Ivanov and B. Ostanin (Moscow: NLO, 2003). Among the names that come up numerous times as both editors and published authors are Dmitrii Volchek (*Mitin Zhurnal, Molchanie*), Arkadii Dragomoshchenko (*Chasy, Mitin Zhurnal, Predlog*), Viktor Krivulin (*37, Servernaia pochta*), Boris Ivanov (*Chasy, Klub-81*), Sergei Stratanovskii (*37, Dialog, Obvodnyi Kanal*), Tatiana Goricheva (*37, Zhenshchina i Rossiia*).

'Leningrad school'.[4] Some published juvenilia notwithstanding, all poets made their debut in the official Soviet and Russian press during the last years of *perestroika* and the early 1990s; as such they were part of the wave of 'lost literature' that reached the general reader with a twenty-year time lag. All these poets continued to write into the 2000s. Krivulin died in 2001, Okhapkin in 2008, Mironov and Shvarts in 2010. Stratanovskii remains active today.

My criteria for defining canonicity in relation to this group of poets are naturally contingent.[5] They are: 1) the number of book-length collections published that do not contain primarily work from the 1970s and 1980s, indicative of the fact that a poet has an established readership eager to read new work and/or that their name is significant enough to draw in new readers, and thus that they are considered a viable investment by a publishing house; 2) the existence of a published collected works; 3) single-author collections published in translation (I have limited my enquiry to translations into English); they indicate that a poet is regarded as representative; foreign editors are unlikely to be interested in publishing translations of work by a minor writer; 4) scholarly interest in both Russia and the English-speaking world — academics play an important role in canon formation because it is they who decide which writers to include in school and university curricula. Shvarts is dominant in all four categories.

The comparative publication data offers scope for empirical analysis as well as speculation. Neither is my main objective for this chapter. Instead, I understand this data as evidence that Shvarts belongs to the canon of the new Russia in a way that her peers do not, and proceed to a discursive exploration of potential reasons for her enduring success.

---

4   Stanislav Savitskii, *Andegraund: Istoriia i mify leningradskoi neofitsial'noi literatury* (Moscow: NLO, 2002), p. 20.

5   Such criteria are always contingent: Per-Arne Bodin in *Language, Canonization and Holy Foolishness* (Stockholm: Stockholm University Press, 2009) justifies his choice of poets for a chapter on 'Contemporary Russian poetry and the Orthodox Tradition' (Shvarts, Ivan Zhdanov, Sergei Stratanovskii, Vsevolod Nekrasov, Dmitrii Prigov, Nina Iskrenko) by defining the canonicity of his authors in the following terms: 'Poets have been selected on the basis of ratings lists: winners of the Andrej Belyj Prize and poets published by the prestigious publishing house *Novoe Literaturnoe obozrenie*. I have also used the website *Vavilon*, which includes a broad spectrum of modern Russian poetry. All of these writers are thus already acknowledged as poets by the Russian public' (p. 283).

As Frank Kermode has pointed out, extra-textual factors play an ever greater role in canon formation.[6] This is reflected in the two-part structure of my discussion: Part One considers qualities that are inherent to Shvarts's poems (without the attempt to make judgements about 'literary quality'), while Part Two focuses on contextual factors.

The defining features of the discourse on Shvarts in the West were established early: Barbara Heldt's article in *World Literature Today*, written in 1989, two years after Shvarts published her first official book-length publication in Russia, a year after she gave her first reading in the main hall of the Leningrad Writers' Union and straight after her first trip abroad to read at a poetry festival in London, praised Shvarts's poetry as 'highly original' and positively ignorant of the rules of patriarchal culture.[7] Nine years later Shvarts was included in Neil Cornwell's seminal *Reference Guide to Russian Literature* (1998), a fact that proves she had attracted a significant amount of attention from Western scholars by this point. Michael Molnar, the author of her entry, identified Shvarts as originating in the 'second culture' of Leningrad but calls her one of the 'leading poets of the post-war generation', indicating that her relevance is not limited to and by her immediate socio-political surroundings.[8]

Part One: Textual Criteria

Shvarts and the Poetic Tradition

A juxtaposition of texts written by Shvarts in different decades reveals no significant changes in either voice or subject matter. Such continuity of style and vision was possibly a result of the fact that Shvarts's work was never defined by her situation as an underground poet. The underground does not feature explicitly in her texts, neither as subject nor backdrop, as it does, for example, in Viktor Krivulin's poems of the

---

6   Frank Kermode, *Pleasure and Change: The Aesthetics of Canon* (New York and Oxford: Oxford University Press, 2004). See p. 15 ff. for how the focus of academics has been shifting away from purely literary factors.
7   Barbara Heldt, 'The Poetry of Elena Shvarts', *World Literature Today*, 63: 3 (1989), 381–83 (p. 381).
8   Michael Molnar, 'Elena Shvarts', in *Reference Guide to Russian Literature*, edited by Neil Cornwell (London and Chicago: Fitzroy Dearborn Publishers, 1998), pp. 737–38.

1970s. She also largely dispenses with hidden references that require a reader initiated into the same cultural context. Her unchanging voice means she could seamlessly build on the reputation she had established with her early work, a factor that was almost certainly conducive to her increasing fame. In her post-Soviet collections, new work sits alongside poems written significantly earlier. To give an example, the volume *Zapadno-vostochnyi veter* (*West-Easterly Wind*, 1997), which brings together several shorter collections, consists almost entirely of works written in 1996, but also features some poems from the early 1980s, 'Probuzhdenie' ('Awakening', 1983), 'Na progulke' ('On a Walk', 1981), and the previously published cycle 'Vozdushnoe Evangelie' ('Air Gospel', 1982). Were it not for the dates given, the reader would not notice that he is dealing with poems written in different decades and different political systems.

Shvarts always has been an openly spiritual poet, defining poetry as 'a way of reaching the non-material (spiritual) by semi-material means'.[9] The setting in which she pursued her spiritual quest was her native city of Leningrad-Petersburg. Like other poets of her generation, such as Iosif Brodskii and Krivulin, she preferred the outskirts of the city to the grand imperial facades, but her predilection for marginal spaces was not limited to geographical settings; she also favoured the outskirts of society over a well-ordered world. Often, she found transcendence in the dirt beneath her feet, and in scenes of violence and debauchery, as in 'Kak eta ulitsa zovetsia' ('What this Street is Called', 1982):

> Ты ломок, тонок, ты крошишься фарфоровою чашкой, в ней
> Просвечивает Бог, наверно. Мне это все видней, видней.
> Он скорлупу твою земную проклевывает на глазах, […]
> Играя вниз,
> С «Славянкой» падает с обрыва
> мой Парадиз.[10]

I, p. 135

---

9 'A Poetics of What is Alive' ('Poetika zhivogo', 1996), in Elena Shvarts, *Sochineniia*, 5 vols. (St Petersburg: Pushkinskii dom, 2002–2008), IV, 272–75 (p. 274). All references to Shvarts's works are to this edition and will be given by volume and page number, where appropriate directly after the quotation unless otherwise stated.

10 Shvarts's insistence on finding vestiges of sacredness is shared by many contemporaries, most famously Venedikt Erofeev in his *Moskva-Petushki* (1973).

You are fragile and dainty, you crumble like a porcelain cup; God shines
through, probably. I see this more and more clearly.
He is pecking through your mortal shell for all to see, [...]
off the precipice it falls, playing the 'Slavianka',
my Paradise.

The same preferences characterise her post-Soviet work:

[...] волки следят за мерцаньем игры
Звёзд, выплывающих снизу, глубокие видят миры. [...]
Если это звезда, то её исказила слеза.
В ней одной есть спасенье, на неё и смотри,
Пока Крест, расширяясь, раздирает тебя изнутри.

'Bol'shaia elegiia na piatuiu storonu sveta'
('Great Elegy on the Fifth Side of the Light')
(1997), I, p. 270.

Wolves observe the twinkle in the game
of stars appearing from below, they see profound worlds. [...]
If this is a star, it has been distorted by a tear.
It alone holds salvation, so look at it
while the widening Cross tears you up from within.

Shvarts is commonly identified as a Petersburg poet, a writer whose texts are steeped in allusions to other texts and who is drawing on two centuries of location-specific literary tradition, both during her underground career and after.[11] One key to the Petersburg myth according to Shvarts is the five-poem cycle *Chernaia Paskha* (*Black Easter*, 1974). It exemplifies how Shvarts uses literary tradition in order to create a complex web of associations for her own images.[12] The result is a highly individual, idiosyncratic representation of the city and its literary myth,

---

11   For example by editor and translator Michael Molnar in his foreword to the bilingual volume *Paradise* (Newcastle upon Tyne: Bloodaxe, 1993), pp. 9–10.
12   For a detailed account of the Petersburg myth see Solomon Volkov's *St. Petersburg: A Cultural History*, translated by Antonina W. Bouis (London: Sinclair-Stevenson, 1996).

although the shadow of Dostoevskii looms large. Just as Dostoevskii's city, Shvarts's Petersburg alienates individuals from both nature and from each other, engendering illness and madness though the resulting duality within the person and society. The cycle, which contains few explicitly religious references apart from its title, establishes Shvarts's vision of Petersburg as a site for spiritual quest by making explicit the 'permeability' of her native city. At the same time, her religious vision is revealed as profoundly pessimistic: none of her attempts to touch upon that which lies beyond the material world is successful; transcendence remains forever outside the poet's reach. This is particularly evident in the second poem of the cycle:

2. Где мы?

[…] Я думала — не я одна,–
Что Петербург, нам родина — особая страна,
Он — запад, вброшенный в восток,
И окружен, и одинок,
Чахоточный, всё простужался он,
И в нем процентщицу убил Наполеон.
Но рухнула духовная стена — Россия хлынула — дурна, темна, пьяна.
Где ж родина? И поняла я вдруг:
Давно Россиею затоплен Петербург.
И сдернули заемный твой парик,
И все увидели, что ты–
Все тот же царственный мужик,
И так же дергается лик,
В руке топор,
Расстегнута ширинка…
Останови же в зеркале свой взор
И ложной красоты смахни же паутинку
О Парадиз! […]
В тебе тамбовский ветер матерится,
И окает, и цокает Нева.

II, p. 10

> Where are We?
>
> I thought — and I am not alone, —
> that Petersburg, our motherland, was a special country,
> It is the West, thrown into the East,
> encircled and all alone,
> Consumptive, with a perennial cold
> And the site where Napoleon murdered the pawnbroker.
> But the spiritual wall has collapsed
> And Russia gushed in, evil, dark and drunk.
> Where is my motherland? And then I got it:
> Russia flooded Petersburg long ago.
> And tore away your borrowed wig, for all to see that you
> have remained that very same regal peasant
> same facial tic
> axe in hand
> your fly undone…
> Stop, rest your gaze in the mirror
> wipe away the web of false beauty
> Oh Paradise! […]
> The wind from Tambov curses inside you
> And the Neva burrs and gurgles.

Shvarts names the city, but the reader would recognise it anyway from the breathtaking array of references: the city features as Peter the Great's 'Paradise' and the capital conceived as a window to the West; we are familiar with the scourge of tuberculosis in the damp, cold climate from countless nineteenth-century literary texts, including Dostoevskii's *Crime and Punishment* (Sonia Marmeladova's stepmother is consumptive). The reference to *Crime and Punishment* thus reinforces the central theme of fatal 'duality', embodied in Dostoevskii's novel by the protagonist, Raskol'nikov, whose very name implies schism. Finally there is the Neva, a landmark well established as shorthand for Petersburg. More pertinently, in the context of a destructive, even apocalyptic, flood the Neva invokes Pushkin's *Bronze Horseman*, the foundation text of the Petersburg myth, which forever linked the image of the city to catastrophe and the destruction of the individual.

Most Petersburg references in the poem cited above hinge on the figure of Peter the Great who, as the 'regal peasant', a Russian emperor irresistibly drawn to the West, embodies the duality that is intrinsic to the city and makes it susceptible to the incursion of elements that do not belong to the realm of the rational. The refined, Western features that Peter and his city are proudly parading are vulnerable to the onslaught of forces beyond Peter's control. His own 'borrowed wig' is torn off to reveal an uncouth Russian peasant who, wielding an axe, once again invokes Dostoevskii's Raskol'nikov, who committed murder after persuading himself he was a Napoleon, a man standing above the law of morality. Ominous foreboding is a trait of many Petersburg texts. In Shvarts's poem, however, the catastrophe has already happened. Russia has flooded Petersburg, the site that epitomises alien, Western, influence. 'Russia' represents more than the accumulation of unsavoury national stereotypes as displayed by the violent peasant with his fly unbuttoned. It is an external force, an amorphous flood, breaking down and submerging the cultural values that constitute the city's 'spiritual wall'. These values are Western in essence, and literary culture is foremost among them, as the web of literary associations in this poem demonstrates. By presenting culture as a *spiritual* bulwark, now breached ('the spiritual wall collapsed'), Shvarts forges an inseparable connection between culture and spirituality, in effect identifying the two. Culture as an entry point into, or even replacement for, lost spiritual values is a trait that links Shvarts firmly to her contemporaries.[13]

The Petersburg Shvarts presents to her readers is as much a spiritual landscape as an actual geographical site. The map to this spiritual landscape is contained in the cycle's title. The collocation *Chernaia Paskha* (*Black Easter*) is a contradiction in terms. Easter, the feast which in the Christian tradition commemorates the resurrection of Jesus from

---

13 For statements to this effect see, for example, Viktor Krivulin, 'Peterburgskaia spiritual'naia lirika vchera i segodnia', in *Istoriia leningradskoi nepodtsensurnoi literatury*, edited by B. Ivanov and B. Roginskii (SPb: DEAN, 2000), pp. 99–110; Ol'ga Sedakova, 'Muzyka glukhogo vremeni', *Vestnik novoi literatury*, 2 (1990), 257–63; 'A Dialogue on Poetry: Olga Sedakova and Slava Yastremski', in *Poems and Elegies*, edited by Slava I. Yastremski (Lewisburg: Bucknell University Press, 2003), pp. 11–20.

the dead, is associated with the colour white, symbolising hope. In the northern hemisphere, Easter coincides with spring, the season in which nature renews itself. Shvarts negates this message when she paints her Easter entirely in black.[14] Her Petersburg has become the site that resists the resurrection, a site where the all-encompassing pain of crucifixion, of Good Friday, reigns supreme ('Мы ведь–где мы?–в России, / Где от боли чернеют кусты' ('Where are we after all? In Russia / where the shrubs blacken with pain'), 'Where are We?'). Blackness is woven into every lyric of the cycle, with the fifth and final poem ending on the ultimate triumph of death over life. There, the poet encounters Life and Death in the guise of two old women but fails to tell one from the other. Consequently, her Petersburg remains confined to its mortally wounded (collapsed, submerged) present state, without hope of transformation. Literary culture, its greatest hope, is doomed, too, as it is no longer a 'spiritual wall', a stepping stone towards transcendence. In a final pessimistic note, Shvarts presents the literary word, 'Slovo', spelled with a capital S to recall its original kinship with the Logos, the creative Word of God, as powerless: 'Бумагу Слово не прожжет, / Но поджелтит края' ('The Word can't burn through the page / it merely singes the edges').[15] The literary word fails to transform the world of which it is a part, remaining firmly bound to its material realm, the page, rather than transforming the page into flame.

The cycle *Portret Blokady cherez zhanr, natiurmort i peizazh* (*A Portrait of the Blockade through a Genre Painting, a Still Life and a Landscape*) was written twenty-five years later, in 1999, yet exhibits a number of striking similarities. The most obvious is the setting of Leningrad/Petersburg, once again presented as both a geographical and a spiritual landscape. *Portret Blokady* too, is a work in which Good Friday fails to give way to Easter, negating any hope for transformation.

---

14 A similar negation of spring and new life can be found in Innokentii Annenskii's short poem 'Chernaia vesna' ('Black Spring') (1906), in *Stikhotvoreniia i tragedii* (Leningrad: Sovetskii pisatel', 1990), p. 131.
15 'Obychnaia oshibka' ('An Ordinary Mistake'), vol. II, p. 83.

8. From Underground to Mainstream: The Case of Elena Shvarts

3. Смещенный пейзаж. Лестница, двор, церковь.
(бумага, уголь, воронья кровь)

За этой сырой синей краской — желтая, за ней зеленая,
До пустоты не скреби, не надо,
Там штукатурка и испарения ада.
На, жри, картофельный розовый цвет.
Больше у тебя ничего нет, кость моя, блокада! [...]
А во дворе человека зарезали без ножа
Запросто просто.
Из раны, дымясь, вытекал голос.
Он пел о горчичном зерне и крошечке хлеба,
О душе крови.
Под слабым северным сияньем
Желваками ходило небо.
Блокада жрала
Душу, как волк свою лапу в капкане...

Великая пятница. Пустая голодная церковь.
У дьякона высох голос, он почти неживой,
Тени гулко выносят плащаницу–
Священник раскачивает головой:
'О, теперь я прозрел, я понял–
Ты очнулся от смерти больной,
Тебе не поправиться, погибель всем вам'.
Кровь моя стала льдяным вином,
Уробор прокусил свой хвост.
Зубы разбросаны в небе
Вместо жестоких звезд.

Misaligned Landscape. Stairs, Yard, Church.
(Paper, Coal, Raven's Blood)

Behind this wet blue paint comes yellow and then green
Don't scrape down to the void, really don't
There you find plaster and hell fumes.

> There, eat, the colour pink, like potatoes.
> That's all you have, my bones, the blockade! […]
> In the court yard they stabbed a man without using a knife
> All too easy.
> His voice flowed from the steaming wound.
> He sang about the mustard seed and a crumb of bread,
> About the soul of blood.
> Under the pale Northern light
> The sky is grinding like a set of jaws
> The Blockade devoured
> The Soul, like a trapped wolf chewing his own paw…
>
> Good Friday. An empty, hungry church.
> The deacon's voice has dried up, he is hardly alive,
> Shadows are bearing the shroud of Christ —
> The priest shakes his head:
> 'Oh now I see, I understand —
> You woke up from death as a sick man,
> You won't get better, you are all doomed'.
> My blood turned into icy wine,
> The ouroboros bit through his tail
> Teeth are scattered in the sky
> In place of the merciless stars.

As in *Chernaia Paskha*, Leningrad is evoked in *Portret Blokady* through references, in this case the Blockade of the winter of 1941 (the Blockade lasted from 8 September 1941 to 1927 January 1944). And once again, the city is described as permeable to outside forces, inexplicable and sinister ('There you find plaster and hell fumes'). The poem depicts a post-apocalyptic landscape in which the violence of the Blockade has annihilated respect for human life — the basis of all culture — as well as culture itself. In the first poem a crowd indulges in an act of cannibalism — something that happened during the Blockade but had been a taboo subject during the Soviet period. In the second poem somebody boils a pet cat for food. In this third and last scene we witness the gratuitous stabbing of an innocent man whose final song, replete with references to Gospel teachings, links him to the figure of Jesus. The identification of culture, in a broad sense, and spirituality is central to this cycle, and the explicitly Christian imagery of the final lyric lends it a poignant religious gravity.

Images related to 'devouring' permeate the entire cycle: humanity is being devoured, literally, when people attempt to still their hunger with a fellow human being's flesh, culture is devoured when the frescoes of a church are scraped off so that the starving person can eat the paint (yet another literalised metaphor); finally even heaven succumbs to hunger when it turns into a giant set of jaws, with teeth taking the place of the stars. But the pivotal image is 'The blockade devoured the Soul'. It fulfils a similar function to the collapsed spiritual wall we saw in *Chernaia Paskha*, marking an apocalyptic event. The Blockade — an event particular to Leningrad — has devoured the human soul, and the consequences are more catastrophic than the Blockade itself. While Leningrad remains mired in the stern Blockade winter, with no hope of spring, its spiritual expanse is locked in the pain and death that is Good Friday. Once the soul is dead, Easter and resurrection become impossible. *Portret Blokady* ends on an eerie Good Friday celebration in an anthropomorphised, *hungry*, church. A clergyman diagnoses Christ's resurrection as failed, foreboding the death of all humanity. The Easter message, which promises fullness of life to those who believe in the risen Christ, is thus once again turned on its head.

Chernaia Paskha and *Portret Blokady* are Petersburg poems that broaden the traditional association of the city with apocalypse and destruction to include a sense of desolation that is explicitly spiritual. Concerns that are contemporary and/or the poet's own, above all the fascination with madness and violence, are given weight by the vicinity of tradition. This weaving together of the traditional and the topical, the highbrow and the vulgar, and the old and the new, is a typical feature of Shvarts's poetic vision, on the level of imagery as well as poetic technique. Shvarts's trademark style, exemplified in the examples above, comes close to the type of versification known as 'raeshnyi stikh' used in folk theatre, in which lines carrying varying numbers of stresses are brought into formal cohesion through strong and memorable rhymes at the end of each phrase. The dazzling variety and vitality of her rhythmic features she explains with her dream 'to find a rhythm that would change with every change in my train of thought, with every new emotion or sensation'.¹⁶ In combination with her characteristic imagery, this technical device makes her voice instantly recognisable; however, the idea of rhythm mirroring thought was suggested by Osip Mandel'shtam in 1933.¹⁷ Rhyme used as the glue for rhythmically diverse poems was a common occurrence in futurist poetry.¹⁸ Her versification thus exhibits the same combination of eccentric individuality and reassuring gestures towards her literary predecessors that characterises her lexicon and choice of subject matter.

In fact Shvarts, an outspoken adversary of free verse, which she vilified as 'an abattoir — bad prose'¹⁹ richly orchestrated her poetry, using the devices of cycle, stanza, line, rhyme and rhythm in a traditional manner. We can thus read her poetry successfully with the help of the usual hermeneutic tools honed by reading Russian poetry of the nineteenth and twentieth centuries. This makes her work instantly accessible, giving her a definitive advantage over more experimentally minded peers such as Arkadii Dragomoshchenko, whose experiments with free verse have few, if any, predecessors in Russian poetry, or the notoriously opaque octaves of Mikhail Eremin.

Shvarts's multilayered references to Russian and European predecessors will earn her the appreciation of the discerning, erudite poetry lover who is able to decode them. The provocative power of her images, capable of shocking the reader, and perhaps specifically created in order to shock, can make us momentarily forget that these images nevertheless remain poetic images in the classical sense. As such they stand for themselves, remaining accessible even when their resonance with the Russian tradition is lost. Shvarts's reliance on images rather than subtle variations of language alone also minimises translation loss, making her an attractive candidate for publication in a foreign language.

---

16   'A Poetics of What is Alive', p. 275.
17   'The internal image of a poem is inseparable from the countless changes of expression that flicker across the narrator's face when he speaks and is agitated'. Osip Mandel'shtam, 'Razgovor o Dante' (1933), *Sochineniia*, 2 vols. (Moscow: Khudozhestvennaia literatura, 1990), II, 214–54 (p. 216).
18   Maiakovskii heightened this effect by setting out his poems as 'stepladders', forcing the reader to pause in certain places.
19   'A Poetics of What is Alive', p. 275. Also in 'Interv'iu s Elenoi Shvarts (1990)', in *Iosif Brodskii glazami sovremennikov. Kniga pervaia (1987–1992)*, edited by Valentina Polukhina (St Petersburg: Zvezda, 2006), pp. 226–46 (p. 229).

It seems that Shvarts has managed to position herself at the advantageous crossroads of tradition and innovation, as if following the advice of Aristotle, according to whom the perfect poetic style combines rare and commonplace words.[20] It seems thus appropriate to conclude that Shvarts's choice of subject matter, lexicon and style, in combination with the fact that her voice did not undergo major changes and was already mature and recognisable by the time the Soviet Union collapsed, were vital factors contributing to her post-Soviet fame.

Part Two. Contextual Criteria: Three Keys to Shvarts's Work

Having established the general picture, I will use the remainder of this chapter to delineate three specific areas of Shvarts's work and life that may afford us further insight into why she was privileged over her peers when it came to entering the post-Soviet canon. These areas are the use of her underground credentials, gender and its reflection on her work, and her extra-literary persona.

Shvarts as an Underground Poet

Literature in nineteenth- and twentieth-century Russia was more than just literature. The radical intelligentsia of the nineteenth century looked to writers for moral leadership; literature thus became a platform for political and ethical debate.[21] The Bolsheviks followed in this tradition when they attempted to utilise literature as a tool for forging the new Soviet man.[22]

---

20 'A diction that is made up of strange (or rare) terms is a jargon. A certain infusion, therefore, of these elements is necessary to style; for the strange (or rare) word, the metaphorical, the ornamental, and the other kinds above mentioned, will raise it above the commonplace and mean, while the use of proper words will make it perspicuous'. Aristotle, *Poetics*, chapter XXII, http://classics.mit.edu/Aristotle/poetics.3.3.html

21 These views are summarised by Vissarion Belinskii in his 'Letter to N. V. Gogol'' (1847), in N. V. Gogol', *Polnoe sobranie sochinenii*, 14 vols. (Moscow and Leningrad: Izdatel'stvo AN SSSR, 1937–1952), XIV, pp. 500–10.

22 Compare the statement that 'writers are engineers of the human soul', popularized by and attributed to Stalin, who used it in 1932 at a meeting with Soviet writers. In fact he was quoting the novelist Iurii Olesha. See http://dic.academic.ru/dic.nsf/dic_wingwords/1087/Инженеры

This concept of literature invests the written word with an enormous degree of power, and explains why different authorities, and the Soviet regime in particular, operated a tight censorship regime. As Svetlana Boym has observed, the quasi-religious cult of the poet as voice of truth thrives on political oppression.[23] In this sense, the underground poet is the quintessential Russian poet, a Romantic outsider who is persecuted by the state for the sake of the 'truth' he or she has to tell. Underground culture added a further notion to this myth, namely that of the (underground) writer as the preserver of authentic literary culture in an age that was doing everything to stifle this culture with a barrage of tendentious and formulaic prescriptions.[24] It is precisely this commitment to literary authenticity (cynics might point out that it is a cliché, and one that has been peddled relentlessly by the underground poets themselves) that now, more than thirty years later, makes the underground so attractive as a topic of research, both in the West and, increasingly, in Russia itself. For the first ten years after the fall of the Soviet Union it was researched predominantly as a sociocultural phenomenon, and most of those who wrote about it were former underground writers themselves.[25] This has changed now. Primary sources are readily available, and enough research has been carried out to enable a new generation of scholars to examine the poetry written by

---

23 Svetlana Boym, *Death in Quotation Marks: Cultural Myths of the Modern Poet* (Cambridge, MA and London: Harvard University Press, 1991), p. 120.

24 In their theoretical and critical writings many underground writers made conscious use of this stance. Relevant examples, published in *samizdat*, are Boris Ivanov, 'Kul'turnoe dvizhenie kak tselostnoe iavlenie', 37, 19 (1979); 'K materialam 2-oi konferentsii kul'turnogo dvizheniia', *Chasy*, 24 (1980), 256–78 and A. Kalomirov (a pseudonym of Viktor Krivulin), 'Dvadtsat' let noveishei russkoi poezii', *Severnaia pochta*, 1: 2 (1979). After the fall of the Soviet Union, the same people developed this direction of research: V. Krivulin, 'U istochnikov nezavisimoi kul'tury', Zvezda, 1 (1990), 184–88; 'Peterburgskaia spiritual'naia lirika vchera i segodnia', in *Istoriia leningradskoi nepodtsenzurnoi literatury* edited by Boris Ivanov and Boris Roginskii (St Petersburg: DEAN, 2000), pp. 99–110; B. Ivanov, 'Evoliutsiia literaturnykh dvizhenii v piatidesiatye-vos'midesiatye gody', in *Istoriia leningradskoi nepodtsensurnoi literaratury*, pp. 17–28.

25 As is evident from one of the first collections devoted to this topic: *Samizdat. Po materialam konferentsii '30 let nezavisimoi pechati. 1950–80 gody'* (St Petersburg: NITs 'Memorial', 1993).

underground writers as an integral part of the evolution of twentieth-century poetry.²⁶

Her provenance from the underground lends Shvarts's poetry a certain amount of credibility by default. She is a 'serious', 'true' poet who has suffered for her 'truth' by being deprived of a broad readership for twenty years. She is also part of the 'underground mainstream', with both her texts and her lifestyle following certain established models. At the same time, she exhibits the same obsession with literary culture, expressing itself in highly complex imagery and a proclivity for intertext and citation that Mikhail Epshtein identified as the trademark sign of one of the major currents of Russian postmodernism ('metarealism').²⁷

However, Soviet underground poetry is notoriously opaque and inaccessible to Russian readers of post-Soviet generations (let alone Westerners) who lack the requisite referential framework. I have argued that one of the factors that makes Shvarts a supremely accessible poet is her independence from the underground paradigm as subject matter. Her quasi-religious vision of poetry did not depend, as did that of Krivulin, for example, on the late Soviet context as a setting in which persecuted poets could be likened to the early Christians hounded by the Romans; nor was her lyrical 'I' the quintessential 'underground man/poet' who features so prominently in the work of Krivulin. This fact, in conjunction with Shvarts's otherwise impeccable underground credentials, makes her a convenient deputy figure, capable of standing in for the entire underground in the eyes of readers and non-specialist scholars.

The Perspective of Women's Studies

Shvarts's gender provides us with an additional angle from which to approach her work, namely that of women's studies, and it is this angle that has shaped Western scholarship of Shvarts from the beginning.

---

26 These scholars include Marco Sabbatini (Italy), Stephanie Sandler (US), Emily Lygo (UK), Iuliia Valieva (Russia), Aleksandr Skidan (Russia), Stanislav Savitskii (Russia).

27 Mikhail Epshtein, *Postmodern v russkoi literature* (Moscow: Vysshaia shkola, 2005), p. 127 ff. For a recent study of the phenomenon see A. A. Zhitenev, *Poeziia neomodernizma* (St Petersburg: Inapress, 2012).

Shvarts has found entry in several anthologies — scholarly as well as poetic — that are specifically dedicated to female Russian writers.[28] Anthologisation is an important step towards canonicity: it signifies that a writer is considered exemplary enough to be included in a representative sample. Poetry anthologies are read by more people than individual collections; this is likely to be even more significant in the case of foreign poets. In picking up an anthology, the reader implicitly accepts the editor's choice of material.

Shvarts's gender-specific poems are a magnet for academics: she grapples with the persona of the female poet. The author of the first significant article on Shvarts in English, Barbara Heldt, identified Shvarts's poetry as feminine in a way that defies the patriarchal order and mocks the tradition of the woman poet, especially in attitudes towards her body.[29] Shvarts introduces this thematic field with imagery that seems highly topical from a feminist point of view, centring as it does on violence, often of a sexual nature. A prime example is the cycle 'Grubymi sredstvami ne dostich' blazhenstva' ('You Won't Reach Bliss by Rough Means'), with its subtitle 'Horror eroticus', which presents male sexuality as inherently demonic and violent:

> Верно, хочется тебе
> Деву разломать, как жареную курицу,
> Как спелый красный апельсин,
> И разорвать, и разодрать,
> И соком смерти напитать
> До самых жизни до глубин.
> Разве ты виноват?
>
> II, p. 90

---

28 Academic anthologies in English that mention Shvarts include: Catriona Kelly, *A History of Russian Women's Writing, 1820–1992* (Oxford: Oxford University Press, 1994) and *A History of Women's Writing in Russia*, edited by Adele Barker and Jehanne Gheith (Cambridge, UK: Cambridge University Press, 2002). A comprehensive literary anthology is *An Anthology of Contemporary Russian Women Poets*, edited by Valentina Polukhina and Daniel Weissbort (Iowa City: University of Iowa Press, 2005). N.B., though, footnote 491: the first time Shvarts was 'canonised' in any context was her inclusion in *Contemporary Russian Poetry: A Bilingual Anthology*, edited by G. S. Smith (Bloomington: Indiana University Press 1993), 246–57.

29 Heldt, 'The Poetry of Elena Shvarts', pp. 381–83.

8. From Underground to Mainstream: The Case of Elena Shvarts 243

> True, you want
> to break the girl open like a fried chicken,
> like a ripe red orange,
> tear her to pieces, split her
> and soak her with the juice of death
> down to the deep recesses of life.
> Is that really your fault?

This is not merely an example of *chernukha*, the preoccupation with the dark aspects of life that features prominently in the work of women writers such as Liudmila Petrushevskaia who gained prominence in the later 1980s and 1990s. The all-encompassing, grossly exaggerated violence of these lines borders on the vision of a madwoman; it is plausible that the aim of these lines is neither a description of actual circumstances, nor, in fact, gender politics. Instead, the poet delights in challenging taboos, a feature pioneered by Shvarts's heroine Marina Tsvetaeva.[30] On the other hand the demonisation of male sexuality, which is presented here as exclusively driven by subconscious urges aiming at the violation and subjugation of the female, alongside a proliferation of phallic imagery ('Против воли–тупое жало / Вздымается из брюха кинжалом / И несет томительную смерть' (Against your will the blunt sting / rises from your belly, dagger-like / bringing agonising death)) evoke the theories of Sigmund Freud. While psychoanalysis was no longer a new or unchallenged approach either in the 1970s or in the 1990s, it might have had a greater impact on Soviet/Russian readers, to whom this discourse had not been readily available for a long time. Popular in the experimental early 1920s, psychoanalysis was discredited after Lenin's death and denounced in 1929; Freud's works were not published after 1925.[31]

A scene that is more emphatically centred on domestic violence can be found in 'Where are We?', the second poem of *Chernaia Paskha*, already discussed above:

---

30 The adolescent Shvarts adored Tsvetaeva, stating that she wished to be like her: 'Diaries' ['Dnevniki'], Sochineniia vol. V, p. 346. The adult Shvarts hailed Tsvetaeva as the most technically accomplished poet in the Russian language (Polukhina, 'Interv'iu s Elenoi Shvarts', p. 233).

31 For details see Martin Miller, *Freud and the Bolsheviks: Psychoanalysis in Imperial Russia and the Soviet Union* (New Haven: Yale University Press, 1998).

> Вот пьяный муж
> Булыжником ввалился [...]
> Он весь как божия гроза;
> «Где ты была? С кем ты пила? [...]»
> И кулаком промежду глаз
> Как жахнет.
> И льется кровь, и льются слезы.

II, p. 78

> My drunk husband
> barges in like a rock [...]
> and thunders like the wrath of God:
> 'Where have you been? With whom have you been drinking? [...]'
> And his fists lands between
> my eyes.
> Blood flows, and so do tears.

This scene doubtlessly constitutes an instance of *chernukha*. Yet again we have to concede that the depiction of circumstance is not the poet's main or sole aim. As we have already seen, the cycle of which this scene forms part provides concentric circles of broader context. The inner circles of context are national or religious, owing to the setting and the Easter theme given in the title. All these associations are encompassed by the widest contextual circles, which is literature: *Chernaia Paskha* is a modern-day Petersburg text that ingeniously develops the traditional notions of the genre, received through the work of Dostoevskii, Gogol' and others — and the question of the power and/or impotence of literary culture in late twentieth-century Russia.

Everyday life is rarely the focus of Shvarts's gender-specific poems. Some of them are downright otherworldly (for example 'Vospominanie o strannom ugoshchenii' ('Memory of a Strange Treat', I, p. 54), in which the heroine tastes a friend's breast milk). Her woman poet is a mutable heroine who usually appears in the guise of a first-person lyrical 'I'. Well-known poems that employ this device include 'Tantsuiushchii David' ('Dancing David', I, p. 79), 'Elegiia na rentgenovskii snimok moego cherepa' ('Elegy on an X-Ray of my Skull', I, p. 28) and many others. This first-person narrator tempts us to read the texts as autobiography.

Yet we learn close to nothing about Shvarts from her poems; in this she sharply differs from her Silver Age predecessors Akhmatova and Tsvetaeva, who displayed a similar narcissistic fixation on the persona of themselves-as-poet, but supplied plenty of (carefully edited) personal detail.[32] I will use Akhmatova and Tsvetaeva as points of comparison for the following discussion, perhaps unfairly prioritising these most famous among women poets and forfeiting the opportunity for a more nuanced analysis of Shvarts's female poetic lineage. Yet there are good reasons for choosing these two figures — their rank among Russia's main poets of the twentieth century is undisputed, they were unabashedly feminine voices who refused to be belittled as *poetessa*, and last but not least Shvarts had strong opinions on both of them (see notes 667 and 688)[33].

Given the predominance of men in the poetic canon, readers are more used to looking at the world, and at women (especially women-as-objects) through the eyes of a male poet, but Shvarts, just as Akhmatova and Tsvetaeva had done before her, inverted the gendered perspective, instead evoking a world seen through the eyes of the gifted female. This is particularly evident in her bold re-imagining of poetic inspiration in 'Ia rodilas' s ladon'iu gladkoi' ('I was Born with an Unlined Hand', I, p. 110), where the female poet replaces the male poet's muse by the grammatically and behaviourally masculine 'Fatum', who tries to inscribe her virgin hands with a challenging fate, and with poetry. This poem exhibits clear parallels with Tsvetaeva's long poem 'Na krasnom kone' ('On a Red Steed', 1921), where the gentle muse takes the guise of a fierce knight who demands of the poet self-sacrifice and submission to the poetic calling.[34] A less well-known version of the male muse we find in Anna Radlova's 'Angel pesnopeniia' ('Angel of Song', 1922).[35]

Some of Shvarts's first-person narrators are elaborately crafted fictional alter egos, with their own history, in whose names Shvarts

---

32 Examples that can be traced back to events in the respective poet's life include Akhmatova's 'Rekviem' (on her son's arrest and Gulag sentence) and Tsvetaeva's cycles of love poetry, e.g. 'Georgii' (to her husband Sergei Efron), 'Poema kontsa' ('Poem of the End') (to her lover, Konstantin Rodzevich), and 'Provoda' ('Wires') (to Boris Pasternak).
33 Shvarts, 'Diaries', p. 346.
34 Marina Tsvetaeva, *Stikhotvoreniia i poemy* (Moscow: Ripol Klassik, 2002), pp. 621–25.
35 Anna Radlova, *Bogoroditsyn korabl', krylatyi gost', povest' o Tatarinovoi* (Moscow: 'Its-Garant', 1997), pp. 83–84.

produced entire collections.³⁶ One of them is 'Kinfiia', purportedly a first-century Roman poetess whose 'poems did not survive, nevertheless I shall try to translate them into Russian' (II, p. 5) and who shocks her readers with a graphic description of imaginary patricide in poem two of the cycle. A similarly colourful alter ego is Lavinia, heroine of Shvarts's most important religious work, the cycle *Trudy i dni Lavinii, monakhini iz ordena obrezaniia serdtsa. Ot Rozhdestva do Paskhi* (*The Works and Days of Lavinia, a Nun in the Order of the Circumcision of the Heart: From Christmas to Easter*, 1984). Lavinia is a nun, and as the purported author of the cycle, she is by definition also a poet. The cycle is presented, in best Romantic manner, as a 'found manuscript': it is preceded by a letter from a fictitious editor and a lyric by Lavinia's fictitious sister, explaining how this cycle came into being. *Trudy i dni Lavinii* includes elements of biblical motifs that Shvarts adapted to create a birth myth of the female poet. In 'Temnaia rozhdestvenskaia pesn'' ('A Dark Christmas Song' (poem eleven, II, p. 174)), a child is born in the desert. Yet this child is not Jesus Christ, born of the Virgin Mary, but Mary herself, who then, curiously, joins Venus, Roman goddess of love, in the Christian heaven. 'Leviafan' ('Leviathan' (poem thirteen, II, p. 176)) is an adaptation of the story of Jonah and the whale (Jonah 1–2). The Leviathan, a (grammatically) masculine figure, invites the heroine to 'enter my womb'. He swallows her and she rather enjoys the ride in his belly until the monster goes into labour and expels her in a fountain of blood. In the Old Testament, the expulsion from the belly of the whale marks the beginning of Jonah's path as a prophet. Shvarts is harnessing this notion for her heroine Lavinia: the whale is thus giving birth to the woman poet, her birth marking her as special.

Lavinia's tremendous energy and prophetic gift are inspired by an irrational source; she exhibits traits of the Holy Fool, driven out of the convent by her fellow nuns because of her erratic behaviour: 'Выгоняли меня, говорили: "Иди! / Спасайся, сестра, где знаешь, / А нас ты, сестра, ужасаешь"' (They drove me out, they told me: 'Go! / Save your soul where you want, sister / But we, sister, are horrified by you'.

---

36   These poems were collected in the aptly titled volume *Mundus imaginalis* (St Petersburg: Ezro, 1996). Not all of them were female: the 'Estonian poet' Arno Tsart, became a pseudonym under which Shvarts published two *samizdat* collections in the early 1980s. See http://libverse.ru/barkova/dyrochka.html

(poem 52), II, p. 206). While Lavinia exhibits a particularly prominent prophetic desire tinged with madness, evocative of Anna Barkova's 'Durochka' ('The Fool', 1954),[37] this trait is common to most of Shvarts's first-person narrators. By creating female versions of the Holy Fool, both Barkova and Shvarts invoke a literary archetype: the Holy Fool has been a staple figure in Russian religious literature since the Middle Ages; subsequently he entered secular literature as the quintessential outsider who challenges established structures.[38] In donning the mask of the Holy Fool, Shvarts thus claims her place within a tradition that is explicitly linked to extravagance and the exploration of taboos, be they political, religious, social or sexual. Consciously or not, she thus created a female genealogy of influence, appropriating and developing techniques used, once again, by Akhmatova and Tsvetaeva, who habitually highlighted the female poet's involvement with that which is considered taboo. The familiarity with taboo is often indicated by the presence of folk motifs, as in Tsvetaeva's 'Akhmatovoi' ('To Akhmatova', 1921, not to be confused with her earlier eponymous cycle), a poem with a gypsy theme evident in lexicon and the song-like rhythm. Akhmatova with the raven plait ('chernokosyn'ka') is addressed as a woman familiar with black magic ('chernoknizhnitsa'), and assonance and consonance between the two lend weight to the poem's suggestion that Tsvetaeva's famous colleague might indeed be a gypsy sorceress.

The use of named mythical figures as a mouthpiece is yet another trait Shvarts inherited, consciously or not, from Akhmatova and Tsvetaeva. All three poets lent their voice to mythical female heroines whom the usual sources describe as passive and silent.[39] To give just

---

37 Available at http://libverse.ru/barkova/dyrochka.html
38 For a study that considers the roots of the tradition but also includes secular literature and culture is S. A. Ivanov, *Blazhennye pokhaby: kul'turnaia istoriia iurodstva* (Moscow: Iazyki slavianskikh kul'tur, 2005). Also Ewa M. Thompson, *Understanding Russia: The Holy Fool in Russian Culture* (Lanham, MD: University Press of America, 1987). Per-Arne Bodin is focusing on the application of the tradition in contemporary Russia: *Language, Canonization and Holy Foolishness: Studies in Postsoviet Russian Culture and the Orthodox Tradition* (Stockholm: Stockholm University, 2009). Marco Sabbatini argues that for holy foolishness can be seen as a form of inner emigration among underground poets: 'The Pathos of Holy Foolishness in the Leningrad Underground', in *Holy Foolishness in Russia: New Perspectives*, edited by Priscilla Hunt and Svitlana Kobets (Bloomington: Slavica Publishers, 2011), pp. 337–52.
39 A contemporary English poet who exploits a very similar device to great effect is Carol Ann Duffy, the British Poet Laureate, with her collection *The World's Wife* (London: Picador, 1999).

two select examples, both Akhmatova and Tsvetaeva re-imagined a Hamlet story in which Ophelia, rather than suffering in silence, answers back to Hamlet.[40] In turn, Tsvetaeva and Shvarts each produced their own version of the myth of Orpheus and Eurydice, allowing Eurydice to expound on her reasons for remaining in Hades. These reasons are particular to the individual poet's vision, and they have little to do with the disobedience Orpheus exhibits in the source myth.[41]

Unsurprisingly, the poems centred on the female voice in literature are particularly attractive to scholars studying Russian literature from a feminist perspective.[42] The gender aspect thus broadens academic interest in Shvarts's work, which in turn heightens the poet's chance of being considered canonical.

Zhiznetvorchestvo and Celebrity Culture

A poet's popularity depends to a not insignificant degree on the way they present themselves to their readers. Pushkin's tragic fate moved his audience; Silver Age figures such as Akhmatova or Maiakovskii invested considerable effort in their self-presentation. In other words, it is not enough to write good poetry, it is also necessary to be attractive, intriguing and in some ways newsworthy. Shvarts was aware of the impact of a poet's personal myth on his or her reception. While she stated that it was the forces around the poet, rather than the poet herself, who created this myth, she certainly offered her readers plenty of relevant material.[43]

In the remainder of this article I will give a brief overview of ways in which Shvarts staged her own persona. It is clear that the celebrity of Shvarts, whose reluctance to read in public dates back

---

[40] Akhmatova's 'Chitaia Gamleta' ('Reading Hamlet', 1909), in *Sochineniia*, 2 vols. (Moscow: Khudozhestvennaia literatura, 1986), I, pp. 21–22; Tsvetaeva's 'Ofeliia-Gamletu' ('Ophelia to Hamlet', 1923), in *Stikhotvoreniia i poemy*, p. 373.

[41] Tsvetaeva's 'Evridika-Orfeiu' ('Euridice to Orpheus', 1923) celebrates death as a state free of attachment and sexual passion, and introduces an uncomfortable notion of incest, presenting Orpheus and Eurydice as siblings (in *Stikhotvoreniia i poemy*, p. 384). In Shvarts's 'Orfei' ('Orpheus', I, p. 154), Orpheus's doubt in his beloved's reality leads to her decision to slip back into the underworld.

[42] For example, Catriona Kelly discusses birth-myth poems in her chapter on Shvarts in *A History of Russian Women's Writing*, pp. 411–22.

[43] For a statement to this effect see Polukhina, 'Interv'iu s Elenoi Shvarts', p. 239.

to her underground days, was not a product of present-day Russian popular culture.⁴⁴ Russian celebrity culture now is little different from its Western counterpart and driven by TV shows, glossy magazines, performance and (self-)publication on social media and platforms such as YouTube.⁴⁵ There are writers who exploit the media age very successfully, often by supplementing traditional poetry with a performance aspect. One of Shvarts's contemporaries who managed the transition to the new media age, and who arguably reached canonical status precisely because of his media presence, was the extremely versatile Dmitrii Aleksandrovich Prigov, the central figure of Moscow conceptualism in the late 1970s and 1980s.⁴⁶ A contemporary example is the omnipresent Dmitrii Bykov with his hugely successful *Grazhdanin poet* (*Citizen Poet*) project, or younger performance poets such as Andrei Rodionov or Vera Polozkova.⁴⁷ Shvarts's media presence was minimal; she relied entirely on traditional channels of publication. Traditional are also her modes of self-presentation, which have their precedent in modernist *zhiznetvorchestvo*, the fusion of life and text.⁴⁸ Shvarts created her public persona — who bore traits of the *femme fatale*, the mystic seer, and the holy fool — through a process of self-mystification that strongly resembles the techniques employed, once again, by Akhmatova and Tsvetaeva.⁴⁹

---

44 'Kratkaia istoriia dopotopnykh chtenii' ('A Short History of Antediluvian Readings', III, pp. 193–96) details Shvarts's dislike of public readings. For a visual impression of a younger Elena Shvarts reading her poetry see http://www.youtube.com/watch?v=TOaJnTqpzhk. Recordings of her readings can be found at http://asiaplus.ru/cgi-bin/mp3.cgi?id=30&sid=492884ca-027b-4202-8bf8-32dc9b1fb547

45 A study touching on some of these points that is not yet entirely out of date is Birgit Beumers's *Pop Culture Russia!: Media, Arts, and Lifestyle* (Santa Barbara: ABC-CLIO, 2005).

46 Some of the wide variety of his work can be appreciated on http://prigov.ru

47 Polozkova promotes herself via social media, including Zhivoi Zhurnal (Life Journal), Facebook and VKontakte. Her official page on VKontakte mixes the private and the public, featuring family photographs as well as poems and multimedia files of her performing her poetry. See https://vk.com/vera_polozkova. For a film portrait of Polozkova, see http://www.youtube.com/watch?v=1GVlDslpLBA

48 A good description of *zhiznetvorchestvo* can be found in *Cultural Mythologies of Russian Modernism: From the Golden Age to the Silver Age*, edited by B. Gasparov, Robert P. Hughes and Irina Paperno (Berkeley and Oxford: University of California Press, 1992), p. 3 ff.

49 See Catriona Kelly, *A History of Russian Women's Writing*, p. 210 for a definition of the process of self-mystification in Akhmatova's case.

When asked what Shvarts looks like, readers will recall a beautiful, sad-eyed young woman, never smiling, who looks into the camera defiantly, sometimes drawing on a cigarette and overall resembling a film noir heroine.[50] These are the images of Shvarts that precede each of the volumes of her *Sochineniia* (*Collected Works*); it seems significant that she should have chosen the iconic pictures of her youth, although by the time the *Sochineniia* came out she was well into her fifties.[51] Shvarts professed that she could not stand Akhmatova, whom she met when she was a young woman.[52] Yet when looking at the photographs by which Shvarts became known, it is Akhmatova's pictures, and her policy in using them, that come to mind — a striking profile, an enigmatic gaze into the distance.

The richest source of self-mystifying material is her autobiographical prose, published in two collections entitled *Vidimaia storona zhizni* (*The Visible Side of Life*, 1997) and *Opredelenie v durnuiu pogodu* (*Definition in Foul Weather*, 2003). These collections consist of anecdotal, witty, bite-sized vignettes that are rarely longer than one page. They give the impression of being diary entries, especially the pieces in *Vidimaia storona zhizni*, a collection which begins with the poet's childhood. However, the episodes were in all likelihood written retrospectively; they are

---

50 Elena Shvarts is known to have had a professional picture taken once a year (interview with Kirill Kozyrev, executor of Shvarts's estate, July 2015). A Google search for 'Images' of 'Елена Шварц', in Cyrillic, will give access to many of these iconic images, plus other similar ones, taken by friends, which have proliferated in works by and about Shvarts, e. g. the encyclopaedia *Samizdat Leningrada* and the translated volume *Paradise*. The above-mentioned picture of the sad-eyed woman drawing on a cigarette illustrates Darra Goldstein's essay 'The Heart-Felt Poetry of Elena Shvarts', in *Fruits of her Plume: Essays on Contemporary Russian Woman's Culture*, edited by Helena Goscilo (Armonk, N.Y.: M.E. Sharpe), 1993, pp. 239–50 (p. 240). This photo is particularly striking when contrasted with the photograph of Iuliia Voznesenskaia (p. 229), a contemporary and acquaintance of Shvarts.

51 For an analysis of the role of photography in the creation of celebrity, see Leo Braudy, *The Frenzy of Renown: Fame & its History* (New York: Vintage Books, 1997), in particular pp. 491–99. See also Chris Rojek, *Celebrity* (London: Reaktion, 2008). Beth Holmgren's essay 'Gendering the Icon: Marketing Women Writers in Fin-de-siècle Russia', in *Russia-Women-Culture*, edited by Helena Goscilo and Beth Holmgren (Bloomington: Indiana University Press, 1996), pp. 321–46, provides a useful history of women writers' portraits.

52 'Today I went to see Akhmatova. I thought she was a saint, a great woman. She is a fool and overvalued. She sees nothing apart from herself' ('Diaries', V, p. 346). The dislike was mutual; Akhmatova's impressions of Shvarts are published in Emily Van Buskirk, 'Lidiia Ginzburg on Elena Shvarts', *Slavonica*, 16: 2 (2010), 139–41.

stylistically homogenous and present a consistent, highly stylised image of the first-person heroine.[53] While they are doubtlessly intriguing, the entries do not divulge factual information about Shvarts's life, or inner life for that matter; the reader does not have the usual impression of getting closer to the poet, however deceptive this impression might be. Some of the pieces (e.g. 'Neskol'ko osobennostei moikh stikhov' ('A Few Peculiarities of My Poems')) treat Shvarts's vision of poetry, but they describe rather than explain, in stark contrast to the essays of Shvarts's friend Ol'ga Sedakova, for example, which evince an almost scholarly interest in the reasons for writing in a particular way. The function of Shvarts's prose is fundamentally different — her vignettes are the primary instrument with which she 'ghosts' her persona, fine-tuning the light in which her readers see her.[54]

An unkind reader might be tempted to point out that the elements of the poetic myth to which Shvarts pandered have been over-used by Russian poets throughout the ages to the point that they have become clichés. The first of these clichés is the romantic image of the poet-as-seer, whose gift makes her stand apart from the crowd (see Pushkin's 'Poet i tolpa' ('The Poet and the Crowd', 1828)). Shvarts's exalted vision of poetry as a quasi-religious practice reinforces the cliché: 'I regard the composition of verse as a sacral, sacred act'[55] and 'I have always looked to the poet giving a reading as a priest'.[56] The consistency with which Shvarts promoted this version of herself is remarkable: in the prose piece 'Luch' ('The Ray') she describes how she came to faith (*poverila*) as a teenager when a ray of light fell onto her temple, elevating her to a new level of cognition. Later, she saw a miniature of King David in prayer, with a ray touching his temple, and too it as an illustration for what had happened to her — she had come into contact with the divine (III, pp. 229–30). In an earlier poem, 'Bokovoe zrenie pamiati' ('The Lateral Vision of Memory', 1985) the same ray of light is explicitly identified as

---

[53] Shvarts's actual adolescent diaries, published posthumously in *Novoe literaturnoe obozrenie*, 115 (2012), and subsequently in volume V of her *Sochineniia* (2013), reveal that she began honing this style very early in her life.

[54] Aleksandr Ulanov identifies Shvarts's autobiographical pieces as a 'portrait of the poet as romantic genius who is not a normal human being', http://magazines.russ.ru/znamia/1998/4/nabl1.html

[55] Polukhina, 'Interv'iu s Elenoi Shvarts', p. 235.

[56] 'A Short History of Antediluvian Readings', III, p. 194.

poetic inspiration. We find a similar image in the prose piece 'Sumerki' ('Twilight', III, p. 185).

The emergent child-prodigy theme falls in the same category of cliché, and once again Shvarts seems to follow in the footsteps of her prominent predecessors — both Akhmatova and Tsvetaeva published their first collection at a precocious age. However, writing poetry from a tender age was common among Soviet poets, including many of Shvarts's underground peers. The cult of literature in the Soviet Union facilitated this: many children and young people in the 1960s attended writing circles at school, at the Young Pioneers, and later at university.[57] In Shvarts's own description, which should be read with the necessary degree of critical distance, her status as an outcast, marked by her peculiar understanding of narrative and poetry, was cemented while she was still a child. When she told other adolescents at a poetry seminar (of all places) about a freak accident her mother had, falling into the Neva, the other children refused to believe her, 'having decided that my madness had reached a new stage' indicating that she already had a reputation for being out of her mind.[58] When she read her own poetry for the first time as a young pioneer, the other children reportedly laughed at her. The teacher alone sat still, with tears streaming down her face comforting the distraught Elena with the magic words 'don't pay attention to them, they have no idea. You are a real poet'.[59] Now that we have access to Shvarts's adolescent diaries, we can see that she used this technique long before she became a fully-fledged writer: 'Not long ago Iu. A. and I went to see two old ladies. They love my poems. They prophesied I would be famous'.[60] This is a very powerful act of self-certification: rather than calling herself an accomplished poet outright, Shvarts quotes other people's appreciation of her gift, directing the light of other people's authoritative scrutiny at her craft. For an underground poet — a writer who, as a result of the authenticity of her gift and the integrity of her character, will be scorned by the literary establishment — this kind of validation assumes particular poignancy.

---

57 See Lygo, *Leningrad Poetry 1953–75*; entries on individual poets in *Samizdat Leningrada*. Details are also given by Aleksandr Skidan in his introduction to Shvarts's diaries in *Novoe literaturnoe obozrenie*, 115 (2012), 236.
58 'The Cruiser' ('Kreiser'), III, p. 176.
59 'First Reading' ('Pervoe chtenie'), III, p. 188.
60 'Diaries', V, p. 318.

There is an another aspect to Shvarts's public persona, one that exploits her gender. The persona she presents in her prose is a highly strung *femme fatale*, confirming what her photographs suggest: an unpredictable whirlwind with a penchant for histrionics and scandal. We get a taste of this in vignettes such as 'Zhestko nakazannyi antisemit' ('A Harshly Punished Anti-Semite'), in which she pours boiling water on the belly of an artist who had insulted a Jewish guest (III, p. 203), and 'Izbienie slepogo' ('Beating Up a Blind Man'), where friends struggle to break up a fist fight between her and a blind, male acquaintance (III, pp. 214–15), and most shockingly, in 'Bog spas' ('God Saved Me'), where the poet relates: 'it was night, I was drunk and desperate and standing on the roof of a nine-storey house, on one leg and on the wrong side of the barrier' (III, p. 217). Upon examining more closely the scene as Shvarts describes it, we might conclude that it lacks substance: we are not given any reason for the existential despair other than her drunkenness. The dramatic gesture of the act (the first association most people will have with a person on a roof is that of a suicide) and the similarly dramatic title are out of tune with the rather banal context — yet another drunken party among the literary bohemia. But the episode adds another facet to the poet's already complicated personality. The effect seems to conform to an observation made by James Hopgood with regard to the behaviour of saints (and performers who become secular quasi-saints): 'the human desire and "impulse" to find and fashion what is desired in the other often settles on someone outside normal bounds'.[61]

Her exalted feminine antics and her attractive exterior notwithstanding, Shvarts's behaviour was in many aspects more typical of the male poets that dominated the Leningrad underground.[62] In the male bastion that was underground literature, most women tended to play the role of muse, facilitator and preserver, following in the footsteps of Nadezhda Mandel'shtam, who preserved her persecuted husband's poetry for posterity. One example is Tat'iana Goricheva, Krivulin's former wife. Herself a keen translator and prolific religious philosopher, she is nevertheless best known for her role as hostess of

---

61 In the introduction to the volume *The Making of Saints: Contesting Sacred Ground*, edited by James F. Hopgood (Tuscaloosa: University of Alabama Press, 2005), p. xv.
62 A visual impression of this dominance can be gleaned from the group photos at the back of *Samizdat Leningrada*.

innumerable get-togethers of the literary boheme, co-founder and editor of the *samizdat* journal 37, and later, after her forced emigration in 1980s, of the publishing house *Beseda* in Paris, which introduced many *samizdat* poets to a wider public.[63] Another example is Alena Basilova, the wife of Leonid Gubanov, who was a poet in her own right but is described as someone who contributed to the underground as a hostess, someone who made her flat available to Moscow's underground poets.[64] Shvarts, on the other hand, was a full-blown participant, an active agent rather than a facilitator for others. She drank and smoked heavily, failed to turn up for readings and was known among her friends for her proclivity for 'scandals and blows'.[65] She also publicised her notorious love life, thus claiming a male domain as her own. A few such episodes she describes laconically in 'Pazukhin-Shafer' how she got married aged twenty, 'myself not knowing why', while another friend, himself in love with her, had to wake her up for the wedding and drive her to the registry office; she then goes on to describe domestic life with her new husband, including a graphic scene of domestic violence when he almost strangles her in a fit of jealousy (III, p. 209). The gender inversion that we can see in her poetic perspective and behaviour, contrasted with her striking appearance, may paradoxically have helped her storm the bastion and become one of the few female underground voices who was truly heard — without allowances being made for her gender: a real *poet*, not a *poetessa*.

Conclusion

Shvarts's entry into the poetic canon of post-Soviet Russia was the result of her producing a large body of new, first rate poetry. The discussion above demonstrates that she had an advantage over her underground peers because her work was more accessible to a general readership; at the same time her poetry, as well as her personality, were

---

63 Beseda produced thirty issues of the eponymous literary journal; it also published single author collections of the Leningrad samizdat poets, introducing many of them to a broader readership for the first time. Shvarts's first official collection, Stikhi, was published by Beseda in 1987.
64 For details see http://rvb.ru/np/publication/sapgir5.htm#67
65 Evgenii Pazukhin, 'Antisotsium', in *Sumerki 'Saigona'*, edited by Iuliia Valieva (St Petersburg: Samizdat, 2009), pp. 163–70 (pp. 168–69).

unusual enough to stand out and attract attention. Shvarts could not be pigeonholed as an underground poet. At the same time she was tarred with the underground brush; this paradox is at the centre of her fame. She was not a poet of the media age; her celebrity was old-fashioned and in essence close to that of the highly popular prose-writer Viktor Pelevin, who professed in the year 2000 that he never gave interviews and avoided literary circles, maintaining that an author should be famous for his books alone, and he seems not to have changed his stance.[66] While Shvarts did not take elusiveness to the same (carefully staged) extreme, in the final analysis her own status is similarly grounded more exclusively on literary merit. Her eccentric personality and the inclination to perform it notwithstanding, she remains a highbrow writer who appeals to literary readers rather than those seeking entertainment or acute political commentary. As such, she may be one of the last poets to enter the canon as 'classical' poets who were not famous for anything else. Time will tell whether she can maintain that position.

---

66 See http://www.guardian.co.uk/books/2000/apr/30/fiction; also http://pelevinlive.ru/17

Unofficial Leningrad Poets: Selected Comparative Bibliography

Officially published collections

[Titles in ***bold italic*** indicate that the poems in the collection were written after 1991]

Elena Shvarts (1948–2010)	Viktor Krivulin (1944–2001)	Aleksandr Mironov (1948–2010)	Oleg Okhapkin (1944–2008)	Sergei Stratanovskii (*1944)
Tantsuiushchii David: stikhi raznykh let (New York: Russica Publishers, 1985)	Stikhi (Paris: Ritm, 1981)	Metafizicheskie radosti Stikhotvoreniia 1964–1982 (SPb: Prizma-15, 1993)	Stikhi (Leningrad-Paris: Beseda, 1989)	Stikhi (SPb: Assotsiatsiia Novaia literatura, 1993)
Stikhi (Leningrad; Paris; Munich: Beseda, 1987) [Poems from the early 1980s, most from 1982]	Stikhi, 2 vols. (Paris and Leningrad: Beseda, 1988)	Izbrannoe. Stikhotvoreniia i poemy 1964–2000 (SPb: INAPRESS, 2002)	Pylaiushchaia kupina (Leningrad: Sovetskii pisatel', 1990) [Nature poems from the 1970s]	***T'ma dneonaia. Stikhi devianostykh godov*** (Moscow: Novoe literaturnoe obozrenie, 2000)
Trudy i dni Lavinii, monakhini iz Ordena Obrezaniia Serdtsa: ot Rozhdestva do Paskhi (Ann Arbor: Ardis, 1987)	Obrashchenie (Leningrad: Sovetskii pisatel', 1991) [Poems undated, but most of these circulated in 1970s samizdat, print run 5700]	Bez ognia (Moscow: Novoe izdatel'stvo, 2009) [Poems from the 1970s–2000s]	Vozvrashchenie Odisseia (SPb: Mitkilibris, 1994) [The title poem was written in 1973]	***Riadom s Chechnei: Novye stikhtvoreniia i dramaticheskoe deistvo*** (SPb: Pushkinskii fond, 2002) [Poems on the Chechen war]
Storony sveta (Leningrad: Sovetskii pisatel', 1989)	***Kontsert po zaiavkam*** (SPb: Izdatel'stvo Fonda russkoi poezii, 1993) [Three short collections with poems from 1990–1992, print run 1000]		Molenie o chashe (SPb: Mitkilibris, 2004) [Dedicated to Iosif Brodskii, written in 1970]	***Na reke neprozrachnoi: Kniga novykh stikhtvorenii*** (SPb: Pushkinskii fond, 2005)

Stikhi (Leningrad: Novaia literatura, 1990) [Excerpts from five 'collections' composed in 1976, 1978, 1980, 1982, 1987, print run 10,000]	*Posledniaia kniga* (SPb: [n.p.], 1993)	*Ozhivlenie bulma* (Moscow: Novoe izdatel'stvo, 2009)
Lotsiia nochi: kniga poem (Leningrad: Sovetskii pisatel', 1993) [Poems from the early 1980s, print run 1000]	*Predgranich'e* (SPb: Borei Art, 1994) [Poems from 1993–1994]	*Izbrannoe* (2009) [Posthumous edition; selected work from four decades, published only online http://www.religare.ru/25_861.html]
Pesnia ptitsy na dne morskom (SPb: Pushkinskii fond, 1995) [Mostly poems from 1992–1995; print run 1000]	*Rekviem* (Moskva: ARGO-RISK, 1998) [Dedicated to his son, Lev Krivulin (1980–1998), print run 300]	*Lampada* (SPb: Russkaia kul'tura, 2010) [Posthumous edition; Okhapkin's poetic diary of the years 1991–1992]
		Smokovnitsa (SPb: Pushkinskii fond, 2010) [Poems on religious themes from four decades]
Mundus imaginalis: kniga otvetvlenii (SPb: Ezro, 1996) [Poems from the 1970s and 80s written under a lyrical hero's pseudonym]	*Kupanie v iordani* (SPb: Pushkinskii fond, 1998) [Three short collections from 1996, 1997 and 1998, as well as the full text of Requiem, print run 1000]	*Liubovnaia lirika* (SPb: Russkaia kul'tura / Soiuz pisatelei Rossii, 2013) [Posthumous thematic edition]
Zapadno-vostochnyi veter: novye stikhotvoreniia (SPb: Pushkinskii fond 1997) [Print run 1000]	*Stikhi iubileinogo goda* (Moskva: OGI, 2001)	*Graffiti: Kniga stikhov raznykh let* (SPb: Pushkinskii fond, 2011)
		Iov i Arab: kniga stikhov (SPb: Pushkinskii fond, 2012)
		Filosofskaia lirika (SPb: Russkaia kul'tura, 2014) [Posthumous thematic edition]
Solo na raskalennoi trube: novye stikhotvoreniia (SPb: Pushkinskii fond, 1998) [Written after her mother's death; poems themselves undated, print run 1000]	*Stikhi posle stikhov* (SPb: Peterburgskii pisatel' — Russko-Baltiiskii tsentr "BLITs", 2001) [Posthumous edition, poems from 1994–2000, print run 1000]	*Molotkom Nekrasova: kniga novykh stikhtvorenii* (SPb: Pushkinskii fond, 2014)
		http://stratanovskys.chat.ru [All poems on this website are from the 1970s–early 1980s but are entitled *Современная русская поэзия Санкт-Петербурга*]

Elena Shvarts (1948–2010)	Viktor Krivulin (1944–2001)	Aleksandr Mironov (1948–2010)	Oleg Okhapkin (1944–2008)	Sergei Stratanovskii (*1944)
Stikhotvoreniia i poemy Eleny Shvarts (SPb: INAPRESS, 1999) [Selected works, print run 2000]	***Kompozitsii*** (Moscow: ARGO-RISK, Knizhnoe obozrenie, 2010) [Posthumous edition: slim volume containing cycles from the 1970s; print run 500]			***Nestroinoe mnogogolosie. Stikhi 2014–2015*** (SPb: Pushkinskii fond, 2016)
Dikopis' poslednego vremeni: novaia kniga stikhotvorenii (SPb: Pushkinskii fond, 2001) [Written after her mother's death; poems themselves undated]	***Voskresnye oblaka*** (SPb: Palmyra, 2017) [Posthumous edition, containing early poems from the late 1960s–1980s]			
Trost' skoropistsa: kniga novykh stikhotvorenii (SPb: Pushkinskii fond, 2004) [Most poems undated, some earlier ones (1974, 1993) with dates, print run 1000]				
Vino sed'mogo goda: kniga novykh stikhotvorenii (SPb: Pushkinskii fond, 2007)				
Pereletnaia ptitsa (SPb: Pushkinskii fond, 2011) [Her last poems, posthumous collection]				
Sochineniia Eleny Shvarts, vols I–V (SPb: Pushkinskii fond, 2002–2013)*				

* Shvarts is one of the very few underground writers who had Collected Works published and, what is more, during her lifetime. One of the few others who have achieved this extent of 'completeness' is Shvarts's Moscow-based contemporary and friend Olga Sedakova. Two Leningrad poets whose Collected Works were published posthumously are Leonid Aronzon (*Sobranie proizvedenii*, 2 vols, SPb: Izd. Ivana Limbakha, 2006) and Roal'd Mandel'shtam (*Sobranie stikhotvorenii*, SPb: Izd. Ivana Limbakha, 2006), but both died before underground culture reached its zenith in the 1970s.

Translations into English
[Titles in ***bold italic*** indicate a single-author collection]

Elena Shvarts (1948–2010)	Viktor Krivulin (1944–2001)	Aleksandr Mironov (1948–2010)	Oleg Okhapkin (1944–2008)	Sergei Stratanovskii (*1944)
Paradise: Selected Poems, translated by Michael Molnar and Catriona Kelly (Newcastle upon Tyne: Bloodaxe, 1993)	*In the Grip of Strange Thoughts: Russian Poetry in a New Era*, ed. by J. Kates and M. Aizenberg (London: Bloodaxe, 1998)			*In the Grip of Strange Thoughts: Russian Poetry in a New Era*, ed. by J. Kates and M. Aizenberg (London: Bloodaxe, 1998)
Birdsong on the Seabed, translated by Sasha Dugdale (Tarset: Bloodaxe Books, 2008)				***Muddy River***, translated by J. Kates (London: Carcanet, 2016)
Contemporary Russian Poetry: a Bilingual Anthology, ed. by G. S. Smith (Bloomington: Indiana University Press, 1993)				
In the Grip of Strange Thoughts: Russian Poetry in A New Era, ed. by J. Kates and M. Aizenberg (London: Bloodaxe, 1998)				
Contemporary Russian Poetry: An Anthology ed. by Evgenii Bunimovich and J. Kates (Champaign: Dalkey Archive Press, 2008)				

Selected scholarship after 2000 — articles that are not primarily reviews

Elena Shvarts (1948–2010)	Viktor Krivulin (1944–2001)	Aleksandr Mironov (1948–2010)	Oleg Okhapkin (1944–2008)	Sergei Stratanovskii (*1944)
Catriona Kelly, 'Elena Shvarts', in *A History of Russian Women's Writing 1820–1992* (Oxford: Oxford University Press, 1994), pp. 411–22	Marco Sabbatini, 'Shto rifmovalos' (1990) — refleksiia krizisa neofitsial'noi kul'tury', *NLO*, 83 (2007), 710–70	Anton Nesterov, 'Germenevtika, metafizika i "drugaia kritika". O stikhakh Aleksandra Mironova', *NLO*, 61 (2003), 75–97 [Focused on early work]	Sergei Stratanovskii, 'Poeticheskii mir Olega Okhapkina', *Zvezda*, 8 (2010), 197–205	Oleg Rogov, 'O poezii Sergeia Stratanovskogo', *Volga*, 9 (1999), http://magazines.russ.ru/volga/1999/9/rogov.html
Sarah Clovis Bishop, 'In Memoriam: Elena Andreevna Shvarts (17 March 1948–11 March 2010)', *Slavonica*, 16: 2 (November 2010), 112–30	Smith, Alexandra 'Viktor Borisovich Krivulin', in *Dictionary of Literary Biography, Vol. 285: Contemporary Russian Writers*, ed. by Marina Balina and Mark Lipovetsky (Detroi, New York, San Diego, London and Munich: Gale Research Inc. and Bruccoli Clark Layman Books, Thompson-Gale, 2003)	Nikolai Nikolaev, 'Vospominaniia o poezii Aleksandra Mironova', *NLO*, 101 (2010), 263–79		Rein Karasti, 'Pust' on zapishet', *Zvezda*, 5 (2005), 219–28
Dunja Popovic, 'Symbolic Injury and Embodied Mysticism in Elena Shvarts's "Trudy i Dni Lavinii"', *The Slavic and East European Journal*, 51 (2007), 753–71	Walker, Clint 'The Spirit(s) of the Leningrad Underground', *The Slavic and East European Journal*, 43: 4 (1999), 674–98	Valerii Shubinskii, 'V luchashchikhsia adakh: vvedenie v poetiku Aleksandra Mironova', *NLO*, 106 (2010), 193–201 [Introduction to Mironov's poetics, part of a special section in the leading literary journal dedicated to Mironov after his death]		Kirill Butyrin (Mamontov), 'Strasti po smokovnitse', *Zvezda*, 12 (2010), 195–208 [Long scholarly review]

			Anna Orlitskaia, Mikroistoriia velikikh sobytii', *Oktiabr'*, 2 (2012), 169–72 [Long review of his last three collections]
		Natalia Chernykh, 'Kontsert dlia geniia pervonachal'noi nishchety', on http://nattch.narod.ru/nbmironov.html	
Arina Kuznetsova, 'Voskresenie vnutri dukha', *Zvezda*, 12 (1990), 161–63			
	Maria Khotimsky, 'Singing David, Dancing David: Olga Sedakova and Elena Shvarts Rewrite a Psalm', *The Slavic and East European Journal*, 51 (2007), 737–52 Stephanie Sandler, 'Cultural Memory and Self-Expression in a Poem by Elena Shvarts', in *Rereading Russian Poetry*, ed. by Stephanie Sandler (New Haven and London: Yale University Press, 1999), pp. 256–69 Ol'ga Sedakova, 'L'antica fiamma Elena Shvarts'; Boris Vantalov, 'Pamiati nevozmozhnogo'; Dmitrii Panchenko, '"Kinfiia" Eleny Shvarts'; Tomas Epstain, 'Velikansha malen'koi poemy', All in *Novoe literaturnoe obozrenie*, 103 (2010) [Leading literary journal dedicating a special section to Shvarts after her death]		

Selected Publications on the Leningrad Underground as a Literary Phenomenon, in Chronological Order

Mikhail Epshtein, 'Kontsepty... metaboly... o novykh tendentsiakh v poezii', *Oktiabr'*, 4 (1988), 194–203.

Viacheslav Dolinin and Boris Ivanov, eds, *Samizdat. Po materialam konferentsii '30 let nezavisimoi pechati. 1950–80 gody'. S.-Peterburg, 25–27 aprelia 1992* (SPb: NITs 'Memorial', 1993).

Mikhail Berg, *Literaturokratiia. Problema prisvoeniia i pereraspredeleniia vlasti v literature* (Moscow: NLO, 2000).

Boris Ivanov and Boris Roginskii, eds, *Istoriia leningradskoi nepodtsenzurnoi literatury* (SPb: DEAN, 2000).

Stanislav Savitskii, *Andegraund. Istoriia i mify leningradskoi neofitsial'noi literatury* (Moscow: NLO, 2002).

Viacheslav Dolinin and Dmitrii Severiukhin, eds, *Preodolenie nemoty: Leningradskii samizdat v kontekste nezavisimogo kul'turnogo dvizheniia (1953–1991)* (SPb: Izdatel'stvo Novikovoi, 2003).

Dmitrii Severiukhin, Viacheslav Dolinin, Boris Ivanov and Boris Ostanin, eds, *Samizdat Leningrada 1950e-1980e. Literaturnaia entsiklopediia* (Moscow: NLO, 2003).

Marco Sabbatini '"Leningradskij tekst" i ekzistencializm v nezavisimoj kul'ture 1970-ch godov. Seminary, samizdat i poezija', in *Atti del convegno internazionale: Pietroburgo, capitale della cultura russa, Università degli studi di Salerno, 28–31 Ottobre 2003* (Salerno: Europa Orientalis, 2004), pp. 221–46.

Marco Sabbatini, *Poesia e cultura underground a Leningrado* (Salerno: Europa Orientalis, 2008).

Iuliia Valieva, ed., *Sumerki 'Saigona'* (SPb: Samizdat, 2009).

Boris Ivanov, ed., *Peterburgskaia poeziia v litsakh* (Moscow: NLO, 2011).

Marco Sabbatini, 'The Pathos of Holy Foolishness in the Leningrad Underground', in *Holy Foolishness in Russia: New Perspectives*, ed. by Priscilla Hart Hunt and Svitlana Kobets (Bloomington, IN: Slavica Publishers), 2011.

Iuliia Valieva, ed., *Litsa peterburgskoi poezii. 1950–1990-e.* (SPb: Zamizdat, 2011).

Aleksandr Zhitenev, *Poeziia neomodernizma* (SPb: Inapress, 2012).

Jean-Philippe Jaccard, ed., *Vtoraia kul'tura: Neofitsial'naia poeziia Leningrada v 1970-e–1980-e gody* (SPb: Rostok, 2013).

Iuliia Valieva, ed., *K istorii neofitsial'noi kul'tury i sovremennogo russkogo zarubezh'ia: 1950–1990-e.* (SPb: [n.p.], 2015)

Josephine von Zitzewitz, *Poetry and the Leningrad Religious-Philosophical Seminar 1974–1980: Music for a Deaf Age* (Oxford: Routledge and Legenda, 2016).

The sizeable anthology *Russkie stikhi 1950–2000 godov. Antologiia (pervoe priblizhenie)*, 2 vols, ed. by I. Akhmet'ev, G. Lukomnikov, V. Orlov and A. Uritskii (Moscow: Letnii sad, 2010) features a large number of poets from the unofficial sphere.

A brand new encyclopaedia, *Literaturnyi Sankt-Peterburg. XX vek. Entsiklopedicheskii slovar*, 3 vols, ed. by O. Bogdanova (SPb: Beresta, 2015) includes long entries on most significant unofficial writers.

9. Boris Slutskii: A Poet, his Time, and the Canon

Katharine Hodgson

Boris Slutskii lived his entire life (1919–1986) in the Soviet era. Many of the significant events of Soviet history played an important role in his life and creative development, especially his experiences as a soldier between 1941 and 1945, his rise to fame as a poet of the post-Stalin Thaw, and his efforts to understand the phenomenon that was Stalinism. Slutskii was intimately bound up with his times. His role as a chronicler of the Soviet experience was underlined by the publication of many previously unknown poems from his archive in the final years of the Soviet Union's existence. Gorbachev's *glasnost'* policy prompted a confrontation with uncomfortable aspects of the past: the poetry by Slutskii that appeared for the first time in the late 1980s spoke about Stalinism, guilt, anti-semitism, the brutal cost of victory. Daniil Danin wrote in 1990 that: 'Boris Slutskii was organically — to the core of his being and poetic gift — made for an era which he did not live to see'.[1]

This mass of previously unpublished work meant that earlier assessments of Slutskii needed to be revisited. On the basis of what was available in 1978, Deming Brown described him as someone who:

> seems a model of what the Soviet poet is expected to be — patriotic, affirmative, down to earth, fully committed to the Revolution, and one who stresses the moral value of hard work, self-sacrifice, and social

---

1   Daniil Danin, 'Khorosho ushel — ne oglianulsia', *Voprosy literatury*, 5 (2006), 168–79 (p. 168).

dedication. At the same time he manages to preserve an air of wary independence, of striving to expand the limits of orthodoxy, which places him unmistakably in the liberal camp.²

In the poetry which emerged from Slutskii's archive there was ample confirmation of the inner tensions that Brown had detected earlier: the 'discontent of a strongly frustrated moral sense' and fears about 'the destructive effects of rigid institutions on the human soul'.³ The circumstances in which the poet's unknown work came to light made it inevitable that the post-Soviet reception of Slutskii was dominated by his role as a chronicler of his times. G. S. Smith wrote that:

> his work stands indisputably as the most valuable body of individual poetic testimony to the experience of the Russians under Soviet rule, comparable in importance to that of Solzhenitsyn and Grossman in prose. He was the best poet it was possible for him to be in his place and time.⁴

In his appreciation of Slutskii, Evgenii Evtushenko claims that 'a great poet embodies his epoch', and Irina Plekhanova describes Slutskii as 'one of the most vivid poets of the Soviet epoch'.⁵ The identification of Slutskii with the Soviet era, which has a strong foundation in the poet's work, can, however, be seen as a limitation. For Stanislav Kuniaev, as for Evtushenko, Slutskii was 'a poet of his epoch', but his significance is diminished as a result: 'I never considered him a great poet, for a great poet is always higher, more profound, more significant than his time'.⁶

The version of Slutskii that has been canonised by repetition is one that, as Marat Grinberg puts it, privileges 'the Soviet variable in his

---

2   Deming Brown, *Soviet Russian Literature Since Stalin* (Cambridge: Cambridge University Press, 1979), p. 88.
3   *Ibid.*, p. 89.
4   G. S. Smith, 'Soldier of Misfortune', in Boris Slutsky, *Things That Happened*, edited and translated and with an introduction and commentaries by G. S. Smith (Moscow and Birmingham: Glas, 1999), pp. 1–23 (p. 23).
5   Evgenii Evtushenko, 'Obiazatel'nost' pered istoriei', in *Boris Slutskii: vospominaniia sovremennikov*, compiled by Petr Gorelik (St Petersburg: Zhurnal Neva, 2005), pp. 377–83 (p. 379); I. Plekhanova, 'Igra v imperativnom soznanii: lirika Borisa Slutskogo v dialoge s vremenem', *Voprosy literatury*, 1 (2003), 46–72 (p. 47).
6   Stanislav Kuniaev, *Poeziia, Sud'ba, Rossiia*, 2 vols. (Mosow: Nash sovremennik, 1991), I, 231.

poetic equation'.⁷ Viewing Slutskii, a member of the Communist Party from 1943, through the prism of political ideology reveals a poet who was undoubtedly shaped by his times, a would-be commissar who fell prey to disillusion. For some commentators, the most prominent illustration of Slutskii's political loyalties is his contribution to the public condemnation of Boris Pasternak in 1957, an act that, some argue, left him irreparably compromised.⁸ Nevertheless, other variables have come into play which make it possible to explore Slutskii's relationship to his times in ways that were not feasible during the Soviet period. One is his Jewish identity, the subject of many poems from Slutskii's archive, significant numbers of which were left out of his 1991 collected works. Grinberg's study of Slutskii's writing as a project of self-canonisation as a writer of scripture in the Judaic tradition situates the poet as an artist who was bound not just to his time but also to eternity.⁹ The times in which Slutskii lived made Jewish identity a matter of pressing and immediate personal significance: he lived through the post-war 'anti-cosmopolitan' campaign, and lost relatives to the Holocaust. In the Soviet Union, where the Holocaust was not acknowledged as a campaign directed towards the annihilation of the Jews, and home-grown anti-semitism became a taboo topic, Slutskii wrote about both. The other variable that has contributed to an evolving post-Soviet understanding of Slutskii is the question of his poetics, always at odds with the Soviet 'grand style' (*bol'shoi stil'*), now seen in the context of a poetic canon that has expanded to admit underground poets such as Ian Satunovskii and others associated with the Lianozovo group, with whom Slutskii was acquainted. This shifting context offers a different perspective on a poet whose frame of reference extends well beyond the norms of socialist realism, back to the early twentieth-century avant-garde, and whose influence on others stretches to the poetry of the late- and post-Soviet era. Oleg Chukhontsev sees Slutskii as the essential link between

---

7   Marat Grinberg, '*I Am to Be Read not from Left to Right, But in Jewish, from Right to Left': The Poetics of Boris Slutsky*, Borderlines: Russian and East European-Jewish Studies (Boston: Academic Studies Press, 2011), p. 16.
8   For representative versions of Slutskii's condemnation of Pasternak, see David Samoilov, 'Drug i sopernik', in *Boris Slutskii: vospominaniia sovremennikov*, pp. 77–105 (pp. 96–97) and Aleksandr Matskin, 'Boris Slutskii, ego poeziia, ego okruzhenie', *ibid.*, pp. 307–23 (pp. 310–11).
9   Grinberg, *The Poetics of Boris Slutsky*, p. 15, pp. 27–31.

Vladimir Maiakovskii and Iosif Brodskii, the three of them making up the trio of avant-garde classics of the twentieth century.[10] This chapter will explore Slutskii in relation to all three of these variables: the poet's relationship with the Soviet system, his Jewish identity, and his poetics. It will assess the extent to which the most prominent interpretation of Slutskii, as the author of poetic testimony to the upheavals of the times in which he lived, has been challenged, or at least supplemented by the view of Slutskii as the link between the early twentieth-century avant-garde and the Soviet underground.

Slutskii's position in the post-Soviet canon is still evolving. One of the main reasons for this is the fact that, as Igor' Shaitanov remarked in 2000, Slutskii has simply not been read.[11] An overwhelming proportion of what Slutskii wrote was unpublished and largely unknown during his lifetime. Gerald Smith estimates that up to 60% of his work remained unpublished at the time of his death in 1986.[12] Even when vast quantities of his poetry emerged from the archives after his death, thanks to the efforts of Iurii Boldyrev to whom Slutskii entrusted his literary legacy, Slutskii's work reached the reading public as part of a deluge of literature from underground and émigré authors. This, combined with a growing unwillingness to go back over the Soviet past, and a tendency to sideline writers who had been regularly published during the Soviet period, meant that there was little appetite for a sustained engagement with Slutskii's poetry. Furthermore, as Smith points out, 'Slutsky was denied the widow and heirs whose efforts have helped to secure other men's reputations'.[13] He remains a figure who is invariably included in literary histories and textbooks, but his reputation is based on a relatively small range of texts. In addition to the 1991 collected works, and subsequent collections of both his prose and poetry, the main efforts to secure Slutskii's position in the canon consist of accounts by people who knew him. As a result, the picture that emerges is shaped to a large degree by his biography, so that his poetry has been discussed

---

10   Oleg Chukhontsev, 'V storonu Slutskogo', *Znamia*, 1 (2012), 130–50 (p. 149).
11   Igor' Shaitanov, 'Boris Slutskii: povod vspomnit'', *Arion*, 3 (2000), para. 17, http://magazines.russ.ru/arion/2000/3/shaitan.html
12   G. S. Smith, 'Boris Slutskii', *Dictionary of Literary Biography*, vol. 359, Russian Poets of the Soviet Era, edited by Karen Rosneck (Detroit: Gale, 2011), pp. 255–64 (p. 261).
13   G. S. Smith, 'Soldier of Misfortune', in Boris Slutsky, *Things That Happened*, p. 8.

principally as an expression of his complex relationship with the Soviet system, and with the Soviet literary world.

Memoir accounts reveal that Slutskii was deeply concerned by the question of canons and literary hierarchies, and his own position within them. According to Lev Ozerov: 'he was interested by literary reputations. How they were formed, how they changed, how they disappeared'.[14] Several accounts recall his habit of questioning friends and acquaintances to hear their views on who the best nineteenth-century and the best contemporary poets were; according one account, he annotated a 1947 collection of young writers' poetry, ranking contributors (while leaving some unplaced).[15] He is said to have found considerable amusement in devising, with friends, a 'Table of Ranks' for members of the Writers' Union, with associated rules about the impermissibility of a junior member criticising a more senior one, for example, a 'lieutenant of criticism' doing anything except praising a 'marshall of prose'.[16] Such a playful approach was not always evident when it came to Slutskii's assessment of his own status in the literary world. In the late 1950s, it seems, he confidently placed himself second among contemporary poets (behind Leonid Martynov).[17] According to Lazar' Lazarev, however, Slutskii was not always so certain about his position, wondering whether his work would in fact still be read after his death; Lazarev interprets Slutskii's concern for helping 'second-rate' poets to mean that he may, at times, have considered himself one.[18] Slutskii made this realistic assessment of his position in the Soviet canon at some point between the early 1960s and the early 1970s:

---

14 Lev Ozerov, 'Rezkaia liniia', in *Boris Slutskii: vospominaniia sovremennikov*, pp. 327–46 (p. 331).

15 See, for example, Samoilov, 'Drug i sopernik', p. 81, for Slutskii's interest in how others ranked contemporary poets, Russian poets, world poets; also Viktor Maklin, 'Boris Slutskii, kak ia ego pomniu', *Boris Slutskii: vospominaniia sovremennikov*, pp. 496–504 (p. 499). According to Gorelik, the anthology Slutskii annotated was *Molodaia Moskva* (Moscow: Moskovskii rabochii, 1947). See Gorelik's footnote to Nina Koroleva, 'Poeziia tochnogo slova', in *Boris Slutskii: vospominaniia sovremennikov*, pp. 401–14 (p. 411).

16 Slutskii's 'Table of Ranks' for Writers' Union members is recalled by Lazar' Lazarev, 'S nadezhdoi, pravdoi i dobrom…', in *Boris Slutskii: vospominaniia sovremennikov*, pp. 169–201 (p. 183).

17 For Slutskii's assessment of his own importance as a poet in the late 1950s, see Samoilov, 'Drug i sopernik', p. 96.

18 Lazarev, 'S nadezhdoi, pravdoi i dobrom…', p. 200.

> Я слишком знаменитым не бывал,
> Но в перечнях меня перечисляли,
> В обоймах, правда, вовсе не в начале,
> К концу поближе — часто пребывал.[19]

> I was never all that famous,
> but I was included in lists,
> admittedly, not as the first named in a group,
> most often somewhere towards the end.

Slutskii's position in the post-Soviet canon, to judge by a selection of literary histories and anthologies, has not changed significantly since this poem was written. He is often placed alongside other poets who were Party members and war veterans, and who were able to publish their work regularly. Yet Slutskii's own literary horizons went far beyond what was available in libraries and bookshops during his lifetime. He was a voracious reader and book-collector from his youth. According to Semen Lipkin, Slutskii was familiar with the work of Khlebnikov, Tsvetaeva, Belyi, Kuzmin, Khodasevich, and Bunin.[20] Petr Gorelik, who knew Slutskii when both were still at school in Khar'kov, remembered Slutskii owning a copy of the 1925 anthology compiled by Ezhov and Shamurin, and knew that Slutskii had taken the opportunity presented to him as a Soviet officer in Eastern Europe during the closing stages of the war to collect any poems he could find in émigré publications.[21] The canon in which Slutskii tends to be located, however, is usually restricted to the poets who were published through the 1950s to the 1970s. He stands alongside other war veterans, such as Aleksandr Mezhirov, Sergei Narovchatov, Sergei Orlov, Konstantin Vanshenkin, and Evgenii Vinokurov, and is associated with poets of an older generation such as Nikolai Aseev, Leonid Martynov, Iaroslav Smeliakov, and Pavel Antokol'skii.[22]

---

19 Boris Slutskii, 'Ia slishkom znamenitym ne byval', *Sobranie sochinenii*, compiled by Iurii Boldyrev, 3 vols. (Moscow: Khudozhestvennaia literatura, 1991), II, 374. Reproduced with permission.
20 Semen Lipkin, 'Sila sovesti', in *Boris Slutskii: vospominaniia sovremennikov*, pp. 212–18 (pp. 212–13).
21 Gorelik, Petr, 'Drug iunosti i vsei zhizni', in *Boris Slutskii: vospominaniia sovremennikov*, pp. 26–66 (p. 28, p. 47).
22 V. A Zaitsev, *Lektsii po istorii russkoi poezii XX veka (1940–2000)* (Moscow: Izdatel'stvo moskovskogo universiteta, 2009), p. 109.

Life and Times: The 'Soviet Variable'

In his 2011 study of Slutskii's work, Grinberg sets out the key features of what he sees as the post-Soviet consensus on Slutskii, and the standard account of his career.[23] This account, repeated in textbooks, literary histories, memoirs, or as a preface to selections of his poems in anthologies, foregrounds his relationship with the time in which he lived, and categorises him primarily as a Soviet poet whose writing can be interpreted as: 'a kind of poetic chronicle of the war and the post-war period'.[24] Slutskii is closely identified with the hopes of the Thaw, but also with the disillusion of the Brezhnev years. His death, after nine years of silence, came when the Soviet Union itself was close to disintegration, but before Gorbachev's reforms gained momentum. Yet although Slutskii is widely seen as a poet of his times, and a loyal Party member, his career does not entirely correspond to what might be expected of a successful official Soviet writer. The sense of belatedness mentioned above in connection with the impact of Slutskii's previously unpublished poetry in the late 1980s and early 1990s is something that was present from the start of his moderately successful career as a published Soviet poet. His debut was significantly delayed, his first collection appearing only in 1957. In the post-war years his poems were known only to those who read them in manuscript, circulated unofficially. Many of these poems would not appear in print for decades. In the 1960s Slutskii was eclipsed by a younger generation of poets whose readings drew huge audiences, and he became, in Il'ia Falikov's words, 'something like a backdrop or piece of scenery on the set of their never-ending performances'.[25]

Most accounts of Slutskii's life focus on two particular episodes: his participation in the public condemnation of Boris Pasternak in 1958 over the publication abroad of *Doktor Zhivago* (*Doctor Zhivago*), and his mental breakdown following the death of his wife in 1977. The latter is seen as a personal tragedy and the principal cause of the poet's long silence in the final years of his life. The former is commonly treated as the moment when Slutskii's conscience lost its battle with his political loyalties.

---

23 Grinberg, *The Poetics of Boris Slutsky*, pp. 14–15.
24 Zaitsev, *Lektsii po istorii russkoi poezii XX veka*, p. 112.
25 The first critical article on Slutskii to appear was written by Il'ia Erenburg. See Il'ia Erenburg, 'O stikhakh Borisa Slutskogo', *Literaturnaia gazeta*, 28 July 1956; and Il'ia Falikov, 'Krasnorechie po-Slutski', *Voprosy literatury*, 2 (2000), 62–110 (p. 84).

Although other poets who, like Slutskii, were not functionaries in the apparatus of cultural control also spoke against Pasternak, it is Slutskii who is singled out for his actions. The reasons for Slutskii's apparent scapegoating are discussed by Omri Ronen, who finds that Slutskii's membership of progressive literary circles meant that his actions were deemed, in those circles, to be all the more abhorrent.[26] It is Ronen's view that the significance of Slutskii's speech condemning Pasternak has been exaggerated in accounts that interpret his long silence as a self-imposed act of penance.

Slutskii's own view of his role as a poet seems to have been shaped by a sense of obligation in relation to the time in which he lived. Irina Plekhanova states that he saw it as his duty to inform his time with meaning.[27] Discussions about what that meaning actually was are inevitably influenced by questions of Slutskii's ideological point of view, with the poetry itself relegated to second place. Because a majority of accounts emphasise his biography, his poetry is often presented as an illustration of his experiences of, and reflections on, contemporary Soviet reality. As Oleg Dark comments:

> It's hard to imagine an article about him that did not quote 'I believed all the slogans completely' ('Vsem lozungam ia veril do kontsa...'), a poem in which Slutskii reflects on his previous ideological certainty and accepts his share of the blame, should the whole edifice he has helped to build collapse.[28]

Along with many on active service in wartime, Slutskii joined the Communist Party in 1943, and remained a member for the rest of his life, though he was increasingly disillusioned and became explicitly anti-Stalinist in his views. Slutskii was not one of the writers who chose

---

26 Omri Ronen, 'Grust'', *Zvezda*, 9 (2012), para. 49, http://magazines.russ.ru/zvezda/2012/9/rq9.html, Ronen quotes from the Russian Wikipedia entry on Slutskii: 'Борис Слуцкий имеет неоднозначную репутацию в литературных кругах' (Boris Slutskii has an ambiguous reputation in literary circles), and points out that the adjective 'неоднозначный' (ambiguous), as currently used, hints at something unfavourable, but non-specific. The Wikipedia article on Slutskii can be found at para. 6, http://ru.wikipedia.org/wiki/Слуцкий_Борис_Абрамович

27 Plekhanova, 'Igra v imperativnom soznanii: lirika Boris Slutskogo v dialoge s vremenem', p. 48.

28 Oleg Dark, 'V storonu mertvykh (mezhdu Smeliakovym i Sapgirom)', *Russkii zhurnal*, 14 July 2003, para. 6, http://old.russ.ru/krug/20030714_od.html; 'Vsem lozungam ia veril do kontsa', *Sobranie sochinenii*, I, 172.

to pursue careers as literary functionaries, or to churn out work that was utterly conventional, both ideologically and formally. Yet his political loyalties remain a problem for his post-Soviet interpreters. The fact that he is strongly identified as a spokesman of the Thaw means that in the post-Soviet period he has been criticised as one of the would-be reformers who could only allow themselves to express half-truths and were incapable of viewing the world outside the framework of socialist ideas.[29] It has been argued that his speech against Pasternak was motivated by his fear that the Thaw might be endangered if officials came to think that liberalisation had been allowed to go too far.[30] The question of the poet's Party loyalties reinforces the view of Slutskii as a poet of, and for a particular time, a time that has now passed. Most of the poets now accorded a prominent place in the evolving post-Soviet canon can be portrayed either as victims of the Party, or resolutely independent of it. Slutskii does not fit easily into either category.

Interpretations of Slutskii's ideological standpoint do, however, vary considerably. He is depicted by Stanislav Rassadin as someone who was unchanging in his Communist convictions, by Valerii Shubinskii and Stanislav Kuniaev as someone who continued to identify himself with the Soviet state even after he had become fully aware of the true nature of that state, and by Il'ia Falikov as someone who left ideology behind in his later life.[31] David Samoilov believed that Slutskii remained true to his ideals, although he did eventually become disillusioned with both politics and reality. Dmitrii Sukharev declares that he never revised his fundamental values of social justice, internationalism, and sympathy for the unfortunate.[32] Danin sees him as a victim of his times; others, for example Iosif Brodskii and Falikov, see him as a victim of his assumed role

---

29 See Vladislav Zubok, *Zhivago's Children: The Last Russian Intelligentsia* (Cambridge, MA and London: The Belknap Press of Harvard University Press, 2009), pp. 356–62, for post-Soviet views of the Thaw generation. Ronen points out that Slutskii's view of the Thaw was not in fact as uncritically naive as has been claimed; 'Grust'', *Zvezda*, 9 (2012), and goes on to say: 'There is no need to apologise for Slutskii' (para. 22).

30 Samoilov argues that this was the case: 'Drug i sopernik', p. 96.

31 Stanislav Rassadin, *Samoubiitsy: povest' o tom, kak my zhili i chto chitali* (Moscow: Tekst, 2007), p. 427; Valerii Shubinskii, 'Semeinyi al'bom: zametki o sovetskoi poezii klassicheskogo perioda', *Oktiabr'*, 8 (2000), 150–68 (p. 167); Stanislav Kuniaev, *Poeziia. Sud'ba. Rossiia.*, I, 234; Falikov, 'Krasnorechie po-Slutski', p. 83.

32 Samoilov, 'Drug i sopernik', p. 93; Dmitrii Sukharev, 'Skrytopis' Borisa Slutskogo', *Voprosy literatury*, 1 (2003), 22–45 (pp. 24–25).

of 'commissar'.³³ Kuniaev proffers the opinion that Slutskii's ideological drama was only resolved by his mental breakdown, which came about when he realised that his ideal of social justice was unattainable.³⁴

A good deal of what has been published about Slutskii over the last couple of decades consists of personal accounts by friends, keen to champion his cause, to attempt to explain the pressures that may have led him to speak against Pasternak, and to see his remorse over this incident as one of the main causes of his eventual lapse into profound depression. In their defence of the poet they are concerned to explain Slutskii's complex involvement with the Communist Party, to show that he was not a careerist party hack and sloganiser. His work does show the inner drama of disillusion, the mismatch between the poet's sense of pity for the unfortunate and the system's neglect or ill-treatment of them, and his struggle with censorship.³⁵ Yet the post-Soviet relationship to that time does not make it easy for Slutskii to be assessed objectively. The Soviet epoch has still to be transformed into a piece of the past which demands neither to be rejected nor uncritically celebrated. Boris Paramonov stated in 2007 that it would take some time before this epoch receded into the past sufficiently to allow Slutskii to be seen as a classic author.³⁶ In the meantime, as Paramonov points out, Slutskii satisfies neither the pensioners who carry portraits of Stalin to demonstrations, nor the aesthetes who see him as a commissar. Slutskii is a poet 'not for veterans, but for Brodskii', in other words, he does not offer simply-expressed and comforting ideological formulas, but something altogether more complex and ambivalent, both in terms of ideas and aesthetics.³⁷ Paramonov acknowledges Slutskii's connection with his times, but suggests that this connection is rather more complex

---

33 Danin, 'Khorosho ushel. Ne oglianulsia…', p. 179; Iosif Brodskii's comment attributed to him by Nikita Eliseev. See Nikita Eliseev, 'Boris Slutskii i voina', *Neva*, 5 (2010), para. 49, http://magazines.russ.ru/neva/2010/5/el20.html; Falikov, 'Krasnorechie po-Slutski', p. 108.
34 Stanislav Kuniaev, *Poeziia, Sud'ba, Rossiia*, I, 241.
35 For examples of Slutskii's poems on censorship, see 'Lakiruiu deistvitel'nost'…', *Sobranie sochinenii*, I, 247; 'Byl pechal'nyi, a stal pechatnyi', I, 245; 'Zapakh lzhi, pochti neusledimyi', III, 151. Poems demonstrating Slutskii's sympathy for the unfortunate include 'Okazyvaetsia, voina', III, 47; 'Bessplatnaia snezhnaia baba', I, 286, and 'Pesnia', I, 375.
36 Boris Paramonov, 'Russkii evropeets Boris Slutskii', October 2007, para. 9, http://www.svobodanews.ru/content/article/419149.html
37 *Ibid.*

than often imagined: '[...] his link to his epoch is not so direct and, most importantly, it is not ideological in nature'. He continues, citing the ideas of Viktor Shklovskii: 'It has been known for a long time that one should not take an artist's ideology at face value. For an artist ideology is just a pretext, the motivation [*motirovka*] for an artistic construction'.[38] Paramonov draws on Shklovskii's view that works of art become classics when their ideological content becomes politically harmless, and claims that

> communist ideology was significant to him [Slutskii] principally, if not solely, precisely as the justification for his artistic structures. He gave aesthetic expression to communist ideas. But he only succeeded in doing this because at the point of his arrival on the literary scene — after Stalin, in the Khrushchev Thaw — these ideas were no longer current. Communism was set at a certain temporal distance, it had ceased to be part of the present. It had already become in part a museum piece — and, like everything that belongs to the past, had begun to evoke nostalgia.[39]

The claim that Slutskii's aesthetic, rather than ideological attachment to Communism rests on the assumption that the poet's political attitudes were shaped at the time his first collection appeared, rather than in the late 1930s and early 1940s. Paramonov's interpretation has not offered a serious challenge to the widely accepted account of the poet's drama of genuine idealism and disillusion.

A more convincing alternative reading of Slutskii's relationship with ideology is offered by Oleg Dark. In his interpretation, Slutskii was torn between hopes for greater democracy following on from the Thaw and the evidence of his own experience, which gave no grounds for any such hopes. This led him to realise that there were no firm foundations on which to base any kind of judgement.[40] Dark argues that Slutskii's awareness of the arbitrary nature of existence has been obscured by the way in which he is usually presented to the reading public: 'To allow the public to take Slutskii on board [*chtoby obshchestvennost' usvoila Slutskogo*] he had to be distorted, using the peaceable idea of political opposition'.[41] In fact Dark even suggests that Slutskii may have turned

---

38   Ibid., para. 2.
39   Ibid., para. 3.
40   Ibid., para. 16.
41   Ibid., para. 35.

with some relief to writing political poetry, finding in his disillusion with the system a reassuring explanation for his idiosyncratic and painful vision of the world.[42] It, however, is not political disillusion that characterises Slutskii, argues Dark, it is his existential anxiety in the face of the disturbing truth about how things actually are that finds expression in his poetics. Dark is not alone in linking Slutskii's aesthetics to the poet's confrontation with extreme experiences:

> Slutskii's aesthetics emerge from the beauty of life-creation in its most extreme manifestations. Death looks out from the pit at Cologne, but the poet looks death in the face. [...] horror, turned into the subject of poetry. That is where the eloquence of overcoming non-existence originates.[43]

For Shubinskii, Slutskii's outlook, confronting and accepting the loss of all illusions, sits close alongside that of one of the favourite poets of his youth, Vladislav Khodasevich, yet his aesthetics are closer to those of the futurist tradition.[44] The role played by Slutskii's poetics in his post-Soviet canonisation will be explored in the second section of this chapter.

While there is a broad consensus about the importance of political ideology for Slutskii, the poet's Jewish identity is something that presents a problem for the authors of many post-Soviet accounts. Few writing inside Russia deal with the topic in explicit terms, perhaps anticipating a hostile reaction from anti-semitic nationalist critics who might question Slutskii's right to a place in the Russian literary canon. Slutskii's Jewish identity is treated tentatively by most memoirists. In the 2005 volume of contemporaries' accounts of Slutskii, only David Shraer-Petrov foregrounds the poet's Jewishness.[45] A similar reticence can be seen in some of the editorial decisions made by Boldyrev in compiling Slutskii's collected works in 1991. Grinberg explains that

---

42   *Ibid.*, para. 18.
43   Falikov, 'Krasnorechie po-Slutski', p. 75. The reference to 'the pit at Cologne' alludes to Slutskii's poem 'The Pit at Cologne' ('Kel'nskaia iama', *Sobranie sochinenii*, I, 85–86), relating the treatment of Soviet prisoners of war by their German captors.
44   Shubinskii, 'Semeinyi al'bom: zametki o sovetskoi poezii klassicheskogo perioda', p. 167.
45   David Shraer-Petrov, 'Ierusalimskii kazak', in *Boris Slutskii: vospominaniia sovremennikov*, pp. 456–60. Vladimir Kornilov does give some consideration to the Jewish theme in Slutskii's poetry in 'Pokuda nad stikhami plachut...', in *Boris Slutskii: vospominaniia sovremennikov*, pp. 106–20 (pp. 114–15).

Boldyrev published many of Slutskii's poems with Jewish themes in 'specifically Jewish periodicals or collections', but did not include them in the collected works.[46] Ronen regrets Boldyrev's editorial decisions which left many of Slutskii's 'paired' poems in the collected works without their Jewish partner (for example 'Sel'skoe kladbishche' ('The Village Cemetery') without 'Piatikonechnaia zvezda s shestikonechnoi' ('The Five-pointed and Six-pointed Stars').[47] While the three volumes compiled by Boldyrev show a good deal about Slutskii's response to his time, they are less forthcoming about the poet's response to events and attitudes that had a bearing on his sense of identity as a Jew.

What is striking is that many accounts which define Slutskii as a poet of his epoch fail to consider his poetic response to being Jewish in that particular time. Those that see Slutskii's close connection to his times as a factor that limits his significance as a poet are assuming that Jewish culture and tradition did not, or could not offer Slutskii a frame of reference that might take him beyond the confines of his age. The nationalist critic Kuniaev gives an account of Slutskii in which the poet is doubly marginalised, first by his political idealism, then by his Jewish identity. Kuniaev claims that Slutskii was not interested in 'the Russian-Jewish question' during the first half of his life, but became increasingly preoccupied with it once he realised that his internationalist dreams of complete assimilation would never be fulfilled.[48] The claim that Slutskii had no interest in Jewish matters until later in life ignores the poetry Slutskii wrote on the Holocaust, and, indeed, his 1940–1941 cycle *Stikhi o evreiakh i tatarakh* (*Verses about Jews and Tatars*), including 'Rasskaz emigranta' ('An Emigrant's Tale'), a poem written in response to the Nazi persecution of the Jews before the mass killings began.[49] Slutskii's poetry records Soviet anti-semitism too. While Kuniaev interprets

---

46 Grinberg, *The Poetics of Boris Slutsky*, p. 191.
47 Ronen, 'Grust'', *Zvezda*, 9 (2012), para. 13. Ronen also points out (para. 7) that Slutskii's editorship of the first Soviet anthology of Israeli poetry *Poety Izrailia* (Moscow: Inostrannaia literatura, 1963) is seldom mentioned.
48 *Poeziia, Sud'ba, Rossiia*, I, 236–37.
49 See Petr Gorelik and Nikita Eliseev, '"Ia vse eto slyshal s detstva": k 90-letiiu so dnia rozhdeniia Borisa Slutskogo', *Evreiskoe slovo*, 15 (2009), http://www.e-slovo.ru/433/10pol1.htm, for a discussion of the Jewish theme in Slutskii's poetry, including his pre-1941 poems on German anti-semitic persecution. Grinberg offers a detailed analysis of Slutskii's Holocaust poems, pp. 154–73, and compares them to Holocaust poems by Il'ia Sel'vinskii, pp. 330–46.

Slutskii's interest in his Jewish identity as a dead end, it has been convincingly argued, by Grinberg, and by Harriet Murav, that Slutskii's poetry drew fruitfully on Jewish tradition, reaching back to the distant past of biblical tradition, juxtaposed with details of the present day, so as to find ways of expressing the absolute loss of the Holocaust.[50] Slutskii's breadth of reading, as Grinberg repeatedly argues in his study, included a knowledge of Yiddish literature (his home town Kharkov was a centre of publishing in Yiddish in the 1920s) and the Hebrew bible.[51]

The downplaying or avoidance of Slutskii's Jewish identity suggests anxieties about the place in the Russian literary canon of a Jewish poet writing in Russian. As far back as 1977 Kuniaev had hinted that it was ethnicity that decided whether a writer should be considered a Russian writer.[52] Orthodox believer Boldyrev was motivated, suggests Grinberg, to remove from the collected works poems where the Jewish theme was too evident, so that his selection of Slutskii's work would present the poet as a 'child of his time, who at the end of his journey came to repentance'.[53] There is no evidence, however, that Slutskii made any attempt at converting to Orthodox Christianity. Kuniaev laments Slutskii's stubborn atheism, and his failure to follow other poets such as Pasternak, Zabolotskii and Akhmatova towards the Orthodox faith. His view that Slutskii would never be able to transcend the limitations of being a poet of his times to achieve greater profundity seems to bear out a trend in Russian thinking that Grinberg sees as entrenched: 'a major Russian poet must be a Christian; the only legitimate sense of religiosity is a Christian one'.[54] Nevertheless, Slutskii's contribution as a Russian Jewish poet has received growing recognition, particularly outside Russia, with the publication of Grinberg's study, but also, for instance, in Maxim D. Shrayer's anthology of Jewish-Russian literature.[55]

---

50   Harriet Murav, *Music from a Speeding Train*, pp. 203–06; Grinberg, *The Poetics of Boris Slutsky*, particularly p. 158 on the poem 'Rodstvenniki Khrista', and pp. 160–08 on 'Ia osvobozhdal Ukrainu'.
51   Grinberg, *The Poetics of Boris Slutsky*, p. 23.
52   Kuniaev's contribution to the 'Klassika i my' debate of December 1977 has been interpreted as evidence of his views on ethnicity and canonicity. For a transcript of proceedings, see *Moskva*, 1–3 (1990); Kuniaev's contribution can be found on pp. 190–93 of no. 1.
53   Grinberg, *The Poetics of Boris Slutsky*, p. 191.
54   *Ibid.*, p. 252.
55   English translations of poems by Slutskii can be found in *An Anthology of Jewish-Russian Literature: Two Centuries of Dual Identity in Prose and Poetry*, edited by Maxim

The exploration of Slutskii's relationship with Communist ideology and with his Jewish identity has shown a poet whose involvement with his times was intense and disturbing. In post-Soviet Russia, however, a Jewish Communist poet risks being seen as irrelevant or peripheral, too closely linked with divisive questions of politics and ethnicity. When the focus is switched to questions of poetics, as will be shown below, Slutskii's role in the canon becomes that of a figure who bridges the Stalin era to connect different generations, as well as official and underground poetry.

Slutskii's Poetics: Between Maiakovskii and Brodskii

Having considered the ways in which the 'Soviet variable' is dealt with in accounts of Slutskii's life and career, the remainder of this chapter will address the question of his poetics. Grinberg summarises the post-Soviet consensus on this subject, saying that Slutskii is now recognised as a major poet, perhaps the major poet of post-war Soviet poetry, whose work influenced the sound of Russian prosody and was a major influence on Iosif Brodskii's early development as a poet. Slutskii's poetics were inspired by the futurists, constructivists, and early Soviet avant-garde.[56] This focus on poetics places Slutskii in a rather different relationship with his times, setting him in a context that includes, but goes beyond, mainstream Soviet culture. Slutskii's distinctive diction links his work with the kind of formal experimentation that was largely suppressed during the 1920s, but which later re-emerged in the Soviet literary underground. Slutskii's poetry shows few of the formal characteristics that might be expected from the work of a Soviet socialist realist poet: a smoothly melodic style, regular rhythm, unobtrusively conventional rhyme, and a tendency towards poetic rather than everyday vocabulary. Read alongside the published work of his contemporaries, Slutskii's poetry looks closer to prose than poetry. Its rhythms are irregular, it lacks metaphor and melody, it uses language which is often colloquial, sometimes employing non-standard variants from everyday speech.

D. Shrayer, 2 vols. (Armonk, NY and London: M. E. Sharpe, 2007), II, 639–47 and 795–96. A volume of Slutskii's writing on Jewish themes has appeared in Russia: B. A. Slutskii, *'Teper' Osventsim chasto snitsia mne'*, compiled by P. Gorelik (St Petersburg: Zhurnala Neva, 1999).

56 Grinberg, *The Poetics of Boris Slutsky*, pp. 14–15.

Lazar' Lazarev highlights both the artful and deliberate construction of Slutskii's verse, and its studied avoidance of easy harmoniousness:

> the awkwardness and unfinished quality of Slutskii's poetry are deceptive — he is one of those poets who place a great emphasis on form, 'technique', instrumentation — this is not the result of carelessness but of the desire to destroy, explode smoothness and slickness.[57]

Igor' Shkliarevskii's notes that Slutskii made significant, and largely successful efforts to suppress the melodic qualities of his writing.[58] Slutskii's avoidance of obvious ornament goes together with an emphasis on reasoned reflection rather than emotional effusiveness. In a poem of 1973 Ian Satunovskii, a writer belonging to the unofficial Lianozovo group, recognised Slutskii's sober rationality, declaring:

> Люблю стихи Бориса Слуцкого–
> толковые суждения
> прямого харьковского хлопца,
> как говорит Овсей;
> веские доказательства
> недоказуемого.[59]

> I love Boris Slutskii's poems —
> sensible opinions of a plain
> Khar'kov lad,
> as Ovsei says;
> weighty proofs of something
> that cannot be proved.

---

57 Lazar' Lazarev, 'S nadezhdoi, pravdoi i dobrom...', p. 195.
58 Igor' Shkliarevskii, 'On ne zaigryval s nebom', in *Boris Slutskii: vospominaniia sovremennikov*, pp. 390–91 (p. 391).
59 Ian Satunovskii, 'Liubliu stikhi Borisa Slutskogo', *Khochu li ia posmertnoi slavy: izbrannye stikhi*, compiled by I. Akhmet'ev and P. Satunovskii (Moscow: Biblioteka al'manakha 'Vesy', 1992), http://www.vavilon.ru/texts/satunovsky1-3.html. The reference to 'Ovsei' is likely to be to the poet Ovsei Driz, who wrote in Yiddish, and was translated into Russian by, among others, Genrikh Sapgir and Slutskii. A poem by Slutskii, 'Optimisticheskie pokhorony' ('An optimistic funeral') on Driz's funeral in 1968 is included in Lev Frukhtman's memoir of Driz, 'Zhil-byl skazochnik', http://velelens.livejournal.com/879503.html

Compared with the work of most of the mainstream Soviet poets with whom Slutskii is usually associated in literary histories, his work might well be described as 'not-quite poetry' ('nedopoeziia'), the word Oleg Dark uses to describe the perception of Slutskii's work as anomalous.[60] Yet while it cannot reasonably be claimed that Slutskii's position in the poetry canon has changed significantly since 1991, even though readers have access to a much wider range of his work, it is nevertheless fair to say that the canon has changed around him, making it possible to view Slutskii in a new context. By placing emphasis on his poetics, Slutskii can be read beyond the confines of the Soviet/anti-Soviet binary. The poets associated with the Lianozovo school such as Satunovskii, Evgenii Kropivnitskii, Sapgir, and Igor' Kholin, who are gradually and tentatively being included in the canon, adopted minimalist aesthetics which resemble Slutskii's own. By tracing Slutskii's connections with such poets of the Soviet underground along the axis of poetic form, it becomes easier to recover him first and foremost as a poet. This point is well made by Dark, who reminds readers that a poet's work may seem very different when viewed in a new context. Slutskii set alongside canonical Soviet poets Iaroslav Smeliakov, Konstantin Simonov, and David Samoilov is one thing, but next to Satunovskii and the émigré Georgii Ivanov, whose work existed outside that canon, he has the potential to appear as something quite different.[61]

In his anti-normative poetics Slutskii shows himself to be a poet following in the footsteps of the writers of the Russian avant-garde of the early twentieth century, including the futurists and the constructivists of the 1920s. Benedikt Sarnov refers to him as 'the last lawful heir of Maiakovskii'.[62] Slutskii's personal library included the work of many avant-garde poets which became difficult to get hold of during the 1930s.[63] He made contact with some prominent representatives of the avant-garde while studying in Moscow in the late 1930s. At the Literary

---

60 Oleg Dark, 'V storony mertvykh: mezhdu Smeliakovym i Sapgirom', *Russkii zhurnal*, 14 July 2003, para. 9, http://old.russ.ru/krug/20030714_od.html
61 Ibid., para. 11.
62 Benedikt Sarnov, 'Zanimatel'naia dialektika', in *Boris Slutskii: vospominaniia sovremennikov*, pp. 236–54 (p. 247).
63 These names are among the poets listed by Semen Lipkin in his recollections of Slutskii, 'Sila sovesti', in *Boris Slutskii: vospominaniia sovremennikov*, pp. 212–18 (pp. 212–13).

Institute in 1939 he enrolled in Il'ia Sel'vinskii's poetic seminar, choosing a leading figure of the constructivist movement as his teacher. The young poets with whom he studied at IFLI (the Institute of Philosophy, Literature and History) including Pavel Kogan and Mikhail Kul'chitskii, a close friend from Khar'kov, shared an admiration for the work of Maiakovskii and Khlebnikov.[64] Slutskii also attended a poetry seminar run by Osip Brik, and made the acquaintance of Lili Brik who, according to Vladimir Ognev, presented him with a bed that had belonged to Maiakovskii.[65] He would later serve for a time as the chair of the commission handling Khlebnikov's legacy.[66]

When it comes to situating Slutskii in relation to his poetic descendants, it is striking that his influence extends to poets active in the literary underground as well as published poets. Shubinskii claims Slutskii, with his emphasis on poetic language as a medium which does not permit the superfluous, as a precursor of conceptualism, without whom Vsevolod Nekrasov and Lev Rubinshtein might not have become poets at all, or would have been very different; Brodskii, he adds, would not have been the same without Slutskii.[67] It is Brodskii who made one of the most important, and frequently quoted canonising statements on Slutskii. Brodskii foregrounds Slutskii's poetics, identifying the disparate elements that contribute to the poet's distinctive style:

> It is Slutzky who has almost single-handedly changed the diction of post-war Russian poetry. His verse is a conglomeration of bureaucratese, military lingo, colloquialisms and sloganeering, and it employs with equal ease assonance, dactylic and visual rhymes, sprung rhythms and vernacular cadences.[68]

---

64 Falikov notes that the young IFLI poets were also influenced by the work of Nikolai Gumilev, which was excluded from the published canon until the late 1980s; 'Pust' budet', *Voprosy literatury*, 5 (2006), 180–201 (p. 183).
65 Vladimir Ognev, 'Moi drug Boris Slutskii', in *Boris Slutskii: vospominaniia sovremennikov*, pp. 274–89 (p. 280). Lili Brik's gift of Maiakovskii's bed must have been made considerably later, as Slutskii was without a secure base in Moscow for many years after the war, and lived in a succession of rented rooms.
66 Petr Miturich, *Boris Slutskii: vospominaniia sovremennikov*, pp. 546–47. Slutskii's poem, 'Perepokhorony Khlebnikov', *Sobranie sochinenii*, II, 286–87, refers to the reburial of Khlebnikov's remains in 1960.
67 Shubinskii, 'Semeinyi al'bom: zametki o sovetskoi poezii klassicheskogo perioda', p. 167.
68 Joseph Brodsky, 'Literature and War: A Symposium', *TLS*, 17 May 1985, 11–12 (p. 12).

Brodskii acknowledged Slutskii's influence on his own early development; his creative dialogue with Slutskii is discussed in some detail by David MacFadyen.[69] Falikov claims that the list of poets who had read Slutskii 'productively' is too long to ennumerate.[70] Nevertheless, various critics have named the following as in some way shaped by Slutskii: Evgenii Vinokurov, Nikolai Panchenko, Vladimir Kornilov, Aleksandr Mezhirov, Mikhail Aizenberg, together with later poets who emerged at roughly the same time as many of Slutskii's works found their way out of his archive into print.[71] He was certainly known as a generous mentor of young poets, and taught at the Literary Institute for many years. His generous moral and financial support for younger colleagues was well known and is mentioned by many memoirists, though Kuniaev, a former protégé, suggests that Slutskii's generosity was motivated principally by his wish to establish a group of loyal disciples, and claims that those who did not agree with him were marginalised.[72]

The reach of Slutskii's influence across a wide range of poets must be ascribed primarily to his poetics, which he had formed under the influence of the early twentieth-century avant-garde. At a time when the legacy of this movement had been largely suppressed, Slutskii was one of the few published poets who continued with formal experimentation and so helped to link two generations separated by socialist realism. Certainly Maiakovskii's style left its traces in Slutskii's rhythm. Barry P. Scherr sees a similar use of variable and mixed meters, particularly the frequent insertion of trochaic lines into poems that are predominantly iambic.[73] Other features of Slutskii's poetics that align him with the tradition of futurist poetry include his use of word-play; Tat'iana Bek sees his fondness for bringing together words which are etymologically

---

69   See David MacFadyen, *Joseph Brodsky and the Soviet Muse* (Montreal: McGill-Queen's University Press, 2000), pp. 55–75.
70   Falikov, 'Krasnorechie po-Slutski', p. 104.
71   See *Sovremennye russkie poety* (Moscow: Nauchno-prakticheskii tsentr Megatron, 1998), compiled by V. Agenosov, K. Ankudinov, pp. 296–303 (pp. 296–97).
72   Stanislav Kuniaev, *Poeziia, Sud'ba, Rossiia*, II, 227–28. Vladimir Kornilov, however, states that Slutskii had no interest in being part of a literary clique. See Kornilov, 'Pokuda nad stikhami plachut...', p. 113.
73   Barry P. Scherr, 'Martynov, Slutskii and the Politics of Rhythm', *Paragraph*, 33: 2 (2010), 246–59 (p. 257), and *Russian Poetry: Meter, Rhythm, and Rhyme* (Berkeley: University of California Press, 1986), pp. 107–08.

related by having the same root as a feature that links him with the futurists.⁷⁴ In the area of rhyme, too, Slutskii shows his connection with futurist word-play by using homonym rhyme, in which the rhyming words sound the same but have different meanings, and repetend rhyme, in which the words in a rhyming pair are identical in both sound and meaning. Bek sees Slutskii very much as continuing along the path laid down by the futurists, and describes his work as a rewriting of Russian classics 'in the language handed to him by his times (passing his unique experience through the intermediate filters of Khlebnikov and other Futurists)'.⁷⁵ Oleg Khlebnikov finds echoes of earlier predecessors in Slutskii's 'not-quite-poetry':

> When reading Slutskii's poetry you need to remember that as well as Pushkinian harmony there exists in our poetry the harmony of Derzhavin and Maiakovskii, and if you tune your ear accordingly the accusations of Slutskii's 'inelegance' vanish all by themselves.⁷⁶

Mikhail Gasparov, meanwhile, sees a connection between Slutskii and another formally innovative twentieth-century poet whose work is distinguished by an intensely emotional pitch, Marina Tsvetaeva. The similarity with Slutskii lies elsewhere: 'If you set aside Tsvetaeva's hyperbolism and passion, while retaining the same precision with which phrases are formulated, as well as the emphasis on the way words echo one another, you get Slutskii's poetics'.⁷⁷

In its apparent simplicity Slutskii's poetry clearly echoes, too, the concerns of the Literary Centre of Constructivists, who wanted writers to produce work which would be simply formulated so as to be intelligible to the masses. It draws on what the constructivists termed the 'local method', which meant that every level of a literary work (such as sound, imagery, lexicon) should be selected so as to form an integral part of its meaning. Sel'vinskii had led the way in using slang and regional expressions when the theme of a poem called for it. Slutskii's own

---

74 Tat'iana Bek, 'Rasshifruite moi tetradi...', in *Boris Slutskii: vospominaniia sovremennikov*, pp. 255–66 (p. 256).
75 *Ibid.*, p. 258.
76 Oleg Khlebnikov, 'Vysokaia bolezn' Borisa Slutskogo', in *Boris Slutskii: vospominaniia sovremennikov*, pp. 202–11 (p. 211).
77 Mikhail Gasparov, quoted in Marat Grinberg, 'Vychityvaia Slutskogo: Boris Slutskii v dialoge s sovremennikami', *Kreshchatik*, 3, 2008, para. 39, http://magazines.russ.ru/kreschatik/2008/3/gr23.html

early years were spent in Khar'kov, a city where Russian, Ukrainian and Yiddish co-existed. His childhood home, right next to the city's main market, exposed the poet to a mixture of languages, colloquial and substandard forms of expression, which he later found their way into his work. Simplicity is a word that needs to be used in relation to Slutskii's poetry with caution, however, as Slutskii's simplicity is plainly not of the same variety as that of Dem'ian Bednyi or Vasilii Lebedev-Kumach. Kuniaev, for a while one of Slutskii's poetic protégés, seems to have been influenced in his decision to part company with his mentor because of what he describes as the 'refined atmosphere' around his work.[78] In the view of Lev Anninskii, the simplicity of Slutskii's work conceals its subtleties: 'this simplicity is aimed at a conoisseur who is far from simple'.[79] Dmitrii Sukharev finds it appropriate to describe Slutskii's poetics as 'cryptographic'; the deceptive simplicity of his style directs attention away from complex sound patterning which generates associations and layers of meaning.[80] Lev Mochalov also sees hidden depths in Slutskii's poetry:

> its secret explosive power lay in its anti-normative, disruptive qualities of rough, unworked stone or rusty metal; its rhythmical breaks are there to give the living intonation of conversation, its incorrect usage provides expressiveness.[81]

A significant element that contributes towards the impression of simplicity produced by Slutskii's poetry is what G. S. Smith describes as its 'a low-pitched conversational tone'.[82] Slutskii's conversational tone of voice when reading his own work clearly stood out from the reading style of his contemporaries. One memoirist recalls hearing Slutskii read his famous 'Loshadi v okeane' ('Horses in the Ocean', 1956) at a seminar for young writers in the late 1950s; his tone of voice did not change as he

---

78 Vladimir Bondarenko, *Poslednie poety imperii: ocherki literaturnykh sudeb* (Moscow: Molodaia gvardiia, 2005), p. 138.
79 Lev Anninskii, 'Ia rodilsia v zheleznom obshchestve', *Druzhba narodov*, 2 (2006), para. 60, http://magazines.russ.ru/druzhba/2006/2/an16.html
80 Dmitrii Sukharev, '"Skrytopis" Borisa Slutskogo', pp. 31–32.
81 Lev Mochalov, 'V znake starinnoi druzhby', in *Boris Slutskii: vospominaniia sovremennikov*, pp. 392–400 (p. 394).
82 G. S. Smith, *Dictionary of Literary Biography*, vol. 359, p. 258.

began to recite his poem, remaining matter-of-fact throughout, much to the puzzlement of at least some of his audience.[83]

The tone of Slutskii's poetry does not rely merely on its avoidance of declamation and adoption of colloquial language. It is, as Scherr points out, built in through his use of variable meters, mixing binary and ternary feet, and the varying length of his lines.[84] The fact that it is hard to make out a predictable pattern reinforces the impression that Slutskii's poetry is just one remove from everyday speech. Scherr's analysis of Slutskii's use of the four-foot *dolnik* shows that he avoids regular rhythms, in a deliberate departure from nineteenth-century norms, and demonstrates the highest degree of rhythmical experimentation in poems which deal with the subject of poetry.[85] It is perhaps because of the close affinity between Slutskii's poetics and everyday speech that little of what he wrote seems to have been taken up as phrases in common usage, although Bek recalls her parents often using phrases from Slutskii's poems as part of their everyday conversations.[86] Slutskii's pairing of *fiziki i liriki* (physicists and lyric poets) established itself firmly from the late 1950s, but the phrase was often used by people who were not aware of its origins.[87] Perhaps Slutskii's conversational tone made his poetry resistant to memorisation; in contrast to the sonorous and predictably-patterned verse of the Stalinist 'grand style', it was simply too close to the texture of everyday speech to take root in it.

Even though Slutskii's poetics point towards his association with artistic currents of the twentieth century which did not originate in official Soviet culture and were generally at odds with that culture, the identification of Slutskii with the ideology of the era in which he lived still features in discussions of the formal characteristics of his works.

---

83 Dmitrii Sukharev, 'Dlia ponimaniia Slutskogo nuzhny miagkie nravy i eshche kakoi-nikakoi professionalizm', in *Boris Slutskii: vospominaniia sovremennikov*, pp. 267–73 (p. 271).
84 Vladimir Kornilov notes that Slutskii used the same tone of voice for normal conversation and for reciting his poetry. See Vladimir Kornilov, 'Pokuda nad stikhami plachut...', in *Boris Slutskii: vospominaniia sovremennikov*, pp. 106–20 (p. 106). See also Scherr, *Russian Poetry: Meter, Rhythm, and Rhyme*, pp. 107–08.
85 Scherr, *Russian Poetry*, pp. 137–78.
86 According to Marina Krasnova, 'Slutskii's poetry did not produce any quotations'. See Marina Krasnova, 'Vladelets shestisot istorii', *Novyi mir*, 8 (2006), 177–82 (p. 181). Bek, 'Rasshifruite moi tetradi...', p. 264.
87 'Fiziki i liriki', *Sobranie sochinenii*, I, 351.

The poet Evgenii Rein describes Slutskii's poetry as 'a phenomenon of rhythm, poetics, sound, and it is this sound in Slutskii's work that most corresponds to the peculiar Soviet era'.[88] Rein pursues his point by restating the close relationship between Bolshevik ideology and avant-garde culture, describing Slutskii's closeness to 'the avant-garde as a movement and project connected to the Soviet utopia, Stalinism'.[89] Aleksei Smirnov also hears echoes of Slutskii's times in the sound of his poetry, claiming that Slutskii's work is 'a pure echo of his epoch', but gives his opinion that the disharmony to be found in his work originates in the times and not in the poet himself.[90]

An exploration of Slutskii's poetics makes it possible to see him in a relation to a canon that is not constructed according to binary concepts such as Soviet/anti-Soviet, but which foregrounds poetic form and language in a tradition that connects him with Derzhavin, the post-war underground poets, Maiakovskii and Brodskii.

Conclusion

The case of Slutskii shows that the position of an individual poet within the literary canon may begin to shift not so much as a result of any new discoveries of that poet's texts, or of attempts by advocates of that poet to transform readers' perceptions, but by a process of gradual canonical change which alters the context in which the poet is viewed. In the late-Soviet version of literary history, Slutskii was firmly embedded alongside his contemporaries, war veterans and party members, a chronicler of wartime heroism and duty. This picture was disrupted in the final years of the Soviet Union's existence by the publication of poems which revealed Slutskii's struggle with censorship and anti-semitism, the complex, often dramatic relationship between the poet and his times. When those times came to a sudden end, the legacy of a poet seen as intimately bound up with the Soviet experience lost much of its immediate interest. Through the 1990s and 2000s the

---

88 Evgenii Rein, 'Samyi krupnyi poet pozdnego sovetizma', in *Boris Slutskii: vospominaniia sovremennikov*, pp. 387–89 (pp. 388–89).
89 *Ibid.*, p. 388.
90 Aleksei Smirnov, 'Blizhnee ekho', in *Boris Slutskii: vospominaniia sovremennikov*, pp. 461–67 (pp. 464–65).

history of twentieth-century poetry has gradually been assembled from its apparently disparate elements. This has enabled Slutskii to emerge in the company of other poets from outside the Soviet-era canon. The familiar narrative of the poet and his times remains in place, and Slutskii can still be compared with poets such as Ol'ga Berggol'ts and Aleksandr Tvardovskii, who, like him, tried to reconcile party loyalties with poetic integrity. The changing canon, however, reveals Slutskii as a figure who demonstrates the inadequacy of simplistic divisions between official and unofficial poetry as a way of understanding twentieth-century Russian poetry, and the power of poetic innovation.

10. The Diasporic Canon of Russian Poetry: The Case of the Paris Note

Maria Rubins

Reclaiming Diasporic Voices: Unity or Difference?

The canonical shifts that defined Russian literary history in the late twentieth century entailed not only a massive reassessment of Soviet-era verse and the reintegration into the canon of previously silenced voices and texts, but also the recovery of diaspora poets. The rhetoric of a unified literature and canon that emerged in Russian criticism then and which prevails to this day constructs émigrés as prodigal sons, finally readmitted into the fold of national culture. Typical titles of émigré anthologies and prefaces to émigré works published since the *glasnost'* period recycle a familiar repertoire, spelling out the myth of return: 'Returning to Russia in Verse', 'Homecoming', etc. This celebration of unity was understandable after many decades of division and isolation. The dialogue that was re-launched between the metropolitan and diasporic branches of Russian culture focused on shared elements and common origins in the pre-revolutionary tradition. This perspective was facilitated by the publishing dynamic itself: among the émigré poets first to be printed after the relaxation of censorship were such key figures of the Silver Age as Marina Tsvetaeva, Zinaida Gippius, Dmitrii Merezhkovskii, Georgii Ivanov, Irina Odoevtseva, Vladislav Khodasevich, Konstantin Bal'mont, and Igor' Severianin, whose pre-exile works were for the most part 'sanctioned' during the Soviet period, even if available in limited quantities. In addition to introducing broad reading audiences to their more mature émigré verse, this dissemination offered Russians an opportunity to reconnect to the Silver Age in a new way and to establish continuity between pre- and post-Soviet culture.

However, when the time came to reclaim the second generation of émigré poets, who left Russia at a young age and began their literary careers already in the West, this approach became a handicap: rather than seeking nuance, it glossed over the 'foreign' and 'strange' elements that fit uncomfortably into the native poetic paradigm. As a result, the diasporic specificity of particular poets whose verse was generated as much by their experience of migration, dislocation, and transcultural flows as by the national cultural tradition, has been de-emphasised.

The idea of a fundamental aesthetic homogeneity and parallel development of metropolitan and émigré branches had already been voiced previously in the diaspora itself, provoking a certain resistance on the part of younger poets who argued that their distinct poetic identity could not be circumscribed by a straightforward affiliation with Russian literature. Originally articulated in Gleb Struve's book *Russian Literature in Exile* (1956), the idea of a unified Russian literature was reinforced at the 1972 Geneva conference 'One or Two Russian Literatures?'.[1] As Efim Etkind stated at that forum, the separation of Russian poetry into Soviet and foreign was artificial, caused entirely by politics, and bound to give rise to a convergence of both in one literary mainstream once ideological barriers were removed. Moreover, Etkind insisted that 'poetry within and outside the country developed according to the same or similar laws, solving common aesthetic tasks'.[2] Characteristically, to illustrate his position Etkind drew on a limited number of examples, such as the alleged coherence between Tsvetaeva, Pasternak and Maiakovskii, or between pamphlet poems by Gippius and Dem'ian Bednyi. In passing he commented on the differentiation of the younger generation ('poets of the second émigré generation deviated, it seems, from the common path of Russian literature'[3]) but did not elaborate. Etkind's declaration of

---

1   In the diaspora this position challenged Soviet ideological discourse, which excluded émigré voices from the Russian canon.
2   Efim Etkind, 'Russkaia poeziia XX veka kak edinyi protsess', in *Odna ili dve russkikh literatury?*, edited by Georges Nivat (Lausanne: L'Age d'Homme, 1981), pp. 9–30 (p. 16).
3   Ibid., p. 29.

aesthetic unity across borders was countered by Zinaida Shakhovskaia, on behalf of the younger interwar generation. She insisted on the *sui generis* character of their literary production, quite different, in her view, from developments in metropolitan Russia.[4]

Such contrasting estimations of the role of the native tradition for émigrés, driven by the empirical material at hand, is another confirmation that émigré literature was far from monolithic and consisted of diverse streams. The optic that highlights the parallelism of twentieth-century Russian poetry inside and outside Soviet borders on the basis of their common origins in the classical tradition is perhaps valid for a number of poetic phenomena of Russia Abroad. It is particularly appropriate for many of the senior poets of the First Wave whose artistic beginnings stemmed from the Silver Age and who continued to cultivate national literary identities in exile.[5] Geographical displacement of course introduced certain changes into their art, such as new themes, settings or nostalgic retrospection, but these modifications remained rather superficial and inconsequential for their deeper poetic matrix. The older generation of Russian émigré writers, especially those grouped around the Merezhkovskii-Gippius literary *salon*, regarded themselves as guardians of pre-revolutionary Russian culture. Consequently, rather than exploring new aesthetic dimensions and engaging with opportunities offered by their new locale and with contemporary European art, they often limited themselves to the reproduction of familiar models drawn from the classical Russian canon. But at the same time, in Russia Abroad, there emerged voices that transcended the national framework and produced poetry generated by the very experience of life in the diaspora with its inevitable interstitiality, transcultural diversity and plurality of aesthetic and linguistic idioms. Therefore, discussing such works exclusively from the perspective of the Russian national canon appears problematic.

National canons, at least as they took shape in Western European literatures in the early nineteenth century, articulate certain aesthetic

---

4   Zinaida Shakhovskaia, 'Literaturnye pokoleniia', in *Odna ili dve russkikh literatury?*, pp. 52–62.
5   On the contribution of émigré writers to the construction of Russian national identity, see Greta Slobin, *Russians Abroad: Literary and Cultural Politics of Diaspora (1919–1939)* (Boston: Academic Studies Press, 2013).

and cultural values, provide an authoritative (albeit constantly revised) set of key models, and thereby promote a vision of a distinct national literary tradition that reflects (and perhaps also informs) a specific version of national identity. This approach fails to account for a large and ever-growing corpus of diasporic narratives that engage with cross-cultural sensibilities and practices and articulate emerging, fluid, often conflicted, hybrid and hyphenated identities. Explaining why diasporic discourse has become an object of intense study only now, Igor Maver writes:

> Diasporic subjectivities have always coexisted within and outside the long migrant history of a nation but their experience as a text had long been disregarded. However, diasporic (trans)cultural experiences and practices have become today a mode of everyday existence [...][6]

Due to specific historical circumstances, as a result of almost a hundred years of dispersion Russia has also acquired a global cultural diaspora. Its literary legacy has gradually reached critical mass, calling attention to the emergence of the diasporic canon of Russian literature. Although a great many studies have been written on individual authors and various aspects of émigré writing, the Russian diasporic canon as such has not yet found sufficient conceptual articulation. In what follows, I will present preliminary considerations regarding the taxonomy of the Russian diasporic production, and then develop some of the relevant criteria, focusing on the interwar poetic group known as the Paris Note.

Plurality of Canons and Russian Diasporic Experience

Although the examination of the distinct character of Russian diasporic culture is long overdue, the plurality of canons more generally has been a conspicuous topic in Western critical writing since the late twentieth century. Many newly-formed canon varieties have been articulated, including postcolonial, transnational, feminist, and Afro-American. These new discourses contest the conception of a unified national canon, dismissing it as elitist and totalitarian, as the heated debates

---

6   Igor Maver, 'Introduction: Positioning Diasporic Literary Cultures', in *Diasporic Subjectivity and Cultural Brokering in Contemporary Post-colonial Literatures*, edited by Igor Maver (Lanham and Plymouth: Lexington Books, 2009), pp. ix–xiv, xi.

around Harold Bloom's *The Western Canon: The Books and School of the Ages* have demonstrated. At the same time, the canon is reconfigured as a repository of specific values, ideologies, and sensibilities germane to a particular group or a subculture.

The emergence of multiple canonical paradigms is perhaps a natural consequence of mobility, the increasingly porous nature of various geographical, social and cultural boundaries, the empowering of previously marginalised social or ethnic groups, and the resulting fragmentation and hybridization of aesthetic experiences and practices. The mono-national framework is simply no longer sufficient to capture the entire range of cross-cultural and transnational artistic production. And even if, as in contemporary Russia, for example, we witness the opposite tendency to reinforce the nationalist discourse by recycling an old set of aesthetic and ideological symbols, this is most likely just a stubborn reaction against the world's shift beyond the physical and conceptual borders of the nation-state. Rather than simply resisting or embracing this canonical diversity, we should further extend our inquiry, addressing the following questions: what kind of realities and viewpoints do these newly-formed canons represent? What are their fundamental criteria? On what basis are works included or excluded from a canon? And most importantly, how do we expand and deepen the interpretation of a literary text if we approach it from the perspective of a specific canon?

As opposed to newly-articulated canons associated with particular subcultures, diasporic literatures have evolved over thousands of years in extremely diverse contexts, generating an infinite number of diasporic literary models. But contemporary criticism has often framed the discussion of diasporic literary production with the tenets of postcolonial theory, addressed primarily to the work of authors from former colonies who live outside their homeland and write in the language of the former coloniser (such as the Anglophone work of immigrants from India now living in the British Isles, or francophone narratives of North African authors). This postcolonial paradigm does not quite fit the situation of Russian émigrés, despite a number of parallels with postcolonial writers in their way of seeing and representing the world, a nostalgic focus on geographies, the mythic image of the homeland, and the way of inscribing divided or conflicted identities. In particular, the difference lies in the fact that most authors of Russia Abroad continued to write in Russian, and the primary point of reference for their narratives is the Russian metropolitan literary tradition rather than that of the host country. Furthermore, the entire colonial context is replaced in Russian émigré imagination by the pain and longing of exile, caused by an oppressive political regime. Indeed, in the Russian experience, the exilic condition has in most cases served as a stepping stone to diasporic identity. Exilic narratives, much like the Ovidian lament, are informed by acute memory of the suffering caused by involuntary departure from home and the desire of return. To use Svetlana Boym's terminology, they are often predicated on 'restorative' nostalgia, on a futile dream of exact reconstitution of the past. Diasporic literature proper, on the other hand, tends to practice a 'reflective' nostalgia that delays homecoming, lingers on the ruins, and engenders an understanding of the irrevocability of the past.[7] While mindful of the place of origin, a diasporic literary subject mitigates his nostalgia by conceiving of life and belonging as an itinerary rather than as a fixed locus, and creates a complex transitory identity for himself, drawing on his experience of a different place and time to reflect on the present. In other words, diasporic narratives are predicated to a greater extent on the condition of migration, various border-crossings, in-between areas, and transcultural encounters than on the pain of exile and the dream of return.

Diasporic studies see migrancy 'in terms of adaptation and construction — adaptation to changes, dislocations and transformations, and the construction of new forms of knowledge and ways of seeing the world'.[8] It is worth specifying that 'adaptation' should not be equated with assimilation in a host culture, as in this case one national identity would be simply exchanged for another. Meanwhile, the diasporic 'way of seeing the world' implies not a new, but an extra pair of eyes, a transnational experience of fragmentation, fusion and hybridity. While from the position of a monolithic nation state, diasporic narratives can be read as a subversive counter-discourse, with regard to the Russian artistic experience diasporic and national cultural formations do not establish a

---

7   See Svetlana Boym, *The Future of Nostalgia* (New York: Basic Books, 2001).
8   *Diasporic Literature and Theory — Where Now?* edited by Mark Shackleton (Newcastle upon Tyne: Cambridge Scholars Publishing, 2008), p. ix.

strict binary opposition. Rather, diasporic and metropolitan culture form a complementary relationship; without negating the national legacy, diaspora offers additional vistas, alternative routes of development and patterns of interpretation, constructing an ambivalent and fluid 'third space'[9]—a peculiar blend of the memories of the homeland, experience of and reflection on the host culture(s), and imaginary trajectories between the two. Diasporic identities cannot be assigned as stable and fixed entities, rather diasporic belonging is enacted through narrative. When diasporic characters perform themselves through narration, they render national identifications unreliable or irrelevant. This challenge to the protocols of essentialist and homogeneously constructed versions of national identity often takes form not of direct confrontation and negation but as veering off, sidestepping, adding variations to the theme, defamiliarising, or proceeding in a 'knight's move', according to Viktor Shklovskii's famous metaphor.

The origins of contemporary diasporic Russian literary culture can be found in the work of a number of interwar émigrés who gradually turned away from the 'mission' of preserving the national legacy and the teleology of return to exploring the diasporic imaginary, stimulated by mobility, displacement and new cultural experiences. Most of such verbal artists belonged to a younger and more dynamic generation, who refused to live by past alone. Their émigré peers were quick to accuse these younger writers of betraying their origins and writing 'like foreigners' (a frequent charge levelled against Vladimir Nabokov and Gaïto Gazdanov, among others), without delving deeper into the reasons for such a turn. Indeed, there were few attempts at the time to define the distinct character of this new writing, even on the part of the younger émigrés themselves. Deeper reflection came much later,

---

9   'Third space' has become a trendy concept in interdisciplinary sources on postmodernist cultural production. In *Location of Culture* (London: Routledge, 1994), Homi Bhabha interprets 'third space' as a creative form of cultural identity produced on the boundaries between forms of difference, in particular in overlaps across the spheres of nation and location. For Edward Soja, *third spaces* are simultaneously material and mental, or real and imagined, resulting from negotiations between physical realities and mental or cultural constructions. More importantly, *third spaces* are spaces of transition between localities and over time (Edward Soja, *Thirdspace: Journey to Los Angeles and Other Real-and-Imagined Places* (Oxford: Blackwell, 1996)).

as for example in Zinaida Shakhovskaia's articulation of the diasporic specificity of Vladimir Nabokov:

> The pinnacle of émigré literature is Vladimir Nabokov, a writer who could not have appeared in the Soviet Union. [...] In the airless space of emigration, Nabokov created an airless and signal literature, a soulless world of symbols, grotesques and parodies — non-beings. He also created his own language, mastering it with years, mixing all languages known to him, transforming geographical names and proper nouns into puns. This restlessness, which he consciously chose after it had been pressed upon him by history, Nabokov brought to perfection and became a free-floating island, separated from the native continent.[10]

Similarly, Vladimir Markov defined the poetics of Georgii Ivanov as informed primarily by the experience of emigration:

> Georgii Ivanov is a poet of Russian emigration because in emigration and thanks to it, he became a singular and original poet. It is also important that in his poems he wrote more than others about emigration and from the émigré point of view. Many writers and poets of Russia Abroad tried to blur this point of view and conceived of their often remarkable tableaux of the past as part of the great and majestic preceding tradition. In Georgii Ivanov, this past is an openly nostalgic (or ironic) reminiscence, and it is 'subjectively local', i.e. not only personal 'in general' but also written down by a person located in a particular spot. This endows his verse with distinct concrete lyricism. In this sense, Georgii Ivanov is perhaps the most unquestionable jewel of emigration.[11]

In the same article, Markov comments on Paris Note poetry as constituting merely a 'footnote' to Ivanov's verse.[12] While this opinion was hardly intended as a compliment to Ivanov's disciples, a reference to them in the same context confirms their affinity with the premier poet of Russia Abroad. Perhaps falling short of Ivanov's artistic excellence, the Paris Note poets responded to the challenges and anxieties inherent in their condition as uprooted migrants, suspended between the distant Russian homeland and the immediate reality of interwar France. And arguably, they did this even more starkly than their *maître*, stripping their verse of anything extraneous to crystallise the diasporic condition of deracination and hybridity.

---

10   Shakhovskaia, p. 61.
11   Vladimir Markov, 'O poezii Georgiia Ivanova', *Opyty*, 8 (1958), p. 85.
12   *Ibid.*, p. 85.

The Paris Note: Diasporic Imagination in the Making

What came to be known as the Paris Note (*Parizhskaia Nota*) was a loose group that formed around Georgii Adamovich in the 1930s. While there is no definitive list of its members, most critics agree that the ethos and poetics of the Paris Note were expressed most consistently by Anatolii Shteiger and Lydiia Chervinskaia, in addition to Adamovich himself and, as mentioned earlier, Ivanov, who was for them an important inspirational figure. Among other names mentioned in this context are Igor' Chinnov, Raisa Blokh, Irina Knorring, Perikl Stavrov, and, to a limited extent, Boris Bozhnev, Dovid Knut, and Odoevtseva. Meanwhile, the verse of Boris Poplavskii, who may have even coined the group's name, deviated significantly from Paris Note poetics.

The distinct position of Paris Note poets in Russia Abroad has been highlighted in a number of studies on émigré verse. Roger Hagglund even considers the Paris Note 'the very antithesis' of Russian literature of exile. Echoing Claudio Guillén,[13] Hagglund defines the Paris Note legacy as 'literature of counter-exile' because their verse transcended autobiographical reflection on loss to convey 'a metaphysical concern with the eternal themes of life, the so-called "final questions" of man's origin, destiny, and purpose'.[14] According to Vadim Krejd, 'The Paris Note is one of the pages of poetry that cannot be overlooked. With regards to émigré literature, the "Note" in it is not a mere page, but a whole chapter, and one of the most conceptual'.[15] The group's original character was obvious to those who witnessed the evolution of émigré literature at close range. In his 1942 survey of Russian Parisian poetry, Georgii

---

13 Claudio Guillén proposed to differentiate between 'literature of exile' and 'literature of counter-exile'. The former focuses on 'an autobiographical conveyance of the actual experience of exile itself', whereas the latter refers to writers moving beyond their experience of exile 'toward integration, increasingly broad vistas or universalism'. Triumphing over 'the separation from place, class, languages, or native community', the literature of counter-exile, according to Guillén, offers 'wide dimensions of meaning that transcend the earlier attachment to place of native origin' (Claudio Guillén, 'On the Literature of Exile and Counter-Exile', *Books Abroad*, 50 (1976), 271–80 (p. 272)). In essence, this opposition captures the distinction that I draw here between exilic and diasporic literature.

14 Roger Hagglund, *A Vision of Unity: Adamovich in Exile* (Ann Arbor: Ardis, 1985), pp. 38–39.

15 Vadim Krejd, 'Chto takoe "Parizhskaia nota"', *Slovo/Word*, 43–44 (2004), http://magazines.russ.ru/slovo/2004/43/kr41.html

Fedotov suggested that the original and independent character of the Paris Note stands in sharp relief against the backdrop of epigone verse duplicating Russian (mostly Petersburg) poetics: 'Take away the School [Paris Note — M.R.] and only separate voices will remain, continuing to rehash pre-revolutionary — mostly Petersburg — poetry'.[16]

This is not to say that the Paris Note members were weakly connected to the Russian tradition. After all, their mentors, Adamovich and Ivanov, themselves represented Petersburg modernism, and they were keen to engage in an intertextual dialogue with the Russian classics and the Silver Age.[17] However, their main *raison d'être* was to express a sense of anxiety and alienation in the dehumanised contemporary metropolis, to articulate the perceived entropy of European civilisation, and to leave a testimony of their existence through a creative act. The interwar Parisian *chronotope* offers crucial context for their verse. Rather than reminisce nostalgically about forsaken Russia as a 'paradise lost', in the vein of some of their older peers, the poets of the Paris Note inscribed their experience of exile into the interwar modernist crisis narrative. They created poetic language adapted to addressing the key concerns of the time, writing in a style reminiscent of the human document, a genre pervasive in the prose and verse of the Western 'lost generation'. In this way, Paris Note members defied the mono-national construction of their poetic identity and transcended the Russian canon without abandoning it. In order to appreciate the hybrid character of their poetry, we need to reconstruct the contemporaneous cultural context, to provide insight into the challenges that these texts sought to address.

---

16   Georgii Fedotov, 'O parizhskoi poezii', *Voprosy poezii*, 2 (1990), pp. 231–38 (p. 237).
17   This perspective, framing Paris Note poetry exclusively within the Russian tradition, and in particular as a continuation and 'conclusion' of the Silver Age, has been frequently recycled in Russian critical literature today (e.g. Oleg Korostelev, '"Parizhskaia Nota" russkogo Monparnasa', http://institut-est-ouest.ens-lsh.fr/spip.php?article302 and '"Bez krasok i pochti bez slov…" (poeziia Georgiia Adamovicha)', in Georgii Adamovich, *Stikhi, proza, perevody* (St Petersburg: Aleteia, 1999), pp. 5–74; Kirill Ratnikov, 'Sud'ba "Parizhskoi noty" v poezii russkogo zarubezh'ia', http://zhurnal.lib.ru/p/petrushkin_a_a/ratnikov.shtml; Ol'ga Kochetkova, 'Ideino-esteticheskie printsipy "parizhskoi noty" i khudozhestvennye poiski Borisa Poplavskogo' (unpublished doctoral thesis, Moscow State University, 2010), http://www.dissercat.com/content/ideino-esteticheskie-printsipy-parizhskoi-noty-i-khudozhestvennye-poiski-borisa-poplavskogo

The Crisis of Poetry

Considered broadly, the literary context of the interwar period was informed by the general existential crisis provoked by World War One (intensified in the Russian émigré case by the trauma of revolution and exile); transformation of the aesthetic paradigm all across European literature; and the increasingly precarious position of the artist in a world of mass culture and mechanical reproduction, which, as Walter Benjamin argued in his seminal essay, threatened to compromise the uniqueness and authenticity of artwork by decoupling the creator and his creation.[18] One of the corollary effects of these tendencies was a crisis of poetry, actively debated by diaspora poets and critics.

The feeling that poetry was no longer possible was pervasive in the diaspora. This was one of the rare points on which the two leading émigré critics, Adamovich and Khodasevich, who engaged in an energetic polemic on various other subjects, were content to agree. One of Khodasevich's articles bore the straightforward title: 'Krizis poezii' ('The Crisis of Poetry', 1934). As for Adamovich, the crisis of poetry was his recurring topic for years, and he often quoted Valerii Briusov's words, 'Gentlemen, write prose!' ('Пишите прозу, господа!') when discussing in the press the deplorable condition of émigré literature. Writing in the newspaper *Mech* on April 5, 1936, Alfred Bem stated unambiguously that émigré poetry had reached a dead end. Vladimir Veidle, who in his book *Umiranie iskusstva* (*The Dying of Art*, 1937) came to the sad conclusion that Western art and literature in general were not viable, was no less pessimistic when evaluating the condition of émigré poetry: 'Émigré verse is written at a time profoundly unpropitious for poetry'.[19] In practice, this crisis translated into a dramatic decrease in the volume of poetic production and publications, even among the older and well-established poets. Gippius, for example, released only one collection, *Siianiia* (*Radiance*, 1938), during the two post-revolutionary decades. After publishing *Rozy* (*Roses*, 1931), Georgii Ivanov practically

---

18 Walter Benjamin, 'The Work of Art in the Age of Mechanical Reproduction', in *Illuminations*, edited by H. Arendt, translated by H. Zohn (New York: Schocken, 1969), pp. 217–51.

19 Vladimir Weidle, 'Antologiia zarubezhnoi poezii', in *Iakor'*: *antologiia russkoi zarubezhnoi poezii*, edited by Oleg Korostelev, Luigi Magarotto and Andrei Ustinov (St Petersburg: Alateia, 2005), pp. 218–22, 219.

stopped writing verse until well into the 1940s.[20] His nihilist 'Raspad atoma' ('Disintegration of an Atom', 1938), which Ivanov himself preferred to define as a *poema* (the term usually denotes a long poem with narrative elements), inaugurated a long period of complete silence. Odoevtseva, who during her Petrograd days could not conceive of trading the 'high' status of a poet for prose, switched to the genre of short stories and eventually to the novel from the middle of the 1920s, composing verse only occasionally. Nor were the interwar decades terribly prolific for Viacheslav Ivanov, whose cycle 'Rimskie sonety' ('Roman Sonnets') created in the mid-1920s as a *postscriptum* to his pre-émigré period, was published eleven years later (in *Sovremennye zapiski*, 62, 1936). Poetic revival began for Ivanov only in 1944 with 'Rimskii dnevnik' ('Roman Diary'), but by then his distinct manner had undergone a drastic change (its new, diaristic aspect was signalled by the key word in the title). Khodasevich's only new cycle composed in emigration and included in his 1927 *Sobranie stikhov* (*Collection of Poems*) was suggestively titled 'Evropeiskaia noch'' ('The European Night'). Thereafter he wrote mostly criticism and memoirs. According to Iurii Mandel'shtam, Khodasevich was 'broken by the prose of life, the un-transfigured matter'.[21] Contemplating Khodasevich's poetic silence, Struve comes essentially to the same conclusion:

> Khodasevich's path [...] anticipated this end, this hopeless poetic dead end. Perhaps this path [...] is a path of ripening and perfection. But this ripening is linked with the ever increasing realization of a tragic split and just as tragic discord with the world — and no less keen realization of poetry's impotence. [...] our epoch pressed down upon his poetry like some terrible nightmare.[22]

Adamovich also published only one book of poetry after emigration, *Na Zapade* (*In the West*, 1939), which comprised some poems from the pre-exile period.

---

20 Ivanov's book *Otplytie na ostrov Tsiteru* (*Departure for the Island of Cythera*) although it came out in 1937, contained for the most part previously published poems, including some from his early, pre-émigré period.

21 Iu. Mandel'shtam, 'Gamburgskii schet: po povodu *Antologii zarubezhnoi poezii*', in *Iakor': antologiia russkoi zarubezhnoi poezii*, pp. 230–36 (p. 233).

22 Gleb Struve, *Russkaia literatura v izgnanii* (Paris: YMCA, 1984), p. 144. See also Tania Galcheva, 'Krizis molchaniia v poezii Vladislava Khodasevicha i v proze Georgiia Ivanova', *Slavia Orientalis*, 44: 4 (1995), pp. 503–13.

This obvious decline in poetic potential among the most authoritative members of the Russian diaspora, including those who regarded themselves as mentors of the younger generation (Gippius, Ivanov, Khodasevich, Adamovich), hardly served as an inspiring example. Therefore, the significance of their mentorship for the new voices of the diaspora should not be overestimated. It is quite plausible that the aesthetics of the younger Parisian poets was developing not so much under the tutelage of the iconic figures of the Silver Age as in reaction to their 'death throes'.[23]

More importantly, the crisis was accompanied by general disillusionment with the core values associated with the classical Russian canon. The discourse that promoted the cult of the poet; his sacred, prophetic status; his function as a mediator between the transcendental world and visible reality, and, consequently, the conception of poetry as a mystical, theurgical activity, was rapidly losing its credibility in the eyes of those who had lived through national catastrophe and then witnessed the collapse of European civilisation. From their point of view, Pushkinian aesthetics could no longer offer sustenance in distress and had been revealed to be untrustworthy (this feeling of deception was accentuated in the refrain of Ivanov's 'Raspad atoma': 'Pushkin's Russia, why have you deceived us, Pushkin's Russia, why have you betrayed us?').[24]

There were certainly more basic causes for the plummeting prestige of poetry and, indeed, intellectual literature, in the diaspora. With the exception of the literary situation in Berlin at the beginning of the 1920s, émigré writers were barred from the Soviet book market. The circle of diaspora readers was progressively shrinking, and their purchasing power was diminishing as well, especially after the outbreak of the global economic crisis. Russian-language periodicals often closed after just a few issues, and only a handful of Russian-language publishing houses were able to endure for more than several years. The general profile of the émigré audience, its level of education and literary tastes also changed considerably. In his article 'Bez chitatelia'

---

23 Iu. V. Zobnin, *Poeziia beloi emigratsii: 'Nezamechennoe pokolenie'* (St Petersburg: SPbGUP, 2010), p. 16.
24 Georgii Ivanov, 'The Atom Explodes', translated by Justin Doherty, *Slavonica*, 8: 1 (2002), 42–67, p. 64.

('Without a Reader', published in *Chisla*, 5, 1931), Ivanov lamented the disappearance of the intellectual reader. Gazdanov elaborated on this problem in his controversial article 'O molodoi emigrantskoi literature' ('On young émigré literature', published in *Sovremennye zapiski*, 60, 1936). He explained that the former intelligentsia — lawyers, doctors, and journalists — had been cut off from the 'cultural stratum' in exile, forced to join the ranks of manual workers and cab drivers. In his article 'Literatura v izgnanii' ('Literature in Exile', published in *Vozrozhdenie* on 27 January and 4 May, 1933), Khodasevich also focused on limited readership as one of the reasons for the tragic lot of émigré literature. The first draft of this article bore the eloquent title: 'Otchego my pogibaem?' ('Why are we perishing?'). Clearly, this situation was detrimental for poetry to a far greater extent than for prose. While in *fin-de-siècle* Russia poetry reading might have been a routine activity for the educated general public, it was no longer in high demand in a shrinking and impoverished émigré community with the precarious legal status of *apatrides* (stateless persons), either unemployed or eking out an existence by hard labour. Those who continued to read during rare moments of leisure required light and entertaining fare, prompting émigré editors to give preference to *belletristika* (middlebrow, rather than high literature) and mass fiction.

Avant-Garde versus Art Deco

In addition to the particular Russian historical circumstances, the crisis of émigré poetry can be traced to specific socio-cultural trends on the contemporary European scene. The post-World War One period was characterised by several contrasting (although occasionally overlapping) aesthetic models. At one end of the spectrum there was extreme avant-garde experimentation, provocative liberation of the literary form from any conventional norms, unrestricted self-expression of unique individuality and the subconscious. The other end was distinguished by the efforts to re-create a uniform, universal style, drawing on the new visions of realism and neoclassicism, on the principles of utility, technological progress, and standardisation of living, to re-focus on the physicality of the world and the vitality of the human body. Avant-garde tendencies, expressed most vocally through Dadaism and surrealism, clashed with the rising mass culture and the spirit of consumerism, which eventually crystallised in the transnational Art Deco style. Yet, these two seemingly antithetical trends explored a number of similar areas, sharing an interest in urbanism, cinema, and syncopated rhythms, which expressed so well the tremendous acceleration of life during the Jazz Age. Ultimately, these contrasting phenomena jointly contributed to the articulation of a new concept of modernity. This rapidly evolving, eclectic and vibrant modern culture formed the context to which Russian Parisian poets were indirectly responding and against which they should be read and interpreted, in addition to the native poetic legacy.

In the 1920s, many Russian émigrés were toying with avant-garde movements and establishing their own avant-garde groups, such as Gatarapak, Cherez, and Palata Poetov. Poet and painter Serge Sharshun was an active member of Dada and took part in their public performances, masterminded by Tristan Tzara. In his artwork, Sharshun not only synthesised visual and verbal media, but also fused random fragments of Russian and French, thereby increasing its transrational quality (*zaum'*). In 1921, he published his first Dadaist poem in French, 'Foule immobile' ('The Immobile Crowd'). Later Sharshun joined the poetic association Cherez. Many of his Dada and avant-garde texts in Russian were collected in *Nebo kolokol. Poeziia v proze, 1919–1928* (*The Sky Bell. Poetry in Prose, 1919–1928*, 1938). A genre particularly favoured by Sharshun was the *listovka* (leaflet). He produced and duplicated leaflets himself and usually hand-delivered them to his bohemian acquaintances. Although some leaflets contained a paragraph or even a page-long text, most commonly Sharshun produced aphoristic, puzzling one-liners, for example: 'Аэроплан — зажег в небе свечку' ('Airplane — lit up a candle in the sky'); 'Небо — полно ангелов' ('Sky — full of angels'); 'Голуби — искупались в радуге' ('Pigeons — took a swim in the rainbow').[25]

Another poet who was avidly assimilating the style of Dada and surrealism was Poplavskii. His verse is steeped in surrealist imagery, illogical sequences, and hyper-metaphors, which can be illustrated by

---

25 'Iz listovok S. Sharshuna. Publikatsiia R. Gerra', *The New Review*, 163 (1986), pp. 127–39 (p. 132).

such characteristic examples as 'Бледнолицые книги склонялись к железным рукам'[26] ('Pale-faced books bent down to iron hands') or:

> А ночной король на солнце ходит
> С мертвой головой,
> Бабочек он тонкой сеткой ловит
> Голубой.[27]
> ('Мистическое рондо III').

> Meanwhile the King of Night walks on the sun
> With a dead head.
> He is catching butterflies in a fine net,
> A fine, pale blue net.
> ('Rondo Mystique III')[28]

The title *Avtomaticheskie stikhi* (*Automatic Verses*, 1999), given to Poplavskii's posthumous collection by its late twentieth-century editors, seems to point to the Surrealist *écriture automatique* created by transcribing random utterances articulated from a trance-like state.[29] Eventually Poplavskii began to tone down his Surrealist imagery, making it more comprehensible. His brief but intense poetic evolution was punctuated by a steady movement away from avant-garde excesses, even if he never reached the verbal asceticism characteristic of the Paris Note.

One of the factors that contributed to the crisis of poetry in the late 1920s may therefore be excessive avant-garde experimentation that pushed the language to the limits of intelligibility, weakening its communicative function, transforming poetry into a solipsistic

---

26 Boris Poplavskii, *Avtomaticheskie stikhi* (Moscow: Soglasie, 1999), p. 65.
27 *Idem*, *Sochineniia* (St Petersburg: Letnii sad, 1999), p. 92.
28 Boris Poplavsky, 'Rondo Mystique III', translated by Ron Loewinsohn, in *The Bitter Air of Exile: Russian Writers in the West 1922–1972*, edited by Simon Karlinsky and Alfred Appel Jr. (Berkeley, Los Angeles and London: University of California Press, 1973), p. 291.
29 However, in Dmitrii Tokarev's opinion, Poplavskii's approach to composition differed significantly from the tenets of the Surrealists, and therefore his affinity to the French movement should not be pushed beyond acknowledgement of a certain similarity of *topoi* (Dmitrii Tokarev, *'Mezhdu Indiei i Gegelem': Tvorchestvo Borisa Poplavskogo v komparativnoi perspektive* (Moscow: NLO, 2011), p. 79).

performance, or a 'corporate' activity addressed to a narrow circle of the initiated. As a result, by and large poetry lost its appeal for 'lay' readers. This tendency was common across the Soviet/diaspora divide, although each side proposed its own way out of the poetic dead-end. Contemplating this problem in the Soviet context, Kevin Platt suggests that the increased complexity of poetry during the avant-garde period led to the collapse of traditional engagement with verse among broad reading audiences, and that the institutionalisation of Socialist realism was a way to save poetry as a mass art.[30] It would be fair to assume that in the diaspora, instead of Socialist realism, it was the younger poets' verbal practice, with its emphasis on formal poverty, thematic simplicity, and understated lyricism, that represented a potential mechanism for rescuing poetry from the linguistic and semantic violence of the avant-garde. New minimalism called for a return to a new version of classicism, a trend that Iurii Terapiano detects in émigré verse from 1925.[31] This poetics was crystallised several years later in the output of the Paris Note, which can be regarded as the prime example of the solution provided in emigration to the important aesthetic dilemma of the time.

Another threat to the traditionally 'elevated' status of poetry was presented by the up-beat ethos of the Jazz Age. The rise of mass culture in the 1920s brought to an unprecedented level the artist's dependence on public taste, which was shaped by the culturally programmed desire for entertainment, constant movement, and enjoyment of life through travel, dance, jazz music, film, and sports. New technological achievements put automobiles, transatlantic liners, planes, trains, gramophones, and movie theatres at the disposal of a large number of consumers. Advertisements, radio and movies were actively promoting this dynamic way of life around the globe, advocating universal reconciliation and a carefree, urban and libidinous culture based on a hedonistic mindset. Art Deco art and literature quickly assimilated the spirit of the age, offering a universal vocabulary and a new model for interpreting reality, and creating a corresponding set of aesthetic

---

30   Kevin Platt, 'O iambakh i posledstviiakh, prichinakh i trokheiakh', *Novoe literaturnoe obozrenie*, 114 (2012), pp. 264–68.
31   See Iurii Terapiano, *Vstrechi* (New York: izd-vo Chekhova, 1958), pp. 150–51.

patterns and themes.[32] Characterised by fusion and eclecticism, Art Deco transcended all boundaries: between high and low culture; different arts and spheres of human activity; social and ethnic groups; past and present; archaic, classical and avant-garde; tradition and innovation; public and private; monumental and human-scale dimensions. The only context required for the new style was provided by the urban metropolis, which facilitated the removal of barriers between the individual and the city through new principles of architecture and interior design. Behind a highly decorative and carefree veneer, Art Deco, ostensibly devoid of any ideological dimension, hid an aesthetic mechanism for shaping social practices and private routine.

Dislocated by mass culture, literature was rapidly losing its autonomy; the boundaries separating high art from popular entertainment became blurred. Meanwhile, the strong emphasis on the physical body and the environment eclipsed readers' interest in introspection and the exploration of spirituality, which had been a conventional domain of poetry. Intelligentsia of the interwar period questioned the very possibility of creative activity in the post-apocalyptic world of mass consumption and mechanical reproduction that duplicated art, stripping it of its sacred aura.

Poetry versus Cinema: Rivalry and Imitation

During the Jazz Age, the main challenge to literature came from cinema, perceived as the epitome of modernity, capable of displacing and replacing traditional artistic media. Gradually, the rivalry between literature and cinema evolved into fusion and imitation, as texts began to draw on film-script techniques and to adopt cinematographic poetics. The 'cinematographization' of aesthetic reality affected both the avant-garde and Art Deco in equal measure, conflating their poetic practices and creating overlapping stylistic affiliations for texts that engaged with the seventh art. This modern kind of *ekphrasis* was exemplified, for instance, by *poèmes cinématographiques*, composed by Philippe Soupault and other Surrealists. In 'Charlot mystique' (1918), Louis Aragon

---

[32] On Art Deco as a literary style see Michel Collomb, *Littérature Art Deco* (Paris: Méridiens Klincksieck, 1987) and the chapter 'Challenges of the Jazz Age' in Maria Rubins, *Russian Montparnasse: Transnational Writing in Interwar Paris* (London: Palgrave Macmillan, 2015), pp. 113–61.

welcomed Charlie Chaplin as a harbinger of modernity and the silver screen as another channel of communication with mystical *sur*reality.

Such enthusiasm for cinema contrasts markedly with the attitudes cultivated by some of the more conservative poets, who still resisted the pervasive practice of border crossing, either between national canons or between 'high' and 'mass' art. For example, in 'Ballada' ('Ballad', 1925), Khodasevich dismisses Chaplin's performances as sheer 'idiocy':

> Мне невозможно быть собой,
> Мне хочется сойти с ума,
> Когда с беременной женой
> Идет безрукий в синема.
>
> Мне лиру ангел подает,
> Мне мир прозрачен, как стекло, —
> А он сейчас разинет рот
> Пред идиотствами Шарло.[33]

> I can't be myself,
> I feel like going mad
> When with his pregnant wife
> An armless man goes to the cinema.
>
> An angel hands me a lyre,
> The world is clear to me, like glass,-
> And he will now open his mouth wide
> At the idiocy of Charlot.

Restating the canonical Russian myth of the poet as prophet, the second of the quoted stanzas posits an unbridgeable gap between poetry writing as communing with the angels and the cheap antics of an American comedian, destined for the primitive entertainment of the simple-minded. Yet, at the end of this poem the lyrical persona acknowledges that his cultural snobbery will prevent him (as opposed to the unassuming consumer of American movies) from entering the kingdom of heaven. The reference to cinema serves in this poem as an indication that the time

---

33 Vladislav Khodasevich, *Stikhotvoreniia* (St Petersburg: Akademicheskii proekt, 2001), p. 150.

of 'sacred' creativity and high spirituality is gone, and the poet-prophet has lost his place in a world of kitsch and crude entertainment.

However, not all poets in Russian Paris were as entrenched in classical national axiologies. Odoevtseva, one of the most flexible and culturally open-minded authors of the Parisian diaspora, was quite keen to imitate popular Western models in prose (this is particularly evident in her novel *Zerkalo* (*The Mirror*, 1939)), but occasionally the cinematographic context is apparent in her verse as well. For example, 'Pod lampoi elektricheskoi' ('Under an Electric Lamp') reconstructs a cinematic melodrama in a poetic medium:

> Под лампой электрической
> С улыбкой истерической
> В подушку головой.
>
> Подстреленная птица,
> Нет, это только снится,
> Нет, это скверный сон...
>
> И казино, и Ницца,
> И звездный небосклон.
>
> И все ж она гордится
> Богатством и собой
> И горькою судьбой,
> Она такая странная,
> Прелестная и пьяная –
> И вдребезги стакан.
>
> –Вы из далеких стран?
> Вам хочется любить?
> Вам хочется пожить
> На маленькой земле
> В печали и тепле?[34]

> Under an electric lamp
> With a hysterical smile
> and head in the pillow.

---

34   *Iakor'*, p. 66.

> A bird brought down by a gunshot,
> No, this is only a dream,
> A bad dream...
>
> Casino and Nice
> And starry firmament.
>
> And yet she is proud
> of her riches and herself
> And her bitter destiny,
> She is so strange,
> So pretty and drunk –
> And the glass is broken into shards.
>
> –Are you from distant lands?
> Do you want to love?
> Do you want to live
> On this small planet
> In sadness and warmth?

Odoevtseva evokes the hysterical state of the heroine through a rapid succession of images which suggests the accelerated pace of silent movies. Temporal and spatial boundaries are disrupted by elements of montage and juxtaposition as the poet plays with a variety of angles, and combines close-ups with a panoramic view (shifting from the intimate environment of a bedroom to the starry firmament). The boundaries between the real and the imaginary are also blurred by the near-simultaneous depiction of scenes which offer both external and internal perspectives on the heroine's situation (reporting on her behaviour from the outside and then offering insight into her subjective assessment). The poem has an elliptical structure. Not just a graphic glyph, ellipsis was possibly the most common rhetorical figure in Art Deco literature, as it was best suited to convey the sense of acceleration that was pervasive during this era, which was distinguished by the cult of speed. Ellipses also made it possible to cut out all extraneous details and descriptions, inviting the reader to fill in the omitted details, and thereby to move more quickly to the dramatic denouement. Furthermore, Odoevtseva borrows from expressionistic films a melodramatic gesture (the breaking of the glass by the distressed heroine). Concise and evocative, gestures routinely served as filters, a way to avoid psychologising or dwelling on feelings. The heightened visual quality and carefully chosen allusions to the most telling markers of modernity (electric light) complete the stage sets.

Odoevtseva's poem is an experiment in adapting Russian verse to the new cultural and material reality, something that many émigré poets, bound by conventional hierarchies, were still reluctant to do. It is nonetheless representative of a certain shift in the cultural discourse of the diaspora: in the 1930s even the established literary 'gurus' began to express the opinion that poetry should more actively respond to the rapidly evolving environment. As Bem stated at a poetic evening in 1933, contemporary émigré poetry 'is forced to reconquer for itself whole new areas of life. *Things stamp upon the throat of poetry.* [...] It is impossible to protect oneself with the old world of images that have already lost any touch with reality'.[35]

Deracination, Elective Genealogies and Translocal Imagination

'Pod lampoi elektricheskoi' was included in the only anthology of émigré poetry published during the interwar period, *Iakor'* (*Anchor*, 1936). Initiated and edited by Adamovich, the volume included seventy-seven poets from diverse regions of the international Russian diaspora, dominated by the Paris Note. In the preface, Adamovich articulates one of the objectives of the collection, which sounds like an expression of the ethos of the Paris Note:

> The poet at first blush is talking to himself, often he talks only about himself; the era of oratory has passed and, I would add, to some extent the spiritual energy of this volume is directed precisely at confirming the right to 'agendalessness' and its value, liquidating any belated quixotic pretensions.[36]

The title of the anthology was inspired by Evgenii Baratynskii's poem 'Piroskaf' ('Steamship'), in which the anchor is referred to as a symbol of hope. Baratynskii's image of weighing anchor is recontextualised

---

35 Al'fred Bem, 'Vstupitel'noe slovo na vechere "Skita" 25 aprelia 1933 g.', *Skit. Praga 1922–1940. Antologiia. Biografii. Dokumenty* (Moscow: Russkii put', 2006), p. 668.
36 *Iakor'*, p. 6.

here as a 'navigational'[37] or itinerant construction of diasporic identity, emancipated from the place of origin. However, a string of rhetorical questions in the preface suggests a notable vein of self-doubt that Adamovich voices on behalf of the deracinated group, suspended between two worlds, alienated from their homeland and not quite at ease in their adopted country. This sense of vulnerability compels him to resort to the 'letter in a bottle' trope, appealing to the judgment of future generations:

> Sometimes we ask ourselves: why didn't we force ourselves to stay there? What is it that we don't accept? In what do we refuse to participate? And what are we doing here anyway? There are many ready-made, reassuring explanations, — but still 'doubt is gnawing at our souls'. The answer is contained in the poems. [...] To express it without pompous phrases — this volume is directed at the future rather than the present, and perhaps the future will find our justification where most of our contemporaries, so eager to discuss various 'missions', saw only light-mindedness, mischief and boredom.[38]

Adamovich's preface reflects internal ambivalence: between the conventional definition of emigration as a 'broken piece' of the homeland ('У нас же не страна, а осколок ее') and the assertion of the autonomy of the new poetic voices that emerge in exile and seek to 'inhabit' immediate reality.[39] It was crucial for the evolution of the Paris Note, caught between various types of discourse, past and present, Russia and the West, to realise and eventually to break out of this dichotomy. Their sense of belonging to more than one place at a time (inevitably accompanied by a sense of alienation from both places) lends itself to interpretation through the concept of translocality, which designates by a 'place' not only a geographical location but practices, ideas, styles, images, or cultural constructs. Translocal imagination integrates the notions of discontinuity and fluidity that are implicit in the process of migration, with a focus on particular settings, and visualises linkages between them. Ultimately, translocality is a space where diverse

---

37 Stephen Clingman has argued that the trope of navigation is central to the expression of transnational identities (Stephen Clingman, *The Grammar of Identity: Transnational Fiction and the Nature of the Boundary* (Oxford: Oxford University Press, 2009), p. 21).
38 *Iakor'*, p. 7.
39 *Ibid.*, p. 6.

localised narratives establish a dialogic relationship and are thereby transcended, and where hybrid, transnational identities are constituted. For the Paris Note practitioners, the primary locus of these fractured identities was Paris, regarded not only as a cosmopolitan capital and specific place on the map of Western Europe, but above all as an open and dynamic field of inter-cultural exchanges. As Poplavskii summed this up in his article 'Vokrug "Chisel"':

> New émigré literature, which has been formed in exile, honestly acknowledges that it does not know anything else and that its best years, the years of the most intense response to the surrounding reality, are spent here, in Paris. Its homeland is neither Russia nor France but Paris. [...] We are the literature of truth about today, which resounds for us like the eternal music of hunger and happiness on Boulevard Montparnasse, as it would have resounded on Kuznetskii Most. [...] We write about our own experience, neither Russian nor French, but Parisian experience.[40]

The translocal imagination of the Paris Note poets shaped their vision of cultural transmission. Under Adamovich's guidance they revised the classical Russian canon, creating for themselves such literary genealogy as would reflect their sensibilities, informed by their experience of modernity as dislocation and cross-cultural alienation. Dismissing Pushkin and the social, religious, philosophical and moral pathos of the nineteenth-century literary mainstream, they turned to Lermontov as the most 'modern' among the Russian classics. Needless to say, using Lermontov as a precursor for the Paris Note was far from straightforward. Glossing over his use of Romantic irony, the émigré poets defined him as a 'tragic', 'lonely', 'misunderstood' and 'rejected' genius. Moreover, the young writers presented him as an archetypal exile and 'cursed poet' ('гонимый миром странник' ('a wanderer chased away by the world')), emphasised the metaphysical content of his texts and pictured him as a forerunner of existentialism. Such reading of Lermontov by émigré poets transformed him from a 'national poet' to 'a diasporic voice in a culture subsisting increasingly on adaptation, hybridity, and live interaction with Western literature, art, and philosophy'.[41]

---

40 Poplavskii, 'Vokrug "Chisel"', in *Russkii Parizh* (Moscow: MGU, 1998), pp. 288–91 (p. 288).
41 Galin Tihanov, 'Russian Émigré Literary Criticism and Theory between the World Wars', in *A History of Russian Literary Theory and Criticism: The Soviet Age and Beyond*, edited by Evgenii Dobrenko and Galin Tihanov (Pittsburgh: University of Pittsburgh Press, 2011), pp. 144–62 (p. 162).

Innokentii Annenskii was another voice claimed by the Paris Note, perhaps with more legitimacy. As Bem points out, Annenskii was appealing to these poets, whose style was distinguished by 'extreme simplicity' of poetic form.[42] More problematic was their appropriation of Nikolai Gumilev. Given the authority of Adamovich and Ivanov for the Paris Note, the role attributed to Gumilev in the group's self-definition is unsurprising. But in reality, this was a case of false pedigree. Gumilev's flair for exoticism, bright, bold colours, his positive outlook and firm religious beliefs, his preference for epic genres during his later period, and even his occasional mystical and surrealist insights (as in 'Zabludivshiisia tramvai' ('The Tram That Lost Its Way') or 'Ia i vy' ('Me and you')) were a far cry from the colourless, subdued and plaintive tone of the Parisian poets, and of Adamovich himself. The value of craftsmanship, central to the Acmeist conception of poetry, was also dismissed by Adamovich and his disciples, who instead favoured formal imperfection as a path to ultimate sincerity. Paying lip service to Gumilev, Adamovich copied his *maître's* organisational, rather than poetic style.[43]

Along with establishing a list of literary models, Adamovich can also be credited with the articulation of canonical principles that would inform the poetics and thematic focus of the Paris Note. The group's texts generally resonated with the 'human document' style of contemporary European writing.[44] Marked by subjectivity, intimacy, and immediacy, this diary-style poetry was conceived as a private affair, i.e. ostensibly written for oneself, as a means of self-expression and engaging only with the personal world of the lyrical persona, as illustrated by the title of Knorring's collection, *Stikhi o sebe* (*Poems About Myself*, 1931). The prevailing tone of confession defined a particular vocabulary, with extensive use of such key words as 'sincerity', 'truth', etc. Lexical poverty and the absence of elaborate rhyme patterns or metaphors corresponded to the existentialist agenda of conveying only the most essential human experience, while also promoting the negative value of personal failure

---

42 Al'fred Bem, 'Russkaia literatura v emigratsii', in *Pis'ma o literature*, edited by M. Bubenikova and L. Vakhalovskaia (Prague: Euroslavia, 1996), p. 336.

43 In 1923 Adamovich founded a Guild of Poets in Paris, and mentored his young disciples through regular discussion meetings dedicated to the rigorous analysis of their texts.

44 Obviously, the anti-novelistic and anti-fictional trend was most relevant for émigré prose. But even poetry, especially in the case of the Paris Note, was affected by this radical shift towards a new understanding of literature as testimony and ego-document.

and creative impotence, a loss of faith in the power of the word, and the poet's anxiety over his inability to express himself adequately. The overuse of dashes, parentheses, elliptical sequences and unfinished sentences suggested disrupted communication, attempts to redefine a feeling or thought ever more accurately, and permanent incompletion. The disjointed, fragmentary nature of the poetic text found organic expression in the genre of lyrical fragment, with its conflation of the 'singular' and the 'universal' and allusions to multiple contexts.[45] The archetypal emotion of the Paris Note was pity for the 'helpless tongue' and the dream of writing 'without colours and almost without words', as Adamovich declares in the poem 'Stikham svoim ia znaiu tsenu' ('I know the price of my poems'):

> Стихам своим я знаю цену.
> Мне жаль их, только и всего.
> Но ощущаю как измену
> Иных поэзий торжество.
>
> Сквозь отступленья, повторенья,
> Без красок и почти без слов,
> Одно, единое виденье,
> Как месяц из-за облаков,
>
> То промелькнет, то исчезает,
> То затуманится слегка,
> И тихим светом озаряет,
> И непреложно примиряет
> С беспомощностью языка.[46]

> I know the price of my poems.
> I'm sorry for them, that's all.
> But the glory of the verse of others
> I experience as betrayal.
>
> Through digressions, repetitions,
> Without colours and almost without words,

---

[45] See I. A. Tarasova, 'Zhanr fragmenta v poezii "Parizhskoi noty"', *Zhanry rechi*, 1: 11 (2015), pp. 111–16.

[46] Georgii Adamovich, 'Stikham svoim ia znaiu tsenu', in *Poety parizhskoi noty: v Rossiiu vetrom strochki zaneset*, compiled by Vadim Kreid (Moscow: Molodaia gvardiia, 2003), p. 51.

> One single vision,
> Like the moon through the clouds.
>
> Now it shows, now it's gone,
> Now it fogs up slightly
> And sheds quiet light
> And brings inevitable reconciliation
> With the tongue's helplessness.

With regard to this self-effacing stance of the lyrical voice, Lev Gomolitskii remarked: 'The Parisian poet's ideal would have been achieved if poetry could do completely without words'.[47] An alternative way of obliterating the conventional markers of poetry was 'prosaisation', an aspiration captured by the following lines from Shteiger: 'Who has risked to call himself a poet / Must speak seriously in prose here' ('Тут должен прозой говорить всерьез / Тот, кто рискнул назвать себя поэтом').[48]

In another iconic poem, Adamovich expressed the sense of entropy engulfing not only poetry but the entire diaspora, depleted of energy and doomed quietly to expire in the midst of Paris. But here, this total despair is welcomed by the lyric persona as a precondition for inspiration and spiritual ascent:

> За все, за все спасибо. За войну,
> За революцию и за изгнанье.
> За равнодушно-светлую страну,
> Где мы теперь «влачим существованье».
> Нет доли сладостней — все потерять.
> Нет радостней судьбы — скитальцем стать,
> И никогда ты к небу не был ближе,
> Чем здесь, устав скучать,
> Устав дышать,
>   Без сил, без денег,
>   Без любви,
>   В Париже...[49]

---

47 Lev Gomolitskii, 'Nadezhdy simvol', in *Iakor'*, pp. 223–27, p. 224.
48 Anatolii Shteiger, 'Ne do stikhov... Zdes' slishkom mnogo slez', http://gostinaya.net/?p=8387
49 Adamovich, 'Za vse, za vse spasibo. Za voinu', in *Poety parizhskoi noty*, p. 66. This poem contains transparent intertextual allusions to Georgii Ivanov's nihilist text

>   Thank you for everything. For the war,
>   For the revolution and exile.
>   For the indifferent bright country
>   Where we now 'drag out our existence'.
>   There is no sweeter destiny than to lose everything.
>   There is no happier fate than to become a vagabond.
>   And you've never been closer to heaven
>   Than here, tired of boredom
>   Tired of breathing,
>   Without strength, without money,
>   Without love,
>   In Paris…

Anatolii Shteiger, who published three books of poetry during his short life, *Etot den'* (*This Day*, 1928), *Eta Zhizn'* (*This Life*, 1932), and *Neblagodarnost'* (*Ingratitude*, 1936), was the most devoted adept of the Paris Note, and arguably he expressed the ethos of the group even more faithfully than Adamovich himself.[50] Choosing several lines from the second poem of Annenskii's dyptich 'Iiul'' ('July', 1900) ('Подумай, на руках у матерей / Все это были розовые дети' ('Just think, in mothers' arms / They were all pink babies')) as an epigraph to one of his short texts, he explicitly confirmed his poetic genealogy:

>   Никто, как в детстве, нас не ждет внизу.
>   Не переводит нас через дорогу.
>   Про злого муравья и стрекозу
>   Не говорит. Не учит верить Богу.

'Khorosho, chto net tsaria' ('It is good that there is no czar'), rejected for publication in the leading émigré journal *Sovremennye zapiski* where Ivanov was otherwise a regular contributor. Its dark irony was lost on the journal's editor, Mark Vishniak, who considered the poem too subversive. As Ivanov recalled in a letter to Roman Gul' of February 14, 1957: 'By the way the only poem that the esteemed Vishniak returned to me back then was "It's good that there is no czar." — "We are against monarchy, but we can't publish such provocation" — these are his genuine words!' (*Georgii Ivanov, Irina Odoevtseva, Roman Gul': troistvennyi soiuz* (Perepiska 1953–1958), edited by A. Ar'ev and S. Guan'elli (St Petersburg: Petropolis, 2010), p. 436).

50 See Vadim Kreid, 'V liniiakh notnoi stranitsy…', in *Poety parizhskoi noty*, pp. 5–30, 12.

10. The Diasporic Canon of Russian Poetry: The Case of the Paris Note

До нас теперь нет дела никому —
У всех довольно собственного дела.
И надо жить, как все, но самому...
(Беспомощно, нечестно, неумело).[51]

Nobody waits at the foot of the stairs any more
Or takes our hand crossing a street, the way they did
When we were young. Nobody tells us about the mean
Ant and the Grasshopper. Or teaches us to believe in God.

Nowadays nobody thinks of us at all —
They all have enough just thinking of themselves,
So we have to live as they do — but alone...
(Impotent, dishonest, and inept.)[52]

In fact, the two lines in Annenskii's poem immediately preceding those quoted in the epigraph would have defined Shteiger's mood even more precisely: 'Doesn't one get scared sometimes in this world? / Doesn't one want to run and quickly find shelter?' ('Не страшно ль иногда становится на свете? / Не хочется ль бежать, укрыться поскорей?') Annenskii's metaphysical horror before the ugliness, degradation, and brutality to which uncontrollable 'wild forces' subject human beings in the course of their lives is reduced in Shteiger to recurring motifs of fear of life, suffering, lack of vitality, and illness:

Брат мой, друг мой, не бойся страданья,
Как боялся всю жизнь его я...[53]

My brother, my friend, don't be afraid of suffering,
As I feared it all my life...

---

51   Anatolii Shteiger, 'Iul'', *Poety parizhskoi noty*, p. 131.
52   *Idem*, 'Nobody waits at the foot of the stairs any more', translated by Paul Schmidt, in *The Bitter Air of Exile*, p. 338.
53   Shteiger, 'Esli dni moi milost'iu Boga', in *Poety parizhskoi noty*, p. 130.

> Этот к вечеру легкий жар,
> Кашель ровный и суховатый[...]
> Сырость. Сумрак. Последний тлен
> И последняя в сердце жалость...
> –Трудно книгу поднять с колен,
> Чтобы уйти, такова усталость...[54]

> This light fever towards the evening,
> Even and dry cough [...]
> Humidity. Twilight. The last decay
> And the last pity in the heart...
> –It's hard to lift the book from the knees
> In order to leave, so strong is the fatigue...

The hospital is a pervasive *topos* in his verse, which can be defined as 'consumptive' poetry (Shteiger did in fact suffer from tuberculosis, and was treated in a sanatorium for many years before finally succumbing to the disease in Bern during World War Two). It is therefore rather difficult to agree with Struve, who perceived in Shteiger's poetry 'great avidity toward life' ('большая жадность к жизни').[55] Rather, it would be fair to suggest that Shteiger's mood correlates with Semen Nadson's plaintive and sorrowful line in Russian poetry, labelled *nadsonovshchina* (Nadsonovism) by nineteenth-century readers and critics. There are striking parallels between the two poets, even on a biographical level: Nadson also suffered from consumption, was treated in Nice and Bern, and died young. Nadson's confessional intonation, motifs of suffering, ennui, and lament, and even his typical vocabulary (e.g. doubt, ennui, darkness, heavy, futile, difficult, fatal, cruel, insane, beyond one's strength, severe (сомнение, тоска, мгла, тяжкая, напрасная, трудная, роковая, жестокая, безумная, непосильная, суровая)) are echoed in Shteiger's own work and in Paris Note poetry more generally. But as often was the case with the

---

54   Idem, 'Sentiabr", in *ibid.*, p. 133.
55   Struve, *Russkaia literatura v izgnanii*, p. 334.

output of the Paris Note practitioners, plausible Russian pedigree is conflated with references to the cultural realities of contemporary Europe. Literalising the metaphor, Shteiger's motif of physical sickness makes manifest the condition of spiritual and philosophical malaise of the 'European Hamlets', as the post-World War One generation came to be identified in Paul Valéry's 'The Crisis of the Mind' (1919).[56] Adamovich coined an analogous phrase 'Eastern Hamlets' for young émigré men in his poem 'Kogda my v Rossiiu vernemsia... o, Gamlet vostochnyi, kogda?' ('When Will We Return to Russia... oh, Eastern Hamlet, When?', 1936), intertwining the *topos* of the hospital, dying and pre-mortem hallucinations with the doom of exile and the unrealisable dream of return. In this way, Adamovich created a more obvious parallel between malady and the émigré condition, whereas in Shteiger it figures as part of his generational experience and perhaps of the human lot more generally.

Shteiger's lyrical persona emerges as a helpless and sick child — frightened, hurt and lonely, quietly lamenting his fate and crying into his pillow at night (the word offence (обида) is recurrent, as well as pain, impotence, boredom, helplessly, tears, children, childish, fear, more frightening (боль, бессилье, скука, беспомощно, слезы, дети, детский, страх, страшнее).

Есть что-то детское и птичье
В словах, делах и снах туберкулезных.[57]

There is something childish and bird-like
In tuberculosis words, acts and dreams.

---

56 Marcel Arland reintroduced the concept of the 'new malady of the century' in relation to the post-World War One generation in his article 'Sur un nouveau mal du siècle', *Nouvelle revue française*, 125 (February 1924). On the 'Russification' of this concept and Russian émigrés' fashioning themselves as 'émigré Hamlets' see Leonid Livak, *How It Was Done in Paris: Russian Émigré Literature and French Modernism* (Madison: Wisconsin University Press, 2003), pp. 26–41.

57 Shteiger, 'Uzhe ne strakh, skoree bezrazlich'e', in *Poety parizhskoi noty*, p. 140.

> Скоро и глупый плач
> Ночью (во сне) пройдет.[58]

> Soon silly crying
> At night (in sleep) will also pass.

> Но детский страх и наши боль и страх
> Одно и то же, в сущности, конечно.[59]

> But childish fear and our pain and fear
> Are in essence one and the same, of course.

The motifs of infantilism, tears, and futile attempts to revert to the puerile condition were also apparent in Boris Bozhnev's early verse, which in certain respects anticipates the Paris Note:

> Чтоб стать ребенком, встану в темный угол,
> К сырой стене заплаканным лицом,
> И буду думать с гневом и испугом —
> За что наказан я, и чьим отцом…[60]

> In order to become a child, I will stand in a dark corner,
> My tear-stained face toward the moist wall,
> And will think with rage and fear —
> Why am I punished and by whose father…

Like a meek child, the lyric voice frequently encountered in the poetry of the Paris Note is ready to surrender in the face of misfortune, incapable of resistance. For Shteiger, love is always unhappy, and he unfailingly assumes a passive, effeminate position. Always expecting to be abandoned, his persona lacks even the energy for jealousy ('We even

---

58 *Idem*, 'Vremia iskusnyi vrach', in *ibid.*, p. 153.
59 *Idem*, 'Net v etoi zhizni tiagostnei minut'', in *ibid.*, p. 155.
60 Boris Bozhnev, *Bor'ba za nesushchestvovan'e* (St Petersburg: INAPRESS, 1999), p. 73.

forgot how to be jealous' ('Мы отучились даже ревновать')).⁶¹ His only aspiration is to fall into bed and to escape into oblivion:

> Отдыхает во сне человек.⁶²

> Man rests as he sleeps

> Неужели опять, чуть стемнело,
>   ничком на кровать —
> Чтобы больше не думать, не слышать
>   И вдруг не заплакать.⁶³

> Shall I again, as soon as it starts getting dark
>   Fall face down on the bed —
> So as no longer to think or hear
>   And not to burst out crying suddenly.

When sleep no longer soothes his suffering, the lyric hero entertains suicidal thoughts:

> А если уж правда невмочь —
> Есть мутная Сена и ночь.⁶⁴

> When you can bear it no longer —
> There is the muddy Seine and the night.

There is hardly anything mature or 'masculine' in this verse, and Struve's comparison of Shteiger to Anna Akhmatova is partially justified.⁶⁵ Their styles are indeed distinguished by density, clarity, terseness, and abrupt endings. But the heroine of Akhmatova's earlier period at times exudes more vitality, and fashions herself as a *femme fatale* who makes

---

61 Shteiger, 'My otuchilis' dazhe revnovat'', in *Poety parizhskoi noty*, p. 144.
62 Idem, 'Otchego, kak stikhaet rech'', in *ibid.*, p. 110.
63 Idem, 'Neuzheli sentiabr'', in *ibid.*, p. 151.
64 Idem, 'Kryl'ia? Oblomany kryl'ia?', in *ibid.*, p. 116.
65 Struve, *Russkaia literatura v izgnanii*, p. 334.

her admirers suffer. By contrast, Shteiger's persona is always on the receiving end:

> Где-то теперь мой друг?
> Как-то ему живется?
> Сердце, не верь, что вдруг
> В двери раздастся стук:
> Он никогда не вернется.[66]

> Where is he now, I wonder?
> And what's his life like?
> Don't let me sit by the door
> Expecting a sudden knock:
> He will never come back.[67]

> Как нам от громких отучиться слов:
> Что значит «самолюбье», «униженье»
> (Когда прекрасно знаешь, что готов
> На первый знак ответить, первый зов,
> На первое малейшее движенье).[68]

> How do we break the habit of big words:
> What does 'pride' mean? What's 'humiliation'?
> (When you know perfectly well I'm ready
> to respond to the first sign, the first call,
> the first slight gesture.)…[69]

Shteiger generously plies elliptical closures. Unfinished lines iconically represent his persona's inability to complete any action, his permanent failure in life, hesitation, fatigue and lack of self-confidence. Ellipses also

---

66 Shteiger, 'Gde-to teper' moi drug?', in Anatolii Shteiger, *Dvazhdy dva chetyre: stikhi 1926–1939* (Paris: Rifma, 1950), p. 16.
67 *Idem*, 'Friendship', translated by Paul Schmidt, in *The Bitter Air of Exile*, p. 337.
68 *Idem*, 'Kak nam ot gromkikh otuchit'sia slov', in *Poety parizhskoi noty*, p. 158.
69 Shteiger, 'How do we break the habit of big words', translated by Paul Schmidt, in *The Bitter Air of Exile*, p. 337.

appeal to some common experience that the reader may share, indicate a potential plurality of interpretation, or symbolise the death of poetry and its return to silence:

> Мы несчастны. Очень. Боже, Боже,
> Отчего Ты с нами не добрей…[70]

> We are unhappy. Very. God, God,
> Why aren't You kinder to us…

> Только память с нами остается,
> Точно крест на брошенной могиле,
> И тоска о том, что не вернется,
> Что из рук мы сами упустили…[71]

> Only memory stays with us,
> Like a cross over an abandoned grave,
> And yearning for what will not come back,
> For what we let escape from our hands…

Parentheses, another prominent graphic device of the Paris Note, are used by Shteiger to define each emotion in the most precise way, to convey the 'ultimate' truth, to attain complete sincerity. This goal can be achieved only through careful selection of the simplest words and by suppressing all pathos:

> Слова печальны и просты,
> Не хочет сердце слов заумных.[72]

> Words are sad and simple,
> The heart wants no highbrow words.

---

70 Idem, 'Ty osudish'. My ne vinovaty', in *Poety parizhskoi noty*, p. 134.
71 Idem, 'Vstrecha', in *ibid.*, p. 109.
72 Shteiger, 'Prostoi peizazh', in *ibid.*, p. 118.

> Можно о многом сказать односложно.[73]

Most things can be said in monosyllables.

Along with Shteiger, Akhmatova's émigré double was often identified in the likeness of the beautiful Lydiia Chervinskaia, whose verse was distinguished by 'chamber' tonality, psychological precision, brevity and evocative detail. A friend of Poplavskii, Chervinskaia was also notorious for recreational drug use. Before World War Two, she published two books of poetry, *Priblizheniia* (*Approaches*, 1934) and *Rassvety* (*Sunrises*, 1937), and contributed verse to a range of émigré journals. A distinctive feature of her style is the extensive use of compound adjectives and rhetorical questions. The Parisian *chronotope* is easily perceptible in her verse, and the city is represented through restrained but telling details serving as necessary backdrop for the existential drama of Chervinskaia's heroine:

> С тобой и с ним, с дождями, с тишиной,
> С Парижем в марте, с комнатой ночной,
> С мучительно-знакомыми словами,
> Неровными, несчитаными днями,
> Почти вся молодость...[74]

With you and him, with rain, with silence,
With Paris in March, with a nocturnal room,
With painfully familiar words,
Uneven, uncounted days,
Almost all my youth...

> Город. Огни. Туман.
> Все-таки мы умрем.
> В комнате темный диван,
> Лучше побудем вдвоем.[75]

---

73 *Idem*, 'Bessarabiia', in *ibid.*, p. 171.
74 Lydiia Chervinskaia, 'S toboi i s nim', in *Poety parizhskoi noty*, p. 177.
75 *Idem*, 'Gorod. Ogni. Tuman', in *ibid.*, p. 183.

> City. Lights. Fog.
> But we'll die anyway.
> A dark sofa in the room,
> Let's better be here together.

In addition to ennui, metaphysical solitude, and unhappy love, her topic of choice is death and failure, and her weak poetic voice tends to fade into whispers and silence:

> Вспомнилось... нет, помолчим, подождем.

> A recollection... no, let's be silent, let's wait.

> Жизнь пройдет и тихо оборвется
> В море, в неудачу, в ничего...[76]

> Life will pass and quietly drop off
> Into the sea, into misfortune, into nothing...

The most characteristic poems of the Paris Note suppress any kind of (auto)biographical information, focusing on pure feeling, emotion, or state of mind in the almost complete absence of specifying context. As in some of Chervinskaia's texts cited above, the lyric voice often simply mentions a place, condition, mood, or the process of recollection, which anyone can access as part of the general human experience. Despite its universal dimension, this conception of poetry arose in the specific environment of the interwar Russian diaspora in Europe.

Conclusion

The Paris Note corpus embodied the existentialist poetics of the time in its most distilled form. Reflecting the experience of modernity as deracination, marginalisation, and skepticism about any positive teleology, these poets' work was predicated on a mechanism of self-destruction, as it not only systematically suppressed the classical master

---

76 Chervinskaia, 'Zhizn' proidet i tikho oborvetsia', *ibid.*, p. 185.

narrative of Russian literature, with its ideal of the poet as a sage, moral guide and spiritual authority, and the émigré rhetoric of national revival and cultural continuity, but sought to cancel out conventional poetic tropes and even the verbal medium itself. As Igor Chinnov, who identified himself as a 'hanger-on' of the Paris Note, later explained:

> Its [Paris Note's — M.R.] hallmark was simplicity — a limited vocabulary, pared down to only the most essential words. We were so eager to replace the specific with the generalized that sea gulls, larks, and nightingales were all reduced to 'birds', while birches, oaks, and weeping willows became 'trees'. We believed that we should write as if there would be no more poetry after us, that what we would write in exile would be the last Russian poetry, and that we should add no ornamentation, nothing superfluous.[77]

The focus of the Paris Note on the entropy of culture and language was an implicit reaction to a variety of socio-historical phenomena and artistic trends, including exile, the instability of publishing networks in the diaspora, the avant-garde, the supremacy of mass culture, ideological crises, and the existentialist discourse of the interwar decades. Their poetry represented a transition between the Silver Age, i.e. *fin-de-siècle* modernism in its Russian incarnation, and interwar modernism, which informed the artistic vocabulary of most Western artists of their generation. In the words of Modris Eksteins, 'Modernism, which in its prewar form was a culture of hope, a vision of synthesis, would turn to a culture of nightmare and denial'.[78] Even if, when applied to prewar Russian modernism, its definition as the 'culture of hope' appears reductive, Silver Age poetry conveys the ecstatic expectation of an impending universal transformation, and its eschatological element is inseparable from the intense quest for mystical revelations. After the Revolution, metropolitan Russian literature gradually deviated from European aesthetic trends, and as a result the second phase of modernism was curtailed in the Soviet Union. But this 'culture of nightmare and denial' affected the output of diaspora poets, the Paris Note in the first

---

77 *Conversations in Exile: Russian Writers Abroad*, edited by John Glad (Durham, NC, and London: Duke University Press, 1993), p. 33.
78 Modris Eksteins, *The Rites of Spring: The Great War and the Birth of the Modern Age* (New York: Anchor Books Doubleday, 1990), p. 237.

instance.⁷⁹ Against the backdrop of metropolitan Russian poetry, the Paris Note strikes a unique chord. Granted, poetry conceived within Soviet borders was extremely diverse, expressing pro-Soviet or dissident sentiments, heroic opposition to tyranny, as well as loneliness and the fear of an oppressive regime, suffering induced by isolation from European civilisation and yearning for a reconnection to world culture, etc. But Paris Note verse is testimony to the profound loneliness and despair of an individual who is located in the epicentre of this 'world culture' and understands that the previously nourishing European civilisation has become a cultural 'wasteland'. The realisation of the emptiness of all conventional notions and words, and of the senselessness of life itself, accounts for the profound introspection of Paris Note poetry as a way to experience this global catastrophe on personal level while 'struggling for non-existence' (in Bozhnev's words). Akhmatova's *Rekviem* could not have appeared in emigration, just as the meaninglessness of freedom, permeating many lines of the Paris Note, cannot be appreciated by someone who suffers from totalitarian oppression.

Compared to literary developments in the Soviet Union, Paris Note poems embody a different *chronotope*, expressing cultural and philosophical currents that shaped European modernist culture of the interwar period and in particular the Russian diasporic experience. But some of these texts also transcend their time, place, and individual circumstances, opening themselves to diverse critical readings that can potentially expand their semantics. Without such intense interpretive work, as Mikhail Yampolsky observes, a text cannot attain canonical status.⁸⁰ At the time of publication, Paris Note poems were accompanied by reviews, articles and polemics.⁸¹ Critics of later periods have likewise

---

79 Among other prominent examples of diasporic poetic production that expressed this *Zeitgeist* is Khodasevich's cycle 'Evropeiskaia noch'', distinguished by a jarring discontinuity between the 'classical' form cultivated by the poet against all odds and the profoundly modern expression of the collapse of civilisation.

80 Mikhail Iampolskii, 'Literaturnyi kanon i teoriia "sil'nogo avtora"', *Inostrannaia literatura*, 12 (1998), magazines.russ.ru/inostran/1998/12/iamp.html

81 In post-Soviet Russia, however, the Paris Note has so far enjoyed limited interest beyond the circle of scholars of émigré literature. There have been occasional publications of the Paris Note poems in various collections of émigré lyrics, and at least one book has been released for individual poets, including Shteiger, Chervinskaia, and Chinnov. The Paris Note certainly has not entered the school curriculum, although it is usually introduced as part of university courses on émigré literature.

agreed that Parisian poets were not epigones of the classical tradition, but trend-setters. Kreid even extended the chronological parameters of the movement far beyond the interwar decades, arguing for its viable and lasting influence:

> The idea that the 'Note' existed only in the thirties is false. It was not short-lived, it lasted with diverse modulations for almost half a century — from the 1920s to the 1970s, but most fruitful were the pre-war and postwar decades. 'Note' did not repeat itself, it varied and sounded in various arrangements.[82]

The diasporic canon, inaugurated by the Paris Note along with other émigré authors of the interwar period, opens up new areas of twentieth-century Russian experience, as explored in literary texts. It fosters different approaches to Russian literary identities that cannot be adequately captured from a strictly nationalist perspective on writing, authorship, language, and the poet's status and mission. While it appears to play a provocative role, undermining the fundamental narratives and tropes associated with the mainstream cultural conception of Russianness, it also works against the 'cultural inertia' of the national canon, suggesting an alternative and implicitly contributing to its reconfiguration.[83]

---

82 Kreid, 'Chto takoe "Parizhskaia nota"', http://magazines.russ.ru/slovo/2004/43/kr41.html

83 Igor' Sukhikh observes that any established national canon is characterised by 'powerful cultural inertia' (Igor' Sukhikh, *Russkii kanon: Knigi XX veka* (Moscow: Vremia, 2013)). Although Sukhikh deliberately stays away from poetry in this book, it is nonetheless noteworthy that on his list of thirty canonical figures of twentieth-century Russian literature he includes several émigrés (among those, the selected texts of Gazdanov and Nabokov clearly belong to the Russian diasporic canon). This demonstrates that canonical boundaries are sufficiently porous for a text to fall within more than one canon, and for diasporic works to be admitted also into a unified, and more comprehensive, canon of Russian literature.

11. The Thaw Generation Poets in the Post-Soviet Period

Emily Lygo

During the Khrushchev Thaw, poetry became a popular means of expressing ideas of renewal, hope, optimism and sincerity associated with de-Stalinisation and the USSR's increasing openness to the West.[1] The establishment of the 'Day of Poetry' in 1956 is indicative of the prominent place that poetry came to occupy in culture and arts during the Thaw that was, in many ways, launched at the Twentieth Party Congress that year. A group of poets who came to prominence at this time identified strongly with both the politics of de-Stalinisation and the sincerity and truthfulness that imbued much cultural production of the period. These *estrada* (podium) poets, who reached a wide audience both in the USSR and abroad through mass public readings, domestic and foreign publications and foreign trips, achieved fame and notoriety with works that were published thanks to the Thaw.[2] They were criticised as well as praised, but they became the most famous

---

1   On poetry during the Thaw period see Marc Slonim, *Soviet Russian Literature: Writers and Problems 1917–67* (New York: Oxford University Press, 1967), pp. 315–17; Ol'ga Carlisle, *Poets on Street Corners: Portraits of Fifteen Russian Poets* (New York: Random House, 1968), pp. 2–6; Suzanne Massie, *The Living Mirror. Five Poets from Leningrad* (London: Victor Gollancz Ltd, 1972), pp. 22–43; Emily Lygo, *Leningrad Poetry 1953–75: The Thaw Generation* (Oxford and Bern: Peter Lang, 2010).

2   Anna Akhmatova used this term to describe Evtushenko and others. See, for example, Aleksandr Kushner, 'U Akhmatovoi', in *'Svoiu mezh vas eshche ostaviv ten'…': Akhmatovskie chteniia*. Vypusk 3, edited by N. V. Koroleva and S. A. Kovalenko (Moscow: Nasledie, 1992), pp. 133–41 (p. 137).

poets of their generation whose story was intimately bound up with the narrative of the de-Stalinisation of the arts under Khrushchev. The most famous figures were Evgenii Evtushenko, Andrei Voznesenskii, Bella Akhmadulina, Robert Rozhdestvenskii and Bulat Okudzhava, but alongside them, bards also became very popular, as did some older poets, such as Boris Slutskii and Aleksandr Tvardovskii, whose work chimed with the cultural and political Thaw.

This chapter is concerned with how the reputations of these poets and the narrative about poetry in the Thaw period altered after the radical political and cultural changes in the USSR and then Russia of the late 1980s and early 1990s. After analysing the state of the canon for the Thaw Generation in the late-Soviet period, I will proceed to examine how the Thaw Generation has been positioned in the canon in the post-Soviet period. I will draw upon three main areas of canon formation: educational syllabuses and textbooks, anthologies, and prominent literary critics and commentators. Questions of literary quality, of course, play a significant role in canon formation, but in this article I am concerned primarily with extra-literary factors, since it seems to me that these have proved fundamental to the establishment of a narrative about poetry during the Thaw period which has influenced the canonisation of the individual members of this generation.

Any examination of the canon in the post-Soviet period must take as its starting point the canon as it existed in various contexts before the collapse of the USSR in 1991. Dealing with the question of the canon of Soviet poetry for the Thaw period is complicated by the existence of censorship, state control, and the difficulty of measuring the readership of unofficial publications. There has been a significant shift in thinking about canon that has led to the acknowledgement of more popular literature as constituting either part of a broad canon, or a competing canon of its own.[3] The Soviet experience poses the question of a popular canon a little differently, however: the challenge is whether literature that was popular in the sense of being read widely can be recognised as canonical even if it was largely ignored by state-controlled institutions of canon formation. Publications such as textbooks prescribed for the

---

3   See, for example, *The Popular and the Canonical: Debating Twentieth-century Literature 1940–2000*, edited by David Johnson (Abingdon: Routledge, 2005), especially pp. 3–12.

teaching of literature and official histories of Soviet writing represent the highest level of canonicity — official approval and endorsement — but, especially from the Thaw period onwards, they were only part of the picture in the USSR, with *samizdat* (self-published) literature and *magnitizdat* recordings (amateur recordings using tape recorders) of guitar poetry making literature available through independent channels. *Samizdat* was not confined to the publication of new literature by unpublished poets. In the conditions of paper deficit, fixed print-runs, and a changing political climate that could see a work approved for publication but never re-printed, *samizdat* supplied what was in demand but not available. This 'other' canon is not necessarily one of so-called 'popular literature', but it is one that found expression only in its popularity. Labels such as 'unofficial', 'alternative', 'underground' and 'uncensored' have all been applied to it, or to a smaller subset, for example, prose works or poetry, but none really covers its variety.[4]

In the last decade of Soviet power, the official canon did not include many poets of the Thaw Generation beyond Evtushenko and Voznesenskii. The conservatism and hierarchical nature of the Soviet literary establishment meant that official statements about the canon of Soviet poetry, which included histories of Soviet literature and school syllabuses, were slow to incorporate younger poets. In the 1982 university textbook *Istoriia russkoi sovetskoi literatury* (*The History of Russian Soviet Literature*), L. F. Ershov's chapter on the 1960s to the early 1980s covers the period that the new generation of Thaw poets belong to, but concentrates on the older generation of writers predominantly: Tvardovskii, Vasilii Fedorov, Leonid Martynov, Sergei Vikulov, Mikhail Dudin, Sergei Orlov, Iaroslav Smeliakov. Of the poets who made names for themselves during the Thaw, Ershov includes only Evtushenko, Voznesenskii, Rozhdestvenskii, and Nikolai Rubtsov.[5] When he comes to the 1970s, there are no new entries into his canon, only the significant

---

4 For example, *Istoriia leningradskoi npodtsenzurnoi poezii: 1950e–1980e gody*, edited by B. Ivanov (St Petersburg: Dean, 2000); Stanislav Savitskii, *Andegraund: Istoriia i mify leningradskoi beofitsial'noi literatury* (Moscow: NLO, 2002); and Robert Porter, *Russia's Alternative Prose* (London: Bloomsbury, 1994); although in the latter book Robert Porter arguably presents writers united by a common reaction to the lifting of censorship in Russia and an aesthetic response to the new conditions.

5 L. F. Ershov, *Istoriia russkoi sovetskoi literatury: uchebnoe posobie dlia universitetov* (Moscow: Vysshaia shkola, 1982), pp. 255–70.

departures of a generation of poets. The period is — in classic Soviet euphemistic language — said to have been a 'difficult one' for poetry: 'there were searches, but they did not always yield results'.⁶

The Thaw Generation poets had a similarly low profile in a textbook for students of Russian language and literature at Pedagogical Institutes that focuses specifically on Russian Soviet literature of the 1950s to 1970s. Two out of twelve chapters are devoted to poetry, a proportion of the study that already suggests poetry is not considered to be the most important genre of the period.⁷ One chapter focuses exclusively on poetry that takes the countryside as its theme, while the other deals only with the work of Martynov and Tvardovskii. Owing to the choice of themes to be explored in poetry of the period, this study does not make mention of Evtushenko, Voznesenskii or Rozhdestvenskii, names that were almost synonymous with Russian poetry of the Thaw in the West, and which were certainly well known and associated with the period in the USSR as well.

One has to look beyond official Soviet publications to find evidence of the popular canon that existed among readers in the USSR. In 1978, Edward Brown wrote that contemporary Soviet poets were those 'who create the greatest stir and receive widest acclaim both at home and abroad',⁸ and listed these as Evtushenko, Voznesenskii, Akhmadulina, Slutskii, Novella Matveeva, Tvardovskii, Okudzhava, Iosif Brodskii and Martynov.⁹ This is an indication of a canon perceived by a Western visitor trying to get beyond the official level of the conservative Soviet literary establishment, to an understanding of which poets mattered to Soviet, predominantly intelligentsia readers.

In such Western studies of Soviet literature and anthologies of Soviet poetry that predate the fall of the USSR, there is much consensus about the key figures of the Thaw Generation. A selection of Soviet

---

6   *Ibid.*, p. 267.
7   *Russkaia sovetskaia literatura 50–70kh godov*, edited by V. A. Kovalev (Moscow: Prosveshchenie, 1981).
8   Edward Brown, *Russian Literature Since the Revolution* (London: Collier-MacMillan Ltd, 1963, revised edn 1969), p. 318.
9   Notably, almost all these poets are featured in an anthology of Soviet Russian poetry taken from the journal *Sovetskaia literatura* translated and published in English in 1981. Only Akhmadulina and Brodskii are absent. See *Soviet Russian Poetry of the 1950s–1970s*, compiled by Nina Kupriianova and Ariadna Ivanovskaia (Moscow: Progress Publishers, 1981).

and Russian literature covering the period of the Thaw all included Evtushenko, Voznesenskii and Akhmadulina among the major figures of the generation.[10] All but the earliest one published in 1963, include Brodskii. That these four figures were, by the end of the 1960s, the most canonical poets of their generation, is underscored by the number of publications of their work in English translation.[11] Other figures included in three or four of the studies are Okudzhava, Tvardovskii, Slutskii and Matveeva. The names of Aleksandr Galich, Viktor Sosnora, Evgenii Vinokurov, Gennadii Aigi and Rozhdestvenskii appear in only two of the studies and appear to form a group of poets that are not the core of the canon found in the more general surveys, but which belong in that which is described in studies of Soviet poetry aimed at a more specialist and specifically academic audience.

The narrative of poetry of the Thaw period found in Soviet publications plays down the *estrada* phenomenon that brought poetry to popular culture. Ershov acknowledges that literature underwent significant change during the Khrushchev Thaw, however, and when he describes the advent of Evtushenko and Voznesenskii, he is quick to point out the shortcomings of their style.[12] A sober evaluation of much poetry of the Thaw appeared as early as the late 1960s in various official statements indicating a return to more conservative norms.[13] There was also a tendency to downplay the significance of poetry for this historical period. In contrast, narratives found in Western studies of

---

10 See *Soviet Literature in the Sixties*, edited by Max Hayward and Edward L. Crowley (London: Methuen, 1963); Johannes Holthusen, *Twentieth-Century Russian Literature: A Critical Introduction* (New York: Ungar Publishing Co., 1968); Edward Brown, *Russian Literature Since the Revolution* (Cambridge, MA: Harvard University Press, 1969); Deming Brown, *Soviet Russian Literature Since Stalin* (Cambridge: Cambridge University Press, 1979); Peter France, *Poets of Modern Russia* (Cambridge: Cambridge University Press, 1982); Geoffrey Hosking, 'The Twentieth Century: In Search of New Ways, 1953–80', in *The Cambridge History of Russian Literature*, edited by Charles Moser (Cambridge: Cambridge University Press, 1992), pp. 520–94; Carlisle, *Poets on Street Corners*; George Reavey, *The New Russian Poets 1953–1968: An Anthology* (New York: October House Inc., 1968).

11 The *Reference Guide to Russian Literature* lists for the period 1962–1991 at least sixteen significant publications of Evtushenko's work in English, nine of Voznesenskii's, four of Akhmadulina's and eleven of Brodskii's. See *Reference Guide to Russian Literature*, edited by Neil Cornwell (London and Chicago: Fitzroy Dearborn Publishers, 1998).

12 Ershov, *Istoriia russkoi sovetskoi literatury*, pp. 223 and 213.

13 See, for example, Lygo, *Leningrad Poetry 1953–75*, pp. 86–94.

Thaw literature from the late Soviet period underline that lyric poetry, which had virtually disappeared from official publications during the Stalin period, experienced a revival and rehabilitation in the 1950s. Poetry is connected to de-Stalinisation, to the growth of dissidence and non-conformism, and to the development of an underground and the phenomenon of *samizdat*. The range of Thaw Generation poets recognized as significant is far wider than that found in Soviet publications.

Changes to the Canon During and After *Perestroika*

During *perestroika*, the range of published poets belonging to the Thaw Generation expanded to include émigrés and poets who had remained 'unofficial' in the USSR. The removal of Soviet ideology from narratives about Thaw poetry changed the way that this generation of poets was conceived and interpreted in Russia.

Émigré poets introduced to Russia during *perestroika* include Brodskii, Dmitrii Bobyshev, Natal'ia Gorbanevskaia, and Lev Losev. By far the most significant of these was Brodskii, and the return of his work to Russia was a huge corrective to the canon. From about 1995, and especially after his death, there were a large number of publications about Brodskii, mostly by academics.[14] To a large extent, however, he has been seen as an individual: his identity as a Russian poet is in no doubt, but he is not seen as a representative of third-wave émigré literature.[15] He is seen more as a part of the Leningrad poetry of the post-Stalin era, but even then his work is discussed largely divorced from this context.[16] Another context for him is the transnational canon that, through his essays and articles, he was instrumental in forging.[17] When his poetry returned to Russia in the late 1980s, it did not open

---

14   This is suggested in the Russian language bibliography by Lev Losev, *Iosif Brodskii: Opyt literaturnoi biografii*, Zhizn' zamechatel'nykh liudei (Moscow: Molodaia gvardiia, 2006). See also Chapter 2 by Aaron Hodgson in this volume.

15   See, for example, Maxim Shrayer's article 'Russian American Literature', in *The Greenwood Encyclopedia of Multiethnic American Literature*, edited by Emmanuel S. Nelson, 5 vols. (Westport CT: Greenwood Publishing Group, 2005), IV, 1940–1951.

16   Exceptions include David MacFadyen, *Joseph Brodsky and the Soviet Muse* (Montreal: McGill-Queen's University Press, 2000); Lygo, *Leningrad Poetry 1953–75*; and Losev, *Iosif Brodskii, Opyt literaturnoi biografii*.

17   See the bibliography in Losev, *Iosif Brodskii, Opyt literaturnoi biografii*.

the door for the reception of third-wave émigré poets more generally, and the narrative of the Thaw Generation has yet to assimilate a good number of poets.[18]

The previously unofficial poets who now appeared in print and on the internet were more numerous. In anthologies published in both the West and Russia, three widely included figures from unofficial literature are Evgenii Rein, Genrikh Sapgir, and Dmitrii Prigov.[19] Boris Chichibabin and German Plisetskii also appear in several anthologies, as does Vladimir Kornilov, who belonged to official literature but fell from grace in the 1970s. However, a much more extensive list of unofficial poets emerges from comprehensive collections and studies that aimed to make accessible this underground stratum of literature. In the 1990s, a powerful narrative about the evolution of underground poetry and poets of the Thaw era developed, informed by Konstantin Kuz'minskii's *Blue Lagoon Anthology* published in the United States in the 1980s,[20] and then by studies, anthologies and web-based projects in Russia in the following decade, including *Samizdat veka* (*Samizdat of the Century*),[21] and the web site 'Russkaia poeziia 60-kh godov' ('Russian Poetry of the 1960s'), created in 1999.[22] Dmitrii Kuz'min's website *Vavilon* (*Babylon*) is not necessarily put forward as an attempt at canon definition,[23] but a comprehensive anthology *Russkie stikhi 1950–2000* (*Russian Poetry*

---

18   To a greater or lesser extent this includes: Lev Losev, Dmitrii Bobyshev, Naum Korzhavin (as a dissident he is more assimilated), Maria Temkina, Vladimir Gandel'sman, Konstantin Kuz'minskii, and Vadim Kreps. Other lesser-known poets listed by Shrayer are Pavel Babich, Ina Bliznetsova, Mikhail Iupp, Aleksandr Ocheretianskii, Sergei Petrunis, and Viktor Urin; see 'Russian American Literature', p. 1949.

19   Included in S*trofy veka*. edited by Evgenii Evtushenko (Moscow: Polifakt, 1995); *Russkaia poeziia 1950–2000*, edited by Uritskii, Akhmetev, Orlov, Lukomnikov (Moscow: Letnii sad, 2010); and *Sovremennye russkie poety*, edited by V. Agenosov, K. Ankudinov (Moscow: Naucho-prakticheskii tsentr 'Megatron', 1998) all published in Russia, and in G. S. Smith, *Contemporary Russian Poetry: A Bilingual Anthology* (Bloomington: Indiana University Press, 1993) and J. Kates, *In the Grip of Strange Thoughts* (Newcastle-upon-Tyne: Bloodaxe Books, 1999) with the exception that Sapgir does not appear in *Contemporary Russian Poetry*.

20   *The Blue Lagoon Anthology of Modern Russian Poetry*, edited by Konstantin Kuz'minskii and Grigorii Kovalev, 5 vols. (Newtonville: Oriental Research Partners, 1986).

21   *Samizdat veka*, edited by Andrei Strelianyi (Moscow: Polifakt, 1999).

22   Mariia Levchenko, 'Russkaia poeziia 60kh godov', *Ruthenia*, http://ruthenia.ru/60s/poets/index.htm

23   Dmitrii Kuz'min, *Vavilon*, http://www.vavilon.ru

1950–2000), which includes unofficial, émigré and official Soviet poets, seems to be putting forward a version of the canon.²⁴

In contrast to the lack of a narrative about émigré poetry in this period, the narrative of unofficial poetry of the 1950s onwards has become well established. It identifies 'forefathers' in poets such as Nikolai Glazkov,²⁵ and Roal'd Mandel'shtam, who spurned official Soviet culture.²⁶ It also describes the mentoring of younger poets by members of the older generation of intelligentsia, of whom some had experienced the Gulag and some were associated with the pre-revolutionary period. Anthologies and studies of the period describe the associations and groups of poets that together make up a patchwork of the generation as a whole. Significantly, the emphasis on groups is distinct from the official Soviet canon of poets which deliberately avoided the organization of poets into the kinds of sub-groups that were outlawed in the early 1930s.

Canon-Forming Processes

Educational Syllabuses

The poets and narratives about poetry of the Thaw Generation have undergone processes of canonisation to varying extents in the fields of educational syllabuses, anthologies, and influential commentators. These processes are distinct, but not unrelated. There is usually a delay before the publication and critical reception of contemporary literature settles down enough to be incorporated into the educational canon; Mikhail Gasparov has suggested, indeed, that the incorporation of a work of literature into educational syllabuses is a sign that the work no longer pertains to the category of 'contemporary'.²⁷ While the Thaw clearly no longer belongs to the category of contemporary literature, the newcomers to the corpus of poetry from this era are in some sense

---

24 On this see Katharine Hodgson, 'Two Post-Soviet Anthologies of the 1990s and the Russian 20th-Century Canon', *Slavonic and East European Journal*, 90 (2012), 642–70.
25 'Nikolai Glazkov', *Samizdat veka*, p. 372.
26 Roal'd Mandel'shtam, *Sobranie stikhotvorenii* (St Petersburg: Izdatel'stvo Ivana Limbakha, 2006).
27 Mikhail Gasparov, 'Stoletie kak mera, ili Klassika na fone sovremennosti', *Novoe literaturnoe obozrenie*, 62 (2003), http://magazines.russ.ru/nlo/2003/62/gaspar-pr.html

still new, and it is not surprising that although returned literature has been published and received critical attention, it has yet to be fully assimilated by educational syllabuses.

There are post-Soviet government prescriptions for literature to be studied in general and specialised ('middle') schools. In the second half of the 1990s, the general syllabus for literature of the second half of the twentieth century set the minimum requirement as the study of three to four works drawn from Fedor Abramov, Viktor Astaf'ev, Vasilii Belov, Valentin Rasputin, Evgenii Nosov, Vasilii Shukshin, Iurii Kazakov, Rubtsov, Mikhail Isakovskii, Nikolai Zabolotskii, Aleksandr Iashin, Rozhdestvenskii and others.[28] In the syllabus for middle schools published two years later, the choice of works for study from the second half of the twentieth century is explained as taking in those which 'were acclaimed as significant by their contemporaries'. Here, Kazakov, Isakovskii, Zabolotskii, Iashin and Rozhdestvenskii from the general level list are replaced with Viktor Nekrasov, Aleksandr Solzhenitsyn, Vasil Bykov, Konstantin Vorob'ev, Iurii Trifonov, Evtushenko, Aleksandr Vampilov, Akhmadulina, Voznesenskii, Brodskii, Okudzhava, Vladimir Vysotskii.[29] This selection introduces writers whose work opens up the possibility of discussing more complex questions of the historical period such as emigration, dissidence, the individual, and problems in Soviet society that were, as a rule, excluded from mainstream Soviet literature. It also introduces a few more poets to a list that is certainly dominated by prose writers.

The syllabuses that were set out ten years later were more narrowly prescriptive about the range of poets from the Thaw Generation to be studied. The general level prescribed Brodskii, Voznesenskii, Vysotskii, Evtushenko, Okudzhava, and Rubtsov, and named, albeit in vague formulations, the themes characterising their poetry: 'the critical problems of their times' and 'the search for solid moral values in the life

---

28 'Ob obiazatel'nom miminume soderzhaniia obrazovatel'nykh programm osnovnoi obshcheobrazovatel'noi shkoly. Pis'mo. Ministerstvo obshchego i professional'nogo obrazovaniia RF', 18 June 1997, N 974/14–12 (D), p. 19, http://www.innovbusiness.ru/pravo/DocumShow_DocumID_52815.html

29 'Srednego (polnogo) obshchego obrazovaniia. Prikaz. Ministerstvo obrazovaniia RF', 30 June 1999, N 56 (NTsPI), p. 5, http://www.businesspravo.ru/Docum/DocumShow_DocumID_71939.html

of the people and the discovery of distinctive national characteristics'.[30] While the inclusion of Brodskii makes clear that the canon has undergone a shift since the Soviet period, the themes identified are still rather conservative, concentrating on the history of Thaw poetry, and the theme of national character. The middle school syllabus is similarly prescriptive in spite of the fact that it is aimed at students at a higher level.[31] The choice of poets put forward is only a suggestion, and others may be substituted, but as it stands it recommends including Tvardovskii, Rubtsov, the Dagestan national poet of the Soviet period Rasul Gamzatov, Brodskii and Okudzhava. The themes identified for discussion go beyond rather vague and nationalist concerns, and introduce questions about the past: the influence of the Thaw on the development of literature; literary journals and their place in social consciousness; the 'camp' theme; and 'village' prose.

The government prescriptions make clear that alongside the *estrada* poets and older figures such as Tvardovskii, the canon for the Thaw Generation now includes Brodskii and some other figures that have gained recognition since *perestroika*. Interestingly, however, the themes and concerns of Brodskii's work in particular have not come to be seen as indicative of the Thaw years. Indeed, since 2000, Rubtsov has become identified as more representative of the Thaw period and the principal concerns that preoccupied the literature of that time: the themes of Russia, Russianness and rural life. Such recommendations give a distinctly nationalist bent to the government syllabuses, which is not surprising in the least, and also imply that while Brodskii cannot be ignored, he is not typical or representative of his time.

Alongside the government syllabuses for schools are textbooks and curricula for both school and university courses that are published by academics and teachers. There is considerable variation between textbooks, and there has not been a steady progress of change to the canon put forward by them; rather, while in 1998 a Moscow University

---

30 'Standart osnovnogo obshchego obrazovaniia po literature', from 'Dokumenty i materialy deiatel'nosti federal'nogo agenstva po obrazovaniiu za period 2004–2010 (vplot' do ego uprazdneniia na osnovanii Ukaza Prezidenta RF ot 4 marta 2010 goda No. 271)', pp. 86–102 (p. 94), http://www.mccme.ru/edu/oficios/standarty/2004/standart.edu/p1/09.doc

31 'Primernaia programma srednego (polnogo) obshchego obrazovaniia po literature, bazovyi uroven'', http://www.edu.doal.ru/predm/laws7/prog_sb_lit.doc

textbook shows considerable influence of the changes to the canon in the post-Soviet period, a 2007 syllabus from Voronezh University on the 'History of Russian Literature of the Twentieth Century' sticks quite closely to the Soviet canon. It may be that there is a tendency for the capital to be more up-to-date than the provinces; on the other hand, the influence of the individuals writing the textbooks is also crucial.

Two of the more conservative examples of syllabuses include the programme for prospective university students (*abiturienty*) published by Ulianovsk Pedagogical College in 2001,[32] and educational materials produced by Voronezh State University for higher education institutions in 2007.[33] In the Ulianovsk document, the Thaw Generation poets appear under the heading *Poeziia poslednikh desiatiletii* (Poetry of the recent decades) and are represented by Evtushenko, Voznesenskii, Rozhdestvenskii, and Akhmadulina. With the addition of Okudzhava, the same figures appear as a group in the Voronezh syllabus, and here they are identified as one of two reactions to the Stalinism of the preceding decades. This emphasis on the *estrada* poets is distinct from the Soviet canon that was wary of promoting these poets and their de-Stalinising work, but does not move beyond the bounds of Soviet published poetry. The Voronezh syllabus also includes the poetry of Rubtsov: he is presented here as a representative of a contrasting tradition, an alternative response to the Stalinist past that involved a return to the village and Russian nineteenth-century tradition and a position that was 'outside' the Thaw politics.

Other curricula reflect the changes to the field of Russian poetry that have taken place since the late 1980s. A Moscow University textbook introduces Brodskii to the heart of the Thaw Generation, devoting a chapter to him; Vysotskii is the only other Thaw poet whose work receives a chapter of its own, while in the introductory chapter, other names from this period mentioned are Rubtsov, Galich, Iulii Kim,

---

[32] O. K. Rybitskaia, 'Metodicheskie rekomendatsii po literature dlia abiturientov 2001 goda (polnoe srednee obshchee obrazovanie)', Ulianovsk Pedagogical College, approved by the Ministry of General and Professional Education of the Russian Federation, http://venec.ulstu.ru/lib/2002/1/Rybickaja.pdf

[33] T. A. Nikonova, 'Istoriia russkoi literatury XX veka. Shestidesiatye gody. Uchebnoe posobie dlia vuzov' (Voronezh: Voronezhskii gosudarstvennyi universitet, 2007), *Edinoe okno*, http://window.edu.ru/resource/315/59315

and Okudzhava.³⁴ In this textbook there is at least mention of Losev, Slutskii, Rein, Anatolii Naiman, Prigov, Kushner, Akhmadulina, Fazil Iskander, Voznesenskii, and Rubtsov. The selection of Brodskii and Vysotskii as the two leading figures that merit a chapter of their own suggests several important strands to the history of the poetry of the Thaw Generation: the genuine popularity that Vysotskii enjoyed during his lifetime, the phenomenon of Brodskii's exile, and the phenomena of unpublished and underground poetry. Along with these changes to the canon, however, is a perhaps related assertion that in this period, poetry was not very important as a literary genre. The authors even go as far as dismissing Brodskii's acknowledgement of the great talent of his generation as 'poetic exaggeration'. In common with the Moscow University publication, the textbook *Uroki literatury v 11-om klasse* (*Literature Lessons in Class 11*) places Brodskii at the centre of the canon.³⁵ An essay entitled 'Contemporary literature', written by the prominent literary critic Igor' Shaitanov, states that Brodskii is the only major Russian poet of the second half of the twentieth century. The essay places emphasis on the historical context of the Thaw period and the place of both official and unofficial poetry, and does not entirely reject the former in favour of the latter.

Though they have taken into account the changes to the corpus in the post-Soviet period, even these syllabuses are still relatively conservative in their canonical statements: there is virtually no mention of avant-garde poetry or poets, for example. Shaitanov's essay is notable for its attempt to bring together pre- and post-1991 views of the Thaw Generation. He recognises the historical interest of the *estrada* poets as major, seeing them as importantly provocative (*vozmutiteli*) at the time, and sets them in their historical context. Significantly, it argues that their work now often requires a commentary because it is so closely connected to the historical context of the Thaw. In fact, it was mainly Evtushenko and Rozhdestvenskii who wrote such 'topical' poems, but even the intimate poetry of Akhmadulina or quiet philosophical lyrics

---

34 *Istoriia russkoi literatury XX veka (20–90e gody). Osnovnye imena: Uchebnoe posobie*, edited by S. I. Kormilov (Moscow: Moskovskii gosudarstvennyi universitet, 1998), http://www.hi-edu.ru/e-books/xbook046/01/part-002.htm

35 Igor' Shaitanov, 'O sovremennoi lirike (Opyt analiza)', in *Uroki literatury v 11-om klasse. Kniga dlia uchitelia*, edited by V. P. Zhuravlev (Moscow: Prosveshchenie, [n.d.]). Also available online at http://window.edu.ru/resource/080/28080

of Kushner perhaps lose some of the impact they had when they were written, when read out of the context of their time.

Shaitanov's essay also acknowledges the significance of Thaw Generation poets who were not recognized by the Soviet literary establishment, but this inclusion does not lead to a complete re-casting of the narrative of the generation. He singles out two figures from their contemporaries, Rein and Oleg Chukhontsev, and devotes a section to each.[36] This selection is rare if not unique for the Russian school and university syllabuses, and would appear to be included largely because of Shaitanov's personal judgement: as an influential and prolific literary critic, as well as an academic, Shaitanov brings a view of the canon to the construction of the school syllabus that appears radical against the general inertia in this field. The two poets are not, however, seen as part of a wider narrative about this generation. They are given very little context and discussed almost exclusively in terms of their texts. The chronological narrative moves from Ol'ga Berggol'ts and Smeliakov, to Evtushenko, Voznesenskii, Akhmadulina and Rozhdestvenskii. A divergence thus emerges in this syllabus — and is echoed in others too — between the figures of the history of Thaw poetry, and the main poets of the Thaw Generation. Overall, this tendency suggests that a significant source of inertia within the canon of poetry is the established narrative of a generation that is linked to institutions, historical events, political trends and the history of publication.

Anthologies

If educational syllabuses tend to be limited in terms of the number of works and writers that are included in the canon, anthologies can be far more inclusive and therefore more reflective of the changes that have occurred to the corpus. Nevertheless, either through the selection of poets included, or by the amount of space dedicated to individual poets, anthologies make important statements about canon. Katharine Hodgson points out that two of the most significant anthologies of Russian twentieth-century poets that have been published since 1991

---

36   Notably, these two figures were also singled out for extensive attention in Neil Cornwell, *Reference Guide to Russian Literature* (London and Chicago: Fitzroy Dearborn Publishers, 1998), pp. 227–28 and 693–94.

have claimed to be motivated by the task of the preservation of texts, but that nevertheless the selection of poets and poems have been subject to vigorous criticism because of the perceived assertions about the shape of the canon.[37]

Arguments over the canon that are presented by the anthologies confirm that the main problem for anthologists is the question of whether Soviet literature should now be recognized as a part of Russian literature. As Hodgson shows, both approaches have been advocated by Russian literary critics.[38] Although there are significant voices that advocate the removal of most, if not all, Soviet poetry from the canon, most major published anthologies that aim at anything like a comprehensive picture of Russian poetry of the twentieth century do not make such a wholesale rejection. However, given the politically-charged nature of the twentieth-century canon, this can mean, as Il'ia Kukulin has formulated, that

> any assertion of the canon looks like a re-evaluation of the Soviet picture of new Russian poetry with a bias towards the underground and émigrés, or [...] a confirmation that Soviet aesthetic criteria are valid for the present day.[39]

Hodgson highlights that disagreements over the inclusion or exclusion of poets in the major anthologies have at times focused on the extent to which avant-garde and non-conformist work has been introduced to the canon.[40]

These questions of the balance in the canon of Soviet and unpublished poetry, and of avant-garde and strict form are particularly pointed in the discussion of the Thaw Generation poets. It is complicated to reformulate an understanding of the period without the *estrada* poets, but at the same time in the post-Soviet context there has been a tendency to see their political positions as hopelessly compromised. Poetic form is much debated because the proliferation of underground poetry during the period, especially in Moscow, featured a significant amount of non-classical, avant-garde verse. In the anthologies, as in

---

37 Hodgson, 'Two Post-Soviet Russian Poetry Anthologies', p. 650.
38 *Ibid.*, see especially pp. 650, 654.
39 Il'ia Kukulin, 'Impressionisticheskii monument', *Novoe literaturnoe obozrenie*, 109 (2011), http://magazines.russ.ru/nlo/2011/109/ku26.html
40 Hodgson, 'Two Post-Soviet Russian Poetry Anthologies', p. 657.

the school syllabuses, the question emerges as to whether or not the historical figures are in fact the major poets of the period; the answers presented by the anthologies can articulate a more nuanced positioning of the poets, however, since previously central figures can be retained but shifted to a peripheral position in the overall picture.

Although there have been many anthologies of Russian poetry of the Soviet era published in Russia since 1991, a significant majority of these are confined to poets of the Silver Age.[41] This seems to suggest that this period is seen as the most significant for twentieth-century Russian poetry. Whatever the grounds for this perception are, they mean that the number of anthologies in which the Thaw Generation is represented is quite small. Collections of poetry that are focussed exclusively on underground poets, for example *Samizdat veka*, are by definition not contributing directly to the canon-forming processes under discussion. In particular, they do not engage with the key question of the re-balancing of Soviet and non-Soviet (émigré or unofficial) poetry within the canon. For this study a selection of six anthologies was made, three from Russia and three from the West.[42]

Before looking at the general trends that emerge across the six anthologies, a comparison of the Western and Russian publications points to some distinctions between these sub-groups, and perhaps between the Russian and foreign branches of the canon-forming process. There are a handful of poets included in all the Russian anthologies who are absent from, or given little space in, the Western anthologies, yet the space alloted to them by the Russian compilers suggests they are of some significance. They include figures of Soviet poetry such as Vladimir Sokolov, Iurii Kuznetsov, Konstantin Vanshenkin and Iurii Riashentsev, whose recognition and popularity in the USSR continued into the post-Soviet period with the awarding of prizes, and, in Vanshenkin's and Riashentsev's cases, the continuing popularity of their songs in classic Soviet films. They also include conceptualists such as Vsevolod Nekrasov and Stanislav Krasovitskii, and bards such as

---

41   I am grateful to Joanne Shelton for this information.
42   In order of publication they are: *Contemporary Russian Poetry*; *Sovremennaia russkaia poeziia*; *Twentieth-Century Russian Poetry*, compiled and edited by Evgenii Evtushenko (London: Fourth Estate, 1993); *Strofy veka. In the Grip of Strange Thoughts*; *Russkie stikhi 1950–2000*.

Novella Matveeva, Kim, Aleksandr Gorodnitskii and even Vysotskii. Lastly, both Evtushenko and Voznesenskii are found in Evtushenko's collection in English, but are surely significant exclusions from both *Contemporary Russian Poetry* and *In the Grip of Strange Thoughts*.[43]

The reasons for these poets' absence from the Western-published anthologies are no doubt varied. The Soviet poets, especially those famous as song-writers, and the bards might be described as belonging to sub-genres of poetry that have not been recognized widely as part of Russian lyric poetry outside Russia; the lesser-known conceptualists, on the other hand, may just have missed the 'radar' of Russian poetry readers abroad, eclipsed by their more famous counterpart Prigov. But the editorial decisions not to include Evtushenko and Voznesenskii in two of the Western publications cannot be because these poets are unknown in the West. Instead, it suggests that Western observers of the canon feel more able to make such radical exclusions from a selection of Thaw Generation poets than their Russian counterparts, perhaps because Russian editors are concerned with the question of the preservation of texts and the literary-historical picture: that any selection made should not only reflect the editor's judgement of poetic merit, but also acknowledge that the picture of poetry of this era that has changed over time.

Notwithstanding these differences between the Western and Russian publications, a comparison between the selections of poets featured in the collections and the relative weighting assigned to individual figures suggests that there is no clear dividing line between East and West. Therefore, by treating the six as a sample of anthologies, it is possible to draw some observations and conclusions about canon formation within a reasonable range of publications from the 1990s and 2000s. There are six poets who appear in all of the anthologies, a list which does not include Brodskii: Akhmadulina, Kushner, Iunna Morits, Okudzhava, Prigov and Rein. Brodskii's absence from *In the Grip of Strange Thoughts* may be due to his being so well known, and it would seem unwise to draw conclusions about his canonicity — which is so strongly established in so many ways — from this one omission. The other names here are predominantly

---

43 G. S. Smith has described how both Russians and non-Russians suggested that he should have included Evtushenko and Voznesenskii in the anthology because of their historical importance. Email to the author, 15 June 2013.

poets who were published, albeit only partially, during the Soviet period. Rein hardly counts as such, given that his first collection was published during *perestroika*, so he and Prigov can be said to be the only two of the six who belong to unofficial literature. With the absence of Evtushenko, Voznesenskii and Rozhdestvenskii, the four Soviet-published poets of the list looks like an elite of the more lyrical poets of the Thaw Generation published since the 1950s and 1960s, who are not seen as compromised by their political situations and, even though Akhmadulina and Okudzhava did take part in the stadium poetry readings, are distanced from the phenomenon of *estrada* poetry. These are perhaps seen as more 'authentic' poets who were not such obvious mouthpieces for Khrushchev's de-Stalinising, liberalising agendas.

The following table shows the frequency that poets appear in the selected anthologies:

In all the anthologies	In five out of six	In four out of six
Akhmadulina	Brodskii	Kuznetsov
Kushner	Bobyshev	Losev
Morits	Gorbanevskaia	Matveeva
Okudzhava	Kornilov	Plisetskii
Prigov	Lisnianskaia	Sokolov
Rein	Sapgir	Vanshenkin
	Slutskii	Voznesenskii
	Sosnora	Vysotskii
	Chukhontsev	Evtushenko

Of the poets appearing in five out of six, there are four more Soviet-published poets, and five who belong to unofficial poetry. In four out of the six anthologies we find six more Soviet-published and four unofficial poets. In total, therefore, there is a majority (fourteen) of Soviet-published poets and slightly fewer (eleven) unofficial (including émigré) poets. In view of the drama of the upheaval of the canon and the extensive debates over whether or not any worthwhile poetry was published in the USSR, the number of Soviet poets is perhaps surprisingly high. On the other hand, it bears out the historical narrative that sees the Thaw as a period during which a window of opportunity to become a published Soviet poet opened temporarily for young poets, especially in Moscow, and points to the Writers' Union as having managed to accommodate a significant number of talented poets of the time.⁴⁴

A slightly different view is gained by taking into account also the amount of space given to poets in these anthologies as an indication of their importance (with the caveat that the number of pages is an imprecise measure). In the case of the *In the Grip of Strange Thoughts* and *Contemporary Russian Poetry*, the poets selected are given roughly equal amounts of space, but inclusion in itself is an indication that the poet is considered important; in the others, the difference in the number of poems and pages allotted to each poet is significant. There is a group of poets that emerges as being important in five of the six anthologies (as it happens, none has this status in all six): Akhmadulina, Brodskii, Slutskii, Rein and Okudzhava, which overlaps significantly, of course, with the survey of frequency.⁴⁵ Looking at the anthologies in this way throws up some interesting contrasts with the first, however; while the inclusion of a poet may be considered mandatory, the diminution of that figure achieved by including only a few poems can be an important statement about his or her position in the canon. Evtushenko and Voznesenskii, for example, are given significant coverage in only two and three of the six anthologies respectively, and two of these were edited by Evtushenko himself.

At the other end of the spectrum, there is a group of eight poets who receive significant space in only one anthology: Losev, Nekrasov, Plisetskii, Prigov, Rozhdestvenskii, Rubtsov, Sapgir, and Vladimir Ufliand; in five cases this is in the anthology, *Russkie stikhi 1950–2000*, pointing to this as the most idiosyncratic of the six examined here. The selection of poets given prominence by only this publication (Losev, Nekrasov, Prigov, Sapgir, and Ufliand) clearly points to an emphasis on avant-garde figures. Although overall the anthology is inclusive, featuring all the main poets of the generation, the selections of individual poets reveal its focus on the avant-garde, which is in contrast

---

44 Of the list of Soviet poets, the following were living and publishing in Moscow: Akhmadulina, Okudzhava, Kornilov, Morits, Lisnianskaia, Slutskii, Matveeva, Vanshenkin, Voznesenskii, Vysotskii, Evtushenko. Only Kushner and Sosnora were able to make careers in Leningrad, and the latter had heavy sponsorship from Moscow.

45 For each anthology I identified bands of poets to whom similar amounts of space were allotted, for example 9–11 pages, 4–6 pages.

to the general tendency in the anthologies examined to focus on poetry written in more conventional, 'classical' form.

In the canon that emerges from these anthologies, the poetry is significantly depoliticised. Overall, the generation is still associated with the notes of sincerity and authenticity that were part of the reaction to the Stalin period, but this is expressed through private, intimate lyrics, as distinct from the more political de-Stalinisation associated with Evtushenko and Voznesenskii. Okudzhava and Akhmadulina, for example, although part of the *estrada* phenomenon, are both associated with a quieter and more intimate, lyrical style of work than Evtushenko's public and often polemical poems and Voznesenskii's formal experimentation and verbal play. Poets such as Brodskii and Rein who have been introduced to the canon are significantly apolitical; both were excluded from official literature, but neither is defined by a strongly political position in opposition to the Soviet authorities in the way that some Gulag writers were. They are also identified with the classical tradition of Russian poetry. In spite of quite frequent assertions that the Thaw witnessed a renewed interest in futurist and avant-garde poetics, in the canon as it emerges, they are still peripheral.

The range of poets in these anthologies represents a significantly revised view of the Thaw period. By implication, then, a different narrative about poetry in this era is also emerging, which will revolve around — or at least take in the experience of — these figures. It would be simplistic to assert that this new narrative requires poetry to be free from association with the Soviet authorities — the poets featured in anthologies are clearly not all from the underground and emigration. It is notable, however, that the poets in this reconfigured canon are to a greater or lesser degree distanced from the Soviet authorities, sometimes in literary, but more often in extra-literary terms. Thus, the Soviet literary process, defined largely in terms of publications and privileges, no longer exerts such an influence on the canon. Underground and émigré literary processes are recognised as having produced poets who can be assimilated into Russian poetry of the twentieth century. Instead of having an institutional base, I suggest that the canon, as it is expressed through these anthologies, is now formed of poets who can broadly be seen to share the renewal of poetry associated with the Thaw, mostly, though with some exceptions, through the foregrounding of intimacy, informality and sincerity in their work. This common thread has undermined the positions of Evtushenko and Voznesenskii, for their proximity to the authorities now compromises the sincerity and freshness that the form and content of their works seemed to express at the time.

Influential Commentators

A sense of the kinds of narratives emerging about the Thaw Generation can be found in criticism and commentary by influential critics. For the purposes of this study, I have identified Brodskii, Shaitanov, and Aizenberg as important and contrasting in their attitudes; Shaitanov's comments about the Thaw Generation are generally found across a range of articles on contemporary and twentieth-century poetry; Brodskii's are made through his endorsements of poets of the Thaw Generation, and in Aizenberg's case, his essays written during the 1990s draw his own narrative about poetry that he proposes as a replacement for the existing, Soviet-era version. The contrasts between them highlight some of the main questions around poetry of the Thaw Generation that remain in contention. In particular, they disagree about the status of formerly official poets, about the significance of the avant-garde, and the relative importance of the generation in twentieth-century Russian poetry.

Brodskii's statements about the canon for this generation are found not in a polemic on this subject, but in his support and endorsement of poets of his own generation, and in his important assertion of this generation's significance found in his Nobel Prize acceptance speech. In the latter, he asserted that

> the fact that not everything got interrupted [in those crematoria and in the anonymous common graves of Stalin's archipelago], at least not in Russia, can be credited in no small degree to my generation, and I am no less proud of belonging to it than I am of standing here today.[46]

Ludmila Stern has described how, in the last decade of his life, Brodskii was inundated with requests for his endorsement of contemporaries' poetry, and was regarded as holding the key to unlocking recognition

---

46 'Uncommon Visage' in Joseph Brodsky, *On Grief and Reason* (London: Hamish Hamilton, 1996), pp. 44–58 (p. 55).

and success in the West.⁴⁷ Notwithstanding the somewhat *ad hoc* way in which his endorsements of poets may have been elicited, his introductions to, statements about, and translations of Russian poets of his generation bear out the pride in his generation that he first mentioned in the 1987 speech. From Losev's bibliography of Brodskii's articles from the period, one can find endorsements made during the *perestroika* period of Kushner, Ufliand, Rein, Akhmadulina, Inna Lisnianskaia, Tatiana Shcherbina, Naiman, and Gandel'sman.⁴⁸

While this list is not exhaustive, it is an indication of Brodskii's approach to the canon. He does not provide an explicit narrative, but through the selection it is immediately clear that his view of the Thaw Generation is not dominated by the history of poetry closely associated with politics of the period: neither the official policies of Khrushchev nor the resistance of the underground and unofficial literature. Brodskii apparently does not give weight to the distinction between poets officially published and those unofficial in the USSR: Lisnianskaia, Kushner and Akhmadulina feature alongside Ufliand, Rein and Naiman. In this respect, he is typical of his generation: in the early 1960s when he emerged as a poet in Leningrad, there was not a strong divide between official and unofficial poets. The selection is also dominated by Leningraders, suggesting that Brodskii saw the Leningrad school of poetry as a significant element of Russian poetry during the Thaw Generation. Since it is notable that Brodskii gave endorsements primarily to his own generation, and not to those a little younger than him, it seems that Brodskii's choice was dictated in part by personal acquaintance, making his selection of poets also personal.

In contrast with Brodskii's statements and endorsements, Aizenberg's essays collected in 'Alternative Chronicles of Russian Poetry' put forward a view of Russian poetry that is concentrated in Moscow, in the 1960s and 1970s, and in the underground.⁴⁹ If Brodskii seems

---

47 Ludmila Stern, *Joseph Brodskii: A Personal Memoir* (Fort Worth: Baskerville Publishers, 2004), pp. 304–05.
48 Losev, *Iosif Brodskii. Opyt literaturnoi biografii*, pp. 432–43. Evgenii Rein was identified by Brodskii as his main teacher.
49 These essays dating from 1991–1996 were collected, translated and published as a special edition of a journal: 'Alternative Chronicles of Russian Poetry. Essays by Mikhail Aizenberg', edited by Michael Makin, *Russian Studies in Literature*, 32: 2 (1996), 4–9.

unconcerned with whether a poet was, during the Thaw period, official or unofficial, then for Aizenberg, this is a starting point. In his view, two bodies of work that can be defined as official and unofficial literature are mutually exclusive on the grounds that this status is always indicative of the aesthetic principles of the work and the poetic tradition it belongs to. 'Unofficial', for Aizenberg, denotes not just something that remained unpublished in the USSR. The term, as he defines it, implies poetry with a particular history and 'genealogy': it begins with the OBERIU poets, and it is continued through the late works of Osip Mandel'shtam and Georgii Obolduev, and in the 1950s works of Roal'd Mandel'shtam.[50] It is interesting that, in contrast to the OBERIU, Vladimir Maiakovskii is not seen as a 'teacher' or precursor for these poets due to his involvement with Soviet publishing and power. Aizenberg suggests that the works of these writers varied hugely, and they are not united by a common aesthetic; rather, they share in common a rejection of all that was Soviet. In opposition to this 'tainted' literature is posited a 'pure' position that was opposed to Soviet power and therefore, it is assumed, was a more genuine development of Russian poetry.

Aizenberg's selection of poets is clearly influenced by his own position in the generation, and, like Brodskii's, must be seen as highly personal. It is dominated by conceptualism, which is given roots and a history here, apparently intended to strengthen its claim to be the most genuine expression of Russian poetry in the period. By avoiding aesthetic criteria and concentrating on what he deems to be moral choices about publishing in the USSR, Aizenberg would appear to be trying to re-cast conceptualism in a new mould. Rather than see it as a phenomenon peculiar to Moscow and as one of various directions that poetry developed in during the 1960s and later, he seeks to assert its predominance. Clearly the essays are polemical and challenge the perceived consensus that the 'classical' tradition in Russian poetry remained the central current in the Thaw period and beyond. It remains

---

50 The name OBERIU stood for 'Ob'edinenie real'nogo iskusstva' (Association for Real Art), a group of avant-garde writers, artists and musicians founded in 1928. They ceased to perform in public in the early 1930s. Writers associated with OBERIU included Daniil Kharms, Konstantin Vaginov, Aleksandr Vvedenskii and Nikolai Zabolotskii.

a radical challenge to the canon, one of the chief voices among critics and poets who complain that the avant-garde tradition in Russian poetry is sidelined.

As chief editor of *Voprosy literatury* (*Questions of Literature*) and major contributor to literary criticism on contemporary poetry, Shaitanov has, in the post-Soviet period, been an influential figure in canon formation in Russia. In 1998, he wrote three essays on contemporary poetry that deal in a variety of ways with the subject of the canon.[51] Across these essays he addresses what are perhaps the key questions about the canon for this period: Brodskii's position, the Soviet past, and the avant-garde. Shaitanov sees that the canon must draw on both unofficial and official poetry — especially since Brodskii is an 'unofficial' poet — but he is also dismissive of the rhetoric that prioritises unofficial poetry and makes assumptions about its superior quality. In comments about the English-language *Reference Guide to Russian Literature*, he notes that this publication includes poets from the avant-garde who are peripheral and known only to small, interested groups, yet omits Kuznetsov, Rubtsov, Aleksei Prasolov, Arsenii Tarkovskii, Morits, Martynov, Aleksandr Mezhirov, and Sokolov, and the poets of the Lianozovo school.[52] These poets who have not made it into Cornwell's *Reference Guide* are very different in school and style, yet without them, Shaitanov argues, there can be no overview of Russian poetry of the second half of the twentieth century. He sees in this western version of the Russian canon a tendency to prioritise the avant-garde in a way that distorts the picture of Russian poetry as it is seen and understood in Russia. On the other hand, he does not suggest that the Evtushenko and Voznesenskii should occupy a central position in the canon, and sees them as largely historical figures who wrote a handful of poems that should be preserved in anthologies.[53]

---

51 Igor' Shaitanov, 'O byvshem i nesbyvshemsia', *Arion*, 1 (1998), http://magazines.russ.ru/arion/1998/1/014.html; 'Poet v Rossii...', *Arion*, 2 (1998), http://magazines.russ.ru/arion/1998/2/shaitan.html; 'Grafoman, brat epigona', *Arion*, 4 (1998), http://magazines.russ.ru/arion/1998/4/shaitan.html

52 *Idem*, 'Grafoman, brat epigone'.

53 *Idem*, 'Poet v Rossii...'.

Conclusions

From this range of statements about the canon, it is apparent that the syllabuses from educational institutions are more conservative than commentators and editors working in the field of literary publishing and literary criticism. That said, even in most educational syllabuses and textbooks, the changes that have occurred to the corpus of poetry for the Thaw Generation since 1991 have had some impact on the choice of poets for discussion, reading and study. Anthologies and literary comments and criticism from influential individuals have introduced more significant changes to the canon; taken together, these statements highlight the borderlines and disputed areas of this still-difficult territory.

Major questions apparently remain about the shape of the canon of poetry of this era. *Estrada* poetry was prominent at the time and remained firmly in the Soviet canon, in terms of poets, poems and also the history of poetry. Now, the problem has emerged of how to re-conceive the history of poetry during the Thaw, acknowledging its prominence in official culture, but also its flowering beyond the bounds of Soviet publication and literary process. While syllabuses have tended to stick to the established narrative, accounts such as Aizenberg's alternative narratives of Russian poetry propose a radical reassessment that replaces entirely Soviet publications with avowed underground and avant-garde poetry. Aizenberg's position is certainly polemical and perhaps not widely shared, but it raises an important question about the significance of the avant-garde for this generation, and about the inertia of literary criticism and history in relation to it. In contrast to him, Shaitanov remains highly critical of the underground, not just in this period but also of the OBERIU, for example, endowed by many with sacrosanct status as persecuted geniuses beyond reproach. His defence of figures of the Soviet canon who have been marginalised in the post-Soviet period casts him somewhat in the role of gatekeeper defending the canon against incursions from aesthetic and formal extremes, but also from arguments founded on anti-Soviet sentiment. For some, such as Brodskii, an individual's relationship to Soviet power seems not to figure in the estimation of a poet, and the division between official and unofficial literature is ignored, even as many narratives about literature of the period and especially those focussing specifically on the phenomenon of underground or unofficial literature, preserve this distinction. But it may be that to ignore it is also to ignore its formative influence upon poets, such that a part of the history of the generation is lost.

As well as the question of which poets are canonical for this generation, there is a wider question, raised by these various configurations of the canon, about the significance of this poetic generation in the context of Russian and especially twentieth-century Russian poetry. In the Soviet era, the Khrushchev Thaw was closely associated with poetry chiefly in the form of *estrada*, but there have also been claims that the unofficial flowering of poetry made it a great poetic generation: as well as Brodskii's claims in his Nobel Prize speech referred to above, the term 'Bronze Age' has quite frequently been adopted to refer to this period, claiming a position behind, but nonetheless associated, with the Golden and Silver Ages of Russian poetry. Yet syllabuses in particular indicate that this status is not universally accepted, and that in fact the generation is seen by some as insignificant for poetry. This rhetoric about Thaw poetry having limited interest is reminiscent of the most conservative critics of the late Soviet period, who focused, for example, more on the deaths of established poets than the emergence of new ones in the 1970s. It could be, therefore, that such assertions hark back to this attitude of the early 1980s. On the other hand, it may be that the removal of the *estrada* poets leaves a vacuum that looks like a dearth of good poetry, and also an uncomfortable question about the pedigree of the poets who might replace them: a mixture of underground and émigré figures whose Russianness is questioned not only in terms of their ethnicity (there is a striking number of Jewish poets among the Thaw Generation) but also in their opposition to the Soviet state that might be seen as unpatriotic.

It may also be that the close association of poetry and politics in the period is uncomfortable. In comparison with the Silver Age, Thaw poetry is hardly published at all. This may have something to do with the fact that the location of the Silver Age outside and on the cusp of the Soviet period renders it free from political associations. The complexity of the relationship between poetry and power in the Thaw period may create a sense that it is compromised and therefore less 'genuine' and less worthy of attention. It is interesting to note, for example, the recent interest in poets of the 1970s underground, coming after the Thaw Generation, who were much more cut off from and in opposition to the authorities. In this respect, they too are less tainted by association with the authorities and are perhaps more attractive because of this.

12. The Post-Soviet Homecoming of First-Wave Russian Émigré Poets and its Impact on the Reinvention of the Past

Alexandra Smith

Following the collapse of the Soviet Union in 1991, the re-assessment of Soviet literature's role in disseminating national identity and promoting socialist ethics became a part of the widespread re-evaluation of cultural elites, including writers, responsible for the formation of national identity constructs. In the early 1990s the inflated political value of literature in the Soviet Union became significantly discredited by numerous philological wars in Russian literary journals.[1] Sadly, the withering away of the communist ideology triggered the rise of an explicitly ultra-nationalist course and a more elaborate Russophile ideology based on the notion of transnational identity. New intellectual centres in Russia began to emerge from the mid-1990s onwards and their influence on cultural policies in Putin's Russia is becoming increasingly evident.[2] Thus, for example, in December 2012, Gennadii A. Ziuganov,

---

1   Henrietta Mondry, '"Philological Wars": Nationalism in Russian Literary Periodicals (1993–1996)', in *In Search of Identity: Five Years Since the Fall of the Soviet Union*, edited by Vladimir Tikhomirov (Melbourne, Centre for Russian and Euro-Asian Studies, University of Melbourne Press, 1996), 133–43.

2   Maria Engström describes post-Soviet conservatism (also known as new Russian conservatism or neoconservatism) as 'a metapolitical, intellectual movement, which acts at the junction of art, literature, philosophy, and politics'. See Maria Engström, 'Contemporary Russian Messianism and New Russian Foreign Policy', *Contemporary Security Policy*, 35: 3 (2014), 356–79 (p. 358).

© 2017 Alexandra Smith, CC BY 4.0   https://doi.org/10.11647/OBP.0076.12

the leader of the Communist Party of the Russian Federation, who had appropriated various ideas of leading Russian and European right-wing thinkers including, for instance, the émigré monarchist political theorist Ivan Il'in' (1883–1954), started chairing the Russian creative movement *Russkii lad* (*Russian Order*). It comprises some 300 patriotic and religious associations. The proclaimed aim of the movement is to protect the Russian identity against the corruption of globalisation and to unite Russians and other indigenous people in their efforts to preserve the Russian language as the most important basis 'for unity and creativity in the country'.[3] This reference to the Russian language invokes the use of Russian literature as a tool of cultural hegemony during the Late Imperial and Soviet periods. As Alexander Etkind noted, 'Russian literature proved to be an extremely successful instrument of cultural hegemony', especially because it enabled the standardisation of the language and the integration of a multi-ethnic community of readers on an enormous scale. As Etkind put it, 'the Empire collapsed, but the literature outlived it'.[4] The utilisation of the concept of Russia beyond borders in post-Soviet Russia — which contributed to the integration of the first wave Russian émigré culture both into the present day politics and into the pedagogical canon — might be viewed therefore as a part of the emergence of the Russophone canon which overcomes Soviet classification of literary traditions by nationality. The term *russkofoniia* is well described in Mikhail Gusman's 2002 article in which it is applied to an emerging unified information space of the Russian language that characterises the community of people 'raised in the system of the Russian language and culture' who live or work together, irrespective of their place of residence, national boundaries and religious beliefs.[5] The emergence of the Russophone canon inside and outside Russia in the 2000s has its roots in the nostalgic reinvention of the Late Imperial culture in the 1990s and in the tradition of state messianism associated

---

3   Kerry Bolton, 'Zyuganov Communists Continue Stalin's Fight Against "Rootless Cosmopolitanism"', *Foreign Policy Journal*, December 12, 2012, http://www.foreignpolicyjournal.com/2012/12/12/zyuganov-communists-continue-stalins-fight-against-rootless-cosmopolitanism/2
4   Alexander Etkind, *Internal Colonisation: Russia's Imperial Experience* (Cambridge: Polity Press, 2011), p. 250.
5   Mikhail Gusman. 'Russkofoniia mirovogo informatsionnogo polia', *Nezavisimaia gazeta*, 7 October 2002, http://www.ng.ru/project/2002-07-10/9_field.html

with the sixteenth-century doctrine of Moscow as the Third Rome. It is largely supported by contemporary radical conservatives in Russia who aspire to achieve cultural hegemony in the collective consciousness with the help of a new mythology of the empire capable of uniting people in a new historical situation.

The present chapter will outline the history of the post-Soviet reception of émigré poetry of the first wave, with the aim of demonstrating the absence of the homogenising entity called the canon in today's Russia, and will point to the co-existence of competing views on the role of the canon as an important aid in the production of works of art and in the formation of both national and transnational identities.

In the West, the ongoing debate about the canon triggered by the postmodernist critique of high culture tends to focus on the issue of its inclusions and exclusions. It highlights the role of institutional forms of syllabus and curriculum (administered by schools and universities) in the process of canon formation which is often defined as pedagogical canon.[6] It has been argued that the mechanisms of the canonisation of various authors should be best understood 'as a problem of the constitution and distribution of cultural capital' and 'as a problem of access to the means of literary production and consumption'.[7] In his commentary on the recent revision of the English canon, which legitimised the moderns and re-evaluated the metaphysical poets, John Guillory notes that the redefinition of cultural capital, comprising both linguistic capital known as standard English and symbolic capital that the well-educated person is expected to possess, became possible due to literary study in universities where the use of the technique of close reading enabled students to appreciate the conceptual and linguistic difficulty of the metaphysical and modern poets.[8] Yet, as Jan Gorak elucidates, nowadays the issue of the intrinsic value of works included

---

6   Alan Golding, *From Outlaw to Classic: Canons in American Poetry* (Wisconsin-Madison: University of Wisconsin Press, 1995); Harold Bloom, *The Western Canon: The Books and School of the Ages* (New York: Riverhead Books, 1994); *English Literature: Opening Up the Canon*, edited by Leslie Fiedler and Houston Baker (Baltimore: Johns Hopkins University Press, 1981); Joan Lipman, 'Constructing our Pedagogical Canon', *Pedagogy*, 10: 3 (2010), 535–53.

7   John Guillory, *Cultural Capital: The Problem of Literary Canon Formation* (Chicago and London: The University of Chicago Press, 1994), p. ix.

8   *Ibid.*, p. xi.

in the canon is overshadowed by discussion of the role of educationalists and public intellectuals in the process of canon formation:

> The conviction that the canon survives only by virtue of institutional control and sponsorship has made it difficult to argue for the intrinsic merit and genuine worth of the works included in it. It is traditional to suggest that some works are more linguistically or aesthetically rewarding or more humanly moving than others [...]. This appeal to emotional or evaluative criteria has fallen out of favour.[9]

Guillory thinks that the issue of value is difficult to abandon altogether, even if the educational system should stop claiming a monopoly over the consecration of past and present day cultural consumers. In Guillory's view, cultural producers would continue to compete for the reader and the spectator with the aim that their products be read, studied and heard. Subsequently, they would still

> accumulate cultural capital in the form of 'prestige' or fame' and 'social distinctions' reinstated on such an aesthetic basis would have to be expressed in social relations as distinctions in 'life style', [...] as a vast enlargement of the field of aesthetic judgment.[10]

Guillory believes that in a cultural space of universal access, canonical works would cease to be perceived as lifeless monuments if critics were able to reform the conditions of cultural practice by using judgments in a different way.[11] Guillory's vision of the formation of canon/s in contemporary societies is only partly applicable to post-Soviet Russia because the collapse of the Soviet Union in 1991 created a void in Russian society and led to the emergence of independent newspapers, publishing houses and internet publications which made the cultural landscape highly diverse and eclectic. At the same time, in the 1990s many conservative forces became eager to revive Russian cultural imperial hegemony and promote Russia's role in the Eurasian space in a reinvented messianic manner. The commercialisation of Russian cultural production also became inseparable from the promotion of cultural icons and celebrities as part of the growing fascination with the glamour aspects of globalisation. The sensationalist nature of some

---

9   Jan Gorak, *The Making of the Modern Canon: Genesis and Crisis of a Literary Idea* (London and Atlantic Highlands: Athlone Press, 1991), p. 3.
10 Guillory, *Cultural Capital*, p. 339.
11 *Ibid.*, p. 340.

publications created a distorted view of many writers and performers, so the traditional notion of a Soviet cultural elite located in such cultural centres as Moscow and Petersburg became undermined by the existence of several elites (comprising powerful businessmen, television producers and local authorities) residing both in the centre and at the peripheries, and involved in the formation of cultural values through the mass media, television broadcasts and cultural tourism. This process can be well illustrated by the evolution of Vladimir Nabokov's image from one of a subversive émigré author to that of a fully canonised writer, to the effect that two museums dedicated to Nabokov opened in the 1990s — in St Petersburg and in Rozhdestveno. Yuri Leving elucidates: 'We became full witnesses during the 1990s to the full crystallisation of Nabokov's heritage, from hot, half-legal and ambiguous intellectual goods to an object of a heightened semiotic and marketable value'.[12] After the collapse of the Soviet Union, Nabokov became a best-selling author able 'to compete with Pushkin, the pivot of Russian culture, and what is a more important barometer of popular culture, he has become a character of anecdotes'.[13] Due to an increasingly popular vision of cultural activities as being autonomous from politics in the 1990s, Nabokov 'was transformed into a shining myth of a dissident and aesthete whose subversive discourse was undermining the basis of socialist realism'.[14] Likewise, the legacy of other émigré authors was turned into a useful antidote to the poisonous effects of socialist realism on the formation of the Russian national identity.

The post-Soviet revaluation of the literary canon illustrates well how the issue of canonicity can be traced to institutions (including schools, academia, critics, editors and publishers) on the one hand, and on the other hand to the notion of personal choices, lifestyles and preferences articulated by influential authors and critics involved in the creation of anthologies, textbooks and life-writing projects. Alastair Fowler's thesis that the formation of canon pertains to the issue of genres is also relevant to the current broadening of the definition of literature in the post-Soviet period that is marked by a growing interest in memoirs, diaries, letters, occasional pieces and confessions produced by modernists inside and

---

12 Yuri Leving, 'Plaster, Marble, Canon: The Vindication of Nabokov in Post-Soviet Russia', *Ulbandus Review*, vol. 10: 'My Nabokov', 2007, 101–22 (p. 103).
13 *Ibid.*, p. 107.
14 *Ibid.*, pp. 112–13.

outside Russia.¹⁵ Modernist impressionistic and fragmented literary output has been accepted as a manifestation of different kinds of written communication that enables the reader to engage in the demystification of literary production. By contrast with the post-Soviet canon/s, the Soviet canon promoted the epic and monumental genres, especially the novel that served 'as the official repository of state myths'.¹⁶ Party watchdogs in charge of literary activities suppressed any experimental modes of artistic expressions deviating from the norms of cultural production controlled by the state. While the canon created during Soviet times by institutions and ideologists collapsed in the 1990s, the history of post-Soviet canon formation does not amount to a story of an evolving and stabilising consensus.

The integration of Russian émigré poetry into the current process of canon formation entails a reassessment of the term *canon* perceived by critics and practitioners today in a variety of ways — as a sublime truth, as an artistic model, as a master work, or as a book list for educational use. The first important debates about the emergence of several coexisting twentieth-century Russian literary traditions took place in the 1970s–80s and were followed by the subsequent merger of Russian émigré literature with the output of Soviet writers after the collapse of the Soviet Union in 1991, yet the issue of the legitimacy of a single encompassing twentieth-century canon remains problematic. This chapter will assess the reception of several major Russian émigré poets of the first wave in the post-Soviet period in the context of current debates about the canon and the notion of canonicity. It will also demonstrate how absorption of first-wave Russian émigré literature into the post-Soviet cultural landscape has led to the creation of new myths and new reductionist approaches to twentieth-century literary developments as a whole.

One prevalent approach to Russian contemporary culture pivots around the notion of nostalgia associated with the reinvention of the imperial past. Svetlana Boym, in her discussion of Iosif Brodskii's autobiographical works, affirms that the preservation of Russian poetic language, together with its classical metrics and stanzas, functioned for

---

15   Alastair Fowler, *Kinds of Literature: An Introduction to the Theory of Genres and Modes* (Oxford: Oxford University Press, 1982).
16   Katerina Clark, *The Soviet Novel: History as Ritual* (Bloomington: Indiana University Press, 2000), p. xii.

Brodskii as 'a survivalist mnemonic device'. It enabled him to create 'an alternative space of cultural memory'.[17] Such a vision of Russian language as a mnemonic device is not only relevant to Brodskii. It can be easily applied to other émigré poets as well as to post-Soviet poets who found themselves displaced in today's Russia due to various political and social factors. Furthermore, the vision of Russian language as an embodiment of cultural memory has become widespread in a post-Soviet Russia that is generally defensive of her literary heritage in opposition to the destabilisation of the language and the existing canon undertaken by many authors, young people and media personalities who embraced the wave of liberalisation in the 1990s by creating their own alternative virtual communities with the help of the internet. Radical experiments with the Russian linguistic and literary heritage in the early 2000s triggered concerns about the destabilisation of the standard language and of the established literary canon. Many leading Russian educationalists, representatives of the Russian Orthodox Church and government officials responded with their own projects related to the spread of traditional values via the Russian media and the internet, including the television channel *Culture*, and such sites as http://polit.ru and *Priamaia rech'* (*Direct Speech*) at http://www.pryamaya.ru. As Kåre Johan Mjør's 2009 analysis of Russian internet resources shows, several internet libraries and web portals in Russia, including the Fundamental Electronic Library of Russian Literature and Folklore (FEB) and the http://www.gramota.ru site, became government sponsored.[18] It was done as part of the reinforcement of the policy of *kul'turnost'* (culturedness) that had been previously employed in the Soviet Union. Russian policy makers and educationalists think that the notion of culturedness had been forgotten in the 1990s when many disparate internet sites started to offer a variety of texts promoting their own idiosyncratically compiled canons and preferences.[19]

---

17 Svetlana Boym, *The Future of Nostalgia* (New York: Basic Books, 2001), p. 293.
18 The Fundamental Electronic Library of Russian Literature and Folklore, in Russian the Fundamental'aia elektronnaia biblioteka: Russkaia literatura i fol'klor (FEB) was launched on 1 June 2001 at http://www.feb-web.ru
19 In a talk delivered at the Moscow bookshop *Dodo* on 19 October 2013 on teaching Russian literature today, Marietta Chudakova, one of the most influential critics and public figures in Russia, stated that Russian classical literature is an important brand for Russians all over the world, together with oil exports, and that cultural standards in Russia should be raised. She also voiced her opposition to the

While the aim of the Fundamental Electronic Library is to create the most comprehensive and accurate library of Russian literary and folklore texts on line, including unofficial Soviet literature, it is largely oriented towards the Soviet canon, comprising a selection of Russian literature and folklore preserved and circulated during the Soviet period through scholarly and authoritative editions of literary works. Mjør explains:

> Having become a fundamental value in Soviet society, *kul'turnost'* was not only propagated by the authorities, but also supported by the intelligentsia. In particular in the post-Stalin period, *kul'turnost'* came above all to be seen as manifesting itself in the reading of books.[20]

Mjør links the notion of culturedness existing in Russia and outside Russia before the post-Soviet period to the creation of the Russian canon. The version of the canon that is currently transmitted and preserved in the FEB has its roots in late Imperial Russia and was maintained with some adjustments during the Soviet period. Mjør elucidates:

> As argued by Jeffrey Brooks, its emergence was tightly connected to quests for a new secular Russian national identity, in which educated Russians such as Vissarion Belinskii saw nineteenth-century literature as well-suited for drawing the common man into a unified Russian culture.[21]

The appropriation of Russian émigré poets' outputs in today's Russia might be seen as a vivid manifestation of the Russian cultural elite's longing for pre-revolutionary values, institutions, national unity and educational practices. This trend might be explained by the striking analogy between displaced Russian intellectuals of the 1920s who fled Russia after the 1917 October Revolution and Russian intellectuals in the 1990s who had to adjust themselves to the loss of Soviet imperial culture.

Greta Slobin's 2001 examination of how works written in the 1920s–1950s in the Russian diaspora have been integrated into the literary landscape in the late 1980s–1990s also points to the presence

---

government's idea of creating one textbook for all Russian schools as well as her opposition to the exclusion of Mikhail Bulgakov's novel *Master and Margarita* from the school curriculum. A recording of this talk is available at http://www.youtube.com/watch?v=uu_pXWxo62w

20 Kåre Johan Mjør, 'The Online Library and the Classic Literary Canon in Post-Soviet Russia: Some Observations on "The Fundamental Electronic Library of Russian Literature and Folklore"', *Digital Icons*, 2 (2009), http://www.digitalicons.org/wp-content/uploads/2009/12/Kare-Johan-Mjor-DI-2.6.pdf

21 *Ibid.*

of nostalgic overtones in Russia's quest for a new national identity. Slobin attests: 'We see the complexity of this process in the contested versions of nationalism, tinged with a heady mix of imperial, orthodox, and postcommunist nostalgia, that are shaping both the memory and the history of the past'.[22] Slobin goes on to say that 'in the absence of a coherent political ideology, Russia's transformation is haunted by meta-narratives and cultural systems that can be defined as "prerevolutionary, Soviet and émigré"'.[23] She argues that the heterogeneous makeup of the first-wave émigré community might have been instrumental in the post-Soviet quest for unity and points to similarities between celebrations of Pushkin's 1937 anniversary that took place both in Russia and outside Russia. It appears that émigré rituals aimed at preserving the Russian canon served as models imitated in post-Soviet Russia, so superseding the sense of the rupture of the cultural tradition when seen through the prism of Soviet ideology.

The post-Soviet reception of émigré authors turned them into heroes due to their sense of moral duty, and their efforts to preserve the classical nineteenth-century canon have been perceived as a symbol of a nation able to counteract the rupture caused by the division of Russian culture. Slobin states:

> The cult of Aleksandr Pushkin was central for this purpose, and in 1925 a host of educational institutions issued an appeal to organize an annual 'Day of Russian Culture' to be celebrated on the poet's birthday. Holding an annual cultural celebration helped to provide a sense of unity and continuity for the émigré communities across the globe from Berlin to Shanghai.[24]

According to Mark Raeff, members of the Russian diaspora were determined to carry on in their adopted countries 'a meaningful Russian life'.[25] The focus on unity highlighted in Raeff's and Slobin's studies derives from the established framework favoured by many historians and social scientists who link nation-building tendencies to the formation of modern states. As William Robinson observes, the

---

22 Greta Slobin, 'The "Homecoming" of the First Wave Diaspora and Its Cultural Legacy', *Slavic Review*, 60: 3 (Autumn 2001), 513–29 (p. 513).
23 *Ibid.*, p. 514.
24 *Ibid.*, p. 515.
25 Marc Raeff, *Russia Abroad: A Cultural History of the Russian Emigration, 1919–1939* (Oxford and New York: Oxford University Press, 1990), p. 10.

nation-state framework of analysis 'continues to guide much macro-social inquiry despite recognition among scholars that globalization involves fundamental change in our paradigmatic reference points'.[26] Robinson thinks that scholars do not take account of 'the truly *systemic* change represented by globalisation' and, consequently, their research into transnationalism unfolds 'within the straitjacket of a nation-state framework'.[27] He points to the limitations of nation-state conceptualisations as useful tools for explaining a phenomenon that is transnational in nature. This observation resonates well with the reception of works by Russian diaspora writers in the post-Soviet period because many critics and scholars fail to see the impact of globalisation on the patterns of readership and the construction of identity inside and outside Russia today.

In order to understand the post-Soviet reception of first-wave Russian émigré culture, it is necessary to deconstruct the myth of the prevalence of unifying tendencies of the Russian diaspora in the 1920s–1940s. It was reinforced by the television documentary series *Russkie bez Rossii, 2003–2005* (*Russians Without Russia, 2003–2005*) directed and presented by Nikita Mikhalkov, a prominent Russian filmmaker known for his nationalistic views, not least his admiration for the Russian monarchy and the White Army movement. One film from the series entitled *Russkii vybor* (*The Russian Choice*) features Viktor Leonidov's song 'Son' ('The Dream')[28] in which the lyric hero encounters in his dream many participants in the White Army movement dispersed all over the world and living parallel lives in France and China simultaneously with present-day Russians. The use of montage in the film helps to promote the message of the simultaneous existence of different historical epochs. Leonidov's song, sung in the style of Vladimir Vysotskii's ballads, portrays White Army officers as one collective body united by their loyalty to the Tsar and their Motherland, invoking thereby a sense of nostalgia and patriotic sentiments. Leonidov's song functions as a nostalgic gesture in the film and illustrates the hybrid nature of

---

26 William Robinson, 'Beyond Nation-State Paradigms: Globalization, Sociology, and the Challenge of Transnational Studies', *Sociological Forum*, 13: 4 (December 1998), 561–94 (p. 562).
27 Ibid.
28 The episode from Mikhalkov's film featuring Viktor Leonidov's song is available on YouTube at http://www.youtube.com/watch?v=7MjnojUZ1Kg

post-Soviet melancholy permeated with postmodernist overtones which are often entwined with apocalyptic rhetoric. The song creates an imaginary community of Russian heroes who need to protect Russian values from the corruptive influences of globalisation and from the oblivion of the legacy of Russian diaspora. Yet it does not call for any radical change of the post-Soviet cultural situation characterised by the co-existence of competing processes of remembering and forgetting. One can even detect in Leonidov's song a self-ironising gesture that mocks modern Russian men as lacking the characteristics of true heroes due to a crisis of masculinity in post-Soviet Russia. 'Despite the apocalyptic rhetoric that often accompanies it', states Linda Hutcheon, 'the postmodern marks neither a radical Utopian change nor a lamentable decline to hyperreal simulacra'.[29] Hutcheon's thesis about the ironising and self-ironising discourses produced by postmodernist texts implies that they do not shatter culture but contest and challenge it from within. Indeed, both Leonidov's song in particular and the post-Soviet cultural landscape as a whole encompass several disparate tendencies related to the idea of modernisation and the recycling of the usable past which results in the ironising of the inability of the post-Soviet audience to reinvent grand narratives in a non-totalising way.

Mikhalkov's series devoted to the life of Russian émigré communities of the first wave failed to produce a coherent image of the Russian diaspora. The project highlights the existence of conflicting ideological and cultural trends and articulates the discontinuities of cultural memory in Russia shaped by memory wars and various interpretations of the past. Yet we can see that the idea of the unity of the Russian émigré community in the 1920s–1940s was celebrated in Mikhalkov's series in such a way that the emphasis on Russian spiritual values became reinforced. Such a vision of the Russian diaspora as a homogenious group preoccupied with the preservation of Russian spiritual values could easily be exposed as a post-Soviet myth, especially because Russian émigré communities were located in many parts of the world. Furthermore, many cultural groups were divided due to political, religious and personal beliefs. Despite the search for unity in the 1920s–1940s and the establishment of many publishing houses,

---

29   Linda Hutcheon, *A Poetics of Postmodernism: History, Theory, Fiction* (New York and London: Routledge, 1988), p. xiii.

churches, schools and centres responsible for promoting Russian culture abroad, there were many tensions and disagreements even within seemingly coherently organised associations and groups. Even such a well-established Parisian émigré journal as *Sovremennye zapiski* (*Contemporary Annals*), defined by Simon Karlinsky as 'the finest Russian literary journal of the post-revolutionary period', relied on the expertise and aesthetic sensibilities of many prominent editors, including Vadim Rudnev, who were determined to make idiosyncratic modernist writing to fit their notions of realistic and accessible literature. 'The five Socialist Revolutionary politicians who started *Contemporary Annals* in 1920, and the editors of *The Latest News*, like the majority of pre-revolutionary radicalized intelligentsia', writes Karlinsky, 'were not affected by the broadening of cultural horizons brought about by Sergei Diaghilev and the symbolist movement at the turn of the century'.[30]

The cultural roots of the editors of several émigré publications were comparable to the roots of Lenin and Lev Trotskii. They were shaped by the radical utilitarianism found in the works of nineteenth-century critics and writers, including Belinskii, Nikolai Dobroliubov and Nikolai Chernyshevskii. Karlinsky lists a few examples of severe censorship undertaken by émigré editors in relation to the works of Marina Tsvetaeva, Nabokov and Dmitrii Chizhevskii. While Nabokov was asked to delete one chapter from his novel *Dar* (*The Gift*), because its satirical portrayal of Chernyshevskii was not to the liking of the editors of *Sovremennye zapiski*, Chizhevskii's book on Nikolai Gogol' (published by the journal in 1938) appeared in such a form that all references to devils were removed, although most of them were mentioned in quotations from Gogol's works.[31]

It would be wrong therefore to understand the views of those émigré critics and authors who worked towards autonomy of national culture and its separation from the state as being representative of the whole community of Russian intellectuals abroad. Given that many Russian émigré authors had close contacts with their European counterparts and were engaged in many cultural activities organised by French, German and British writers, it would be better to see Russian émigré literature of the 1920s–1940s as a tradition complementing Soviet

---

30 Simon Karlinsky, *Marina Tsvetaeva: The Woman, Her World, and Her Poetry* (Cambridge: Cambridge University Press, 1985), pp. 220–21.
31 *Ibid.*, p. 221.

and European cultural developments of that period. In his 1937–1939 notes on Russian émigré culture, Vladislav Khodasevich highlights the differences between Soviet and émigré literary developments and focuses on the different understanding of artistic sensibilities: 'The differences are deeper and much more striking: they are in the language, in style, in the voice, in the very concepts of the nature and function of artistic creativity'.[32] Khodasevich's observation of the differences of the two traditions has been forgotten today. It can be argued that for contemporary readers and educationalists one attraction to the works of Russian émigré authors of the first wave lies in how their literary output provides additional links to the past and to alternative visions of Russian twentieth-century history which were largely muted and suppressed in the Soviet period. In Slobin's opinion, the most valuable link offered by Russian émigré writings 'to the pre-revolutionary renaissance of philosophy and the arts during the so-called Silver Age that was curtailed under Iosif Stalin yet continued abroad' has been the eagerness of post-Soviet authors to expand their linguistic and cultural knowledge in order to promote their innovations and engagements with the tradition.[33] Yet many post-Soviet interpretations of Russian first-wave culture offer a useful insight into the existence of competing discourses related to the search for national unity today. The post-Soviet re-evaluation of the literary output of the Russian diaspora of the 1920s–1950s, maintains Slobin, 'presents an interesting case of "partisan" appropriation of the past and of its suppressed history and memory'.[34] The re-examination of Russian religious philosophical thought of the 1880s–1920s by post-Soviet critics, artists and thinkers is subordinated to the traditional Russian spirituality that today is also seen as an antidote to Soviet culture and to globalisation.

Furthermore, in the last twenty years the imaginary community created by Russian nationalists and conservatives has become entwined with the notion of imaginary geographies. According to Edith Clowes,

---

32 Vladislav Khodasevich, 'Untitled Notes', The Manuscript Collection of M. M. Karpovich, Papers on V. I. Khodasevich, Bakhmeteff Archive, Columbia University. Quoted in Greta N. Slobin, 'The "Homecoming" of the First Wave Diaspora and Its Cultural Legacy', p. 519.
33 *Ibid.*, p. 513.
34 *Ibid.*, p. 514.

unlike the Soviet identity 'linked to a vision of the Soviet state at the vanguard of history', major Russian cultural figures and public intellectuals tend to present their vision of post-Soviet identity with the help of spatial metaphors.[35] The tendency to spatialise cultural memory and historical continuity discussed in Clowes's book can be well illustrated by the existence of several Tsvetaeva monuments erected in Moscow, Bashkiriia, Tatarstan, Tarusa and France as well as by the special commemorations known as 'the Tsvetaeva fires' that take place all over the world around her birthday in October. Although no works written by Tsvetaeva were published widely or studied by schoolchildren in Russia before 1991, today they are being appropriated for the formation of local, national and global identities.

The reception of Tsvetaeva in today's Russia is very different from the more personal engagements with Tsvetaeva's poetry found in Russian émigré writing of the third wave émigré community and in the works of Russian dissidents of the 1970s–1980s. In general, their works related to Tsvetaeva were more oriented towards philosophical and metaphysical themes rather than ideological concerns. Thus Brodskii, in contrast to post-Soviet nationalists, comments on Tsvetaeva's use of the tradition of lamentation in her long poem 'Novogodnee' ('Happy New Year'), dedicated to Rainer Maria Rilke. He highlights Tsvetaeva's ability to express modern sensibility rather than Russian national identity. He says that the poem endeavours 'to transmit the psychology of modern man by means of traditional folk poetics' and 'it gives an impression of linguistic justification for any fracture or dislocation of the modern sensibility'.[36] The Scottish contemporary poet Christopher Whyte (currently residing in Budapest), who recently translated this poem into English, affirms that Tsvetaeva's 'Novogodnee' is 'a crucial event in European poetry between the wars'.[37]

By contrast with Brodskii and Whyte, Sofia Gubaidulina, an important Russian-German composer of the post-war period, talks in spatial terms about her personal connection with Tsvetaeva (whose poetry she used

---

35 Edith W. Clowes, *Russia on the Edge: Imagined Geographies and Post-Soviet Identity* (Ithaca and New York: Cornell University Press, 2011), xi.
36 Joseph Brodsky, 'Footnote to a Poem', *Less Than One: Selected Essays* (Harmondsworth: Penguin Books, 1987), 195–267 (pp. 209–10).
37 Christopher Whyte, 'The English for an Anti-Elegy: Translating Tsvetaeva on Rilke', *Translation and Literature*, 21 (2012), 196–212 (p. 197).

for her vocal music on several occasions in the 1970s–1990s). In a 1995 interview with Vera Lukomsky, Gubaidulina states:

> I feel a very special connexion to Marina Tsvetaeva. Marina ended her own life (in suicide) in the small town Elabuga, very close to Chistopol', my place of birth. Both cities are located between two rivers, the Volga and the Kama. I lived in Chistopol' for the first seven months of my life. Nevertheless I feel a significant symbol in our geographic closeness: I started where she finished'.[38]

At the same time, for Gubaidulina Tsvetaeva stands out as a symbol of resistance to Soviet ideology and vulgarity.

Like Brodskii, Gubaidulina is interested in the metaphysical aspects of Tsvetaeva's poetry but she does not link them to the transnational and cosmopolitan identities embedded in her poems. The composer proclaims Tsvetaeva as a saint-like figure concerned with metaphysical and spiritual values:

> Her fate was extremely tragic: she was destroyed by the vulgarity of Soviet ideology, the aggressiveness of the Soviet system. I decided to make percussion the medium representing Marina's soul, her irrationality and mysticism. Her musical antagonists are Soviet popular and patriotic songs, representing vulgarity and the aggressiveness of the common crowd as bred by the Soviet system.[39]

A stronger verdict regarding Tsvetaeva's victimhood is inserted into the concluding paragraph of Irma Kudrova's biography of Tsvetaeva:

> Gumilev who was shot; Kliuev and Mandel'shtam who disappeared in the Gulag; Meierkhol'd and Babel' who were executed… Marina Tsvetaeva who was noble, independent and brilliant belongs to the same group of victims of the great socialist revolution.[40]

Kudrova's and Gubaidulina's views on Tsvetaeva's legacy are representative of the large group of the post-Stalin readers who were inspired by the Thaw cultural liberalisation and who see the post-Soviet period as a continuation of the de-Stalinisation of the 1960s.

Yet Tsvetaeva's physical displacement — cultivated in her poetry as an important trope and as an existential condition of any poet — appears

---

[38] Sofia Gubaidulina and Vera Lukomsky, '"The Eucharist in My Fantasy": Interview with Sofia Gubaidulina', *Tempo*, New Series, 206 (September 1998), 29–35 (p. 30).
[39] *Ibid.*, pp. 30–31.
[40] Irma Kudrova, *Put' komet*, 3 vols. (St Petersburg: Izdatel'stvo 'Kriga', 2007), III, 293.

to accord with the portrayal of Russian identity constructed from spatial metaphors that extends beyond the traditional sense of identity confined to geographical borders. In Clowes's opinion,

> Many major voices in the contemporary debate move beyond the traditional concepts of nation defined by language, kinship, ethnic group, shared history, though virtually all either cling to or interrogate a crucial characteristic of national identity — geographical territory and its symbolic meanings.[41]

Clowes finds this type of identity comparable to the notion of hybrid identity foregrounded in postcolonial theory and suggests that its emergence takes place through the metaphors of territorial border and periphery. This tendency is visible in the attempt by many post-Soviet performers and critics to present Tsvetaeva as a multicultural figure that stimulates the creation of communities of like-minded individuals inside and outside Russia with the help of various museums, commemorative plaques, and monuments located in Tarusa, Moscow, Elabuga, Aleksandrov, Feodosiia, Bolshevo, Prague and Vshenory as well as in locations in Germany and France.

Fig. 12.1 Commemorative plaque in Elabuga. © Alexandra Smith, CC BY 4.0.

---

41   Clowes, *Russia on the Edge*, p. xi.

A more recent monument to Tsvetaeva created by Zurab Tsereteli was unveiled in the town of St Gilles-Croix-de-Vie in western France on 16 June 2012. As one newspaper reports, 'the resort has been one of the favourite places of Russian celebrities, in various years it was visited by the composer Sergey Prokofiev, poet Konstantin Bal'mont, Alexander Solzhenitsyn and others'.[42] As can be seen from the description of the French resort, a cultural landmark associated with the life of Russian émigré writers and composers is perceived as the rightful place for a monument to Marina Tsvetaeva who wrote many poems and letters to Boris Pasternak there in which she immortalised her own vision of an imagined Russian creative identity beyond geographical borders.

At the same time, one poem dedicated to the Tsvetaeva monument in Moscow penned by Ol'ga Grigor'eva, a Russian poet and journalist from Kazakhstan (Pavlodar) — who received the Tsvetaeva prize organised by the Tsvetaeva museum in Elabuga in 2008 — reinstates Moscow as an important cultural centre featuring a monument to Tsvetaeva located next to the Tsvetaeva museum on Borisoglebskii Avenue. In her 2008 poem 'Vstretimsia u Mariny' ('We'll See Each Other at Marina's Place') Grigor'eva describes an imaginary meeting with her friend near the Tsvetaeva monument in Moscow and suggests that they should read together a volume of Tsvetaeva's poems on the bench near the monument. The poem concludes with the belief that Tsvetaeva's verse will elevate them to higher realms of being and, subsequently, the two characters will join their beloved poet in heaven:

> Рано иль поздно встретимся —
> Там, у Марины. Там, у нее в гостях.[43]

> Sooner or later — We'll meet each other at Marina's place.
> Over there. We'll visit her over there.

In metaphysical vein, the poem refers to the otherworldly realm, suggesting that the notion of displacement is an essential part of the poetic self and that those whose sense of national belonging is neither

---

42   [N.a.], 'Unveiling Ceremony for the Monument to Marina Tsvetaeva by Zurab Tsereteli in France', Press service, 18 June 2012, http://en.rah.ru/news/detail.php?ID=24266

43   Ol'ga Grigor'eva, 'Vstretimsia u Mariny', *Reka i rech'* (Pavlodar: 'TOO "Dom pechati"', 2009), p. 77.

axiomatic nor unproblematic could be offered a different vantage point: their everyday life can be seen as part of their spiritual evolution guided by Tsvetaeva.

The examples above demonstrate a shift from de-Stalinisation to the de-ideologisation linked to the reinvention of the canon. It advocates the inclusion of metaphysical poems into the canon. To this end, the rediscovery of émigré literature enabled post-Soviet readers to see cultural tradition itself as their imaginary spiritual homeland. In Slobin's view,

> The émigré sense of its 'sacred' mission, now combined with postcommunist nostalgia, appeared to inspire a longing for an impossible return to some version of a 'misty' pre-revolutionary Russia, with the 'originary tradition' still intact.[44]

Russian émigré authors' dedication to the continuity of Russian cultural tradition, used to a large extent as a compensation for their loss of motherland, appeals to Russian nationalists today. Yet their heterogeneous cultural longings and encoded practices of accommodation of cultural norms of their host countries do not appear completely compatible with a post-Soviet mainstream culture mourning the loss of the empire. According to Slobin, the post-Soviet literary canon continues to be associated with Russian realism, due to the suppression of the modernist tradition in the Soviet Union over several decades. As she puts it, the rejection of the modernist literary experiment does not seem to be compatible 'with a nationalist conception of the canon-traditionally identified with Russian realism'.[45]

In a more optimistic manner, Natalia Ivanova's 2007 article welcomes the merger into one narrative of different branches of Russian literature, including émigré, Soviet official and underground literatures, as one of the most important features of the post-Soviet period. She also talks about the emergence of postmodernist literature as a mainstream literature rooted in the Thaw-era cultural experiments of the 1960s. For Ivanova, the initial merger of different trends and alternative canon/s has resulted in a more vibrant cultural landscape. She sees the explosive clashes of

---

44 Slobin, 'The "Homecoming" of the First Wave Diaspora and Its Cultural Legacy', p. 523.
45 Ibid., p. 525.

different styles and worldviews triggering further diversification of Russian literature and the hybridisation of contemporary culture as an extension of the postmodern condition.[46] Yet the reception of the modernist tradition, including Russian émigré poetry, continues to be shaped by Russian intellectuals and cultural figures of the 1960s–1980s who promote their own values, taste and their own version of the canon through memoirs, biographies, scholarly studies and intertextual links embedded in their poetry, vocal music and performances. The attitudes to Tsvetaeva expressed by Gubaidulina and Kudrova, discussed above, are representative of the displacement experienced by Russian intellectuals in the Soviet Union. It is not surprising that they turned to Tsvetaeva as an embodiment of displacement and of opposition to Soviet ideology. The influential Russian dissident critic, translator and scholar Efim Etkind also perceived Tsvetaeva's works as an important antidote to Soviet ideology and vulgarity. As will be demonstrated below, his views regarding Tsvetaeva were extended to other émigré poets, including Khodasevich and Ivanov.

Etkind's contribution to the collection of articles published and edited by Georges Nivat in 1981 — based on a conference devoted to the role of the émigré literature in Russian twentieth-century cultural developments — was a courageous attempt to challenge the Soviet canon and broaden it through the inclusion of many modernist and émigré texts. The 1981 volume provided an important forum for the Russian diaspora and presented it as a significant alternative to the cultural elite in the Soviet Union. It offers a range of approaches to émigré works that challenge the Soviet canon and question the mechanisms of inclusion and exclusion applied to Soviet and Russian émigré anthologies. In his article 'Russian Twentieth-century Poetry As a Single Movement', Etkind names sixteen significant Russian poets who lived abroad in the 1920s–1950s and suggests that Georgii Ivanov, Khodasevich and Tsvetaeva should be viewed as the most important poets produced by the first-wave emigration.[47] While Etkind agrees with the list of

---

46 Natalia Ivanova, '"Uskol'zaiushchaia sovremennost'": Russkaia literatura XX–XXI vekov: ot "vnekomplektnoi" k postsovetskoi, a teper' i vsemirnoi', *Voprosy literatury*, 3 (2007), http://magazines.russ.ru/voplit/2007/3/iv7.html

47 Efim Etkind, 'Russkaia poeziia XX veka kak edinyi process', in *Odna ili dve russkikh literatury?*, edited by Georges Nivat (Lausanne: l'Âge d'Homme, 1981), 9–30 (p. 15).

canonical twentieth-century poets created by Gleb Struve that includes, in addition to the above-mentioned three major poets of the Russian diaspora, seven more names (Valerii Briusov, Anna Akhmatova, Nikolai Gumilev, Fedor Sologub, Mikhail Kuzmin, Boris Pasternak, and Osip Mandel'shtam); he asserts that a further fifteen poets of the Soviet period (including Vladimir Maiakovskii, Sergei Esenin and Nikolai Kliuev) should be also regarded as major twentieth-century poets. Curiously, the list of poets discussed in Etkind's article omits Elena Guro, Aleksei Kruchenykh, Boris Poplavskii and Velimir Khlebnikov, suggesting thereby that Russian versions of surrealism and futurism were seen by him as been alien to the Russian canon.

Despite disagreements with Struve, Etkind shares the view that in the future the Russian émigré poetic output will be integrated into the mainstream of Russian literature and will significantly enrich the canon.[48] Etkind rightly points out that Russian émigré poetry absorbed many aesthetic principles and innovations of European culture and suggests that it is up to future cultural historians to assess whether the contribution of Russian émigré poets to the overall development of Russian literature was more significant than the impact on it produced by Soviet poets.[49] For Etkind, the most important criterion of the vitality of Russian émigré poetry was embodied in the works of Tsvetaeva who managed to overcome 'émigré snobbery' and 'provincial narrow-mindedness' by incorporating in her works many experiments undertaken by Maiakovskii and Pasternak and by enriching her poetic language.[50] Etkind's emphasis on Tsvetaeva's ability to attune herself to Soviet everyday language and poetic practice demonstrates his adherence to Aleksandr Potebnia's belief that poetry embodies the most creative aspects of language, contributes to the sustainability of cultural memory and helps the reader to cognise life.[51]

Etkind mentions Tsvetaeva and Khodasevich as the two most significant poets of the Russian diaspora who maintained a strong interest in Soviet literary developments and whose poetry had similar

---

48 Gleb Struve, *Russkaia literature v izgnani* (New York: Izdatel'stvo Chekhova, 1956), p. 7.
49 Etkind, 'Russkaia poeziia XX veka kak edinyi process', p. 16.
50 *Ibid.*, p. 17.
51 A. Potebnia, *Mysl' i iazyk* (Kharkov: Tipografiia Adol'fa Darre, 1892), p. 176.

traits to the output of such poets as Pasternak, Akhmatova and Mandel'shtam. In his opinion, the gap between the two strands of Russian twentieth-century poetry created by political circumstances was not very substantial. Such a view downplays the effect of the socialist realist aesthetic on poets living in the Soviet Union in the 1920s–1940s. While Etkind's suggestion, that the formal devices used by poets inside and outside Russia were independent from the everyday life with which they engaged, might appear to be ahistorical it does reveal his view that canonicity is systemic. In accordance with such a view, all excluded texts are potentially includable in the canon. As Ross Chambers rightly points out, 'when we accede to the idea that certain texts are in the canon while others are not, we are in fact acceding to the system of canonicity, of which the canon is a product'.[52] Chambers's thesis that 'the supposedly canonical texts are so only by virtue of there being texts excluded from that category' and 'that the noncanonical works are an indispensable part of the whole system of which the canon is another part' resonates well with Etkind's critique of the twentieth-century literary canon created by Soviet critics and educationalists.

Given that 'every excluded text is potentially included in the canon and every included text is a possible candidate for exclusion'[53], Georges Nivat's collection of articles about a new literary canon comprising literary texts produced both in Russia and outside Russia can be seen as a pioneering attempt to conceptualise the legacy of the Russian diaspora.[54] It anticipated the debate about the Russian twentieth-century canon in the late 1980s–early 1990s. Thus the publication of works by Russian poets featured in the Soviet popular weekly *Ogonek* that had been initiated by Evgenii Evtushenko during *perestroika* raised many questions about the stability of the Soviet poetic canon. Likewise, the publication of memoirs by Irina Odoevtseva (born Iraida Heinike) that feature Odoevtseva's participation in important pre-revolutionary cultural developments (including the Institute of the Living Word and Acmeist gatherings), her life in France and her contacts with many prominent cultural figures, including Georgii Ivanov and Georgii Adamovich, created an impression that the notion of one single Russian

---

52 Ross Chambers, 'Irony and the Canon', *Profession* (1990), 18–24 (p. 18).
53 Ibid.
54 Ibid.

poetic canon had its validity. Even though Odoevtseva's memoirs were written in the 1960s and were published by émigré publishing houses in the US and in France, her status as a living embodiment of the Silver Age was achieved largely not by her émigré writings but by her return to St Petersburg at the invitation of the Union of Writers in 1987. The fact of her return to Russia had a symbolic meaning for Russian writers and readers and influenced the subsequent rediscovery of her fiction, poetry and memoirs in the late 1980s and in the 1990s. Odoevtseva's memoirs and her interviews with Soviet journalists and critics on her return to Russia after many years in emigration reinforced the sense of unity between the different branches of Russian twentieth-century literature. A volume of Odoevtseva's collected writings, including her poetry and memoirs, appeared in Moscow in 1998: it was meant to promote a sense of continuity of Russian culture. Prior to this, in her 1989 interview with *Ogonek*, Odoevtseva mentions her wish to reconcile the two branches of Russian literature as the main reason for her return to Russia. It gave an impression that she aspired to fulfill the missionary role of the Russian diaspora to preserve and develop further Russian cultural traditions of the pre-Soviet period. 'One cannot have a separate Russian émigré literature', says Odoevtseva. 'As I pointed out before, there is only one great Russian literature'. Odoevtseva's authentic account of twentieth-century literary and cultural developments published in Russia triggered widespread interest among Russian readers who saw her as a Silver Age celebrity. While the print run of the 1988 edition of the book *On the Banks of the Neva* was 250,000, the 1989 edition of the book about Russian émigré culture —*On the Banks of the Seine* — was 500,000. In his introduction to the 1988 edition of *On the Banks of the Neva*, the influential Russian poet and critic Konstantin Kedrov defined Odoevtseva as a chronicler of pre-revolutionary culture and a herald of Acmeism. He also mentions Georgii Ivanov, commenting that Ivanov's poetry has become an important part of Russian contemporary culture.[55]

---

55 Irina Odoevtseva, *Na beregakh Nevy* (Moscow: Khudozhestvennia literatura, 1988); *Na beregakh Seny* (Moscow: Khudozhestvennia literatura, 1989); Oleg Khlebnikov, 'S voskhishcheniem zhivu: Interv'iu s Irinoi Odoevtsevoi', *Ogonek*, 11 (11–18 March 1989), 22–23; Konstantin Kedrov, 'Vozvrashchenie Iriny Odoevtsevoi', in Irina Odoevtseva, *Na beregakh Nevy* (Moscow: Khudozhestvennaia literatura, 1988), pp. 5–12.

Following several decades of oblivion in the Soviet Union, at the end of the 1980s Georgii Ivanov was declared a leading poet of the Russian diaspora. While a volume containing Ivanov's poetry and memoirs was published in the Soviet Union in 1989, in 1994 a three-volume edition of his works appeared in Moscow and in 2006 the prestigious series *New Poet's Library* published a collection of his poetry. The first biography of Georgii Ivanov — written by Vadim Kreid, the Russian-American poet, scholar, critic and editor-in-chief of the émigré journal *The New Review* — was published in Russia in 2007 in the famous series *Zhizn' zamechatel'nykh liudei* (*Lives of Remarkable People*). It was followed by the publication of a second biography of Ivanov in 2009 penned by Andrei Ar'ev, St Petersburg critic and editor of a collection of Ivanov's poetry.[56] Shortly after the publication of his collections of poetry in post-Soviet Russia, Ivanov's poetry was also appropriated by Russian popular culture. In 2012 the St Petersburg musician Aleksandr Vetrov produced a disc featuring his performance of songs based on Ivanov's poetry and told his fans about the next project that would also transfer Khodasevich's poetry into songs.[57] Vetrov's homage to émigré poets might be seen as a part of a larger trend to revive the modernist tradition in Russia, especially the Silver Age, that has become glamourised by contemporary films, mass media and popular culture.[58]

Due to a growing interest in the 1990s–2000s to the Silver Age, the terms 'modernism' and 'the Silver Age' have become interchangeable in the post-Soviet popular imagination. This tendency has its roots in Russia's non-conformist artistic circles in the 1950s and 1960s. Boris Ivanov wrote that Russian non-conformist poets of the 1970s, including Petersburg poet Viktor Krivulin, embraced the legacy of the Silver Age in the same way as European medieval artists and writers had created

---

56 Georgii Ivanov, *Stikhotvoreniia*, edited by Andrei Ar'ev (Moscow: DNK, Progress-Pleiada, 2010); Georgii Ivanov, *Sobranie sochinenii v trekh tomakh*, edited by Evgenii Vitkovskii (Moscow: Soglasie, 1994); Georgii Ivanov, *Stikhotvoreniia*, edited by Andrei Ar'ev (Moscow: DNK, Progress-Pleiada, 2010).

57 Sasha Vetrov, *Led. Al'bom pesen na stikhi poeta Georgiia Ivanova* (St Petersburg: Peterburgskaia studiia gramzapisi, 2012), http://proektvetrov.kroogi.com/ru/download/2470196-Lyod.html. Vertov is planning to produce a collection of songs based on the poetry of Vladislav Khodasevich, http://culture.ru/press-centre/news/9857

58 Galina Rylkova, *The Archaeology of Anxiety: The Russian Silver Age and Its Legacy* (Pittsburgh: Pittsburgh University Press, 2007).

their own image of antiquity. Elena Ignatova's article 'Who are we?', first published in the literary journal *Neva* in 1992, also identifies the presence of a nostalgic longing for the Silver Age among the dissidents of the 1960s–1980s.[59]

Galina Rylkova's study features several writers and poets (including Akhmatova, Mikhail Kuzmin, Vladimir Nabokov, Boris Pasternak and Viktor Erofeev) who have contributed to the mythologising of historical and cultural developments associated with the Silver Age. She argues that, despite its occupation of a unique place in the Russian collective memory for several decades, its distinct function as an enigmatic 'other' during the Soviet period prevented it from becoming a sustainable realm of memory in post-Soviet times. In Rylkova's view, the Silver Age's role in the Russian collective memory has been downplayed by the erasure of the Bolshevik Revolution from the political and cultural landscape of today's Russia. Thus the celebration of the anniversary of the 1917 Bolshevik Revolution on 7 November was replaced by the *Den' narodnogo edinstva* (Day of Popular Unity), celebrated for the first time on 4 November 2005. Rylkova thinks that the Silver Age, which was seen as the main enemy of the 1917 Revolution, might 'sink into oblivion not because of the revolution but together with the revolution' as a result of such an association with one of the major political events in twentieth-century history.[60]

The tendency to see Russian émigré writing as part of the Silver Age and its legacy continues visibly in today's Russia. It is strongly felt in Nikolai Bogomolov's review of Ar'ev's biography of Georgii Ivanov, which benefits from well-researched contextual details of Ivanov's life, thereby serving as an insightful account of cultural life of the Silver Age and of the Russian diaspora in France.[61] Bogomolov concludes that Ar'ev's publications enabled Ivanov to return to Russia, after a long period of oblivion in his native land and of limited recognition outside Russia, as 'a rightful creator of Russian literature'.[62] D. D. Nikolaev's review highlights the canonical status of Georgii Ivanov

---

59 Elena Ignatova, 'Kto my? Leningradskii andegraund semidesiatykh', *Interpoeziia*, 3 (2010), http://magazines.russ.ru/interpoezia/2010/3/ig11.html
60 Rylkova, *The Archaeology of Anxiety*, p. 209.
61 N. A. Bogomolov, 'Andrei Ar'ev. Zhizn' Georgiia Ivanova. Dokumental'noe povestvovanie ', *Znamia*, 4 (2010), http://magazines.russ.ru/znamia/2010/4/bo25.html
62 *Ibid.*

in the post-Soviet period more boldly: it claims that the task of any biography published in the series *Lives of Remarkable People* is not to engage in literary debates with fellow critics but to put the subject of one's study on a pedestal.[63] It should be noted here that the vision of poets as biographical subjects — which stems from the recognition of a new poet-hero in the early modern period — constitutes a relatively new development in the history of Russian biography.[64] The inclusion of biographies of Russian émigré poets in the series *Lives of Remarkable People* — run by F. F. Pavlenkov in 1890–1924 and re-started by Maxim Gor'kii in 1933 — suggests that the post-Soviet culture is still oriented towards the canon formation which became solidified during the pre-Soviet and Soviet periods. This might be explained by how Russian cultural traditions were largely shaped by the emergence of the secular culture in Russia in the eighteenth century, which was oriented towards the preservation of many cultural values of antiquity. In the last three hundred years, the neo-classical themes were often used by early modern and modern Russian authors for self-canonisation purposes. Anna Makolkin also points to the link between biographies and eulogies:

> At least through the end of the eighteenth century, change is the defining quality of Russian biography, as heroic blends into postheroic and preheroic phases, and a new subject — the poet — emerges. Russian biography during this period was awaiting the new saint, the poet, but remains deeply rooted in the eternal mourning song, the eulogy, and the transhistoric, transcultural praise of the departed.[65]

Likewise, the presentation of Georgii Ivanov as a friend of Nikolai Gumilev and as a saint-like hero victimised by the 1917 October Revolution in post-Soviet biographies, suggests that a representation of a life has a definite pattern and is closely linked to the reshaping of the existing canon. Given that Kreid and Ar'ev were familiar with Georgii Ivanov's works during the Soviet period, either through foreign publications (*tamizdat*) or through the journals and books published in Russia in the 1910s–1920s, it would appear natural to them to consider

---

63 D. D. Nikolaev, 'Kreid V. P. Georgii Ivanov. Moscow, Molodaia gvardiia, 2007', *Novyi istoricheskii vestnik*, 2 (2009), 18, http://www.nivestnik.ru/2009_2/18.shtml

64 Anna Makolkin, 'Probing the Origins of Literary Biography: English and Russian Versions', *Biography*, 19: 1 (Winter 1996), 87–104 (p. 87).

65 *Ibid.*, p. 100.

Ivanov as a living embodiment of the displacement of the Silver Age in the post-Soviet period and to include him in the twentieth-century poetic canon.[66]

Following the celebration of the 100th anniversary of Georgii Ivanov's birth in Russia in 1994 and the subsequent publication of his books, his biographies and several Ph.D. theses, it is not surprising that his poetry has become part of the contemporary cultural landscape characterised by a search for new saint-like heroes. It is not coincidental that for biographies like Kreid's, Ivanov's poetry appears permeated with the idea of spiritual quest and religious attitudes towards creativity, despite the many nihilist overtones embedded in his works.[67] The post-war generation of critics and poets influenced by the Thaw period sees the widespread nihilism and commercialisation of Russian culture in the 1990s as something that should be remedied. In their eyes, Russian émigré poetry of the 1920s–1950s, including the poetry of Georgii Ivanov, serves as a repository of cultural and spiritual values of the pre-revolutionary period that could reconnect post-Soviet readers with Russian pre-Soviet culture. At the same time, the widespread appeal of Georgii Ivanov's poetry to post-Soviet readers and musicians of the younger generation (including Tat'iana Aleshina, who included her songs based on his poetry in a special double-disc album dedicated to the 300th anniversary of St Petersburg, and Aleksandr Vetrov[68]) lies in how its ironic and decadent overtones, inseparable from the perception of life as part of the collapse of grand narratives, accord well with Russian contemporary poetry's manifestations of the crisis of humanism which, according to Mikhail Epstein, 'reached its maturity'. Epstein explains:

> The movement of lyric poetry beyond the sphere of the lyric 'I' reveals the depths of a new experience, which is more primordial, more originary, and hence more holistic. Its structuredness and trans-subjectivity [...] are best described in religious terms, even if this description has no immediate connection to any concrete religious tradition. The essential

---

66 Elena Dubrovina, 'O poezii i proze Georgiia Ivanova. Interv'iu s Vadimom Kreidom', *Gostinaia, vypusk* 53, Literaturnyi Parizh (September 2013), http://gostinaya.net/?p=8398; Ivan Tolstoi, 'Veter s Nevy: Zhizn' Georgiia Ivanova', *Radio Svoboda*, 11: 10 (2009), http://www.svoboda.org/content/transcript/1849756.html
67 Elena Dubrovina, 'O poezii i proze Georgiia Ivanova'.
68 Tat'iana Aleshina, *Peterburgskii al'bom* [CD] (St Petersburg: studiia 'Aziia-plius', 2003).

thing is not the object of representation, but the subject of enunciation […] The elusive subject, as a consequence of all the processes of disembodiment and 'depersonalisation', cannot help manifesting the characteristics of a transcendental subjectivity.[69]

Commenting on such poets as Ol'ga Sedakova, Ivan Zhdanov, Alexei Parshchikov and Il'ia Kutik, Epstein suggests that they have incorporated into their poetry those words that have not turned yet into clichés and 'placed them under high tension' in order 'to reveal the structure of a multidimensional reality'.[70]

Certainly, these authors belong to the generation of poets who achieved prominence in the 1970s and 1980s. That is why their vision of the Russian cultural tradition deviates from the binary oppositions of the Soviet period which pivot around the Soviet and anti-Soviet attitudes towards culture. Their vision of culture might be defined as neo-classical or even neo-Acmeist. It includes many allusions not only to Russian modernist and Romantic poets but also to eighteenth-century Russian poets, European poets (especially to Dante, Goethe and Rilke), and to classical poets (including Catullus, Ovid, and Horace). Their works foreground the notion of metarealism, which indicates the shift from the vision of poetry as a means of political resistance to the understanding of poetry as an important tool of the preservation of cultural memory.

In his 2007 book on Russian poetry, Igor' Shaitanov also detects many signs of alienation from society, and self-alienation, in post-Soviet poetry that show in the language of silence. It is revealed through the expression of autodestruction or self-transcendence. Shaitanov's definition of the language of silence derives from Ihab Hassan's description of postmodern art as an embodiment of reflexive energy and of the introversion of the alienated will that give rise to 'the arts of silence, of the void, and of death' as well as to 'the languages of omission, ambiguity, games, and numbers'.[71] According to Shaitanov,

---

69 Mikhail Epstein, 'Like a Corpse in the Desert: Dehumanisation in the New Moscow Poetry', in *Russian Postmodernism: New Perspectives on Post-Soviet Culture*, edited by Mikhail Epstein, Alexander A. Genis, Slobodanka M. Vladiv-Glover (New York and Oxford: Berghahn Books, 1999), 134–44 (pp. 135–36).
70 *Ibid.*, p. 137.
71 Ihab Habb Hassan, *The Dismemberment of Orpheus: Toward a Postmodern Literature* (Wisconsin-Madison: University of Wisconsin Press, 1982), p. 12.

the emergence of postmodern tendencies in the post-Soviet period resulted in a different attitude towards tradition which is invoked in contemporary poetry either through palimpsest-like writing or through the employment of centos. He refers to the prevalence of a hybrid mode of writing that comprises both palimpsest and centos. It enables the reader to recognise the humorous juxtaposition of famous lines in a new semantic matrix and appreciate the diversity of sources of various poetic texts. In Shaitanov's opinion, this type of poetic expression subverts the notion of continuity and cultural memory since it is oriented towards amnesia and absurdity and makes the meaning of the poem unstable.[72] Viewed in this light, Ivanov's poetry accords well with the post-Soviet sense of disorientation, amnesia and self-ironising discourse manifested in the work of many leading authors, including Elena Shvarts, Genrikh Sapgir and Timur Kibirov, to name just a few.

As Eric Laursen points out, Ivanov's highly autobiographical and confessional émigré poetry contains a dialogue conducted by a split self acting like a two-headed Janus 'who simultaneously gazes at the beloved past and the hopeless present'.[73] In Laursen's opinion, a striking feature of Ivanov's paradoxical and distinctive lyric poetry is the co-existence of two opposing visions of hope and despair that 'merge into distorting reflections of one another'.[74] Ivanov's ability to express his melancholic longing for the past and his inability to revive it might be especially appealing to a post-Soviet reader grappling with the revision of the Soviet and pre-Soviet past. To a large extent, the first-wave émigré poets serve as role models for contemporary authors attempting the construction of a transnational identity and for overcoming the sense of discontinuity of the tradition interrupted by Soviet cultural policies.

The above-discussed treatment of the works of Tsvetaeva and Ivanov in the post-Soviet period exemplifies Theodor Adorno's thesis that 'artworks have a life sui generis': they 'constantly divulge new layers', grow old and die, and, as products of social labour, they 'speak by virtue of the communication of everything particular to

---

72 Igor' Shaitanov, *Delo vkusa. Kniga o sovremenoi poezii* (Moscow: Vremia, 2007), p. 30.
73 Eric Laursen, 'The Talent of Double Vision: Distorting Reflection in Georgii Ivanov's Émigré Poetry', *Russian literature*, 43 (1998), 481–93 (p. 481).
74 Ibid.

them' and 'communicate with the empirical experience that they reject and from which they draw their content'.[75] In Adorno's view, 'art perceived strictly aesthetically is art aesthetically misperceived' since art is both autonomous and not autonomous.[76] Evgenii Evtushenko's 1994 anthology of twentieth-century Russian poetry comprising 875 poets exemplifies Adorno's thesis about the limitations of strictly aesthetic criteria applied to literary and artistic production.[77] Although Evtushenko envisaged his anthology as a poetic textbook on Russian twentieth-century history, many critics found his selection of poems and commentaries highly subjective and arbitrary.[78] Mikhail Gasparov defined it as a book for easy reading rather than an anthology due to its eccentric selection of poems that do not represent all the poetic trends and literary developments of the twentieth century.

Gasparov's review poses an important question about the notion of canonicity and suggests that Evtushenko's system of cultural values reflects the taste of the generation of readers and authors born in the 1930s. Furthermore, Gasparov thinks that the inclusion of many poets of the Soviet period into Evtushenko's anthology indicates how most of the twentieth-century literary output was inseparable from Soviet experiences and historical events.[79] Given that Evtushenko's desire to produce an anthology of Russian twentieth-century poetry was inspired by his conversations with Georgii Adamovich, a minor Acmeist poet but influential critic of the Russian diaspora in Paris, it might be possible to see how Evtushenko's anthology was shaped by the creative dialogue between two important representatives of different currents of Russian twentieth-century poetry. The anthology also exemplifies Evtushenko's personal desire to create a new national literary canon, fulfilling thereby his own messianic role as poet-prophet and poet-educator dedicated to

---

75 Theodor W. Adorno, *Aesthetic Theory*, edited by Gretel Adorno and Rolf Tiedemann (London and New York: Continuum, 1997), p. 5.
76 *Ibid.*, p. 7.
77 *Strofy veka. Antologiia russkoi poezii*, edited by Evgenii Evtushenko (Moscow: Polifakt, 1994).
78 Evgenii Evtushenko, 'Poet v Rossii bol'she, chem poet...', *Novye izvestiia*, 16 September 2005, http://www.newizv.ru/culture/2005-09-16/31782-tolko-v-ni.html
79 Mikhail Gasparov, 'Kniga dlia chteniia', *Novyi mir*, 2 (1996), http://magazines.russ.ru/novyi_mi/1996/2/zar1.html

the nineteenth-century ideal of linking poetic activities with the notions of civic and moral duty.[80]

The striking presence of Russian twentieth-century émigré poets on the internet, including Brodskii, Georgii Ivanov and Tsvetaeva, suggest that there might be some aesthetic as well as extra-literary factors that have contributed to the promotion of these poets in today's Russia. It is plausible that Georgii Ivanov and Tsvetaeva occupy an important place in the post-Soviet cultural landscape not only because their poetry accords well with today's search for a new national identity but also because their poetic selves represent the manifestation of the subjectivity, individualism, dialogicity and the lyric 'I' entwined with elegiac overtones that were largely suppressed in the Soviet period. The melancholic mode of expression was seen as something that stood in sharp contrast to the socialist realist aesthetic oriented towards an optimistic, futuristic and heroic representation of reality.

In her recent study on lyric poetry and modern politics in Russia and in Poland, Clare Cavanagh provides a good summary of many views antagonistic to the expression of individualism in Soviet times. She notes that Aleksandr Bogdanov's post-revolutionary manifesto welcomes the replacement of the lyric 'I' with the notion of lyric comradeship and claims that Soviet proletarian poetry foregrounded the collective as the most basic creator of poetry. She goes on to say:

> By the end of the twenties, Boris Eikhenbaum laments, both 'personal poetry' (the lyric) and 'the lyric "I"' were virtually taboo'. [...] In his speech, Bukharin derides the 'anti-realistic lyric', with its unsocialist attachment to otherworldly imaginings. Bakhtin was very much Bukharin's comrade-in-arms in this, if little else.[81]

Cavanagh's analysis of the construction of the self in Soviet poetry suggests that the polyphonic mode of poetic speech that became evident in Russian poetry in the 1930s might have been influenced by the rise of the Soviet novel. These novels were oriented towards the construction of epic modes of artistic expression and the glorification of contemporary heroes who devoted their lives to the attainment of

---

[80] Pavel Basinskii, 'Eto bylo nedavno...', *Rossiiskaia gazeta*, 26 August 2013, https://rg.ru/2013/08/26/basinsky.html

[81] Clare Cavanagh, *Lyric Poetry and Modern Politics: Russia, Poland, and the West* (New Haven and London: Yale University Press, 2010), p. 13.

a radiant socialist future. In contrast, Tsvetaeva's and Georgii Ivanov's works offer a different vision of the notions of the heroic and of the lyric from those found in socialist realist canonical narratives. That is why their popularity among post-Soviet readers might be partially explained by the radical departure from Soviet literary practices and by the search for a more sophisticated mode of artistic expression attuned with the anxieties of post-Soviet readers affected by the experience of discontinuity caused by the collapse of the Soviet Union in 1991.

Given the didactic nature of socialist realism, it is not surprising that many theoretical studies devoted to it highlight the role of the positive hero in Soviet canonical texts. Comparing the representation of the positive hero in Soviet mainstream fiction to the self-representation of gladiators in ancient Rome, Régine Robin suggests that the positive hero found in Soviet fiction in particular, and in the aesthetic of socialist realism in general, accomplished an important task that enabled the writer 'to maintain enthusiasm at the level of the great historical tragedy' and conceal not 'the narrow content of the struggle' but 'rather the price to be paid for the construction of socialism, the lost generation, the uncertainty of the future'.[82] Having taken a cue from Mikhail Bakhtin on dialogicity and polyphony as prerequisites for the novelistic genre, Robin explains her theoretical position about the impossibility of writing socialist realist narratives in these terms:

> 'Impossible' refers to the theoretical contradictions, to the aporias of that aesthetic, to the nature of the particular combination that it puts into figures: epics, heroic narratives, legendary verse-chronicles that take on the forms of verisimilitude, realism, and representation.[83]

Robin's conviction that 'the postulates of realism as aesthetic constraint and textual convention are incompatible' with socialist realism's insistence on the use of 'revolutionary Romanticism', 'certainty in the vector of history', 'control of the imaginary' and 'mandatory monologism' is strongly felt in her verdict suggesting that the death of socialist realism as an aesthetic 'preceded the death of the Soviet Union by twenty to thirty years' due to how it 'has been replaced by all sorts of

---

82   Régine Robin, *Socialist Realism: An Impossible Aesthetic*, translated by Catherine Porter (Stanford: Stanford University Press, 1992), pp. xxvi–xxvii.
83   *Ibid.*, p. xxxiii.

genres and writings, from country prose to a new urban prose than no longer conceals the harsh conditions of everyday life'.[84] In her comments on the post-*perestroika* diversification of genres and narratives, Robin offers an apt assessment of the way the past reconstructs itself in today's Russia: 'From silence and taboo to lapse of memory, from repression to censorship, from the political rewriting of history to re-readings of public opinion and fiction'.[85] Likewise, the post-Soviet poetic canon in making is inevitably associated either with lamenting the death of socialist realism or with reinventing the past. Such a mythopoeic reinvention of the past enables post-Soviet readers to come to terms with the collapse of grand narratives (including Marxism and socialist realism).

As has been demonstrated above, many contemporary interpretations of the present state of Russian literature are still expressed in binary terms and highlight either the official-dissident or Soviet-émigré divisions of Russian twentieth-century literary traditions. In his book on post-Soviet literature, N. N. Shneidman suggests that the binary opposition applicable to late Soviet literary developments has been transformed into another set of oppositions that manifest two distinct literary ideological trends in Russia. He writes:

> In the late Soviet era there were two distinct streams of literature: official Soviet literature and underground, anti-Soviet *samizdat* and *tamizdat* literature. In the USSR Soviet underground literature was taboo, but it was published, recognized, and studied in the West, regardless of its artistic merit.[86]

Shneidman also talks about the ideological split between the conservatives and liberals in post-Soviet Russia that is reflected in the organisational framework of the writers' community and the existence of two antagonistic unions of Russian writers which has been partially overcome by the efforts of some writers and cultural figures to gain access to the Russian state's financial and political support. Shneidman provides this summary of the latest divergent ideological literary streams:

---

84 *Ibid.*, p. xxxii.
85 *Ibid.*, p. iv.
86 N. N. Shneidman, *Russian Literature, 1995–2002: On the Threshold of the New Millenium* (Toronto, Buffalo and London: University of Toronto Press, 2004), p. 5.

One includes all liberal writers, regardless of their artistic inclinations; the other incorporates all Russian conservative, 'patriotic' writers. Since there is no censorship in Russia, and the country has a multi-party political system, the literature of both streams is published without interference from, or censorship by, state authorities. The literature of each stream has its own readership, and representatives of the two groups criticise and attack each other on political and ideological grounds. Most western Slavists and literary scholars ignore the literature of Russian 'patriotic' writers, despite the fact that this literature represents an important social and cultural, albeit not artistic, phenomenon.[87]

Shneidman's description of post-Soviet literary trends does not take account of the appropriation and reassessment of the usable past, including socialist realist canonical texts and Russian émigré literature of the first wave. It seems that the aesthetic concerns of Russian writers in the post-Soviet period are not always bound up with a clear-cut political outlook. They tend to change in accordance with dominant commercial trends, spontaneously-arising fashionable fads, and social concerns. Shneidman overlooks how post-Soviet subjectivity is an important factor that affects many literary and cultural developments in today's Russia, especially because of its immense influence on the eclectic state of the post-Soviet memory wars, sites of memory and the reinvention of tradition. Barret Watten explains that 'the break-up of official culture, even the "official/unofficial" dialectic that was a part of it, in the Soviet Union led to aesthetic developments characterised by an intense, utopian, and metaphysically speculative subjectivity' that derives from the early postmodern tendencies that were visible in the 1960s.[88] Watten identifies the eclectic and all-inclusive nature of post-Soviet subjectivity and affirms that it incorporates both western and Russian aesthetic trends, including American pop culture (exemplified by Andy Warhol's paintings) and Reagan-era consumerism (illustrated by Jeff Koons's works).

It is difficult not to agree with Watten's observation that the culture of Russian modernism has been refracted through Western connoisseurship and that its reinterpretation in the new post-Soviet context created a new sense of discontinuity because the vision of

---

87   Ibid., pp. 5–6.
88   Barrett Watten, 'Post-Soviet Subjectivity in Arkadii Dragomoshchenko and Ilya Kabakov', *Postmodern Culture*, 3: 2 (January 1993), https://muse.jhu.edu/article/27402

it which has emerged does not correspond to its historical origins.[89] Thus Aleksei German Junior's illusion of unity inscribed into his film *Garpastum* with the help of the depiction of Silver Age poets, who appear as close friends in his film (despite the physical impossibility of this fact), creates an imaginary space in the style of the photography and cinematography of the 1910s. The group of poets and performers shown in this film includes Akhmatova, Aleksandr Blok, Mandel'shtam, Khodasevich, Nikolai Gumilev, Aleksandr Vertinskii and Tsvetaeva. In Antony Anemone's opinion, a central theme of the film is the role of art in social and political life:

> The final crisis of the film concerns the status of art in the modern world. For Andrei, Anitsa's salon is about the sexual, not artistic, revolution, and his inability to recognize the significance of Blok (Gosha Kutsenko) and the other members of the salon suggests a growing gap between artist and audience. Both Blok and Anitsa, by comparison, recognize that the war represents the end of an era. And Blok goes on to suggest the possibility that his generation's assumptions about the centrality of art and the intelligentsia are mistaken: if they suddenly were to disappear, would anyone notice?[90]

The crisis of individualism entwined with the crisis of masculinity in *Garpastum* enables the post-Soviet director to demystify several taboo subjects of the Soviet period, including sexuality and mental problems. The film touches upon many unresolved issues that contributed to the utopian thinking of the early Soviet period. Anemone rightly points to how German Junior's imagined community of the pre-revolutionary period invokes many images from the post-Soviet period. He asserts:

> In this vision of a Russia marked by poverty and criminality, middle-class apathy towards the poor, the hedonistic cult of sport, the decline of traditional morality and of the prestige of art, and heading towards an unimaginable historical calamity, German has created a double image: not only a snapshot of Russia on the eve of 1917, but an allegory of the contemporary post-Soviet world as well. But German refuses to resolve the central question raised by the film: does the brothers' attempt to escape from the political problems of the larger society contribute to the tragedies that Russia will experience? Or is private life the only refuge for

---

89 Ibid.
90 Tony Anemone, 'Aleksei German Junior: Garpastum, 2005', *Kinokultura*, 12 (April 2006), http://www.kinokultura.com/2006/12r-garpastum.shtml

ordinary people caught up in historical calamities beyond their control? What is clear, however, is German's consistently tragic sense that life is more about suffering and surviving than about attaining dreams.⁹¹

German Junior's film is laced with elegiac overtones and laments the demise of the Russian creative intelligentsia who, in order to succeed in the post-Soviet period, have had to account of market forces as well as the new type of readership seeking entertainment rather than spiritual guidance.

It can be argued that the aesthetic values of the leading Russian émigré authors of the 1920s–1940s related to the nature and function of artistic creativity of Russian diaspora — identified in Khodasevich's aforementioned statement as being strikingly different from Soviet literature — have come to be of central importance to Russian contemporary poets, critics and performers who are eager to move away from the ideological and utilitarian aesthetic concerns of the Soviet period. That is why the rediscovery of the writing of Russian émigré authors enables a post-Soviet reader to assess the development of modernist ideas in the post-revolutionary period preserved by different branches of Russian twentieth-century literature. It is also interesting to observe a hidden dialogicity embedded in post-Soviet textbooks on history and literature, suggesting the existence of a creative impulse to reinvent tradition and rewrite the past. Thus a 2008 textbook on Russian twentieth-century literature produced for university students of Russian philology mentions the names of several Russian émigré poets that had been erased from Soviet textbooks for decades. V. V. Losev's chapter devoted to Khodasevich describes him as an heir of Pushkin who followed Pushkin's advice not to seek fame or the acceptance of contemporary readers.⁹²

Furthermore, Losev writes about Khodasevich's loyalty to Russian culture in the style of the aforementioned song by Leonidov featuring White movement officers who had fled abroad as being true Russian patriots. Losev portrays Khodasevich as a person who, despite many travels during his years of emigration, managed to preserve the image

---

91 Ibid.
92 V. V. Losev, 'V. F. Khodasevich (1886–1939)', in *Izbrannye imena: Russkie poety. XX vek. Uchebnoe posobie*, edited by N. M. Malygin (Moscow: Flinta, Nauka, 2008), pp. 145–55 (p. 145).

of his motherland in his heart.⁹³ He talks about Khodasevich's desire to emulate the Apollonian qualities of Pushkin's poetry based 'on the harmonious coordination between semantic and sound elements' and affirms that 'in anticipation of his forthcoming death, Khodasevich emigrated spiritually to Pushkin'.⁹⁴ Losev's description of Khodasevich's poetic persona exemplifies the process, discussed above, of re-imagining Russian identity without borders and the continuing association of the canon with nineteenth-century classical literature.

The description by Losev of Russian émigré poets who long for an imagined community of Russian readers is similar to the traditional representation of Tsvetaeva in criticism and the media of the 1960s–1990s. They usually represent Tsvetaeva as a true Russian poet. Many film makers, performers and critics state that her literary output is firmly rooted in the Russian poetic tradition and suggest that she was capable of appropriating European cultural models in her works in the style of the universalised image of Pushkin, as depicted in Fedor Dostoevskii's 1880 Pushkin Speech. Dostoevskii's speech moulds Pushkin into a poet who can empathise with other countries and cultural traditions. Likewise, the universal qualities of Tsvetaeva's artistic outlook and all-inclusive poetic language is reflected in the introductory note to a recent edition of her poetry by A. Dmitriev:

> 'The poet's speech takes him far away...' — it transfers him into the year 1610 in order to meet with Marina Mnishek; it leads him to an imaginary meeting with Russian generals taking part in the 1812 Borodino battle; it takes him to Paris and Prague (which results in the desire to return the ticket to the Creator) and it makes him seek otherworldly reality in order to enter the river Styx in the last day of summer 1941 spent in Elabuga.⁹⁵

Dmitriev's analysis of Tsvetaeva's imaginary world containing fragments of Russian history, culture and European travels might be seen as an allegorical depiction of the state of the Russian poetic canon today. It alludes to the existence of many different views on the notion of canonicity linked not only to the notion of national identity but also to intertextuality and sublimity. The ambiguity of the post-Soviet cultural

---

93 *Ibid.*, p. 146.
94 *Ibid.*, p. 152.
95 A. Dmitriev, 'Predislovie', in M. I. Tsvetaeva, *Zakon zvezdy i formula tsvetka...* (Moscow: Eksmo, 2010), p. 4.

landscape resembles the eclectic nature of the physical landscape comprising remnants of the Soviet and the pre-Soviet past.

It is worth pointing here to a striking analogy between attitudes towards monuments and street naming in post-Soviet Russia and to the reassessment of the twentieth-century poetic canon. Graeme Gill, in his study of the pattern of name changes in Moscow in the post-Soviet period, highlights how the transition from communism to capitalism remains a highly ambiguous process.[96] Gill asserts:

> The generation of new symbols like flags, coats of arms, and anthems, the destruction of old and the construction of new monuments, the creation of new rituals or the injection of new context into the existing rituals, and even the reworking of the language (through the injection of new words, the changing of the meaning of the existing terms, and the elimination of some words) in order to invest it with a new ethos have all been important to the creation of the new regime's symbolic culture.[97]

According to Gill, most of the street name changes in Russia since 1990 were meant to replace the memory of any associations with Soviet heroes and *homo soveticus* by new names that celebrate the notion of *homo economicus*. It is not surprising that out of 152 street name changes in Moscow in the last 20 years 102 of them were clearly linked to the desire to eradicate any memory of the communist past associated with revolutionary violence and utopian ideology. The change of street names, affirms Gill, was often triggered by the desire to erase those street names that were closely linked to political figures of the Soviet regimes, their associates (in Soviet Russia and outside Russia), the regime's forefathers and various prominent members of the international revolutionary movement.[98] Likewise, the twentieth-century poetic canon will continue to be contested for many years to come. The process of the construction of the new canon/s is likely to rely heavily on the existence of shared cultural values — shaped by the notion of culturedness created during the Soviet period — and to the growing desire to preserve the role of the Russian language as the basis of unity and creativity inside and outside Russia.

---

96 Graeme Gill, 'Changing Symbols: The Renovation of Moscow Place Names', *The Russian Review*, 64 (July 2005), 480–503 (p. 495).
97 *Ibid.*, p. 480.
98 *Ibid.*, p. 485.

Such a desire to construct an image of Russia without borders appears to be indicative of the emerging Russophone poetic canon. It is not coincidental perhaps that a street in Kiev is renamed after Marina Tsvetaeva and that an underground stations due to open in the city in 2019 will be named 'Tsvetaeva street'.[99] Other existing streets named after Tsvetaeva are located in Russia, including such places as Krasnodar, Kazan', Korolev, Koktebel', Griazi (near Lipetsk), Uchaly (Baskiriia), Plodovyi village (near Kalinin), and Ekaterinburg. The list of streets associated with Tsvetaeva invokes Aleksandr Dugin's concept of the Eurasian empire and imperial utopianism. Viewed in this light, the new Russophone canon seems inseparable from the post-Soviet geopolitical imagination. Furthermore, Tsvetaeva's popularity in post-Soviet Russia can be partly explained by the Eurasianist overtones embedded in her poetry and fiction.[100] Needless to say, Tsvetaeva's poetry's strong emotional appeal to the post-Soviet reader can also be seen as another sign of the return of emotionality. According to Maria Engström, the return of emotionality in today's Russia exemplifies a search for 'new forms of collectivity and commonness' advocated by Russian neoconservative thinkers and writers whose promotion of 'a passionate, emotional citizen'[101] (as opposed to a rational citizen) is becoming alarmingly more popular than ever.

---

99 [N.a.], 'Levoberezhnaia liniia', https://ru.wikipedia.org/wiki/Левобережная_линия
100 Alexandra Smith. 'Tsvetaeva's Story "The Chinaman" and Its Link with the Eurasian Movement in Prague and in Paris in the 1920–1930s', *The Soviet and Post-Soviet Review*, 28: 3 (2001 [2002]), 269–86.
101 Maria Engström, 'Contemporary Russian Messianism and New Russian Foreign Policy', p. 358.

13. Creating the Canon of the Present

Stephanie Sandler

Assessing a poetic canon, as it is emerging, is probably impossible, but provisional judgements can offer valuable insights and the poetry of the present has important lessons to teach about how canons form. Coming to judgements about the present sheds new light on earlier moments of canonisation. The instability and variability of the contemporary canon can act as a cautionary tale, slowing down our confident glance of retrospection at the past. Our judgements can and should change, as the many case studies in this volume happily attest.

Contemporary material, then, which obviously has not settled into anything like a canon, has a methodological advantage for scholars alongside its obvious challenges. It prevents us from regarding *a* canon as *the* canon. Moreover, it makes us see canon creation as the work of culture, as a process that is open-ended, and as an activity of persons and institutions with a diverse and conflicting set of interests.

Two distinctive features of contemporary poetry should be noted at the outset. First, in ways that became acute after 1991 but which began in the 1980s, the movement of bodies and texts across borders makes it difficult to use the geographical and political entity known as Russia as the sole site for canon-formation. We now see vividly that a model of Russian culture in the homeland versus Russian culture in emigration is inadequate and misleading — it can be useful in identifying specific cultural contexts, like the interactions of Russian poets with their Czech counterparts in Prague in the inter-war period, or the effects of ideological demands (what was known as *sotsial'nyi zakaz*) on Soviet-era poets — but it equally obscures such cross-cultural mechanisms as the work of translation, the complexly orchestrated creation of an evolving national cultural identity, and the forms of interaction among poets living in different parts of the world. Obviously, the internet has now radically changed those last possibilities, which is one reason why even a formulation like 'texts moving across borders' begins to sound faintly anachronistic. Still, the permeability of most geographic borders is a defining feature of the contemporary cultural moment, and it plays itself out in poetry-creation in terms of linguistic possibilities, cultural markers, and available forms of poetic self-creation.

A second distinctive feature also involves a form of blending. The incorporation of multiple forms of aesthetic and cultural material makes it similarly difficult to build a fence around Russian poetry. How poems present themselves as visual artefacts, how they interact with other art forms and with a full range of cultural activities — visual arts, journalism, performance art, to name only three possibilities — are matters we are only beginning to understand. Poems have always drawn on other cultural and political spheres, from the psalm-translation contests of the eighteenth century to the album inscriptions of the nineteenth century and the agitprop visual texts of the early twentieth, so this is not a new cultural feature so much as a newly emphasised one. And in that new emphasis, we may reconsider the proportions we assign to different forms of cultural activity; the lessons of the present can help us review our assumptions and judgements about the past. Vladimir Maiakovskii's brutal, visually arresting alphabet books or memoirs of Daniil Kharms's performances can float up more vividly before our gaze, for instance, leading us to an account of early twentieth-century Russian poetry that is not just a recitation of one 'ism' replacing another.

In order to explore these distinctive features, here I will take up five large rubrics: language, aesthetic category, textual boundaries, story-telling, and performance. As I consider each topic, I will focus on poets whose work is especially illustrative and whose achievements, I am implying, will almost surely place them within canons of the present we will form at future moments. That is not to say that these are in any absolute sense the best current poets (although each is definitely worthy of serious study), nor do they represent an exhaustive set of current trends. Rather, their work speaks to central concerns of Russian poetry today, and shows us canon-formation as it is happening.

Language

Language would seem the most obvious given: if we speak about Russian poetry, then surely we speak about poetry that is written in Russian. But what is a national language, exactly? If we have learned anything from the post-structuralist intervention into cultural theory, it is the uncertainty that any of our human productions is stable, fixed, or entirely knowable. Linguists told us long ago, anyway, that languages change profoundly over time, and that those changes are the result of interaction with other national languages as much as they are the fruit of historical change and political or social needs (new tools need new names as much as invading armies or descending nomads bring foodstuffs, weapons, and behaviours that generate new terms). So the language is always changing, but perhaps it is poetry's gift to us that we get a series of linguistic snapshots? If this were true, we could still believe that national language is crystallised, held still in the work of poetry.

To some extent, the snapshot theory of poetry is useful, but most texts seek not to give an overall picture of the language, but to focus on a discrete corner of the picture. Aleksandr Pushkin may have created a linguistic encyclopaedia of Russian life in *Evgenii Onegin* but it is more likely that a contemporary poem grabs hold of a scene where the language of marketing collides with the lexicon of Romantic elegies (Kirill Medvedev), or the structure of computer codes unnervingly shapes a peculiarly philosophical outpouring of self-assertion (Nika Skandiaka).

To reframe my question about language, then, and to put it in terms that relate to canon formation: how does poetry, that most language-driven art form, explore the territory at the remotest edges of a national language? Let me sketch out three mappings of that terrain. First, the macaronic, where national languages mix; second, the assertion of text as translation, often by publishing poems alongside apparent 'originals'; third, and most radically, the production of 'Russian' poetry in another language entirely.

The Macaronic

Mixed languages have long appeared in Russian texts, famously and impudently in *Evgenii Onegin*, outrageously and with an admixture of neologisms and *zaum'* in the writings of the futurists. Recent writings return interest to several forms of linguistic bricolage; while the casual introduction of foreign words has escalated in the post-Soviet period, it began at least three decades earlier, in the 1960s, most prominently and most productively in the work of Leningrad poet Mikhail Eremin (b. 1936). A member of the *Filologicheskaia shkola* (Philological School) that also gave us Lev Losev, Vladimir Ufliand, Sergei Kulle, among others, Eremin remains a powerful and strange presence in contemporary poetry. His publications continue to emerge from the excellent *Pushkinskii fond* (Pushkin foundation) publishing house, each book called only *Stikhotvoreniia* (*Poems*). As of this writing, the most recent is book six, which appeared in 2016 in St Petersburg. Each book offers work in only one form: eight-line poems, almost always untitled. In the face of such radical formal consistency, the poet creates miniature poetic worlds that contain whole lexicons of botany, astronomy, ornithology, mathematics, metallurgy, chemistry, mythology, and more. It is common for poems to use terms that the poet annotates in what may constitute effectively a ninth or tenth line, explaining that two words were at the heart of theological controversies in the seventeenth century or that a phrase comes from the title of William Hogarth's aesthetic essay. (Eremin annotates some items but leaves countless others to be chased down by industrious readers — not for nothing did Mikhail Aizenberg famously call him a poet of the dictionary.)[1] Some poems directly link the use of neologisms to the question of translatability between languages, or between experience and linguistic rendering: a fine example would be 'Neudivitelen, kogda zaliv podoben arsenalu' ('Unsurprising, when a gulf resembles an arsenal', 1983), with its mixed-language line about translation 'na russkii or *from Russian*' ('into Russian or *from Russian*').[2]

---

[1] Mikhail Aizenberg, 'Literatura za odnim stolom: O poetakh "filologicheskoi shkoly"', *Novaia kamera khraneniia* (2008), http://www.litkarta.ru/dossier/aizenberg-o-filologicheskoi-shkole/dossier_940

[2] Mikhail Eremin, *Stikhotvoreniia* (St Petersburg: Pushkinskii fond, 1998), p. 25.

Another excellent instance is a slightly earlier poem, which has one of Eremin's annotations alongside many mysteries:

> Топь–зыбь. Твердь–зябь. Мель–
> Рябь. Даль–гладь. Хлябь.
> Кривую замыкает ель. Ветвь.
> The line of beauty–овидь. Над заливом–
> Изложницею неба–зеркалом небес,
> Над полем, над болотом–в окнах звезды,–месяц–
> Злат–хлад–млад–
> Gold–cold–old.[3]

1979

'The line of beauty' — W.Hogarth.

> Bog–ripple. Earth–field. Shoal–
> Dazzle. Distance–glade. Mud.
> Locks closed the crooked fir. Branch.
> The line of beauty–horizon. Above the gulf–
> Heaven's form–heavens' mirror–
> Above field, above swamp–in the windows of a star,–moon–
> Gold–cold–young–
> Gold–cold–old.[4]

1979

'The line of beauty' — W.Hogarth.

---

3   Mikhail Eremin, *Stikhotvoreniia*, edited by Lev Losev (Tenafly, NJ: Hermitage Press, 1986), p. 94. The translation here and elsewhere in the chapter, unless otherwise indicated, is mine.

4   The translation is mostly word-for-word, but takes one liberty: in line 2, the word 'glad'' a 'smooth surface', usually referring to water. To keep to the noun sequence, I choose 'glade', which repeats the sounds in the Russian because of the common Indo-European root. Historically, 'glade' did mean 'bright, smooth place': see *Webster's New World Dictionary of the American Language* (New York: The World Publishing Co., 1972), p. 592.

By identifying the source of the phrase 'the line of beauty', Eremin asks readers to imagine the S-shaped form it represents (and to connect that form to some of the nouns that open the poem, with their rippled surfaces). He hopes we will attend to the way in which foreign phrases come into languages, and can function in a text. Those four English words, 'the line of beauty', slip gracefully into the iambic rhythm of Eremin's lines — the iambs are challenged by the potential spondees of lines 1–2 and 7–8, one should note, which may let us hear the lilting rhythm of this English phrase all the more clearly. The phrase 'the line of beauty' is as lovely as the imagery of the poem, including the extraordinary picture of the firmament arching over the open seas, the swamps and the fields, mirror-like and moulded. The final line is seductively absorbed into the Russian fabric of the lines quite similarly. A perfect formal equivalent of line 7, line 8 uses monosyllables that seem a strangely wonderful refraction of the CCVC phonological structure of Church Slavonic words, at least as far as 'gold' and 'cold' go. The words 'gold' and 'cold' word golf, to use Vladimir Nabokov's famous game, perfectly, in one step, and the Russian line golfs perfectly, too, in two steps, then one. But the outlier in the game of word golf, as well as in the semantics of the sequence, is 'old'. If we think of line 8 as a translation of line 7, then 'old' is at once a semantic error and a stroke of acoustic genius. It stays within the same semantic field of the word it is meant to translate ('mlad' ('young')), but moves in the opposite direction, toward age rather than toward youth. Eremin presents these two lines as a forceful demonstration of the logic of translation: one can translate from Russian to English with the greatest formal accuracy, he suggests, when the translation risks considerable semantic freedom.

Poems as Translations

Several contemporary Russian poets are also outstanding translators, including Ol'ga Sedakova, Anna Glazova, and the late poets Arkadii Dragomoshchenko, Natal'ia Gorbanevskaia, and Grigorii Dashevskii. Also important, in terms of the connections between translation and canon formation, is the Moscow poet Stanislav L'vovskii (b. 1972). He is admired as a versatile writer, and an influential poet and critic. He has integrated translation into his publications (as did Grigorii Dashevskii, one should note) in ways that ask implicitly whether works of translation really differ from supposedly 'original' works.

Some poets include a section called 'Translations' in their published books, and such a gesture is potentially unmarked as an aesthetic statement about translation and originality. L'vovskii does something different, however, particularly in his 2008 book *Camera rostrum*. We might take the Latin title of the book as itself a signal of curiosity about and connection to foreign languages. But is it Latin? The words exist in English as well: a rostrum camera is one that is mounted on a platform for use in creating animated films. The Latin words, however, while not constituting a fixed phrase, suggest a strange coupling of the private room of the Latin *camera* and the public speaking platform, the *rostrum*, a raised section of the Forum. L'vovskii's poetry is itself perched at that spot where public and private discourse meet — he is, among other things, an outstanding poet of contemporary history, one who catches lived experience in snatches of overheard conversation and espied glances.

Which brings us to one of the poems presented as a translation in *Camera rostrum*, George Oppen's 'Quotations', translated into Russian as 'Tsitaty'.[5] Oppen's poetry is marked by an unusual (for American poetry) density of quoted material, and by a wonderful freeness in using those quotations to sometimes startling ends. In this poem, the citations punningly refer to the inclusion in the text of quoted speech. The speaker heard in 'Quotations' exemplifies Oppen's way with these insertions: a very old man answers a question about the age of a village in the Bahamas with the slightly off-kilter words, 'I found it'. L'vovskii somewhat normalizes those words, translating them as 'Ia ee osnoval', which actually means 'I founded it', a possible pun suggested

---

5   The turn to Oppen's work is itself an important signal to readers. His conversational diction stretches across an estranged syntax and a poetic surface roughened by italicised and quoted words; his presentation of seemingly random facts about the external world is marked by an equally careful presentation of the effects of that world on the consciousness that perceives it. These elements of Oppen's work, which made him so important to later American poets, are nearly all trademarks of L'vovskii's poetry; L'vovskii in turn has had a tremendous impact on contemporary Russian poets.

in the English but a more limited and less surprising response than Oppen presents. Later in the text, Oppen quotes another speaker, saying, 'Therefore they are welcome', which is nearly incongruous as a description of children, animals, and insects staring 'at the open'. It's the word 'therefore' that makes this rejoinder peculiar, and L'vovskii retains it, although shifting the rest of the line: 'Poetomu im mozhno'. He retains the open-endedness of the original — what is it precisely that they are permitted to do, one wonders. What indeed could be equally permitted animals, children, insects, as they stare at something 'open'?

L'vovskii displays a normalising impulse of the translations, which is entirely usual in translators, but his decision to include the facing English originals is a powerful way of destabilising his own versions. Many of his readers know English, so the texts will arrive in doubled form, all the more so since, in this book (*Camera rostrum*), there is also a section of song lyrics translated into Russian. These appear only in Russian, perhaps because readers will have ringing in their ears the famous English-language originals of songs like Frank Sinatra's 'It Was a Very Good Year', or Nina Simone's 'Sinnerman'. In any case, L'vovskii chooses a different variegation of the text for those songs, presenting the English-language title, with name of performer and name of song, at the top of the Russian translated lyrics.

The porous borders between 'original' and 'translated' poetry are another important lesson to take away from L'vovskii's poetry. The turn to translation seems to offer an old lesson, as old for Russia as the medieval scribes who were creating Church Slavonic versions of rituals, prayers, and Biblical texts. What is new in L'vovskii's poems is the proposition of equivalent status, the presentation to readers of versions as texts worthy of equally close attention, versions as models, in other words, for future work in Russian poetry.

In L'vovskii's 'Tsitaty', as in Oppen's 'Quotations', a minimalist form of poetic expression treats speech acts as verbal objects. The poems fracture the syntax of sense and description just enough to surprise readers, even though the situations narrated are entirely ordinary. Scrawled words under a subway's advertisement, a child's exclamation during a family trip, and a woman with a closet full of clothes fill out the other part of 'Quotations' / 'Tsitaty', bits of verse that celebrate not the found material of the world (whether verbal or material, for the two are always intertwined), but the poet's attitude toward those discoveries.⁶ L'vovskii is trying to teach Russian poetry the lessons of objectivism, as practiced by Oppen and others (and further exemplified in *Camera rostrum* by his translation of Charles Simic's poem in memory of Oppen, 'The Tiger'). Those lessons base poetry not in the innovations of rhythm or rhyme or stanzaic pattern but in the infinite capacities of the poetic line to register what one scholar has called a fusion into 'one verbal gesture' of the 'familiar and the strange'.⁷ To embrace this poetic work is to push 'Russian' poetry toward models some would find deeply alien to its formal traditions. I could adduce other poets and other foreign models who have had similarly powerful effects (Dragomoshchenko's encounter with the Language poets, for example; Aleksandr Skidan's translation and critical work as well).⁸ Let L'vovskii stand in for a larger trend, one that in his case works by challenging the very language of poetry itself.⁹

Texts in English

What about poems in English penned by poets known and admired for their work in Russian? We have such poems by Aleksei Tsvetkov, Katia Kapovich, and Iosif Brodskii, for instance, including some in English with no Russian originals. Brodskii's 'tunes' are poems of political and ethical sharpness, as in 'Bosnia Tune', 'Belfast Tune', or 'Berlin Wall Tune'. The last is perhaps the most famous, modelled on 'This is the house that Jack built', a rhyme that had generated other important poems in English of similar sharp intent (like Elizabeth Bishop's poem

---

6   I adopt here a point made by James Longenbach, *The Resistance to Poetry* (Chicago: University of Chicago Press, 2004), p. 44.

7   Michael Heller, 'Speaking the Estranged: Oppen's Poetics of the Word', *Chicago Review*, 50 (Winter 2004–2005), 137–50 (p. 137).

8   For a discussion of Dragomoshchenko's work in the context of Language poetry, see Jacob Edmond, *A Common Strangeness: Contemporary Poetry, Cross-cultural Encounter, Comparative Literature* (New York: Fordham University Press, 2012), pp. 44–71.

9   The further question is whether the national tradition is itself the most meaningful way to think about these poems. That challenge has been raised by comparatists, many seeking to re-imagine Comparative Literature as a discipline to study cultural production in the post-internet, globalised world. See, for example, Jahan Ramazani, *A Transnational Poetics* (Chicago: University of Chicago Press, 2009).

about Ezra Pound, 'Visits to St. Elizabeth's'). So an argument could be made that the poems in English are built out of the traditions of English-language poetry, not Russian. Perhaps, but it would be a loss to our understanding of Brodskii and of contemporary political processes were we to leave it at that. Consider the opening stanzas of one of his 'Tunes':

> Bosnia Tune
>
> As you pour yourself a scotch,
> crush a roach, or scratch your crotch,
> as your hand adjusts your tie,
> people die.
>
> In the towns with funny names,
> hit by bullets, caught in flames,
> by and large not knowing why,
> people die.
>
> In small places you don't know
> of, yet big for having no
> chance to scream or say good-bye,
> people die.[10]

Here are several trademark Brodskii poetic practices, like the dramatic use of enjambment (lines 9–10, 'know / of'), the insistent rhyming, the casually introduced vulgarity in a poem with serious political aims, the recognizable images of statues, time, the rephrased clichés, like the later references to a place where 'cherubs dread to fly'. To anyone who knows his poetry in Russian, the lines bear Brodskii's signature, right down to the unapologetic and explicit argument about free men distracted by their pleasures and thus blind to the violence and harm in the world around them.

A different test case would be a poem by a poet for whom we do not have such standard notions of poetic signature in Russian, a poet who writes entirely in English, Ilya Kaminsky. Here, for example, is what he wrote about Brodskii:

---

10 Joseph Brodsky, *Collected Poems in English*, edited by Ann Kjellberg (New York: Farrar, Straus & Giroux, 2000), p. 490. The poem first appeared 20 November 1992 in the *Baltimore Sun*.

Elegy for Joseph Brodsky

i

In plain speech, for the sweetness
between the lines is no longer important,
what you call immigration I call suicide.
I am sending, behind the punctuation,
unfurling nights of New York, avenues
slipping into Cyrillic
winter coils words, throws snow on a wind.
You, in the middle of an unwritten sentence, stop,
exile to a place further than silence.

ii

I left your Russia for good, poems sewn into my pillow
rushing towards my own training
to live with your lines
on a verge of a story set against itself.
To live with your lines, those where sails rise, waves
beat against the city's granite in each vowel, –
pages open by themselves, a quiet voice
speaks of suffering, of water.

iii

We come back to where we have committed a crime,
we don't come back to where we loved, you said;
your poems are wolves nourishing us with their milk.
I tried to imitate you for two years. It feels like burning
and singing about burning. I stand
as if someone spat at me.
You would be ashamed of these wooden lines
how I don't imagine your death
but it is here, setting my hands on fire.[11]

---

11 Ilya Kaminsky, *Dancing in Odessa* (Dorset, VT: Tupelo Press, 2004), p. 44. Reproduced with permission.

When this poem was published in Kaminsky's prize-winning book *Dancing in Odessa* (2004), it was accompanied by a prose text. Elements of fantasy and searchingly revealed truth are inextricable here:

> Joseph Brodsky
> Joseph made his living by giving private lessons in everything from engineering to Greek. His eyes were sleepy and small, his face dominated by a huge mustache, like Nietzsche's. He mumbled. Do you enjoy Brahms? I cannot hear you, I said. How about Chopin? I cannot hear you. Mozart? Bach? Beethoven? I am hard of hearing, could you repeat that please? You will have a great success in music, he said.
> To meet him, I go back to Leningrad of 1964. The streets are devilishly cold: we sit on the pavement, he begins abruptly (a dry laugh, a cigarette) to tell me the story of his life, his words change to icicles as we speak. I read them in the air.[12]

Kaminsky's poem merits a detailed and subtle reading, but without some knowledge of the Russian poetic tradition, that reading would be little more than a loose appreciation of its beauty. Pushkin's description of Petersburg in the first chapter of *Evgenii Onegin* generates the image of waves beating against a city's granite; Osip Mandel'shtam's honey-tinged words, his command to preserve his speech, give verbal energy to the poem's opening lines; Mandel'shtam again, from the prose of 'Egipetskaia marka' ('Egyptian Stamp'), supplies those words legible in the air. That last is one of Mandel'shtam's most memorable images, words created by the hand gestures of deaf people signing to one another — Kaminsky, himself deaf, thus motivates his phrase 'I am hard of hearing' not only biographically but also via Mandel'shtam. My small point about this complex text is that it stakes its own subtle claim to having emerged from under the overcoat of the Russian poetic tradition. It shows that tradition to be strangely porous, and an inspiring presence in world literature. The canon of early twenty-first-century Russian poetry, if we follow the logic of Kaminsky's work, extends beyond the boundaries of the language toward other linguistic domains, toward the many places around the globe where contemporary poets, like Brodskii, Kaminsky and many others, have come to live.[13]

---

12 Ibid., p. 45.
13 In an article about Orhan Pamuk's novel *Snow*, Andrew Wachtel makes a similar argument, pinning that novel in a variety of ways to Russian models. See Wachtel,

Reception in Russia

Here is a test that Kaminsky would have failed until the middle of 2012, when his poetry was translated into Russian:[14] should canonisation depend on the adulation and attention toward a poet's work from Russian audiences? Is it a limiting condition, in other words, for a poet to be recognised in his or her homeland? That question persists even in these days of diaspora, but was it present earlier, in a time of firmer fantasy of home versus abroad, of the motherland versus emigration? A perfect case study presents itself in the work of Gennadii Aigi (1934–2006).

Aigi is extremely well regarded by Western — especially American and French — critics and poets. In the United States, he is published by the prestigious New Directions Press; in the United Kingdom, he has been championed by his translator, Peter France; in 1972, he was awarded a prize by the *Académie Française,* and he is both well-translated into French and highly regarded as a translator from French to Chuvash, his native language. Aigi's allegiance to European modernist poetics cannot be underestimated. His labours as a translator mean that he thought about how the poems were made in French, and about how these poems' techniques and habits of mind could work in another language. His poetry especially shows the lessons of French surrealist poetry, with its elliptical syntax, semantic gaps, and near-mystical representations of nothingness as a meaningful, apprehensible category of being.[15] Just as we might ask the question, 'How Russian Is It?' with respect to English-language or macaronic 'Russian' poetry, so it is the case that, even when all the words of an Aigi poem are in Russian, the poetics and even the look of the poem on the page depart radically from Russian norms.

Consider the minuscule poem 'tishina' ('silence', 1973):

'Orhan Pamuk's Snow as a Russian Novel', *Slavic and East European Journal,* 56 (2012), 91–108.

14   Kaminskii, *Muzyka narodov vetra,* translated by Anastasiia Afanas'eva (New York: Ailuros Publishing, 2012).

15   On the varieties of silence in Aigi's work, see Gerald Janecek, 'Poeziia molchaniia u Gennadiia Aigi', in *Minimalismus zwischen Leere und Exzess,* edited by Mirjam Goller and Georg Witte. *Wiener slawistischer Almanach,* vol. 51 (Vienna: Gesellschaft zur Förderung slawistischer Studien, 2001), pp. 433–46. See also Sarah Valentine, 'Music, Silence, and Spirituality in the Poetry of Gennady Aigi', *Slavic and East European Journal,* 51 (2007), 675–92.

тишина

(стихи для одновременного чтения двух голосов)

– ма-á ... –

(а во сне те же самые
ж и в ы
г л а з а)

........................, а-má[16]

silence

(verses for simultaneous reading in two voices)

– ma- á... –

(but in sleep these same
e y e s
are alive)

– .... a-má[17]

Such a poem challenges readers by its visual layout, with the splitting across several lines of the sound formation 'ma-a ... a-ma' (an extended pronunciation of the word 'mama'), its use of spaced lettering for the parenthetical intervention, as if the words were to be all the more emphasised, and the lineation of that parenthetical comment, with 'alive' ('zhivy') and 'eyes' ('glaza') on separate lines, adding still more emphasis. The short-form adjective 'zhivy' seems grammatically wrong, in the attributive position where we expect a long-form adjective; such 'errors', as well as the markedly accented voice heard when Aigi read his work, contribute to the reaction of some Russian readers that there is something not quite Russian about the poetry.

16 Gennadii Aigi, *Sobranie sochinenii v semi tomakh*, 7 vols. (Moscow: Gileia, 2009), II, p. 95. Reproduced with permission.
17 My translation, but see also the translation in *Into the Snow: Selected Poems of Gennady Aygi*, translated by Sarah Valentine (Seattle and New York: Wave Books, 2011), p. 24.

This poem is typical of Aigi's work in many ways. The mother is one of the rare human figures to appear in his landscapes — and most of the poems are landscapes, often snowy, silent, stirred to motion by wind or fleeting birds. Many poems refer to dreams or are presented as the transcription of a dream. The term 'tishina' ('silence') recurs so often as to have generated some discussion as to the difference in his work between two forms of silence, 'tishina' and the less-often mentioned 'molchanie'.[18] The ellipses bear mention, too, an example of Aigi's unconventional use of punctuation.[19] The poem's subtitle, instructing us that it is meant to be read by two voices, points to another key feature of Aigi's work, its directions for performance.

Whereas in reading Kaminsky's work, or Brodskii's poems in English, one wanted to think about ways to draw them closer to the norms of Russian poetry, Aigi's poems invite in us the opposite response. Here is a poem that shows even more dramatically how resistant he is to the expected poetic forms of Russia's traditions. In this poem, he abandons all syntactic markers:

моцарт: 'кассация I'
[*с. губайдулиной*]

моцарт божественный моцарт соломинка
циркуль божественный лезвие ветер бумага
инфаркт богородица ветер жасмин операция
ветер божественный моцарт кассация ветка
жасмин операция ангел божественный роза
соломинка сердце кассация моцарт[20]
1977

---

18 See Valentine, 'Music, Silence'.
19 See Gerald Janecek, 'The Poetics of Punctuation in Gennady Aygi's Free Verse', in Janecek, *Sight and Sound Entwined: Studies of the New Russian Poetry* (New York: Berghahn Books, 2000), pp. 91–109.
20 Aigi, *Sobranie sochinenii*, vol. II, p. 101. Reproduced with permission.

> mozart: cassation I
> [for s. gubaidulina]
>
> mozart   divine   mozart   straw
> compass divine razoredge wind paper
> heartattack madonna wind jasmine surgery
> wind   divine   mozart   cassation   twig
> jasmine   surgery   angel   divine   rose
> straw heart cassation mozart
> 1977

Mozart's name here points toward a Western, foreign model for artistic creation. The poem's only adjective, 'divine' ('bozhestvennyi') acts as a partial calque for the second half of Mozart's middle name, Amadeus. And the poem is dedicated to the contemporary composer Sofia Gubaidulina, who represents both musical creativity and high Russian modernism in its most spiritual incarnation. (That positioning in fact applies well to Aigi himself.) Like 'tishina', this poem is a kind of performance, but with more explicit references to music.

In 'motsart: kassatsiia I' ('mozart: cassation I'), Aigi uses musical clues to teach a reader how to comprehend the poem's horizontally sequenced words, each of which (and they are mostly nouns) rings out like a single note in a pattern of rhythmic repetition and sound echoing. The words constitute an extended and evolving musical phrase. That propelled forward movement, one word coming after the next as if without pause, challenges one of poetry's defining traits, the use of an unjustified right margin, but it does not present the challenge, as otherwise is more common, by means of a prose paragraph (as was seen in Kaminsky's prose text on Brodskii) — there is no syntax to organize a story here, and the impulse toward narrative, if present, is minimal. But we are not without resources to imagine such a story: the implied poetic world takes that music out into the natural environment, where twigs and straw, jasmine and rose are metonymically linked, as are references to the divinity and the Mother of God, or to surgery and a razor's edge. The poem's work seems restorative, a response to bodily harm that invokes both spiritual salvation and the calming embrace of nature. The poem is mysterious, in other words, but not illegible, and in its unusual presentation on the page, it pushes our thinking about poetry but not so far that we cannot follow it onto this new terrain.

To suggest that such a poem is potentially canonical is to point toward a venerable tradition of verbal and visual innovation. The brick-like arrangement of these lines is perhaps the opposite of Maiakovskii's 'stairstep' poems, which sprawl over the page, and most of Aigi's poems in fact take up that airier presentation, with the white spaces between and around the lines expanded in ways that seem visually to embody the silences often mentioned in the texts. The point of Aigi's experimentation with visual form, as for his invocations of musical performance, is to lead readers out of the norms of metered, rhymed verse, and away from predictable stanzaic arrangements, toward new possibilities that are now found in the work of dozens of important contemporary Russian poets. Aigi is a touchstone for many of them — Natal'ia Azarova, Anna Al'chuk, for example.[21] Poets whose work looks completely different have, in their reviews of his work or in their responses to his death in 2006, argued that he figures prominently in any plausible picture of contemporary Russian poetry.[22] These critics and poets are coming around to a view that perhaps more readers within Russia will share, but it has been a long process. I am glad of the shift, but I persist in believing that we cannot use readers' acceptance of a poet's work as a required first step for canonisation.

Other models of critical review, including widespread translation and an international audience, are indispensable as we assess the norms and structures of contemporary canonisation. I hesitate to add a further reason that we must look beyond Russian readership, but perhaps it has to be said that critics have noted repeatedly that readership of poetry in general has diminished within Russia.[23] I am not a fan of the droopy assessments of the state of contemporary poetry that often

---

21 See Anna Al'chuk, *Sobranie stikhotvorenii*, edited by Natal'ia Azarova and M. K. Ryklin (Moscow: NLO, 2011); Natal'ia Azarova, *Solo ravenstva: Stikhotvoreniia* (Moscow: NLO, 2011).

22 To cite two examples, see Stanislav L'vovskii, 'Gennadiiu Aigi: Ob"iasnenie v liubvi', *Vozdukh*, 1 (2006), 6–7; Ol'ga Sedakova, 'Aigi: Ot'ezd', *Novoe literaturnoe obozrenie*, 79 (2006), 200–04.

23 See for example Igor' Shaitanov, 'Poet v Rossii', *Arion*, 2 (1998); Al'chuk, *Sobranie stikhotvorenii*; Azarova, *Solo ravenstva*; 'Russkaia poeziia v kontse veka: Neoarkhaisty i neonavotory', *Znamia*, 1 (2001), http://magazines.russ.ru/znamia/2001/1/kritika.html. For a radically different assessment of current poetry, see Dmitrii Kuz'min, 'Russkaia poeziia v nachale XXI veka', *Rets*, 48 (2008), http://www.litkarta.ru/dossier/kuzmin-review; Il'ia Kukulin, 'Aktual'nyi russkii poet kak voskresshie Alenushka i Ivanushka', *Novoe literaturnoe obozrenie*, 53 (2002), 273–97.

accompanies such announcements, nor of their high-handed dismissal of the 'masses'; there are several camps within contemporary poetry, and these sad prognostications often come from traditionalists, who also disparage much of what is published. But these comments alert us to the problem of actually knowing who is in the audience as well as whether it is numerous. It becomes all the more important that we think broadly about the mechanisms of canon-formation. Institutions like prizes, translations, comments on blogs, Facebook posts, re-tweeting, university study in and beyond Russia's borders, and inclusion in anthologies can all be useful signals of who is finding what kind of readership, and whose voice is heard by those who listen in a range of educated contexts.

Visual Poetry

Let me return to the questions of visual format. Consider a poem by Aigi that presents itself on the page as a visual transcription of a performance:

Без названия

ярче сердца любого единого дерева

и:

(Тихие места — опоры наивысшей силы пения. Она отменяет там слышимость, не выдержав себя. Места не-мысли, — если понято «нет»).[24]
1964

---

[24] Gennadii Aigi, *Razgovor na rasstoianii: Stat'i, esse, besedy, stikhi* (St Petersburg: Limbus Press, 2001), p. 32. Reproduced with permission.

Untitled

brighter than the heart of any single tree

and:

(Quiet places — are the strongest fulcrum for song. It cancels all that is heard, unable to restrain itself. Places of non-thought — if «no» can be understood)[25]

These red squares 'quote' the artwork of Kasimir Malevich (1879–1935), not least his 'Red Square' (1915). In Malevich's painting, the red square is not in fact perfectly square, and its slight misalignment suggests the dynamism found in his other Suprematist works. Aigi reproduces the effort of balancing with his two squares not visually aligned with each other or with the written text. The careful placement of the two red squares, their diminishing size, and the intermittent verbal text seize our attention as intensely as Malevich's painting. Malevich's geometrical shapes, as Camilla Gray aptly put it, offer a 'sensation of infinity', of 'a new space in which there is no human measure'.[26] Aigi seeks the contemplation of the infinite but also the idea of a person engaged in that act of contemplation, even in poems like this one which do not represent the person in any direct way. Instead it presents human activities, abstract capacities of the senses, and negations whose effects inevitably evoke the very thing negated ('slyshimost'' (sound's capacity to be heard); 'mysl'' (thought)). Like Malevich, Aigi challenges notions of representation in art, but he also explores the relationships among sensory perception, the natural world, and thought.

---

25 See also the version in *Into the Snow*, tr. Valentine, p. 16.
26 Camilla Gray, *The Russian Experiment in Art, 1863–1922* (New York: H. N. Abrams, 1971), p. 166.

To include such texts in the corpus of contemporary poetry is to return to our first question, about language, as if from a different direction. We ask now not about national languages, but about written language itself. What of texts that refuse to limit themselves to referential language, to the denotative work of signs with semantic value? Aigi's red square requires us to think about referential, verbal signs as part of a larger process of symbol-making. This is a tremendously productive move, one that resonates even with poets who would seem to be emphatically, insistently verbal, like Eremin. He has poems that incorporate chemical formulae, for instance, and hieroglyphics.[27] Such poems, I would argue, should change one's belief that Eremin, or any other poet, lives by and for the dictionary.[28]

Allowing for the importance of visual poetry would also draw our attention to the book art of Elizaveta Mnatsakanova (b. 1922). Her creation of hand-lettered artist books alongside type-faced books seems very much in the Russian futurist tradition. But some design and book-creation elements press in other directions, for instance her use of decorative calligraphy, the large body of work in pastels that exists alongside her book art, her reliance on music as a principle of rhythmic organisation and genre designation, and the incorporation of other languages, sometimes in quite large bits. Mnatsakanova's body of work is like that of no other living poet, in other words; here, there is no way around the ambiguous, intense attitude toward the word and toward language's sounds in a context filled with shapes, colours, textures, and unnerving rhythmic patterns.

Consider one example from her work, a page from the poem 'Das Hohelied'. The typed text represents one page in 'Das Hohelied', which itself is one part of the book-length poem *Das Buch Sabeth* (1988).[29]

---

27   See, for example, the chemical formula in 'Edva l' ne samyi dostoslavnyi' (1972) in Mikhail Eremin, *Stikhotvoreniia, Kniga 2* (St Petersburg: Pushkinskii fond, 2002), p. 8.

28   An antecedent for such sweeping gestures of meaning-making is again to be found within the Russian tradition, for example in the writings of the OBERIU. Daniil Kharms's famous window-shape comes to mind as one such model. And elsewhere in the futurist corpus we would find the thematisation of this kind of deciphering work. An excellent source on this work is Gerald Janecek, *The Look of Russian Literature: Avant-garde Visual Experiments, 1900–1930* (Princeton: Princeton University Press, 1984).

29   Elisabeth Netzkowa, *Das Buch Sabeth* (Vienna: [n. pub.], 1988), p. 151. Mnatsakanova, as here, often publishes as 'Netzkowa', a name she took when she moved to Vienna.

Fig. 13.1 Elisabeth Netzkowa (Mnatsakanjan). *Das Buch Sabeth,* first page of poem No. 1 in Part 5, *Pesn' pesnei. Das Hohelied,* p. 129. © and courtesy Elizaveta Mnatsakanova, all rights reserved.

The words and pieces of words in this one-page text are repeated and rearranged on other pages of the poem. The semantics overall are also consistent: love endures, in the face of loss, separation, even death.[30] In everything she writes, Mnatsakanova takes words apart, recombines their elements, and puts syllables next to each other based on sound

---

30 For a fuller reading of these themes in Mnatsakanova's work, see Stephanie Sandler, 'Visual Poetry after Modernism: Elizaveta Mnatsakanova', *Slavic Review,* 67 (2008), 610–41.

rather than semantics, all the while advancing a meaningful if elliptical narrative about loyalty and loss.

These lines are spread across and diagonally down the page in a harmonious, intriguing way, but what really qualifies Mnatsakanova's work as visual poetry is the way she creates ancillary, accompanying artistic material. Here is a hand-written version of some elements of this typed text, a reordered sequence where the theme of mortality is prominent.

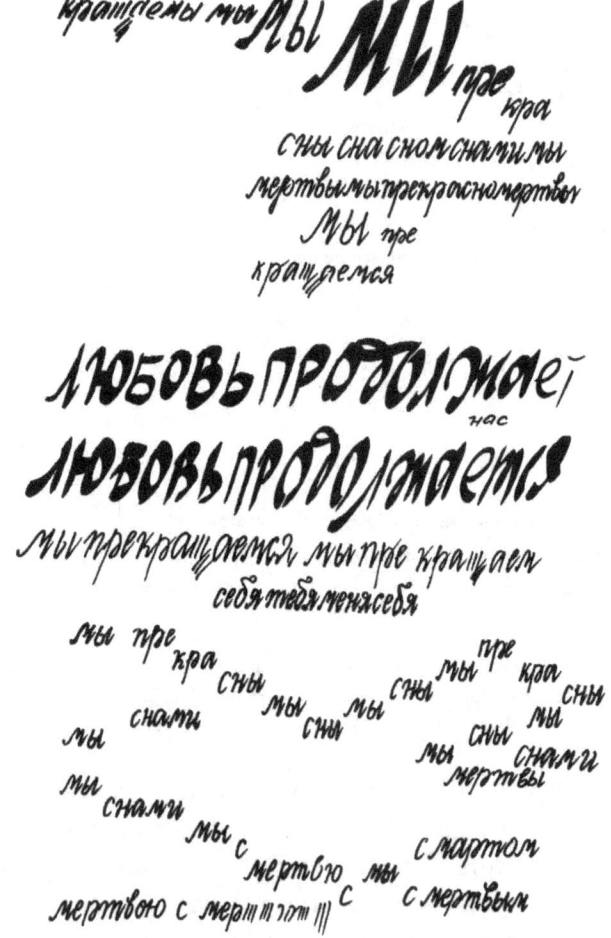

Fig. 13.2 Elisabeth Netzkowa (Mnatsakanjan), *Das Buch Sabeth, VI. Anhang: Bilder zum Finale (Das Hohelied)*, unpaginated image. © and courtesy Elizaveta Mnatsakanova, all rights reserved.

As always in Mnatsakanova's work, pronouns play across the lines. Throughout 'Das Hohelied', the speaker and an addressee, 'I' ('ia') and 'you' ('ty'), sometimes join as 'we' ('my') and sometimes are painfully kept apart. Multiple case declensions appear, implicitly creating little dramas where speaker and addressee have fleeting powers of agency only to be turned into the object or means of some unnamed action.

The last line in this calligraphic text abandons semantics to let the letters break apart into the curves and lines that make alphabets possible. Just as Mnatsakanova creates a kind of centrifugal force within words to split morphological elements into spaced out or recombined syllables, so she looks at the letter that can denote the phoneme 't' or 'sh' and strips it down to a vertical line or two, a marker of echoing sound that has only its own visual artistry to recommend it. Elsewhere, she renders letters as lines or curves even more freely, from which we may conclude that she wants her readers to see the visual forms of letters and words as aesthetic artefacts, in the same way that she wants us to hear the sounds of poetic speech as a complex form of music.[31]

In drawing the world of music into her visual poetry, Mnatsakanova returns us to questions of language, source material, and the boundaries around poetic creative work. Mnatsakanova stands as a superb example of poetic creativity pushing against those boundaries, and as richly as she mixes the discourses of the visual and musical arts, so she confidently crosses boundaries of national languages, playing freely with long insertions of Latin, German, and Italian into her poems. (The German title of the poem discussed here is one such resonant example.) To foreground the linguistic elements of her work is not to diminish its value as visual poetry, but rather to indicate how the questions addressed here are interconnected and mutually reinforcing.

Stories, Not Poems

What, then, does it mean for our notion of poetry that elements of other aesthetic modes have successfully infiltrated poetic production? (The example I will pursue here is prose, but similar questions could be posed about drama and film, and in effect I have been asking this question

---

31 See Gerald Janecek, 'Paronomastic and Musical Techniques in Mnacakanova's Rekviem', *Slavic and East European Journal*, 31 (1987), 202–19.

about the visual arts in the previous section.) To ask such a question is to go to the very heart of our assumptions about canon formation. We have a sense of the poetic function as the crucial element in Russian poetry, and it is worth considering whether this is a good thing.[32] That belief sometimes masquerades as a preference for regular meter, stanzaic patterns, and rhyme. To the extent that Brodskii is the most canonised contemporary poet, in fact, he represents the view of poetry as the supreme form of artistic expression (expressed, for instance, in his frequent claim that poets serve the language, rather than the other way around).[33]

Several significant poets have challenged the primacy of the poetic function in poetry in the last several decades. Some, like Mariia Stepanova, do so even as they demonstrate aesthetic virtuosity, but there are now many superb poems that are aesthetically rich but also chatty and discursive, as if their true motive is the revelation of plot. The work of L'vovskii, discussed above for its fascination with gestures of translation, is one such example, although my focus will be on the work of Elena Fanailova, Fedor Svarovskii and, very briefly, Stepanova.[34] These poets all tell stories. How new or canon-defying is this trend? Narrative poetry is a long-standing and admired form, well-developed in the ballads of Vasilii Zhukovskii, the southern poems of Pushkin, and the long poems of Nikolai Nekrasov. It is that tradition that Stepanova develops, following variants of ballad form, for instance, in her *Pesni severnykh iuzhan* (*Songs of Northern Southerners*, 1999), with its ternary meters and compelling stanzas.[35] Where she deviates, perhaps, is in her

---

32 The 'poetic function' is Jakobson's term, discussed most succinctly as the defining feature of poetry in 'What is Poetry?' in Roman Jakobson, *Language in Literature*, edited by Krystyna Pomorska and Stephen Rudy (Cambridge, MA: Harvard University Press, 1987), pp. 368–78.

33 See, for example, 'The Condition We Call Exile' in Joseph Brodsky, *On Grief and Reason: Essays* (New York: Farrar, Straus & Giroux, 1995), p. 33.

34 Also pertinent is the glorious long poem 'Gnedich' by Mariia Rybakova, which won, in the prose category, the 2011 Andrei Belyi Prize. See Mariia Rybakova, *Gnedich: Roman* (Moscow: Vremia, 2011).

35 Mariia Stepanova, *Pesni severnykh iuzhan: 20 sonetov k M* (Moscow and Tver': Argo-Risk/Kolonna, 2001). Stepanova plays at the boundaries of strict poetic form and narrative prose: compare the title of another whose text is poetic, *Proza Ivana Sidorova* (Moscow: Novoe izdatel'stvo, 2008).

reliance on supernatural, particularly vampiric, apparitions, although even that has its source in the Romantic ballad tradition to some extent.

The poetry of Svarovskii takes us further away from such norms, however, and as a result we have fewer ideas how to approach it. With Stepanova, in other words, we can fall back on our ideas of rhyme and ballad form as a starting point, but with Svarovskii, there is no obvious formal way in. He practices free verse, and has an acute ear for conversational rhythms and contemporary lexicon. Both these poets are associated with what has been called a 'new form of epic' ('novyi epos').[36] The supernatural is present in Svarovskii's work as a fascination with science fiction, particularly with robots and time travel. His book *Vse khotiat byt' robotami* (*Everyone Wants to Be a Robot*, 2007) abounds in tales of intergalactic wars and doomed machinery. Like Stepanova's ballads, his poems feature a powerful psychological element, and there is a spiritual dimension as well. Angels circle around dying men and robots as both 'die'. (In Stepanova's work, the aura of magic also seems to embrace ordinary objects, as Anna Glazova has noticed.)[37] Svarovskii's depictions of life on the moon or wars fought decades into the future are rife with the strong emotions of loneliness and fear. Anxieties about what it means to be human can be projected onto cyborgs and machines, or onto humans whose bodies have absorbed mechanical prostheses. All are then pressed into contemplation of their evolving status at the boundaries of animacy and agency (in the poem from which Svarovskii's volume takes its name, for instance).[38]

In the poem 'Dva robota plyli' ('Two robots were swimming'), Svarovskii goes further in the direction of exploring how robots may be treated as persons.[39] This work may be theorised and discussed in multiple ways — by Barbara Johnson, on persons and things; Eric Santner, on stranded objects; Daniel Tiffany, on toys as medium; and Victoria Nelson, on the secret life of puppets and other inanimate,

---

36 On which, see Il'ia Kukulin, 'Ot Svarovskogo k Zhukovskomu i obratno: O tom, kak metod issledovaniia konstruiruet literaturnyi kanon', *Novoe Literaturnoe Obozrenie*, 89 (2008), 228–40.

37 See 'Otzyvy', *Vozdukh*, 4 (2008), 22–23.

38 Fedor Svarovskii, *Vse khotiat byt' robotami* (Moscow: Argo-Risk, 2007), pp. 5–7.

39 *Ibid.*, pp. 42–44.

person-like entities.[40] But Svarovskii's profound spirituality, felt in this first collection but which really emerges into the foreground in his next book, *Puteshestvenniki vo vremeni* (*Time-Travellers*, 2009), disrupts many of the premises of these post-modernist readings. For those theorists, subjectivity is always already under suspicion, and our turn to puppets or dolls reveals a desire for our own impossible reanimation in the face of the fictions of legitimation and authority with which we must live. Svarovskii recovers personhood through faith, we might say, and his faith means he never imagines personhood as lost in the first place. The act of recovery, and the real brilliance of his writing, is in the language, in the infiltration of the speech and rhythms of daily life, in the plaintive questions and ironic self-reflections that pepper his acts of storytelling and self-expression. In that sense, he is recovering the poetic function, but toward ends that take poetry toward previously unimagined stories of self and soul.

Even more than is the case with Svarovskii, the long poems of Fanailova conventionally fulfil the requirements of prose — development and disclosure of character gradually over the course of a text, use of language to replicate a character's way of thinking or speaking, suggestion of plotlines that sketch in quickly an idea of contemporary public and private life. I want to pursue this account of Fanailova's longer poems in order to argue that however we canonise contemporary poetry, we must make room for work that achieves many of its goals by means normally associated with prose, not poetry.

Fanailova, Moscow journalist and outspoken political activist, has written narrative poems exposing flesh-and-blood people's stories of love, loss, sex, politics, commerce, and travel in a vividly set post-Soviet world of daily life. Fanailova is more scandalous than Svarovskii, readier to play against the expectations of how poets represent their own lives in their work. Svarovskii and Stepanova are credited with creating the 'Novyi epos' ('New form of epic') because they distanced themselves from lyric poetry, but Fanailova takes the further step of

---

40 Barbara Johnson, *Persons and Things* (Cambridge, MA: Harvard University Press, 2008); Eric L. Santner, *Stranded Objects: Mourning, Memory, and Film in Postwar Germany* (Ithaca: Cornell University Press, 1990); Daniel Newton Tiffany, *Toy Medium: Materialism and Modern Lyric* (Berkeley: University of California Press, 2000); Victoria Nelson, *The Secret Life of Puppets* (Cambridge, MA: Harvard University Press, 2001).

compromising lyric poetry itself. She creates not the fanciful names of Svarovskii's robots and not the folklore-inspired mythical creatures of Stepanova's ballads (although she sometimes turns to folklore, with memorable results).[41] Instead, she gives us a strong admixture of seemingly personal experiences, and multiple characters named, as she herself is, Lena.[42] Ironically gazing out at the desire of readers to know the inner experiences of the poet, particularly to know the woman poet whose amorous adventures are imagined to supply immensely rich poetic material, she parades a dizzying series of possibilities. In the long poem 'Lena i liudi' ('Lena and the People', 2008), a night-store clerk named Lena reads the work of a poet also named Lena; the poet offers tired self-reflections on how her life has brought her to this moment, but also reflections on lazy publishers, and the strangely revolting wish to be liked by one's readers.[43] In the next poem in the series, 'Lena i Lena' ('Lena and Lena', 2010), the working life of a poet is less visible, replaced by sexual adventures, travel, illness, and friendship. Here, the second Lena is a Slavist, the intellectual opposite of the uncomprehending night clerk from the earlier poem. 'Lena i Lena' fantasises about wild sex but also about the connections of friendship with a reader who 'gets' it.[44]

The work of canonisation in Russian poetry in the first decades of the twenty-first century particularly requires us to expand beyond our criterion of density of aesthetic features, or rich rhetorical experimentation. Like Svarovskii, Fanailova unfolds a performance of language creation that is organised by the dynamic of the story. In her case, the rhythms and diction are not so much those of speech and dialogue as of interior monologue, which is entirely appropriate given her deep engagement with lyric poetry. But this is a kind of performance, attested by her readings (there is a CD with *Russkaia versiia*, for instance, putting the poet's voice into the ears of anyone who has that book; and

---

41 See for example, 'Lesnoi tsar'' in Elena Fanailova, *Lena i liudi* (Moscow: Novoe izdatel'stvo, 2011), pp. 12–13.
42 The narrative impulse is powerfully felt in other ways in the poems of *Russkaia versiia*. See Elena Fanailova, *Russkaia versiia* (Moscow: Zapasnyi vykhod, 2005), pp. 8–9, pp. 68–83.
43 See Fanailova, *Lena i liudi*, pp. 68–73. For a translation, see 'Lena, or the Poet and the People', *Aufgabe* (2009), pp. 13–18.
44 Elena Fanailova, 'Lena i Lena', *Zerkalo* (2011), 35–36, http://magazines.russ.ru/zerkalo/2010/35/4fa.html. For a translation, see Elena Fanailova and Stephanie Sandler, 'Lena and Lena', *Jacket2* (2013), https://jacket2.org/article/lena-and-lena

as with nearly all contemporary poets, there are multiple recordings of her readings up on YouTube).

Performing the Self

The mention of Fanailova as a performer of her poetry raises the final question I want to pose to theories of canonisation, and that has to do with performance and visual self-representation. The proliferation of live readings in multiple venues across the globe, and more important, the availability of recorded performances in libraries and on the internet, have guaranteed that our experience of contemporary poetry need not be limited to the printed page. It is now the exception when we cannot get access to the sound of the poet's voice or the sight of the person reading from the work. All performances also add an element of instability our apprehensions of a poetic text, since performances vary, contributing nuances and often quite dramatic changes to the printed text, and layering it with acts of improvisation.[45]

Consider the work of Dmitrii Prigov, master performer, who, even without the performances I will treat, would pose an unusual challenge to the work of canonisation. I note the title of a massive volume of essays about Prigov, *Nekanonicheskii klassik* (*Uncanonical Classic*), which appeared in 2010.[46] How can a writer be a classic but be outside the canon? The editors of that volume compared praise of Prigov as the most talented and best poet of the post-Soviet period to Stalin's similarly worded praise of Maiakovskii, but they also claimed for him a major role in shaping that culture. To read Prigov has been mostly to theorise him: scholars have established both his own deep knowledge of social theories and philosophy, and typically placed him in the contexts of postmodernism or conceptualism.[47]

---

45 A particularly vivid instance of such a changed and changing text is Polina Barskova's performance of her 2011 poem 'Bitva', https://www.youtube.com/watch?v=gtcv3jnUqHw

46 *Nekanonicheskii klassik: Dmitrii Aleksandrovich Prigov*, edited by E. Dobrenko *et al.* (Moscow: NLO, 2010). Compare the argument of Maria Maiofis in 'Prigov i Derzhavin: Poet posle prizhiznennoi kanonizatsii', in this volume, pp. 281–304.

47 A very good example of this approach is Jacob Edmond, *A Common Strangeness*, pp. 125–63. Edmond's chapter is entitled 'Dmitri Prigov and Cross-Cultural Conceptualism'.

A different way to approach the poet, even though his voluminous output works against such close reading, is to work outward from the texts and images, rather than beginning with theoretical paradigms. To begin in any one place is of course to risk distorting that text's or object's position with regard to the whole, but Prigov left some aesthetic objects that might safely allow us to generalise productively. I have in mind his strange representations of persons, in the series 'Liki' ('Faces') and especially 'Portrety' ('Portraits'), also known as 'Bestiarii' ('The Bestiary').[48] I also urge our attention to the images as a way to open out our idea of performance — Prigov was not just a master in chanting and intoning his texts, he was a master of visual representation and performed selfhood. These two series, 'Liki' and 'Portrety' have the potential to alter our reading of Prigov's poetics — suggesting, for example, that he did not abandon the notion of personhood in his work, as most intensely postmodernist readings would argue, but rather transformed it into a species of monstrosity. If we can learn to read this aspect of his poetry more astutely, we get the benefit not only of a better understanding of Prigov's works, but also of the interactions between performed selfhood and the formation of the poetic canon.

The images at hand are typical of his work in important ways, then. Prigov's creative output, across both poetic and prose writings and across the visual arts, emerged in series.[49] The structural and format similarity within the series is not unique to him among conceptualists, although the massive quantity of items in any given series is perhaps distinctive. In the 'Bestiary', for example, the key elements of foliage, lettering, goblet, egg, sphere, hands, proboscis, avian features on a furry body, and richly textured shading are nearly always present in each image. Genitalia, breasts, ears, and orifices for nourishment are often shown. The facial expression is almost uniformly sad, pensive, with eyes staring off into a distance or vaguely askew. The main Prigov web

---

48   The name 'Portrety' appears as the category, most likely, at http://www.prigov. ru. The name 'Bestiarii' is used at http://www.prigov.org, the English-language website, and in *Grazhdane! Ne zabyvaites' pozhaluista*, catalogue from the exhibit at the Moscow Museum of Contemporary Art, 2008, curated by Ekaterina Degot' (Moscow: Izdatel'skaia programma Moskovskogo muzeia sovremennogo iskusstva, 2008), [n.p.].

49   See Dzheral'd Ianechek, 'Seriinost' v tvorchestve D. A. Prigova', in *Nekanonicheskii klassik*, pp. 501–12.

site has many of these images (at one point there were eighty-two of them; there are twenty as of this writing), an astonishingly productive instance of the poet spinning multiple instances of a glowing, effective key idea. So, what we know to say about Prigov is to comment on the amount of work, the manic multiplication of images.

Yet (and this is not unlike the work of Fanailova), these images also start to create the psychologies and typologies of contemporary personhood in late Soviet and post-Soviet Russia. They merge with Prigov's photographic, video, and dramatic projects of self-portraiture.[50] These acts of self-representation are also somewhat monstrous, including strange markers (like the big ears) of a poet who refuses to take himself seriously. The pacifier in the mouth of the faces represented in the 'Liki' series has a similar function, like the teddy bear that renders the poet childlike in the series entitled 'Bez nazvaniia' ('Untitled').[51] There is even a self-portrait in the 'Bestiary' series, which is to say that the poet chose to create as grotesque a version of himself as he had done with figures as different as Gertrude Stein, fellow conceptualist Grisha Bruskin, and Nikolai Gogol'. The self-portrait as beast was chosen in fact as the cover image of Prigov's and Sergei Shapoval's book of conversations and prose, *Portretnaia galereia D. A. P.*[52]

Prigov's self-representations let me end with the idea of the poet as monster, not just the kind of monster made by Mary Shelley's scientist Victor Frankenstein, but one that all makers of art risk becoming. This is a decidedly post-Romantic and perhaps also post-Soviet way of rereading the figure of the poet. It reflects back to readers what they have been suspected of projecting onto the poet. And it rejects that most cherished of all Russian cultural notions, the poet as hieratic figure, as repository for all otherwise lost cultural achievements and memories, as testimony to dangerous truths. Not all contemporary poets would reject that beloved myth, indeed some of the very best contemporary poets still embody it — among those mentioned here, poets who are challenging the rules of the canon in other ways, Mnatsakanova and

---

50 See, for example, 'Rekonstruktsiia po kasatel'noi ili sem'ia navsegda', a series of black-draped figures, some with huge, added ears, http://prigov.ru/action/foto.php
51 All of the series mentioned can be found at http://prigov.ru
52 Dmitrii Prigov and Sergei Shapoval, *Portretnaia galereia D. A. P.* (Moscow: NLO, 2003).

Aigi, Eremin and Stepanova come to mind; among those I have not been able to include, I would mention Sedakova, Elena Shvarts, and many others. Each of these poets will, if one wants to risk predictions, be seen as canonical when time has advanced enough for us to cast retrospective glances back at this moment. But even now, we can see how some poets are pressing us to rethink what we mean by the canon and how it is formed. My goal here has been to look at those who are at the boundaries, who offer new ways to see the changing totality that is Russian poetry today.

Bibliography

[N.a.], 'A Selected Vacation Reading List', *New York Times*, 2 June 1974, F31–37.

—, *Aleksandr Blok v illiustratsiiakh I. Glazunova*, a set of 16 postcards (Moscow: Iskusstvo, 1982).

—, 'An Underworld Classic: R. W. B. Lewis, *Dante, A Penguin Life: The Poet's Dante*, ed. by Peter Hawkins and Rachel Jacoff; *The Inferno*, translated by Robert and Jean Hollander', *The Economist*, 17 February 2001.

—, 'Angliiskaia metafizicheskaia poeziia', *Voprosy literatury*, 4 (2004), 78–79.

—, 'Bank Slavianskii, Poety: Mandel'shtam, Pasternak, Blok, Pushkin', http://www.sostav.ru/columns/mmfr20/nominantCard.php?IDNominant=125

—, 'Blok Aleksandr Aleksandrovich', Telekanal 'Rossiia' (2008), http://top50.nameofrussia.ru/person.html?id=106

—, 'Bunin Ivan Alekseevich', Telekanal 'Rossiia' (2008), http://top50.nameofrussia.ru/person.html?id=62

—, 'Bunin, Ivan Alekseevich', Wikipedia, http://ru.wikipedia.org/wiki/Бунин,_Иван_Алексеевич

—, 'Commentary', *Times Literary Supplement*, 15 February 1974.

—, 'Editorial', *PN Review*, 63 (September–October 1988).

—, 'Editorial', *PN Review*, 74 (July–August 1990).

—, 'Esenin Sergei Aleksandrovich', Telekanal 'Rossiia' (2008), http://top50.nameofrussia.ru/person.html?id=68

—, 'Gospodin iz Efremova', *Literaturnaia gazeta*, 42–43 (27 October 2010), http://www.lgz.ru/article/N42-43--6297---2010-10-27-/Gospodin-iz-Efremova14296/

—, 'Imia Rossiia [*sic*]. Istoricheskii vybor 2008', Telekanal 'Rossiia' (2008), http://top50.nameofrussia.ru

—, 'Interv'iu s Elenoi Shvarts', in Valentina Polukhina, ed., *Iosif Brodskii glazami sovremennikov: kniga pervaia (1987–1992)* (St Petersburg: Zvezda, 2006), pp. 226–46.

—, 'Joseph Brodsky's Flat Opens as Museum in St Petersburg', *Russian Art + Culture*, 24 May 2015, http://www.russianartandculture.com/news-joseph-brodskys-flat-opens-as-museum-in-saint-petersburg

—, 'Kak pravil'no delat' uroki', *Izvestiia*, 16 February 2006, http://izvestia.ru/news/311276

—, 'Khudozhniki-Buninu: Raboty sovremennykh khodozhnikov', Muzei Rossii (2011), http://www.museum.ru/N41906

—, *Kodifikator elementov soderzhaniia i trebovanii k urovniu podgotovki vypusknikov obshcheobrazovatel'nykh uchrezhdenii dlia edinogo gosudarstvennogo ekzamena 2010 goda po literature* (Moscow: Federal'nyi institut pedagogicheskikh izmerenii, 2010).

—, 'Otkrylas' vystavka, posviashchennaia 140-letiiu so dnia rozhdeniia Ivana Bunina', *Rossiiskaia gazeta* (22 October 2010), http://www.rg.ru/2010/10/22/bunin-anons.html

—, 'Poets at Peace', http://www.ikewrites.com/tag/jack-kerouac

—, 'Primernaia programma srednego (polnogo) obshchego obrazovaniia po literature, bazovyi uroven'', http://www.edu.doal.ru/predm/laws7/prog_sb_lit.doc

—, *Programmy srednei obshcheobrazovatel'noi shkoly. Literatura 4–10 klassy* (Moscow: Prosveshchenie, 1983).

—, *Programmy vos'miletnei i srednei shkoly na 1969/70 uchebnyi god. Russkii iazyk i literatura* (Moscow: Ministerstvo prosveshcheniia RSFSR, 1969).

—, 'Rezul'taty Internet golosovaniia', Telekanal 'Rossiia' (2008), http://www.nameofrussia.ru/rating.html

—, 'Ob obiazatel'nom miminume soderzhaniia obrazovatel'nykh programm osnovnoi obshcheobrazovatel'noi shkoly. Pis'mo. Ministerstvo obshchego i professional'nogo obrazovaniia RF', 18 June 1997, N 974/14–12 (D), http://www.innovbusiness.ru/pravo/DocumShow_DocumID_52815.html

—, *Skhemy programmy po literature dlia srednei shkoly. Proekt. Dlia obsuzhdeniia na biuro otdeleniia didaktiki i chastnykh metodik* (Moscow: Akademiia pedagogicheskikh nauk SSSR, 1983).

—, 'Vysotskii Vladimir Semenovich', Telekanal 'Rossiia' (2008), http://top50.nameofrussia.ru/person.html?id=63

—, 'Slutskii, Boris Abramovich', http://ru.wikipedia.org/wiki/Слуцкий_Борис_Абрамович

—, Solovyov, Dmitry, 'Poet of Post-Stalin Thaw Voznesensky Dies at 77', Reuters Online, 1 June 2010, http://in.reuters.com/article/2010/06/01/idINIndia-48968820100601

—, 'Srednego (polnogo) obshchego obrazovaniia. Prikaz. Ministerstvo obrazovaniia RF', 30 June 1999, No. 56 (NTsPI), http://www.businesspravo.ru/Docum/DocumShow_DocumID_71939.html

—, 'Standart osnovnogo obshchego obrazovaniia po literature', in 'Dokumenty i materialy deiatel'nosti federal'nogo agenstva po obrazovaniiu za period 2004–2010 (vplot' do ego uprazdneniia na osnovanii Ukaza Prezidenta RF ot 4 marta 2010 goda No. 271)', pp. 86–102.

—, 'The Nobel Prize in Literature 1933: Ivan Bunin', Nobelprize.org [n.d.], http://www.nobelprize.org/nobel_prizes/literature/laureates/1933

—, 'Uglubliaiushchiisia krizis: knigoizdanie Rossii v 2012 godu', Rossiiskaia knizhnaia palata [n.d.], http://www.bookchamber.ru/download/stat/stat_2012.zip

—, 'Unveiling Ceremony for the Monument to Marina Tsvetaeva by Zurab Tsereteli in France', Press service, 18 June 2012, http://en.rah.ru/news/detail.php?ID=24266

—, 'V stolitse vruchili literaturnuiu premiiu imeni Ivana Bunina', Newsru.com, 24 October 2005, http://www.newsru.com/cinema/24oct2005/bunin.html

[no ed.], *A. A. Blok-Andrei Belyi: Perepiska* (Munich: Wilhelm Fink Verlag, 1969).

—, *I. A. Bunin i russkaia literatura XX veka: po materialam mezhdunarodnoi konferentsii, posviashchennoi 125-letiiu so dnia rozhdeniia I. A. Bunina* (Moscow: Nasledie, 1995).

—, '*Posmotrim, kto kogo pereuptriamit...*'. *Nadezhda Iakovlevna Mandel'shtam v pis'makh, vospominaniiakh, svidetel'stvakh* (Moscow: Izdatel'stvo ACT, 2015).

—, *Samizdat. Po materialam konferentsii '30 let nezavisimoi pechati: 1950–80 gody'* (St Petersburg: NITs 'Memorial', 1993).

XIV konferentsiia Rossiiskoi Kommunisticheskoi partii (bol'shevikov): stenograficheskii otchet (Moscow-Leningrad: Gosizdat, 1925).

Adamovich, Georgii, 'Stikham svoim iz znaiu tsenu', in *Poety parizhskoi noty: v Rossiiu vetrom strochki zaneset*, comp. Vadim Kreid (Moscow: Molodaia gvardiia, 2003).

Adorno, Theodore W., *Aesthetic Theory*, ed. by Gretel Adorno and Rolf Tiedemann (London and New York: Continuum, 1997).

Agenosov, Vladimir, *Russkaia literatura XX veka. 11 klass. Chast' I*, 2 vols (Moscow: Drofa, 1996).

—, and Kirill Ankudinov, comp., *Sovremennye russkie poety* (Moscow: Nauchno-prakticheskii tsentr Megatron, 1998).

Aigi, Gennadii, *Razgovor na rasstoianii: Stat'i, esse, besedy, stikhi* (St Petersburg: Limbus Press, 2001).

—, *Sobranie sochinenii v semi tomakh*, 7 vols (Moscow: Gileia, 2009).

Aizenberg, Mikhail, 'In Lieu of an Introduction', *Russian Studies in Literature*, 4 (1993), 8–24, https://doi.org/10.2753/rsl1061-197529048

—, 'Literatura za odnim stolom: O poetakh "filologicheskoi shkoly"', *Novaia kamera khraneniia* (2008), http://www.litkarta.ru/dossier/aizenberg-o-filologicheskoi-shkole/dossier_940

Akhmatova, Anna, *Sochineniia*, 2 vols (Moscow: Khudozhestvennaia literatura, 1986).

—, *Sochineniia*, ed. by M. M. Kralin, 2 vols (Moscow: Pravda, 1990).

—, *The Complete Poems of Anna Akhmatova*, ed. by Roberta Reeder, trans. by Judith Hemschemeyer, 2 vols (Somerville, MA: Zephyr Press, 1990).

—, *Sochineniia*, 2 vols, ed. by M. M. Kralin (Moscow: Tsitadel', 1997).

—, *The Complete Poems of Anna Akhmatova*, ed. by Roberta Reeder, trans. by Judith Hemschemeyer, updated and expanded ed. (Boston: Zephyr Press, 1997).

—, *Sobranie sochinenii*, 6 vols (Moscow: Ellis Lak, 1998).

Akhmet'ev, Ivan, *et al.*, eds, *Russkie stikhi 1950–2000 godov: antologiia (pervoe priblizhenie)*, 2 vols (Moscow: Letnii sad, 2010).

Akimov, Boris, comp., *Poeziia Serebrianogo veka* (Moscow: Eksmo, 2007).

Al'chuk, Anna, *Sobranie stikhotvorenii*, ed. by Natal'ia Azarova and M. K. Ryklin (Moscow: NLO, 2011).

Alekseev, Aleksandr, '350 tysiach rublei za talant: Ezhegodnaia Buninskaia premiia smenila format', *Rossiiskaia gazeta*, 15 April 2008, http://www.rg.ru/2008/04/15/premia.html

Aleshina, Tat'iana, *Peterburgskii al'bom* [CD] (St Petersburg: Studiia 'Aziia-plius', 2003).

Alter, Robert, 'Introduction', in Frank Kermode, *Pleasure and Change: The Aesthetics of Canon* (Oxford: Oxford University Press, 2004), 3–12, https://doi.org/10.1093/acprof:oso/9780195309355.001.0001

Alvarez, A., 'From Russia with Passion', *The Observer*, 9 July 1967.

Andrushchenko, E., *Vlastelin 'chuzhogo': tekstologiia i problema poetiki D. S. Merezhkovskogo* (Moscow: Vodolei, 2012).

Anemone, Tony, 'Aleksei German Junior: Garpastum, 2005', *Kinokultura*, 12 (April 2006), http://www.kinokultura.com/2006/12r-garpastum.shtml

Annenskii, Innokentii, *Stikhotvoreniia i tragedii* (Leningrad: Sovetskii pisatel', 1990).

Anning, Nicholas J., 'The Wolfhound Age', *Times Literary Supplement*, 2 July 1971.

Anninskii, Lev, '"Ia rodilsia v zheleznom obshchestve"', *Druzhba narodov*, 2 (2006), http://magazines.russ.ru/druzhba/2006/2/an16.html

Antologiia poezii Serebrianogo veka: 1890–1940, comp. by Karen Dzhangirov, http://anthology.karendjangirov.com/sereb.html

Arkhangel'skii, Aleksandr, and Vladimir Agenosov, *Metodicheskie rekomendatsii po ispol'zovaniiu uchebnikov 'Russkaia literatura XIX veka' pod redaktsiei A. N. Arkhangel'skogo, 'Russkaia literatura XX veka' pod redaktsiei V. V. Agenosova* (Moscow: Drofa, 2006).

Aristotle, *Poetics*, ch. XXII, trans. by S. H. Butcher, http://classics.mit.edu/Aristotle/poetics.3.3.html

Arland, Marcel, 'Sur un nouveau mal du siècle', *Nouvelle revue française*, 125 (February 1924).

Ar'ev, A. and S. Guan'elli, eds, *Georgii Ivanov, Irina Odoevtseva, Roman Gul': troistvennyi soiuz (Perepiska 1953–1958)* (St Petersburg: Petropolis, 2010).

Asmus, V. F., *Izbrannye filosofskie trudy*, 2 vols (Moscow: Moscow University, 1969).

Astrachan, Anthony, 'Powerful, Beautiful and Incomplete: Book World: The Living Mirror', *The Washington Post*, 29 November 1972.

—, 'Requiem Service for W. H. Auden', *The Washington Post*, 5 October 1973.

Atamonova, E., *et al.*, eds, *I. A. Bunin i russkii mir: materialy Vserossisskoi nauchnoi konferentsii, posviashchennoi 75-letiiu prisuzhdeniia Nobelevskoi premii pisateliu* (Elets: Eletskii gosudarstvennyi universitet im. I. A. Bunina, 2009).

—, N. V. Borisova, A. M. Podoksenov, eds, *I. A. Bunin i XXI vek: materialy mezhdunarodnoi konferentsii, posviashchennoi 140-letiiu so dnia rozhdeniia pisatelia* (Elets: Eletskii gosudarstvennyi universitet im. I. A. Bunina, 2011).

—, ed., *Ivan Bunin: filologicheskii diskurs. Kollektivnaia monografiia k 135-letiiu so dnia rozhdeniia I. A. Bunina* (Elets: Eletskii gosudarstvennyi universitet im. I. A. Bunina, 2005).

Averintsev, Sergei, *et al.*, 'Final "Dvenadtsati" — vzgliad iz 2000 goda', *Znamia*, 11 (2000), 190–206.

A. V., 'Novaia shkola-novye traditsii', *Nezavisimaia gazeta* (13 September 2001).

Avramenko, A., *A. Blok i russkie poety XIX veka* (Moscow: MGU, 1990).

Aygi, Gennady, *Into the Snow: Selected Poems of Genady Aygi*, trans. by Sarah Valentine (Seattle and New York: Wave Books, 2011).

Azadovski, Konstantin, 'Russia's Silver Age in Today's Russia', http://www.pum.umontreal.ca/revues/surfaces/vol9/azadovski.htm

Azarov, Iurii, 'Polnoe sobranie sochinenii Bunina nuzhno podgotovit' k ego 150-letiiu', *Russkii mir*, 22 October 2010, http://www.russkiymir.ru/publications/87865/?sphrase_id=704486

Azarova, Natal'ia, *Solo ravenstva: Stikhotvoreniia* (Moscow: NLO, 2011).

Baimukhametov, Sergei, 'Ekho okaiannykh stoletii', *Literaturnaia gazeta*, 12–18 July 2000.

Baines, Jennifer, 'Mandelstam, Poems', *Slavonic and East European Review*, 57: 3 (1979), 439.

—, 'Clarence Brown, *Mandelstam*', *The Modern Language Review*, 69: 4 (October 1974), 954.

Barannikov, Anatolii, *Russkaia literatura XX veka. Khrestomatiia dllia 11 kl. sr. shk.*, 2 vols (Moscow: Prosveshchenie, 1993).

—, *Russkaia literatura XX veka. 11 klass. Khrestomatiia. Chast' I*, 2 vols (Moscow: Prosveshchenie, 1997).

—, *Russkaia literatura XX veka. 11 klass. Khrestomatiia dlia obshcheobrazovatel'nykh uchrezhdenii*, 2 vols (Moscow: Prosveshchenie, 2000).

Barker, Adele Marie, 'Rereading Russia', in *Consuming Russia: Popular Culture, Sex, And Society Since Gorbachev*, ed. by Adele Marie Barker (Durham and London: Duke University Press, 1999), 3–11.

—, 'The Culture Factory: Theorising the Popular in the Old and New Russia', in *Consuming Russia: Popular Culture, Sex, And Society Since Gorbachev*, ed. by Adele Marie Barker (Durham and London: Duke University Press, 1999), 12–48.

—, and Jehanne Gheith, eds, *A History of Women's Writing in Russia* (Cambridge: Cambridge University Press, 2002), https://doi.org/10.1017/cbo9780511485930

Barkovskaya, Nina, 'Poet and Citizen: Canon Game in Contemporary Russian Poetry', in *Russian Classical Literature Today: The Challenges/Trails of Messianism and Mass Cuture*, ed. by Hristo Manolaked Lyutskanov and Radostin Rusev (Newcastle Upon Tyne: Cambridge Scholars Publishing, 2014), pp. 10–25.

Barskova, Polina, 'Bitva', https://www.youtube.com/watch?v=gtcv3jnUqHw

Barthes, Roland, 'The Death of the Author', in *Authorship: From Plato to the Postmodern*, ed. by S. Burke (Edinburgh: Edinburgh University Press, 1995).

Basinskii, Pavel, 'Eto bylo nedavno…', *Rossiiskaia gazeta*, 26 August 2013, https://rg.ru/2013/08/26/basinsky.html

Basovskaia, Evgeniia, Literatura. Sochineniia. 11 klass. Kniga dlia uchenika i uchitelia (Moscow: Olimp, 1997).

Bayley, John, 'Mandelstam and the Bitch-Pack', *The Listener*, 6 December 1973.

—, 'The Dangerous Poet', *New York Times Book Review*, 4 March 1979.

—, 'Nightingales', *London Review of Books*, 15 April 1982.

Bek, Tat'iana, '"Rasshifruite moi tetradi…"', in *Boris Slutskii: vospominaniia sovremennikov*, comp. by Petr Gorelik (St Petersburg: Zhurnal Neva, 2005), 255–66.

Beketova, M. A., ed., *Pis'ma Aleksandra Bloka k rodnym*, 2 vols (Moscow-Leningrad: Akademiia, 1927–1932).

Bel'chevichen, S. P., *Problema vzaimosviazi kul'tury i religii v filosofii D. S. Merezhkovskogo* (Tver': Izdatel'stvo Tverskogo universiteta, 1999).

Bel'chikov, N. F., ed., *Istoriia russkoi literatury*, 10 vols (Moscow-Leningrad, Akademiia Nauk SSSR, 1941–1956).

Belen'kii, Gennadii, 'Informoprobezhka ili izuchenie?', *Literatura v shkole*, 9 (2003), 26–29.

—, ed., *Literatura. Russkaia klassika (izbrannye stranitsy). Uchebnik-praktikum dlia obshcheobrazovatel'nykh uchrezhdenii* (Moscow: Mnemozina, 1997).

Belinskii, Vissarion, 'Pis'mo N. V. Gogoliu' (1847), in N. V. Gogol', *Polnoe sobranie sochinenii*, 14 vols (Mokva and Leningrad: Izdatel'stvo AN SSSR, 1937–1952), XIV, pp. 500–10.

Bem, Al'fred, 'Russkaia literatura v emigratsii', in *Pis'ma o literature*, ed. by M. Bubenikova and L. Vakhalovskaia (Prague: Euroslavia, 1996).

—, 'Vstupitel'noe slovo na vechere "Skita" 25 aprelia 1933 g.', *Skit. Praga 1922–1940. Antologiia. Biografii. Dokumenty* (Moscow: Russkii put', 2006).

Benjamin, Walter, 'The Work of Art in the Age of Mechanical Reproduction', in *Illuminations*, ed. by H. Arendt, trans. by H. Zohn (New York: Schocken, 1969), 217–51.

Berlin, Isaiah, 'A Great Russian Writer'. Review, *The Prose of Osip Mandelstam*, trans. by Clarence Brown, *New York Review of Books*, 23 December 1965, 1–2.

—, 'Anna Akhmatova: A Memoir', in Akhmatova, Anna, *The Complete Poems of Anna Akhmatova*, ed. by Roberta Reeder, trans. by Judith Hemschemeyer, updated and expanded ed. (Boston: Zephyr Press, 1997), 35–55.

Bethea, David, *Joseph Brodsky and the Creation of Exile* (Princeton: Princeton University Press, 1994), https://doi.org/10.1163/221023997x00285

Beumers, Birgit, *Pop Culture Russia!: Media, Arts, and Lifestyle* (Santa Barbara: ABC-CLIO, 2005).

Bhabha, Homi, *Location of Culture* (London: Routledge, 1994).

Blok, Aleksandr, 'Rossiia i intelligentsiia', *Zolotoe runo*, 1 (1909).

—, 'Dvenadtsat'', *Znamia truda*, 3 March 1918, p. 2.

—, *Sobranie sochinenii*, 8 vols, ed. by V. N. Orlov, A. A. Surkov and K. I. Chukovskii (Moscow-Leningrad: Khudozhestvennaia literatura, 1960–1963).

—, *Polnoe sobranie sochinenii i pisem v 20 tomakh*, ed. by A. N. Grishunin (Moscow: Nauka, 1997–1999).

—, Blok, Alexander, *The Twelve*, trans. by Avil Pyman (Durham, UK: University of Durham Press, 1989).

Bloom, Harold, *The Western Canon: The Books and School of the Ages* (New York: Riverhead Books, 1994; 1995).

Bodin, Per-Arne, *Language, Canonization and Holy Foolishness: Studies in Postsoviet Russian Culture and the Orthodox Tradition* (Stockholm: Stockholm University Press, 2009).

Bogomolov, N. A., 'Andrei Ar'ev. Zhizn' Georgiia Ivanova. Dokumental'noe povestvovanie', *Znamia*, 4 (2010), http://magazines.russ.ru/znamia/2010/4/bo25.html

Boiko, Svetlana, '"Divnyi vybor vsevyshnikh shchedrot...": filologicheskoe samosoznanie sovremennoi poezii', *Voprosy literatury*, 1 (2000), 44–73.

Bolton, Kerry, 'Zyuganov Communists Continue Stalin's Fight Against "Rootless Cosmopolitanism"', *Foreign Policy Journal*, 12 December 2012, http://www.foreignpolicyjournal.com/2012/12/12/zyuganov-communists-continue-stalins-fight-against-rootless-cosmopolitanism/2/

Bondarenko, Vladimir, *Poslednie poety imperii: ocherki literaturnykh sudeb* (Moscow: Molodaia gvardiia, 2005).

Bonfel'd, Moris, 'Moshch' i "nevesomost"', *Voprosy literatury*, 5 (2003), 91–99.

Bonnefoy, Yves, 'On the Translation of Form in Poetry', *World Literature Today*, 53: 3 (1979), 374–79.

Borisova, Natalia, 'Buninskii tsentr', Eletskii gosudarstvennyi universitet im. I. A. Bunina [n.d.], http://www.elsu.ru/news/2899-o-centre-buninskaya-rossiya.html

Bourdieu, Pierre, *Distinction: A Social Critique of the Judgement of Taste*, trans. by Richard Nice (London: Routledge, 1984).

—, *The Field of Cultural Production: Essays on Art and Literature*, ed. by Randal Johnson (Cambridge: Polity Press, 1993).

Bowra, Maurice, 'Poets of Russia', *Times Literary Supplement*, 2 April 1949, 222.

Boym, Svetlana, *Death in Quotation Marks: Cultural Myths of the Modern Poet* (Cambridge, MA and London: Harvard University Press, 1991).

—, *The Future of Nostalgia* (New York: Basic Books, 2001).

Bozhnev, Boris, *Bor'ba za nesushchestvovan'e* (St Petersburg: INAPRESS, 1999).

Braudy, Leo, *The Frenzy of Renown: Fame and Its History* (New York: Vintage Books, 1997).

Braun, Rebecca, 'Fetishising Intellectual Achievement: The Nobel Prize and European Literary Celebrity', *Celebrity Studies*, 2: 3 (2011), 320–34.

Brik, Lili, *Pristrastnye rasskazy* (Moscow: Dekom, 2011).

Brik, O. M., 'Ritm and sintaksis (Materialy k izucheniiu stikhotvornoi rechi)', *Novyi LEF*, 3 (1927), 15–20; 4 (1927), 23–29; 5 (1927), 32–37; 6 (1927) 33–39.

Briusov, Valerii, 'Vtoraia kniga', *Pechat' i revoliutsiia*, 6 (1923).

Brodskii, Iosif, *Sochineniia* (Ekaterinburg: U-Faktoriia, 2002).

Brodsky, Joseph, 'Introduction', in Osip Mandelstam, *Fifty Poems*, trans. by Bernard Meares (New York: Persea Books, 1977).

—, 'The Art of Poetry', *Paris Review*, 24 (1982), 83-126.

—, 'Literature and War: A Symposium', *Times Literary Supplement*, 17 May 1985, 11–12.

—, '"S mirom derzhavnym ia byl lish' rebiacheski sviazan..."', in *Mandelstam Centenary Conference*, ed. by Robin Aizlewood and Diana Myers (Tenafly: Hermitage Publishers, 1994), pp. 9–17.

—, 'The Condition We Call Exile', in *On Grief and Reason* (New York: Farrar, Straus & Giroux, 1995).

—, *On Grief and Reason* (London: Hamish Hamilton, 1996).

—, *Collected Poems in English*, ed. by Ann Kjellberg (New York: Farrar, Straus & Giroux, 2000).

—, 'The Keening Muse', in *Less Than One: Selected Essays*, ed. by Joseph Brodsky (London: Penguin, 2011), pp. 34–52.

Broitman, S. N., *Russkaia lirika XIX-nachala XX veka v svete istoricheskoi poetiki* (Moscow: RGGU, 1997).

Brown, Clarence, *Mandelstam* (Cambridge: Cambridge University Press, 1973).

—, 'Ashes and Crumbs', *Times Literary Supplement*, 7 January 1984, 8.

—, 'Every Slightest Pebble', *London Review of Books*, 25 May 1995, 24, 26–27.

—, and Nadezhda Mandelstam, 'The Nature of the Miracle', *New York Review of Books*, 22 October 1970, 24–27.

Brown, Deming, *Soviet Russian Literature Since Stalin* (Cambridge: Cambridge University Press, 1979).

Brown, Edward, *Russian Literature Since the Revolution* (London: Collier-MacMillan Ltd, 1963; revised ed. 1969).

—, *Russian Literature Since the Revolution* (Cambridge, MA: Harvard University Press, 1969).

Buneev, Rustem, and Ekaterina Buneeva, *Shag za gorizont. Uchebnik-khrestomatiia po literature. 5 klass. Kniga 2*, 2 vols (Moscow: Balass, 1998; 2004).

—, *Istoriia tvoei literatury. Uchebnik-khrestomatiia po literature. 9 klass. Kniga 2*, 2 vols (Moscow: Balass, 2005).

Bunin, Ivan, *Stories and Poems by Ivan Bunin*, trans. by Olga Shartse and Irina Zheleznova (Moscow: Progress, 1979).

—, *Stikhotvoreniia* (Moscow: Khudozhestvennaia literatura, 1985).

—, *Stikhotvoreniia* (Moscow: Molodaia gvardiia, 1990).

—, *Stikhotvoreniia. Perevody* (Moscow: Olma-Press, 1999).

—, *Stikhotvoreniia* (Moscow: Profizdat, 2007).

Burbank, Jane, *Intelligentsia and Revolution: Russian Views of Bolshevism, 1917-1922* (Oxford: Oxford University Press, 1986).

Burliuk, David, Aleksandr Kruchenykh, Vladimir Maiakovskii, Viktor Khlebnikov, 'Poshchechina obshchestvennomu vkusu', http://www.futurism.ru/a-z/manifest/slap.htm

Burukina, A. F., 'Formy avtorskogo prisutstviia v proze A. Bloka', *Gummanitarnye issledovaniia*, 4 (2007), 56–62.

Bykov, Dmitrii, *Sovetskaia literatura: kratkii kurs* (Moscow: Prozaik, 2012).

—, *Sovetskaia literatura: rasshirennyi kurs* (Moscow: Prozaik, 2014).

—, and Mikhail Efremov, 'Dvadtsat' let — ni khrena net', from 'Grazdhanin poet', https://www.youtube.com/watch?v=f6zxSQny4Bg

—, and Mikhail Efremov, 'Grazhdanin poet', onGar, http://ongar.ru/grazhdanin-poet

—, and Mikhail Efremov, 'Grazhdanin poet', https://www.youtube.com/user/GrazhdaninPoet

Carlisle, Olga, *Poets on Street Corners: Portraits of Fifteen Russian Poets* (New York: Random House, 1968).

—, 'Speaking of Books: Anna Akhmatova', *New York Times*, 11 September 1966, section VII, pp. 2, 28, 30.

—, 'Speaking of Books: Through Literary Russia', *New York Times*, 26 May 1968, section VII, pp. 2–7.

Carson, Anne, 'TV Men: Akhmatova (Treatment for a Script)', *PN Review*, 126 (March–April 1999), 14–15.

Caute, David, *The Dancer Defects: The Struggle for Cultural Supremacy During the Cold War* (New York and Oxford: Oxford University Press, 2003).

Cavanagh, Clare, *Lyric Poetry and Modern Politics: Russia, Poland, and the West* (New Haven and London: Yale University Press, 2009).

Chamberlain, Lesley, *Lenin's Private War: The Voyage of the Philosophy Steamer and the Exile of the Intelligentsia* (New York: St Martin's Press, 2007).

Chambers, Ross, 'Irony and the Canon', *Profession* (1990), 18–24.

Charques, R. D., 'Russian Poems', *Times Literary Supplement*, 9 January 1930, 23.

—, 'Soviet Literature', *Times Literary Supplement*, 19 October 1933, 707.

Chernysheva, Veronika, 'Nesovremennyi i nesvoevremennyi', *Nezavisimaia gazeta*, 12 November 2004, http://www.ng.ru/style/2004-11-12/24_bunin.html

Chudakova, Marietta, 'Marietta Chudakovo v novom "Dodo" na Solianke o knige *Literatura v shkole i ne tol'ko*, chast' I', 20 October 2013, http://www.youtube.com/watch?v=uu_pXWxo62w

Chukhontsev, Igor', 'V storonu Slutskogo', *Znamia*, 1 (2012), 130-50.

Chukovskaia, Lidiia, *Zapiski ob Anne Akhmatovoi*, 3 vols (Moscow: Vremia, 1987; 2013).

Chukovskii, Kornei, *Sobranie sochinenii*, 6 vols (Moscow: Khudozhestvennaia literatura, 1965-1969).

—, *Sovremenniki. Portrety i etiudy* (Moscow: Molodaia gvardiia, 1967).

Clark, Katerina, *The Soviet Novel: History as Ritual* (Bloomington: Indiana University Press, 2000).

Clingman, Stephen, *The Grammar of Identity: Transnational Fiction and the Nature of the Boundary* (Oxford: Oxford University Press, 2009), http://dx.doi.org/10.1093/acprof:oso/9780199278497.001.0001

Clowes, Edith W., *Russia on the Edge: Imagined Geographies and Post-Soviet Identity* (Ithaca and London: Cornell University Press, 2011).

Coetzee, J. M., 'Osip Mandelstam and the Stalin Ode', *Giving Offence: Essays on Censorship* (Chicago: University of Chicago, 1993), 104-16.

Collomb, Michel, *Littérature Art Deco* (Paris: Méridiens Klincksieck, 1987).

Cornwell, Neil, ed., *Reference Guide to Russian Literature* (London and Chicago: Fitzroy Dearborn Publishers, 1998).

Danin, Daniil, 'Khorosho ushel — ne oglianulsia', *Voprosy literatury*, 5 (2006), 168-79.

Dark, Oleg, 'V storonu mertvykh (mezhdu Smeliakovym i Sapgirom)', *Russkii zhurnal*, 14 July 2003, http://old.russ.ru/krug/20030714_od.html

Davenport, Guy, 'The Man Without Contemporaries', *The Hudson Review*, 27: 2 (1974).

Davie, Donald, 'From the Marches of Christendom: Mandelstam and Milosz', *PN Review*, 109 (May-June 1996), 13-24.

Davydov, Iu. N., *Begstvo ot svobody: filosofskoe mifotvorchestvo i literaturnyi avangard* (Moscow: Khudozhestvennaia literatura, 1978).

Dawkins, Richard, *The Selfish Gene*, 30th Anniversary Edition (Oxford: Oxford University Press, 2006).

Depretto, Katrin, *Formalizm v Rossii: predshestvenniki, istoriia, kontekst* (Moscow: Novoe literaturnoe obozrenie, 2015).

Dinega, Alyssa W., *A Russian Psyche: The Poetic Mind of Marina Tsvetaeva* (Madison: University of Wisconsin Press, 2001).

D'Israeli, Isaac, 'Literary Fashions', in *Curiosities of Literature*, 3 vols (Boston: Lilly, Wait, Colman and Holden, 1833), III, 35-39.

Dmitriev, A., 'Predislovie', in Marina Tsvetaeva, *Zakon zvezdy i formula tsvetka* (Moscow: Eksmo, 2010).

Dnevnik ego zheny, dir. by Aleksei Uchitel' (Goskino Rossii, 2000).

Dobrenko, Evgenii, *et al.*, eds, *Nekanonicheskii klassik: Dmitri Aleksandrovich Prigov* (Moscow: NLO, 2010).

Dobrenko, Evgeny, *The Making of the State Writer: Social and Aesthetic Origin of Soviet Literary Culture*, trans. by Jesse M. Savage (Stanford: Stanford University Press, 2001).

—, and Galin Tihanov, eds, *A History of Russian Literary Theory and Criticism: The Soviet Age and Beyond* (Pittsburgh: University of Pittsburgh Press, 2011).

Dolgopolov, L. K., *Poema Bloka 'Dvenadtsat'* (Leningrad: Khudozhestvennaia literatura, 1979).

Dolinin, Viacheslav and Boris Ivanov, eds, *Samizdat. Po materialam konferentsii '30 let nezavisimoi pechati. 1950–80 gody'* (St Petersburg: NITs 'Memorial', 1993).

Dubrovina, Elena, 'O poezii i proze Georgiia Ivanova. Interv'iu s Vadimom Kreidom', *Gostinaia*, vypusk 53, Literaturnyi Parizh (September 2013), http://gostinaya.net/?p=8398

Duffy, Carol Ann, *The World's Wife* (London: Picador, 1999).

Eagleton, Terry, 'International Books of the Year for 1996', *Times Literary Supplement*, 29 November 1996, 12.

—, *How to Read a Poem* (Oxford: Blackwell, 2007).

Edmond, Jacob, *A Common Strangeness: Contemporary Poetry, Cross-cultural Encounter, Comparative Literature* (New York: Fordham University Press, 2012).

Eikhenbaum, B. M., *O poezii* (Leningrad: Sovetskii pisatel', 1969).

—, 'Anna Akhmatova: Opyt analiza', in *O poezii*, pp. 75–147.

Eksteins, Modris, *The Rites of Spring: The Great War and the Birth of the Modern Age* (New York: Anchor Books Doubleday, 1990).

Eliot, T. S., 'Tradition and the Individual Talent', in *Points of View* (London: Faber & Faber, 1941), 23–34.

Eliseev, Nikita, 'Boris Slutskii i voina', *Neva*, 5 (2010), http://magazines.russ.ru/neva/2010/5/el20.html

Elliot, David, *New Worlds: Russian Art and Society 1900–1937* (London: Thames and Hudson Ltd., 1986).

Ellis, Frank, *From Glasnost to the Internet: Russia's New Infosphere* (Basingstoke: Macmillan, 1999).

Engdahl, Horace, 'The Nobel Prize: Dawn of a New Canon?' (2008).

Engström, Maria, 'Contemporary Russian Messianism and New Russian Foreign Policy', *Contemporary Security Policy*, 35: 3 (2014), 356–79, http://dx.doi.org/10.1080/13523260.2014.965888

Epshtein, Mikhail, *Postmodern v russkoi literature* (Moscow: Vysshaia shkola, 2005).

Epstein, Mikhail, 'Like a Corpse in the Desert: Dehumanisation in the New Moscow Poetry', in *Russian Postmodernism: New Perspectives on Post-Soviet Culture*, ed. by Mikhail Epstein, Alexander A. Genis and Slobodanka M. Vladiv-Glover (New York and Oxford: Berghahn Books, 1999), 133–44.

—, Alexander A. Genis, Slobodanka M. Vladiv-Glover, eds, *Russian Postmodernism: New Perspectives on Post-Soviet Culture* (New York and Oxford: Berghahn Books, 1999).

—, 'The Philosophical Implications of Russian Conceptualism', *Journal of Eurasian Studies*, 1 (2010), 64–71, http://doi.org/10.1016/j.euras.2009.11.008

Eremin, Mikhail, *Stikhotvoreniia*, ed. by Lev Losef (Tenafly, NJ: Hermitage Press, 1986).

—, *Stikhotvoreniia* (St Petersburg: Pushkinskii fond, 1998).

—, *Stikhotvoreniia, Kniga 2* (St Petersburg: Pushkinskii fond, 2002).

Erenburg, Il'ia, 'O stikhakh Borisa Slutskogo', *Literaturnaia gazeta*, 28 July 1956.

Erhart, W. E., 'An Indomitable Poetic Spirit', *The Virginia Quarterly*, 65: 1 (1989), 175–82.

Erlich, Victor, 'Russian Formalism — In Perspective', *Journal of Aesthetics and Art Criticism*, 2 (December 1954), 215–25.

Erofeev, Viktor, 'Soviet Literature: in Memoriam', *Glas*, 1 (1991), 225–34.

Ershov, L. F., *Istoriia russkoi sovetskoi literatury: uchebnoe posobie dlia universitetov* (Moscow: Vysshaia shkola, 1982).

Esenin, Sergei, *Sobranie sochineni*, 7 vols, ed. by Iu. L. Prokushev (Moscow: Nauka-Golos, 1995–2002).

Etkind, Aleksandr, *Eros nevozmozhnogo: Istoriia psikhoanaliza v Rossii* (St Petersburg: Meduza, 1994).

—, *Sodom i psikheia. Ocherki intellektual'noi istorii Serebrianogo veka* (Moscow: Its-Garant, 1996).

—, *Khlyst: Sekty, literatura i revoliutsiia* (Moscow: NLO, 1998).

—, *Internal Colonisation: Russia's Imperial Experience* (Cambridge: Polity Press, 2011).

Etkind, Efim, 'Russkaia poeziia XX veka kak edinyi protsess', in *Odna ili dve russkikh literatury?*, ed. by Georges Nivat (Lausanne: L'Age d'Homme, 1981), 9–30.

—, 'Kopengagenskaia vstrecha deiatelei kul'tury' [roundtable contribution], *Voprosy literatury*, 5 (1989), 14–20.

—, *Tam vnutri: O russkoi poezii XX veka* (St Petersburg: Maksima, 1997).

Evtushenko, Evgenii, 'Obiazatel'nost' pered istoriei', in *Boris Slutskii: vospominaniia sovremennikov*, comp. by Petr Gorelik (St Petersburg: Zhurnal Neva, 2005), 377–83.

—, 'Poet v Rossii bol'she, chem poet...', *Novye izvestiia*, 16 September 2005, http://www.newizv.ru/culture/2005-09-16/31782-tolko-v-ni.html

—, ed., *Strofy veka: antologiia russkoi poezii* (Moscow: Polifakt, 1994; 1995; 1997).

Fainlight, Ruth, 'Touching the String', *Times Literary Supplement*, 8 February 2002, 25.

Falikov, Il'ia, 'Krasnorechie po-Slutski', *Voprosy literatury*, 2 (2000), 62–110.

—, 'Pust' budet', *Voprosy literatury*, 5 (2006), 180–201.

Fanailova, Elena, *Russkaia versiia* (Moscow: Zapasnyi vykhod, 2005).

—, 'Lena i Lena', *Zerkalo* (2011), http://magazines.russ.ru/zerkalo/2010/35/4fa.html

—, *Lena i liudi* (Moscow: Novoe izdatel'stvo, 2011).

—, 'Lena, or the Poet and the People', *Aufgabe* (2009), pp. 13–18.

—, 'Lena and Lena', trans. by Stephanie Sandler, *Jacket2* (2013), https://jacket2.org/article/lena-and-lena

Fediakin, Sergei, 'Dali Ivan Bunina', *Nezavisimaia gazeta*, 24 October 2000, http://www.ng.ru/culture/2000-10-24/7_bunin.html

—, et al., eds, *Russkaia poezii. XX vek. Antologiia* (Moscow: OLMA Press, 1999).

Fedotov, Georgii, 'O parizhskoi poezii', *Voprosy poezii*, 2 (1990).

Fenton, James, 'Hell Set to Music', *The Guardian*, 16 July 2005.

Fiedler, Leslie, and Houston Baker, eds, *English Literature: Opening Up the Canon* (Baltimore: Johns Hopkins University Press, 1981).

Figes, Orlando, 'A Double Game with Stalin', *New York Review of Books*, 12 January 2012, 33.

Fitzpatrick, Sheila, 'Culture and Politics under Stalin: A Reappraisal', *Slavic Review*, 35 (1976), 211–31.

Fleming, Mike, 'The Literary Canon: Implications for the Teaching of Language as Subject', in *Text, literature and 'Bildung'*, ed. by Irene Pieper (Strasbourg: Council of Europe, 2007), pp. 31–38, http://www.coe.int/t/dg4/linguistic/Source/Prague07_LS_EN.doc

Fokin, Pavel (ed.), *Akhmatova bez gliantsa* (Petersburg: Amfora, 2008).

Fowler, Alastair, 'Genre and the Literary Canon', *New Literary History*, 11: 1, Anniversary Issue II (Autumn 1979), 97–119.

—, *Kinds of Literature: An Introduction to the Theory of Genres and Modes* (Oxford: Oxford University Press, 1982).

France, Peter, 'Four Troubled Lives', *Times Literary Supplement*, 12 March 1982, 275.

—, *Poets of Modern Russia* (Cambridge: Cambridge University Press, 1982).

Freidin, Gregory, *A Coat of Many Colors: Osip Mandelstam and his Mythologies of Self-Presentation* (Berkeley and Los Angeles: University of California Press, 1987).

Friedberg, Maurice, 'Socialist Realism: Twenty-Five Years Later', *The American Slavic and East European Review*, 2 (1960), 276–87.

Frukhtman, Lev, 'Zhil-byl skazochnik', http://velelens.livejournal.com/879503.html

Galcheva, Tania, 'Krizis molchaniia v poezii Vladislava Khodasevicha i v proze Georgiia Ivanova', *Slavia Orientalis*, 44: 4 (1995), pp. 503–13.

Gandel'sman, Vladimir, '"Stalinskaia oda" Mandel'shtama', *Novyi zhurnal*, 215 (1999), 133–41.

Gandlevskii, Sergei, 'Sochineniia Timura Kibirova', *Poeticheskaia kukhnia* (St Petersburg: Pushkinskii fond, 1998), pp. 18–22.

Gasparov, Boris, 'Introduction', in Iurii M. Lotman, Lidiia Ia. Ginsburg and Boris A. Uspenskii, *The Semiotics of Russian Cultural History: Essays*, ed. by Alexander D. Nakhimovsky and Alice Stone Nakhimovsky (Ithaca, NY: Cornell University Press, 1985), 13–29.

—, Robert P. Hughes, and Irina Paperno, eds, *Cultural Mythologies of Russian Modernism: From the Golden Age to the Silver Age* (Berkeley and Oxford: University of California Press, 1992).

Gasparov, Mikhail, 'Metricheskoe sosedstvo "Ody" Stalinu', in *Mandelstam Centenary Conference*, ed. by Robin Aizlewood and Diana Myers (Tenafly: Hermitage Publishers, 1994), pp. 99–111.

—, *Akademicheskii avangardizm: priroda i kul'tura u pozdnego Briusova* (Moscow: RGGU, 1995).

—, 'Kniga dlia chteniia', *Novyi mir*, 2 (1996), http://magazines.russ.ru/novyi_mi/1996/2/zar1.html

—, 'Stoletie kak mera, ili Klassika na fone sovremennosti', *Novoe literaturnoe obozrenie*, 62 (2003), http://magazines.russ.ru/nlo/2003/62/gaspar-pr.html

Gathmann, Moritz, 'Satire Against Cynicism', *Russia Behind the Headlines*, 13 March 2012, http://rbth.com/articles/2012/03/13/satire_against_cynicism_15054.html

Genette, Gérard, *Paratexts: Thresholds of Interpretation*, trans. by Jane E. Lewin (Cambridge: Cambridge University Press, 1997).

Gifford, Henry, 'Mandelstam Whole. Review of Sidney Monas, *Osip Mandelstam: Selected Essays*, Jennifer Baines, *Mandelstam. The Later Poetry*', *New York Review of Books*, 9 March 1978.

—, 'The Use of Poetry in Twentieth-century Russia', *PN Review*, 3 (April–June 1978), 4.

—, 'Pound, Mayakovsky and the Defence of Human', *PN Review*, 6 (January–March 1979), 15–19.

—, 'A Witness Between Two Worlds', 14 March 1980, 283.

—, 'Dante and the Modern Poet', *PN Review*, 12 (March–April 1980), 13.

—, 'Origins and Recognitions', *Times Literary Supplement*, 25 July 1980, 827.

—, 'Surrounded with Fire', *Times Literary Supplement*, 19 June 1981, 700.

—, 'On Modesty and Boldness', *Times Literary Supplement*, 23 August 1985, 915.

—, 'The Flinty Path', *Times Literary Supplement*, 20 October 1978, 1227.

—, 'Binocular Vision: Review of Donald Davie, *Czeslaw Milosz and the Insufficiency of Lyric*', *PN Review*, 55 (May–June 1987), 83–84.

—, 'Hearing Close-Knit Harmonies: Mandel'stam's Essential Music Translated', *Times Literary Supplement*, 24 May 1991, 9.

—, 'The Staying Power of Russian Poetry', *Times Literary Supplement*, 24 May 1991, 9.

Gill, Graeme, 'Changing Symbols: The Renovation of Moscow Place Names', *The Russian Review*, 64 (July 2005), 480–503. http://dx.doi.org/10.1111/j.1467-9434.2005.00371.x

Ginzburg, Lidiia, *O lirike* (Leningrad: Sovetskii pisatel', 1964).

Gippius, Zinaida N., *Stikhotvoreniia. Zhivye litsa* (Moscow: Khudozhestvennaia literatura, 1991).

Glad, John, ed., *Conversations in Exile: Russian Writers Abroad* (Durham and London: Duke University Press, 1993).

Glazova, Anna, 'Otzyvy', *Vozdukh*, 4 (2008), 22–23.

Glazunova, Ol'ga, 'Buninskie iabloki', *Rossiiskaia gazeta*, 28 October 2010, http://rg.ru/2010/10/28/reg-roscentr/bunin.html

Glinin, G. G., *Avtorskaia pozitsiia v poeme A. Bloka 'Dvenadtsat''* (Astrakhan': Izdatel'stvo Astrakhanskogo pedagogicheskogo instituta, 1993).

—, *Avtor i geroi v poemakh Bloka* (Astrakhan': Izdatel'stvo Astrakhanskogo universiteta, 2006).

Gogol', N. V., *Polnoe sobranie sochinenii*, 14 vols (Moscow and Leningrad: Izdatel'stvo A. N. SSSR, 1937–1952).

Golding, Alan, *From Outlaw to Classic: Canons in American Poetry* (Madison: The University of Wisconsin Press, 1995).

Goldstein, Darra, 'The Heart-Felt Poetry of Elena Shvarts', in *Fruits of her Plume: Essays on Contemporary Russian Women's Culture*, ed. by Helena Goscilo (Armonk, NY: M. E. Sharpe, 1993), 239–50.

Golubkov, V. V. and M. A. Rybnikova, *Izuchenie literatury v shkole II stupeni. Metodika chteniia* (Moscow: Gosizdat, 1929).

Gomolitskii, Lev, 'Nadezhdy simvol', in *Iakor': antologiia russkoi zarubezhnoi poezii*, ed. by Oleg Korostelev, Luigi Magarotto, Andrei Ustinov (St Petersburg: Aleteia, 2005), 223–27.

Gorak, Jan, *The Making of the Modern Canon: Genesis and Crisis of a Literary Idea* (London and Atlantic Highlands: Athlone Press, 1991).

Gorbachev, Oleg, 'The *Namedni* Project and the Evolution of Nostagia in Post-Soviet Russia', *Canadian Slavonic Papers*, 3–4 (2015), 180–94. http://dx.doi.org/10.1080/00085006.2015.1083358

Gorelik, Petr, comp., *Boris Slutskii: vospominaniia sovremennikov* (St Petersburg: Zhurnal Neva, 2005).

—, 'Drug iunosti i vsei zhizni', in *Boris Slutskii: vospominaniia sovremennikov*, comp. by Petr Gorelik (St Petersburg: Zhurnal Neva, 2005), 26–66.

—, and Nikita Eliseev, '"Ia eto slyshal s detstva": k 90–letiiu so dnia rozhdeniia Borisa Slutskogo', *Evreiskoe slovo*, 15 (2009), http://www.e-slovo.ru/433/10pol1.htm

Gor'kii, Maksim, *Sobranie sochinenii*, 30 vols (Moscow: Khudozhestvennaia literatura, 1949–1955).

Gorky, Maxim, *Reminiscences of Lev Nikolayevich Tolstoy*, trans. by S. S. Koteliansky and Leonard Woolf (New York: B. W. Huebsch, Inc., 1920).

Goscilo, Helena, 'Playing Dead: The Operatics of Celebrity Funerals, or, the Ultimate Silent Part', in *Imitations of Life: Two Centuries of Melodrama in Russia*, ed. by Louise McReynolds and Joan Neuberger (Durham, NC and London: Duke University Press, 2002), 283–319.

—, ed., *Fruits of her Plume: Essays on Contemporary Russian Women's Culture* (Armonk, NY: M. E. Sharpe, 1993).

—, and Beth Holmgren, eds, *Russia-Women-Culture* (Bloomington: Indiana University Press, 1996).

Goshko, John, 'The Exiles: No Escaping Literary Wars', *The Washington Post*, 29 December 1974, B5.

Gratsiadei, Katerina [Caterina Graziadei], 'Enjambement kak figura: bitva v predstavlenii Al'tdorfera i Brodskogo', *Voprosy lilteratury*, 3 (1998), 324–28.

Gray, Camilla, *The Russian Experiment in Art, 1863–1922* (New York: H. N. Abrams, 1971).

Grechanik, I. V., 'Osobennosti liriki Bloka: filosofskie osnovy, stil'', in *Religiozno-filosofskie motivy russkoi liriki rubezha XIX–XX vekov* (Moscow: Sputnik, 2003), 59–111.

Grigor'eva, Ol'ga, *Reka i rech'* (Pavlodar: TOO 'Dom pechati', 2009).

Grinberg, Marat, 'Vychitivaia Slutskogo: Boris Slutskii v dialoge s sovremennikami', *Kreshchatik*, 3 (2008), http://magazines.russ.ru/kreschatik/2008/3/gr23.html

—, *'I Am to Be Read not from Left to Right, But in Jewish, from Right to Left': The Poetics of Boris Slutsky*, Borderlines: Russian and East European Jewish Studies (Boston: Academic Studies Press, 2011).

Gronas, Mikhail, *Cognitive Poetics and Cultural Memory: Russian Literary Mnemonics* (New York and London: Routledge, 2011).

Groys, Boris, *The Total Art of Stalinism: Avant-garde, Aesthetic Dictatorship, and Beyond*, trans. by Charles Rougle (Princeton, NJ: Princeton University Press, 1992).

Gubaidulina, Sofia, and Vera Lukonsky, '"The Eucharist in My Fantasy": Interview with Sofia Gubaidulina', *Tempo*, New Series, 206 (September 1998), 29–35.

Guershoon Collin, Andrew, 'Ivan Bunin in Retrospect', *The Slavonic and East European Review*, 34 (1955), 156–73.

Guest, Harry, 'Cantos at Kantô', *PN Review*, 62 (July–August 1988), 23.

Guillén, Claudio, 'On the Literature of Exile and Counter-exile', *Books Abroad*, 50 (1976), 271–80.

Guillory, John, *Cultural Capital: The Problem of Literary Canon Formation* (Chicago: University of Chicago Press, 1993).

Gusman, Mikhail, 'Russkofoniia mirovogo informatsionnogo polia', *Nezavisimaia gazeta*, 7 October 2002, http://www.ng.ru/project/2002-07-10/9_field.html

Gustafson, Richard F., 'Ginzburg's Theory of the Lyric', *Canadian-American Slavic Studies*, 2 (1985), 135–39.

Hackel, Sergei, *The Poet and the Revolution* (Oxford: Clarendon Press, 1975).

Hagglund, Roger, *A Vision of Unity: Adamovich in Exile* (Ann Arbor: Ardis, 1985).

Haight, Amanda, *Anna Akhmatova: A Poetic Pilgrimage* (Oxford: Oxford University Press, 1976).

Harrington, Alexandra, 'Anna Akhmatova's Biographical Myth-Making: Tragedy and Melodrama', *Slavonic and East European Review*, 89 (2011), 455–93, http://doi.org/10.5699/slaveasteurorev2.89.3.0455

—, 'Anna Akhmatova', in *Russia's People of Empire: Life Stories from Eurasia, 1500 to the Present*, ed. by Stephen M. Norris and Willard Sunderland (Bloomington and Indianapolis: Indiana University Press, 2012).

—, 'Melodrama, Feeling, and Emotion in the Early Poetry of Anna Akhmatova', *The Modern Language Review*, 108 (2013), 241–73, http://doi.org/10.5699/modelangrevi.108.1.0241

Hassan, Ihab Habb, *The Dismemberment of Orpheus: Toward a Postmodern Literature* (Wisconsin-Madison: University of Wisconsin Press, 1982).

Hayward, Max, and Edward L. Crowley, eds, *Soviet Literature in the Sixties* (London: Methuen, 1963).

Heaney, Seamus, 'Osip and Nadezhda Mandelstam', *London Review of Books*, 20 August 1981, 3–6.

—, 'International Books of the Year', *Times Literary Supplement*, 29 November 1996, 11.

—, *The Redress of Poetry: Oxford Lectures* (London and Boston: Faber & Faber, 1995).

Heldt, Barbara, 'The Poetry of Elena Shvarts', *World Literature Today*, 63: 3 (1989), 381–83.

Heller, Michael, 'Speaking the Estranged: Oppen's Poetics of the Word', *Chicago Review*, 50 (Winter 2004–2005), 137–50.

Hill, Geoffrey, 'Unpublished Lecture Notes', in Kenneth Haynes and Andrew Kahn, 'Difficult Friend: Geoffrey Hill and Osip Mandelstam', *Essays in Criticism*, 63 (2013), 51–80, https://doi.org/10.1093/escrit/cgs028

Himmelman, Jeff, 'Peter Matthiessen's Homegoing, *New York Times Magazine*, 3 April 2014, http://www.nytimes.com/2014/04/06/magazine/peter-matthiessens-homegoing.html

Hodgson, Katharine, 'Two Post-Soviet Anthologies of the 1990s and the Russian 20th-Century Canon', *Slavonic and East European Review*, 90 (2012), 642–70, http://dx.doi.org/10.5699/slaveasteurorev2.90.4.0642

Holak, Susan, Alexei Matveev, and William Havlena, 'Nostalgia in Post-Socialist Russia: Exploring Applications to Advertising Strategy', *Journal of Business Research*, 60 (2007), 649–55, http://doi.org/10.1016/j.jbusres.2007.06.013

Holmgren, Beth, *Women's Works in Stalin's Time: On Lidiia Chukovskaia and Nadezhda Mandelstam* (Bloomington: Indiana University Press, 1993).

—, ed., *The Russian Memoir: History and Literature* (Evanston: North Western University Press, 2003).

—, 'Gendering the Icon: Marketing Women Writers in Fin-de-siècle Russia', in *Russia-Women-Culture*, ed. by Helena Goscilo and Beth Holmgren (Bloomington: Indiana University Press, 1996), 321–46.

Holthusen, Johannes, *Twentieth-Century Russian Literature: A Critical Introduction* (New York: Ungar Publishing Co., 1968).

Hood, Stuart, 'As If Winter Had Not Touched', *PN Review*, 22 (November–December 1981), 62–63.

Hopgood, James F., ed., *The Making of Saints: Contesting Sacred Ground* (Tuscaloosa: University of Alabama Press, 2005).

Hunt, Priscilla, and Svitlana Kobets, eds, *Holy Foolishness in Russia: New Perspectives* (Bloomington: Slavica Publishers, 2011).

Hutcheon, Linda, *A Poetics of Postmodernism: History, Theory, Fiction* (New York and London: Routledge, 1988).

—, *A Theory of Parody: The Teachings of Twentieth-Century Art Forms* (Urbana and Chicago: University of Illinois Press, 2000).

Huyssen, Andreas, 'Geographies of Modernism in a Globalizing World', in *Geographies of Modernism: Literatures, Cultures, Spaces*, ed. by Peter Brooker and Andrew Thacker (London and New York: Routledge, 2005), pp. 6–18. https://doi.org/10.1215/0094033X-2006-023

Iampolskii, Mikhail, 'Literaturnyi kanon i teoriia "sil'nogo avtora"', *Inostrannaia literatura*, 12 (1998), http://magazines.russ.ru/inostran/1998/12/iamp.html

Ignatieff, Michael, 'The Beloved'. Review of J. M. Coetzee, *Giving Offence: Essays on Censorship, London Review of Books*, 6 February 1997, 14.

Ignatova, Elena, 'Kto my? Leningradskii andegraund semidesiatykh', *Interpoeziia*, 3 (2010), http://magazines.russ.ru/interpoezia/2010/3/ig11.html

Igosheva, T. V., *Ranniaia lirika A. A. Bloka (1898–1904): poetika religioznogo simvolizma* (Moscow: Global Kom, 2013).

Il'enkov, A. I., 'O skrytoi kompozitsii liricheskoi trilogii Aleksandra Bloka', in *Arkhetipicheskie struktury khudozhestvennogo soznaniia*, ed. by E. K. Sozina (Ekaterinburg: Izdatel'stvo Ural'skogo Universiteta, 2002), 124–38.

Il'inskii, Igor', I. A. Bunin i sovremennaia poeziia: Press-konferentsiia, posviashchennaia ob"iavleniiu konkursa Buninskoi premii 2007 goda' (2007), http://ilinskiy.ru/activity/public/bunin/2007

Imlah, Mick, 'Poetry Publishing and Publishers', *Times Literary Supplement*, 27 April 1984, 455.

Ivanov, Boris, 'Kul'turnoe dvizhenie kak tselostnoe iavlenie' (Samizdat, 1979).

—, 'K materialam 2-oi konferentsii kul'turnogo dvizheniia', *Chasy*, 24 (1980), 256–78.

—, 'Evoliutsiia literaturnykh dvizhenii v piatidesiatye-vos'midesiatye gody', in *Istoriia leningradskoi podtsenzurnoi literatury*, in B. Ivanov, ed., *Istoriia leningradskoi nepodtsenzurnoi poezii: 1950–e–1980–e gody* (St Petersburg: Dean, 2000), 17–28.

—, ed., *Istoriia leningradskoi nepodtsenzurnoi poezii: 1950–e–1980–e gody* (St Petersburg: Dean, 2000).

Ivanov, Georgii, *Sobranie sochinenii v trekh tomakh*, ed. by Evgenii Vitkovskii (Moscow: Soglasie, 1994).

—, 'The Atom Explodes', trans. by Justin Doherty, *Slavonica* 8: 1 (2002), 42–67.

—, *Stikhotvoreniia*, ed. by Andrei Ar'ev (Moscow: DNK, Progress-Pleiada, 2010).

Ivanov, S. I., *Blazhennye pokhaby: kul'turnaia istoriia iurodstva* (Moscow: Iazyki slavianskikh kul'tur, 2005).

Ivanova, Natal'ia, 'Uskol'zaiushchaia sovremennost'': Russkaia literatura XX–XXI vekov. Ot "vnekomplektnoi" k postsovetskoi, a teper' i vsemirnoi', *Voprosy literatury*, 3 (2007), http://magazines.russ.ru/voplit/2007/3/iv7.html

—, 'Mythopoesis and Mythoclasticism', *Russian Studies in Literature*, 45: 1 (2008–2009), 82–91.

Jaffe, Aaron, *Modernism and the Culture of Celebrity* (Cambridge: Cambridge University Press, 2005).

Jakobson, Roman, 'What is Poetry?', in *Language in Literature*, ed. by Krystyna Pomorska and Stephen Rudy (Cambridge, MA: Harvard University Press, 1987), 368–78.

Janecek, Gerald, *The Look of Russian Literature: Avant-garde Visual Experiments, 1900–1930* (Princeton: Princeton University Press, 1984).

—, 'Paronomastic and Musical Techniques in Mnacakanova's Rekviem', *Slavic and East European Journal*, 31 (1987), 202–19.

—, 'The Poetics of Punctuation in Gennady Aygi's Free Verse', in *Sight and Sound Entwined: Studies of the New Russian Poetry* (New York: Berghahn Books, 2000), 91–109.

—, 'Poeziia molchaniia u Gennadiia Aigi', in *Minimalismus zwischen Leere und Exzess*, ed. by Mirjam Goller and Georg Witte, *Wiener slawistischer Almanach*, 51 (Vienna: Gesellschaft zur Förderung slawistischer Studien, 2001), 433–46.

Jefferson, Margo, 'On Writers and Writing: Texts for Our Time', *New York Times Books Review*, 30 September 2000, http://www.nytimes.com/2001/09/30/books/on-writers-and-writing-texts-for-our-time.html

Johnson, Barbara, *Persons and Things* (Cambridge, MA: Harvard University Press, 2008).

Johnson, David, *The Popular and the Canonical: Debating Twentieth-century Literature 1940–2000* (Abingdon: Routledge, 2005).

Josipovici, Gabriel, 'The Book of the Book', *Times Literary Supplement*, 17 June 1988, 684.

Kahn, Andrew, 'Introduction', in *The Cambridge Companion to Pushkin*, ed. by Andrew Kahn (Cambridge: Cambridge University Press, 2006), pp. 1–7. https://doi.org/10.1017/CCOL0521843677

—, 'Lidiya Ginzburg's Lives of the Poets: Mandel'shtam in Profile', in *Lydia Ginzburg's Alternative Literary Identity*, ed. by Andrei Zorin and Emily van Buskirk (Oxford: Peter Lang, 2012), 163–91.

Kaiser, Robert, 'Panovs Have 5 Days to Leave', *The Washington Post*, 9 June 1974, A13.

Kalomirov, A. [pseud. of Viktor Krivulin], 'Dvadtsat' let noveishei russkoi poezii', *Severnaia pochta*, 1: 2 (1979).

Kaminskii, Il'ia, *Muzyka narodov vetra*, trans. by Anastasiia Afanas'eva (New York: Ailuros Publishing, 2012).

Karabchievskii, Iurii, *Voskresenie Maiakovskogo* (Moscow: Enas, 2008).

Karlinsky, Simon, and Alfred Appel, Jr., eds, *The Bitter Air of Exile: Russian Writers in the West 1922–1972* (Berkeley, Los Angeles and London: University of California Press, 1973).

—, *Marina Tsvetaeva: The Woman, Her World, and Her Poetry* (Cambridge: Cambridge University Press, 1985).

Kataeva, Tamara, *Anti-Akhmatova* (Moscow: Ellis Lak, 2007).

—, *Otmena rabstva: Anti-Akhmatova 2* (Moscow: Astrel', 2012).

Katanian, Vasilii, *Maiakovskii: khronika zhizni i deiatel'nosti* (Moscow: Sovetskii pisatel', 1985).

Kates, J., ed., *In the Grip of Strange Thoughts* (Newcastle-upon-Tyne: Bloodaxe Books, 1999).

Kelly, Aileen, 'Brave New Worlds', *New York Review of Books*, 6 December 1990, 60–67.

Kelly, Catriona, *A History of Russian Women's Writing 1820–1992* (Oxford: Clarendon Press, 1994).

—, 'New Boundaries for the Common Good', in *Constructing Russian Culture in the Age of Revolution 1881–1940*, ed. by Catriona Kelly and David Shepherd (Oxford: Oxford University Press, 1998), 238–55.

—, *Russian Literature: A Very Short Introduction* (Oxford: Oxford University Press, 2001).

Kemp-Welch, Anthony, *Stalin and the Literary Intelligentsia, 1928–1939* (Basingstoke: Macmillan, 1991).

Kermode, Frank, *Pleasure and Change: The Aesthetics of Canon* (Oxford: Oxford University Press, 2004).

Khagi, Sofya, 'Art as Aping: The Uses of Dialogism in Timur Kibirov's "To Igor" Pomerantsev. Summer Reflections on the Fate of Belles Lettres', *The Russian Review*, 4 (2002), 579–98, http://doi.org/10.1111/1467-9434.00251

Khanzen-Lieve, Oge, *Russkii formalizm: metodologicheskaia rekonstruktsiia razvittiia na osnove printsipa ostraneniia* (Moscow: Iazyki russkoi kul'tury, 2001).

Kharitonov, M., 'Apologiia literatury', *Literaturnaia gazeta*, 19 June 1991, 11.

Khlebnikov, Oleg, 'S voskhishcheniem zhivu: Interv'iu s Irinoi Odoevtsevoi', *Ogonek*, 11 (11–18 March 1989), 22–23.

—, 'Vysokaia bolezn' Boris Slutskogo', in *Boris Slutskii: vospominaniia sovremennikov*, comp. by Petr Gorelik (St Petersburg: Zhurnal Neva, 2005), 202–11.

Khodasevich, Vladislav, *Stikhotvoreniia* (St Petersburg: Akademicheskii proekt, 2001).

—, *Sobranie sochinenii v vos'mi tomakh*, ed. by John Malmstad and Robert Hughes (Moscow: Russkii put', 2009–2010).

Kuniaev, Stanislav, 'Klassika i my', *Moskva*, 1 (1990), 190–93.

Kniazhitskii, Aleksandr, *Metodicheskie rekomendatsii i prakticheskie materialy k provedeniiu ekzamena po literature*, 2 vols (Moscow: Mezhdunarodnaia shkola distantsionnogo obucheniia, 2003).

Kochetkova, Ol'ga, 'Ideino-esteticheskie printsipy "parizhskoi noty" i khudozhestvennye poiski Borisa Poplavskogo' (unpublished candidate dissertation, Moscow State University, 2010), http://www.dissercat.com/content/ideino-esteticheskie-printsipy-parizhskoi-noty-i-khudozhestvennye-poiski-borisa-poplavskogo

Koehler, Ludmila, 'New Trends in Soviet Literary Criticism', *Russian Review*, 27 (1968), 54–67.

Kolokol'tsev, Nikolai, *Sochineniia v obshcheobrazovatel'noi politekhnicheskoi shkole (iz opyta raboty uchitelei-slovesnikov)* (Moscow: Gosudarstvennoe uchebno-pedagogicheskoe izdatel'stvo ministerstva prosveshcheniia, 1961).

Komaromi, Ann, 'The Material Existence of Soviet Samizdat', *Slavic Review*, 63 (2004), 597–618, http://doi.org/10.2307/1520346

Kommissiia Ts. K. VKP (b) (ed.), *Istoriia VKP (b): kratkii kurs* (Moscow: OGIZ, 1945; first ed. 1938).

Kondrashov, Aleksandr, 'Gody okainstva, ili Zagadka N. B. I', *Literaturnaia gazeta*, 27 August 2013, http://www.lgz.ru/article/-33-34-6427-27-08-2013/gody-okayanstva-ili-zagadka-n-b-i/

Kormilov, S. I. (ed.), *Istoriia russkoi literatury XX veka (20–90–e gody). Osnovyne imena. Uchebnoe posobie* (Moscow: Moscow State University, 1998) http://www.hi-edu.ru/e-books/xbook046/01/part-002.htm

Korneichuk, Vladislav, 'Kniga v provintsii i ee chitateli', *Nezavisimaia gazeta*, 3 August 2006, http://www.ng.ru/tendenc/2006-08-03/4_kniga.html

Kornilov, Vladimir, 'Pokuda nad stikhami plachut...'. in *Boris Slutskii: vospominaniia sovremennikov*, comp. by Petr Gorelik (St Petersburg: Zhurnal Neva, 2005), 106–20.

Korniukhina, A. V., 'Misticheskii anarkhizm kak stadia formirovaniia russkogo simvolizma', *Vestnik Moskovskogo Gosudarstvennogo oblastnogo universiteta. Seriia Filosofskie nauki*, 2 (2006), 176–81.

Koroleva, Nina, 'Poeziia tochnogo slova', in *Boris Slutskii: vospominaniia sovremennikov*, comp. by Petr Gorelik (St Petersburg: Zhurnal Neva, 2005), 401–14.

Koroleva. N. V. and S. A. Kovalenko, eds, *Tainy remesla*, Akhmatovskie chteniia 2 (Moscow: Nasledie, 1992).

Korostelev, Oleg, '"Bez krasok i pochti bez slov..." (poeziia Georgiia Adamovicha)', in Georgii Adamovich, *Stikhi, proza, perevody* (Saint Petersburg: Aleteia, 1999), 5–74.

—, Luigi Magarotto, Andrei Ustinov, eds, *Iakor': antologiia russkoi zarubezhnoi poezii* (St Petersburg: Aleteia, 2005).

—, '"Parizhskaia Nota" russkogo Monparnasa', [n.d.], http://institut-est-ouest.ens-lsh.fr/spip.php?article302

Kostomarova, Inna, 'Muzei', Bunin Ivan Alekseevich (1870–1953), [n.d.], http://bunin.niv.ru/bunin/museum/museum.htm

—, 'Muzei I. A. Bunina v Orle', Bunin Ivan Alekseevich (1870–1953), [n.d.], http://bunin.niv.ru/bunin/museum/museum-orel.htm

Koupovykh, Maxim, *The Soviet Empire of Signs: A Social and Intellectual History of the Tartu School of Semiotics* (unpublished doctoral dissertation, University of Illinois at Urbana-Champaign, 2005).

Kovalev, Valentin, *Russkaia sovetskaia literatura*, 11th ed. (Moscow: Prosveshchenie, 1989).

—, ed., *Russkaia sovetskaia literatura 50–70–kh godov* (Moscow: Prosveshchenie, 1981).

Kozlov, Vladimir, 'Neperevodimye gody Brodskogo: dve strany i dva iazyka v poezii i proze I. Brodskogo 1972–1977 godov', *Voprosy literatury*, 3 (2005), 155–85.

Krasnova, Marina, 'Vladelets shestisot istorii', *Novyi mir*, 8 (2006), 177–82.

Kreid, Vadim, 'Chto takoe "Parizhskaia nota"', *Slovo/Word*, 43–44 (2004), http://magazines.russ.ru/slovo/2004/43/kr41.html

—, comp., *Poety parizhskoi noty: v Rossiiu vetrom strochki zaneset* (Moscow: Molodaia gvardiia, 2003).

Krivulin, Viktor, 'U istochnikov noveishei kul'tury', *Zvezda*, 1 (1990), 184–88.

—, 'Peterburgskaia spiritual'naia lirika vchera i segodnia', in *Istoriia leningradskoi nepodtsensurnoi literatury*, ed. by B. Ivanov and B. Roginskii (St Petersburg: DEAN, 2000), 99–110.

Kudrova, Irma, *Put' komet*, 3 vols (St Petersburg: Izdatel'stvo 'Kniga', 2007).

Kukulin, Il'ia, 'Ot Svarovskogo k Zhukovskomu i obratno: O tom, kak metod issledovaniia konstruiruet literaturnyi kanon', *Novoe literaturnoe obozrenie*, 89 (2008), 228–40.

—, 'Aktual'nyi russkii poet kak voskresshie Alenushka i Ivanushka', *Novoe literaturnoe obozrenie*, 53 (2002), 273–97.

—, 'Impressionisticheskii monument', *Novoe literaturnoe obozrenie*, 109 (2011), http://magazines.russ.ru/nlo/2011/109/ku26.html

Kuniaev, Stanislav, *Poeziia, Sud'ba, Rossiia*, 2 vols (Moscow: Nash sovremennik, 1991).

Kupriianova, Nina, and Ariadna Ivanovskaia, comp., *Soviet Russian Poetry of the 1950s–1970s* (Moscow: Progress Publishers, 1981).

Kurdiumova, Tamara, ed., *Literatura. Uchebnoe izdanie. 9 klass* (Moscow: Drofa, 1998).

Kutuzov, Aleksandr, ed., *V mire literatury: 6 klass* (Moscow: Drofa, 1996; 2005).

Kuz'min, Dmitrii, 'Atmosfernyi front', *Vozdukh: zhurnal poezii*, 1 (2006), 11.

—, 'Russkaia poeziia v nachale XXI veka', *Rets*, 48 (2008), http://www.litkarta.ru/dossier/kuzmin-review

—, *Vavilon*, http://vavilon.ru

Kuz'minskii, Konstantin, and Grigorii Kovalev, eds, *The Blue Lagoon Anthology of Modern Russian Poetry*, 5 vols (Newtonville: Oriental Research Partners, 1986).

Kuznetsov, Feliks, *Russkaia literatura XX veka. Ocherki. Portrety. Esse. Kniga dlia uchashchikhsia 11 klassa srednei shkoly*, 2 vols (Moscow: Prosveshchenie, 1991).

Kuznetsov, Sergei, 'Raspadaiushchaia amal'gama: o poetike Brodskogo', *Voprosy literatury*, 3 (1997), 24–49.

Lahusen, Thomas, 'Socialist Realism in Search of Its Shores: Some Historical Remarks on the "Historically Open Aesthetic System of the Truthful Representation of Life"', in *Socialist Realism Without Shores*, ed. by Thomas Lahusen and Evgenii Dobrenko (Durham and London: Duke University Press, 1997), 5–26.

Laursen, Eric, 'The Talent of Double Vision: Distorting Reflection in Georgii Ivanov's Emigre Poetry', *Russian Literature*, 43 (1998), 481–93.

Lauter, Paul, *Canons and Contexts* (New York and Oxford: Oxford University Press, 1991).

Lavrov, A. V., 'Neskol'ko slov o Zare Grigor'evne Mints, redaktore i vdokhnovitele taruskikh "Blokovskikh sbornikov"', *Blokovskii sbornik*, 12 (1993), 6–10.

Lazarenko, Galina, *Khrestomatiia po otechestvennoi literature XX veka* (Moscow: Metodicheskii kabinet zapadnogo okruga g. Moskvy, 1995).

Lazarev, Lazar', 'S nadezhdoi, pravdoi i dobrom...', in *Boris Slutskii: vospominaniia sovremennikov*, comp. by Petr Gorelik (St Petersburg: Zhurnal Neva, 2005), 169–201.

Lebedeva, Natal'ia, 'Gil'otina dlia zvezdy: kak zashchitit' geniev ot masskul'ta', *Rossiiskaia gazeta*, 22 August 2007, http://www.rg.ru/printable/2007/08/22/chukovskaya.html

Lehmann-Haupt, Christopher, 'The Good Woman of Mandelstam', *Books of the Times*, 19 October 1970, [n.p.].

Leiderman, N. L. and A. V. Tagil'tsev, *Poeziia Anny Akhmatovoi: ocherki* (Ekaterinburg: Slovesnik, 2005).

Lenin, Vladimir, *Pamiati Gertsena* (Moscow: Politizdat, 1980).

Levchenko, Marina, 'Russkaia poeziia 60–kh godov', *Ruthenia*, http://ruthenia.ru/60s/poets/index.htm

Leving, Yuri, 'Plaster, Marble, Canon: The Vindication of Nabokov in Post-Soviet Russia', *Ulbandus Review*, 10 (2007) [special issue 'My Nabokov'], 101–22.

Lévi-Strauss, Claude, *La Pensée sauvage* (Paris: Librarie Plon, 1962).

Lipkin, Semen, 'Iskusstvo ne znaet starosti', *Voprosy literatury*, 3 (1998), 253–77.

—, 'Sila sovesti', in *Boris Slutskii: vospominaniia sovremennikov*, comp. by Petr Gorelik (St Petersburg: Zhurnal Neva, 2005), 212–18.

Lipking, Laurence, *The Life of the Poet: Beginning and Ending Poetic Careers* (Chicago: University of Chicago Press, 1981).

Lipman, Joan, 'Constructing Our Pedagogical Canon', *Pedagogy*, 10: 3 (2010), 535–53.

Lipovetsky, Mark, 'Russian Literary Postmodernism in the 1990s', *Slavonic and East European Review*, 1 (2001), 31–50.

Livak, Leonid, *How It Was Done in Paris: Russian Émigré Literature and French Modernism* (Madison: Wisconsin University Press, 2003).

Ljunggren, Magnus and Lazar' Fleishman, 'Na puti k Nobelevskoi nagrade (S. M. Bowra, N. O. Nil'sson, Pasternak)', in *Rossiia i Zapad: Sbornik statei v chest' 70–letiia K. M. Azadovskogo*, comp. by M. Bezrodnyi, N. A. Bogomolov, A. Belkina (Moscow: Novoe Literaturnoe Obozrenie, 2011).

Lloyd, Rosemary, *The Poet and his Circle* (Ithaca: Cornell University Press, 1999).

Loewen, Donald, 'Twentieth-Century Russian Literature and the North American Pedagogical Canon', *Slavic and East European Journal*, 50 (2006), 172–86, http://doi.org/10.2307/20459241

—, *The Most Dangerous Art: Poetry, Politics, and Autobiography after the Revolution* (Plymouth, Lexington Books, 2008).

Lominadze, S., 'Pustynia i oazis', *Voprosy literatury*, 2 (1997), 337–44.

Longenbach, James, *The Resistance to Poetry* (Chicago: University of Chicago Press, 2004).

Lootens, Tricia, *Lost Saints: Silence, Gender, and Victorian Literary Canonization* (Charlottesville and London: University Press of Virginia, 1996).

Losev, Lev, *Iosif Brodskii: opyt literaturnoi biografii*, Zhizn' zamechatel'nykh liudei (Moscow: Molodaia gvardiia, 2006).

—, 'V. F. Khodasevich (1886–1939)', ed. by N. M. Malygin, *Izbrannye imena: russkie poety. XX Vek. Uchebnoe posobie* (Moscow: Flinta, Nauka, 2008), 145–55.

Lotman, Juri, *Culture and Explosion*, ed. by Marina Grishakova, trans. by Wilma Clark (Berlin and New York: Mouton de Gruyter, 2009).

Lotman, Iu. M., *et al.*, eds, *Blokovskii sbornik, Trudy nauchnoi konferentsii, posviashchennoi izucheniiu zhizni i tvorchestva A. A. Bloka, mai 1962* (Tartu: Tartu State University, 1964).

—, *O poetakh i poezii* (Petersburg: Iskusstvo, 1996).

—, Lidiia Ia. Ginsburg and Boris A. Uspenskii, *The Semiotics of Russian Cultural History: Essays*, ed. by Alexander D. Nakhimovsky and Alice Stone Nakhimovsky (Ithaca: Cornell University Press, 1985).

L'vovskii, Stanislav, 'Gennadiiu Aigi: Ob"iasnenie v liubvi', *Vozdukh*, 1 (2006), 6–7.

Lygo, Emily, *Leningrad Poetry, 1953–1975. The Thaw Generation* (Oxford: Peter Lang, 2010).

Lyssyi, Iurii, *Russkaia literatura XX veka. 11 klass: praktikum dlia obshcheobrazovatel'nykh uchrezhdenii* (Moscow: Mnemozina, 1998).

MacFadyen, David, *Joseph Brodsky and the Soviet Muse* (Montreal: McGill-Queen's University Press, 2000).

MacKinnon, Lachlan, 'A Last Testament', *Times Literary Supplement*, 6 September 1996, 6.

Maiakovskii, Vladimir, *Polnoe sobranie sochinenii*, 13 vols, ed. by E. I. Naumov (Moscow: Khudozhestvennaia literatura, 1955–1961).

Makin, Michael, ed., 'Alternative Chronicles of Russian Poetry. Essays by Mikhail Aizenberg', special issue of *Russian Studies in Literature*, 32: 2 (1996), 4–9.

Maklin, Viktor, 'Boris Slutskii, kak ia ego pomniu', in *Boris Slutskii: vospominaniia sovremennikov*, comp. by Petr Gorelik (St Petersburg: Zhurnal Neva, 2005), 496–504.

Makolkin, Anna, 'Probing the Origins of Literary Biography: English and Russian Versions', *Biography*, 19: 1 (Winter 1996), 87–104.

Mallarmé, Stéphane, 'Crise de Vers', in *Divagations* (Paris: Bibliotèque Charpentier, 1897), 235–51.

Malykhina, Svitlana, *Renaissance of Classical Allusions in Contemporary Russian Media* (Lanham, NY: Lexington Books, 2014).

Mandel'shtam, Iu., 'Gamburgskii schet: po povodu *Antologii zarubezhnoi poezii*', in *Iakor': antologiia russkoi zarubezhnoi poezii*, ed. by Oleg Korostelev, Luigi Magarotto and Andrei Ustinov (St Petersburg: Aleteia, 2005), 230–36.

Mandelstam, Nadezhda, *Hope Against Hope*, trans. by Max Hayward (New York: Atheneum, 1970).

—, *Hope Against Hope*, trans. by Max Hayward (London: Collins and Harvill Press, 1971).

Mandelstam, Osip, *The Selected Poems of Osip Mandelstam*, trans. by Clarence Brown and W. S. Merwin (New York: New York Review of Books, 1971; 2004).

—, *Fifty Poems*, trans. by Bernard Meares, with an Introduction by Joseph Brodsky (New York: Persea Books, 1977).

—, *Journey to Armenia*, trans. by Clarence Brown with an Introduction by Bruce Chatwin (London: Nest Editions in Association with Faber, 1980).

Mandel'stam, Osip, *Sobranie sochnenii* (New York: Izdatel'stvo imeni Chekhova, 1955).

—, *Sobranie sochnenii v dvukh tomakh*, ed. by G. P. Struve and B. A. Filippov (Washington and New York: Inter-Language Associates, 1964–1968).

—, 'Nine Poems', trans. by Robert Lowell and Olga Carlisle, *New York Review of Books*, 23 December 1965, 3–7.

—, *Poems from Mandelstam*, trans. by R. H. Morrison (London and Toronto: Associated University Press, 1990).

—, *Sochineniia*, 2 vols (Moscow: Khudozhestvennaia literatura, 1990).

—, *Sobranie sochnenii*, 4 vols, ed. by P. Nerler (Moscow: Artbiznestsentr, 1993).

—, *Polnoe sobranie sochinenii i pisem v trekh tomakh*, ed. by A. G. Mets (Moscow: Progress-Pleiada, 2011).

Mandel'shtam, Roal'd, *Sobranie stikhotvorenii* (St Petersburg: Izd. Ivana Limbakha, 2006).

Marchenko, Alla, *et al.*, 'Russkaia poeziia v kontse veka: neoarkhaisty i neonovatory', *Znamia*, 1 (2001), http://magazines.russ.ru/znamia/2001/1/kritika.html?

Marchenko, Tat'iana, 'Izbranie i ne', *NG Ex Libris*, 11 May 2000, http://www.ng.ru/ng_exlibris/2000-05-11/3_nobellius.html

Markov, Vladimir, 'O poezii Georgiia Ivanova', *Opyty*, 8 (1958), 83–92.

Marsh, Rosalind, *Literature, History, and Identity in Post-Soviet Russia, 1991–2006* (Bern, Switzerland: Peter Lang, 2007).

Marshall, David P., *Celebrity and Power: Fame in Contemporary Culture* (Minneapolis and London: University of Minnesota Press, 1997).

Massie, Suzanne, *The Living Mirror: Five Poets from Leningrad* (London: Victor Gollancz Ltd, 1972).

Masterova, Galina, 'Sculpture of Exiled Poet Brodsky Graces U. S. Embassy', 4 July 2011, http://rbth.ru/articles/2011/07/04/sculpture_of_exiled_poet_brodsky_graces_us_embassy_13113.html

Matskin, Aleksandr, 'Boris Slutskii, ego poeziia, ego okruzhenie', in *Boris Slutskii: vospominaniia sovremennikov*, comp. by Petr Gorelik (St Petersburg: Zhurnal Neva, 2005), 307–23.

Maver, Igor, 'Introduction: Positioning Diasporic Literary Cultures', in *Diasporic Subjectivity and Cultural Brokering in Contemporary Post-colonial Literatures*, ed. by Igor Maver (Lanham, MD and Plymouth: Lexington Books, 2009), ix–xiv.

McCauley, Karen A., 'Production Literature and the Industrial Imagination', *The Slavic and East European Journal*, 42: 3 (Autumn, 1998), 444–66.

McDuff, David, 'The Prosody of Fate', *Times Literary Supplement*, 1 July 1983, 703.

Medish, Vadim, and Elisiavetta Ritchie, 'Writers in Exile: Planting New Roots — Planting Roots in Foreign Soil', *The Washington Post*, 24 February 1974, C1, C5.

Medvedev, P. N., ed., *Dnevnik Al. Bloka* (Leningrad: Izdatel'stvo leningradskikh pisatelei, 1928).

Meilakh, Mikhail, 'Mandelstam in London', *Times Literary Supplement*, 6 September 1991, 13.

Mel'nikov, N., ed., *Klassik bez retushi: Literaturnyi mir o tvorchestve I. A. Bunina* (Moscow: Knizhnitsa; Russkii put', 2010).

Merezhkovskii, D. S., *Sobranie sochinenii*, 4 vols, ed. by O. Mikhailov (Moscow: Pravda, 1990).

Mikhailov, Oleg, *I. A. Bunin: Ocherk tvorchestva* (Moscow: Izdatel'stvo 'Nauka', 1967).

—, 'Moi Bunin', *Literaturnaia gazeta*, 14 December 2011, http://www.lgz.ru/article/ N50--6350---2011-12-14-/Moy-Bunin17885/

Miller, Chris, 'The Mandelstam Syndrome and the "Old Heroic Bang"', *PN Review*, 162 (March–April 2005), 14–22.

Miller, Martin, *Freud and the Bolsheviks: Psychoanalysis in Imperial Russia and the Soviet Union* (New Haven: Yale University Press, 1998).

Milner-Gulland, Robin, 'Mandelshtam and Zabolotsky: Two Russian Rediscoveries', *Times Literary Supplement*, 11 May 1967, 398.

Milosz, Czeslaw, 'On Pasternak Soberly', in *Emperor of the Earth: Modes of Eccentric Vision* (Berkeley: University of California Press, 1977), 69–77.

Ministerstvo obrazovaniia Rossiiskoi Federatsii, 'Obiazatel'nyi minimum soderzhaniia srednego (polnogo) obshchego obrazovaniia', 30 June 1999, http://www.businesspravo.ru/Docum/DocumShow_DocumID_71939.html

—, 'Standart srednego (polnogo) obshchego obrazovaniia po literature. Bazovyi uroven'', Federal'nyi komponent gosudarstvennogo standarta obshchego obrazovaniia. Chast' II-Srednee (polnoe) obshchee obrazovanie (2004), http://window.edu.ru/resource/276/39276/files/29.pdf

—, 'Standart osnovnogo obshchego obrazovaniia po literature', Federal'nyi komponent gosudarstvennogo standarta obshchego obrazovaniia. Chast' I (2004), http://window.edu.ru/resource/259/39259/files/09.pdf

—, 'Standart srednego (polnogo) obshchego obrazovaniia po literature. Profil'nyi uroven", Federal'nyi komponent gosudarstvennogo standarta obshchego obrazovaniia. Chast' II-Srednee (polnoe) obshchee obrazovanie (2004), http://window.edu.ru/resource/277/39277/files/30.pdf

Ministerstvo obshchego i professional'nogo obrazovaniia RF, 'Ob obiazatel'nom minimume soderzhaniia obrazovatel'nykh programm osnovnoi obshcheobrazovatel'noi shkoly' (18 July 1997), http://www.businesspravo.ru/Docum/DocumShow_DocumID_52815.html

Mints, Zara, *Poetika Aleksandra Bloka* (St Petersburg: Iskusstvo, 1999).

Miturich, Petr, *Zapiski surovogo realista epokha avangarda* (Moscow: Literaturno-khudozhestvennoi agenstvo 'ga', 1997), quoted in *Boris Slutskii: vospominaniia sovremennikov*, comp. by Petr Gorelik (St Petersburg: Zhurnal Neva, 2005).

Mjør, Kåre Johan, 'The Online Library and the Classic Literary Canon in Post-Soviet Russia: Some Observations on "The Fundamental Electronic Library of Russian Literature and Folklore"', *Digital Icons*, 2 (2009), http://www.digitalicons.org/wp-content/uploads/2009/12/Kare-Johan-Mjor-DI-2.6.pdf

Mnatsakanian, Sergei, 'Bratskaia mogila', *Literaturnaia gazeta*, 8 September 2010, http://www.lgz.ru/article/N35--6289---2010-09-08-/Bratskaya-mogila13774/

Mochalov, Lev, 'V znak starinnoi druzhby', in *Boris Slutskii: vospominaniia sovremennikov*, comp. by Petr Gorelik (St Petersburg: Zhurnal Neva, 2005), 392–400.

Mole, John, 'Daisy chains and trains', *Times Literary Supplement*, 1 February 2002, 11.

Mole, Tom, *Byron's Romantic Celebrity: Industrial Culture and the Hermeneutic of Intimacy* (Basingstoke: Palgrave, 2007).

Molnar, Michael, 'Elena Shvarts', in *Reference Guide to Russian Literature*, ed. by Neil Cornwell (London and Chicago: Fitzroy Dearborn Publishers, 1998).

Monas, Sidney, 'Poets on Street Corners: Portraits of Fifteen Russian Poets', *New York Times*, 26 January 1969, section VII, 6, 40.

—, 'An Introduction to Osip Mandelstam's Essays', *New Literary History*, 6: 3 (1975), 629–32.

Mondry, Henrietta, '"Philological Wars": Nationalism in Russian Literary Periodicals (1993–1996)', in *In Search of Identity: Five Years Since the Fall of the Soviet Union*, ed. by Vladimir Tikhomirov (Melbourne, Centre for Russian and Euro-Asian Studies: University of Melbourne Press, 1996), 133–43.

Montefiore, Simon Sebag, *Young Stalin* (London: Phoenix, 2008).

Moser, Charles (ed.), *The Cambridge History of Russian Literature* (Cambridge: Cambridge University Press, 1992).

Murav, Harriet, *Music from a Speeding Train: Jewish Literature in Post-Revolution Russia* (Stanford: Stanford University Press, 2011).

Nabokov, Vladimir, 'The Art of Fiction', *Paris Review*, 4 (1967), 92–111.

Naiman, Anatoly, 'From Prayer to Howl', *Times Literary Supplement*, 4 September 1992, 4.

—, *Remembering Anna Akhmatova*, trans. by Wendy Rosslyn (New York: Henry Holt, 1991).

Nappel'baum, Moisei, *Nash vek*, ed. by Il'ia Rudiak (Ann Arbor: Ardis, 1984).

Nauchnyi tsentr 'Buninskaia Rossiia', 'Itogi deiatel'nosti nauchnogo tsentra 'Buninskaia Rossiia' v 2010 godu', Buninskii tsentr (2010), http://www.elsu.ru/bunincnt_osnov_rezul.html

Nefedov, Valerii, *Poeziia Ivana Bunina: etiudy* (Minsk: Vysheishaia shkola, 1975).

Nekrasov, Nikolai, 'Poet i grazhdanin', *Izbrannye sochineniia* (Moscow: OGIZ, 1945), 47–51.

Nelson, Victoria, *The Secret Life of Puppets* (Cambridge, MA: Harvard University Press, 2001).

Nepomniashchii, V., 'Pushkin cherez dvesti let', *Novyi mir*, 6 (1993), 230–38.

Nerler, Pavel, 'V poiskakh kontseptsii: kniga Nadezhdy Mandel'shtam ob Anne Akhmatovoi na fone perepiski s sovremennikami', in *Nadezhda Mandel'shtam, Ob Akhmatovoi* (Moscow: Novoe izdatel'stvo, 2007), 7–108.

Nesterova, K. F., ed., *Serebrianyi vek russkoi poezii* (Moscow: IMA-Kross, 1994).

Netzkowa, Elisabeth [pseud. of Elizaveta Mnatsakanova], *Das Buch Sabeth* (Vienna: [n. pub.], 1988).

Newman, Charles, 'A People Does Not Choose its Poets', *Harpers*, 248 (1974), 83–84.

Nikolaev, D. D., 'Kreid V. P., Georgii Ivanov. Moscow, Molodaia gvardiia, 2007', *Novyi istoricheskii vestnik*, 2 (2009), http://www.nivestnik.ru/2009_2/18.shtml

Nikonova, T. A., 'Istoriia russkoi literatury XX veka. Shestidesiatye gody. Uchebnoe posobie dlia vuzov' (Voronezh: Voronezh State University, 2007), *Edinoe okno*, http://window.edu.ru/resource/315/59315

Nivat, Georges, ed., *Odna ili dve russkikh literatury?* (Lausanne: L'Age d'Homme, 1981).

Novikov, Vladimir, 'Puti sovremennoi poezii', *Voprosy literatury*, 1 (1994), 9–16.

Novikova, Liza, 'Poeticheskoe stolpotvorenie. Ob"iavleny pretendenty na Buninskuiu premiiu', *Kommersant'* (7 August 2007), http://www.kommersant.ru/doc/793345

Obatin, G., *Ivanov-mistik: Okkul'tnye motivy v poezii i proze Viacheslava Ivanova* (Moscow: NLO, 2000).

Odoevtseva, Irina, *Na beregakh Nevy* (Moscow: Khudozhestvennaia literatura, 1988).

—, *Na beregakh Seny* (Moscow: Khudozhestvennaia literatura, 1989).

O'Driscoll, Dennis, 'Going a-roving', *Times Literary Supplement*, 12 June 1998, 24.

Ogorodnikov, Ivan, *Pedagogika* (Moscow: Prosveshchenie, 1964).

Ognev, Vladimir, 'Moi drug Boris Slutskii', in *Boris Slutskii: vospominaniia sovremennikov*, comp. by Petr Gorelik (St Petersburg: Zhurnal Neva, 2005), 274–89.

Ogryzko, Viacheslav, '"Vosslavim, bratsy, sumerki svobody", ili kak dogmatik Aleksandr Dymshits dobil partiinye vlasti i vypustil v 'Biblioteke poeta' tomik poluzapreshchennogo Osipa Mandel'shtama', *Literaturnaia Rossiia*, 11 March 2016, http://litrossia.ru/item/8721-vosslavim-brattsy-sumerki-svobody.

Okaiannye dni, Ivan Bunin, dir. Aleksei Denisov (Vserossiisaia gosudarstvennaia televizionaaia i radioveshchatel'naia kompaniia, Studiia istoricheskogo dokumental'nogo kino, 2007), http://russia.tv/brand/show/brand_id/10345

Orlov, V. N., *Gamaiun: Zhizn' Aleksandra Bloka* (Leningrad: Sovetskii pisatel', 1980).

—, *Zhizn' Bloka* (Moscow: Tsentrpoligraf, 2001).

—, ed., 'Iz literaturnogo naslediia Aleksandra Bloka. Iunosheskii dnevnik', in *Literaturnoe nasledstvo* (Moscow: Zhurnal'no-gazetnoe ob"edinenie, 1937), XXVII–XXVIII, 299–370.

—, ed., 'Literaturnoe nasledstvo Aleksandra Bloka', *Literaturnoe nasledstvo* (Moscow, Zhurnal'no-gazetnoe ob"edinenie, 1937), XXVII–XXVIII, 505–74.

Ostrovskaia, Sophie, *Memoirs of Anna Akhmatova's Years 1944–1950*, trans. by Jesse Davies (Liverpool: Lincoln Davies & Co, 1988).

Ozerov, Lev, 'Rezkaia liniia', in *Boris Slutskii: vospominaniia sovremennikov*, comp. by Petr Gorelik (St Petersburg: Zhurnal Neva, 2005), 327–46.

Pachmuss, Temira, 'Ivan Bunin through the Eyes of Zinaida Gippius', *The Slavonic and East European Review*, 44 (1966), 337–50.

Pakhareva, T. A., 'Obraz "monakhini-bludnitsy" v kul'turnom kontekste serebrianogo veka', *Anna Akhmatova: epokha, sud'ba, tvorchestvo: Krymskii Akhmatovskii nauchnyi sbornik*, 9 (2011), 227–37.

Paperno, Irina, *Stories of the Soviet Experience: Memoirs, Diaries, Dreams* (Ithaca: Cornell University Press, 2009).

—, and Joan Grossman, eds, *Creating Life: The Aesthetic Utopia of Russian Modernism* (Stanford: Stanford University Press, 1994).

Paramonov, Boris, 'Russkii evropeeets Boris Slutskii', October 2007, http://www.svobodanews.ru/content/article/419149.html

Parte, Kaitlin [Kathleen Parthé], 'Chto delaet pisatelia russkim? Puti sovremennoi poezii', *Voprosy literatury*, 1 (1996), 83–120.

Pasternak, Boris, *Poems of Boris Pasternak*, trans. by Lydia Pasternak-Slater (London: Unwin, 1963).

—, *Vozdushnye puti: Proza raznykh let* (Moscow: Sovetskii pisatel', 1982).

—, *Izbrannoe*, 2 vols (Moscow: Khudozhestvennaia literatura, 1985).

—, *Izbrannoe*, ed. by A. Pikach, 2 vols (St Petersburg: Kristall, 1998).

Pazukhin, Evgenii, 'Antisotsium', in *Sumerki 'Saigona'*, ed. by Iuliia Valieva (St Petersburg: Samizdat, 2009), 163–70.

Pelevin, Viktor, *Chapaev i Pustota* (Moscow: Vagrius, 1999).

—, 'I Never Was a Hero', *The Guardian*, 30 April 2000, http://www.guardian.co.uk/books/2000/apr/30/fiction

Peskov, Vasilii, 'Buninskie mesta', *Komsomol'skaia Pravda*, 25 October 2002.

Petrovskii, M., '"Dvenadtsat" Bloka i Leonid Andreev', in *Aleksandr Blok: Literaturnoe nasledstvo* (Moscow: IMLI, 1987), IV, 226.

Pevear, Richard, 'On the Memoirs of Nadezhda Mandelstam', *Hudson Review*, 24: 3 (1971), 427–40.

Pilling, John, 'Before Yesterday and After', *PN Review*, 82 (November–December 1991), 55–56.

Platt, Kevin, 'O iambakh i posledstviiakh, prichinakh i trokheiakh', *Novoe literaturnoe obozrenie*, 114 (2012), 264–68.

Plekhanova, I., 'Igra v imperativnom soznanii: lirika Borisa Slutskogo v dialoge s vremenem', *Voprosy literatury*, 1 (2003), 46–72.

Poety Serebrianogo veka, http://slova.org.ru

Polivanov, Konstantin, ed., *Anna Akhmatova and Her Circle*, trans. by Patricia Beriozkina (Fayetteville, AR: University of Arkansas Press, 1994).

Polonsky, Rachel, 'Beneath the Kremlin Crag', *Times Literary Supplement*, 14 May 2004, 9.

Polozkova, Vera, 'Snova ne my', https://www.youtube.com/watch?v=1GVlDslpLBA

—, http://vera-polozkova/ru

Polukhina, Valentina, 'Poets of Protest', *Times Literary Supplement*, 11 September 1987, 987.

—, ed., *Iosif Brodskii glazami sovremennikov: kniga pervaia (1987–1992)* (St Petersburg: Zvezda, 2006).

—, and Daniel Weissbort, eds, *An Anthology of Contemporary Russian Women Poets* (Iowa City: University of Iowa Press, 2005).

Pomorska, Krystyna, *Russian Formalist Theory and Its Poetic Ambiance* (The Hague: Mouton, 1968).

Ponomareff, Constantin V., *The Time Before Death: Twentieth-Century Memoirs* (Amsterdam: Rodopi, 2013).

Poplavskii, Boris, 'Vokrug "Chisel"', in *Russkii Parizh* (Moscow: Izdatel'stvo MGU, 1998), 288–91.

—, *Avtomaticheskie stikhi* (Moscow: Soglasie, 1999).

—, *Sochineniia* (St Petersburg: Letnii sad, 1999).

Porter, Robert, *Russia's Alternative Prose* (London: Bloomsbury, 1994).

Potebnia, A., *Mysl' i iazyk* (Kharkov: Tipografiia Adol'fa Darre, 1892).

Prigov, Dmitrii, 'Bestiarii', http://www.prigov.org and in *Grazhdane! Ne zabyvaites', pozhaluista*, catalogue from the exhibit at the Moscow Museum of Contemporary Art, 2008, curated by Ekaterina Degot' (Moscow: Izdatel'skaia programma Moskovskogo muzeia sovremennogo iskusstva, 2008).

—, 'Rekonstruktsiia po kasatel'noi ili sem'ia navsegda', http://prigov.ru/action/foto.php

—, and Sergei Shapoval, *Portretnaia galereia D. A. P.* (Moscow: MLO, 2003).

Prikhod'ko, I. S., *Mifopoetika A. Bloka* (Vladimir: Vladimirskii pedagogicheskii universitet, 1994).

Pushkin, Aleksandr, *Sobranie sochinenii*, 10 vols (Leningrad: Nauka, 1977).

—, *Complete Works* (Downham Market: Milner and Company Ltd, 1999–2003).

—, *A. Pushkin: Selected Verse*, ed. and trans. by John Fennell (London: Bristol Classical Press, 2001).

Pyman, Avril, *The Life of Aleksandr Blok*, 2 vols (Oxford: Oxford University Press, 1979).

—, 'The Last Romantic', *Russian Life* (Nov.–Dec. 2000), 34–43.

—, ed., *The Twelve* (Durham: University of Durham Press, 1989).

Radlova, Anna, *Bogoroditsyn korabl', Krylatyi gost', Povest' o Tatarinovoi* (Moscow: 'Its-Garant', 1997).

Raeff, Marc, *Russia Abroad: a Cultural History of the Russian Emigration, 1919–1939* (Oxford: Oxford University Press, 1990).

Ramazani, Jahan, *A Transnational Poetics* (Chicago: University of Chicago Press, 2009).

Rassadin, Stanislav, *Samoubiitsy: povest' o tom, kak my zhili i chto chitali* (Moscow: Tekst, 2007).

Ratnikov, Kirill, 'Sud'ba "Parizhskoi noty" v poezii russkogo zarubezhi'a', http://zhurnal.lib.ru/p/petrushkin_a_a/ratnikov.shtml

Rawson, Claude, 'Escaping the Irish Labyrinth', *Times Literary Supplement*, 24 January 1992, 19.

Rayfield, Donald, 'The Great Unfathomable', *Times Literary Supplement*, 2 July 1999, 13.

—, 'Stalin, Beria and the Poets', *PN Review*, 92 (July–August 1993), 22–30.

Reavey, George, *The New Russian Poets 1953–1968. An Anthology* (New York: October House Inc., 1968).

Reeder, Roberta, *Anna Akhmatova: Poet and Prophet* (London: Allison & Busby, 1994).

Rein, Evgenii, 'Samyi krupnyi poet pozdnego sovetizma', in *Boris Slutskii: vospominaniia sovremennikov*, comp. by Petr Gorelik (St Petersburg: Zhurnal Neva, 2005), 387–89.

Robin, Régine, *Socialist Realism: An Impossible Aesthetic*, trans. by Catherine Porter (Stanford: Stanford University Press, 1992).

Robinson, William, 'Beyond Nation-State Paradigms: Globalization, Sociology, and the Challenge of Transnational Studies', *Sociological Forum*, 13: 4 (December 1998), 561–94.

Rodionov, Andrei, 'a_rodionoff's Journal', http://a-rodionoff.livejournal.com

—, 'Poeticheskii vecher Dmitriia Tonkonogova i Andreia Rodionova', *Virtual'nyi klub poezii*, http://www.ctuxu.ru/article/report/tonkonogov_rodionov.htm

Rogatchevski, Andrei, 'Staging the Unstageable: Casper Wrede's production of *Hope Against Hope* at the Royal Exchange Theatre (1983)' in *When the Elephant Broke Out of the Zoo: A Festschrift for Donald Rayfield*, ed. by A. Schönle, O. Makarova and J. Hicks, *Stanford Slavonic Studies*, 39 (2012), 108–28.

Rojek, Chris, *Celebrity* (London: Reaktion Books, 2001).

Ronen, Omry, *The Fallacy of the Silver Age in Twentieth-Century Russian Literature* (Amsterdam: Harwood Academic, 1997).

—, 'Grust'', *Zvezda*, 9 (2012), http://magazines.russ.ru/zvezda/2012/9/rq9.html

Rowse, A. L., 'The Mandelstam Experience', *Contemporary Review*, 249 (1986), 21–26.

Rubins, Maria, 'Challenges of the Jazz Age', *Russian Montparnasse: Transnational Writing in Interwar Paris* (London: Palgrave Macmillan, 2015), 113–61. https://doi.org/10.1057/9781137508010

Russkaia poeziia: Stikhi serebrianogo veka, http://rupoem.ru/silver.aspx

Russkaia poeziia 1960–kh godov, http://www.ruthenia.ru/60s

Rybakova, Mariia, *Gnedich: Roman* (Moscow: Vremia, 2011).

Rybitskaia, O. K., 'Metodicheskie rekomendatsii po literature dlia abiturientov 2001 goda (polnoe srednee obshchee obrazovanie)', Ulianovsk Pedagogical College, approved by the Ministry of General and Professional Education of the Russian Federation, http://venec.ulstu.ru/lib/2002/1/Rybickaja.pdf

Rybnikova, M. A., *A. Blok-Gamlet* (Moscow: Svetlana, 1923).

—, *Russkaia literatura. Voprosnik po russkoi literature dlia zaniatii 7, 8 i 9 grupp shkol 2–i stupeni i dlia pedtekhnikumov* (Moscow: Mir, 1928).

Rylkova, Galina, *The Archaeology of Anxiety: The Russian Silver Age and its Legacy* (Pittsburgh: University of Pittsburgh Press, 2007).

—, 'Saint or Monster? Akhmatova in the 21st Century', *Kritika: Explorations in Russian and Eurasian History*, 11: 2 (Spring 2010), http://muse.jhu.edu/journals/kritika/v011/11.2.rylkova.html

Sabbatini, Marco 'The Pathos of Holy Foolishness in the Leningrad Underground', in Holy Foolishness in Russia: New Perspectives, ed. by Priscilla Hunt and Svitlana Kobets (Bloomington: Slavica Publishers, 2011), pp. 337–52.

Samizdat veka: neofitsial'naia poeziia, http://rvb.ru/np

Samoilov, David, 'Drug i sopernik', in *Boris Slutskii: vospominaniia sovremennikov*, comp. by Petr Gorelik (St Petersburg: Zhurnal Neva, 2005), 77–105.

Sandler, Stephanie, 'Introduction: Myths and Paradoxes of the Russian Poet', in *Rereading Russian Poetry*, ed. by Stephanie Sandler (New Haven and London: Yale University Press, 1999), 1–28.

—, 'Poetry after 1930', in *The Cambridge Companion to Twentieth-Century Russian Literature*, ed. by Evgeny Dobrenko and Marina Balina (Cambridge: Cambridge University Press, 2011). 115–34.

—, 'Sex, Death and Nation in the "Strolls with Pushkin" Controversy', *Slavic Review*, 51: 2 (1992), 294–308.

—, 'Visual Poetry after Modernism: Elizaveta Mnatsakanova', *Slavic Review*, 67: 3 (2008), 610–41.

Santner, Eric L., *Stranded Objects: Mourning, Memory, and Film in Postwar Germany* (Ithaca: Cornell University Press, 1990).

Sapozhkov, S., 'Russkaia poeziia 1880–1890-kh godov: "konstruktivnost" khaosa ili "esteticheskii immoralizm"?', *Novoe literaturnoe obozrenie*, 75 (2005), 338–47.

Sarnov, Benedikt, 'Zanimatel'naia dialektika', in *Boris Slutskii: vospominaniia sovremennikov*, comp. by Petr Gorelik (St Petersburg: Zhurnal Neva, 2005), 236–54.

Satunovskii, Ian, *Khochu li ia posmertnoi slavy: izbrannye stikhi*, comp. by I. Akhmet'ev and P. Satunovskii (Moscow: Biblioteka al'manakha 'Vesy', 1992), http://www.vavilon.ru/texts/satunovsky1-3.html

Savitskii, Stanislav, *Andegraund: Istoriia i mify leningradskoi neofitsial'noi literatury* (Moscow: NLO, 2002).

Scammell, Michael, 'Writers in a Cage', *New York Review of Books*, 14 January 2010, 55.

Scherr, Barry P., *Russian Poetry: Meter, Rhythm, and Rhyme* (Berkeley: University of California Press, 1986).

—, 'Martynov, Slutskii and the Politics of Rhythm', *Paragraph*, 33: 2 (2010), 246–59.

Schmidt, Rachel, *Critical Images: The Canonization of Don Quixote through Illustrated Editions of the 18th Century* (Montreal: McGill-Queen's University Press, 1999).

Schweitzer, Viktoria, 'Spustia pochti polveka', *Russica* (1981), 229–56.

Schweitzer, Vivien, 'Poetry and Song to Plumb the Russian Soul's Depths', *The New York Times*, 14 February 2008, http://www.nytimes.com/2008/02/14/arts/music/14krem.html

Schwerter, Stephanie, *Northern Irish Poetry and the Russian Turn: Intertextuality in the work of Seamus Heaney, Tom Paulin and Medbh McGuckian* (London: Palgrave Macmillan, 2013).

Sedakova, Ol'ga, 'Aigi: Ot"ezd', *Novoe literaturnoe obozrenie*, 79 (2006), 200–04.

—, 'Konchina Brodskogo', http://olgasedakova.com/Poetica/239

—, 'Muzyka glukhogo vremeni', *Vestnik novoi literatury*, 2 (1990), 257–63.

—, 'Zametki i vospominaniia o raznykh stikhotvoreniiakh, a takzhe Pokhvala poezii', in *Proza* (Moscow: NFQ/Tu Print, 2001).

—, and Slava Yastremski, 'A Dialogue on Poetry', in Sedakova, *Poems and Elegies*, ed. by Slava I. Yastremski (Lewisburg: Bucknell University Press, 2003), 11–20.

Severiukhin, D, V. Dolinin, B. Ivanov and B. Ostanin, eds, *Samizdat Leningrada 1950e–1980e: literaturnaia entsiklopediia* (Moscow: NLO, 2003).

Shackleton, Mark, ed., *Diasporic Literature and Theory — Where Now?* (Newcastle upon Tyne: Cambridge Scholars Publishing, 2008).

Shaitanov, Igor', 'Grafoman, brat epigona', *Arion*, 4 (1998), http://magazines.russ.ru/arion/1998/4/shaitan.html

—, 'O byvshem i nesbyvshemsia', *Arion*, 1 (1998), http://magazines.russ.ru/arion/1998/1/014.html

—, 'Poet v Rossii...', *Arion*, 2 (1998), http://magazines.russ.ru/arion/1998/2/shaitan.html

—, 'Boris Slutskii: povod vspomnit'', *Arion*, 3 (2000), http://magazines.russ.ru/arion/2000/3/shaitan.html

—, *Delo vkusa: kniga o sovremennoi poezii* (Moscow: Vremia, 2007).

—, 'O sovremennoi lirike. (Opyt analiza)', in *Uroki literatury v 11–om klasse. Kniga dlia uchitelia*, ed. by V. P. Zhuravlev (Moscow: Prosveshchenie, [n.d.]), http://window.edu.ru/resource/080/28080

Shakhovskaia, Zinaida, 'Literaturnye pokoleniia', in *Odna ili dve russkikh literatury?*, ed. by Georges Nivat (Lausanne: L'Age d'Homme, 1981), 55–62.

Shapoval, Sergei, 'Otdushina dlia politika', *Nezavisimaia gazeta*, 14 February 2003, http://www.ng.ru/saturday/2003-02-14/13_lukyanov.html

Sharshun, Serge, 'Iz listovok S. Sharshuna. Publikatsiia R. Gerra', *The New Review*, 163 (1986), 127–39.

Shcherbina, V., 'O gruppe estetstvuiushchikh kosmopolitov v kino', *Iskusstvo kino*, 1 (1949), 14–16.

Sheldon, Richard Robert, 'Viktor Borisovich Shklovsky: Literary Theory and Practice, 1914–1930' (unpublished Ph.D dissertation, University of Michigan, 1966).

Shepelev, V. L. and V. N. Liubimov, '"On budet pisat' stikhi protiv nas". Pravda o bolezni i smerti Aleksandra Bloka (1921)', *Istochnik*, 2 (1995), 33–45.

Shkliarevskii, Igor', 'On ne zaigryval s nebom', in *Boris Slutskii: vospominaniia sovremennikov*, comp. by Petr Gorelik (St Petersburg: Zhurnal Neva, 2005), 390–91.

Shlapentokh, Vladimir, 'The Justification of Political Conformism: The Mythology of Soviet Intellectuals', *Studies in Soviet Thought*, 39 (1990), 111–35.

Shneidman, N. N., *Literature and Ideology in Soviet Education* (Toronto: University of Toronto Press, 1973).

—, *Russian Literature 1995–2002: On the Threshold of the New Millenium* (Toronto, Buffalo and London: University of Toronto Press, 2004).

Shraer-Petrov, David, 'Ierusalimskii kazak', in *Boris Slutskii: vospominaniia sovremennikov*, comp. by Petr Gorelik (St Petersburg: Zhurnal Neva, 2005), 456–60.

Shrayer, Maxim, 'Russian American Literature', in *The Greenwood Encyclopedia of Multiethnic American Literature*, ed. by Emmanuel S. Nelson, 5 vols (Westport, CT: Greenwood Publishing Group, 2005), IV, 1940–51.

— (ed.), *An Anthology of Jewish-Russian Literature: Two Centuries of Dual Identity in Prose and Poetry*, 2 vols (Armonk, NY and London: M. E. Sharpe, 2007).

Shteiger, Anatolii, *Dvazhdy dva chetyre: stikhi 1926–1939* (Paris: Rifma, 1950).

—, 'Ne do stikhov... Zdes' slishkom mnogo slez', '"My govorim o rozakh i stikhakh...": stikhi', http://gostinaya.net/?p=8387

Shubinskii, Valerii, 'Semeinyi al'bom: zametki o sovetskoi poezii klassicheskogo perioda', *Oktiabr'*, 8 (2000), 150–68.

Shvarts, Elena, 'Dnevniki', *Paradise* (Newcastle upon Tyne: Bloodaxe, 1993), ed., trans. and foreword by Michael Molnar and Catriona Kelly.

—, *Mundus imaginalis* (St Petersburg: Ezro, 1996).

—, 'Neobiazatel'nye poiasneniia', http://www.vavilon.ru/texts/shvarts1-6.html

—, *Sochineniia*, 4 vols (St Petersburg: Pushkinskii dom, 2002–2008).

—, Birdsong on the Seabed, translated by Sasha Dugdale (Tarset: Bloodaxe Books, 2008).

—, 'Dnevniki', *Novoe literaturnoe obozrenie*, 115 (2012), 239–79.

—, *Sochineniia*, 5 vols (St Petersburg: Pushkinskii dom, 2002–2013).

Siniavskii, Andreii, *Progulki s Pushkinym* (London: Overseas Publications Interchange, 1975).

Slobin, Greta, 'The "Homecoming" of the First Wave Diaspora and its Cultural Legacy', *Slavic Review*, 60: 3 (Autumn 2001), 513–29.

—, *Russians Abroad: Literary and Cultural Politics of Diaspora (1919–1939)* (Boston: Academic Studies Press, 2013).

Slobodniuk, S. L., *Idushchie putiami zla* (St Petersburg: Aleteia, 1998).

—, *Solov'inyi ad: trilogiia vocheloveheniia Aleksandra Bloka* (St Petersburg: Aleteia, 2002).

Slonim, Marc, *Soviet Russian Literature: Writers and Problems 1917–67* (New York: Oxford University Press, 1967).

Slutskii, Boris, ed., *Poety Izrailia* (Moscow: Inostrannaia literatura, 1963).

—, *Sobranie sochinenii*, 3 vols, comp. by Iurii Boldyrev (Moscow: Khudozhestvennaia literatura, 1991).

—, *Teper' Osventsim chasto snitsia mne,* comp. by Petr Gorelik (St Petersburg: Izdatel'stvo zhurnala Neva, 1999).

Slutsky, Boris, *Things that Happened*, ed., trans. and with an introduction by G. S. Smith (Moscow and Birmingham: Glas, 1999).

Smirnov, Aleksei, 'Blizhnee ekho', in *Boris Slutskii: vospominaniia sovremennikov*, comp. by Petr Gorelik (St Petersburg: Zhurnal Neva, 2005), 461–67.

Smith, Alexandra, 'Tsvetaeva's Story "The Chinaman" and its Link with the Eurasian Movement in Prague and in Paris in the 1920s–30s', *The Soviet and Post-Soviet Review*, 28: 3 (2001 [2002]), 269–86.

Smith, G. S., 'Soldier of Misfortune', in Boris Slutsky, *Things that Happened*, ed., trans. by, and with an introduction by G. S. Smith (Moscow and Birmingham: Glas, 1999).

—, 'Russian Poetry: The Lives or the Lines?', *The Modern Language Review*, 95 (2000), xxix–xli.

—, 'Joseph Brodsky: Summing Up', *Literary Imagination*, 7: 3 (2005), 399–410.

—, 'Boris Slutskii', *Dictionary of Literary Biography*, vol. 359, Russian Poets of the Soviet Era, ed. by Karen Rosneck (Detroit: Gale, 2011), 255–64.

—, 'Russian Poetry Now', http://www.aatseel.org/resources/stateofthefield/poetry.htm

—, ed., *Contemporary Russian Poetry: A Bilingual Anthology* (Bloomington: Indiana University Press, 1993).

Smola, O., *'Chernyi vecher. Belyi sneg…'. Tvorcheskaia istoriia i sud'ba poemy Aleksandra Bloka 'Dvenadtsat'* (Moscow: Nasledie, 1993).

Sobolev, Olga, 'Appropriated by the Revolution: Blok and the Socialist Realist Cinema', unpublished paper presented at the AAASS Conference, Boston, November 2013.

Soja, Edward, *Thirdspace: Journey to Los Angeles and Other Real-and-Imagined Places* (Oxford: Blackwell, 1996).

Solov'ev, S. M., G. I. Chulkov, A. D. Skaldin and V. N. Kniazhnin, eds, *Pis'ma Aleksandra Bloka* (Leningrad: Kolos, 1925).

Steiger, Andrew J., 'Soviet Poetry-Dynamized Incarnate Sound', *Books Abroad*, 3 (1935), 247–50.

Steiner, George, 'A Terrible Exactness', *Times Literary Supplement*, 11 June 1976, 709.

—, 'An Enclosure of Time', *Times Literary Supplement*, 4 February 1977, 132.

—, 'Songs of a Torn Tongue', *Times Literary Supplement*, 28 September 1984, 1093.

Stepanova, Mariia, *Pesni severnykh iuzhan: 20 sonetov k M.* (Moscow and Tver': Argo-Risk/Kolonna, 2001).

—, *Proza Ivana Sidorova* (Moscow: Novoe izdatel'stvo, 2008).

Stern, Ludmila, *Joseph Brodskii: A Personal Memoir* (Forth Worth: Baskerville Publishers, 2004).

Strelianyi, Andrei, ed., *Samizdat veka* (Moscow: Polifakt, 1999).

Strizhneva, Svetlana, *'V tom, chto umiraiu, ne vinite nikogo'?…: sledstvennoe delo V. V. Maiakovskogo* (Moscow: Ellis Lak, 2000, 2005).

Struve, Gleb, 'The Art of Ivan Bunin', *Slavonic and East European Review*, 11 (1933), 423–36.

—, 'Nadezhda Mandelstam's remarkable memoirs', *Books Abroad*, 45: 2 (Winter 1971), 18–25.

—, *Russkaia literatura v izgnanii* (Paris: YMCA, 1984).

Sukharev, Dmitrii, 'Dlia ponimaniia Slutskogo nuzhny miagkie nravy i esche kakoi-nikakoi professionalizm', in *Boris Slutskii: vospominaniia sovremennikov*, comp. by Petr Gorelik (St Petersburg: Zhurnal Neva, 2005), 267–73.

—, 'Skrytopis' Borisa Slutskogo', *Voprosy literatury*, 1 (2003), 22–45.

Sukhikh, Igor', *Russkii kanon: knigi XX veka* (Moscow: Vremia, 2013).

Svarovskii, Fedor, *Vse khotiat byt' robotami* (Moscow: Argo-Risk, 2007).

Sverdlov, M., and E. Staf'eva, 'Stikhotvorenie na smert' poeta: Brodskii i Oden. Rozhdenie "metafizicheskogo" Brodskogo iz stikhotvoreniia na smert' poeta', *Voprosy literatury*, 3 (2005), 220–44.

Svetlikova, I. Iu., *Istoki russkogo formalizma: traditsiia psikhologizma i formal'naia shkola* (Moscow: Novoe literaturnoe obozrenie, 2005).

Szamuely, Helen, review of Sonia Ketchian, 'The Poetic Craft of Bella Akhmadulina', *Times Literary Supplement*, 23 September 1994, 26.

Tabachnikova, Olga, 'Akhmatova on Chekhov: A Case of Animosity?', *Russian Literature*, 66: 2 (2009), 235–55.

Takho-Godi, E. A, 'Vladimir Solov'ev i Konstantin Sluchevskii. K istorii vzaimootnoshenii', in *Kontekst: 1993. Literaturno-istoricheskie issledovaniia* (Moscow: Nasledie, 1996), 323–40.

—, ed., *Vladimir Solov'ev i kul'tura Serebrianogo veka* (Moscow: Nauka, 2005).

Tarasova, I. A., 'Zhanr fragmenta v poezii "Parizhskoi noty"', *Zhanry rechi* 1: 11 (2015), 111–16.

Tazhidinova, Irina G., '"Declaration of Emotional Independence" in Soviet Poetry in the 1930s: A Historical-Sociological Analysis', *History and Historians in the Context of the Time*, 1 (2014), 48–54.

Terapiano, Iurii, *Vstrechi* (New York: izdatel'stvo Chekhova, 1958).

Terts, Abram (pseudonym of Andrei Siniavskii), *Chto takoe sotsialisticheskii realizm* (Paris: Syntaxis, 1988).

Thomas, D. M., 'The Weaponry of Poets', *Times Literary Supplement*, 17 February 1978, 186.

—, 'Catching Up — Poetry: 3; Poetry in Translation', *Times Literary Supplement*, 18 January 1980, 66.

Thompson, Ewa M., *Understanding Russia: the Holy Fool in Russian Culture* (Lanham MD: University Press of America, 1987).

Tiffany, Daniel Newton, *Toy Medium: Materialism and Modern Lyric* (Berkeley: University of California Press, 2000).

Tikhomirov, Vladimir, ed., *In Search of Identity: Five Years Since the Fall of the Soviet Union* (Melbourne, Centre for Russian and Euro-Asian Studies: University of Melbourne Press, 1996).

Timenchik, Roman, 'K semioticheskoi interpretatsii "Poemy bez geroia"', *Trudy po znakovym sistemam*, 6 (1973), 438–42.

—, 'Rozhdenie stikha iz dukha prozy: "Komarovskie kroki" Anny Akhmatovoi', in L. Flejshman, C. Gölz, A. A. Hansen-Löve, eds, *Analysieren als Deuten: Wolf Schmid zum 60. Geburtstag* (Hamburg: Hamburg University Press, 2004), 541–62.

Todd, Uil'iam Mills III, 'Otkrytiia i proryvy sovetskoi teorii literatury v poslestalinskuiu epokhu', in *Istoriia russkoi literaturnoi kritiki*, ed. by Evgenii Dobrenko and Galin Tikhanov (Moscow: Novoe literaturnoe obozrenie, 2011), 571–607.

Tokarev, Dmitrii, *'Mezhdu Indiei i Gegelem': Tvorchestvo Borisa Poplavskogo v komparativnoi perspektive* (Moscow: NLO, 2011).

Tolstoi, Ivan, 'Veter s Nevy: Zhizn' Georgiia Ivanova', Radio Svoboda, 11 October 2009, http://www.svoboda.org/content/transcript/1849756.html

Tomashevskii, Boris, *O stikhe* (Leningrad: Priboi, 1929).

Tomlinson, Charles, and John Bayley, 'An Involuntary Witness', *Times Literary Supplement*, 21 November 1986, 1295.

Toporov, Viktor, 'No, Bozhe, kak ikh zamolchat' zastavit'!', *Vzgliad*, 18 August 2007, http://vz.ru/columns/2007/8/18/101677.html

Trotsky, Leon, *Literature and Revolution* (Chicago, IL: Haymarket Books, 2005).

Tsvetaeva, Marina, *Sochineniia*, 2 vols (Moscow: Khudozhestvennaia literatura, 1980).

—, *Sochineniia*, ed. by Anna Saakiants, 2 vols (Moscow: Khudozhestvennaia literatura, 1988).

—, *Stikhotvoreniia i poemy* (Moscow: Ripol Klassik, 2002).

—, *Zakon zvezdy i formula tsvetka* (Moscow: Eksmo, 2010).

Tvardovskii, Aleksandr, 'About Bunin', in *Stories and Poems by Ivan Bunin*, trans. by Olga Shartse and Irina Zheleznova (Moscow: Progress, 1979), 9–29.

Tynianov, Iurii, *Arkhaisty i novatory* (Leningrad: Priboi, 1929).

Ulanov, Aleksandr, 'Elena Shvarts: *Opredelenie v durnuiu pogodu'*, *Znamia*, 4 (1990), http://magazines.russ.ru/znamia/1998/4/nabl1.html

Valentine, Sarah, 'Music, Silence, and Spirituality in the Poetry of Gennady Aigi', *Slavic and East European Journal*, 51 (2007), 675–92.

Valieva, Iuliia, ed., *Sumerki 'Saigona'* (St Petersburg: Samizdat, 2009).

Vaughan, Richard, 'Literature — Why Dostoyevsky is One of Russia's Best Teachers', *The Times Educational Supplement*, 24 January 2014, 8.

Van Buskirk, Emily, 'Lidiia Ginzburg on Elena Shvarts', *Slavonica*, 16: 2 (2010), 139–41. http://dx.doi.org/10.1179/136174210X12814458213808

Van Het Reve, K., 'Samizdat: The Sudden Flowering of Underground Literature in Russia', *The Observer*, 29 March 1970, 21.

Vavilon: sovremennaia russkaia literatura, http://www.vavilon.ru

Vendler, Helen, 'False Poets and Real Poets', *The New York Times Book Review*, 7 September 1975 [n. p.].

Vetrov, Sasha, *Led: Al'bom pesen na stikhi poeta Georgiia Ivanova* (St Petersburg: Petersburgskaia studiia gramzapisi, 2012), http://proektvetrov.kroogi.com/ru/download/2470196-Lyod.htm

Vilenskii, Semen, comp., *Poeziia uznikov Gulaga. Antologiia* (Moscow: Materik. Mezhdunarodnyi fond, 2005).

Virabov, Igor', 'Vakson vo mgle', *Rossiiskaia gazeta*, 2 November 2016, https://rg.ru/2016/11/02/serial-tainstvennaia-strast-novye-pohozhdeniia-poetov-shestidesiatnikov.html

Volchenko, Natal'ia, '"A vy noktiurn sygrat' smogli by na fleite vodostochnykh trub?": o probleme vypusknogo sochineniia', *Russkaia slovesnost'*, 6 (2005), 2–7.

Volgina, Arina, 'Sravnitel'naia poetika: Iosif Brodskii/Joseph Brodsky', *Voprosy literatury*, 3 (2005), 186–219.

Volkov, Solomon, *St. Petersburg: A Cultural History*, trans. by Antonina W. Bouis (London: Sinclair-Stevenson, 1996).

—, *The Magical Chorus: A History of Russian Culture from Tolstoy to Solzhenitsyn*, trans. by Antonina W. Bouis (New York: Vintage Books, 2009).

Vol'pe, T. S., ed., *Pis'ma Al Bloka k E. P. Ivanovu* (Moscow-Leningrad: AN SSSR, 1936).

Wachtel, Andrew, *Remaining Relevant After Communism: The Role of the Writer in Eastern Europe* (Chicago and London: University of Chicago Press, 2006).

—, 'Orhan Pamuk's *Snow* as a Russian Novel', *Slavic and East European Journal*, 56 (2012), 91–108.

—, and Ilya Vinitsky, *Russian Literature* (Cambridge: Polity Press, 2009).

Watchel, Michael, *The Cambridge Introduction to Russian Poetry* (Cambridge: Cambridge University Press, 2004).

Wainright, Jeffrey, 'On Anna Akhmatova', *PN Review*, 2 (January–March 1978), 1–2.

Watten, Barrett, 'Post-Soviet Subjectivity in Arkadii Dragomoshchenko and Ilya Kabakov', *Postmodern Culture*, 3: 2 (January 1993), http://muse.jhu.edu/article/27402

Weber, Max, *On Charisma and Institution Building*, ed. by S. N. Eisenstadt (Chicago: University of Chicago Press, 1968).

Webster's New World Dictionary of the American Language (New York: The World Publishing Co., 1972).

Weidle, Vladimir, 'Antologiia zarubezhnoi poezii', in *Iakor': antologiia russkoi zarubezhnoi poezii*, ed. by Oleg Korostelev, Luigi Magarotto and Andrei Ustinov (St Petersburg: Aleteia, 2005), 218–22.

Wells, David, 'The Function of the Epigraph in Akhmatova's Poetry', in *Anna Akhmatova 1889–1989: Papers from the Akhmatova Centennial Conference, Bellagio*, ed. by Sonia Ketchian (Oakland, CA: Berkeley Slavic Specialties, 1993), 266–81.

Werth, Alexander, 'New Russian Poetry', *Times Literary Supplement*, 22 March 1963, 200.

Whyte, Christopher, 'The English for an Anti-Elegy: Translating Tsvetaeva on Rilke', *Translation and Literature*, 21 (2012), 196–212.

Wilmer, Clive, 'Song and Stone', *Times Literary Supplement*, 6 May 2005, 12.

Winter, Jay, and Emmanuel Sivan, 'Setting the Framework', in *War and Remembrance in the Twentieth Century*, ed. by Jay Winter and Emmanuel Sivan (Cambridge: Cambridge University Press, 1999), 6–39.

Yershov, Peter, 'Soviet National Literature in the New Soviet Encyclopedia', *American Slavic and East European Review*, 13 (1954), 89–99.

Zaitsev, V. A., *Lektsii po istorii russkoi poezii XX veka (1940–2000)* (Moscow: Izdatel'stvo moskovskogo universiteta, 2009).

Zhdanov, Andrei, 'O zhurnalakh "Zvezda" i "Leningrad": Iz postanovleniia TsK VKP (b) ot 14 avgusta 1946 g.', in *Sovetskaia pechat' v dokumentakh*, ed. by N. Kaminskaia (Moscow: Gosudarstvennoe izdatel'stvo politicheskoi literatury, 1961), pp. 94–98.

Zhirmunskii, V. M., 'Anna Akhmatova i Aleksandr Blok', in *Izbrannye trudy. Teoriia literatury. Poetika. Stilistika* (Leningrad: Nauka, 1977), 323–52.

Zhitenev, A., *Poeziia neomodernizma* (St Petersburg: Inapress, 2012).

Zholkovskii, Aleksandr, 'Anna Akhmatova: Piat'desiat let spustia', *Zvezda*, 9 (1996), 211–27.

—, 'K pereosmysleniiu kanona: sovetskie klassiki nonkonformisty v postsovetskoi perspektive', http://www-bcf.usc.edu/~alik/rus/ess/reth.htm

—, 'Strakh, tiazhest', mramor (iz materialov k zhiznetvorcheskoi biografii Akhmatovoi)', *Wiener Slawistischer Almanakh*, 36 (1996), 119–54.

Zholkovsky, Alexander, 'Anna Akhmatova: Scripts, Not Scriptures', *Slavic and East European Journal*, 40 (1996), 135–41.

—, 'The Obverse of Stalinism: Akhmatova's Self-Serving Charisma of Selflessness', in *Self and Story in Russian History*, ed. by Laura Engelstein and Stephanie Sandler (Ithaca and London: Cornell University Press, 2000), 46–68.

Zinin, Sergei, and Viktor Chalmaev, *Literatura XX veka. Khrestomatiia. 11 klass. Chast' I*, 2 vols (Moscow: Russkoe slovo, 2005).

Zobnin, Iu. V., *Poeziia beloi emigratsii: 'Nezamechennoe pokolenie'* (St Petersburg: SPbGUP, 2010).

Zubok, Vladislav, *Zhivago's Children: The Last Russian Intelligentsia* (Cambridge, MA and London: The Belknap Press of Harvard University Press, 2009).

Index

abiturienty (prospective university students) 339
Abramov, Fedor 337
academia 82, 85, 359
acmeism 23, 161, 376, 381
 acmeists 32, 71, 162, 163, 313, 375, 381, 383
Adamovich, Georgii 47, 207, 297, 298, 299, 300, 301, 310, 311, 312, 313, 314, 315, 316, 319, 375, 383
 'Kogda my v Rossiiu vernemsia... o, Gamlet vostochnyi, kogda?' ('When will we return to Russia ... oh, Eastern Hamlet, when?') 319
 Na Zapade (In the West) 300
Adorno, Theodor 382, 383
Aeroflot 60
Afro-American 292
Agenosov, Vladimir 117, 118, 119, 120, 211, 283, 335
Aigi, Genadii 22, 39, 333, 405, 406, 407, 408, 409, 410, 411, 412, 423
 'motsart: kassatsiia I' ('mozart: cassation I') 408
Aizenberg, Mikhail 18, 19, 283, 348, 349, 350, 352, 396
Aizlewood, Robin 175
Akhmadulina, Bella 12, 22, 54, 189, 206, 330, 332, 333, 337, 339, 340, 341, 344, 345, 346, 347, 349
Akhmatova, Anna 5, 9, 22, 23, 37, 40, 43, 49, 50, 61, 63, 64, 65, 66, 67, 68, 69, 70, 71, 72, 73, 74, 75, 76, 77, 78, 80, 81, 82, 83, 84, 85, 86, 87, 88, 89, 90, 91, 92, 93, 110, 119, 140, 141, 142, 158, 161, 164, 166, 168, 171, 174, 180, 182, 185, 186, 191, 192, 195, 196, 197, 207, 245, 247, 248, 249, 250, 252, 278, 321, 324, 327, 329, 374, 375, 378, 388
 Chetki (Rosary) 69
 'Nas chetvero' ('The Four of Us') 73, 76
 'Na shee melkikh chetok riad...' ('On the Neck a String of Fine Beads') 69
 Rekviem (Requiem) 78, 79, 80, 82, 83, 84, 245, 415
 'Slava miru' ('In Praise of Peace') 87
 Vecher (Evening) 68
 'Venok mertvym' ('A Wreath for the Dead') 74
Akhmet'ev, I. 218, 280
Aksenov, Vasilii 12
 Tainstvennaia strast' (Secret Passion) 12
Akunin, Boris x
Al'chuk, Anna 409
Aleksandrov 370
Alekseev, Aleksandr 215
Aleshina, Tat'iana 380
Alkonost Publishing House 140
All-Russia Union of Poets 129
Alter, Robert 64, 71, 73, 84
Al'tman, Natan 69
Alvarez, A. 50, 165
America 45, 47, 115

American 25, 29, 33, 43, 49, 54, 61, 83, 157, 158, 159, 160, 166, 173, 175, 177, 181, 182, 183, 185, 186, 189, 190, 191, 194, 202, 292, 307, 334, 335, 357, 377, 387, 397, 399, 405
Andrushchenko, E. 146
Anemone, Anthony 388
Anglo-American 25, 158, 160, 166, 189, 191
Anglo-Irish 181
Anglophone 293
Anglo-Soviet relations viii
Ankudinov, K. 283, 335
Annenkov, Iurii 140
Annenskii, Inokentii 33, 207, 234, 313, 316, 317
Anning, Nicholas J. 193
Anninskii, Lev 285
anthology 2, 36, 37, 40, 108, 135, 147, 161, 163, 187, 202, 206, 213, 218, 219, 226, 242, 269, 270, 271, 277, 278, 289, 310, 330, 332, 335, 336, 341, 342, 343, 344, 345, 346, 347, 351, 359, 373, 383, 410
Antokol'skii, Pavel 270
Apollinaire, Guillaume 162
Apollonian and Dionysian 153
Aragon, Louis 306
  'Charlot mystique' 306
Aranovich, Semen 71
Arbenina, Diana 59
archives 3, 6, 12, 58, 154, 160, 195, 265, 266, 267, 268, 283
Arendt, Hannah 299
Ar'ev, Andrei 316, 377, 378, 379
Aristotle 239
Arkhangel'skii, Aleksandr 120
Arkhangelsk region 43
Arland, Marcel 319
Art Deco 302, 303, 305, 306, 309
Arts and Humanities Research Council vii, viii, x
Aseev, Nikolai 29, 76, 103, 270
Asmus, Valentin 137
Astaf'ev, Viktor 337

Astrachan, Anthony 50
Atamanova, E. 216
Auden, W. H. 50, 167
audience 14, 18, 28, 42, 148, 169, 191, 196, 213, 248, 286, 301, 329, 333, 365, 388, 409, 410. *See also* readers
avant-garde 90, 302, 412
Avramenko, Al'bert 149
Azadovski, Konstantin 79
Azarova, Natal'ia 409
Azarov, Iurii 206, 224
Azhgikhina, Nadezhda 4

Babich, Pavel 335
Bagritskii, Eduard 161
Baimukhametov, Sergei 220
Baines, Jennifer 157, 165, 174, 176, 186, 188
Baker, Houston 357
Bakhtin, Mikhail 153, 384, 385
  dialogicity 384, 385, 389
    dialogic 20, 312
  polyphony 39, 385
    polyphonic 153, 384
Balina, Marina 28
Bal'mont, Konstantin 27, 47, 124, 127, 289, 371
Barannikov, Anatolii 108, 110, 211
Baratynskii, Evgenii 196, 310
  'Piroskaf' ('Steamship') 310
Barker, Adele 10, 11, 242
Barkova, Anna 247
  'Durochka' ('The Fool') 247
Barkovskaya, Nina 14, 15
Barskova, Polina 420
Barthes, Roland 23, 65
Basilova, Alena 254
Basinskii, Pavel 384
Basovskaia, Evgeniia 111
Bayley, John 164, 167, 174, 175, 177, 179
Bednyi, Dem'ian 285, 290
Beevor, Anthony 193
Beketova, M. A. 138
Bekmambetov, Eksender 59, 148

Bek, Tat'iana 283, 284, 286
Bel'chevichen, S. P. 146
Bel'chikov, N. F. 126
Belen'kii, Gennadii 109, 210, 211, 212
Belinskii, Vissarion 239, 362, 366
Belkina, A. 161
Bell, Alexander Graham 184, 303
belletristika (middlebrow literature) 302
Belov, Vasilii 337
Belyi, Andrei 33, 124, 127, 132, 147, 153, 161, 270, 416
Bem, Al'fred 299, 310, 313
Benjamin, Walter 18, 299
Berdiaev, Nikolai 139
Berestov, Valentin 206
Berggol'ts, Ol'ga 288, 341
Beriozkina, Patricia 67
Berlin 178, 301
Berlin, Isaiah 63, 64, 65, 72, 87, 91, 92, 182, 185
Bern 84, 318
Bethea, David 44
Beumers, Birgit 249
Bezrodnyi, M. 161
Bhabha, Homi 295
Biblioteka poeta (The Poet's Library) 31, 36, 195
Binet, Laurent 193
  HHhH 193
biography 23, 43, 45, 46, 47, 51, 52, 54, 55, 58, 62, 65, 67, 71, 84, 87, 97, 101, 103, 104, 181, 191, 198, 220, 268, 272, 369, 377, 378, 379
Bliznetsova, Ina 335
Blok, Aleksandr 7, 18, 33, 34, 40, 68, 73, 82, 100, 102, 109, 113, 120, 123, 124, 127, 128, 129, 130, 131, 132, 133, 134, 135, 136, 137, 138, 139, 140, 141, 142, 143, 144, 145, 146, 147, 148, 149, 150, 151, 152, 153, 154, 155, 164, 170, 186, 196, 203, 207, 211, 213, 222, 388
  Collected Verse 152
  Collected Works 137
  'Devushka pela v tserkovnom khore' ('A Girl Sang in a Church Choir') 148
  Diaries 137
  'Druz'iam' ('To My Friends') 136
  Dvenadtsat' (The Twelve) 134, 135, 143, 149, 150
  'Fabrika' ('The Factory') 131
  'Golos iz khora' ('A Voice from the Chorus') 132
  Gorod (The City) 131
  'Ia prigvozhden k traktirnoi stoike' ('I Am Nailed to the Bar in the Tavern') 133
  'I vnov' — poryvy iunykh let' ('And Again — The Impulses of Youth') 132
  'Miry letiat. Goda letiat' ('Worlds fly past. Years fly past') 132
  Na pole Kulikovom (On the Field of Kulikovo) 131
  Narod i intelligentsia (The People and the Intelligentsia) 132
  'Na zheleznoi doroge' ('On the Railway') 109, 131
  'Neznakomka' ('The Unknown Woman') 131, 140
  'O naznachenii poeta' ('On the Poet's Calling') 129
  'O, vesna bez kontsa i bez kraiu' ('Oh, Spring Without an End and Without a Limit') 132
  Pesnia sud'by (Song of Fate) 145
  'Pliaski smerti' ('Dances of Death') 132
  Rodina (Native Land) 131, 145
  'Rossiia' ('Russia') 131
  'Rus'' ('Russia') 140
  'Skify' ('The Scythians') 133, 134
  Stikhi o Prekrasnoi dame (Verses on the Beautiful Lady) 131, 153
  'V chas, kogda p'ianeiut nartsissy' ('In the Hour when Narcissi are Intoxicated') 133
  Vozmezdie (Retribution) 133

Blokh, Raisa 297
Bloom, Harold 72, 124, 293, 357
Bobyshev, Dmitrii 5, 334, 335, 345
Bodin, Per-Arne 227, 247
Bogdanov, Aleksandr 384
Bogomolov, N. A. 161, 378
Boiko, Svetlana 54
Bokov, Viktor 206
Boldyrev, Iurii 268, 270, 276, 277, 278
Bolshevik 10, 127, 128, 129, 135, 139, 148, 152, 178, 239, 287, 378
Bolshevik Revolution 10, 128, 133, 134, 135, 143, 150, 178, 193, 210, 220, 265, 326, 362, 378, 379
Bolshevo 370
bol'shoi stil' (grand style) 267
Bolton, Kerry 356
Bondarenko, Vladimir 285
Bonfel'd, Moris 53
Bonnefoy, Yves 165
Borisova, N. V. 216, 217, 223
Boroditskaia, Marina 195
Bouis, Antonina W. 71, 230
Bourdieu, Pierre 65, 66, 125, 148
Bowra, Maurice 161
Boym, Svetlana 64, 240, 294, 360, 361
Bozhnev, Boris 297, 320, 327
Braque, Georges 162
Braudy, Leo 65, 68, 250
Braun, Rebecca 71
Brecht, Bertolt 18
Brezhnev, Leonid 143, 145, 271
   Brezhnev era 145
Brik, Lili 103, 114, 115, 116, 119, 282
Brik, Osip 26, 96, 103, 282
Britain 41, 173
British 159, 165, 168, 173, 174, 177, 178, 181, 186, 247, 293, 366
British Isles 293
Briusov, Valeri 33, 102, 124, 127, 128, 204, 207, 213, 299, 374
   Dali (Horizons) 128
   Speshi! (Hurry up!) 128
Brodskii, Iosif (Brodsky, Joseph) 5, 21, 36, 38, 39, 43, 44, 45, 46, 47, 48, 49, 50, 51, 52, 53, 54, 55, 56, 57, 58, 59, 60, 61, 62, 66, 80, 83, 158, 159, 160, 165, 167, 169, 171, 175, 180, 186, 188, 189, 190, 191, 193, 194, 196, 198, 218, 229, 268, 273, 274, 279, 282, 283, 287, 332, 333, 334, 337, 338, 339, 340, 344, 345, 346, 347, 348, 349, 350, 351, 352, 353, 360, 361, 368, 369, 384, 401, 402, 403, 404, 407, 408, 416
   American Poet Laureate 43
   'Bosnia Tune' 401
   'Brodskiimania' 45, 46, 56, 61
   'Niotkuda s liubov'iu' ('Out of Nowhere with Love') 59
   'Ot okraini k tsentru' ('From the Margins to the Mainstream') 59, 60
   'Pis'mo v oazis' ('Letter to an Oasis') 55
   Potomu chto iskusstvo poezii trebuet slov: vecher-posviashchenie Iosifu Brodskomu (*Because the Art of Poetry Requires Words: An Evening Dedicated to Joseph Brodsky*) 57
Broitman, S. N. 146
'Bronze Age' 353
Brooker, Peter 18
Brooks, Jeffrey 362
Brown, Archie 177
Brown, Clarence 128, 161, 164, 165, 166, 167, 171, 177, 183, 184, 185, 187, 197, 332
Brown, Deming 265, 266, 333
Brown, Edward 333
Bruskin, Grisha 422
Bulgakov, Mikhail 114, 120, 362
   Master and Margarita 362
Buneeva, Ekaterina 210
Buneev, Rustem 210
Bunin, Ivan 39, 47, 201, 202, 203, 204, 205, 206, 207, 208, 209, 210, 211, 212, 213, 214, 215, 216, 217, 218, 219, 220, 221, 222, 223, 224, 270
   I. A. Bunin Elets State University 216
      'Buninskaia Rossiia' ('Bunin's Russia') 216, 223
   Ivan Bunin Literary Prize 215

Okaiannye dni (Cursed Days) 220
*Pod otkrytym nebom. Stikhotvoreniia
(Under the Open Sky. Poems)* 204
Sobranie sochinenii (Collected Works)
205
*Stikhotvoreniia. 1903–1906 (Poems.
1903–1906)* 203, 204
'Sviatogor i Il'ia' ('Sviatogor and Il'ia') 210
'Zmeia' ('Snake') 210
Burbank, Jane 145
Burke, S. 65
Burliuk, David 101, 102, 113, 119, 142
Burukina, A. F. 153
Bykov, Dmitrii 13, 14, 15, 16, 19, 41, 42, 91, 249, 337
'Skazka prodolzhaetsia' 15, 16
*Sovetskaia literatura: kratkii kurs
(Soviet Literature: A Short Course)*
42
*Sovetskaia literatura: rasshirennyi
kurs (Soviet Literature: Extended
Course)* 42

Cambridge 168
canon formation 2, 4, 5, 10, 36, 64, 74, 79, 82, 84, 125, 158, 187, 201, 202, 203, 208, 211, 214, 215, 216, 217, 218, 222, 224, 227, 228, 330, 344, 351, 357, 358, 360, 379, 395, 398, 416
    canon change 1, 2
    canonical diversity 2, 29, 293
    dogmatic approach 2, 99, 111, 112
    model 8, 10, 43, 65, 68, 71, 87, 88, 121, 192, 201, 202, 203, 206, 208, 211, 214, 215, 216, 217, 221, 222, 226, 265, 305, 360, 393, 408, 412
    reshaping 1, 3, 6, 9, 38, 44, 47, 52, 379
canonical status 2, 5, 44, 45, 50, 53, 54, 62, 64, 68, 71, 72, 73, 80, 88, 92, 114, 124, 142, 157, 159, 173, 176, 197, 201, 207, 208, 220, 226, 249, 252, 255, 269, 300, 301, 302, 305, 327, 328, 346, 348, 350, 352, 353, 376, 378, 388, 400, 417
Carlisle, Olga 50, 182, 329, 333

Catullus 381
Cavanagh, Clare 26, 43, 78, 79, 83, 84, 161, 384
Celan, Paul 158, 159, 166
censorship 2, 3, 4, 6, 25, 79, 86, 130, 138, 146, 183, 184, 208, 240, 274, 287, 289, 330, 331, 366, 386, 387
Central Committee of the Communist Party of the Soviet Union 28
Chalmaev, Viktor 211
Chamberlain, Lesley 127
Chambers, Ross 375
Chaplin, Charlie 307
Chatwin, Bruce 176, 177
Chekhov, Anton x, 41, 72, 207
Cherdyn' 163, 199
Cherez 303
chernukha 243, 244
Chernysheva, Veronika 221
Chernyshevskii, Nikolai 366
Chervinskaia, Lydiia 297, 324, 325, 327
    Priblizheniia (Approaches) 324
    Rassvety (Sunrises) 324
Chichibabin, Boris 335
China 364
Chinnov, Igor' 297, 326, 327
Chisla 302
Chistopol' 369
Chizhevskii, Dmitrii 366
Christ 84, 88, 134, 151, 237, 246
Christian 88, 150, 167, 172, 233, 237, 246, 278
Christianity 154
Christian, Nicole 88, 150, 167, 172, 233, 237, 246, 278
Christians 241
Christiansen, Broder 36
Christmas 57, 246
Chudakov, Aleksandr 25
Chudakova, Marietta 25, 361
Chukhontsev, Oleg 199, 267, 268, 341, 345
Chukovskaia, Lidiia 70, 85, 86
Chukovskii, Konstantin 102
Chukovskii, Kornei 129, 140, 195
Chulkov, G. I. 138

Church Slavonic 398, 400
Clark, Wilma 8, 360
clichés 18, 29, 251, 381, 402
Clingman, Stephen 311
Clowes, Edith W. 21, 367, 368, 370
Coetzee, J. M. 184, 191, 192
Cold War 41, 49, 50, 158, 160, 174, 181, 183, 184
Colin, Andrew 207
Collomb, Michel 306
Cologne 276
Communism 28, 29, 46, 86, 124, 127, 267, 272, 273, 274, 275, 279, 356
Communist Party 28, 46, 59, 127, 130, 131, 267, 270, 271, 272, 273, 274, 329, 356, 360
Communist Party Conference 130
Communist Party of the Russian Federation 356
conceptualism 18, 32, 282, 344, 350, 420, 422
   Russian conceptualism 18
constructivism 279, 281, 282, 284
Contemporary Russian Poetry 14, 242, 335, 343, 344, 346
Cornwell, Neil 228, 333, 341, 351
   Reference Guide to Russian Literature 228, 351
Costello, D. P. 183
Costlow, Jane ix
critical theory 170
critics 5, 8, 23, 24, 25, 27, 29, 31, 32, 33, 35, 36, 38, 39, 40, 42, 46, 87, 125, 134, 136, 147, 155, 162, 165, 168, 169, 175, 177, 190, 198, 202, 204, 205, 208, 212, 223, 276, 283, 297, 299, 318, 330, 342, 348, 351, 353, 358, 359, 360, 361, 364, 366, 367, 370, 375, 376, 379, 380, 383, 389, 390, 405, 409
Crowley, Edward L. 333
culture 20
Culture 361
curriculum 95, 97, 99, 105, 108, 109, 112, 120, 121, 135, 139, 143, 148, 208, 209, 212, 213, 214, 215, 327, 357, 362

Cyrillic 250, 403

Dada 303
Dadaism 302, 303
Danin, Daniil 265, 273, 274
Dante 62, 72, 171, 172, 173, 178, 238, 381
Dark, Oleg 246, 272, 275, 276, 281
Darwin, Charles 82, 169
Dashevskii, Grigorii 398, 399
Davenport, Guy 164, 165
David (Bible) 155, 181, 251
Davie, Donald 166, 174, 191, 192, 193
Davies, Jesse 68
Dawkins, Richard 80
'Day of Russian Culture' 363
Decembrists 126
de Chirico, Giorgio 162
Degot', Ekaterina 421
Deleuze, Gilles 23
demonism 145, 149
Denisov, Aleksei 222
Denisova, Maria 114
Den' narodnogo edinstva (Day of Popular Unity) 378
Den' Poezii (Poetry Day) 162
Depretto, Katrin 25
Derrida, Jacques 23
Derzhavin, Gavrila 155, 191, 284, 287, 420
de-Stalinisation 329, 330, 334, 347, 369, 372
Diaghilev, Sergei 366
diaspora 38, 41, 160, 289, 290, 291, 292, 295, 299, 301, 305, 308, 310, 315, 325, 326, 362, 363, 364, 365, 367, 373, 374, 375, 376, 377, 378, 383, 389, 405
   diasporic narratives 292, 294
   diasporic studies 294
Dinega, Alyssa W. 77
D'Israeli, Isaac 125
Dmitriev, A. 390
Dobrenko, Evgeny 19, 24, 27, 28, 312, 420
Dobroliubov, Nikolai 366

Doherty, Justin 301
Dolgopolov, Leonid 150
Dolinin, V. 226
Donne, John 53
Dostoevskii, Fedor (Dostoevsky, Fyodor) x, 41, 71, 72, 102, 135, 222, 231, 232, 233, 244, 390
   Crime and Punishment 232
      Raskol'nikov 232, 233
      Sonia Marmeladova 232
Dovlatov, Sergei 58
   Zapovednik (Pushkin Hills) 58
Dragomoshchenko, Arkadii 226, 238, 387, 398, 401
Driz, Ovsei 280
Dubrovina, Elena 380
Dudin, Mikhail 331
Duffy, Carol Ann 247
Dugin, Aleksandr 392
Dymshits, Aleksandr 31, 33

Eagleton, Terry 83, 157
Easter 233, 234, 237, 244
Eastern Europe 64, 270
Economist, The 172
editors 2, 22, 36, 138, 201, 211, 212, 213, 225, 226, 227, 302, 304, 344, 352, 359, 366, 420
Edmond, Jacob 401, 420
education 2, 11, 41, 95, 96, 97, 98, 99, 102, 108, 109, 110, 112, 120, 121, 125, 126, 127, 130, 135, 136, 139, 147, 214, 301, 339
Efremov, Mikhail 13, 14, 16, 219
Eikhenbaum, Boris 25, 26, 70, 384
   'Melodika russkogo liricheskogo stikha' ('The Melody of Russian Lyric Verse') 25
   Moi vremennik (My Chronicle) 25
Eisenstadt, S. N. 88
Eksteins, Modris 326
Elabuga 369, 370, 371, 390
Elets 220
Eliot, T. S. 72, 162, 166, 167, 170, 171, 172
   'The Waste Land' 167

Eliseev, Nikita 274, 277
Elliot, David 131
Ellis, Frank 4
émigré 4, 24, 26, 34, 36, 37, 38, 39, 44, 54, 62, 157, 162, 163, 164, 178, 195, 201, 208, 213, 224, 268, 270, 281, 289, 290, 291, 292, 293, 294, 295, 296, 297, 299, 300, 301, 302, 303, 305, 310, 312, 313, 316, 319, 324, 326, 327, 328, 334, 335, 336, 342, 343, 345, 347, 353, 356, 357, 359, 360, 361, 362, 363, 364, 365, 366, 367, 368, 371, 372, 373, 374, 376, 377, 378, 379, 380, 382, 384, 386, 387, 389, 390. *See also* Russia Abroad
   apatrides (stateless persons) 302
   authors 268, 328, 359, 363, 366, 367, 372, 389
   circles 164
   critics 162, 299, 366
   emigration 2, 86, 127, 128, 157, 205, 210, 212, 213, 223, 247, 254, 296, 300, 305, 311, 327, 337, 347, 373, 376, 389, 390, 393, 405
   poets 3, 334
   Russian Parisian 297, 303
   writers 291, 301, 371
Engdahl, Horace 214
Engels, Friedrich 202
Engelstein, Laura ix, 66
England 24, 179
English 53, 55, 59, 157, 160, 162, 163, 164, 165, 169, 181, 182, 184, 186, 187, 188, 190, 192, 195, 196, 227, 242, 333, 344, 351, 357, 368, 398, 399, 400, 401, 402, 405, 407
English metaphysical poetry 53
Engström, Maria 355, 392
Epshtein, Mikhail (Epstein, Mikhail) 31, 32, 241, 380, 381
Eremin, Mikhail 238, 396, 397, 398, 412, 423
   'Neudivitelen, kogda zaliv podoben arsenalu' ('Unsurprising, when a gulf resembles an arsenal') 396
   Stikhotvoreniia (Poems) 396

Erenburg, Il'ia 162, 195, 271
Erhart, W. D. 183
Erlich, Victor 24
Ermilov, Vladimir 104
Erofeev, V. 147, 229, 378
Ershov, L. F. 331, 333
Esenin, Sergei 9, 15, 100, 115, 135, 140, 141, 148, 161, 222, 374
Estonia 24, 25
estrada (podium) poets 329, 333, 338, 339, 340, 342, 345, 347, 353
Etkind, Efim 47, 51, 147, 226, 290, 356, 373, 374, 375
  'Russian Twentieth-century Poetry As a Single Movement' 373
Eurasian 22, 358, 392
Eurasianist 392
Euripides 72
Europe 64, 72, 158, 170, 172, 180, 270, 312, 319, 325
European x, 17, 24, 35, 157, 160, 175, 186, 193, 194, 226, 238, 291, 298, 299, 300, 301, 302, 313, 319, 326, 327, 356, 366, 367, 368, 374, 377, 381, 390, 405
Evtushenko, Evgenii 12, 13, 15, 17, 30, 37, 50, 135, 206, 218, 266, 329, 330, 331, 332, 333, 335, 337, 339, 340, 341, 343, 344, 345, 346, 347, 348, 351, 375, 383
  Strofy veka (Stanzas of the Century) 37, 218
exile 20, 39, 43, 44, 45, 46, 47, 49, 50, 51, 54, 55, 58, 60, 163, 168, 172, 173, 175, 200, 213, 289, 291, 294, 297, 298, 299, 300, 302, 311, 312, 316, 319, 326, 340, 403
  exilic condition 294
  exilic narratives 294
Ezhov Terror 84

Facebook 410
Fadeev, Aleksandr 100
Fainlight, Ruth 170, 171
Falikman, Mariia 196
Falikov, Il'ia 271, 273, 274, 276, 282, 283

Fanailova, Elena 39, 416, 418, 419, 420, 422
  'Lena i Lena' ('Lena and Lena') 419
  'Lena i liudi' ('Lena and the People') 419
Federal'noe agenstvo po pechati i massovym kommunikatsiiam (Federal Agency for Press and Mass Communications) 220
Fediakin, Sergei 218, 221
Fedorovskii, Natan 57
Fedorov, Vasilii 331
Fedotov, Georgii 38, 298
feminism 242, 248, 292
Fenton, James 171, 172
Feodosiia 370
Fet, Afanasii 27, 33, 111
Fiedler, Leslie 357
Figner, Vera 126
Filippov, B. A. 163, 164, 166
Finland 129
Fitzpatrick, Sheila 7, 85, 86
Fleishman, Lazar' 157, 161
Flejshman, L. 76
Fleming, Mike 212, 213
Fofanov, Konstantin 146
Fokin, Pavel 77
Fontannyi Dom 63, 92
formalism 2, 22, 23, 24, 25, 26, 32, 35, 89
  Russian formalism 22, 24, 25, 32
Fowler, Alastair 3, 125, 130, 153, 359, 360
France 24, 47, 176, 181, 186, 296, 312, 364, 368, 370, 371, 375, 376, 378, 405
France, Peter 333
Frangulian, Georgii 60
Frankel, Edith 167, 177
Frank, Semen 139
free speech 4, 179
Freidin, Gregory 68, 177, 192, 196
  A Coat of Many Colors 68, 177, 192
French 158, 166, 303, 304, 312, 319, 366, 371, 405

Freud, Sigmund 243
Friedberg, Maurice 29
Frolova, Elena 59
Frukhtman, Lev 280
Fundamental Electronic Library of Russian Literature and Folklore (FEB) 361, 362
futurism 24, 32, 71, 76, 126, 158, 238, 276, 279, 281, 283, 284, 347, 374, 396, 412

Gadaev, Lazar 199
Galcheva, Tania 300
Galich, Aleksandr 333, 339
Gal', Iurii 34
Gamzatov, Rasul 338
Gandel'sman, Vladimir 193, 335, 349
Gandlevskii, Sergei 19, 58
Gasparov, Boris 64, 128, 137, 138, 177, 190, 249, 284, 336, 383
Gatarapak 303
Gathmann, Moritz 13
Gazdanov, Gaito
  'O molodoi emigrantskoi literature' ('On young émigré literature') 302
Gazdanov, Gaïto 295, 302, 328
generation 11, 38, 40, 49, 121, 127, 144, 155, 157, 174, 189, 196, 228, 229, 240, 270, 271, 273, 290, 291, 295, 298, 301, 319, 326, 330, 331, 332, 333, 334, 336, 340, 341, 346, 347, 348, 349, 350, 352, 353, 380, 381, 383, 385, 388, 391
  lost generation 298, 385
  new generation 196, 240, 331
  older generation 11, 127, 189, 270, 291, 331, 336
  poetic generation 353
  post-Soviet generation 121
  post-war generation 228, 380
Generation 332
Genette, Gérard 70, 77, 78
  epitext 70
Genis, Alexander A. 381

German 57, 129, 143, 158, 188, 276, 277, 366, 368, 415
German Junior, Aleksei 18, 388, 389
  Garpastum 18, 388
Germany 24, 370, 418
Gershtein, Emma 197
Gheith, Jehanne 242
Gifford, Henry 165, 167, 169, 171, 174, 175, 176, 177, 178, 180, 193, 197
Gill, Graeme 391
Ginzburg, Lidiia 32, 33, 64, 173, 180, 250
  O lirike (On Lyric Poetry) 32
Gippius, Zinaida 5, 47, 124, 127, 128, 146, 204, 289, 290, 291, 299, 301
  Siianiia (Radiance) 299
Glad, John 44, 326
  Conversations in Exile: Russian Writers Abroad 44
glasnost' 44, 147, 157, 164, 265, 289
Glazkov, Nikolai 336
Glazova, Anna 398, 417
Glazunova, Ol'ga 142, 219
Glazunov, Il'ia 142
Glinin, Gennadii 149, 153
gnostic 149
Goethe, Johann Wolfgang von 155, 158, 381
Gogol', Nikolai 135, 150, 239, 244, 366, 422
  Vii 150
Golden Age 20, 21, 206, 249, 353
Golding, Alan 202, 206, 357
Goldstein, Darra 250
Goliath 181
Golubkov, V. V. 131
Gölz, C. 76
Gomolitskii, Lev 315
Good Friday 234, 236, 237
Google 250
Gorak, Jan 357, 358
Gorbachev, Oleg 13, 44, 147, 265, 271
Gorbanevskaia, Natal'ia 334, 345, 398
Gorelik, Petr 266, 269, 270, 277, 279
Goricheva, Tatiana 226, 253

Gor'kii Literary Institute 30, 281, 283
Gor'kii Literary Institute 30
Gor'kii, Maxim 27, 30, 99, 100, 102, 105, 107, 113, 119, 120, 126, 129, 207, 379
　'Chelovek' ('Human') 102
Gorodnitskii, Aleksandr 344
Goscilo, Helena 70, 250
Goshko, John 50
Gray, Camilla 411
Grazhdanin poet (*Citizen Poet*) 13, 14, 15, 16, 19, 41, 42, 249
Graziadei, Caterina 56
Great Patriotic War 100
Grebenshchikov, Boris 22
Grechanik, I. V. 152
Greene, James 164, 165, 174
Gribachev, Nikolai 206
Grigor'eva, Ol'ga 371
　'Vstretimsia u Mariny' ('We'll see each other at Marina's place') 371
Grinberg, Marat 266, 267, 271, 276, 277, 278, 279, 284
Grishakova, Marina 8
Grishunin, A. N. 138
Gromov, Pavel 137
Gronas, Mikhail 79, 80, 82, 83
Grossman, Joan 67, 193, 266
Groys, Boris 90
Gubaidulina, Sofia 368, 369, 373, 408
Gubanov, Leonid 17, 254
Guillén, Claudio 297
Guillory, John 79, 82, 84, 85, 125, 357, 358
Gulag 34, 37, 38, 245, 336, 347, 369
　Gulag poetry 34, 37
　Gulag writers 347
Gumilev, Nikolai 66, 84, 87, 161, 162, 207, 210, 282, 313, 369, 374, 379, 388
　'Ia i vy' ('Me and You') 313
　'Zabludivshiisia tramvai' ('The Tram That Lost Its Way') 313
　'Zmei' ('Dragon') 210
Guro, Elena 374

Gusman, Mikhail 356
Gustafson, Richard 33

Hackel, Sergei 134, 136, 138
　The Poet and the Revolution 134
Hagglund, Roger 297
Haight, Amanda 70, 80
Hamlet 76, 136, 248, 319
Hampstead 165
Hansen-Löve, A. A. 76
Harrington, Alexandra vii, 40, 66, 67, 71, 90
Harris, Jane Gary 164, 169
Hassan, Ihab 381
Havlena, William 11
Hawkins, Peter 172
Haynes, Kenneth 162, 176
Hayward, Max 3, 79, 184, 333
Heaney, Seamus 159, 160, 167, 168, 169, 170, 171, 172, 173, 175, 176, 177, 178, 186, 187, 189, 190
　The Redress of Poetry 178
Hebrew 278
Heldt, Barbara 228, 242
Heller, Michael 401
Hemschemeyer, Judith 63, 142
Herbert, Zbigniew 176, 178
Herzen, Aleksandr 126
Hesiod 72
Heydrich, Reinhard 193
Hicks, J. 179
hierarchical 15, 331
hierarchy 10, 17, 203, 205, 218, 223
high culture 7, 17, 18, 26, 132, 159, 166, 357
Hill, Geoffrey 162, 170, 174, 176, 179, 180, 191
Hingley, Ronald 167, 174, 177
history 5, 6, 9, 10, 12, 14, 15, 22, 23, 27, 33, 44, 46, 52, 57, 63, 64, 65, 79, 85, 98, 103, 118, 125, 126, 130, 134, 138, 139, 154, 155, 157, 158, 160, 161, 167, 170, 171, 173, 178, 181, 185, 186, 191, 195, 198, 199, 202, 222, 223, 245, 250, 265, 274, 287, 288, 289, 292, 296, 302, 326, 333, 337,

338, 340, 341, 343, 344, 345, 349,
350, 351, 352, 353, 357, 360, 363,
364, 367, 368, 370, 378, 379, 383,
385, 386, 388, 389, 390, 395, 399
  cultural 52, 64, 185
  human 134
  literary 5, 44, 46, 63, 157, 158, 170,
    195, 223, 287, 289
  national 5
  recent 6
  Russian 5, 63, 65, 390
  shared 12, 370
  twentieth-century 12, 367, 378
Hodgson, Aaron 38
Hodgson, Aaron Tregellis viii
Hodgson, Katharine vii, 39, 40, 334,
  336, 341, 342
Hogarth, William 396, 397
Holak, Susan 11
Hollander, Jean 172
Hollander, Robert 172
Holmgren, Beth 85, 89, 250
Holocaust 267, 277, 278
Holthusen, Johannes 333
holy fool 179, 249
Holy Spirit 151
Homer 72
  Iliad 155
homo economicus 391
homo soveticus 391
Hood, Stuart 167
Hopgood, James F. 70, 88, 253
Horace 72, 199, 381
Hosking, Geoffrey 333
Hudson Review 164
Hughes, Robert 162, 249
Hunt, Priscilla 247
Hutcheon, Linda 14, 365
Huyssen, Andreas 17, 18

Iagoda, Genrikh 79
Iakor' (Anchor) 299, 300, 310, 311, 315
Iakovleva, Tat'iana 104, 115
Iakovlevna, Nadezhda 179, 195, 197
Iakubovich, Petr 126, 204
Iampolskii, Mikhail 327

Ianechek, Dzheral'd 421
Iashin, Aleksandr 337
Iazyki russkoi kul'tury (Languages of Russian Culture) 25
identity 2, 6, 11, 12, 17, 21, 28, 41, 78,
  85, 86, 88, 112, 124, 132, 154, 166,
  214, 267, 268, 276, 277, 278, 279,
  290, 291, 292, 294, 295, 298, 311,
  334, 355, 356, 359, 362, 363, 364,
  368, 370, 371, 382, 384, 390, 394
  collective identity 17, 41
  crisis of identity 21
  cultural identity 11, 154, 295, 394
  diasporic identity 294, 311
  identity formation 28
  national identity 112, 124, 291, 292,
    294, 295, 355, 359, 362, 363, 368,
    370, 384, 390
  poetic identity 166, 290, 298
  post-Soviet identity 12, 368
  Russian identity 41, 356, 370, 390
  shared identity 6, 12, 132
  Soviet identity 12, 368
  transnational identity 355, 382
ideology 3, 4, 17, 20, 25, 32, 85, 96, 97,
  98, 99, 125, 130, 135, 138, 143, 174,
  178, 181, 202, 208, 272, 273, 274,
  275, 290, 293, 306, 326, 365, 368,
  386, 387, 389, 394
  Bolshevik 287
  communist 8, 40, 87, 131, 178, 193,
    212, 267, 273, 275, 276, 279, 286,
    287, 334, 355, 363, 369, 373, 391
  glamour 40
  political 267, 276, 363
  Russophile 355
  Soviet 334, 363, 369, 373
  totalitarian 193
  utopian 391
Ignatieff, Michael 183, 184, 192
Ignatova, Elena 378
Igosheva, T. V. 152
Il'enkov, A. I. 153
Il Flauto Magico (The Magic Flute).
  See *Die Zauberflöte*
Il'in', Ivan 356

Imlah, Mick 173
Imperial Russia 243, 362
India 293
Institute of the Living Word 375
internet 4, 6, 7, 13, 37, 84, 335, 358, 361, 384, 394, 401, 420
Iron Curtain 161, 184, 193
Isakovskii, Mikhail 29, 337
Iskander, Fazil 340
Iskrenko, Nina 227
Israel ix
Istoriia russkoi sovetskoi literatury (The History of Russian Soviet Literature) 331
Italian 92, 158, 415
Iunost' (Youth) 30
Iupp, Mikhail 335
Ivanova, Natal'ia 91, 223, 296, 300, 372, 373, 377, 378, 380
Ivanov, Boris 377
Ivanov, Georgii 36, 38, 47, 74, 124, 127, 140, 147, 196, 203, 226, 233, 240, 247, 281, 289, 296, 297, 298, 299, 300, 301, 302, 313, 315, 316, 373, 375, 376, 377, 378, 379, 380, 382, 384, 385
  'Bez chitatelia' ('Without a Reader') 301
  'Raspad atoma' ('Disintegration of an Atom') 300, 301
  Rozy (Roses) 299
Ivanovskaia, Ariadna 332
Ivanov, Viacheslav 300
  'Rimskie sonety' ('Roman Sonnets') 300
  'Rimskii dnevnik' ('Roman Diary') 300

Jacoff, Rachel 172
Jaffe, Aaron 66
Jakobson, Roman 26, 416
Janecek, Gerald 405, 407, 412, 415
Janus 382
Jazz Age 303, 305, 306
Jesus 134, 135, 150, 233, 236, 246
Jew 277

Jewish 40, 253, 267, 268, 276, 277, 278, 279, 353
Jews 267, 277
Johnson, Barbara 417
Johnson, Randal 66, 330, 418
Jonah 246
Jones, Elli 119
Josipovici, Gabriel 171
Joyce, James 167
  Ulysses 167

Kafka, Franz 72
Kahn, Andrew viii, 5, 39, 47, 162, 163, 173, 176
Kaiser, Robert 50
Kalomirov, A. 240
Kama river 369
Kamenev, Lev 130, 134
Kaminskaia, N. 70
Kaminsky, Ilya 402, 403, 404, 405, 407, 408
  Dancing in Odessa 403, 404
Kapovich, Katia 401
Karabchievskii, Iurii 118
  Voskresenie Maiakovskogo (Maiakovskii's Resurrection) 118
Karakulina, Natalia viii
Karelia 60
Karlinsky, Simon 304, 366
Karpov, Anatolii 117, 118, 119
Karpovich, M. M. 367
Kataeva, Tamara 40, 77, 90, 91
  Abolition of Slavery 40, 90, 91
  Anti-Akhmatova 40, 90, 91
Katanian, Vasilii 104
Kates, J. 335
  In the Grip of Strange Thoughts 335, 343, 344, 346
Kazakov, Iurii 337
Kelly, Aileen 177
Kelly, Catriona 64, 66, 68, 83, 145, 242, 248, 249
Kemp-Welch, Anthony 139
Kermode, Frank 64, 71, 74, 82, 83, 84, 88, 187, 228

Ketchian, Sonia 78, 189
Khagi, Sofya 19, 20
Khanzen-Lieve, Oge 25
Khardzhiev, Nikolai 195
Kharitonov, M. 147
Khar'kov 270, 280, 282, 285
Kharms, Daniil 22, 148, 350, 394, 412
Khlebnikov, Velimir 101, 102, 113, 119, 158, 161, 164, 170, 189, 198, 270, 282, 284, 374, 376
Khodasevich, Vladislav 47, 162, 207, 270, 276, 289, 299, 300, 301, 302, 307, 327, 367, 373, 374, 377, 388, 389, 390
  'Ballada' ('Ballad') 307
  'Evropeiskaia noch'' ('The European Night') 300
  'Literatura v izgnanii' ('Literature in Exile') 302
  Sobranie stikhov (Collection of Poems) 300
Kholin, Igor' 281
Khrushchev, Nikita 138, 195, 275, 329, 330, 333, 345, 349, 353. *See also* Thaw
Khrzhanovskii, Andrei 58
  Poltora kota (A Cat and a Half) 58
  Poltory komnaty, ili sentimental'noe puteshestvie na Rodinu (A Room and a Half, or a Sentimental Journey to the Homeland) 58
Kibirov, Timur 18, 19, 20, 21, 382
  Kogda byl Lenin malen'kim (When Lenin Was a Little Boy) 18
  'Letnie razmyshleniia o sud'bakh iziashchnoi slovesnosti' ('Summer Reflections on the Fate of Belles Lettres') 20
  Santimenty (Sentiments) 19
Kiev 392
Kim, Iulii 339, 344
Kirsanov, Semen 29
Kliachkin, Evgenii 59
Kliuev, Nikolai 369, 374
Kniazhitskii, Aleksandr 120

Kniazhnin, V. N. 138
Knorring, Irina 297, 313
  Stikhi o sebe (Poems About Myself) 313
Knut, Dovid 297
Kobets, Svitlana 247
Koehler, Ludmila 202
Kogan, Pavel 282
Kolokol'tsev, Nikolai 106
Komaromi, Ann 124
Komarovo 92
Komar, Vitalii 32
Komitet gosudarstvennoi bezopasnosti (KGB) 43
Komsomol press 7
Kondrashov, Aleksandr 223
Konstanz school 171
Koons, Jeff 387
Korablev, Vasilii 204
Korinfskii, Apollon 204
Kormilov, S. I. 340
Korneichuk, Vladislav 219, 220
  'Kniga v provintsii i ee chitateli' ('Books in Russian Provinces and their Readers') 220
Kornilov, Vladimir 276, 283, 286, 335, 345, 346
Korniukhina, A. V. 153
Koroleva, N. V. 68, 269, 329
Korostelev, Oleg 298, 299
Korzhavin, Naum 335
Kostomarova, Inna 219
Koupovykh, Maxim 35
Kovalenko, S. A. 68, 329
Kovalev, Valentin 98, 101, 103, 105, 332, 335
  Russkaia sovetskaia literatura (Soviet Russian Literature) 98, 101, 105, 108, 332
Kozlov, Vladimir 55
Kozyrev, Kirill 250
Kralin, M. M. 66, 142
Krasnova, Marina 286
Krasovitskii, Stanislav 343

Krejd, Vadim (Kreid, Vadim) 297, 314, 316, 328, 377, 379, 380
Kremlin, the 30, 197
Krentsem, Thomas 57
Kreps, Vadim 335
Kriticheskaia massa (Critical Mass) 25
Krivulin, Viktor 196, 226, 227, 228, 229, 233, 240, 241, 253, 377
Kropivnitskii, Evgenii 281
KR (the Grand Duke Konstantin Konstantinovich Romanov) 146
Kruchenykh, Aleksandr 102, 119, 374
Kruzhkov, Grigorii 181, 195, 196
Kudrova, Irma 369, 373
Kukulin, Il'ia 342, 409, 417
Kul'chitskii, Mikhail 282
Kulle, Sergei 396
kul'turnost' (culturedness) 86, 361, 362
Kuniaev, Stanislav 266, 273, 274, 277, 278, 283, 285
Kupriianova, Nina 332
Kuprin, Aleksandr 47, 102, 224
Kurdiumova, Tamara 210, 211, 212
Kushner, Aleksandr 54, 58, 329, 340, 341, 344, 345, 346, 349
Kustanovich, Konstantin 32
Kutik, Il'ia 381
Kutsenko, Gosha 18, 388
Kutuzov, Aleksandr 210
Kuz'mina-Karavaeva, Elizaveta 34, 47. *See also* Mat' Mariia
Kuz'min, Dmitrii 198, 335, 409
Kuzmin, Mikhail 23, 270, 374, 378
Kuz'minskii, Konstantin 335
  Blue Lagoon Anthology 335
Kuznetsov, Sergei 55, 110, 111, 113, 115, 343, 345, 351

Lahusen, Thomas 19
Lak, Ellis 73, 77, 96
Language poets 401
Latin 399, 415
Latvia 24, 25, 26
Laursen, Eric 382
Lauter, Paul 10, 202

Lavrov, Aleksandr 34
Lazarenko, Galina 109, 110, 117, 118
  Khrestomatiia po otechestvennoi literature XX veka (20th Century Russian Literature Reader) 117
Lazarev, Lazar' 269, 280
Lebedeva, Natal'ia 91
Lebedev-Kumach, Vasilii 285
Lebedev, Vladimir 203
Lehmann-Haupt, Christopher 183
Leiderman, N. L. 74
Leningrad 30, 43, 86, 225, 226, 227, 228, 229, 234, 236, 237, 253, 334, 349, 396, 404
Leninist 99
Lenin, Vladimir Iliich 18, 102, 103, 105, 107, 120, 126, 129, 135, 202, 243, 366
  Pamiati Gertsena (In Memory of Herzen) 126
  Union for the Emancipation of Working People 126
Leonidov, Viktor 364, 365, 389
  'Son' ('The Dream') 364
Lermontov, Mikhail 33, 213, 312
Levchenko, Mariia 335
Leviathan 246
Leving, Yuri 359
Levin, Iu. D. 196
Lévi-Strauss, Claude 73
Lewin, Jane E. 70
Lewis, R. W. B. 172
Lianozovo school 267, 280, 281, 351
Liberov, Roman 57
Lipking, Lawrence 170
Lipkin, Semen 53, 54, 270, 281
Lipman, Joan 357
Lipovetsky, Mark 7, 8
Lisnianskaia, Inna 22, 345, 346, 349
literary criticism 2, 24, 153, 163, 351, 352
literary critics 46, 125, 165, 330, 342
Literaturnaia gazeta (Literary Gazette) 29
Littell, Robert 193
  The Stalin Epigram 193

Litvinov, Vladimir 106
'Literaturno-tvorcheskie sochineniia v starshikh klassakh' ('Creative Literary Compositions in Senior Grades') 106
Liubimov, V. N. 129
Livak, Leonid 319
Livanov, Dmitrii 41
'Lives of Remarkable People' Series 379
Ljunggren, Magnus 161
Lloyd, Rosemary 124
Loewen, Donald 83, 128
Loewinsohn, Ron 304
Lominadze, Sergo 55
London 158, 165, 166, 191, 193, 228
London Review of Books, The 158, 165
Longenbach, James 401
Lootens, Tricia 63, 92, 93
Lopatin, German 126
Losev, Aleksei 137, 138, 334, 335, 340, 345, 346, 349, 389, 390, 396, 397
Losskii, Nikolai 139
Lotman, Iurii 8, 9, 10, 33, 35, 36, 41, 64, 137, 138, 139
  Culture and Explosion 8
Lourie, Arthur
  Dans le temple du rêve d'or (In the Sanctuary of Golden Dreams) 142
Lourié, Arthur 161
Lowell, Robert 49, 182
Luders, Harald 57
Lukomsky, Vera 369
Lunacharskii, Anatolii 127
L'vovskii, Stanislav 398, 399, 400, 401, 409, 416
  Camera rostrum 399, 400, 401
Lygo, Emily viii, 30, 40, 161, 225, 241, 252, 329, 333, 334
lyric 20, 22, 26, 27, 28, 30, 31, 33, 40, 69, 75, 76, 77, 80, 142, 143, 159, 168, 182, 188, 196, 198, 234, 237, 246, 286, 315, 320, 321, 325, 334, 344, 364, 380, 382, 384, 385, 418, 419
Lyssyi, Iurii 111, 211
Lyutskanov, Yordan 14

MacFadyen, David 283, 334
Magarotto, Luigi 299
Maiakovskii, Vladimir 13, 15, 16, 32, 33, 76, 95, 96, 97, 98, 99, 100, 101, 102, 103, 104, 105, 106, 107, 110, 112, 113, 114, 115, 116, 117, 118, 119, 120, 121, 128, 134, 135, 142, 143, 158, 161, 164, 170, 180, 238, 248, 268, 279, 281, 282, 283, 284, 287, 290, 350, 374, 394, 409, 420
  'Chelovek' ('The Man') 105
  'Khorosho!' ('Good!') 103, 105, 107, 117, 118, 120
  'Lilichka! Vmesto pis'ma' ('Lilichka! Instead of a Letter') 104
  'Oblako v shtanakh' ('A Cloud in Trousers') 105, 107, 114, 117, 118
  'Pis'mo Tat'iane Iakovlevoi' ('Letter to Tat'iana Iakovleva') 104
  'Pis'mo tovarishchu Kostrovu iz Parizha o sushchnosti liubvi' ('Letter from Paris to Comrade Kostrov on the Nature of Love') 104
  'Pro eto' ('About This') 104
  'Rasskaz Khrenova o Kuznetskstroe i liudiakh Kuznetska' ('Khrenov's Story about the Construction of Kuznetsk and Its Citizens') 15
  'Skaza prodolzhaetsia' ('The Fairy Tale Continues') 15, 16
  'Skripka i nemnozhko nervno' ('A Violin, and a Little Nervous') 120
  'Vladimir Il'ich Lenin' ('Vladimir Ilyich Lenin') 102, 103, 105, 107, 120
  'Vo ves' golos' ('At the Top of My Voice') 107
Makarevich, Andrei 58
  'Pamiati Iosifa Brodskogo' ('In Memory of Brodskii') 58
Makarova, O. 179
Makin, Michael 349
Maklin, Viktor 269
Makolkin, Anna 379
Maksimov, Dmitrii 137

Malevich, Kasimir 411
  'Red Square' 411
Mallarmé, Stéphane 123, 124, 158
Malmstad, John 162
Malykhina, Svitlana 15
Mamonov, Petr 59
Mandel'shtam, Aleksandr 199
Mandel'shtam, Nadezhda 1, 3, 67, 79, 158, 163, 168, 174, 176, 178, 179, 182, 183, 184, 189, 195, 196, 197, 253
Mandel'shtam, Osip (Mandelstam, Osip) 7, 22, 23, 31, 37, 39, 47, 69, 73, 75, 77, 78, 79, 86, 87, 119, 128, 148, 157, 158, 159, 160, 161, 162, 163, 164, 165, 166, 167, 168, 169, 170, 171, 172, 173, 174, 175, 176, 177, 178, 179, 180, 181, 182, 183, 184, 185, 186, 187, 188, 189, 190, 191, 192, 193, 194, 195, 196, 197, 198, 199, 200, 207, 238, 253, 300, 336, 350, 369, 374, 375, 388, 404
  'Chernozem' ('Black Earth') 175
  Chetvertaia proza (Fourth Prose) 163, 177
  Complete Prose and Letters 164
  'Egipetskaia marka' ('Egyptian Stamp') 404
  'Fedra' ('Phaedra') 179
  'Gumanizm i sovremennost'' ('Humanism and the Present') 178
  Kamen' (*Stone*) 162, 166, 167, 169, 176, 183, 185
  'K nemetskoi rechi' ('To the German Language') 188
  Mandel'shtam Centenary Conference 163
  Mandel'shtamovedy (Mandel'shtam specialists) 189
  'My s toboi na kukhne posidim' ('We Will Sit in the Kitchen') 182
  'My zhivem, pod soboiu ne chuiia strany...' ('We live without feeling the country beneath us...') 79
  'Ne muchinistoi babochkoiu beloi' ('My Body, All that I Borrowed from the Earth') 182
  'Net, ne spriatat'sia mne ot velikoi mury' ('No, I Cannot Escape This Grand Nonsense') 182
  'Oda' ('The Stalin Ode') 159, 187, 189, 190, 191, 192, 193
  'O prirode slova' ('On the Nature of the Word') 171
  'O sobesednike' ('On the Interlocutor') 171
  'Pust' imena tsvetushchikh gorodov' ('Let the Names of Flowering Cities') 185
  Puteshestvie v Armeniiu (*Journey to Armenia*) 176, 177
  'Razgovor s Dante' ('Conversation on Dante') 171, 172
  Shum vremeni (*The Noise of Time*) 176
  'Sokhrani moiu rech'' ('Preserve My Speech') 182
  'Stikhi o neizvestnom soldate' ('Verses on an Unknown Soldier') 159, 169, 189
  'Stikhi o russkoi poezii' ('The Verses on Russian Poetry') 188
  'Sumerki svobody' ('Let Us Praise the Twilight of Freedom') 177
  'the Mandel'shtam syndrome' 193
  Tristia 162, 169, 179, 188, 195
  'Umyvalsia noch'iu na dvore' ('I Am Washing Myself in the Night in the Courtyard') 175
  'Vek' ('Century') 193
  Voronezhskie tetradi (*Voronezh Notebooks*) 79, 168, 188, 189
  'Vpoloborota, o pechal'...' ('Half-Turning, o Grief...') 69
  'Za gremuchiu doblest' griadushchikh vekov' ('For the Ringing Renown of Future Ages') 199

Mandel'shtam, Roal'd 336, 350
Manichean philosophy 149
Manolaked, Hristo 14
Marchenko, Tat'iana 220
Margolin, Leonid 59
market
  cultural marketplace 17, 21
  market conditions 4
  market forces 389
  post-Soviet 7
  Soviet book 301
Markov, Vladimir 296
Marshall, David P. 69
Marsh, Rosalind 84
Martynov, Leonid 269, 270, 283, 331, 332, 351
martyrdom 87, 92, 172, 174, 175, 177
  martyr 7, 38, 39, 67, 84, 86, 89, 173, 183, 185, 189
  'martyrology' 84
Marxism 35, 125, 131, 179, 386
Marx, Karl 202
Mashkov, Vladimir 148
mass culture 18, 30, 79, 91, 299, 303, 305, 306, 326
Massie, Suzanne 329
Masterova, Galina 60
Mat' Mariia 34. *See also* Kuz'mina-Karavaeva, Elizaveta
Matskin, Aleksandr 267
Matveev, Alexei 11
Matveeva, Novella 332, 333, 344, 345, 346
Maver, Igor 292
McCauley, Karen 16
McDuff, David 164, 165, 169
McLaughlin, Martin 172
McReynolds, Louise 70
Meares, Bernard 164, 165, 167
Medish, Vadim 50
Medvedev, Roy 89, 137, 395
Meierkhol'd, Vsevolod 369
Meilakh, Mikhail 175
Meladze, Konstantin 59

Melamid, Aleksandr 32
Mel'nikov, N. 203, 207
  Klassik bez retushi: Literaturnyi mir o tvorchestve I. A. Bunina (A Canonical Author Without Retouch: The Literary World on the Creative Work of I. A. Bunin) 207
memory 6, 10, 11, 12, 13, 16, 17, 19, 24, 33, 38, 41, 59, 61, 63, 65, 67, 73, 74, 78, 79, 80, 82, 83, 99, 106, 124, 142, 172, 175, 194, 202, 270, 284, 294, 323, 361, 363, 365, 367, 368, 374, 378, 381, 382, 386, 387, 391, 401
  collective 6, 11, 12, 13, 17, 38, 59, 378
  cultural 13, 41, 80, 361, 365, 368, 374, 381, 382
  lapse 386
  sites of 387
  wars 365, 387
Merezhkovskii, Dmitrii 47, 123, 127, 139, 146, 147, 224, 289, 291
Merwin, W. S. 164, 165, 171, 185, 187
Mezhirov, Aleksandr 270, 283, 351
Middleton, Christopher 170
Mikhailov, O. 146, 206, 207, 221
Mikhalkov, Nikita
  Russkii vybor (The Russian Choice) 364
Mikhalkov, Sergei 14, 15, 364, 365
Miller, Martin 193, 243
Milner-Gulland, Robin 158, 164, 166
Mints, Zara 33, 34, 35, 137, 138, 139, 145
Mironov, Aleksandr 226, 227
Mirzaian, Aleksandr 59
Mit'ki group 19
Miturich, Petr 282
Mjør, Kåre Johan 361, 362
Mnatsakanian, Sergei 218
Mnatsakanova, Elizaveta 39, 177, 412, 413, 414, 415, 422
  'Das Hohelied' 412, 415
Mobile Tele-Systems (MTS) 148
Mochalov, Lev 285

modernism 2, 7, 8, 10, 17, 18, 22, 24, 26, 27, 31, 37, 73, 74, 90, 128, 138, 166, 170, 226, 249, 298, 326, 327, 366, 372, 373, 377, 381, 389, 405, 418
  Russian modernism 24, 34, 72, 249, 326, 387, 408
Modigliani, Amedeo 162
Mole, Tom 66, 179
Molnar, Michael 228, 230
Monas, Sidney 50, 164, 165, 168, 170, 176
Mondry, Henrietta 355
Montefiore, Simon Sebag 86, 90
Morits, Iunna 91, 344, 345, 346, 351
  'Defekatsiia defektologa K' ('The Defecation of Speech Therapist K') 91
Morozov, Nikolai 126
Morrison, R. H. 184
Moscow 16, 18, 20, 21, 23, 24, 30, 37, 58, 60, 61, 127, 129, 137, 163, 172, 195, 196, 197, 199, 215, 249, 254, 281, 282, 338, 339, 340, 342, 346, 349, 350, 357, 359, 368, 370, 371, 376, 377, 391, 398, 418
Moscow Arts Theatre 58
Moscow Institute of Literature and Arts 127
Moser, Charles 333
Mother Russia 148
Mozart, Wolfgang Amadeus 404, 408
Munts, Elena 199
Muratov, Askol'd 146
Murav, Harriet 278
Mussolini, Benito 180
Myers, Diana 175

Nabokov, Vladimir x, 38, 47, 184, 185, 295, 296, 328, 359, 366, 378, 398
  Dar (The Gift) 366
Nadson, Semen 146, 318
  nadsonovshchina (Nadsonovism) 318
Naiman, Anatoly 67, 84, 168, 340, 349
Nakanune (On the Eve) 178
Nakhimovsky, Alexander D. 64

Nakhimovsky, Alice Stone 64
Napoleon Bonaparte 232, 233
Nappel'baum, Moisei 68, 69
Narkompros circulars 127
Narkompros (People's Commissariat for Education) 127, 129
Narovchatov, Sergei 206, 270
narrative poetry 28, 416, 418
Naumov, F. I. 134, 142
Nazi 277
Nazism 213
Nefedov, Valerii 206, 207
Nekrasov, Nikolai 13, 14, 102, 103, 111, 227, 282, 337, 343, 346, 416
  'Poet i grazhdanin' ('The Poet and the Citizen') 13, 14
Nelson, Victoria 186, 334, 417, 418
Neofitsial'naia poeziia (Unofficial Poetry) 37
Nepomniashchii, Valentin 149, 150
Nerler, P. 128, 190, 196, 197
Netzkowa, Elisabeth 412
Neuberger, Joan 70
Neva 232, 252, 266, 274, 279, 376, 378
new criticism 25, 170, 190
new historicism 170
Newman, Charles 164
New Poet's Library 377
New Review, The 303, 377
New York 51, 57, 61, 165, 176, 181, 183, 185, 403
New York Review of Books 165, 171, 172, 174, 176, 181, 182, 183, 185
Nice, Richard 125, 318
Nietzsche, Friedrich 147, 404
Nikolaev, D. D. 378, 379
Nivat, Georges 290, 373, 375
Nobel Prize for Literature 43, 49, 71, 76, 92, 201, 213, 214, 216, 220, 222, 348, 353
Norris, Stephen M. 67
Nosov, Evgenii 337
nostalgia 2, 6, 11, 12, 13, 15, 16, 18, 20, 22, 183, 275, 294, 360, 363, 364, 372
Novikova, Liza 208
Novikov, Vladimir 48

Novoe literaturnoe obozrenie (New Literary Review) 22
Novyi mir (New World) 46

Obatin, G. 146
OBERIU 350, 352, 412
  OBERIU poets 350
objectivism 401
Obolduev, Georgii 350
obscurity 5, 45, 113, 169
Ocheretianskii, Aleksandr 335
October Revolution 133, 135
Odoevtseva, Irina 47, 289, 297, 300, 308, 309, 310, 316, 375, 376
  'Pod lampoi elektricheskoi' ('Under an Electric Lamp') 308, 310
  Zerkalo (The Mirror) 308
O'Driscoll, Dennis 193
Ognev, Vladimir 282
Ogonek (The Little Light) 37, 375, 376
Ogorodnikov, Ivan 99
  Pedagogika (Pedagogy) 99
Ogryzko, Viacheslav 31
Okhapkin, Oleg 226, 227
Okudzhava, Bulat 22, 54, 58, 330, 332, 333, 337, 338, 339, 340, 344, 345, 346, 347
Old Testament 246
Olesha, Iurii 239
On the Banks of the Neva 376
On the Banks of the Seine 376
Ophelia 248
Oppen, George 399, 400, 401
  'Quotations' ('Tsitaty') 399, 400
Orlov, V. N. 129, 134, 137, 138, 150, 270, 331, 335
Ormond, Leonee x
Orpheus and Eurydice 248
Orthodox Christianity 227, 247, 278, 361
Ostanin, B. 226
Ostrovskaia, Sophie 68
Ostrovskii, Nikolai 100
Ovid 72, 381
Oxford 92, 161, 166, 172
Oxford Book of Russian Verse, The 161

Ozerov, Lev 206, 269
Pachmuss, Temira 204
Pakhareva, T. A. 70
Palata Poetov 303
Pamuk, Orhan 404, 405
Panchenko, Nikolai 283
Paperno, Irina 67, 85, 87, 88, 249
Paramonov, Boris 274, 275
Parfenov, Leonid 12, 13
  Namedni (Not So Long Ago) 12, 13
Paris 38, 104, 127, 181, 185, 194, 254, 292, 308, 311, 312, 313, 314, 315, 316, 318, 319, 320, 323, 325, 326, 327, 328, 383, 390
Parisian 297, 298, 301, 303, 308, 312, 313, 315, 324, 328, 366
Paris Note group 38, 289, 292, 296, 297, 298, 304, 305, 310, 311, 312, 313, 314, 316, 318, 319, 320, 323, 325, 326, 327, 328
Parnassian 162, 182
Parshchikov, Alexei 381
Parthé, Kathleen 52
Pasternak, Boris 7, 32, 33, 49, 58, 73, 75, 76, 77, 78, 86, 103, 123, 140, 144, 148, 158, 160, 161, 164, 168, 174, 183, 184, 186, 189, 195, 207, 218, 245, 267, 271, 272, 273, 274, 278, 290, 371, 374, 375, 378
  Doktor Zhivago (Doctor Zhivago) 271
  'Gamlet' ('Hamlet') 76
  'Nas malo. Nas, mozhet byt', troe' ('We are few. There are, perhaps, three of us...') 76
  Zhivago affair 160
  Zhivago poems 76
past, the 1, 5, 6, 8, 10, 11, 12, 13, 14, 15, 16, 19, 20, 22, 39, 40, 41, 65, 71, 83, 98, 103, 131, 135, 178, 204, 205, 265, 274, 275, 294, 296, 338, 363, 365, 367, 382, 386, 389, 393, 394
Paustovskii, Konstantin 29
Pavlenkov, F. F. 379
Pazukhin, Evgenii 254
Pelevin, Viktor x, 148, 255
  Chapaev i Pustota 148

perestroika 4, 44, 79, 97, 108, 109, 112, 113, 124, 147, 154, 196, 197, 227, 334, 338, 345, 349, 375, 386
performance 57, 249, 305, 377, 394, 407, 408, 409, 410, 419, 420, 421
Peskov, Vasilii 208, 221
Petersburg 23, 57, 58, 59, 60, 61, 63, 67, 131, 197, 199, 229, 230, 231, 232, 233, 234, 237, 244, 298, 359, 376, 377, 380, 396, 404
 river Neva 232, 252, 266, 274, 279, 376
Peter the Great 232, 233
Petrograd 128, 129, 134, 140, 300
Petrovskii, M. 150
Petrunis, Sergei 335
Petrushevskaia, Liudmila 243
Pevear, Richard 183
Picasso, Pablo 162
Pieper, Irene 212
Pilling, John 166, 187, 188
Platonov, Andrei 110, 114, 128, 168
Platt, Kevin 305
Plekhanova, Irina 266, 272
Plisetskii, German 335, 345, 346
Pliukhanov, B.V. 34
PN Review, The 174, 178, 188, 190
Podoksenov, A. M. 216
poema 300
poet-prophet 15, 308, 383
Poggioli, Renato 162, 163, 183, 186
Poland 26, 43, 78, 161, 384
Poleva, Viktoriia 59
 Ars moriendi 59
 Summer Music 59
Polivanov, Konstantin 67
Polonskaia, Veronika 115, 119, 121
Polonsky, Rachel 197
Polozkova, Vera 249
Polukhina, Valentina 192, 238, 242, 243, 248, 251
Pomerantsev, Igor' 20
Pomorska, Kristina 32, 416
Ponomareff, Constantin V. 86

Poplavskii, Boris 47, 297, 303, 304, 312, 324, 374
 Avtomaticheskie stikhi (Automatic Verses) 304
popular culture 11, 18, 38, 40, 46, 58, 62, 125, 148, 249, 333, 359, 377
Porter, Robert 331, 385
postmodernism 365, 381
Postnikova, Ol'ga 53
post-Soviet 6, 7, 9, 10, 11, 12, 13, 18, 20, 21, 25, 26, 36, 38, 39, 40, 44, 45, 46, 48, 50, 51, 54, 58, 60, 61, 63, 64, 73, 88, 92, 96, 97, 108, 110, 112, 113, 114, 115, 118, 120, 121, 146, 147, 159, 197, 198, 199, 201, 202, 206, 207, 208, 212, 213, 217, 222, 223, 229, 230, 239, 241, 254, 266, 267, 268, 270, 271, 273, 274, 276, 279, 290, 327, 330, 337, 339, 340, 342, 343, 351, 352, 355, 356, 357, 358, 359, 360, 361, 362, 363, 364, 365, 367, 368, 369, 370, 372, 377, 378, 379, 380, 381, 382, 384, 385, 386, 387, 388, 389, 390, 391, 392, 396, 418, 420, 422
Potebnia, Aleksandr 374
Pound, Ezra 162, 165, 166, 172, 174, 180, 192, 402
Prague 20, 313, 370, 390, 392, 393
Prasolov, Aleksei 351
Priamaia rech' (Direct Speech) 361
Priboi (The Surf) 138
Prigov, Dmitri 39, 227, 249, 335, 340, 344, 345, 346, 420, 421, 422
 'Bestiarii' ('The Bestiary') 421
 'Liki' ('Faces') 421
 'Portrety' ('Portraits') 421
Prikhod'ko, Irina 149, 150
Prize, Andrej Belyj 227
Prodolzhenie vody (The Extension of Water) 57
Prokofiev, Sergey 371
Prokushev, Iu. L. 141
Proust, Marcel 171
Psalms 155

publishers 4, 5, 29, 139, 214, 217, 359, 419
Punin, Nikolai 84, 87
Pushkin ix
Pushkin, Aleksandr ix, 5, 7, 14, 21, 33, 41, 42, 58, 61, 71, 72, 102, 103, 117, 129, 135, 148, 149, 150, 151, 155, 158, 175, 191, 195, 199, 203, 213, 222, 232, 248, 251, 301, 312, 359, 363, 389, 390, 395, 396, 404, 416
  'Besy' ('Demons') 150
  Bronze Horseman 232
  Evgenii Onegin 395, 396, 404
  'Poet i tolpa' ('The Poet and the Crowd') 251
  Pushkinian 167, 198, 284, 301
Pushkin, Michael 49
Pushkinskii fond (Pushkin foundation) 396
Putin, Vladimir 148, 152, 355
Pyman, Avril 129, 134, 155

Radlova, Anna 245
  'Angel pesnopeniia' ('Angel of Song') 245
Raeff, Mark 363
Raffael, Burton 165
Raikin, Arkadii 166
Ramazani, Jahan 401
Rasputin, Valentin 337
Rassadin, Stanislav 273
Ratnikov, Kirill 298
Rawson, Claude 174
Rayfield, Donald 174, 179, 180
readers 2, 3, 4, 5, 6, 8, 9, 14, 19, 22, 23, 24, 28, 36, 37, 38, 40, 42, 53, 61, 68, 80, 83, 84, 85, 104, 108, 114, 130, 131, 155, 157, 159, 160, 161, 163, 164, 165, 167, 169, 170, 174, 175, 178, 181, 182, 184, 187, 188, 189, 190, 193, 195, 196, 204, 205, 207, 208, 217, 219, 220, 221, 227, 233, 241, 243, 245, 246, 248, 250, 251, 255, 281, 287, 301, 305, 306, 318, 332, 344, 356, 367, 369, 372, 376, 380, 383, 385, 386, 389, 390, 396, 398, 399, 400, 406, 409, 415, 419, 422. *See also* audience
readership 24, 41, 158, 172, 174, 179, 184, 197, 206, 221, 227, 241, 254, 302, 330, 364, 387, 389, 409, 410
would-be readers 5
realism 6, 8, 15, 17, 19, 26, 27, 29, 30, 31, 32, 33, 34, 35, 38, 40, 132, 147, 154, 267, 279, 283, 302, 305, 359, 372, 375, 384, 385, 386, 387
Reavey, George 333
reception 9, 25, 26, 38, 40, 45, 46, 47, 48, 49, 50, 51, 52, 53, 54, 55, 56, 57, 61, 62, 79, 85, 124, 139, 158, 159, 160, 162, 165, 166, 169, 172, 173, 175, 181, 182, 186, 188, 194, 195, 197, 198, 248, 266, 335, 336, 357, 360, 364, 368, 373
Reconfiguring the Canon of Twentieth Century Russian Poetry, 1991–2008 viii
Red Army 134
Reeder, Roberta 63, 72, 76, 142
Rein, Evgenii 287, 335, 340, 341, 344, 345, 346, 347, 349
Repertuar 129
Repin, Il'ia 102, 119
repression 86, 184, 193, 386
Reuters 49
Revolutionary Populists 126
Riashentsev, Iurii 343
Rilke, Rainer Maria 187, 368, 381
Ritchie, Elisavietta 50
Robin, Régine 158, 164, 175, 385, 386
Robinson, William 363, 364
Rodionov, Andrei 249
'Rodivshiesia v SSSR' ('Born in the USSR') 12
Rogatchevski, Andrei 179
Roginskii, Boris 233, 240
Rojek, Chris 68, 88, 250
Romanovskii, Feliks 59
Romans 241

Romanticism 35, 62, 67, 68, 90, 143, 181, 226, 240, 246, 312, 381, 385, 395, 417, 422
Rome 127, 357, 385
Ronen, Omri 72, 272, 273, 277
Roskina, Natalia 67, 72
Rosneck, Karen 268
Rosslyn, Wendy 67, 84
Rostotskii, Stanislav 143
Rougle, Charles 90
Rowse, A. L. 178, 179
Rozhdestveno 359
Rozhdestvenskii, Robert 12, 330, 331, 332, 333, 337, 339, 340, 341, 345, 346
Rubinshtein, Lev 282
Rubins, Maria viii, 38, 306
Rubtsov, Nikolai 331, 337, 338, 339, 340, 346, 351
Rudiak, Il'ia 68
Rudnev, Vadim 366
Rudy, Stephen 416
Rusev, Radostin 14
Russia Abroad 160, 291, 294, 296, 297, 363
Russian Association of Proletarian Writers (RAPP) 121
Russification 52, 319
Russkaia literatura XX veka (20th Century Russian Literature) 113, 114, 115, 118
Russkaia poeziia 60-kh godov (Russian Poetry of the 1960s) 335
Russkaia poeziia 1960x gg. (Russian Poetry of the 1960s) 37
Russkaia poeziia. XX vek. Antologiia (Russian Poetry. Twentieth Century. An Anthology) 218
Russkaia slovesnost (Russian Literature) 108
Russkie bez Rossii, 2003–2005 (Russians Without Russia, 2003–2005) 364
Russkie stikhi 1950–2000 godov. Antologii (Russian Poetry of the 1950s–2000s. An Anthology) 218

Russkie stikhi 1950–2000 (Russian Poetry 1950–2000) 335, 346
russkofoniia 356
RuTube 36
Rybakova, Mariia 416
Rybnikova, M. A. 131, 135, 136
  A. Blok-Hamlet 136
Ryklin, M. K. 409
Rylkova, Galina 10, 17, 72, 87, 90, 377, 378

Sabbatini, Marco 241, 247
Saltykov-Shchedrin, Mikhail 102
samizdat 3, 30, 31, 79, 124, 195, 225, 226, 240, 246, 254, 331, 334, 386
Samizdat veka (The Century's Self-Publishing) 37, 335, 343
Samoilov, David 54, 267, 269, 273, 281
Sandler, Stephanie ix, 22, 23, 28, 30, 39, 42, 66, 177, 241, 413, 419
  Rereading Russian Poetry 22
Santner, Eric 417, 418
Sapgir, Genrikh 280, 281, 335, 345, 346, 382
Sapozhkov, S. 146
Sappho 66
Sarnov, Benedikt 281
Satanism 149, 150
Satunovskii, Ian 267, 280, 281
Savage, Jesse M. 27
Savitskii, Stanislav 226, 227, 241, 331
Scammell, Michael 185, 186
Scherr, Barry P. 283, 286
Schmidt, Rachel 36, 317, 322
Schönle, A. 179
schools 3, 25, 37, 39, 96, 97, 101, 108, 112, 120, 123, 144, 337, 338, 357, 359, 362, 366
Schopenhauer, Arthur 147
Schteiger, Anatolii
  Eta Zhizn' (This Life) 316
  Neblagodarnost' (Ingratitude) 316
Schweitzer, Vivien 59, 195
Schwerter, Stephanie 173

Scriabin, Aleksandr 193
Sedakova, Ol'ga 17, 21, 39, 62, 198, 233, 251, 381, 398, 409, 423
Sel'vinskii, Il'ia 29, 277, 282, 284
Serebrianyi vek russkoi poezii (The Silver Age of Russian Poetry) 218
Severianin, Igor' 47, 148, 289
Severiukhin, D. 226
Shackleton, Mark 294
Shaitanov, Igor' 268, 340, 341, 348, 351, 352, 381, 382, 409
Shakespeare, William 72
Shakhovskaia, Zinaida 291, 296
Shakhovskoi, Dmitrii 199
Shalamov, Varlaam 195
Shanghai 363
Shapoval, Sergei 213, 422
  Portretnaia galeriia D. A. P. 422
Sharshun, Serge 303
  'Foule immobile' ('The Immobile Crowd') 303
  Nebo kolokol. Poeziia v proze, 1919–1928 (The Sky Bell. Poetry in Prose, 1919–1928) 303
Shartse, Olga 205, 211
Shcherbina, Tat'iana 143, 198, 349
Sheldon, Richard 35
Shelton, Joanne ix, 39, 343
Shepelev, V. L. 129
Shepherd, David 145
Shil'kovo 20
Shkapskaia, Mariia 5
Shkliarevskii, Igor' 280
Shklovskii, Viktor (Shklovsky, Viktor) 35, 36, 275, 295
Shlapentokh, Vladimir 85, 86
Shmelev, Ivan 224
Shneidman, Noah Norman 98, 99, 100, 208, 386, 387
Sholokhov, Mikhail 100, 120
  Podniataia tselina (Virgin Soil Upturned) 100
Short Course of Soviet History 42
Shostakovich, Dmitri
  Seven Romances of Aleksandr Blok 142

Shraer-Petrov, David 276
Shrayer, Maxim D. 278, 279, 334, 335
Shteiger, Anatolii 297, 315, 316, 317, 318, 319, 320, 321, 322, 323, 324, 327
  Etot den' (This Day) 316
Shubinskii, Valerii 273, 276, 282
Shukshin, Vasilii 337
Shvarts, Elena 17, 21, 225, 226, 227, 228, 229, 230, 231, 232, 233, 234, 237, 238, 239, 241, 242, 243, 244, 245, 246, 247, 248, 249, 250, 251, 252, 253, 254, 255, 382, 423
  'Bog spas' ('God Saved Me') 253
  'Bokovoe zrenie pamiati' ('The Lateral Vision of Memory') 251
  Chernaia Paskha (Black Easter) 230, 233, 236, 237, 243, 244
  'Elegiia na rentgenovskii snimok moego cherepa' ('Elegy on an X-Ray of My Skull') 244
  'Grubymi sredstvami ne dostich' blazhenstva' ('You Won't Reach Bliss by Rough Means') 242
  'Ia rodilas' s ladon'iu gladkoi' ('I was Born with an Unlined Hand') 245
  'Izbienie slepogo' ('Beating Up a Blind Man') 253
  'Kak eta ulitsa zovetsia' ('What this Street is Called') 229
  'Leviafan' ('Leviathan') 246
  'Luch' ('The Ray') 251
  'Na progulke' ('On a Walk') 229
  'Neskol'ko osobennostei moikh stikhov' ('A Few Peculiarities of My Poems') 251
  Opredelenie v durnuiu pogodu (Definition in Foul Weather) 250
  Portret Blokady cherez zhanr, natiurmort i peizazh (A Portrait of the Blockade through a Genre Painting, a Still Life and a Landscape) 234, 236, 237
  'Probuzhdenie' ('Awakening') 229
  Sochineniia (Collected Works) 250

'Sumerki' ('Twilight') 252
'Tantsuiushchii David' ('Dancing David') 244
'Temnaia rozhdestvenskaia pesn' ('A Dark Christmas Song') 246
Trudy i dni Lavinii, monakhini iz ordena obrezaniia serdtsa. Ot Rozhdestva do Paskhi (The Works and Days of Lavinia, a Nun in the Order of the Circumcision of the Heart: From Christmas to Easter) 246
Vidimaia storona zhizni (The Visible Side of Life) 250
'Vospominanie o strannom ugoshchenii' ('Memory of a Strange Treat') 244
'Vozdushnoe Evangelie' ('Air Gospel') 229
Zapadno-vostochnyi veter (West-Easterly Wind) 229
'Zhestko nakazannyi antisemit' ('A Harshly Punished Anti-Semite') 253
Siberia 16
Silver Age 10, 16, 37, 70, 72, 73, 79, 124, 127, 132, 146, 154, 161, 164, 195, 218, 226, 245, 248, 249, 289, 290, 291, 298, 301, 326, 343, 353, 367, 376, 377, 378, 380, 388
Simic, Charles 401
  'The Tiger' 401
Simone, Nina 400
Simonov, Konstantin 100, 281
Simun, Konstantin 60
  Brodskii priekhal (Brodsky Arrived) 60
Sinatra, Frank 400
Siniavskii, Andrei 31, 32, 33, 42
  Chto takoe sotsialisticheskii realizm (What Is Socialist Realism) 31, 32
  Progulki s Pushkinym (Strolls with Pushkin) 42
Sisson, C. S. 191
Sivan, Emmanuel 12
Skaldin, A. D. 138

Skandiaka, Nika 395
Skidan, Alexander 198, 241, 252, 401
Skuratov, Sergei 60
Slavianskii Bank 7, 148
  Poeziia v reklame (Poetry in Advertising) 148
Slobin, Greta 291, 362, 363, 367, 372
Slobodniuk, Sergei 149, 151, 152
Slonim, Marc 161, 329
Slonimskii, Sergei
  A Voice from the Chorus 132, 142
Sluchevskii, Konstantin 146
Slutskii, Boris 39, 40, 265, 266, 267, 268, 269, 270, 271, 272, 273, 274, 275, 276, 277, 278, 279, 280, 281, 282, 283, 284, 285, 286, 287, 288, 330, 332, 333, 340, 345, 346
  'Loshadi v okeane' ('Horses in the Ocean') 285
  'Piatikonechnaia zvezda s shestikonechnoi' ('The Five-pointed and Six-pointed Stars') 277
  'Rasskaz emigranta' ('An Emigrant's Tale') 277
  'Sel'skoe kladbishche' ('The Village Cemetery') 277
  Stikhi o evreiakh i tatarakh (Verses about Jews and Tatars) 277
Smeliakov, Iaroslav 270, 281, 331, 341
Smirnov, Aleksei 287
Smith, Alexandra vii, ix, 10, 38, 392
Smith, G. S. 46, 47, 64, 85, 161, 181, 198, 242, 266, 268, 285, 335, 344
Smola, Oleg 149, 150
Sobolev, Olga x, 3, 40, 142
Socialist realism 6, 15, 17, 19, 26, 27, 30, 31, 32, 33, 38, 40, 147, 279, 305, 375, 384, 385, 387
Soja, Edward 295
Sokolov, Vladimir 343, 345, 351
Sologub, Fedor 33, 127, 147, 374
Solov'ev, Sergei 138, 146, 203
Solov'ev, Vladimir 33, 131, 133, 146, 147, 203
Solovyov, Dmitry 49

Solzhenitsyn, Aleksandr 71, 72, 175, 197, 266, 337, 371
songs 19, 27, 28, 46, 59, 126, 134, 343, 369, 377, 380, 400
Sophocles 72
Sosnora, Viktor 333, 345, 346
Sots Art 32
Soupault, Phillipe 306
Soviet Union 1, 2, 3, 4, 10, 17, 18, 19, 22, 23, 24, 25, 27, 28, 31, 36, 38, 39, 43, 44, 45, 46, 49, 51, 64, 79, 89, 96, 97, 98, 105, 110, 112, 126, 129, 130, 135, 139, 143, 147, 157, 161, 195, 197, 201, 205, 213, 220, 223, 239, 240, 252, 254, 265, 267, 271, 273, 279, 287, 296, 326, 327, 353, 355, 356, 358, 359, 360, 361, 363, 365, 368, 372, 373, 375, 377, 385, 386, 387, 391, 392, 422
  canon 10, 15, 30, 110, 147, 208, 239, 268, 269, 270, 273, 336, 339, 352, 360, 362, 373
  culture 10, 12, 14, 18, 21, 30, 114, 143, 279, 286, 336, 367, 379, 380
Sovremennye zapiski (*Contemporary Annals*) 300, 302, 316, 366
Sozina, E. K. 153
Spector, Ivar 21
Staf'eva, E. 56
Stalin, Iosif 2, 5, 9, 10, 24, 25, 28, 29, 30, 31, 39, 40, 42, 70, 79, 85, 86, 87, 89, 90, 96, 135, 147, 159, 172, 179, 182, 183, 184, 189, 190, 191, 192, 193, 202, 265, 272, 274, 275, 279, 286, 334, 339, 347, 348, 362, 367, 369, 420
  Stalinism 67, 84, 89, 90, 161, 179, 265, 287, 339
  Stalinist 7, 10, 87, 89, 90, 182, 191, 272, 286, 339
Stanislavskii, Konstantin 133
'Staroe Radio' ('Old Radio') 12
'Starye pesni o glavnom' ('The Main Songs of the Past') 11
State University of St Petersburg 60
Stavrov, Perikl 297
Steiger, Andrew 27, 28

Steiner, George 166
Stein, Gertrude 422
Stepanova, Maria 39, 416, 417, 418, 419, 423
  Pesni severnykh iuzhan (*Songs of Northern Southerners*) 416
Stern, Ludmila 348, 349
St Gilles-Croix-de-Vie 371
Stockholm Syndrome 89
Stone, Jonathan 21, 157
St Petersburg 58, 59, 60, 61, 131, 197, 199, 359, 376, 377, 380, 396
  Pirogovskaia Embankment 59
Strakhovsky, Leonid 162
Stratanovskii, Sergei 226, 227
Strelianyi, Andrei 335
Strofy veka. Antologiia russkoi poezii (*Stanza of the Century: An Anthology of Russian Poetry*) 218
structuralism 24, 171, 185
Struve, Gleb 157, 158, 163, 164, 166, 197, 205, 207, 290, 300, 318, 321, 374
  Russian Literature in Exile 290
Sukharev, Dmitrii 273, 285, 286
Sukhikh, Igor' 328
Sunderland, Willard 67
Suprematist 411
Surganova and Orchestra 59
  'Neuzheli ne ia' ('Surely, It Was Me...') 59
Surkov, Aleksei 29, 100, 129
surrealism 302, 303, 304, 374
Svarovskii, Fedor 39, 416, 417, 418, 419
  'Dva robota plyli' ('Two Robots Were Swimming') 417
  Puteshestvenniki vo vremeni (*Time-Travellers*) 418
  Vse khotiat byt' robotami (*Everyone Wants to Be a Robot*) 417
Sverdlov, M. 56
syllabus 2, 37, 40, 85, 209, 330, 331, 336, 337, 338, 339, 340, 341, 343, 352, 353, 357

symbolism 24, 32, 34, 67, 123, 124, 126, 127, 128, 135, 136, 137, 140, 141, 146, 147, 152, 153, 154, 162, 204, 366
  Russian symbolism 34, 127, 137, 141

Tabachnikova, Olga 72
Tagil'tsev, A. V. 74
Takho-Godi, E. A. 146
tamizdat 31, 379, 386
Tarasova, I. A. 314
Tarkovskii, Arsenii 351
Tartu-Moscow Semiotic school 137
Tarusa 368, 370
Tavener, John 71
Tazhidinova, Irina G. 28
Temkina, Marina 335
Terapiano, Iurii 305
Terts, Abram 31
textbook 3, 40, 96, 97, 98, 99, 100, 101, 102, 103, 104, 105, 106, 107, 108, 109, 110, 111, 112, 113, 114, 115, 116, 117, 118, 119, 120, 121, 206, 209, 210, 211, 212, 213, 223, 268, 271, 330, 331, 332, 338, 339, 340, 352, 359, 362, 383, 389
Thacker, Andrew 18
Thaw 5, 17, 30, 38, 40, 46, 49, 79, 138, 144, 161, 195, 265, 271, 273, 275, 329, 330, 331, 332, 333, 334, 335, 336, 337, 338, 339, 340, 341, 342, 343, 344, 345, 347, 348, 349, 350, 352, 353, 354, 369, 372, 380. *See also* Khrushchev, Nikita
  Generation 30, 161, 225, 329, 330, 331, 334, 335, 336, 337, 338, 339, 340, 341, 342, 343, 344, 345, 348, 349, 352, 353, 354
Thomas, D. M. 19, 57, 166, 167, 168, 174, 176, 186
Thompson, Ewa M. 247
Tiffany, Daniel 417, 418
Tihanov, Galin 312
Tikhomirov, Vladimir 355
Timenchik, Roman 23, 73, 76, 77

Times Educational Supplement, The 41
Times Literary Supplement, The 158, 161, 162, 165, 168, 174, 175, 188, 192
Tiutchev, Fedor 33, 213
Todd III, William Mills 24, 25, 26
Tokarev, Dmitrii 304
Tolmachev, M. V. 68
Tolstoi, Aleksei 100
Tolstoi, Ivan 380
Tolstoi, Lev (Tolstoy, Leo) viii, x, 27, 41, 71, 72, 102, 135, 175, 211
  Petr I (Peter the First) 100
Tomashevskii, Boris 26
Tomlinson, Charles 174
Toporov, Vladimir 23, 91, 92
Tracy, Robert 166, 167, 185
tradition 6, 8, 15, 17, 26, 27, 29, 32, 37, 38, 40, 41, 42, 54, 66, 67, 68, 79, 80, 86, 87, 90, 102, 103, 107, 118, 123, 131, 141, 143, 147, 150, 153, 155, 158, 159, 161, 170, 172, 175, 186, 197, 198, 212, 213, 214, 215, 226, 230, 233, 237, 238, 239, 242, 244, 247, 249, 267, 276, 277, 278, 283, 287, 289, 290, 291, 292, 294, 296, 298, 305, 306, 328, 339, 347, 350, 351, 356, 358, 359, 360, 361, 363, 366, 367, 368, 370, 372, 373, 376, 377, 379, 380, 381, 382, 386, 387, 388, 389, 390, 401, 402, 404, 407, 409, 412, 416, 417
transitory identity 294
transnational 38, 46, 292, 293, 294, 303, 311, 312, 334, 355, 357, 364, 369, 382
Trauberg, Leonid 143
Trenev, Konstantin 100
Tret'iakov, Sergei 18
Trifonov, Yuri 337
Trofimov, Gennadii 59
  Niotkuda s liubov'iu, ili Veselye pokhorony (Out of Nowhere with Love, or The Merry Funeral Party) 59
Trotskii, Lev (Trotsky, Leon) 126, 130, 134, 366

Troy 155
Tsarist 129, 131, 133
Tsarskoe Selo 67
Tsekh Poetov (Guild of Poets) 163
Tsereteli, Zurab 371
Tsivian, Tamara 23
Tsivin, Vladimir 59
Tsvetaeva, Marina 9, 22, 36, 37, 38, 47, 53, 66, 73, 75, 76, 77, 78, 140, 158, 161, 162, 180, 192, 199, 218, 243, 245, 247, 248, 249, 252, 270, 284, 289, 290, 366, 368, 369, 370, 371, 372, 373, 374, 382, 384, 385, 388, 390, 392
  'Akhmatovoi' ('To Akhmatova') 247
  'Buzina tsel'nyi sad zalila!' ('Elderberry Filled the Entire Garden!') 76, 85
  museum 371
  'Na krasnom kone' ('On a Red Steed') 245
  'Novogodnee' ('Happy New Year') 368
  prize 371
  'the Tsvetaeva fires' 368
Tsvetkov, Aleksei 198, 401
Turgenev, Ivan 72, 175
Tvardovskii, Aleksandr 13, 15, 29, 31, 98, 100, 205, 206, 207, 211, 212, 213, 214, 288, 330, 331, 332, 333, 338
  'O Bunine' ('About Bunin') 211
twelve apostles 134
Twentieth Party Congress 46, 329
twenty-first century 64, 152, 222, 419
Tychina, Pavlo 100
Tynianov, Iurii 25, 26, 33, 34, 194, 199
Tzara, Tristan 303

Uchitel', Aleksei 222
Ufliand, Vladimir 346, 349, 396
Ukraine 20
Ulanov, Aleksandr 251
Ulianovsk Pedagogical College 339
Ulitskaia, Liudmila 59
  Veselye pokhorony (*The Funeral Party*) 59

underground 2, 3, 4, 7, 8, 17, 18, 22, 30, 37, 44, 78, 195, 225, 226, 228, 230, 239, 240, 241, 247, 249, 252, 253, 254, 255, 267, 268, 279, 281, 282, 287, 331, 334, 335, 340, 342, 343, 347, 349, 352, 353, 354, 372, 386, 392
Union of Poets 127, 129
Union of Soviet Writers 102
United Kingdom (UK) 179, 194, 405
United States ix
United States of America (US) 24, 43, 45, 60, 61, 186, 241, 335, 376, 405
University of Tartu 34
  Tartu School of Semiotics 35
Urin, Viktor 335
Uroki literatury v 11-om klasse (*Literature lessons in class 11*) 340
Uspenskii, Boris A. 64
USSR vii, 12, 46, 49, 50, 52, 329, 330, 331, 332, 334, 343, 345, 349, 350, 386
Ustinov, Andrei 299

Vaginov, Konstantin 198, 350
Valentine, Sarah 405, 406, 407
Valéry, Paul 319
  'The Crisis of the Mind' 319
Valieva, Iuliia 241, 254
Vampilov, Aleksandr 337
van Buskirk, Emily 173
Van Het Reve, K. 50
Vanshenkin, Konstantin 206, 270, 343, 345, 346
Vasil'ev, Andrei 13, 59
Vaughan, Richard 41
Vavilon (Babylon) 37, 227, 335
Vendler, Helen 169
Venice 51, 57
Vertinskii, Aleksandr 388
Veselovskii, Aleksandr 35
Vetrov, Aleksandr 377, 380
Vikulov, Sergei 331
Vilenskii, Semen 37
Villon, François 165
Vilnius, Lithuania 60

Vimeo 36
Vinitsky, Ilya 66, 84
Vinokurov, Evgenii 206, 270, 283, 333
Virabov, Igor' 12
Virgil 62, 72
Virgin Mary 84
Vishniak, Mark 316
Vitkovskii, Evgenii 377
Vladiv-Glover, Slobodanka M. 381
Vladivostok 199
Volchek, Dmitrii 226
Volchenko, Natal'ia 108, 109
Volga river 369
Volgina, Arina 55
Volgin, Igor' 58
   Igra v biser (A Game of Beads) 58
Volkov, Vadim 7, 57, 71, 230
Vol'pe, T. S. 138
Voltskaia, Tatiana viii
Voprosy literatury (Questions of Literature) 46, 47, 48, 50, 51, 52, 53, 54, 55, 57, 351
Vorob'ev, Konstantin 337
Voronezh 60, 79, 159, 163, 168, 180, 181, 188, 189, 199, 200, 339
Voronezh University 339
Vowles, Judith ix
Vozdhushnye puti (Aerial Ways) 163
Vozdukh (The Air) 197, 198, 409, 417
Voznesenskaia, Iuliia 250
Voznesenskii, Andrei 12, 30, 45, 48, 49, 50, 51, 54, 206, 330, 331, 332, 333, 337, 339, 340, 341, 344, 345, 346, 347, 348, 351
   Order of the Red Banner of Labour 49
   USSR State Prize 49
Vozrozhdenie 302
Vshenory 370
Vvedenskii, Aleksandr 350
Vysotskii, Vladimir 222, 337, 339, 340, 344, 345, 346, 364

Wachtel, Andrew Baruch 64, 66, 84, 404
Wachtel, Michael 6, 7
Wainwright, Jeffrey 174
Walcott, Derek 159, 171, 180
Warhol, Andy 387
Watten, Barret 387
Weber, Max 88
Weidle, Vladimir 299
Weissbort, Daniel 242
Wells, David 78
Werth, Alexander 162
West, the 7, 9, 11, 24, 39, 43, 44, 45, 46, 47, 49, 50, 51, 61, 83, 157, 160, 161, 164, 166, 172, 183, 184, 194, 228, 229, 232, 233, 240, 290, 298, 311, 329, 332, 335, 343, 344, 349, 357, 386
   culture 8, 57
   Western 8, 23, 24, 43, 49, 57, 60, 84, 92, 138, 161, 164, 165, 166, 172, 181, 183, 196, 228, 233, 241, 249, 291, 292, 298, 299, 308, 312, 326, 332, 333, 343, 344, 387, 405, 408
White Army 364
Whyte, Christopher 368
Wikipedia 219, 272
Williams, Hugo 179
Winter, Jay 12, 379, 401
World Literature Today 228
World War One 18, 223, 299, 302, 319
World War Two 28, 100, 213, 220, 223, 318, 324
Wrede, Casper 179
Wrenn, Angus x
Writers' Union, the 28, 30, 54, 228, 269, 346, 376
   1954 Writers' Union Congress 28

Yampolsky, Mikhail 327
Yastremski, Slava I. 233
Yeats, W. B. 170
Yershov, Peter 202

Yiddish 278, 280, 285
YouTube 36, 249, 364, 420

Zabolotskii, Nikolai 22, 158, 198, 278, 337, 350
Zaitsev, Boris 224, 270, 271
zaum' 303, 396
Zhdanov, Andrei 70, 227, 381
Zheleznova, Irina 205, 211
Zhirmunskii, Viktor 137, 141
Zhitenev, A. A. 241
zhiznetvorchestvo 67, 249
Zhizn' zamechatel'nykh liudei (The Life of Remarkable People) 377
Zholkovskii, Aleksandr 58, 66, 67, 71, 87, 89, 90, 91
  'O poniatiiakh invariant i poeticheskii mir': 1-ia lektsiia' ('On Notions of the Invariant and the Poetic World: Lecture 1') 58

Zhukovskii, Vasilii 416
Zhuravlev, V. P. 340
Zinin, Sergei 211
Ziuganov, Gennady A. 355
Znamia (The Banner) 25
Znamia truda 135
Zobnin, Iu. V. 301
Zohn, H. 299
Zorin, Andrei 173
Zoshchenko, Mikhail 114
Zubok, Vladislav 273

This book need not end here...

At Open Book Publishers, we are changing the nature of the traditional academic book. The title you have just read will not be left on a library shelf, but will be accessed online by hundreds of readers each month across the globe. OBP publishes only the best academic work: each title passes through a rigorous peer-review process. We make all our books free to read online so that students, researchers and members of the public who can't afford a printed edition will have access to the same ideas.
This book and additional content is available at:
https://www.openbookpublishers.com/product/294

Customize
Personalize your copy of this book or design new books using OBP and third-party material. Take chapters or whole books from our published list and make a special edition, a new anthology or an illuminating coursepack. Each customized edition will be produced as a paperback and a downloadable PDF. Find out more at:
https://www.openbookpublishers.com/section/59/1

Donate
If you enjoyed this book, and feel that research like this should be available to all readers, regardless of their income, please think about donating to us. We do not operate for profit and all donations, as with all other revenue we generate, will be used to finance new Open Access publications.
https://www.openbookpublishers.com/section/13/1/support-us

Like Open Book Publishers

Follow @OpenBookPublish

Read more at the OBP Blog

You may also be interested in:

In the Lands of the Romanovs
An Annotated Bibliography of First-hand English-language Accounts of the Russian Empire (1613–1917)
By Anthony Cross

https://www.openbookpublishers.com/product/268

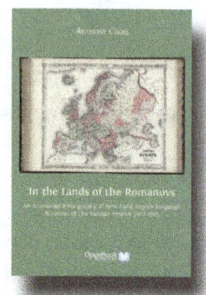

Beyond Holy Russia
The Life and Times of Stephen Graham
By Michael Hughes

https://www.openbookpublishers.com/product/217

A People Passing Rude
British Responses to Russian Culture
Edited by Anthony Cross

https://www.openbookpublishers.com/product/160

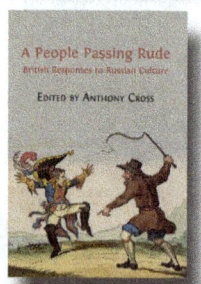

Women in Nineteenth-Century Russia
Lives and Culture
Edited by Wendy Rosslyn and Alessandra Tosi

http://www.openbookpublishers.com/product/98

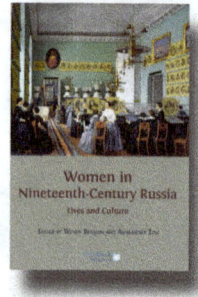